P9-DGV-106

BELMONT UNIVERSITY LIBRARY

BRITISH WRITERS

BRITISH WRITERS

JAY PARINI
Editor

SUPPLEMENT XI

CHARLES SCRIBNER'S SONS
An imprint of Thomson Gale, a part of The Thomson Corporation

THOMSON
GALE

Detroit • New York • San Francisco • San Diego • New Haven, Conn. • Waterville, Maine • London • Munich

British Writers Supplement XI
Jay Parini, Editor in Chief

Project Editor
Maikue Vang

Copyeditors
Robert E. Jones, Linda Sanders

Proofreader
Susan Barnett

Indexer
Wendy Allex

Permissions Researcher
Nicholas Hill, Mark Rzeszutek

Permissions
Margaret Abendroth, Emma Hull, Jessica Schultz

Composition Specialist
Gary Leach

Buyer
Rhonda A. Dover

Publisher
Frank Menchaca

Product Manager
Peg Bessette

© 2006 Thomson Gale, a part of Thomson Corporation.

Thomson and Star Logo are trademarks and Gale and Charles Scribner's Sons are trademarks used herein under license.

For more information, contact
Thomson Gale
27500 Drake Rd.
Farmington Hills, MI 48331-3535
Or you can visit our Internet site at
http://www.gale.com

ALL RIGHTS RESERVED
No part of this book may be reproduced or utilized in any form or by any electronic, mechanical, or other means, now known or hereafter invented including photocopying and recording, or in any information storage or retrieval system, without permission in writing from Charles Scribner's Sons.

For permission to use material from this product, submit your request via Web at http://www.gale-edit.com/permissions, or you may download our Permissions Request form and submit your request by fax or mail to:

Permissions Department
Thomson Gale.
27500 Drake Rd.
Farmington Hills, MI 48331-3535
Permissions Hotline:
248 699-8006 or 800 877-4253, ext. 8006
Fax: 248 699-8074 or 800 762-4058

Since this page cannot legibly accommodate all copyright notices, the acknowledgments constitute an extension of the copyright notice.

LIBRARY OF CONGRESS CATALOGING-IN-PUBLICATION DATA

British Writers Supplement XI / Jay Parini, editor.
    p. cm.
    Includes bibliographical references and index.
    ISBN 0-684-31313-8 (hardcover : alk. paper)
    1. English literature–20th century–Bio-bibliography. 2. English literature–20th century–History and criticism. 3. Commonwealth literature (English)–History and criticism. 4. Commonwealth literature (English)–Bio-bibliography. 5. Authors, Commonwealth–20th century–Biography. 6. Authors, English–20th century–Biography. I. Parini, Jay.
    PR85 .B688 Suppl. 11
    820.9'001–dc22   2004014730

Printed in the United States of America
10 9 8 7 6 5 4 3 2 1

Acknowledgments

Acknowledgment is gratefully made to those publishers and individuals who permitted the use of the following materials in copyright:

IAIN BANKS. Banks, Iain M. From *The State of the Art*. Orbit, 1993 and Nightshade Books, 2004. Reproduced by permission of the author.

THOMAS LOVELL BEDDOES. Beddoes, Thomas Lovell. From "Act Four, Scene II," in *Death's Jest-Book: The 1829 Text*. Edited with an Introduction by Michael Bradshaw. Carcanet-Manchester, 2003. Introduction and editorial matter copyright © Michael Bradshaw, 2003. Reproduced by permission of Carcanet Press Limited. From "Act Two, Song by Isabrand," in *Death's Jest-Book: The 1829 Text* Edited with an Introduction by Michael Bradshaw. Carcanet-Manchester, 2003. Introduction and editorial matter Copyright © Michael Bradshaw, 2003 Reproduced by permission of Carcanet Press Limited. From "Preface of Act Two and Act Three," in *Death's Jest-Book, the 1829 Text*. Edited with an Introduction by Michael Bradshaw. Carcanet-Manchester, 2003. Introduction and editorial matter Copyright © Michael Bradshaw, 2003. Reproduced by permission of Carcanet Press Limited. From "Scene IV: A Retired Gallery in the Ducal Castle," in *Death's Jest-Book: The 1829 Text*. Edited with an Introduction by Michael Bradshaw. Carcanet-Manchester, 2003. Introduction and editorial matter Copyright © Michael Bradshaw 2003. Reproduced by permission of Carcanet Press Limited. From "Albert and Emily, XV," in *The Works of Thomas Lovell Beddoes*. Edited with an Introduction by H. W. Donner. Oxford University Press, 1935. Reproduced by permission of Taylor & Francis Ltd. From "Leopold, VI," in *The Works of Thomas Lovell Beddoes*. Edited with an Introduction by H. W. Donner. Oxford University Press, 1935. Reproduced by permission of Taylor & Francis Ltd. From "Rain, XXXVIII.," in *The Works of Thomas Lovell Beddoes*. Edited with an Introduction by H. W. Donner. Oxford University Press, 1935. Reproduced by permission of Taylor & Francis Ltd. From "Rodolph the Wild, XV," in *The Works of Thomas Lovell Beddoes*. Edited with an Introduction by H. W. Donner. Oxford University Press, 1935. Reproduced by permission of Taylor & Francis Ltd. From "To B.W. Procter, XXIX. (7 March 1826)," in *The Works of Thomas Lovell Beddoes*. Edited with an Introduction by H. W. Donner. Oxford University Press, 1935. Reproduced by permission of Taylor & Francis Ltd.

EDMUND BLUNDEN. Blunden, Edmund. From *Poems 1930-1940*. Macmillan Company, 1940. Copyright © 1940 Estate of Mrs. Clare Blunden. Reprinted by permission of PFD (www.pfd.co.uk) on behalf of the Estate of Mrs. Claire Blunden. From *Poems of Many Years*. Collins, 1957. Copyright © Estate of Mrs. Claire Blunden 1937. Reproduced by permission of PFD (www.pfd.co.uk) on behalf of the Estate of Mrs. Claire Blunden. From *Thomas Hardy*. MacMillian and Co., Limited, 1942. Copyright © 1942 Estate of Mrs. Clare Blunden. Reprinted by permission of PFD (www.pfd.co.uk) on behalf of the Estate of Mrs. Claire Blunden. From *Undertones of War*. R. Cobden-Sanderson, 1928. Copyright © Estate of Mrs. Claire Blunden 1928. Reproduced by permission of PFD (www.pfd.co.uk) on behalf of the Estate of Mrs. Claire Blunden. From *The Waggoner and Other Poems*. Sidgwick & Jackson, Ltd., 1920. Copyright © Estate of Mrs. Clare Blunden. Reprinted by permission of PFD (www.pfd.co.uk) on behalf of the Estate of Mrs. Claire Blunden.

JOHN CLARE. Clare, John. From "What is Life? (a)," in *The Early Poems of John Clare, 1804-1822, Volume I*. Clarendon Press, 1989. Edited by Eric Robinson and David Powell. Copyright © 1989 Eric Robinson. Reproduced by permission. From "Childhood (The Midsummer Cushion) Vol. IV," in *John Clare: Poems of the Middle Period, 1822-1837, Volume III*. Clarendon Press, 1998. Edited by Eric Robinson, David Powell and P. M. S. Dawson. Copyright © 1998 Eric Robinson. Reproduced by permission. From "The Nightingales Nest, (The Midsummer Cushion) Vol. IV," in John Clare: *Poems of the Middle Period, 1822-1837, Volume III*. Edited by Eric Robinson, David Powell and P. M. S. Dawson. Clarendon Press, 1998. Copyright © 1998 Eric Robinson. Reproduced by permission.

ROBERT CRAWFORD. Crawford, Robert. From *A Scottish Assembly*. Chatto & Windus, 1990. Copyright © Robert Crawford 1990. Reprinted by permission of The Random House Group Ltd. From Masculinity. Cape Poetry, Jonathan Cape, 1996. Copyright © 1996 Robert Crawford. Reproduced by permission of Random House Group Ltd. From *Spirit Machines*. Random House, Jonathan Cape, 1999. Copyright ©

ACKNOWLEDGEMENTS

Robert Crawford, 1999. Reprinted by permission of The Random House Group Ltd. From *Sharawaggi: Poems in Scots*. Polygon, 1990. Copyright © Robert Crawford and W. N. Herbert 1990 Polygon. Reproduced by permission. From *Talkies*. Chatto & Windus, 1992. Copyright © Robert Crawford, 1992. Reprinted by permission of The Random House Group Ltd. Crawford, Robert. From *The Tip of My Tongue*. Jonathan Cape, Random House, 2003. Copyright © Robert Crawford, 2003. Reprinted by permission of The Random House Group Ltd. From "A Poet's Epitah," in *W. H. Davies Selected Poems*. Edited by Jonathan Barker. Oxford University Press, 1985. Introduction, Chronology, and Selection Copyright © Jonathan Barker, 1985. Reproduced by permission of the Literary Estate of the author.

W. H. DAVIES. Davies, W. H. From *The Complete Poems of W. H. Davies*. Edited by with an Introduction by Osbert Sitwell and a Forward by Daniel George. Jonathan Cape Limited, 1963. Copyright © 1963 Jonathan Cape Limited. Reproduced by permission of the Literary Estate of the author.

FULKE GREVILLE. Greville, Fulke. From "Caelica-Section I," in *Selected Writings of Fulke Greville*. Edited by Joan Rees. University of London-The Athlone Press, 1973. Copyright © 1973 by Joan Rees. Reproduced by permission of The Continuum International Publishing Group. From "Caelica-Section 3," in *Selected Writings of Fulke Greville*. Edited by Joan Rees. University of London-The Athlone Press, 1973. Copyright © 1973 by Joan Rees. Reproduced by permission of The Continuum International Publishing Group. From "The Life of Sir Philip Sidney," in *Selected Writings of Fulke Greville*. Edited by Joan Rees. University of London-The Athlone Press, 1973. Copyright © 1973 by Joan Rees. Reproduced by permission of The Continuum International Publishing Group. Winters, Yvor. From *Forms of Discovery*. Alan Swallow, 1967. Copyright © 1967 by Yvor Winters. Reproduced by permission.

KEVIN HART. Hart, Kevin. From *The Departure*. University of Queensland Press, 1978. Copyright © Kevin Hart, 1978. Reproduced by permission of the author. From *Flame Tree: Selected Poems*. Bloodaxe Books, 2002. Copyright © Kevin Hart 2002. Reproduced by permission of the author. From *The Lines of the Hand*. Angus & Robertson Publishers, 1981. Copyright © 1981 by Kevin Hart. Reproduced by permission of the author.

SARA MAITLAND. Maitland, Sara. From "A Feminist Writer's Progress," in *On Gender and Writing*. Edited by Michelene Wandor. Pandora Press, 1983. Selection, editorial matter and nos 1 and 20 Copyright © Michelene Wandor 1983; no. 3 © Sara Maitland 1983. Reprinted by permission of HarperCollins Publishers Ltd.

PHILIP MASSINGER. Massinger, Philip. From "Act 1. Scene I," in *A New Way to Pay Old Debts*. Edited by T. W. Craik. Ernest Benn Limited, 1964. Copyright © Ernest Benn Limited, 1964. Reproduced by permission of A & C Black Publishers Ltd. From "Act I, Scene 2," in *The City-Madam*. Edited by T. W. Craik. Ernest Benn Limited, 1964. Copyright © Ernest Benn Limited 1964. Reproduced by permission of A & C Black Publishers Ltd. From "Act III, Scene 2," in *The City-Madam*. Edited by T. W. Craik. Ernest Benn Limited, 1964. Copyright © Ernest Benn Limited 1964. Reproduced by permission of A & C Black Publishers Ltd. *ELH (English Literary History)* , v. 68, 2001. Copyright © 2001 The Johns Hopkins University Press. Reproduced by permission.

REDMOND O'HANLON. O'Hanlon, Redmond. From *In Trouble Again: A Journey Between the Orinoco and the Amazon*. Hamish Hamilton, 1988. Copyright © 1988 by Redmond O'Hanlon. Reprinted by permission of PFD on behalf of Redmond O'Hanlon.

WILLIAM PLOMER. Plomer, William. From *The Collected Poems of William Plomer*. Jonathan Cape, 1973. This Collection © 1973 by William Plomer. Reproduced by permission of The Random House Group Ltd.

JONATHAN RABAN. Raban, Jonathan. From *Coasting*. Simon & Schuster, 1987. Copyright © 1987 by Foreign Land Ltd. Reproduced by permission of the author.

C. H. SISSON. Sisson, C. H. From *Anglican Essays*. Carcanet-Manchester, 1983. Copyright © 1983 by C. H.Sisson. Reproduced by permission of Carcanet Press Ltd. and in the United Kingdom by Pollinger Limited and the proprietor. From "A Four Letter Word," in *The Avoidance of Literature: Collected Essays*. Edited by Michael Schmidt. Carcanet-Manchester, 1978. Copyright © C. H. Sisson 1978. Reproduced by permission of Carcanet Press Limited. From "Autobiographical Reflections on Politics, (unpublished, January 1954)," in *The Avoidance of Literature: Collected Essays*. Edited by Michael Schmidt. Carcanet-Manchester, 1978. Copyright © C. H. Sisson 1978. Reproduced by permission of Carcanet Press Limited. From "Charles Peguy (14 November 1946)," in *The Avoidance of Literature: Collected Essays*. Edited by Michael Schmidt. Carcanet-Manchester, 1978. Copyright © C. H. Sisson 1978. Reproduced by permission of Carcanet Press Limited. From "Henry Vaughan The Silurist," in *The Avoidance of Literature: Collected*

ACKNOWLEDGEMENTS

Essays. Edited by Michael Schmidt. Carcanet-Manchester, 1978. Copyright © C. H. Sisson 1978. Reproduced by permission of Carcanet Press Limited. From "Natural History," in *The Avoidance of Literature: Collected Essays*. Edited by Michael Schmidt. Carcanet-Manchester, 1978. Copyright © C. H. Sisson, 1978. Reproduced by permission of Carcanet Press Limited. From "Sevenoaks Essays," in *The Avoidance of Literature: Collected Essays*. Edited by Michael Schmidt. Carcanet-Manchester, 1978. Copyright © C. H. Sisson 1978. Reproduced by permission of Carcanet Press Limited. From *Collected Poems, 1943-1983*. Carcanet-Manchester, 1984. Copyright © C. H. Sisson 1959, 1960, 1961, 1965, 1967, 1968, 1974, 1976, 1980, 1983, 1984. Reproduced by permission of Carcanet Press Limited. From *In the Trojan Ditch: Collected Poems & Selected Translations*. Carcanet-Manchester, 1974. Copyright © C. H. Sisson 1974. Reproduced by permission of Carcanet Press Limited.

THOMAS TRAHERNE. Traherne, Thomas. From an appendix to *Christian Ethicks*. Edited by Carol L. Marks and George Robert Guffey. Cornell University Press, 1968. Translation Copyright © 1968 by Cornell University. Used by permission of the publisher, Cornell University Press. From "Adam," in *Thomas Traherne: Poems, Centuries and Three Thanksgivings*. Edited by Anne Ridler. Oxford University Press, 1966. Reproduced by permission of The British Library. X25/0637 DSC. From "An Infant-Ey," in *Thomas Traherne: Poems, Centuries and Three Thanksgivings*. Edited by Anne Ridler. Oxford University Press, 1966. Reproduced by permission of The British Library. X25/0637 DSC. From "The Apprehension," in *Thomas Traherne: Poems, Centuries and Three Thanksgivings*. Edited by Anne Riddler. Oxford University Press, 1966. Reproduced by permission of The British Library. X25/0637 DSC. From "Dumnesse," in *Thomas Traherne: Poems, Centuries and Three Thanksgivings*. Edited by Ann Riddler. Oxford University Press, 1966. Reproduced by permission of The British Library. X25/0637 DSC. From "The Enquirie," in *Thomas Traherne: Poems, Centuries and Three Thanksgivings*. Edited by Anne Ridler. Oxford University Press, 1966. Reproduced by permission of The British Library. X25/0637 DSC. From "The Improvement," in *Thomas Traherne: Poems, Centuries and Three Thanksgivings*. Edited by Anne Ridler. Oxford University Press, 1966. Reproduced by permission of The British Library. X25/0637 DSC. From "My Spirit," in *Thomas Traherne: Poems, Centuries and Three Thanksgivings*. Edited by Anne Ridler. Oxford University Press, 1966. Reproduced by permission of The British Library. X25/0637 DSC. From "The Person," in *Thomas Traherne: Poems, Centuries and Three Thanksgivings*. Edited by Anne Ridler. Oxford University Press, 1966. Reproduced by permission of The British Library. X25/0637 DSC. From "Poems from the Church's Year Book," in *Thomas Traherne: Poems, Centuries and Three Thanksgivings*. Edited by Anne Ridler. Oxford University Press, 1966. Reproduced by permission of the Bodleian Library, University of Oxford. From "The Review," in *Thomas Traherne: Poems, Centuries and Three Thanksgivings*. Edited by Anne Ridler. Oxford University Press, 1966. Reproduced by permission of The British Library. X25/0637 DSC. From "The Right Apprehension," in *Thomas Traherne: Poems, Centuries and Three Thanksgivings*. Edited by Anne Ridler. Oxford University Press, 1966. Reproduced by permission of The British Library. X25/0637 DSC. From "Sight," in *Thomas Traherne: Poems, Centuries and Three Thanksgivings*. Edited by Anne Ridler. Oxford University Press, 1966. Reproduced by permission of The British Library. X25/0637 DSC. From "The Third Century," in *Thomas Traherne: Poems, Centuries and Three Thanksgivings*. Edited by Anne Ridler. Oxford University Press, 1966. Reproduced by permission of the Bodleian Library, University of Oxford. From "The World," in *Thomas Traherne: Poems, Centuries and Three Thanksgivings*. Edited by Anne Ridler. Oxford University Press, 1966. Reproduced by permission of The British Library. X25/0637 DSC. Martz, Louis L. From *The Paradise Within*. Yale University Press, 1964. Copyright © 1964 by Yale University. Reproduced by permission. From "Poems from the Church's Year Book," in *Thomas Traherne: Poems, Centuries and Three Thanksgivings*. Edited by Anne Ridler. Oxford University Press, 1966. Reproduced by permission of the Bodleian Library, University of Oxford. MS. Eng. th. e. 51. From "The Third Century," in *Thomas Traherne: Poems, Centuries and Three Thanksgivings*. Edited by Anne Ridler. Oxford University Press, 1966. Reproduced by permission of the Bodleian Library, University of Oxford. MS. Eng. th. e. 50.

ALAN WARNER. Warner, Alan. From *Morvern Callar*. Anchor Books, 1997. Copyright © 1997 by Alan Warner. Used by permission of Doubleday, a division of Random House, Inc. From *The Sopranos*. Farrar, Straus, and Giroux, 1998. Copyright © 1998 by Alan Warner. Reprinted by permission of the Random House Group Ltd. and in the U. S. by Farrar, Strauss and Giroux, LLC.

Contents

Introduction

"Books must be read as deliberately and reservedly as they are written," wrote Henry David Thoreau in the chapter of *Walden* called "Reading." The essays in this volume of *British Writers* consider a wide range of well–known authors–poets, novelists, travel writers, essayists—each of whom repays deliberate reading. In Supplement XI we present detailed introductions to eighteen writers, mostly contemporary, although a few of them reach back to the sixteenth and seventeenth centuries. In each case the articles have been written in a way designed to enhance the reading of the work of each subject, and to make the shape of his or her career, its evolution and influence, accessible to general readers.

As a whole, this series brings together a wide range of articles on British writers (or postcolonial writers in the British tradition, including writers from such countries as Australia, New Zealand, India, and South Africa) who have achieved a considerable reputation in the literary world. As in previous volumes, the subjects have been chosen for their significant work in the literary arts (defined broadly to include popular as well as literary fiction, essayists, travel writers, and critics). Each writer included has influenced intellectual life in the English–speaking world in some way. Readers should find these essays lively and intelligent, written to interest readers unfamiliar with their work and to assist those who know the work quite well by providing close readings of individual texts and a sense of the biographical, cultural, and critical context of that work. Detailed bibliographies of work by the given subject and work about this writer are included.

British Writers was originally an off–shoot of a series of monographs that appeared between 1959 and 1972, the Minnesota Pamphlets on American Writers. These pamphlets were incisively written and informative, treating ninety–seven American writers in a format and style that attracted a devoted following of readers. The series proved invaluable to a generation of students and teachers, who could depend on these reliable and interesting critiques of major figures. The idea of reprinting these essays occurred to Charles Scribner, Jr., an innovative publisher during the middle decades of the twentieth century. The series appeared in four volumes entitled *American Writers: A Collection of Literary Biographies* (1974). *British Writers* began with a series of essays originally published by the British Council, and regular supplements have followed. The goal of the supplements has been consistent with the original idea of the series: to provide clear, informative essays aimed at the general reader. These essays often rise to a high level of craft and critical vision, but they are meant to introduce a writer of some importance in the history of British or Anglophone literature, and to provide a sense of the scope and nature of the career under review.

These essays have been written by critics of considerable experience. Most have published books and articles in their field, and several are well–known writers of poetry or fiction as well as criticism. As anyone glancing through this collection will see, these critics have been held to the highest standards of clear writing and sound scholarship. Jargon and theoretical musings have been discouraged, except when strictly relevant. Each of the essays concludes with a select bibliography of works by the author under discussion and secondary works that might be useful to those who wish to pursue the subject further. The essays in supplement XI often treat modern or contemporary writers from various genres and traditions, several of whom have had little sustained attention from critics, although most are well known. Iain Banks, Edmund Blunden, Robert Crawford, W.H. Davies, Kevin Hart, Elizabeth Jane Howard, Hanif Kureishi, Sara Maitland, Redmond O'Hanlon, William Plomer, Jonathan Raban, C.H. Sisson, and Alan Warner have all been discussed in the review pages of newspapers and magazines, often at considerable length, and their work has acquired a substantial following, but their careers have yet to attract

INTRODUCTION

significant scholarship. That will certainly follow, but the essays included in this volume constitute a beginning of sorts, an attempt to map out the particular universe of each writer.

A few writers from the distant past included here are Thomas Lovell Beddoes, John Clare, Fulke Greville, Philip Massinger, and Thomas Traherne. In each case, these are important authors who, for one reason or another, have yet to be treated in previous volumes. It is time they were added to the series.

As ever, our purpose in these presenting these critical and biographical essays is to bring read-ers back to the texts discussed, to help them in their reading, to make it more deliberate, more "reserved," as Thoreau wrote. Readers should fine a good deal to help them in these essays, which will enable students and general readers to enter into the world of these writers with fresh insights and useful information. They should help readers to appreciate the way things are said by these authors, thus enhancing their pleasure in the texts.

—*JAY PARINI*

Chronology

ca. 1342	John Trevisa born
1348	The Black Death (further outbreaks in 1361 and 1369)
ca. 1350	Boccaccio's *Decameron* Langland's *Piers Plowman*
1351	The Statute of Laborers pegs laborers' wages at rates in effect preceding the plague
1356	The Battle of Poitiers
1360	The Treaty of Brétigny: end of the first phase of the Hundred Years' War
1362	Pleadings in the law courts conducted in English Parliaments opened by speeches in English
1369	Chaucer's *The Book of the Duchess*, an elegy to Blanche of Lancaster, wife of John of Gaunt
1369–1377	Victorious French campaigns under du Guesclin
ca. 1370	John Lydgate born
1371	Sir John Mandeville's *Travels*
1372	Chaucer travels to Italy
1372–1382	Wycliffe active in Oxford
1373–1393	William of Wykeham founds Winchester College and New College, Oxford
ca. 1375–1400	*Sir Gawain and the Green Knight*
1376	Death of Edward the Black Prince
1377–1399	**Reign of Richard II**
ca. 1379	Gower's *Vox clamantis*
ca. 1380	Chaucer's *Troilus and Criseyde*
1381	The Peasants' Revolt
1386	Chaucer's *Canterbury Tales* begun Chaucer sits in Parliament Gower's *Confessio amantis*
1399–1413	**Reign of Henry IV**
ca. 1400	Death of William Langland
1400	Death of Geoffrey Chaucer
1408	Death of John Gower
1412–1420	Lydgate's *Troy Book*
1413–1422	**Reign of Henry V**
1415	The Battle of Agincourt
1420–1422	Lydgate's *Siege of Thebes*
1422–1461	**Reign of Henry VI**
1431	François Villon born Joan of Arc burned at Rouen
1440–1441	Henry VI founds Eton College and King's College, Cambridge
1444	Truce of Tours
1450	Jack Cade's rebellion
ca. 1451	Death of John Lydgate
1453	End of the Hundred Years' War The fall of Constantinople
1455–1485	The Wars of the Roses
ca. 1460	Births of William Dunbar and John Skelton
1461–1470	**Reign of Edward IV**
1470–1471	**Reign of Henry VI**
1471	Death of Sir Thomas Malory
1471–1483	**Reign of Edward IV**
1476–1483	Caxton's press set up: *The Canterbury Tales, Morte d'Arthur,* and *The Golden Legend* printed
1483–1485	**Reign of Richard III**
1485	The Battle of Bosworth Field; end of the Wars of the Roses
1485–1509	**Reign of Henry VII**
1486	Marriage of Henry VII and Elizabeth of York unites the rival houses of Lancaster and York Bartholomew Diaz rounds the Cape of Good Hope
1492	Columbus' first voyage to the New World
1493	Pope Alexander VI divides undiscovered territories between Spain and Portugal
1497–1498	John Cabot's voyages to Newfoundland and Labrador
1497–1499	Vasco da Gama's voyage to India
1499	Amerigo Vespucci's first voyage to America Erasmus' first visit to England
1503	Thomas Wyatt born

CHRONOLOGY

CHRONOLOGY

1564 Births of Christopher Marlowe and William Shakespeare

1565 Mary Queen of Scots marries Lord Darnley

1566 William Painter's *Palace of Pleasure*, a miscellany of prose stories, the source of many dramatists' plots

1567 Darnley murdered at Kirk o'Field
Mary Queen of Scots marries the earl of Bothwell

1569 Rebellion of the English northern earls suppressed

1570 Roger Ascham's *The Schoolmaster*

1571 Defeat of the Turkish fleet at Lepanto

ca. 1572 Ben Jonson born

1572 St. Bartholomew's Day massacre
John Donne born

1574 The earl of Leicester's theater company formed

1576 The Theater, the first permanent theater building in London, opened
The first Blackfriars Theater opened with performances by the Children of St. Paul's
John Marston born

1576–1578 Martin Frobisher's voyages to Labrador and the northwest

1577–1580 Sir Francis Drake sails around the world

1577 Holinshed's *Chronicles of England, Scotlande, and Irelande*

1579 John Lyly's *Euphues: The Anatomy of Wit*
Thomas North's translation of *Plutarch's Lives*

1581 The Levant Company founded
Seneca's *Ten Tragedies* translated

1582 Richard Hakluyt's *Divers Voyages Touching the Discoverie of America*

1583 Philip Massinger born

1584–1585 Sir John Davis' first voyage to Greenland

1585 First English settlement in America, the "Lost Colony" comprising 108 men under Ralph Lane, founded at Roanoke Island, off the coast of North Carolina

1586 Kyd's *Spanish Tragedy*
Marlowe's *Tamburlaine*
William Camden's *Britannia*
The Babington conspiracy against Queen Elizabeth
Death of Sir Philip Sidney

1587 Mary Queen of Scots executed
Birth of Virginia Dare, first English child born in America, at Roanoke Island

1588 Defeat of the Spanish Armada
Marlowe's *Dr. Faustus*

1590 Spenser's *The Faerie Queen*, Cantos 1–3
Richard Brome born

1592 Outbreak of plague in London; the theaters closed
Henry King born

1593 Death of Christopher Marlowe

1594 The Lord Chamberlain's Men, the company to which Shakespeare belonged, founded
The Swan Theater opened
Death of Thomas Kyd

1595 Ralegh's expedition to Guiana
Sidney's *Apology for Poetry*

1596 The earl of Essex's expedition captures Cadiz
The second Blackfriars Theater opened

ca. 1597 Death of George Peele

1597 Bacon's first collection of *Essays*

1598 Jonson's *Every Man in His Humor*

1598–1600 Richard Hakluyt's *Principal Navigations, Voyages, Traffics, and Discoveries of the English Nation*

1599 The Globe Theater opened
Death of Edmund Spenser

1600 Death of Richard Hooker

1601 Rebellion and execution of the earl of Essex

1602 The East India Company founded
The Bodleian Library reopened at Oxford

1603–1625 Reign of James I

1603 John Florio's translation of Montaigne's *Essays*
Cervantes' *Don Quixote* (Part 1)
The Gunpowder Plot
Thomas Browne born

1604 Shakespeare's *Othello*

ca. 1605 Shakespears's *King Lear*
Tourneur's *The Revenger's Tragedy*

1605 Bacon's *Advancement of Learning*

1606 Shakespeare's *Macbeth*
Jonson's *Volpone*

xv

CHRONOLOGY

Death of John Lyly
Edmund Waller born

1607 The first permanent English colony established at Jamestown, Virginia

1608 John Milton born

1609 Kepler's *Astronomia nova*
John Suckling born

1610 Galileo's *Sidereus nuncius*

1611 The Authorized Version of the Bible
Shakespeare's *The Tempest*

1612 Death of Prince Henry, King James's eldest son
Webster's *The White Devil*
Bacon's second collection of *Essays*

ca. 1613 Richard Crashaw born

1613 The Globe Theatre destroyed by fire
Webster's *The Duchess of Malfi*

1614 Ralegh's *History of the World*

1616 George Chapman's translation of Homer's *Odyssey*
Deaths of William Shakespeare, Francis Beaumont, and Miguel Cervantes

ca. 1618 Richard Lovelace born

1618 The Thirty Years' War begins
Sir Walter Ralegh executed
Abraham Cowley born

1619 The General Assembly, the first legislative assembly on American soil, meets in Virginia
Slavery introduced at Jamestown

1620 The Pilgrims land in Massachusetts
John Evelyn born

1621 Francis Bacon impeached and fined
Robert Burton's *Anatomy of Melancholy*
Andrew Marvell born

1622 Middleton's *The Changeling*
Henry Vaughan born

1623 The First Folio of Shakespeare's plays
Visit of Prince Charles and the duke of Buckingham to Spain; failure of attempts to negotiate a Spanish marriage

1624 War against Spain

1625–1649 Reign of Charles I

1625 Death of John Fletcher
Bacon's last collection of *Essays*

1626 Bacon's *New Atlantis*, appended to *Sylva sylvarum*

Dutch found New Amsterdam
Death of Cyril Tourneur
Death of Francis Bacon

1627 Ford's *'Tis Pity She's a Whore*
Cardinal Richelieu establishes the Company of New France with monopoly over trade and land in Canada
Buckingham's expedition to the Isle of Ré to relieve La Rochelle
Death of Thomas Middleton

1627–1628 Revolt and siege of La Rochelle, the principal Huguenot city of France

1628 Buckingham assassinated
Surrender of La Rochelle
William Harvey's treatise on the circulation of the blood (*De motu cordis et sanguinis*)
John Bunyan born
Death of Fulke Greville

1629 Ford's *The Broken Heart*
King Charles dismisses his third Parliament, imprisons nine members, and proceeds to rule for eleven years without Parliament
The Massachusetts Bay Company formed

1629–1630 Peace treaties with France and Spain

1631 John Dryden born
Death of John Donne

1633 William Laud appointed archbishop of Canterbury
Death of George Herbert
Samuel Pepys born

1634 Deaths of George Chapman and John Marston

1635 The Académie Française founded
George Etherege born

1636 Pierre Corneille's *Le Cid*
Harvard College founded

ca. 1637 **Thomas Traherne born**

1637 Milton's "Lycidas"
Descartes's *Discours de la méthode*
King Charles's levy of ship money challenged in the courts by John Hampden
The introduction of the new English Book of Common Prayer strongly opposed in Scotland
Death of Ben Jonson

xvi

CHRONOLOGY

CHRONOLOGY

War against Spain

1655　Parliament attempts to reduce the army and is dissolved

Rule of the major-generals

1656　Sir William Davenant produces *The Siege of Rhodes*, one of the first English operas

1657　Second Parliament of the Protectorate

Cromwell is offered and declines the throne

Death of Richard Lovelace

1658　Death of Oliver Cromwell

Richard Cromwell succeeds as Protector

1659　Conflict between Parliament and the army

1660　General Monck negotiates with Charles II

Charles II offers the conciliatory Declaration of Breda and accepts Parliament's invitation to return

Will's Coffee House established

Sir William Davenant and Thomas Killigrew licensed to set up two companies of players, the Duke of York's and the King's Servants, including actors and actresses

Pepys's *Diary* begun

1660–1685　Reign of Charles II

1661　Parliament passes the Act of Uniformity, enjoining the use of the Book of Common Prayer; many Puritan and dissenting clergy leave their livings

Anne Finch born

1662　Peace Treaty with Spain

King Charles II marries Catherine of Braganza

The Royal Society incorporated (founded in 1660)

1664　War against Holland

New Amsterdam captured and becomes New York

John Vanbrugh born

1665　The Great Plague

Newton discovers the binomial theorem and invents the integral and differential calculus, at Cambridge

1666　The Great Fire of London

Bunyan's *Grace Abounding*

London Gazette founded

1667　The Dutch fleet sails up the Medway and burns English ships

The war with Holland ended by the Treaty of Breda

Milton's *Paradise Lost*

Thomas Sprat's *History of the Royal Society*

Death of Abraham Cowley

1668　Sir Christopher Wren begins to rebuild St. Paul's Cathedral

Triple Alliance formed with Holland and Sweden against France

Dryden's *Essay of Dramatick Poesy*

1670　Alliance formed with France through the secret Treaty of Dover

Pascal's *Pensées*

The Hudson's Bay Company founded

William Congreve born

1671　Milton's *Samson Agonistes* and *Paradise Regained*

1672　War against Holland

Wycherley's *The Country Wife*

King Charles issues the Declaration of Indulgence, suspending penal laws against Nonconformists and Catholics

1673　Parliament passes the Test Act, making acceptance of the doctrines of the Church of England a condition for holding public office

1674　War with Holland ended by the Treaty of Westminster

Deaths of John Milton, Robert Herrick, and **Thomas Traherne**

1676　Etherege's *The Man of Mode*

1677　Baruch Spinoza's *Ethics*

Jean Racine's *Phèdre*

King Charles's niece, Mary, marries her cousin William of Orange

1678　Fabrication of the so-called popish plot by Titus Oates

Bunyan's *Pilgrim's Progress*

Dryden's *All for Love*

Death of Andrew Marvell

George Farquhar born

1679　Parliament passes the Habeas Corpus Act

Rochester's *A Satire Against Mankind*

CHRONOLOGY

1680 Death of John Wilmot, earl of Rochester

1681 Dryden's *Absalom and Achitophel* (Part 1)

1682 Dryden's *Absalom and Achitophel* (Part 2)
Thomas Otway's *Venice Preserv'd*
Philadelphia founded
Death of Sir Thomas Browne

1683 The Ashmolean Museum, the world's first public museum, opens at Oxford
Death of Izaak Walton

1685–1688   Reign of James II

1685 Rebellion and execution of James Scott, duke of Monmouth
John Gay born

1686 The first book of Newton's *Principia—De motu corporum*, containing his theory of gravitation presented to the Royal Society

1687 James II issues the Declaration of Indulgence
Dryden's *The Hind and the Panther*
Death of Edmund Waller

1688 James II reissues the Declaration of Indulgence, renewing freedom of worship and suspending the provisions of the Test Act
Acquittal of the seven bishops imprisoned for protesting against the Declaration
William of Orange lands at Torbay, Devon
James II takes refuge in France
Death of John Bunyan
Alexander Pope born

1689–1702   Reign of William III

1689 Parliament formulates the Declaration of Rights
William and Mary accept the Declaration and the crown
The Grand Alliance concluded between the Holy Roman Empire, England, Holland, and Spain
War declared against France
King William's War, 1689–1697 (the first of the French and Indian wars)
Samuel Richardson born

1690 James II lands in Ireland with French support, but is defeated at the battle of the Boyne
John Locke's *Essay Concerning Human Understanding*

1692 Salem witchcraft trials
Death of Sir George Etherege

1694 George Fox's *Journal*
Voltaire (François Marie Arouet) born
Death of Mary II

1695 Congreve's *Love for Love*
Death of Henry Vaughan

1697 War with France ended by the Treaty of Ryswick
Vanbrugh's *The Relapse*

1698 Jeremy Collier's *A Short View of the Immorality and Profaneness of the English Stage*

1699 Fénelon's *Les Aventures de Télémaque*

1700 Congreve's *The Way of the World*
Defoe's *The True-Born Englishman*
Death of John Dryden
James Thomson born

1701 War of the Spanish Succession, 1701–1714 (Queen Anne's War in America, 1702–1713)
Death of Sir Charles Sedley

1702–1714   Reign of Queen Anne

1702 Clarendon's *History of the Rebellion* (1702–1704)
Defoe's *The Shortest Way with the Dissenters*

1703 Defoe is arrested, fined, and pilloried for writing *The Shortest Way*
Death of Samuel Pepys

1704 John Churchill, duke of Marlborough, and Prince Eugene of Savoy defeat the French at Blenheim
Capture of Gibraltar
Swift's *A Tale of a Tub* and *The Battle of the Books*
The Review founded (1704–1713)

1706 Farquhar's *The Recruiting Officer*
Deaths of John Evelyn and Charles Sackville, earl of Dorset

1707 Farquhar's *The Beaux' Stratagem*
Act of Union joining England and Scotland
Death of George Farquhar
Henry Fielding born

1709 The *Tatler* founded (1709–1711)

CHRONOLOGY

Nicholas Rowe's edition of Shakespeare

Samuel Johnson born

Marlborough defeats the French at Malplaquet

Charles XII of Sweden defeated at Poltava

1710 South Sea Company founded
First copyright act

1711 Swift's *The Conduct of the Allies*
The *Spectator* founded (1711–1712; 1714)
Marlborough dismissed
David Hume born

1712 Pope's *The Rape of the Lock* (Cantos 1–2)
Jean Jacques Rousseau born

1713 War with France ended by the Treaty of Utrecht
The *Guardian* founded
Swift becomes dean of St. Patrick's, Dublin
Addison's *Cato*
Laurence Sterne born

1714–1727 Reign of George I
1714 Pope's expended version of *The Rape of the Lock* (Cantos 1–5)

1715 The Jacobite rebellion in Scotland
Pope's translation of Homer's *Iliad* (1715–1720)
Death of Louis XIV

1716 Death of William Wycherley
Thomas Gray born

1717 Pope's *Eloisa to Abelard*
David Garrick born
Horace Walpole born

1718 Quadruple Alliance (Britain, France, the Netherlands, the German Empire) in war against Spain

1719 Defoe's *Robinson Crusoe*
Death of Joseph Addison

1720 Inoculation against smallpox introduced in Boston
War against Spain
The South Sea Bubble
Gilbert White born
Defoe's *Captain Singleton* and *Memoirs of a Cavalier*

1721 Tobias Smollett born
William Collins born

1722 Defoe's *Moll Flanders*, *Journal of the Plague Year*, and *Colonel Jack*

1724 Defoe's *Roxana*
Swift's *The Drapier's Letters*

1725 Pope's translation of Homer's *Odyssey* (1725–1726)

1726 Swift's *Gulliver's Travels*
Voltaire in England (1726–1729)
Death of Sir John Vanbrugh

1727–1760 Reign of George II
1728 Gay's *The Beggar's Opera*
Pope's *The Dunciad* (Books 1–2)
Oliver Goldsmith born

1729 Swift's *A Modest Proposal*
Edmund Burke born
Deaths of William Congreve and Sir Richard Steele

1731 Navigation improved by introduction of the quadrant
Pope's *Moral Essays* (1731–1735)
Death of Daniel Defoe
William Cowper born

1732 Death of John Gay

1733 Pope's *Essay on Man* (1733–1734)
Lewis Theobald's edition of Shakespeare

1734 Voltaire's *Lettres philosophiques*

1736 James Macpherson born

1737 Edward Gibbon born

1738 Johnson's *London*

1740 War of the Austrian Succession, 1740–1748 (King George's War in America, 1744–1748)
George Anson begins his circumnavigation of the world (1740–1744)
Frederick the Great becomes king of Prussia (1740–1786)
Richardson's *Pamela* (1740–1741)
James Boswell born

1742 Fielding's *Joseph Andrews*
Edward Young's *Night Thoughts* (1742–1745)
Pope's *The New Dunciad* (Book 4)

1744 Johnson's *Life of Mr. Richard Savage*
Death of Alexander Pope

1745 Second Jacobite rebellion, led by Charles Edward, the Young Pretender
Death of Jonathan Swift

1746 The Young Pretender defeated at Culloden

CHRONOLOGY

Collins' *Odes on Several Descriptive and Allegorical Subjects*

1747 Richardson's *Clarissa Harlowe* (1747–1748)
Franklin's experiments with electricity announced
Voltaire's *Essai sur les moeurs*

1748 War of the Austrian Succession ended by the Peace of Aix-la-Chapelle
Smollett's *Adventures of Roderick Random*
David Hume's *Enquiry Concerning Human Understanding*
Montesquieu's *L'Esprit des lois*

1749 Fielding's *Tom Jones*
Johnson's *The Vanity of Human Wishes*
Bolingbroke's *Idea of a Patriot King*

1750 The *Rambler* founded (1750–1752)

1751 Gray's *Elegy Written in a Country Churchyard*
Fielding's *Amelia*
Smollett's *Adventures of Peregrine Pickle*
Denis Diderot and Jean le Rond d'Alembert begin to publish the *Encyclopédie* (1751–1765)
Richard Brinsley Sheridan born

1752 Frances Burney and Thomas Chatterton born

1753 Richardson's *History of Sir Charles Grandison* (1753–1754)
Smollett's *The Adventures of Ferdinand Count Fathom*

1754 Hume's *History of England* (1754–1762)
Death of Henry Fielding
George Crabbe born

1755 Lisbon destroyed by earthquake
Fielding's *Journal of a Voyage to Lisbon* published posthumously
Johnson's *Dictionary of the English Language*

1756 The Seven Years' War against France, 1756–1763 (the French and Indian War in America, 1755–1760)
William Pitt the elder becomes prime minister
Johnson's proposal for an edition of Shakespeare

1757 Robert Clive wins the battle of Plassey, in India
Gray's "The Progress of Poesy" and "The Bard"
Burke's *Philosophical Enquiry into the Origin of Our Ideas of the Sublime and Beautiful*
Hume's *Natural History of Religion*
William Blake born

1758 The *Idler* founded (1758–1760)

1759 Capture of Quebec by General James Wolfe
Johnson's *History of Rasselas, Prince of Abyssinia*
Voltaire's *Candide*
The British Museum opens
Sterne's *The Life and Opinions of Tristram Shandy* (1759–1767)
Death of William Collins
Mary Wollstonecraft born
Robert Burns born

1760–1820 Reign of George III

1760 James Macpherson's *Fragments of Ancient Poetry Collected in the Highlands of Scotland*
William Beckford born

1761 Jean-Jacques Rousseau's *Julie, ou la nouvelle Héloïse*
Death of Samuel Richardson

1762 Rousseau's *Du Contrat social* and *Émile*
Catherine the Great becomes czarina of Russia (1762–1796)

1763 The Seven Years' War ended by the Peace of Paris
Smart's *A Song to David*

1764 James Hargreaves invents the spinning jenny

1765 Parliament passes the Stamp Act to tax the American colonies
Johnson's edition of Shakespeare
Walpole's *The Castle of Otranto*
Thomas Percy's *Reliques of Ancient English Poetry*
Blackstone's *Commentaries on the Laws of England* (1765–1769)

1766 The Stamp Act repealed
Swift's *Journal to Stella* first published in a collection of his letters
Goldsmith's *The Vicar of Wakefield*
Smollett's *Travels Through France and Italy*

xxi

CHRONOLOGY

Lessing's *Laokoon*

Rousseau in England (1766–1767)

1768 Sterne's *A Sentimental Journey Through France and Italy*

The Royal Academy founded by George III

First edition of the *Encyclopaedia Britannica*

Maria Edgeworth born

Death of Laurence Sterne

1769 David Garrick organizes the Shakespeare Jubilee at Stratford-upon-Avon

Sir Joshua Reynolds' *Discourses* (1769–1790)

Richard Arkwright invents the spinning water frame

1770 Boston Massacre

Burke's *Thoughts on the Cause of the Present Discontents*

Oliver Goldsmith's *The Deserted Village*

Death of Thomas Chatterton

William Wordsworth born

James Hogg born

1771 Arkwright's first spinning mill founded

Deaths of Thomas Gray and Tobias Smollett

Walter Scott born

1772 Samuel Taylor Coleridge born

1773 Boston Tea Party

Goldsmith's *She Stoops to Conquer*

Johann Wolfgang von Goethe's *Götz von Berlichingen*

1774 The first Continental Congress meets in Philadelphia

Goethe's *Sorrows of Young Werther*

Death of Oliver Goldsmith

Robert Southey born

1775 Burke's speech on American taxation

American War of Independence begins with the battles of Lexington and Concord

Samuel Johnson's *Journey to the Western Islands of Scotland*

Richard Brinsley Sheridan's *The Rivals* and *The Duenna*

Beaumarchais's *Le Barbier de Séville*

James Watt and Matthew Boulton begin building steam engines in England

Births of Jane Austen, Charles Lamb, Walter Savage Landor, and Matthew Lewis

1776 American Declaration of Independence

Edward Gibbon's *Decline and Fall of the Roman Empire* (1776–1788)

Adam Smith's *Inquiry into the Nature & Causes of the Wealth of Nations*

Thomas Paine's *Common Sense*

Death of David Hume

1777 Maurice Morgann's *Essay on the Dramatic Character of Sir John Falstaff*

Sheridan's *The School for Scandal* first performed (published 1780)

General Burgoyne surrenders at Saratoga

1778 The American colonies allied with France

Britain and France at war

Captain James Cook discovers Hawaii

Death of William Pitt, first earl of Chatham

Deaths of Jean Jacques Rousseau and Voltaire

William Hazlitt born

1779 Johnson's *Prefaces to the Works of the English Poets* (1779–1781); reissued in 1781 as *The Lives of the Most Eminent English Poets*

Sheridan's *The Critic*

Samuel Crompton invents the spinning mule

Death of David Garrick

1780 The Gordon Riots in London

Charles Robert Maturin born

1781 Charles Cornwallis surrenders at Yorktown

Immanuel Kant's *Critique of Pure Reason*

Friedrich von Schiller's *Die Räuber*

1782 William Cowper's "The Journey of John Gilpin" published in the *Public Advertiser*

Choderlos de Laclos's *Les Liaisons dangereuses*

CHRONOLOGY

CHRONOLOGY

1793 Trial and execution of Louis XVI and Marie-Antoinette
France declares war against England
The Committee of Public Safety (Comité de Salut Public) established
Eli Whitney devises the cotton gin
William Godwin's *An Enquiry Concerning Political Justice*
Blake's *Visions of the Daughters of Albion and America*
Wordsworth's *An Evening Walk* and *Descriptive Sketches*
John Clare born

1794 Execution of Georges Danton and Maximilien de Robespierre
Paine's *The Age of Reason* (1794–1796)
Blake's *Songs of Experience*
Ann Radcliffe's *The Mysteries of Udolpho*
Death of Edward Gibbon

1795 The government of the Directory established (1795–1799)
Hastings acquitted
Landor's *Poems*
Death of James Boswell
John Keats born
Thomas Carlyle born

1796 Napoleon Bonaparte takes command in Italy
Matthew Lewis' *The Monk*
John Adams elected president of the United States
Death of Robert Burns

1797 The peace of Campo Formio: extinction of the Venetian Republic
XYZ Affair
Mutinies in the Royal Navy at Spithead and the Nore
Blake's *Vala, Or the Four Zoas* (first version)
Mary Shelley born
Deaths of Edmund Burke, Mary Wollstonecraft, and Horace Walpole

1798 Napoleon invades Egypt
Horatio Nelson wins the battle of the Nile
Wordsworth's and Coleridge's *Lyrical Ballads*
Landor's *Gebir*

Thomas Malthus' *Essay on the Principle of Population*

1799 Napoleon becomes first consul
Pitt introduces first income tax in Great Britain
Sheridan's *Pizarro*
Honoré de Balzac born
Thomas Hood born
Alexander Pushkin born

1800 Thomas Jefferson elected president of the United States
Alessandro Volta produces electricity from a cell
Library of Congress established
Death of William Cowper
Thomas Babington Macaulay born

1801 First census taken in England

1802 The Treaty of Amiens marks the end of the French Revolutionary War
The *Edinburgh Review* founded

1803 England's war with France renewed
The Louisiana Purchase
Robert Fulton propels a boat by steam power on the Seine
Thomas Lovell Beddoes born

1804 Napoleon crowned emperor of the French
Jefferson reelected president of the United States
Blake's *Milton* (1804–1808) and *Jerusalem*
The Code Napoleon promulgated in France
Beethoven's *Eroica* Symphony
Schiller's *Wilhelm Tell*
Benjamin Disraeli born

1805 Napoleon plans the invasion of England
Battle of Trafalgar
Battle of Austerlitz
Beethoven's *Fidelio* first produced
Scott's *Lay of the Last Minstrel*

1806 Scott's *Marmion*
Death of William Pitt
Death of Charles James Fox
Elizabeth Barrett born

1807 France invades Portugal
Aaron Burr tried for treason and acquitted
Byron's *Hours of Idleness*

CHRONOLOGY

Charles and Mary Lamb's *Tales from Shakespeare*
Thomas Moore's *Irish Melodies*
Wordsworth's *Ode on the Intimations of Immortality*

1808 National uprising in Spain against the French invasion
The Peninsular War begins
James Madison elected president of the United States
Covent Garden theater burned down
Goethe's *Faust* (Part 1)
Beethoven's Fifth Symphony completed
Lamb's *Specimens of English Dramatic Poets*

1809 Drury Lane theater burned down and rebuilt
The *Quarterly Review* founded
Byron's *English Bards and Scotch Reviewers*
Byron sails for the Mediterranean
Goya's *Los Desastres de la guerra* (1809–1814)
Alfred Tennyson born
Edward Fitzgerald born

1810 Crabbe's *The Borough*
Scott's *The Lady of the Lake*
Elizabeth Gaskell born

1811–1820 Regency of George IV

1811 Luddite Riots begin
Coleridge's *Lectures on Shakespeare* (1811–1814)
Jane Austen's *Sense and Sensibility*
Shelley's *The Necessity of Atheism*
John Constable's *Dedham Vale*
William Makepeace Thackeray born

1812 Napoleon invades Russia; captures and retreats from Moscow
United States declares war against England
Henry Bell's steamship *Comet* is launched on the Clyde river
Madison reelected president of the United States
Byron's *Childe Harold* (Cantos 1–2)
The Brothers Grimm's *Fairy Tales* (1812–1815)
Hegel's *Science of Logic*
Robert Browning born
Charles Dickens born

1813 Wellington wins the battle of Vitoria and enters France
Jane Austen's *Pride and Prejudice*
Byron's *The Giaour* and *The Bride of Abydos*
Shelley's *Queen Mab*
Southey's *Life of Nelson*

1814 Napoleon abdicates and is exiled to Elba; Bourbon restoration with Louis XVIII
Treaty of Ghent ends the war between Britain and the United States
Jane Austen's *Mansfield Park*
Byron's *The Corsair* and *Lara*
Scott's *Waverley*
Wordsworth's *The Excursion*

1815 Napoleon returns to France (the Hundred Days); is defeated at Waterloo and exiled to St. Helena
U.S.S. *Fulton*, the first steam warship, built
Scott's *Guy Mannering*
Schlegel's *Lectures on Dramatic Art and Literature* translated
Wordsworth's *The White Doe of Rylstone*
Anthony Trollope born

1816 Byron leaves England permanently
The Elgin Marbles exhibited in the British Museum
James Monroe elected president of the United States
Jane Austen's *Emma*
Byron's *Childe Harold* (Canto 3)
Coleridge's *Christabel, Kubla Khan: A Vision, The Pains of Sleep*
Benjamin Constant's *Adolphe*
Goethe's *Italienische Reise*
Peacock's *Headlong Hall*
Scott's *The Antiquary*
Shelley's *Alastor*
Rossini's *Il Barbiere di Siviglia*
Death of Richard Brinsley Sheridan
Charlotte Brontë born

1817 *Blackwood's Edinburgh* magazine founded
Jane Austen's *Northanger Abbey* and *Persuasion*
Byron's *Manfred*
Coleridge's *Biographia Literaria*
Hazlitt's *The Characters of Shakespeare's Plays* and *The Round Table*

CHRONOLOGY

Keats's *Poems*
Peacock's *Melincourt*
David Ricardo's *Principles of Political Economy and Taxation*
Death of Jane Austen
Death of Mme de Staël
Branwell Brontë born
Henry David Thoreau born

1818   Byron's *Childe Harold* (Canto 4), and *Beppo*
Hazlitt's *Lectures on the English Poets*
Keats's *Endymion*
Peacock's *Nightmare Abbey*
Scott's *Rob Roy* and *The Heart of Mid-Lothian*
Mary Shelley's *Frankenstein*
Percy Shelley's *The Revolt of Islam*
Emily Brontë born
Karl Marx born
Ivan Sergeyevich Turgenev born

1819   The *Savannah* becomes the first steamship to cross the Atlantic (in 26 days)
Peterloo massacre in Manchester
Byron's *Don Juan* (1819–1824) and *Mazeppa*
Crabbe's *Tales of the Hall*
Géricault's *Raft of the Medusa*
Hazlitt's *Lectures on the English Comic Writers*
Arthur Schopenhauer's *Die Welt als Wille und Vorstellung (The World as Will and Idea)*
Scott's *The Bride of Lammermoor* and *A Legend of Montrose*
Shelley's *The Cenci*, "The Masque of Anarchy," and "Ode to the West Wind"
Wordsworth's *Peter Bell*
Queen Victoria born
George Eliot born

1820–1830   Reign of George IV

1820   Trial of Queen Caroline
Cato Street Conspiracy suppressed; Arthur Thistlewood hanged
Monroe reelected president of the United States
Missouri Compromise
The *London* magazine founded
Keats's *Lamia, Isabella, The Eve of St. Agnes, and Other Poems*

Hazlitt's *Lectures Chiefly on the Dramatic Literature of the Age of Elizabeth*
Charles Maturin's *Melmoth the Wanderer*
Scott's *Ivanhoe* and *The Monastery*
Shelley's *Prometheus Unbound*
Anne Brontë born

1821   Greek War of Independence begins
Liberia founded as a colony for freed slaves
Byron's *Cain, Marino Faliero, The Two Foscari*, and *Sardanapalus*
Hazlitt's *Table Talk* (1821–1822)
Scott's *Kenilworth*
Shelley's *Adonais* and *Epipsychidion*
Death of John Keats
Death of Napoleon
Charles Baudelaire born
Feodor Dostoyevsky born
Gustave Flaubert born

1822   The Massacres of Chios (Greeks rebel against Turkish rule)
Byron's *The Vision of Judgment*
De Quincey's *Confessions of an English Opium-Eater*
Peacock's *Maid Marian*
Scott's *Peveril of the Peak*
Shelley's *Hellas*
Death of Percy Bysshe Shelley
Matthew Arnold born

1823   Monroe Doctrine proclaimed
Byron's *The Age of Bronze* and *The Island*
Lamb's *Essays of Elia*
Scott's *Quentin Durward*

1824   The National Gallery opened in London
John Quincy Adams elected president of the United States
The *Westminster Review* founded
Beethoven's Ninth Symphony first performed
William (Wilkie) Collins born
James Hogg's *The Private Memoirs and Confessions of a Justified Sinner*
Landor's *Imaginary Conversations* (1824–1829)
Scott's *Redgauntlet*

CHRONOLOGY

Death of George Gordon, Lord Byron

1825 Inauguration of steam-powered passenger and freight service on the Stockton and Darlington railway
Bolivia and Brazil become independent Alessandro Manzoni's *I Promessi Sposi* (1825–1826)

1826 André-Marie Ampère's *Mémoire sur la théorie mathématique des phénomènes électrodynamiques*
James Fenimore Cooper's *The Last of the Mohicans*
Disraeli's *Vivian Grey* (1826–1827)
Scott's *Woodstock*

1827 The battle of Navarino ensures the independence of Greece
Josef Ressel obtains patent for the screw propeller for steamships
Heinrich Heine's *Buch der Lieder*
Death of William Blake

1828 Andrew Jackson elected president of the United States
Births of Henrik Ibsen, George Meredith, Margaret Oliphant, Dante Gabriel Rossetti, and Leo Tolstoy

1829 The Catholic Emancipation Act
Robert Peel establishes the metropolitan police force
Greek independence recognized by Turkey
Balzac begins *La Comédie humaine* (1829–1848)
Peacock's *The Misfortunes of Elphin*
J. M. W. Turner's *Ulysses Deriding Polyphemus*

1830–1837 Reign of William IV

1830 Charles X of France abdicates and is succeeded by Louis-Philippe
The Liverpool-Manchester railway opened
Tennyson's *Poems, Chiefly Lyrical*
Death of William Hazlitt
Christina Rossetti born

1831 Michael Faraday discovers electromagnetic induction
Charles Darwin's voyage on H.M.S. *Beagle* begins (1831–1836)
The Barbizon school of artists' first exhibition

Nat Turner slave revolt crushed in Virginia
Peacock's *Crotchet Castle*
Stendhal's *Le Rouge et le noir*
Edward Trelawny's *The Adventures of a Younger Son*
Isabella Bird born

1832 The first Reform Bill
Samuel Morse invents the telegraph
Jackson reelected president of the United States
Disraeli's *Contarini Fleming*
Goethe's *Faust* (Part 2)
Tennyson's *Poems, Chiefly Lyrical*, including "The Lotus-Eaters" and "The Lady of Shalott"
Death of Johann Wolfgang von Goethe
Death of Sir Walter Scott
Lewis Carroll born

1833 Robert Browning's *Pauline*
John Keble launches the Oxford Movement
American Anti-Slavery Society founded
Lamb's *Last Essays of Elia*
Carlyle's *Sartor Resartus* (1833–1834)
Pushkin's *Eugene Onegin*
Mendelssohn's *Italian Symphony* first performed

1834 Abolition of slavery in the British Empire
Louis Braille's alphabet for the blind
Balzac's *Le Père Goriot*
Nikolai Gogol's *Dead Souls* (Part 1, 1834–1842)
Death of Samuel Taylor Coleridge
Death of Charles Lamb
William Morris born

1835 Hans Christian Andersen's *Fairy Tales* (1st ser.)
Robert Browning's *Paracelsus*
Births of Samuel Butler and Mary Elizabeth Braddon
Alexis de Tocqueville's *De la Democratie en Amerique* (1835–1840)
Death of James Hogg

1836 Martin Van Buren elected president of the United States

CHRONOLOGY

Dickens' *Sketches by Boz* (1836–1837)

Landor's *Pericles and Aspasia*

1837–1901   **Reign of Queen Victoria**

1837   Carlyle's *The French Revolution*

Dickens' *Oliver Twist* (1837–1838) and *Pickwick Papers*

Disraeli's *Venetia* and *Henrietta Temple*

1838   Chartist movement in England

National Gallery in London opened

Elizabeth Barrett Browning's *The Seraphim and Other Poems*

Dickens' *Nicholas Nickleby* (1838–1839)

1839   Louis Daguerre perfects process for producing an image on a silver-coated copper plate Faraday's *Experimental Researches in Electricity* (1839–1855)

First Chartist riots

Opium War between Great Britain and China

Carlyle's *Chartism*

1840   Canadian Act of Union

Queen Victoria marries Prince Albert

Charles Barry begins construction of the Houses of Parliament (1840–1852)

William Henry Harrison elected president of the United States

Robert Browning's *Sordello*

Thomas Hardy born

1841   New Zealand proclaimed a British colony

James Clark Ross discovers the Antarctic continent

Punch founded

John Tyler succeeds to the presidency after the death of Harrison

Carlyle's *Heroes and Hero-Worship*

Dickens' *The Old Curiosity Shop*

1842   Chartist riots

Income tax revived in Great Britain

The Mines Act, forbidding work underground by women or by children under the age of ten

Charles Edward Mudie's Lending Library founded in London

Dickens visits America

Robert Browning's *Dramatic Lyrics*

Macaulay's *Lays of Ancient Rome*

Tennyson's *Poems*, including "Morte d'Arthur," "St. Simeon Stylites," and "Ulysses"

Wordsworth's *Poems*

1843   Marc Isambard Brunel's Thames tunnel opened

The Economist founded

Carlyle's *Past and Present*

Dickens' *A Christmas Carol*

John Stuart Mill's *Logic*

Macaulay's *Critical and Historical Essays*

John Ruskin's *Modern Painters* (1843–1860)

1844   Rochdale Society of Equitable Pioneers, one of the first consumers' cooperatives, founded by twenty-eight Lancashire weavers

James K. Polk elected president of the United States

Elizabeth Barrett Browning's *Poems*, including "The Cry of the Children"

Dickens' *Martin Chuzzlewit*

Disraeli's *Coningsby*

Turner's *Rain, Steam and Speed*

Gerard Manley Hopkins born

1845   The great potato famine in Ireland begins (1845–1849)

Disraeli's *Sybil*

1846   Repeal of the Corn Laws

The *Daily News* founded (edited by Dickens the first three weeks)

Standard-gauge railway introduced in Britain

The Brontës' pseudonymous *Poems by Currer, Ellis and Action Bell*

Lear's *Book of Nonsense*

1847   The Ten Hours Factory Act

James Simpson uses chloroform as an anesthetic

Anne Brontë's *Agnes Grey*

Charlotte Brontë's *Jane Eyre*

Emily Brontë's *Wuthering Heights*

Bram Stoker born

Tennyson's *The Princess*

1848   The year of revolutions in France, Germany, Italy, Hungary, Poland

Marx and Engels issue *The Communist Manifesto*

The Chartist Petition

CHRONOLOGY

The Pre-Raphaelite Brotherhood founded
Zachary Taylor elected president of the United States
Anne Brontë's *The Tenant of Wildfell Hall*
Dickens' *Dombey and Son*
Elizabeth Gaskell's *Mary Barton*
Macaulay's *History of England* (1848–1861)
Mill's *Principles of Political Economy*
Thackeray's *Vanity Fair*
Death of Emily Brontë

1849 Bedford College for women founded
Arnold's *The Strayed Reveller*
Charlotte Brontë's *Shirley*
Ruskin's *The Seven Lamps of Architecture*
Death of Anne Brontë
Death of Thomas Lovell Beddoes

1850 The Public Libraries Act
First submarine telegraph cable laid between Dover and Calais
Millard Fillmore succeeds to the presidency after the death of Taylor
Elizabeth Barrett Browning's *Sonnets from the Portuguese*
Carlyle's *Latter-Day Pamphlets*
Dickens' *Household Words* (1850–1859) and *David Copperfield*
Charles Kingsley's *Alton Locke*
The Pre-Raphaelites publish the *Germ*
Tennyson's *In Memoriam*
Thackeray's *The History of Pendennis*
Wordsworth's *The Prelude* is published posthumously

1851 The Great Exhibition opens at the Crystal Palace in Hyde Park
Louis Napoleon seizes power in France
Gold strike in Victoria incites Australian gold rush
Elizabeth Gaskell's *Cranford* (1851–1853)
Meredith's *Poems*
Ruskin's *The Stones of Venice* (1851–1853)

1852 The Second Empire proclaimed with Napoleon III as emperor
David Livingstone begins to explore the Zambezi (1852–1856)
Franklin Pierce elected president of the United States
Arnold's *Empedocles on Etna*
Thackeray's *The History of Henry Esmond, Esq.*

1853 Crimean War (1853–1856)
Arnold's *Poems*, including "The Scholar Gypsy" and "Sohrab and Rustum"
Charlotte Brontë's *Villette*
Elizabeth Gaskell's *Crawford and Ruth*

1854 Frederick D. Maurice's Working Men's College founded in London with more than 130 pupils
Battle of Balaklava
Dickens' *Hard Times*
James George Frazer born
Theodor Mommsen's *History of Rome* (1854–1856)
Tennyson's "The Charge of the Light Brigade"
Florence Nightingale in the Crimea (1854–1856)
Oscar Wilde born

1855 David Livingstone discovers the Victoria Falls
Robert Browning's *Men and Women*
Elizabeth Gaskell's *North and South*
Olive Schreiner born
Tennyson's *Maud*
Thackeray's *The Newcomes*
Trollope's *The Warden*
Death of Charlotte Brontë

1856 The Treaty of Paris ends the Crimean War
Henry Bessemer's steel process invented
James Buchanan elected president of the United States
H. Rider Haggard born

1857 The Indian Mutiny begins; crushed in 1858
The Matrimonial Causes Act
Charlotte Brontë's *The Professor*
Elizabeth Barrett Browning's *Aurora Leigh*

CHRONOLOGY

Dickens' *Little Dorritt*
Elizabeth Gaskell's *The Life of Charlotte Brontë*
Thomas Hughes's *Tom Brown's School Days*
Trollope's *Barchester Towers*

1858   Carlyle's *History of Frederick the Great* (1858–1865)
George Eliot's *Scenes of Clerical Life*
Morris' *The Defense of Guinevere*
Trollope's *Dr. Thorne*

1859   Charles Darwin's *The Origin of Species*
Dickens' *A Tale of Two Cities*
Arthur Conan Doyle born
George Eliot's *Adam Bede*
Fitzgerald's *The Rubaiyat of Omar Khayyám*
Meredith's *The Ordeal of Richard Feverel*
Mill's *On Liberty*
Samuel Smiles's *Self-Help*
Tennyson's *Idylls of the King*

1860   Abraham Lincoln elected president of the United States
The *Cornhill* magazine founded with Thackeray as editor
James M. Barrie born
William Wilkie Collins' *The Woman in White*
George Eliot's *The Mill on the Floss*

1861   American Civil War begins
Louis Pasteur presents the germ theory of disease
Arnold's *Lectures on Translating Homer*
Dickens' *Great Expectations*
George Eliot's *Silas Marner*
Meredith's *Evan Harrington*
Francis Turner Palgrave's *The Golden Treasury*
Trollope's *Framley Parsonage*
Peacock's *Gryll Grange*
Death of Prince Albert

1862   George Eliot's *Romola*
Meredith's *Modern Love*
Christina Rossetti's *Goblin Market*
Ruskin's *Unto This Last*
Trollope's *Orley Farm*

1863   Thomas Huxley's *Man's Place in Nature*

1864   The Geneva Red Cross Convention signed by twelve nations
Lincoln reelected president of the United States
Robert Browning's *Dramatis Personae*
John Henry Newman's *Apologia pro vita sua*
Tennyson's *Enoch Arden*
Trollope's *The Small House at Allington*
Death of John Clare

1865   Assassination of Lincoln; Andrew Johnson succeeds to the presidency
Arnold's *Essays in Criticism* (1st ser.)
Carroll's *Alice's Adventures in Wonderland*
Dickens' *Our Mutual Friend*
Meredith's *Rhoda Fleming*
A. C. Swinburne's *Atalanta in Calydon*

1866   First successful transatlantic telegraph cable laid
George Eliot's *Felix Holt, the Radical*
Elizabeth Gaskell's *Wives and Daughters*
Beatrix Potter born
Swinburne's *Poems and Ballads*

1867   The second Reform Bill
Arnold's *New Poems*
Bagehot's *The English Constitution*
Carlyle's *Shooting Niagara*
Marx's *Das Kapital* (vol. 1)
Trollope's *The Last Chronicle of Barset*
George William Russell (AE) born

1868   Gladstone becomes prime minister (1868–1874)
Johnson impeached by House of Representatives; acquitted by Senate
Ulysses S. Grant elected president of the United States
Robert Browning's *The Ring and the Book* (1868–1869)
Collins' *The Moonstone*

1869   The Suez Canal opened
Girton College, Cambridge, founded
Arnold's *Culture and Anarchy*

CHRONOLOGY

Mill's *The Subjection of Women*
Trollope's *Phineas Finn*

1870 The Elementary Education Act establishes schools under the aegis of local boards
Dickens' *Edwin Drood*
Disraeli's *Lothair*
Morris' *The Earthly Paradise*
Dante Gabriel Rossetti's *Poems*
Saki [Hector Hugh Munro] born

1871 Trade unions legalized
Newnham College, Cambridge, founded for women students
Carroll's *Through the Looking Glass*
Darwin's *The Descent of Man*
Meredith's *The Adventures of Harry Richmond*
Swinburne's *Songs Before Sunrise*
William H. Davies born

1872 Max Beerbohm born
Samuel Butler's *Erewhon*
George Eliot's *Middlemarch*
Grant reelected president of the United States
Hardy's *Under the Greenwood Tree*

1873 Arnold's *Literature and Dogma*
Mill's *Autobiography*
Pater's *Studies in the History of the Renaissance*
Trollope's *The Eustace Diamonds*

1874 Disraeli becomes prime minister
Hardy's *Far from the Madding Crowd*
James Thomson's *The City of Dreadful Night*

1875 Britain buys Suez Canal shares
Trollope's *The Way We Live Now*
T. F. Powys born

1876 F. H. Bradley's *Ethical Studies*
George Eliot's *Daniel Deronda*
Henry James's *Roderick Hudson*
Meredith's *Beauchamp's Career*
Morris' *Sigurd the Volsung*
Trollope's *The Prime Minister*

1877 Rutherford B. Hayes elected president of the United States after Electoral Commission awards him disputed votes
Henry James's *The American*

1878 Electric street lighting introduced in London
Hardy's *The Return of the Native*
Swinburne's *Poems and Ballads* (2d ser.)
Births of A. E. Coppard and Edward Thomas

1879 Somerville College and Lady Margaret Hall opened at Oxford for women
The London telephone exchange built
Gladstone's Midlothian campaign (1879–1880)
Browning's *Dramatic Idyls*
Meredith's *The Egoist*

1880 Gladstone's second term as prime minister (1880–1885)
James A. Garfield elected president of the United States
Browning's *Dramatic Idyls Second Series*
Disraeli's *Endymion*
Radclyffe Hall born
Hardy's *The Trumpet-Major*
Lytton Strachey born

1881 Garfield assassinated; Chester A. Arthur succeeds to the presidency
Henry James's *The Portrait of a Lady* and *Washington Square*
D. G. Rossetti's *Ballads and Sonnets*
P. G. Wodehouse born

1882 Triple Alliance formed between German empire, Austrian empire, and Italy
Leslie Stephen begins to edit the *Dictionary of National Biography*
Married Women's Property Act passed in Britain
Britain occupies Egypt and the Sudan

1883 Uprising of the Mahdi: Britain evacuates the Sudan
Royal College of Music opens
T. H. Green's *Ethics*
T. E. Hulme born
Stevenson's *Treasure Island*

1884 The Mahdi captures Omdurman: General Gordon appointed to command the garrison of Khartoum
Grover Cleveland elected president of the United States

CHRONOLOGY

The *Oxford English Dictionary* begins publishing
The Fabian Society founded
Hiram Maxim's recoil-operated machine gun invented

1885 The Mahdi captures Khartoum: General Gordon killed
Haggard's *King Solomon's Mines*
Marx's *Das Kapital* (vol. 2)
Meredith's *Diana of the Crossways*
Pater's *Marius the Epicurean*

1886 The Canadian Pacific Railway completed
Gold discovered in the Transvaal
Births of Frances Cornford, Ronald Firbank, and Charles Stansby Walter Williams
Henry James's *The Bostonians* and *The Princess Casamassima*
Stevenson's *The Strange Case of Dr. Jekyll and Mr. Hyde*

1887 Queen Victoria's Golden Jubilee
Rupert Brooke born
Haggard's *Allan Quatermain* and *She*
Hardy's *The Woodlanders*
Edwin Muir born

1888 Benjamin Harrison elected president of the United States
Henry James's *The Aspern Papers*
Kipling's *Plain Tales from the Hills*
T. E. Lawrence born

1889 Yeats's *The Wanderings of Oisin*
Death of Robert Browning

1890 Morris founds the Kelmscott Press
Agatha Christie born
Frazer's *The Golden Bough* (1st ed.)
Henry James's *The Tragic Muse*
Morris' *News From Nowhere*
Jean Rhys born

1891 Gissing's *New Grub Street*
Hardy's *Tess of the d'Urbervilles*
Wilde's *The Picture of Dorian Gray*

1892 Grover Cleveland elected president of the United States
Conan Doyle's *The Adventures of Sherlock Holmes*
Shaw's *Widower's Houses*
J. R. R. Tolkien born
Rebecca West born
Wilde's *Lady Windermere's Fan*

1893 Wilde's *A Woman of No Importance* and *Salomé*
Vera Brittain born

1894 Kipling's *The Jungle Book*
Moore's *Esther Waters*
Marx's *Das Kapital* (vol. 3)
Audrey Beardsley's *The Yellow Book* begins to appear quarterly
Shaw's *Arms and the Man*

1895 Trial and imprisonment of Oscar Wilde
William Ramsay announces discovery of helium
The National Trust founded
Conrad's *Almayer's Folly*
Hardy's *Jude the Obscure*
Wells's *The Time Machine*
Wilde's *The Importance of Being Earnest*
Yeats's *Poems*

1896 William McKinley elected president of the United States
Failure of the Jameson Raid on the Transvaal
Housman's *A Shropshire Lad*
Edmund Blunden born

1897 Queen Victoria's Diamond Jubilee
Conrad's *The Nigger of the Narcissus*
Havelock Ellis' *Studies in the Psychology of Sex* begins publication
Henry James's *The Spoils of Poynton* and *What Maisie Knew*
Kipling's *Captains Courageous*
Shaw's *Candida*
Stoker's *Dracula*
Wells's *The Invisible Man*
Death of Margaret Oliphant

1898 Kitchener defeats the Mahdist forces at Omdurman: the Sudan reoccupied
Hardy's *Wessex Poems*
Henry James's *The Turn of the Screw*
C. S. Lewis born
Shaw's *Caesar and Cleopatra* and *You Never Can Tell*
Alec Waugh born
Wells's *The War of the Worlds*
Wilde's *The Ballad of Reading Gaol*

1899 The Boer War begins
Elizabeth Bowen born

CHRONOLOGY

Noël Coward born
Elgar's *Enigma Variations*
Kipling's *Stalky and Co.*

1900 McKinley reelected president of the United States
British Labour party founded
Boxer Rebellion in China
Reginald A. Fessenden transmits speech by wireless
First Zeppelin trial flight
Max Planck presents his first paper on the quantum theory
Conrad's *Lord Jim*
Elgar's *The Dream of Gerontius*
Sigmund Freud's *The Interpretation of Dreams*
V. S. Pritchett born
William Butler Yeats's *The Shadowy Waters*

1901–1910 Reign of King Edward VII

1901 William McKinley assassinated; Theodore Roosevelt succeeds to the presidency
First transatlantic wireless telegraph signal transmitted
Chekhov's *Three Sisters*
Freud's *Psychopathology of Everyday Life*
Rudyard Kipling's *Kim*
Thomas Mann's *Buddenbrooks*
Potter's *The Tale of Peter Rabbit*
Shaw's *Captain Brassbound's Conversion*
August Strindberg's *The Dance of Death*

1902 Barrie's *The Admirable Crichton*
Arnold Bennett's *Anna of the Five Towns*
Cézanne's *Le Lac D'Annecy*
Conrad's *Heart of Darkness*
Henry James's *The Wings of the Dove*
William James's *The Varieties of Religious Experience*
Kipling's *Just So Stories*
Maugham's *Mrs. Cradock*
Stevie Smith born
Times Literary Supplement begins publishing

1903 At its London congress the Russian Social Democratic Party divides into Mensheviks, led by Plekhanov,

and Bolsheviks, led by Lenin
The treaty of Panama places the Canal Zone in U.S. hands for a nominal rent
Motor cars regulated in Britain to a 20-mile-per-hour limit
The Wright brothers make a successful flight in the United States
Burlington magazine founded
Samuel Butler's *The Way of All Flesh* published posthumously
Cyril Connolly born
George Gissing's *The Private Papers of Henry Ryecroft*
Thomas Hardy's *The Dynasts*
Henry James's *The Ambassadors*
Alan Paton born
Shaw's *Man and Superman*
Synge's *Riders to the Sea* produced in Dublin
Yeats's *In the Seven Woods* and *On Baile's Strand*
William Plomer born

1904 Roosevelt elected president of the United States
Russo-Japanese war (1904–1905)
Construction of the Panama Canal begins
The ultraviolet lamp invented
The engineering firm of Rolls Royce founded
Barrie's *Peter Pan* first performed
Births of Cecil Day Lewis and Nancy Mitford
Chekhov's *The Cherry Orchard*
Conrad's *Nostromo*
Henry James's *The Golden Bowl*
Kipling's *Traffics and Discoveries*
Georges Rouault's *Head of a Tragic Clown*
G. M. Trevelyan's *England Under the Stuarts*
Puccini's *Madame Butterfly*
First Shaw-Granville Barker season at the Royal Court Theatre
The Abbey Theatre founded in Dublin
Death of Isabella Bird

1905 Russian sailors on the battleship Potemkin mutiny
After riots and a general strike the czar concedes demands by the

CHRONOLOGY

Duma for legislative powers, a wider franchise, and civil liberties

Albert Einstein publishes his first theory of relativity

The Austin Motor Company founded

Bennett's *Tales of the Five Towns*

Claude Debussy's *La Mer*

E. M. Forster's *Where Angels Fear to Tread*

Richard Strauss's *Salome*

H. G. Wells's *Kipps*

Oscar Wilde's *De Profundis*

Births of Norman Cameron, Henry Green, and Mary Renault

1906   Liberals win a landslide victory in the British general election

The Trades Disputes Act legitimizes peaceful picketing in Britain

Captain Dreyfus rehabilitated in France

J. J. Thomson begins research on gamma rays

The U.S. Pure Food and Drug Act passed

Churchill's *Lord Randolph Churchill*

William Empson born

Galsworthy's *The Man of Property*

Kipling's *Puck of Pook's Hill*

Shaw's *The Doctor's Dilemma*

Yeats's *Poems 1899–1905*

1907   Exhibition of cubist paintings in Paris

Henry Adams' *The Education of Henry Adams*

Henri Bergson's *Creative Evolution*

Conrad's *The Secret Agent*

Births of Barbara Comyns, Daphne du Maurier, and Christopher Fry

Forster's *The Longest Journey*

André Gide's *La Porte étroite*

Shaw's *John Bull's Other Island* and *Major Barbara*

Synge's *The Playboy of the Western World*

Trevelyan's *Garibaldi's Defence of the Roman Republic*

Christopher Caudwell (Christopher St. John Sprigg) born

1908   Herbert Asquith becomes prime minister

David Lloyd George becomes chancellor of the exchequer

William Howard Taft elected president of the United States

The Young Turks seize power in Istanbul

Henry Ford's Model T car produced

Bennett's *The Old Wives' Tale*

Pierre Bonnard's *Nude Against the Light*

Georges Braque's *House at L'Estaque*

Chesterton's *The Man Who Was Thursday*

Jacob Epstein's *Figures* erected in London

Forster's *A Room with a View*

Anatole France's *L'Ile des Pingouins*

Henri Matisse's *Bonheur de Vivre*

Elgar's First Symphony

Ford Madox Ford founds the *English Review*

1909   The Young Turks depose Sultan Abdul Hamid

The Anglo-Persian Oil Company formed

Louis Bleriot crosses the English Channel from France by monoplane

Admiral Robert Peary reaches the North Pole

Freud lectures at Clark University (Worcester, Mass.) on psychoanalysis

Serge Diaghilev's Ballets Russes opens in Paris

Galsworthy's *Strife*

Hardy's *Time's Laughingstocks*

Malcolm Lowry born

Claude Monet's *Water Lilies*

Stephen Spender born

Trevelyan's *Garibaldi and the Thousand*

Wells's *Tono-Bungay* first published (book form, 1909)

1910–1936   **Reign of King George V**

1910   The Liberals win the British general election

Marie Curie's *Treatise on Radiography*

Arthur Evans excavates Knossos

CHRONOLOGY

Edouard Manet and the first post-impressionist exhibition in London
Filippo Marinetti publishes "Manifesto of the Futurist Painters"
Norman Angell's *The Great Illusion*
Bennett's *Clayhanger*
Forster's *Howards End*
Galsworthy's *Justice* and *The Silver Box*
Kipling's *Rewards and Fairies*
Norman MacCaig born
Rimsky-Korsakov's *Le Coq d'or*
Stravinsky's *The Firebird*
Vaughan Williams' *A Sea Symphony*
Wells's *The History of Mr. Polly*
Wells's *The New Machiavelli* first published (in book form, 1911)

1911   Lloyd George introduces National Health Insurance Bill
Suffragette riots in Whitehall
Roald Amundsen reaches the South Pole
Bennett's *The Card*
Chagall's *Self Portrait with Seven Fingers*
Conrad's *Under Western Eyes*
D. H. Lawrence's *The White Peacock*
Katherine Mansfield's *In a German Pension*
Edward Marsh edits *Georgian Poetry*
Moore's *Hail and Farewell* (1911–1914)
Flann O'Brien born
Strauss's *Der Rosenkavalier*
Stravinsky's *Petrouchka*
Trevelyan's *Garibaldi and the Making of Italy*
Wells's *The New Machiavelli*
Mahler's *Das Lied von der Erde*

1912   Woodrow Wilson elected president of the United States
SS *Titanic* sinks on its maiden voyage
Five million Americans go to the movies daily; London has four hundred movie theaters
Second post-impressionist exhibition in London

Bennett's and Edward Knoblock's *Milestones*
Constantin Brancusi's *Maiastra*
Wassily Kandinsky's *Black Lines*
D. H. Lawrence's *The Trespasser*

1913   Second Balkan War begins
Henry Ford pioneers factory assembly technique through conveyor belts
Epstein's *Tomb of Oscar Wilde*
New York Armory Show introduces modern art to the world
Alain Fournier's *Le Grand Meaulnes*
Freud's *Totem and Tabu*
D. H. Lawrence's *Sons and Lovers*
Mann's *Death in Venice*
Proust's *Du Côté de chez Swann* (first volume of *À la recherche du temps perdu*, 1913–1922)
Barbara Pym born
Ravel's *Daphnis and Chloé*

1914   The Panama Canal opens (formal dedication on 12 July 1920)
Irish Home Rule Bill passed in the House of Commons
Archduke Franz Ferdinand assassinated at Sarajevo
World War I begins
Battles of the Marne, Masurian Lakes, and Falkland Islands
Joyce's *Dubliners*
Norman Nicholson born
Shaw's *Pygmalion* and *Androcles and the Lion*
Yeats's *Responsibilities*
Wyndham Lewis publishes *Blast* magazine and *The Vorticist Manifesto*
C. H. Sisson born

1915   The Dardanelles campaign begins
Britain and Germany begin naval and submarine blockades
The *Lusitania* is sunk
Hugo Junkers manufactures the first fighter aircraft
First Zeppelin raid in London
Brooke's *1914: Five Sonnets*
Norman Douglas' *Old Calabria*
D. W. Griffith's *The Birth of a Nation*
Gustav Holst's *The Planets*

CHRONOLOGY

D. H. Lawrence's *The Rainbow*
Wyndham Lewis's *The Crowd*
Maugham's *Of Human Bondage*
Pablo Picasso's *Harlequin*
Sibelius' Fifth Symphony
Denton Welch born

1916 Evacuation of Gallipoli and the Dardanelles
Battles of the Somme, Jutland, and Verdun
Britain introduces conscription
The Easter Rebellion in Dublin
Asquith resigns and David Lloyd George becomes prime minister
The Sykes-Picot agreement on the partition of Turkey
First military tanks used
Wilson reelected president president of the United States
Henri Barbusse's *Le Feu*
Griffith's *Intolerance*
Joyce's *Portrait of the Artist as a Young Man*
Jung's *Psychology of the Unconscious*
Moore's *The Brook Kerith*
Edith Sitwell edits *Wheels* (1916–1921)
Wells's *Mr. Britling Sees It Through*

1917 United States enters World War I
Czar Nicholas II abdicates
The Balfour Declaration on a Jewish national home in Palestine
The Bolshevik Revolution
Georges Clemenceau elected prime minister of France
Lenin appointed chief commissar; Trotsky appointed minister of foreign affairs
Conrad's *The Shadow-Line*
Douglas' *South Wind*
Eliot's *Prufrock and Other Observations*
Modigliani's *Nude with Necklace*
Sassoon's *The Old Huntsman*
Prokofiev's *Classical Symphony*
Yeats's *The Wild Swans at Coole*

1918 Wilson puts forward Fourteen Points for World Peace
Central Powers and Russia sign the Treaty of Brest-Litovsk

Execution of Czar Nicholas II and his family
Kaiser Wilhelm II abdicates
The Armistice signed
Women granted the vote at age thirty in Britain
Rupert Brooke's *Collected Poems*
Gerard Manley Hopkins' *Poems*
Joyce's *Exiles*
Lewis's *Tarr*
Sassoon's *Counter-Attack*
Oswald Spengler's *The Decline of the West*
Strachey's *Eminent Victorians*
Béla Bartók's *Bluebeard's Castle*
Charlie Chaplin's *Shoulder Arms*

1919 The Versailles Peace Treaty signed
J. W. Alcock and A. W. Brown make first transatlantic flight
Ross Smith flies from London to Australia
National Socialist party founded in Germany
Benito Mussolini founds the Fascist party in Italy
Sinn Fein Congress adopts declaration of independence in Dublin
Eamon De Valera elected president of Sinn Fein party
Communist Third International founded
Lady Astor elected first woman Member of Parliament
Prohibition in the United States
John Maynard Keynes's *The Economic Consequences of the Peace*
Eliot's *Poems*
Maugham's *The Moon and Sixpence*
Shaw's *Heartbreak House*
The Bauhaus school of design, building, and crafts founded by Walter Gropius
Amedeo Modigliani's *Self-Portrait*

1920 The League of Nations established
Warren G. Harding elected president of the United States
Senate votes against joining the League and rejects the Treaty of Versailles
The Nineteenth Amendment gives women the right to vote

CHRONOLOGY

White Russian forces of Denikin and Kolchak defeated by the Bolsheviks

Karel Čapek's *R.U.R.*

Galsworthy's *In Chancery* and *The Skin Game*

Sinclair Lewis' *Main Street*

Katherine Mansfield's *Bliss*

Matisse's *Odalisques* (1920–1925)

Ezra Pound's *Hugh Selwyn Mauberly*

Paul Valéry's *Le Cimetière Marin*

Yeats's *Michael Robartes and the Dancer*

Edwin Morgan born

1921 Britain signs peace with Ireland

First medium-wave radio broadcast in the United States

The British Broadcasting Corporation founded

Braque's *Still Life with Guitar*

Chaplin's *The Kid*

Aldous Huxley's *Crome Yellow*

Paul Klee's *The Fish*

D. H. Lawrence's *Women in Love*

John McTaggart's *The Nature of Existence* (vol. 1)

Moore's *Héloïse and Abélard*

Eugene O'Neill's *The Emperor Jones*

Luigi Pirandello's *Six Characters in Search of an Author*

Shaw's *Back to Methuselah*

Strachey's *Queen Victoria*

Births of George Mackay Brown and Brian Moore

1922 Lloyd George's Coalition government succeeded by Bonar Law's Conservative government

Benito Mussolini marches on Rome and forms a government

William Cosgrave elected president of the Irish Free State

The BBC begins broadcasting in London

Lord Carnarvon and Howard Carter discover Tutankhamen's tomb

The PEN club founded in London

The *Criterion* founded with T. S. Eliot as editor

Kingsley Amis born

Eliot's *The Waste Land*

A. E. Housman's *Last Poems*

Joyce's *Ulysses*

D. H. Lawrence's *Aaron's Rod* and *England, My England*

Sinclair Lewis's *Babbitt*

O'Neill's *Anna Christie*

Pirandello's *Henry IV*

Edith Sitwell's *Façade*

Virginia Woolf's *Jacob's Room*

Yeats's *The Trembling of the Veil*

Donald Davie born

1923 The Union of Soviet Socialist Republics established

French and Belgian troops occupy the Ruhr in consequence of Germany's failure to pay reparations

Mustafa Kemal (Ataturk) proclaims Turkey a republic and is elected president

Warren G. Harding dies; Calvin Coolidge becomes president

Stanley Baldwin succeeds Bonar Law as prime minister

Adolf Hitler's attempted coup in Munich fails

Time magazine begins publishing

E. N. da C. Andrade's *The Structure of the Atom*

Brendan Behan born

Bennett's *Riceyman Steps*

Churchill's *The World Crisis* (1923–1927)

J. E. Flecker's *Hassan* produced

Nadine Gordimer born

Paul Klee's *Magic Theatre*

Lawrence's *Kangaroo*

Rainer Maria Rilke's *Duino Elegies* and *Sonnets to Orpheus*

Sibelius' *Sixth Symphony*

Picasso's *Seated Woman*

William Walton's *Façade*

Elizabeth Jane Howard born

1924 Ramsay MacDonald forms first Labour government, loses general election, and is succeeded by Stanley Baldwin

Calvin Coolidge elected president of the United States

Noël Coward's *The Vortex*

Forster's *A Passage to India*

Mann's *The Magic Mountain*

Shaw's *St. Joan*

CHRONOLOGY

1925   Reza Khan becomes shah of Iran
First surrealist exhibition held in Paris
Alban Berg's *Wozzeck*
Chaplin's *The Gold Rush*
John Dos Passos' *Manhattan Transfer*
Theodore Dreiser's *An American Tragedy*
Sergei Eisenstein's *Battleship Potemkin*
F. Scott Fitzgerald's *The Great Gatsby*
André Gide's *Les Faux Monnayeurs*
Hardy's *Human Shows and Far Phantasies*
Huxley's *Those Barren Leaves*
Kafka's *The Trial*
O'Casey's *Juno and the Paycock*
Virginia Woolf's *Mrs. Dalloway* and *The Common Reader*
Brancusi's *Bird in Space*
Shostakovich's *First Symphony*
Sibelius' *Tapiola*

1926   Ford's *A Man Could Stand Up*
Gide's *Si le grain ne meurt*
Hemingway's *The Sun also Rises*
Kafka's *The Castle*
D. H. Lawrence's *The Plumed Serpent*
T. E. Lawrence's *Seven Pillars of Wisdom* privately circulated
Maugham's *The Casuarina Tree*
O'Casey's *The Plough and the Stars*
Puccini's *Turandot*
Jan Morris born

1927   General Chiang Kai-shek becomes prime minister in China
Trotsky expelled by the Communist party as a deviationist; Stalin becomes leader of the party and dictator of the Soviet Union
Charles Lindbergh flies from New York to Paris
J. W. Dunne's *An Experiment with Time*
Freud's *Autobiography* translated into English
Albert Giacometti's *Observing Head*

Ernest Hemingway's *Men Without Women*
Fritz Lang's *Metropolis*
Wyndham Lewis' *Time and Western Man*
F. W. Murnau's *Sunrise*
Proust's *Le Temps retrouvé* posthumously published
Stravinsky's *Oedipus Rex*
Virginia Woolf's *To the Lighthouse*

1928   The Kellogg-Briand Pact, outlawing war and providing for peaceful settlement of disputes, signed in Paris by sixty-two nations, including the Soviet Union
Herbert Hoover elected president of the United States
Women's suffrage granted at age twenty-one in Britain
Alexander Fleming discovers penicillin
Bertolt Brecht and Kurt Weill's *The Three-Penny Opera*
Eisenstein's *October*
Huxley's *Point Counter Point*
Christopher Isherwood's *All the Conspirators*
D. H. Lawrence's *Lady Chatterley's Lover*
Wyndham Lewis' *The Childermass*
Matisse's *Seated Odalisque*
Munch's *Girl on a Sofa*
Shaw's *Intelligent Woman's Guide to Socialism*
Virginia Woolf's *Orlando*
Yeats's *The Tower*
Iain Chrichton Smith born

1929   The Labour party wins British general election
Trotsky expelled from the Soviet Union
Museum of Modern Art opens in New York
Collapse of U.S. stock exchange begins world economic crisis
Robert Bridges's *The Testament of Beauty*
William Faulkner's *The Sound and the Fury*
Robert Graves's *Goodbye to All That*
Hemingway's *A Farewell to Arms*

Ernst Junger's *The Storm of Steel*
Hugo von Hoffmansthal's *Poems*
Henry Moore's *Reclining Figure*
J. B. Priestley's *The Good Companions*
Erich Maria Remarque's *All Quiet on the Western Front*
Shaw's *The Applecart*
R. C. Sheriff's *Journey's End*
Edith Sitwell's *Gold Coast Customs*
Thomas Wolfe's *Look Homeward, Angel*
Virginia Woolf's *A Room of One's Own*
Yeats's *The Winding Stair*
Second surrealist manifesto; Salvador
Dali joins the surrealists
Epstein's *Night and Day*
Mondrian's *Composition with Yellow Blue*

1930 Allied occupation of the Rhineland ends
Mohandas Gandhi opens civil disobedience campaign in India
The *Daily Worker*, journal of the British Communist party, begins publishing
J. W. Reppe makes artificial fabrics from an acetylene base
John Arden born
Auden's *Poems*
Coward's *Private Lives*
Eliot's *Ash Wednesday*
Wyndham Lewis's *The Apes of God*
Maugham's *Cakes and Ale*
Ezra Pound's *XXX Cantos*
Evelyn Waugh's *Vile Bodies*
Ruth Rendell born

1931 The failure of the Credit Anstalt in Austria starts a financial collapse in Central Europe
Britain abandons the gold standard; the pound falls by twenty-five percent
Mutiny in the Royal Navy at Invergordon over pay cuts
Ramsay MacDonald resigns, splits the Cabinet, and is expelled by the Labour party; in the general election the National Government wins by a majority of five hundred seats

The Statute of Westminster defines dominion status
Ninette de Valois founds the Vic-Wells
Ballet (eventually the Royal Ballet)
Coward's *Cavalcade*
Dali's The *Persistence of Memory*
John le Carré born
O'Neill's *Mourning Becomes Electra*
Anthony Powell's *Afternoon Men*
Antoine de Saint-Exupéry's *Vol de nuit*
Walton's *Belshazzar's Feast*
Virginia Woolf's *The Waves*
Caroline Blackwood born

1932 Franklin D. Roosevelt elected president of the United States
Paul von Hindenburg elected president of Germany; Franz von Papen elected chancellor
Sir Oswald Mosley founds British Union of Fascists
The BBC takes over development of television from J. L. Baird's company
Basic English of 850 words designed as a prospective international language
The Folger Library opens in Washington, D.C.
The Shakespeare Memorial Theatre opens in Stratford-upon-Avon
Faulkner's *Light in August*
Huxley's *Brave New World*
F. R. Leavis' *New Bearings in English Poetry*
Boris Pasternak's *Second Birth*
Ravel's *Concerto for Left Hand*
Peter Redgrove born
Rouault's *Christ Mocked by Soldiers*
Waugh's *Black Mischief*
Yeats's *Words for Music Perhaps*

1933 Roosevelt inaugurates the New Deal
Hitler becomes chancellor of Germany
The Reichstag set on fire
Hitler suspends civil liberties and freedom of the press; German trade unions suppressed

CHRONOLOGY

George Balanchine and Lincoln Kirstein found the School of American Ballet
Beryl Bainbridge born
Lowry's *Ultramarine*
André Malraux's *La Condition humaine*
Orwell's *Down and Out in Paris and London*
Gertrude Stein's *The Autobiography of Alice B. Toklas*
Anne Stevenson born

1934   The League Disarmament Conference ends in failure
The Soviet Union admitted to the League
Hitler becomes Führer
Civil war in Austria; Engelbert Dollfuss assassinated in attempted Nazi coup
Frédéric Joliot and Irene Joliot-Curie discover artificial (induced) radioactivity
Einstein's *My Philosophy*
Fitzgerald's *Tender Is the Night*
Graves's *I, Claudius* and *Claudius the God*
Toynbee's *A Study of History* begins publication (1934–1954)
Waugh's *A Handful of Dust*
Births of Alan Bennett, Christopher Wallace-Crabbe, and Alasdair Gray

1935   Grigori Zinoviev and other Soviet leaders convicted of treason
Stanley Baldwin becomes prime minister in National Government; National Government wins general election in Britain
Italy invades Abyssinia
Germany repudiates disarmament clauses of Treaty of Versailles
Germany reintroduces compulsory military service and outlaws the Jews
Robert Watson-Watt builds first practical radar equipment
Karl Jaspers' *Suffering and Existence*
Births of André Brink, Dennis Potter, Keith Roberts, and Jon Stallworthy

Ivy Compton-Burnett's *A House and Its Head*
Eliot's *Murder in the Cathedral*
Barbara Hepworth's *Three Forms*
George Gershwin's *Porgy and Bess*
Greene's *England Made Me*
Isherwood's *Mr. Norris Changes Trains*
Malraux's *Le Temps du mépris*
Yeats's *Dramatis Personae*
Klee's *Child Consecrated to Suffering*
Benedict Nicholson's *White Relief*

1936   Edward VII accedes to the throne in January; abdicates in December

1936–1952   Reign of George VI

1936   German troops occupy the RhinelandNinety-nine percent of German electorate vote for Nazi candidates
The Popular Front wins general election in France; Léon Blum becomes prime minister
Roosevelt reelected president of the United States
The Popular Front wins general election in Spain
Spanish Civil War begins
Italian troops occupy Addis Ababa; Abyssinia annexed by Italy
BBC begins television service from Alexandra Palace
Auden's *Look, Stranger!*
Auden and Isherwood's *The Ascent of F-6*
A. J. Ayer's *Language, Truth and Logic*
Chaplin's *Modern Times*
Greene's *A Gun for Sale*
Huxley's *Eyeless in Gaza*
Keynes's *General Theory of Employment*
F. R. Leavis' *Revaluation*
Mondrian's *Composition in Red and Blue*
Dylan Thomas' *Twenty-five Poems*
Wells's *The Shape of Things to Come* filmed
Reginald Hill born

1937   Trial of Karl Radek and other Soviet leaders

CHRONOLOGY

Neville Chamberlain succeeds Stanley Baldwin as prime minister
China and Japan at war
Frank Whittle designs jet engine
Picasso's *Guernica*
Shostakovich's Fifth Symphony
Magritte's *La Reproduction interdite*
Hemingway's *To Have and Have Not*
Malraux's *L'Espoir*
Orwell's *The Road to Wigan Pier*
Priestley's *Time and the Conways*
Virginia Woolf's *The Years*
Emma Tennant born
Death of Christopher Caudwell (Christopher St. John Sprigg)

1938   Trial of Nikolai Bukharin and other Soviet political leaders
Austria occupied by German troops and declared part of the Reich
Hitler states his determination to annex Sudetenland from Czechoslovakia
Britain, France, Germany, and Italy sign the Munich agreement
German troops occupy Sudetenland
Edward Hulton founds *Picture Post*
Cyril Connolly's *Enemies of Promise*
du Maurier's *Rebecca*
Faulkner's *The Unvanquished*
Graham Greene's *Brighton Rock*
Hindemith's *Mathis der Maler*
Jean Renoir's *La Grande Illusion*
Jean-Paul Sartre's *La Nausée*
Yeats's *New Poems*
Anthony Asquith's *Pygmalion* and Walt Disney's *Snow White*
Ngũgĩ wa Thiong'o born

1939   German troops occupy Bohemia and Moravia; Czechoslovakia incorporated into Third Reich
Madrid surrenders to General Franco; the Spanish Civil War ends
Italy invades Albania
Spain joins Germany, Italy, and Japan in anti-Comintern Pact
Britain and France pledge support to Poland, Romania, and Greece
The Soviet Union proposes defensive alliance with Britain; British military mission visits Moscow
The Soviet Union and Germany sign nonaggression treaty, secretly providing for partition of Poland between them
Germany invades Poland; Britain, France, and Germany at war
The Soviet Union invades Finland
New York World's Fair opens
Eliot's *The Family Reunion*
Births of Ayi Kwei Armah, Seamus Heaney, Michael Longley and Robert Nye
Isherwood's *Good-bye to Berlin*
Joyce's *Finnegans Wake* (1922–1939)
MacNeice's *Autumn Journal*
Powell's *What's Become of Waring?*
Ayi Kwei Armah born

1940   Churchill becomes prime minister
Italy declares war on France, Britain, and Greece
General de Gaulle founds Free French Movement
The Battle of Britain and the bombing of London
Roosevelt reelected president of the United States for third term
Betjeman's *Old Lights for New Chancels*
Angela Carter born
Chaplin's *The Great Dictator*
Bruce Chatwin born
Death of William H. Davies
J. M. Coetzee born
Disney's *Fantasia*
Greene's *The Power and the Glory*
Hemingway's *For Whom the Bell Tolls*
C. P. Snow's *Strangers and Brothers* (retitled *George Passant* in 1970, when entire sequence of ten novels, published 1940–1970, was entitled *Strangers and Brothers*)

1941   German forces occupy Yugoslavia, Greece, and Crete, and invade the Soviet Union
Lend-Lease agreement between the United States and Britain
President Roosevelt and Winston Churchill sign the Atlantic Charter

CHRONOLOGY

Japanese forces attack Pearl Harbor; United States declares war on Japan, Germany, Italy; Britain on Japan
Auden's *New Year Letter*
James Burnham's *The Managerial Revolution*
F. Scott Fitzgerald's *The Last Tycoon*
Huxley's *Grey Eminence*
Derek Mahon born
Shostakovich's *Seventh Symphony*
Tippett's *A Child of Our Time*
Orson Welles's *Citizen Kane*
Virginia Woolf's *Between the Acts*

1942 Japanese forces capture Singapore, Hong Kong, Bataan, Manila
German forces capture Tobruk
U.S. fleet defeats the Japanese in the Coral Sea, captures Guadalcanal
Battle of El Alamein
Allied forces land in French North Africa
Atom first split at University of Chicago
William Beveridge's *Social Insurance and Allied Services*
Albert Camus's *L'Étranger*
Joyce Cary's *To Be a Pilgrim*
Edith Sitwell's *Street Songs*
Waugh's *Put Out More Flags*
Births of Douglas Dunn, and **Jonathan Raban**

1943 German forces surrender at Stalingrad
German and Italian forces surrender in North Africa
Italy surrenders to Allies and declares war on Germany
Cairo conference between Roosevelt, Churchill, Chiang Kai-shek
Teheran conference between Roosevelt, Churchill, Stalin
Eliot's *Four Quartets*
Henry Moore's *Madonna and Child*
Sartre's *Les Mouches*
Vaughan Williams' *Fifth Symphony*

1944 Allied forces land in Normandy and southern France

Allied forces enter Rome
Attempted assassination of Hitler fails
Liberation of Paris
U.S. forces land in Philippines
German offensive in the Ardennes halted
Roosevelt reelected president of the United States for fourth term
Education Act passed in Britain
Pay-as-You-Earn income tax introduced
Beveridge's *Full Employment in a Free Society*
Cary's *The Horse's Mouth*
Huxley's *Time Must Have a Stop*
Maugham's *The Razor's Edge*
Sartre's *Huis Clos*
Edith Sitwell's *Green Song and Other Poems*
Graham Sutherland's *Christ on the Cross*
Trevelyan's *English Social History*
W. G. Sebald born

1945 British and Indian forces open offensive in Burma
Yalta conference between Roosevelt, Churchill, Stalin
Mussolini executed by Italian partisans
Roosevelt dies; Harry S. Truman becomes president
Hitler commits suicide; German forces surrender
The Potsdam Peace Conference
The United Nations Charter ratified in San Francisco
The Labour Party wins British General Election
Atomic bombs dropped on Hiroshima and Nagasaki
Surrender of Japanese forces ends World War II
Trial of Nazi war criminals opens at Nuremberg
All-India Congress demands British withdrawal from India
De Gaulle elected president of French Provisional Government; resigns the next year
Betjeman's *New Bats in Old Belfries*

CHRONOLOGY

Britten's *Peter Grimes*
Orwell's *Animal Farm*
Russell's *History of Western Philosophy*
Sartre's *The Age of Reason*
Edith Sitwell's *The Song of the Cold*
Waugh's *Brideshead Revisited*
Births of Wendy Cope and Peter Reading

1946   Bills to nationalize railways, coal mines, and the Bank of England passed in Britain
Nuremberg Trials concluded
United Nations General Assembly meets in New York as its permanent headquarters
The Arab Council inaugurated in Britain
Frederick Ashton's *Symphonic Variations*
Britten's *The Rape of Lucretia*
David Lean's *Great Expectations*
O'Neill's *The Iceman Cometh*
Roberto Rosselini's *Paisà*
Dylan Thomas' *Deaths and Entrances*

1947   President Truman announces program of aid to Greece and Turkey and outlines the "Truman Doctrine"
Independence of India proclaimed; partition between India and Pakistan, and communal strife between Hindus and Moslems follows
General Marshall calls for a European recovery program
First supersonic air flight
Britain's first atomic pile at Harwell comes into operation
Edinburgh festival established
Discovery of the Dead Sea Scrolls in Palestine
Princess Elizabeth marries Philip Mountbatten, duke of Edinburgh
Auden's *Age of Anxiety*
Camus's *La Peste*
Chaplin's *Monsieur Verdoux*
Lowry's *Under the Volcano*
Priestley's *An Inspector Calls*
Edith Sitwell's *The Shadow of Cain*
Waugh's *Scott-King's Modern Europe*

Births of Dermot Healy, and **Redmond O'Hanlon**

1948   Gandhi assassinated
Czech Communist Party seizes power
Pan-European movement (1948–1958) begins with the formation of the permanent Organization for European Economic Cooperation (OEEC)
Berlin airlift begins as the Soviet Union halts road and rail traffic to the city
British mandate in Palestine ends; Israeli provisional government formed
Yugoslavia expelled from Soviet bloc
Columbia Records introduces the long-playing record
Truman elected of the United States for second term
Greene's *The Heart of the Matter*
Huxley's *Ape and Essence*
Leavis' *The Great Tradition*
Pound's *Cantos*
Priestley's *The Linden Tree*
Waugh's *The Loved One*
Death of Denton Welch

1949   North Atlantic Treaty Organization established with headquarters in Brussels
Berlin blockade lifted
German Federal Republic recognized; capital established at Bonn
Konrad Adenauer becomes German chancellor
Mao Tse-tung becomes chairman of the People's Republic of China following Communist victory over the Nationalists
Peter Ackroyd born
Simone de Beauvoir's *The Second Sex*
Cary's *A Fearful Joy*
Arthur Miller's *Death of a Salesman*
Orwell's *Nineteen Eighty-four*

1950   Korean War breaks out
Nobel Prize for literature awarded to Bertrand Russell

R. H. S. Crossman's *The God That Failed*
T. S. Eliot's *The Cocktail Party*
Fry's *Venus Observed*
Doris Lessing's *The Grass Is Singing*
C. S. Lewis' *The Chronicles of Narnia* (1950–1956)
Wyndham Lewis' *Rude Assignment*
George Orwell's *Shooting an Elephant*
Carol Reed's *The Third Man*
Dylan Thomas' *Twenty-six Poems*
Births of **Sara Maitland,** and A. N. Wilson

1951 Guy Burgess and Donald Maclean defect from Britain to the Soviet Union
The Conservative party under Winston Churchill wins British general election
The Festival of Britain celebrates both the centenary of the Crystal Palace Exhibition and British postwar recovery
Electric power is produced by atomic energy at Arcon, Idaho
W. H. Auden's *Nones*
Samuel Beckett's *Molloy* and *Malone Dies*
Benjamin Britten's *Billy Budd*
Greene's *The End of the Affair*
Akira Kurosawa's *Rashomon*
Wyndham Lewis' *Rotting Hill*
Anthony Powell's *A Question of Upbringing* (first volume of *A Dance to the Music of Time*, 1951–1975)
J. D. Salinger's *The Catcher in the Rye*
C. P. Snow's *The Masters*
Igor Stravinsky's *The Rake's Progress*

1952– Reign of Elizabeth II
At Eniwetok Atoll the United States detonates the first hydrogen bomb
The European Coal and Steel Community comes into being
Radiocarbon dating introduced to archaeology
Michael Ventris deciphers Linear B script

Dwight D. Eisenhower elected president of the United States
Beckett's *Waiting for Godot*
Charles Chaplin's *Limelight*
Ernest Hemingway's *The Old Man and the Sea*
Arthur Koestler's *Arrow in the Blue*
F. R. Leavis' *The Common Pursuit*
Lessing's *Martha Quest* (first volume of *The Children of Violence*, 1952–1965)
C. S. Lewis' *Mere Christianity*
Thomas' *Collected Poems*
Evelyn Waugh's *Men at Arms* (first volume of *Sword of Honour*, 1952–1961)
Angus Wilson's *Hemlock and After*
Births of Rohinton Mistry and Vikram Seth

1953 Constitution for a European political community drafted
Julius and Ethel Rosenberg executed for passing U.S. secrets to the Soviet Union
Cease-fire declared in Korea
Edmund Hillary and his Sherpa guide, Tenzing Norkay, scale Mt. Everest
Nobel Prize for literature awarded to Winston Churchill
General Mohammed Naguib proclaims Egypt a republic
Beckett's *Watt*
Joyce Cary's *Except the Lord*
Robert Graves's *Poems 1953*
Death of Norman Cameron

1954 First atomic submarine, *Nautilus,* is launched by the United States
Dien Bien Phu captured by the Vietminh
Geneva Conference ends French dominion over Indochina
U.S. Supreme Court declares racial segregation in schools unconstitutional
Nasser becomes president of Egypt
Nobel Prize for literature awarded to Ernest Hemingway
Kingsley Amis' *Lucky Jim*
John Betjeman's *A Few Late Chrysanthemums*
William Golding's *Lord of the Flies*

CHRONOLOGY

Christopher Isherwood's *The World in the Evening*
Koestler's *The Invisible Writing*
Iris Murdoch's *Under the Net*
C. P. Snow's *The New Men*
Thomas' *Under Milk Wood* published posthumously
Births of **Iain Banks,** Romesh Gunesekera, **Kevin Hart,** Alan Hollinghurst, and **Hanif Kureishi**

1955 Warsaw Pact signed
West Germany enters NATO as Allied occupation ends
The Conservative party under Anthony Eden wins British general election
Cary's *Not Honour More*
Greene's *The Quiet American*
Philip Larkin's *The Less Deceived*
F. R. Leavis' *D. H. Lawrence, Novelist*
Vladimir Nabokov's *Lolita*
Patrick White's *The Tree of Man*
Patrick McCabe born

1956 Nasser's nationalization of the Suez Canal leads to Israeli, British, and French armed intervention
Uprising in Hungary suppressed by Soviet troops
Khrushchev denounces Stalin at Twentieth Communist Party Congress
Eisenhower reelected president of the United States
Anthony Burgess' *Time for a Tiger*
Golding's *Pincher Martin*
Murdoch's *Flight from the Enchanter*
John Osborne's *Look Back in Anger*
Snow's *Homecomings*
Edmund Wilson's *Anglo-Saxon Attitudes*

1957 The Soviet Union launches the first artificial earth satellite, *Sputnik I*
Eden succeeded by Harold Macmillan
Suez Canal reopened
Eisenhower Doctrine formulated
Parliament receives the Wolfenden Report on Homosexuality and Prostitution

Nobel Prize for literature awarded to Albert Camus
Beckett's *Endgame* and *All That Fall*
Lawrence Durrell's *Justine* (first volume of *The Alexandria Quartet*, 1957–1960)
Ted Hughes's *The Hawk in the Rain*
Murdoch's *The Sandcastle*
V. S. Naipaul's *The Mystic Masseur*
Eugene O'Neill's *Long Day's Journey into Night*
Osborne's *The Entertainer*
Muriel Spark's *The Comforters*
White's *Voss*

1958 European Economic Community established
Khrushchev succeeds Bulganin as Soviet premier
Charles de Gaulle becomes head of France's newly constituted Fifth Republic
The United Arab Republic formed by Egypt and Syria
The United States sends troops into Lebanon
First U.S. satellite, *Explorer 1*, launched
Nobel Prize for literature awarded to Boris Pasternak
Beckett's *Krapp's Last Tape*
John Kenneth Galbraith's *The Affluent Society*
Greene's *Our Man in Havana*
Murdoch's *The Bell*
Pasternak's *Dr. Zhivago*
Snow's *The Conscience of the Rich*

1959 Fidel Castro assumes power in Cuba
St. Lawrence Seaway opens
The European Free Trade Association founded
Alaska and Hawaii become the forty-ninth and fiftieth states
The Conservative party under Harold Macmillan wins British general election
Brendan Behan's *The Hostage*
Golding's *Free Fall*
Graves's *Collected Poems*
Koestler's *The Sleepwalkers*
Harold Pinter's *The Birthday Party*

xlv

CHRONOLOGY

Snow's *The Two Cultures and the Scientific Revolution*
Spark's *Memento Mori*
Robert Crawford born

1960 South Africa bans the African National Congress and Pan-African Congress
The Congo achieves independence
John F. Kennedy elected president of the United States
The U.S. bathyscaphe *Trieste* descends to 35,800 feet
Publication of the unexpurgated *Lady Chatterley's Lover* permitted by court
Auden's *Hommage to Clio*
Betjeman's *Summoned by Bells*
Pinter's *The Caretaker*
Snow's *The Affair*
David Storey's *This Sporting Life*
Ian Rankin born

1961 South Africa leaves the British Commonwealth
Sierra Leone and Tanganyika achieve independence
The Berlin Wall erected
The New English Bible published
Beckett's *How It Is*
Greene's *A Burnt-Out Case*
Koestler's *The Lotus and the Robot*
Murdoch's *A Severed Head*
Naipaul's *A House for Mr Biswas*
Osborne's *Luther*
Spark's *The Prime of Miss Jean Brodie*
White's *Riders in the Chariot*

1962 John Glenn becomes first U.S. astronaut to orbit earth
The United States launches the spacecraft *Mariner* to explore Venus
Algeria achieves independence
Cuban missile crisis ends in withdrawal of Soviet missiles from Cuba
Adolf Eichmann executed in Israel for Nazi war crimes
Second Vatican Council convened by Pope John XXIII
Nobel Prize for literature awarded to John Steinbeck
Edward Albee's *Who's Afraid of Virginia Woolf?*

Beckett's *Happy Days*
Anthony Burgess' *A Clockwork Orange* and *The Wanting Seed*
Aldous Huxley's *Island*
Isherwood's *Down There on a Visit*
Lessing's *The Golden Notebook*
Nabokov's *Pale Fire*
Aleksandr Solzhenitsyn's *One Day in the Life of Ivan Denisovich*

1963 Britain, the United States, and the Soviet Union sign a test-ban treaty
Birth of Simon Armitage
Britain refused entry to the European Economic Community
The Soviet Union puts into orbit the first woman astronaut, Valentina Tereshkova
Paul VI becomes pope
President Kennedy assassinated; Lyndon B. Johnson assumes office
Nobel Prize for literature awarded to George Seferis
Britten's *War Requiem*
John Fowles's *The Collector*
Murdoch's *The Unicorn*
Spark's *The Girls of Slender Means*
Storey's *Radcliffe*
John Updike's *The Centaur*

1964 Tonkin Gulf incident leads to retaliatory strikes by U.S. aircraft against North Vietnam
Greece and Turkey contend for control of Cyprus
Britain grants licenses to drill for oil in the North Sea
The Shakespeare Quatercentenary celebrated
Lyndon Johnson elected president of the United States
The Labour party under Harold Wilson wins British general election
Nobel Prize for literature awarded to Jean-Paul Sartre
Saul Bellow's *Herzog*
Burgess' *Nothing Like the Sun*
Golding's *The Spire*
Isherwood's *A Single Man*
Stanley Kubrick's *Dr. Strangelove*
Larkin's *The Whitsun Weddings*
Naipaul's *An Area of Darkness*

CHRONOLOGY

Peter Shaffer's *The Royal Hunt of the Sun*
Snow's *Corridors of Power*
Alan Warner born

1965 The first U.S. combat forces land in Vietnam
The U.S. spacecraft Mariner transmits photographs of Mars
British Petroleum Company finds oil in the North Sea
War breaks out between India and Pakistan
Rhodesia declares its independence
Ontario power failure blacks out the Canadian and U.S. east coasts
Nobel Prize for literature awarded to Mikhail Sholokhov
Robert Lowell's *For the Union Dead*
Norman Mailer's *An American Dream*
Osborne's *Inadmissible Evidence*
Pinter's *The Homecoming*
Spark's *The Mandelbaum Gate*

1966 The Labour party under Harold Wilson wins British general election
The Archbishop of Canterbury visits Pope Paul VI
Florence, Italy, severely damaged by floods
Paris exhibition celebrates Picasso's eighty-fifth birthday
Fowles's *The Magus*
Greene's *The Comedians*
Osborne's *A Patriot for Me*
Paul Scott's *The Jewel in the Crown* (first volume of *The Raj Quartet*, 1966–1975)
White's *The Solid Mandala*

1967 Thurgood Marshall becomes first black U.S. Supreme Court justice
Six-Day War pits Israel against Egypt and Syria
Biafra's secession from Nigeria leads to civil war
Francis Chichester completes solo circumnavigation of the globe
Dr. Christiaan Barnard performs first heart transplant operation, in South Africa

China explodes its first hydrogen bomb
Golding's *The Pyramid*
Hughes's *Wodwo*
Isherwood's *A Meeting by the River*
Naipaul's *The Mimic Men*
Tom Stoppard's *Rosencrantz and Guildenstern Are Dead*
Orson Welles's *Chimes at Midnight*
Angus Wilson's *No Laughing Matter*

1968 Violent student protests erupt in France and West Germany
Warsaw Pact troops occupy Czechoslovakia
Violence in Northern Ireland causes Britain to send in troops
Tet offensive by Communist forces launched against South Vietnam's cities
Theater censorship ended in Britain
Robert Kennedy and Martin Luther King Jr. assassinated
Richard M. Nixon elected president of the United States
Booker Prize for fiction established
Durrell's *Tunc*
Graves's *Poems 1965–1968*
Osborne's *The Hotel in Amsterdam*
Snow's *The Sleep of Reason*
Solzhenitsyn's *The First Circle* and *Cancer Ward*
Spark's *The Public Image*

1969 Humans set foot on the moon for the first time when astronauts descend to its surface in a landing vehicle from the U.S. spacecraft *Apollo 11*
The Soviet unmanned spacecraft *Venus V* lands on Venus
Capital punishment abolished in Britain
Colonel Muammar Qaddafi seizes power in Libya
Solzhenitsyn expelled from the Soviet Union
Nobel Prize for literature awarded to Samuel Beckett
Carter's *The Magic Toyshop*
Fowles's *The French Lieutenant's Woman*
Storey's *The Contractor*

CHRONOLOGY

1970   Civil war in Nigeria ends with Biafra's surrender
U.S. planes bomb Cambodia
The Conservative party under Edward Heath wins British general election
Nobel Prize for literature awarded to Aleksandr Solzhenitsyn
Durrell's *Nunquam*
Hughes's *Crow*
F. R. Leavis and Q. D. Leavis' *Dickens the Novelist*
Snow's *Last Things*
Spark's *The Driver's Seat*
Death of Vera Brittain

1971   Communist China given Nationalist China's UN seat
Decimal currency introduced to Britain
Indira Gandhi becomes India's prime minister
Nobel Prize for literature awarded to Heinrich Böll
Bond's *The Pope's Wedding*
Naipaul's *In a Free State*
Pinter's *Old Times*
Spark's *Not to Disturb*
Birth of Sarah Kane

1972   The civil strife of "Bloody Sunday" causes Northern Ireland to come under the direct rule of Westminster
Nixon becomes the first U.S. president to visit Moscow and Beijing
The Watergate break-in precipitates scandal in the United States
Eleven Israeli athletes killed by terrorists at Munich Olympics
Nixon reelected president of the United States
Bond's *Lear*
Snow's *The Malcontents*
Stoppard's *Jumpers*

1973   Britain, Ireland, and Denmark enter European Economic Community
Egypt and Syria attack Israel in the Yom Kippur War
Energy crisis in Britain reduces production to a three-day week
Nobel Prize for literature awarded to Patrick White
Bond's *The Sea*

Greene's *The Honorary Consul*
Lessing's *The Summer Before the Dark*
Murdoch's *The Black Prince*
Shaffer's *Equus*
White's *The Eye of the Storm*
Death of William Plomer

1974   Miners strike in Britain
Greece's military junta overthrown
Emperor Haile Selassie of Ethiopia deposed
President Makarios of Cyprus replaced by military coup
Nixon resigns as U.S. president and is succeeded by Gerald R. Ford
Betjeman's *A Nip in the Air*
Bond's *Bingo*
Durrell's *Monsieur* (first volume of *The Avignon Quintet*, 1974–1985)
Larkin's *The High Windows*
Solzhenitsyn's *The Gulag Archipelago*
Spark's *The Abbess of Crewe*
Death of Nancy Mitford
Death of Edmund Blunden

1975   The U.S. *Apollo* and Soviet *Soyuz* spacecrafts rendezvous in space
The Helsinki Accords on human rights signed
U.S. forces leave Vietnam
King Juan Carlos succeeds Franco as Spain's head of state
Nobel Prize for literature awarded to Eugenio Montale

1976   New U.S. copyright law goes into effect
Israeli commandos free hostages from hijacked plane at Entebbe, Uganda
British and French SST Concordes make first regularly scheduled commercial flights
The United States celebrates its bicentennial
Jimmy Carter elected president of the United States
Byron and Shelley manuscripts discovered in Barclay's Bank, Pall Mall
Hughes's *Seasons' Songs*
Koestler's *The Thirteenth Tribe*
Scott's *Staying On*

CHRONOLOGY

Spark's *The Take-over*

White's *A Fringe of Leaves*

1977　Silver jubilee of Queen Elizabeth II celebrated

Egyptian president Anwar el-Sadat visits Israel

"Gang of Four" expelled from Chinese Communist party

First woman ordained in the U.S. Episcopal church

After twenty-nine years in power, Israel's Labour party is defeated by the Likud party

Fowles's *Daniel Martin*

Hughes's *Gaudete*

1978　Treaty between Israel and Egypt negotiated at Camp David

Pope John Paul I dies a month after his coronation and is succeeded by Karol Cardinal Wojtyla, who takes the name John Paul II

Former Italian premier Aldo Moro murdered by left-wing terrorists

Nobel Prize for literature awarded to Isaac Bashevis Singer

Greene's *The Human Factor*

Hughes's *Cave Birds*

Murdoch's *The Sea, The Sea*

1979　The United States and China establish diplomatic relations

Ayatollah Khomeini takes power in Iran and his supporters hold U.S. embassy staff hostage in Teheran

Rhodesia becomes Zimbabwe

Earl Mountbatten assassinated

The Soviet Union invades Afghanistan

The Conservative party under Margaret Thatcher wins British general election

Nobel Prize for literature awarded to Odysseus Elytis

Golding's *Darkness Visible*

Hughes's *Moortown*

Lessing's *Shikasta* (first volume of *Canopus in Argos, Archives*)

Naipaul's *A Bend in the River*

Spark's *Territorial Rights*

White's *The Twyborn Affair*

1980　Iran-Iraq war begins

Strikes in Gdansk give rise to the Solidarity movement

Mt. St. Helen's erupts in Washington State

British steelworkers strike for the first time since 1926

More than fifty nations boycott Moscow Olympics

Ronald Reagan elected president of the United States

Burgess's *Earthly Powers*

Golding's *Rites of Passage*

Shaffer's *Amadeus*

Storey's *A Prodigal Child*

Angus Wilson's *Setting the World on Fire*

1981　Greece admitted to the European Economic Community

Iran hostage crisis ends with release of U.S. embassy staff

Twelve Labour MPs and nine peers found British Social Democratic party

Socialist party under François Mitterand wins French general election

Rupert Murdoch buys *The Times* of London

Turkish gunman wounds Pope John Paul II in assassination attempt

U.S. gunman wounds President Reagan in assassination attempt

President Sadat of Egypt assassinated

Nobel Prize for literature awarded to Elias Canetti

Spark's *Loitering with Intent*

1982　Britain drives Argentina's invasion force out of the Falkland Islands

U.S. space shuttle makes first successful trip

Yuri Andropov becomes general secretary of the Central Committee of the Soviet Communist party

Israel invades Lebanon

First artificial heart implanted at Salt Lake City hospital

Bellow's *The Dean's December*

Greene's *Monsignor Quixote*

1983　South Korean airliner with 269 aboard shot down after straying into Soviet airspace

U.S. forces invade Grenada following left-wing coup

CHRONOLOGY

Widespread protests erupt over placement of nuclear missiles in Europe

The £1 coin comes into circulation in Britain

Australia wins the America's Cup

Nobel Prize for literature awarded to William Golding

Hughes's *River*

Murdoch's *The Philosopher's Pupil*

1984 Konstantin Chernenko becomes general secretary of the Central Committee of the Soviet Communist party

Prime Minister Indira Gandhi of India assassinated by Sikh bodyguards

Reagan reelected president of the United States

Toxic gas leak at Bhopal, India, plant kills 2,000

British miners go on strike

Irish Republican Army attempts to kill Prime Minister Thatcher with bomb detonated at a Brighton hotel

World Court holds against U.S. mining of Nicaraguan harbors

Golding's *The Paper Men*

Lessing's *The Diary of Jane Somers*

Spark's *The Only Problem*

1985 United States deploys cruise missiles in Europe

Mikhail Gorbachev becomes general secretary of the Soviet Communist party following death of Konstantin Chernenko

Riots break out in Handsworth district (Birmingham) and Brixton

Republic of Ireland gains consultative role in Northern Ireland

State of emergency is declared in South Africa

Nobel Prize for literature awarded to Claude Simon

A. N. Wilson's *Gentlemen in England*

Lessing's *The Good Terrorist*

Murdoch's *The Good Apprentice*

Fowles's *A Maggot*

1986 U.S. space shuttle *Challenger* explodes

United States attacks Libya

Atomic power plant at Chernobyl destroyed in accident

Corazon Aquino becomes president of the Philippines

Giotto spacecraft encounters Comet Halley

Nobel Prize for literature awarded to Wole Soyinka

Final volume of *Oxford English Dictionary* supplement published

Amis's *The Old Devils*

Ishiguro's *An Artist of the Floating World*

A. N. Wilson's *Love Unknown*

Powell's *The Fisher King*

1987 Gorbachev begins reform of Communist party of the Soviet Union

Stock market collapses

Iran-contra affair reveals that Reagan administration used money from arms sales to Iran to fund Nicaraguan rebels

Palestinian uprising begins in Israeli-occupied territories

Nobel Prize for literature awarded to Joseph Brodsky

Golding's *Close Quarters*

Burgess's *Little Wilson and Big God*

Drabble's *The Radiant Way*

1988 Soviet Union begins withdrawing troops from Afghanistan

Iranian airliner shot down by U.S. Navy over Persian Gulf

War between Iran and Iraq ends

George Bush elected president of the United States

Pan American flight 103 destroyed over Lockerbie, Scotland

Nobel Prize for literature awarded to Naguib Mafouz

Greene's *The Captain and the Enemy*

Amis's *Difficulties with Girls*

Rushdie's *Satanic Verses*

1989 Ayatollah Khomeini pronounces death sentence on Salman Rushdie; Great Britain and Iran sever diplomatic relations

F. W. de Klerk becomes president of South Africa

CHRONOLOGY

Chinese government crushes student demonstration in Tiananmen Square

Communist regimes are weakened or abolished in Poland, Czechoslovakia, Hungary, East Germany, and Romania

Lithuania nullifies its inclusion in Soviet Union

Nobel Prize for literature awarded to José Cela

Second edition of *Oxford English Dictionary* published

Drabble's *A Natural Curiosity*

Murdoch's *The Message to the Planet*

Amis's *London Fields*

Ishiguro's *The Remains of the Day*

Death of Bruce Chatwin

1990   Communist monopoly ends in Bulgaria

Riots break out against community charge in England

First women ordained priests in Church of England

Civil war breaks out in Yugoslavia; Croatia and Slovenia declare independence

Bush and Gorbachev sign START agreement to reduce nuclear-weapons arsenals

President Jean-Baptiste Aristide overthrown by military in Haiti

Boris Yeltsin elected president of Russia

Dissolution of the Soviet Union

Nobel Prize for literature awarded to Nadine Gordimer

1992   U.N. Conference on Environment and Development (the "Earth Summit") meets in Rio de Janeiro

Prince and Princess of Wales separate

War in Bosnia-Herzegovina intensifies

Bill Clinton elected president of the United States in three-way race with Bush and independent candidate H. Ross Perot

Nobel Prize for literature awarded to Derek Walcott

1993   Czechoslovakia divides into the Czech Republic and Slovakia; playwright Vaclav Havel elected president of the Czech Republic

Britain ratifies Treaty on European Union (the "Maastricht Treaty")

U.S. troops provide humanitarian aid amid famine in Somalia

United States, Canada, and Mexico sign North American Free Trade Agreement

Nobel Prize for literature awarded to Toni Morrison

1994   Nelson Mandela elected president in South Africa's first post-apartheid election

Jean-Baptiste Aristide restored to presidency of Haiti

Clinton health care reforms rejected by Congress

Civil war in Rwanda

Republicans win control of both houses of Congress for first time in forty years

Prime Minister Albert Reynolds of Ireland meets with Gerry Adams, president of Sinn Fein

Nobel Prize for literature awarded to Kenzaburo Õe

Amis's *You Can't Do Both*

Naipaul's *A Way in the World*

Death of Dennis Potter

1995   Britain and Irish Republican Army engage in diplomatic talks

Barings Bank forced into bankruptcy as a result of a maverick bond trader's losses

United States restores full diplomatic relations with Vietnam

NATO initiates air strikes in Bosnia

Death of Stephen Spender

Israeli Prime Minister Yitzhak Rabin assassinated

Nobel Prize for literature awarded to Seamus Heaney

1996   IRA breaks cease-fire; Sein Fein representatives barred from Northern Ireland peace talks

Prince and Princess of Wales divorce

Cease-fire agreement in Chechnia; Russian forces begin to withdraw

CHRONOLOGY

Boris Yeltsin reelected president of Russia

Bill Clinton reelected president of the United States

Nobel Prize for literature awarded to Wislawa Szymborska

Death of Caroline Blackwood

1996 British government destroys around 100,000 cows suspected of infection with Creutzfeldt-Jakob, or "mad cow" disease

1997 Diana, Princess of Wales, dies in an automobile accident

Unveiling of first fully-cloned adult animal, a sheep named Dolly

Booker McConnell Prize for fiction awarded to Arundhati Roy

1998 United States renews bombing of Bagdad, Iraq

Independent legislature and Parliaments return to Scotland and Wales

Booker McConnell Prize for fiction awarded to Ian McEwan

Nobel Prize for literature awarded to Jose Saramago

1999 King Hussein of Jordan dies

United Nations responds militarily to Serbian President Slobodan Milosevic's escalation of crisis in Kosovo

Booker McConnell Prize for fiction awarded to J. M. Coetzee

Nobel Prize for literature awarded to Günter Grass

Deaths of Ted Hughes, Brian Moore, and Iain Chrichton Smith

2000 Penelope Fitzgerald dies

J. K. Rowling's *Harry Potter and the Goblet of Fire* sells more than 300,000 copies in its first day

Oil blockades by fuel haulers protesting high oil taxes bring much of Britain to a standstill

Slobodan Milosevic loses Serbian general election to Vojislav Kostunica

Death of Scotland's First Minister, Donald Dewar

Nobel Prize for literature awarded to Gao Xingjian

Booker McConnell Prize for fiction awarded to Margaret Atwood

George W. Bush, son of former president George Bush, becomes president of the United States after Supreme Court halts recount of closest election in history

Death of former Canadian Prime Minister Pierre Elliot Trudeau

Human Genome Project researchers announce that they have a complete map of the genetic code of a human chromosome

Vladimir Putin succeeds Boris Yeltsin as president of Russia

British Prime Minister Tony Blair's son Leo is born, making him the first child born to a sitting prime minister in 152 years

Death of Keith Roberts

2001 In Britain, the House of Lords passes legislation that legalizes the creation of cloned human embryos

British Prime Minister Tony Blair wins second term

Margaret Atwood's *The Blind Assassin* wins Booker McConnell Prize for fiction

Kazuo Ishiguro's *When We Were Orphans*

Trezza Azzopardi's *The Hiding Place*

Terrorists attack World Trade Center and Pentagon with hijacked airplanes, resulting in the collapse of the World Trade Center towers and the deaths of thousands. Passengers of a third hijacked plane thwart hijackers, resulting in a crash landing in Pennsylvania. The attacks are thought to be organized by Osama bin Laden, the leader of an international terrorist network known as al Qaeda

Ian McEwan's *An Atonement*

Salman Rushdie's *Fury*

Peter Carey's *True History of the Kelly Gang*

Deaths of Eudora Welty and W. G. Sebald

2002 Former U.S. President Jimmy Carter awarded the Nobel Peace Prize

Europe experiences its worst floods

in 100 years as floodwaters force thousands of people out of their homes

Wall Street Journal reporter Daniel Pearl kidnapped and killed in Karachi, Pakistan while researching a story about Pakistani militants and suspected shoe bomber Richard Reid. British-born Islamic militant Ahmad Omar Saeed Sheikh sentenced to death for the crime. Three accomplices receive life sentences.

Slobodan Milosevic goes on trial at the U.N. war crimes tribunal in The Hague on charges of masterminding ethnic cleansing in the former Yugoslavia.

Yann Martel's *Life of Pi* wins Booker McConnell Prize for fiction

Nobel Prize for literature awarded to Imre Kertész

2003 Ariel Sharon elected as Israeli prime minister

Venezuelan President Hugo Chavez forced to leave office after a nine week general strike calling for his resignation ends

U.S. presents to the United Nations its Iraq war rationale, citing its Weapons of Mass Destruction as imminent threat to world security

U.S. and Britain launch war against Iraq

Baghdad falls to U.S. troops

Official end to combat operations in Iraq is declared by the U.S.

Aung San Suu Kyi, Burmese opposition leader, placed under house arrest by military regime

NATO assumes control of peacekeeping force in Afghanistan

American troops capture Saddam Hussein

J.K. Rowling's *Harry Potter and the Order of the Phoenix*, the sixth installment in the wildly popular series, hit the shelves and rocketed up the best-seller lists

Nobel Prize for literature awarded to J. M. Coetzee

Death of C. H. Sisson

2004 NATO admits seven new members—Bulgaria, Estonia, Latvia, Lithuania, Romania, Slovakia, and Slovenia

Terrorists bomb commuter trains in Spain—al-Qaeda claims responsibility

Ten new states join the European Union, expanding it to twenty-five members states total

Muslim terrorists attack a school in Beslan, Russia, resulting in over 300 civilian deaths, many of them schoolchildren

George W. Bush is re-elected president of the United States

Allegations of corruption in the election of Ukraine's Viktor Yanukovych result in the "Orange Revolution" and Parliament's decision to nullify the first election results—the secondary run-off election is closley monitored and favors Viktor Yushchenko for president

A massive 9.0 earthquake rocks the Indian Ocean, resulting in a catastrophic tsunami, devastating southern Asia and eastern Africa and killing tens of thousands of people

Alan Hollinghurst's *The Line of Beauty* wins Man Booker Prize for fiction

List of Contributors

JAMES P. AUSTIN. James P. Austin is a graduate of the MFA program in fiction at the University of California, Irvine, and is presently at work on a collection of stories. **Redmond O'Hanlon**

SUSAN BALÉE. Susan Balée wrote the first biography of Flannery O'Connor (Chelsea House, 1994) and has contributed entries on Percy Bysshe Shelley and Mary Elizabeth Braddon to Scribners' *British Writers* series. Her essays on O'Connor, American Autobiography, and Henry W. Longfellow (co–authored with Dana Gioia) appear in the *Oxford Encyclopedia of American Literature* (2003). **John Clare**

FRED BILSON. Writer. Holds a bachelors in English and a masters in science. He has lectured in English, linguistics, and computer systems and works as a support tutor to university students with dyslexia. **Jonathan Raban**

J.C. BITTENBENDER. J.C. Bittenbender, Ph.D., is an associate professor at Eastern University in St. Davids, Pennsylvania where he teaches 20th century British literature. He specializes in modern Scottish and Irish literature and has published articles on Robert Burns, Alasdair Gray, and James Kelman. His other areas of academic interest include Bakhtinian theory and censorship studies. **Robert Crawford**

DAN BRAYTON. Dan Brayton teaches in the English Department at Middlebury College and the Williams College–Mystic Seaport Program in American Maritime Studies. His fields of specialization include sixteenth and seventeenth–century English literature, utopian literature, and maritime literature. He has published articles on Shakespeare's King Lear, Thomas More's *Utopia*, and on Marlowe, Greene, Brome, and Bradstreet. His work has appeared in the journals *English Literary History* (ELH), *Shakespeare Quarterly* (SQ), Scribners' *British Writers* and *British Classics*,

The Oxford Companion to American Literature, and *WoodenBoat*. **Philip Massinger**

SANDIE BYRNE. Fellow in English at Balliol College, Oxford. Her publications include works on eighteenth–and nineteenth–century fiction and twentieth–century poetry. **Sara Maitland**

STEFANIE K. DUNNING. Stefanie K. Dunning is assistant professor of English at Miami University of Ohio. Her areas of interest are African American Literature, Postcolonial Studies, and Gay and Lesbian Studies. Her work has been published in *African American Review*, *MELUS*, and *Black Renaissance/Renaissance Noire*. **Hanif Kureishi**

JACQUES KHALIP. Jacques Khalip is assistant professor of English at McMaster University, where he teaches Romantic and post–Romantic literature and culture and critical theory. He is currently completing a manuscript on the ethics and aesthetics of anonymous subjectivity from Adam Smith to Percy Shelley. **Kevin Hart**

E. M. KNOTTENBELT. Assistant–professor of English at the University of Amsterdam, Netherlands. She has published numerous essays on modern and contemporary authors (among them, Ford Madox Ford, Eliot, Beckett) and a book on Geoffrey Hill (1990). Other work includes comparative studies of English translations (Dante, Virgil, Ovid, Racine) and articles in the literary, and/or political religious history of the Renaissance. She is presently completing a book on C. H. Sisson and a survey, *Traditions in English Poetry: From the Early Modern Period to the Present*. **C.H. Sisson**

GAVIN MILLER. Research Fellow in the Centre for the History of Ideas in Scotland, University of Edinburgh. Gavin Miller received his MA and later his Ph.D. degrees from the University of Edinburgh. He is the author of numerous articles on Scottish culture and literature as well as two monographs, *R. D. Laing* (2004) and *Alasdair Gray* (2005). **Iain Banks**

HELENA NELSON. Writer and Lecturer. Born in Cheshire, England in 1953, Nelson holds a BA from the University of York and an MA in Eighteenth–Century literature from the University of Manchester. She has written romantic fiction and is a full–time lecturer in English and Communication Studies at Glenrothes College in Scotland. Nelson is the main writer and editor of the further education resource *Core.com 2002*. Her poetry collections include: *Mr and Mrs Philpott on Holiday at Auchterawe (Kettillonia, 2001) and Starlight on Water* (Rialto Press, 2003). **William H. Davies**

NEIL POWELL. Poet, biographer and editor. His books include six collections of poetry—*At the Edge* (1977), *A Season of Calm Weather* (1982), *True Colours* (1991), *The Stones on Thorpeness Beach* (1994), *Selected Poems* (1998), and *A Halfway House* (2004)—as well as *Carpenters of Light* (1979), *Roy Fuller: Writer and Society* (1995), *The Language of Jazz* (1997), and *George Crabbe: An English Life* (2004). He lives in Suffolk, England. **Fulke Greville, Elizabeth Jane Howard**

PETER SCUPHAM. Peter Scupham has published some ten collections of poetry, mostly with Oxford University Press. His *Collected Poems* was published by Carcanet/Oxford in 2002, and he edited a selection from Arthur Golding' Elizabethan translation of Ovid's *Metamorphose* for Carcanet's Fyfield Books in 2005. He is a fellow of the Royal Society of Literature and a Cholmondeley Award winner. **Edmund Blunden**

ANDREW VAN DER VLIES. Andrew van der Vlies has a MA from Rhodes University in South Africa and an M.Phil. and D.Phil degrees from the University of Oxford. He has published on Olive Schreiner and late–nineteenth–century British publishing and reading cultures, and on South African writers. He has research and teaching interests in twentieth–century British and American writing, colonial and postcolonial literatures, book history and the institutions of publishing, transnational modernisms, literary theory, and contemporary fiction. **William Plomer, Alan Warner**

ANDREW ZAWACKI. Andrew Zawacki is the author of two books of poetry, *Anabranch* (Wesleyan, 2004) and *By Reason of Breakings* (Georgia, 2002), as well as a chapbook, *Masquerade* (Vagabond, 2001). Coeditor of *Verse* and editor of *Afterwards: Slovenian Writing 1945–1995* (White Pine, 1999), he has published criticism in the *TLS*, *Boston Review*, *Antioch Review*, *Kenyon Review*, *Notre Dame Review*, *Australian Book Review*, and elsewhere, including in volumes from Harvard University Press and University of Michigan Press. He is a doctoral candidate in the Committee on Social Thought at the University of Chicago. **Thomas Traherne**

BRITISH WRITERS

IAIN BANKS

(1954–)

Gavin Miller

In 1999, BBC Television held an internet poll to discover the greatest writer of the second millennium. In fifth place—after Shakespeare, Austen, Orwell, and Dickens—came Iain Banks, the prolific author of both mainstream and science fiction literature, who has published twenty novels since the mid-1980s. The poll result no doubt reflects deliberate lobbying by a network of fans. But, though Banks may not quite deserve such esteemed company as Shakespeare and Dickens, neither the literary value of his work nor his dedication to writing should be underestimated.

Banks was born in the Scottish town of Dunfermline, in Fife, on February 16, 1954. An only child, he lived until 1963 in North Queensferry, a Fife town close to his father's job with the British Admiralty in the naval dockyard at Rosyth. Banks then moved to the west coast town of Gourock, on the mouth of the River Clyde, when the navy relocated his father. In the towns of Gourock and Greenock, Banks completed his school education and began his early writing career with unpublished juvenilia such as the engagingly titled *The Hungarian Lift-Jet,* a ten-thousand-word miniature thriller in the style of the popular Scottish author Alistair MacLean.

Banks then proceeded to an ordinary degree at the University of Stirling, a qualification he completed in 1975, having studied philosophy, psychology, and English literature. After university, Banks embarked on a series of dead-end jobs: working as a clerk for IBM, as a technician for British Steel, and for a London law firm. These jobs allowed him money to subsist, while writing and traveling in his spare time. It was in 1980, while working for the London lawyers, that he met his future wife, Annie, whom he would marry in 1992. It was also during this period in London that Banks wrote the science

fiction novels that would later be published as *Consider Phlebas* (1987), *The Player of Games* (1988), and *Against a Dark Background* (1993).

Banks's career as a published author began in 1984 with his phenomenally successful first novel, *The Wasp Factory,* and Banks has continued to produce best-seller after best-seller. Since publication of *The Wasp Factory* he has settled into a routine where he spends most of his time pursuing his interests in technology and fast cars before settling down to produce another novel either as Iain Banks or—for science fiction—under the rather transparent pen name Iain M. Banks. After a period living in London and Kent, he returned to Scotland in 1987 and eventually settled in his childhood hometown of North Queensferry. At the time of writing, Banks has published twelve mainstream novels, eight science fiction novels, a collection of short stories, and *Raw Spirit* (2003), a biographical account of a journey around the whisky distilleries of Scotland. Banks is particularly striking for his literary range: he is as comfortable with quirky, emphatically Scottish novels as with the grandest of interstellar utopian science fiction.

THE WASP FACTORY

The Wasp Factory was written, according to Banks, in about ten weeks in the early 1980s. It was finally, and rapidly, accepted by Macmillan, the seventh publisher to which it was submitted. Banks's future editor, James Hale, read the manuscript over a weekend and then phoned him on Monday morning to offer a contract. When published in 1984, the book generated an enormous amount of publicity because of its tongue-in-cheek depiction of violence toward children and animals and because of its bizarre denouement in which the central character discovers that "he" is really a girl. Critical opinion was far from unanimously favorable. Patricia Craig in the *Times Literary Supplement* thought that although Banks showed a "flair for hammed-up horror," he also displayed "all the finesse of a strip cartoon" in his mixture of "ghoulish frivolity" and "preposterous sadism." Overall, she concluded, *The Wasp Factory* was "the literary equivalent of the nastiest brand of juvenile delinquency: inflicting outrages on animals." Andrew Marr in the *Scotsman* was more sympathetic to his fellow national: he argued that "it could not be said that the violence is casual or unnecessary" and heard "a note of maniac, utterly over-the-top humour about even the worst of the violence that effectively robs it of its power to sicken"; he did not, however, recommend that anyone should buy the book. Yet whatever the reviews, *The Wasp Factory* was an astute investment for its publishers: it has sold over a million copies since its publication and has become emblematic of its author's imagination.

The central character (and narrator) of *The Wasp Factory,* Francis ("Frank") Leslie Cauldhame, lives on a small island off the northern coast of Scotland with his scientist father. Frank's brother Eric is a paranoid schizophrenic who, at the beginning of the narrative, escapes from a mental hospital in the central belt of Scotland. As the story progresses—and as Eric gradually closes in on home—we learn more of Frank's extraordinary existence. He has been reared in secrecy, educated at home by his father, and—apart from Jamie, a dwarf—has no friends in the nearby town of Porteneil, to which the island is connected by a bridge.

The Wasp Factory is the center of Frank's bizarre existence: it is a divinatory tool consisting of a covered clock face, each numeral of which leads to an unusual randomized death for the wasps that Frank feeds into the contraption. From their deaths—in the "Boiling Pool," the "Acid Chamber," and so forth—Frank tries to extract meaning and guidance. As if this were not strange enough, Frank lets his audience in on another secret. He is guilty of three child murders—he has killed his cousin Blyth, his younger brother Paul, and his half-cousin Esmeralda—and he has committed these crimes in bizarre and shocking ways: planting an adder in Blyth's artificial limb, encouraging Paul to beat an unexploded bomb with a plank, and allowing Esmeralda the reins of an enormous kite, which carries her away over the North Sea. As Frank's story unfolds we learn something of the psychological background to this behavior. As a child he was castrated in an attack by the family dog, Old Saul, at the moment of his brother Paul's birth. Old Saul is, to Frank, the "Castraitor" (p. 103) who has set him on a path of twisted vengeance upon the world.

When Eric finally returns to the family home, having left a trail of destruction en route, Frank's father is so shaken that he forgets to lock the door of his study, a room that—Bluebeard-style—is normally inaccessible to his sons. There Frank finds male hormones and concludes in shock that his father may be a woman. The truth, though, is even stranger. When confronted, Cauldhame Senior reveals the real story of Frank's origins. Frank was indeed savaged by Old Saul, but there was never anything for the dog to castrate: Francis is really a girl, Frances. Mr. Cauldhame's fabulations, and frequent doses of male hormones, have managed to suppress all evidence of her true sex.

The psychoanalytic significance of *The Wasp Factory* has been noted by many: Mr. Cauldhame has tried to create a Freudian woman—one who (as Freud speculated) believes that her anatomy was formed by castration and who envies and resents the world and society that have made her this way. In a fine Shakespearean pun, Frank reflects on her life of destruction, and concludes that "lacking...one will, I forged another—Talk about penis envy" (p. 183). Yet what Banks has Mr. Cauldhame produce is not woman in her essential form (envying the penis consciously rather than subconsciously) but rather a hypermasculine personality obsessed with outmanning men. Frank's actions are an anxious emulation of the "ruthless soldier-hero almost all I've ever seen or read seems to pay strict homage to" (p. 183). The only people with penis envy, Banks slyly suggests, are men (or at least those who believe they are men).

Standing against Frank's ideal of masculinity is her brother Eric, who is driven into insanity by an experience that shatters his faith in the world. While training as a doctor, Eric takes care of a badly brain-damaged baby. One day he discovers to his horror that what remains of the child's brain has been consumed by maggots lain by flies in the overheated ward. In some ways this scene is a deliberate attempt to shock the reader; indeed, its artificiality is emphasized by its (presumably unwitting) impossibility—Banks forgets that maggots consume only dead flesh, not living tissue, cerebral or otherwise. But what is of importance is Eric's defective, unmanly vulnerability to this experience. To Frank, Eric's disintegration is a sign of "weakness": as she has learned from films and television, only a woman, or a womanly man, would be unable to cope with such an experience.

The Wasp Factory is perhaps a rather awkwardly written novel that gains most of its effect from its surprise ending. However, it may be seen as a useful introduction to Banks's work. Many of the themes it addresses recur in later works, where they are developed with greater subtlety. Frank's futile masculine quest for revenge upon the world that has seemingly so disfigured her is echoed in many of Bank's novels: for this author, the desire for justice at any price is one of man's great delusions—an anthropomorphic projection upon a universe where neither nature nor fate have any interest in human sufferings. Further, for all the dark imagination of *The Wasp Factory,* one can see in it hints of Banks's science fiction utopia the "Culture." Mr. Cauldhame forcibly attempts to alter the gender of his daughter; in the Culture, advanced technology allows individuals to slowly transform into members of the opposite sex. In Mr. Cauldhame's seeming act of arbitrary cruelty, then, there is a hint of—premature—aspiration toward a utopia. Banks returns to such ambivalent possibilities in his science fiction, where the failure of central and eastern European socialism is revealed (from the future perspective of the anarchist-socialist Culture) as that of a noble idea whose time had not yet come.

HUMAN JUSTICE: COMPLICITY, DEAD AIR

The search for justice is at the heart of Banks's 1993 novel *Complicity.* Set in 1992, the novel tells of Cameron Colley, a journalist at a Scottish newspaper, the *Caledonian* (a thinly veiled version of the Edinburgh newspaper the *Scotsman*). Colley finds himself a suspect in the police investigation of a bizarre series of attacks—many of them murderous—committed as acts of poetic justice against various wrongdoers. Most of the victims are not criminals in the technical sense of the word (though one is a peddler of child pornography); rather, they are establishment figures who abuse their positions of power. A judge who gives out lenient sentences to rapists is himself anally raped by a vibrator-wielding intruder; a warmongering politician and profiteer in the arms industry is bled to death in front of his hunting dogs; and so on. The attacks are described to the reader in sections of narration in the second person; these are interpolated within Colley's ongoing first-person narrative.

Colley is eventually arrested and questioned: he has no alibi and has in some of his articles seemed to advocate similar attacks. The real criminal, though, is Colley's childhood friend Andy, who has faked his own death and framed Colley in order to continue his crimes. However, the attacks reach a climax that reveals their true instigator. Among the final killings is the murder of the army major whom Andy feels betrayed him during the Falklands War. Andy also slaughters the doctor who failed to diagnose the heart condition that led to the early death of his sister. Colley himself has the chance to turn in Andy, but he cannot: he allows Andy to escape, perhaps to continue his murderous rampage.

Complicity could be read merely as a polemic against the ruling powers during the 1980s and 1990s in the United Kingdom. Banks has frequently expressed his revulsion at the right-wing Conservative Party, the Tories, who under Margaret Thatcher and John Major were in charge of Britain during this time. There is no doubt that many of the political stances and exposures of perceived hypocrisy in the narrative of *Complicity* reflect Banks's views (though not, one presumes, his preferred manner of retribution).

Of more interest, though, are the complexities of guilt and innocence that the narrative addresses. Colley is no saint. Despite his crusading left-wing pose, he is himself complicit with the society he condemns. A frequent user of drugs and addicted to cigarettes, Colley is aware of his own corruption by his society: "at the end of the day you still light another cigarette and suck in the smoke like you enjoyed it and make more profits for those evil fucks" (p. 54). Colley also whiles away his leisure time consuming madly: high-profile brands such as Toshiba and Peugeot, and the array of gadgets he wields, are his favorite distractions. Even his journalistic impulses are far from unselfish. Although he would like to think of himself as a reporter in the mode of Woodward and Bernstein, who uncovered the Watergate scandal, news-gathering is merely another addiction for Colley. The "news-fix buzz" (p. 27) is a cheap thrill, like those found in buying a laptop computer, playing Despot (Colley's favorite computer game), and driving fast while under the influence of drink and drugs. Even his most intimate relation—with his lover Yvonne—is merely a game of thrilling undercover encounters.

Despite Colley's self-conception as critical outsider, he can be seen as both complicit with Andy and paving the way for him. At times he mimics Andy's activities—at one point he even enacts a mock rape with Yvonne after pretending to break into her house. Banks's narrative technique also plays with the symbiosis and overlap between Colley and Andy. The book ends with Colley reflecting on events but narrating himself in the second person, in the voice that has been used to narrate the murders: "You light a cigarette…and laugh" (p. 313). Although the story rules out the possibility that Colley is directly responsible for the murders, there is a narrative hint that Andy is his double, a lurking Mr. Hyde to Colley's left-wing Dr. Jekyll.

Dead Air (2002) returns to the theme of the journalist who is implicated in the society he claims to criticize. Ken Nott is a "shock jock" for the (fictional) London radio station Capital Live!, a subsidiary of the media conglomerate Mouth Corp. While at a corporate party one evening, he meets Celia, the wife of John Merrial, a London crime lord. Ken and Celia then begin an affair that almost ends in destruction. Although they meet in secrecy, Ken one night drunkenly phones Celia but accidentally calls her home number instead of her cellphone number and leaves a sexually explicit message on the Merrials' answering machine. Although Ken manages to erase the message with Celia's help, Merrial discovers that Ken has intruded in his home and has him kidnapped for interrogation and, if necessary, punishment. Ken—with a lot of help from Celia—manages to escape with his life by convincing Merrial that he has erased only a drunken insulting rant of the kind he would normally issue on the radio.

Ken in many ways echoes the character of Cameron Colley in *Complicity*. Like Colley, Ken seems to collude with the very system that he claims to oppose. He is told by a colleague in the media that "the bad corporate stuff, which Mouth Corp does as much as anybody, gets a lot less publicity than it deserves, thanks to you" (p. 272); Ken is a court jester whose mockery creates a corporate impression of evenhanded tolerance. Furthermore, Ken, despite his moralistic outbursts, has his own latent satisfactions: despite his protestations to Celia that "I don't mean I insult people or their beliefs because I want to hurt those people, because I get some sort of sadistic kick out of it" (p. 89), the reader can read between the lines. As Ken realizes, when looked at from the outside he is "behaving like a masochist with a death wish" (p. 114). Whatever his conscious intentions and rationalizations, his life is a series of invitations to self-destruction: as well as conducting an affair with Celia and baiting every extremist in the land, Ken consumes drinks and drugs to excess, falls into bed with his best friend Craig's estranged wife, nearly seduces Craig's teenage daughter, and attempts to buy a gun from a gangster. The key plot device—Ken's supposedly unwitting phone call to Merrial—seems merely another element in this latent intention to invite destruction. Ken's idolization of truth and logic—however seemingly laudable—is really an expression of his damaged relation to the world. His affair with Celia, though, reveals to him the selfishness of his personal crusade. Like Andy in *Complicity*, Ken cares nothing for the consequences of his (self-) righteous actions. Even his drunken phone call can be seen as an extension of this desire to "tell the truth" to Merrial, regardless of what ensues. It is only Celia's highly developed ability to lie, and Merrial's wish to be deceived, that allows Ken's affair to be concealed.

COSMIC JUSTICE: ESPEDAIR STREET, THE CROW ROAD

Complicity and *Dead Air* both deal with characters who have made a fetish of truth and justice and who unforgivingly assault human society for its failure to attain those ideals. Other of Banks's novels deal with the further absurdity of holding the universe itself morally accountable. The world of reward and punishment is a human creation and a worthy ideal but, implies Banks, it should not be anthropomorphically projected onto a universe of time and chance. As the "Doctor" remarks in Banks's science fiction novel *Inversions* (1998), "The world itself, without us, does not recognize such things [as good and bad], just because they are not things, they are ideas, and the world contained no ideas until people came along" (p. 125).

The Crow Road (1992) distinguishes between the unreasonable expectation that the cosmos should be fair to humans and the more reasonable and modest human aspiration that society should be fair and just. Prentice McHoan is the son of Kenneth, the middle of three brothers—the oldest is Hamish and the youngest is Rory, who has been missing for several years at the start of the narrative. The three brothers had a sister, Fiona, who died in a car crash; she is survived, though, by her husband, Fergus. By the end of the narrative Prentice has exposed Fergus' secret: he murdered Fiona in a deliberate car

crash as revenge for a one-night affair. Prentice's Uncle Rory was also later killed by Fergus; Rory had worked out his brother-in-law's secret and intended to use it as the thinly veiled basis for a novel.

Although Prentice is not driven by a need for revenge, he does regard the universe as if it should contain a neat balance of merits and rewards. When the world cheats Prentice of this moral accountancy he turns to self-destruction in an act of petulance against a cosmos that could not, Banks's text implies, even attempt to comprehend his actions. Prentice's loss of faith begins as resentment at his brother Lewis' relationship with Verity, a beautiful family friend with whom Prentice has long been infatuated. Things worsen, though, when Prentice's friend Darren Watt dies accidentally while riding his motorbike. In protest to a deaf universe, Prentice begins a slide into self-destruction: drinking too much, neglecting his studies, abusing Lewis and Verity at a New Year's party. Ironically his despair distracts him from the one act of justice he can perform: he has before him all the information he needs to recognize his uncle Fergus' guilt but cannot focus on this useful accomplishment.

Espedair Street (1987) also addresses the human desire for cosmic justice and reveals both the fragility and anthropomorphism of this expectation. Daniel Weir is a wealthy former rock star living alone in his bizarre home, an anti-Christian folly that preserves and inverts the architecture of a church. Weird (as he is known), was bassist and songwriter in a 1970s progressive rock band, Frozen Gold, but has retreated into solitude after the death of the band's guitarist, David Balfour, in an onstage accident. Weird's rather chaotic life is interrupted when his manager comes to visit and informs him of the death of Christine Brice, the former vocalist in Frozen Gold. In response, Weird secretly resolves to kill himself.

Weird's suicidal longings stem from his (irrational) sense of responsibility for the deaths of David and Christine. David was killed by a falling dry-ice unit as part of a complicated stage set designed by Weird. Christine was murdered by a fundamentalist Christian in the United States: her assassin was provoked by an onstage mock crucifixion that had been dreamed up by Weird in their Frozen Gold days. Although David's death is accidental and Christine's is murder, Weird locates himself at the beginning of the complicated causal chain that issues in each. The outcomes, to Weird, seem predestined as punishment for the outlandish rewards that have accrued to his modest talents. Although his nickname derives from his surname and initial (Weir, D.), and is used because of his ungainly height and appearance, the name "weird" is most appropriate in its original etymological sense as "fate" and "destiny"—Weird is a latent fatalist who sees cosmic punishment lurking in the shadows.

This attitude is traced in Banks's text to Weird's Christian upbringing. His Catholic culture has given Weird a sense of original sin, a "dreadful, constant, nagging sensation of wracked responsibility" which "could be accounted for just by being *alive*" (p. 13). Music seemed a way out of this sense of pending doom: the theology of Weird's musings is clear: he reflects that despite "my hulking, graceless body, "I could create grace, could *compose* grace, even if I couldn't be graceful myself" (p. 212). The sad, unlucky end of Frozen Gold, though, brings Weird's sense of original sin back to life, and this is later compounded by Christine's death. Weird sees the deaths of David and Christine as the "weird" for his pretensions above his station. He, "the angel of destruction, "had shifted the bad luck on to others, so that they suffered in my place" (p. 212). The folly in which Weird lives contains bizarre images of upside-down Christianity. Weird too is one these images: he is an inverted Christ—others suffer, he believes, so that he might live. What saves him is a purely secular revelation. While walking in Espedair Street in his hometown of Paisley, Weird understands the fictionality of the narrative order—one of tragic punishment for hubris—that he has imposed upon the events of his life. Such genres, he reflects, "were just tags we'd stuck on our hooligan consequences as we stumbled through the world's definitive grotesqueries" (p. 219). He

decides instead to give up his wealth and start again from scratch; he even returns to his first girlfriend, Jean Webb, who is now divorced and who, he learns, almost decided to come with him on his voyage of fame.

BRIDGES BETWEEN BANKS: THE BRIDGE, WALKING ON GLASS

There are two Bankses: Iain and Iain M., one the mainstream author and one the writer of science fiction. Some of Banks's books are literary "bridges" that join the two. The most obvious of these is *The Bridge* (1986). If *The Wasp Factory* was perceived by critics as Banks's overhyped debut, then *The Bridge* was his literary redemption. John Nicholson in the *Times* saw it as "significant progress in the flowering of an exceptional talent," while Isobel Murray in the *Scotsman* compared it in ingenuity to Alasdair Gray's *Lanark* (1981), the touchstone of Scottish literature's revival in the 1980s. Lennox, the protagonist and narrator of *The Bridge,* is lost in a variety of fantasy worlds while he lies unconscious after a drunken car accident. He is at times "John Orr," an amnesiac inhabitant of an enormous living bridge. At other times, he is a warrior figure—who speaks with an urban Scots accent—pursuing adventures in a marvelous world that seems to be a mixture of the supernatural and science fiction. Mixed in with these and other narratives is an account of Lennox's existence before his accident, first as a rather callow young student in Scotland and later as a man addicted to consumerism and changing fashions, unable to find much meaning in his well-off life.

Banks has recalled, in an interview with Isobel Murray, the enormous iconic presence of the Forth Rail Bridge during his childhood: "from the house in North Queensferry…my bedroom window looked slap onto the bridge" (p. 5). This "world symbol," to use Banks's words, permeates Lennox's fantastic worlds. It appears as the giant bridge in which he lives, and it forms a recurring visual motif—he sees its structure, for example, in the stockings of his fantasy lover, Abberlaine Arrol. The Forth Rail Bridge, with its structure of two viaducts, three main sections, and two linking sections, is even imitated in the sizes of the various books that comprise *The Bridge.*

Much of the reader's delight in *The Bridge* is in its pattern of theme and variation as Banks exploits the central symbol in various ingenious ways. Yet, there is also a didactic, cautionary tone to the tale. Like Cameron Colley in *Complicity,* Lennox is a man who has lost sight of his ambitions—a man who has instead been gradually corrupted by wealth and security. The crucial loss of "depth" occurs after University: instead of accompanying his on-and-off girlfriend to Paris, he immediately settles for a highly paid engineering job. His life from that point is merely a movement through ever more conspicuous acts of consumption: he is a pilgrim who progresses from a Saab to a Range Rover to a Ducati to an Audi and then finally to a Jaguar. Even Lennox's political leanings become merely a cash transaction: when his firm takes on a South African contract, he makes a large donation to the African National Congress to show his "solidarity." And, like Colley, Lennox abuses drink and drugs as a distraction from his rather empty life. He reflects: "If there is a design to my own existence then it escapes me" (p. 250).

Lennox, as his fantasy name "Orr" implies, is forced to make a choice between his hospitalized fantasy life and the real world to which he can return, a "choice...not between dream and reality" but "between two different dreams" (p. 283). He eventually chooses to live in "our collective dream" of shared reality (p. 283) even though it includes "Thatcher's Britain and Reagan's world" (p. 283). This choice is motivated by the realization that fantasy offers little escape: it merely replicates, in a distorted form, the personal truths obscured during his earlier existence in consensus reality. In many ways Banks's text resembles Alasdair Gray's novel *1982 Janine* (1984). Banks has been frank about his admiration for Gray and has frequently stated that Gray's first novel, *Lanark,* is a "landmark." Banks's own landmark text imitates Gray's *1982 Janine* in its use of a protagonist who is imprisoned in fantasy and who is incessantly reminded of the real world by the symbols that permeate his imagination. Lennox

in *The Bridge* also eventually comes to see the reminders of reality hidden among his fantasies. The bridge he finally interprets as a message to himself: as "a thing become place, a means become end, a route become destination" (p. 283), it signifies his own dissolution into consumerism and hedonism. As he lies in his hospital bed, he is, he reflects, "a shallow man breathing shallowly and trying to think deeply" (p. 276).

Walking on Glass (1985) is another of Banks's "bridging" novels. It consists of three interrelated narratives. We have the story of a London art student, Graham Park, who is infatuated with the elusive Sara ffitch (*sic*) to whom he has been introduced via an (apparently) gay friend. A second story concerns Steven Grout, a seeming paranoid schizophrenic, and his trials and tribulations in London. Accompanying these two stories is the far more peculiar tale of Quiss and Ajayi, warriors from two sides in the "Therapeutic Wars" who, as punishment for their crimes, have been imprisoned together in an extraordinary castle stuck in a barren landscape. In order to escape, Quiss and Ajayi must play bizarre games such as One-Dimensional Chess and Spotless Dominoes: for each game played to the end, they are allowed an attempt to answer the question, "What happens when an unstoppable force meets an immovable object?" The catch is that Quiss and Ajayi must work out how to play each game as they go along, through trial, error, and inference.

All three stories are of people who must play games to which they do not know the rules. Like Quiss and Ajayi, who spend hundreds of days playing their way through their challenges, Grout finds his world to be an inscrutable game. When he tries to claim unemployment benefits, he is at loggerheads with the Social Security clerk, unable even to remember which is his surname and which is his Christian name. Despite trying to "play safe" (p. 72), Grout soon finds himself "losing out" (p. 75): he lacks documents, and because he resigned from his last job (just on the point of being fired), he is ineligible for benefits. Banks's text also implies that Grout's delusions are a game played to give himself status and importance; many of them started as childhood distractions, "something to make life more interesting, give it some purpose" (p. 28). Graham Park, meanwhile, is stuck in a game whose rules he never properly grasps. When he finally is invited into Sara ffitch's flat, she ends their tenuous relationship and admits to him that he was merely a decoy. He was used to cover up her real relationship, one she did not want to come to the attention of her estranged husband. What Graham does not learn is that her real relationship is not with the biker Stock but with her own brother—who happens to be Graham's supposedly gay friend Richard Slater.

The three narratives collide in a way that also makes it difficult for the reader to work out the rules of Banks's game—above all, to work out which of the worlds in the text are to be taken as (fictionally) real. As the story develops, the reader learns that Quiss and Ajayi are actually stuck on planet Earth in a far-off future, when the sun is dying. Most of the castle's inhabitants are in a subterranean layer, where they can use advanced technology to vicariously reexperience the lives of the earlier inhabitants of Earth. Perhaps, then, Grout is one of these people, and really is, as he believes, an alien warrior imprisoned on planet Earth? The novel ends with Ajayi picking up a book (the walls and furniture of the Castle are filled with various tomes left over from Earth's earlier days). The first lines of the book are those of *Walking on Glass*. If she reads the book through, then she will find the irrational, Zen-like answer that Grout discovers on the back of a matchbook in the hospital grounds: "The unstoppable force stops, the immovable object moves" (p. 216).

On the other hand, when Grout is hospitalized he meets an elderly couple who while away their day playing games: Is the story of Quiss and Ajayi perhaps merely a folie à deux shared by these two? The issue is undecidable: we cannot tell whether *Walking on Glass* is science fiction or whether it merely depicts the delusions of various deranged inhabitants of a world very much like our own. However, although *Walking on Glass* leaves open which is the ultimate fictional reality, Banks does not seem particularly taken with the postmodern idea that even our nontex-

tual reality is itself fictional. His fondness for scientific explanation seems to rule out any conscious implication in his texts that reality is merely an arbitrary construct. *Walking on Glass* does, though, seem to suggest that in the absence of any transcendent purpose in the universe, it is up to humans to make their own games with which to provide meaning in their lives. This idea is taken up in Banks's science fiction Culture novels, where even the necessity for economically productive labor has been removed; this notion is also addressed—more obliquely—in novels such as *A Song of Stone* and *Canal Dreams*.

MARTIAL ARTS: A SONG OF STONE, CANAL DREAMS, *AND* THE PLAYER OF GAMES

The narrator (and rather ineffectual protagonist) of *A Song of Stone* (1997) is Abel, the owner of a castle in a land wracked by a war that has disintegrated into the squabbles of opposing bands of mercenaries. Abel attempts to flee his castle with Morgan, his sister and lover, but is forced to return by Loot, a female lieutenant who compels him to assist in securing the castle against enemy raiders. Abel is almost executed by Loot in punishment for various acts of disobedience and apparent treachery; however, he eventually kills her when she is seriously wounded by an attacking force. This is to no avail, though; the castle is still controlled by the mercenaries, who parade Loot's corpse, murder Morgan, and eventually dispose of Abel by strapping him to the muzzle of an artillery piece and firing a charge through him.

A Song of Stone is unusually written in comparison with the rest of Banks's oeuvre. Although we know from the technological level of the soldiers that the setting is the present day, gone are Banks's usual colloquial language and contemporary references to brands and mass culture. Abel's orotund narration, with its lengthy piling up of clause after clause, instead detemporalizes and de-localizes the narrative: he rightly reflects, "This could be any place or time" (p. 272). Abel's lack of historical location is indicative of his cultural position: he is a guardian of the outmoded forms of the past, which persist in the present as playful or artistic accomplishments. His "song of stone" is the castle, an obsolete defense system that is now a work of art and a repository for various cultural artifacts—painting, books, and so on. *A Song of Stone* emphasizes that culture flows from these leftover forms, which previously were economic and social imperatives—even an abandoned weapon such as the castle may therefore become an artwork. The descent into barbarism, though it undermines Abel's undeserved privileges, is also the reversion of his culture to utilitarian necessity. In a key scene, Abel is forced to play the piano for his captors. Though he is a skillful pianist, he takes his performance back to marching music—a martial technique that abandons the "appearance of natural fluid grace it takes half a lifetime of study and a thousand arithmetically tedious repetitions of sterile scales to acquire" in order to "thump the pavement of the keyboard in a fatuous, one-two, one-two, one-two marching step" (pp. 177–178).

The capacity for art to revert from culture to necessity is captured too in *Canal Dreams* (1989). Hisako Onoda, a plane-phobic Japanese cellist, is trapped in the Panama Canal on a tanker ship in which she is traveling as a passenger. Her ship is captured by a team of Latin American guerrillas led by Sucre. The guerrillas, however, are actually in the employ of the CIA. They are to mount an attack on a plane full of congressmen in order to provide a casus belli by which the United States can step into the region. But the plot fails when, after the slaughter of the other passengers and her own gang rape, Hisako escapes and kills all the hijackers.

During the narrative Hisako is transformed from a mild-mannered virtuoso into an unstoppable assassin. In a piece of symbolic action she kills Sucre with the spike of her cello, which has been previously shot to pieces by the guerrillas. It is as if her musical training and commitment conceal an original and more sinister single-minded dedication. Indeed, Hisako has taken a life already: during a demonstration in her native country, she killed a riot policeman with a punch

to the throat and later escaped from the fracas without further consequences.

Just as today's martial arts are sporting forms of earlier life-and-death skills, so, Banks suggests, other cultural pursuits conceal traces of an earlier, darker purpose, to which they may, if needed, successfully revert. Although Abel in *A Song of Stone* is an incompetent blunderer, Hisako manages to successfully invoke the spirit of martial discipline that underpins her cultural achievements. The height of such a reversion occurs in Banks's science fiction novel *The Player of Games* (1988), part of his Culture series. Jernau Gurgeh, a master of all forms of games, is sent from his own anarchic and socialist civilization to play in the empire of Azad. The Azadians live in a society where status is determined by one's ability to play the complex game of Azad, and where the position of ruler is given to the best player. Indeed, the game is at times life-and-death—players can stake various horrendous mutilations as part of the play.

Banks uses the society of Azad to provide a dystopian image of our own reality. Earthly relations of power and exploitation are reproduced on Azad, though slightly altered to "defamiliarize" them. The Azadians are, for example, sexist across three sexes: male, female, and the egg-carrying "apex" sex. But, as with Earth, the sexism of our own gender roles is maintained, for "the males are used as soldiers and the females as possessions" (p. 75). Acquisitive, competitive, systematically oppressive, and entangling sexuality with dominance, Azadian society, like our own (Banks implies), ascribes every injustice to "'human nature'—the phrase they used whenever they had to justify something inhuman and unnatural" (p. 226).

Gurgeh eventually defeats even the emperor-regent of Azad at his game, precipitating a collapse of the Azadian hierarchy. The game of Azad itself is then free to become nothing more than a harmless pursuit, rather than a sinister mirror image of the competitive structure of capitalist society. This liberation of gaming from life-and-death necessity is a key part of Banks's future vision. In another science fiction novel, *Look to Windward* (2000), Kabe the Homomdan (a three-meter-tall tripedal alien) observes the Culture, the society to which he is an ambassador. He notes that in the Culture, "what used to have to be suffered as a necessity becomes enjoyed as a sport" (p. 115). This observation is a motto for Banks's views on the interplay of technological and cultural development: the endpoint is an escape from necessity in which laws are transformed into freely negotiated anarchic conventions.

SCIENCE FICTION: THE CULTURE NOVELS

Although science fiction is sometimes dismissed as mere "genre" fiction, it is a prominent part of Banks's oeuvre and his first love. He sees it as "important...because it's the only form of literature that copes with the way technological change might affect people, which is the fundamental quality of our lives now" (Hughes, p. 6). Of Banks's eight science fiction novels, six contain his vision of a future almost-utopia, the Culture: *Consider Phlebas* (1987), *The Player of Games* (1988), *Use of Weapons* (1990), *Excession* (1996), *Inversions* (1998), and *Look to Windward* (2000); the Culture also appears in some of the stories in the collection *The State of the Art* (1991).

The Culture is a hybrid civilization whose advanced technology has liberated its citizens from most of the imperatives of previous societies. They are now free to live lives of endless leisurely, playful pursuits. Banks has explained the attraction of the Culture in an interview in the *Guardian* with Phil Daoust: "Briefly, nothing and nobody in the Culture is exploited....It is essentially an automated civilization in its manufacturing processes, with human labour restricted to something indistinguishable from play, or a hobby" (p. 9). Nor are all the Culture's citizens of flesh and blood. In Banks's future society, the free will and sentience of advanced machines is recognized. Worlds (whether planets, vast artificial ring-shaped "Orbitals," or enormous spaceships) are administered by super-intelligent computers ("Hubs" and "Minds"). On a smaller scale, the flesh-and-blood members of the Culture live alongside "drones"—smaller intelligent computers—with whom they interact as friends and colleagues.

The political terms of reference in the Culture have not gone unnoticed. Steven Poole, writing for the *Guardian,* notes that "while most postwar American space opera dreams pleasantly of pan-galactic capitalism, Banks's Culture, because its technology spread infinite productive capacity evenly throughout the occupied volume of the Milky Way, was a communist Utopia." Marxist terminology is clear in, for example, *Consider Phlebas,* where we are told how "the capacity of [the Culture's] means of production ubiquitously and comprehensively exceeded every reasonable...demand its not unimaginative citizens could make" (p. 451). With its advances in industrial technology (or, to use the Marxist term, in the "means of production"), the Culture has overcome all scarcity and abandoned the use of money. The state—which Marxists traditionally regard as a mere reflex of a certain economic order—has also withered away: the Culture is a well-ordered and peaceful socialist anarchy.

In the title story of *The State of the Art,* the narrator, Diziet Sma (who also appears in some of the Culture novels), provides an opportunity for Banks to relate his utopian vision to the current earthly fate of socialism. Sma is a member of the Culture's Contact section, which classifies planets that potentially may be introduced to more advanced technologies and cultures. She and her crewmates have to consider the potential of Earth circa 1977 for contact. The idea is eventually rejected by their superiors, but along the way Sma gets to investigate East Berlin, where she wonders, "Was this farce, this gloomy sideshow trying to mimic the West...the best job the locals could make of socialism?" (p. 141). Banks implies that twentieth-century socialism was an idea that came too early in history: much more automated capacity and technological stability would be required before Earth could host a utopia like the Culture. This future civilization, though, is clearly identified as the inheritor of the twentieth century's failed socialist legacy: Sma gloats, "I wanted to see the junta generals fill their pants when they realised that the future is—in Earth terms—bright, bright red" (p. 137).

One of Banks's characters also draws attention to the enormous material surplus on Earth right now, and declares that "one wonders that the oppressed of Earth don't rise up in flames and anger yesterday! But they don't because they are...infected with the myth of self-interested advancement, or the poison of religious acceptance" (p. 178). The Culture is both a vision of a utopian future and a goading echo of the neglected utopian possibilities that exist at this very moment in our own time and space.

Although the political polemic in the Culture stories is interesting, a further fascination and narrative power comes from the confrontation between Banks's Cultured characters and those who question or challenge the Culture's assumptions about itself. In "The State of the Art" this dialogue is presented through a Culture citizen, Dervley Linter, who decides to "go native" and live on planet Earth. The attraction for Linter is contrast: good seems to him more precious when it is threatened, transitory, and foregrounded against a backcloth of misery and evil—"a single pretty girl in the crowds of Calcutta," he tells Sma, "seems like an impossibly fragile bloom" (p. 136). By the end of the story Linter has converted to Roman Catholicism and informs Sma that "you have to have the potential for wrongness there or you can't live...or you can but it doesn't *mean* anything" (p. 195). Neither Sma nor the Culture ship are particularly impressed by Linter's argument—the latter remarks that "despite what the locals may think, there is nothing intrinsically illogical or impossible about...removing badness without removing goodness, or pain without pleasure, or suffering without excitement" (p. 168). The narrative logic of the tale itself hardly seems more sympathetic—Linter is knifed to death in a mugging in New York City during his last meeting with Sma. His challenge, though, is never answered and endures no matter how much the story itself, and its privileged voices—the narrator and the Culture's Minds—attempt to dismiss his skepticism.

This "dialogic" element also appears in Banks's first Culture novel (and indeed his first published science fiction novel) *Consider Phlebas*. In many ways this novel borrows the elements of "space opera," that grand genre of science fiction that aspires to the epic and typically deals with the founding, or protection from destruction, of a civilization. The motifs of space opera—mighty starships, space ports, abandoned worlds, and so on—occur throughout the narrative. The background to the story is a war between the Culture and the Idirans, a race of practically immortal tripods who despise the Culture for the mortality of its organic citizens and for their seeming subservience to their machines. Although not directly threatened, the Culture goes to war because the Idirans are enslaving any technologically inferior species they encounter. The foreground to this epic tale is the attempt by Bora Horza Gobuchul to recover for the Idirans a Culture ship's Mind, which has ditched on a forbidden planet controlled by an elder civilization. Horza is a Changer: one of a race of shape-changing entities who have limited access to the planet. He opposes the Culture not because he supports the Idirans but because, like Linter in "The State of the Art," he sees opposition to the Culture as being on the side of "life"—"boring, old-fashioned, biological life; smelly, fallible and short-sighted, God knows, but *real* life" (p. 29). Horza eventually fails (and is killed by his supposed allies), and the Culture goes on to win the war; indeed, the story, the reader learns through an epilogue, is told hundred of years later by a drone that has taken the name Bora Horza Gobuchul, seemingly in an act of commemoration.

Banks's text never wholly absorbs and nullifies Horza's opposition. Horza's Culture opponent, Balveda, has herself put in suspended animation after the war, with instructions to be awakened only when the Culture has proven that it saved more lives by fighting the Idirans than by tolerating them. This places the epigraph from the Koran that precedes *Consider Phlebas* in a more ambiguous light: it reads, "Idolatry is worse than carnage." The Culture prefers carnage in a war that is essentially over an issue of principle, "a religious war in the fullest sense" (p. 451), as the historical epilogue tells the reader. Although the trade-off is eventually justified and Balveda reawakened, she is "autoeuthenised" (p. 465)—she kills herself. Her despair, the text implies, is over the irredeemable loss of Horza and his culture: the Changers, we learn at the end of the novel, are entirely wiped out during the Idiran-Culture war. With this elegy for a lost civilization and culture, Banks's novel is a science fiction version of such historical novels as Sir Walter Scott's *Waverley* (1814). Like the Highland clans in Scott's novel, the Changers are destroyed by a bloody process of historical evolution that lays the ground for a better future.

A similar dialogue between optimism and irretrievable loss haunts other of Banks's Culture novels. *Look to Windward,* for example, picks up eight hundred years after the Idiran-Culture war to deal with another narrative of vengeance and loss. The Culture has recently sparked a bloody civil war in the previously caste-based society of the Chelgrans, a vaguely feline warrior race. The Chelgrans, in revenge, have sent one of their warriors, Quilan, to destroy a Culture orbital by detonating a bomb in its "Hub," its controlling mind. Although Quilan fails in this plan, both he and the Hub commit suicide together: Quilan because he can no longer see any point in existence after the death of his lover in the civil war; the Hub because it cannot bear its memories of irredeemable loss from the Idiran-Culture war eight hundred years earlier.

There are various elements of challenge to the Culture in other novels. *Use of Weapons,* for example, is concerned with the activities of the Culture's Special Circumstances division, who employ a mercenary, Cheradenine Zakalwe, as part of their schemes to discreetly alter the historical evolution of more benighted cultures. At the end of the novel, Zakalwe and his Culture employers discover his real identity: behind an amnesiac veil is hidden his earlier life as Elethiomel, a homicidal warrior who sent the real Zakalwe the bones and flesh of his sister made into a chair. The Culture must dirty its hands to achieve its aims and is perhaps (like Cameron Colley in *Complicity*) more involved than it pretends with that which it seems to oppose.

Yet for all his skeptical dialogues with the Culture, Banks has been clear about its personal utopian meaning: it is, he has said, "my secular heaven, the place I'd like to live, my place over the rainbow" (Daoust, p. 9). Banks is in some ways comparable to the modernist poet T. S. Eliot, but a more left-wing, anarchic Eliot. He is creating a modern-day myth for the iconoclastic present, a myth that finds credence because of our own culture's faith in the utopian possibilities of technology. Though supernatural heavens are out, scientific ones are in, and can, Banks believes, perform a similar function. They may provide hope and an ethical orientation in the chaos of the present: "I know the Culture doesn't exist, and it may never, but if enough people believe in it, it might help people think in a better way towards the future" (Daoust, p. 9).

SCIENCE FICTION: AGAINST A DARK BACKGROUND *AND* FEERSUM ENDJINN

The Culture novels show a future society in which humans, no matter how genetically modified and improved, have delegated the running of their society to machines they have created. This downgrading of organic life is particularly clear, for example, in *Excession* (1996); the real action and dialogue of the story is between the Minds of spaceships as they conspire and plot against each other. The humans in the story are essentially dependent upon these almost omniscient intellects. One (human) character reflects that "you had to accept the likelihood that all your secrets would be known to them and trust that they would not misuse that knowledge" (p. 351). The "Minds" and "Hubs" that run the Culture's ships and orbitals are in effect the benevolent deities of that society. With their squabbles and their manipulations of organic life, they are a science fiction version of the gods who preside over classical epic. In Banks's science fiction, the gods really are man-made—not in the traditional humanist sense that they are anthropomorphic illusions but in the sense that they are artificial productions that are intellectually and (in most cases) morally superior to their creators. Banks's two Culture-free science fiction novels, *Against a Dark Background* (1993) and *Feersum Endjinn* (1994), both show societies that are unable to take the Culture's radical step of post-human humility.

Sharrow, the heroine of *Against a Dark Background,* is caught up in a frantic search for the last surviving "Lazy Gun," a capricious weapon of mass destruction created in an earlier and more advanced age by the civilization of her world, Golter. Throughout this bloody quest-narrative, the only element of Golterian society to emerge with any credit is the androids. These artificial persons are also, like the Lazy Gun, relics of an earlier period; unlike the Lazy Gun, however, their production has been legally banned rather than halted by a technological regression. Yet the androids live the most civilized life of all Golterians, painstakingly restoring a radioactive city severely damaged in a previous war. When Sharrow's own band of mercenaries is eliminated in the bloody competition for the Lazy Gun, her only helper is an android, Feril, whose humanity is greater even than that of her erstwhile colleagues.

Banks's posthuman vision is further amplified in *Feersum Endjinn,* which is set in a future Earth where those who remain have forgotten how the technology created by their forebears was made. The achievements of their ancestors—who have left for the stars—litter the planet, their meaning and purpose forgotten. This amnesia poses a problem because Earth is now threatened by an interstellar dust cloud that will eventually blot out the sun. To prevent this catastrophe, the remaining population must take a simple, yet decisive step: they have to accept the two things they renounced in time immemorial: space travel and artificial intelligence. The device of the (artificial) gods that saves Earth is a space travel technology (the "feersum endjinn" of the title), which may be activated—with some human cooperation—by the artificial intelligences that subsist secretly in the data systems still used by humans. The human heroes of this future epic are the characters who can communicate and interact with these unseen powers: prime among them is Bascule the seer, who can adeptly connect with the data system and who is guided and aided by the artificial intelligences. Yet Bascule is at best a useful functionary: the real agents are (like Banks's Culture ships) nonhumans such as Ergates the artificial ant, who has been sent by the artificial intelligences to communicate with the control systems left behind after the "Diaspora" of space-faring humans.

CONCLUSION

The latest of Banks's mainstream fictions have seemed to critics disappointing when compared with the promise of his earlier works. In his review of *Dead Air* (2002) for *The Guardian,* Steven Poole concludes that "Banks is such a naturally gifted story teller that for some years now he has been coasting on this ability, when he might have become a seriously excellent novelist." Poole dismisses *The Business* (1999), for example, as "an excruciating mess" when set against "the excellence of [the] Culture series." The conversational tone of Banks's mainstream writing and its tendency to descend into harangues that are manifestly a platform for his own views are its most unappealing traits. On the other hand, when Banks's setting prevents him from making direct political statements, as with the Culture novels, then he is forced to employ the subtlety and craftsmanship of which he is capable. This is quite evident in *Inversions* (1998), which tells of the Culture's manipulation of a late-feudal alien civilization but does so through unreliable, uncomprehending narratives written by two members of that same society. The reader is forced into action, as he or she tries to puzzle out the story of the Culture's activities (rather than attending passively to a lengthy political statement like those so frequently found in Banks's mainstream novels).

There is, though, no doubting the sincerity of Banks's political lectures: he has found himself increasingly opposed to the U.K. state. In protest of the U.S.-U.K.-led invasion (or liberation) of Iraq in 2003, he and his wife cut up their passports and posted them to Tony Blair, the British prime minister (an incident Banks recounts in his travelogue *Raw Spirit*). As part of this disenchantment with the course of world politics, Banks has shown an increasing alignment with national resistance to global hegemonies. Although *The Business* met with unfavorable reviews, it is notable for Banks's sympathy toward the nation-state in a globalized world. Banks's heroine is Kate Telman, a girl plucked from a deprived area of Scotland in her childhood, who leads a life among a postnational corporate elite. Kate eventually settles in the small kingdom of Thulahn in the Himalayas. The emphatic locality and particularity of the place explain why she accepts the marriage proposal of its ruler, Prince Suvinder: the nation provides for Kate a place of ethical substance where there exists a value greater than the accumulation of capital. This affection for locality and community is also apparent in *Whit* (1995), where the protagonist chooses to return to her small cultic community in Scotland, where technology is proscribed and consumerism disdained.

This late-blooming nationalism, or "communitarianism," may seem odd, even paradoxical, given Banks's anarchic and socialist ideals. The contradiction though, is dissolved in *Raw Spirit* (2003), Banks's travelogue through the distilleries of Scotland, where he comments that whisky's "ability to accept and combine with distinctive flavours from elsewhere, to enhance them and be enhanced by them, is potentially at least, an important symbol" (p. 359). Although whisky might seem a symbol of a pure-blooded, homogenous, and rigidly bounded Scottish nationalism, it is, as Banks points out, a metaphor for quite the opposite. Whisky, an "apparent paradigm of purity," is aged in wooden casks that may have been used for American bourbon, Spanish sherry, French wine, or Cuban rum:

> the whiskies I've really fallen for are those that have taken on the majority of their character from drinks made in other countries....They are still very much single malts, they are still very much Scotch, but it's the interplay between the raw spirit as made in Scotland and those other tastes brought in from abroad that have made the greatest and most enduring impression on me.
>
> (p. 359)

Scotland's national drink is an ideal metaphor for a Scottish national identity that acknowledges and celebrates its hybrid vigor. Whisky, of course, may also be seen as a fine symbol for Banks's

own work. His writing, which moves capably from Scottish ideas and settings to international genres such as science fiction, shows—like the finest single malts—a mixture of "raw spirit made in Scotland" with "those other tastes brought in from abroad."

Selected Bibliography

WORKS OF IAIN (M.) BANKS

NOVELS AND SHORT STORIES

The Wasp Factory. London: Macmillan, 1984; Boston: Houghton Mifflin, 1984.

Walking on Glass. London: Macmillan, 1985; Boston: Houghton Mifflin, 1986.

The Bridge. London: Macmillan, 1986; New York: St. Martin's, 1986.

Consider Phlebas. London: Macmillan, 1987; New York: St. Martin's, 1988.

Espedair Street. London: Macmillan, 1987.

The Player of Games. London: Macmillan, 1988; New York: St. Martin's, 1989.

Canal Dreams. London: Macmillan, 1989; New York: Doubleday, 1991.

The State of the Art. Willimantic, Conn.: M. V. Ziesing, 1989; London: Orbit, 1991.

Use of Weapons. London: Orbit, 1990; New York: Bantam, 1992.

The Crow Road. London: Scribners, 1992.

Complicity. London: Little, Brown, 1993; New York: Doubleday, 1995.

Against a Dark Background. London: Orbit, 1993; New York: Bantam, 1993.

Feersum Endjinn. London: Orbit, 1994; New York: Bantam, 1995.

Whit; or, Isis Amongst the Unsaved. London: Little, Brown, 1995.

Excession. London: Orbit, 1996; New York: Bantam, 1997.

A Song of Stone. London: Little, Brown, 1997; New York: Villard, 1998.

Inversions. London: Orbit, 1998; New York: Pocket Books, 1999.

The Business. London: Little, Brown, 1999; New York: Simon & Schuster, 1999.

Look to Windward. London: Orbit, 2000; New York: Pocket Books, 2001.

Dead Air. London: Little, Brown, 2002.

OTHER WORK

Raw Spirit: In Search of the Perfect Dram. London: Century, 2003.

CRITICAL AND BIOGRAPHICAL STUDIES

Alegre, Sara Martín. "Consider Banks: Iain (M.) Banks' *The Wasp Factory* and *Consider Phlebas.*" *Revista Canaria de Estudios Ingleses* 41:197–205 (November 2000).

Craig, Cairns. *Iain Banks's* Complicity: *A Reader's Guide.* New York: Continuum, 2002.

Craig, Patricia. "Pest Extermination." *Times Literary Supplement,* March 16, 1984, p. 298. (Review of *The Wasp Factory.*)

Daoust, Phil. "Iain Banks Writes Books About Sex and Drugs. Iain M. Banks Is a Sci-Fi Nerd. Are They by Any Chance Related?" *Guardian,* May 20, 1997, pp. 8–9. (Interview with Banks.)

Hughes, Colin. "Doing the Business." *Guardian,* August 7, 1999, pp. 6–7. (Interview with Banks.)

Lippens, Ronnie. "Imachinations of Peace: Scientifictions of Peace in Iain M. Banks's *The Player of Games.*" *Journal of the Society for Utopian Studies* 13, no. 1:135–147 (2002).

MacGillivray, Alan. *Iain Banks'* The Wasp Factory, The Crow Road, *and* Whit. Glasgow: Association for Scottish Literary Studies, 2001.

Marr, Andrew. "Mad, Bad, and Dangerous to Know." *Scotsman,* February 25, 1984, p. 5. (Review of *The Wasp Factory.*)

Melia, Sally Ann. "Very Likely Impossible, but Oh, the Elegance...." *Science Fiction Chronicle* 16, no. 1:7, 42–44 (October–November 1999).

Murray, Isobel. "Either Orr." *Scotsman,* July 12, 1986, p. 5. (Review of *The Bridge.*)

———. "Iain Banks." In *Scottish Writers Talking 2.* Edited by Isobel Murray. East Linton, Scotland: Tuckwell, 2002. Pp. 1–33.

Nairn, Thom. "Iain Banks and the Fiction Factory." In *The Scottish Novel Since the Seventies: New Visions, Old Dreams.* Edited by Randall Stevenson and Gavin Wallace. Edinburgh: Edinburgh University Press, 1993. Pp. 127–135.

Nicholson, John. "Amnesia or Waking Dream." *Times,* July 10, 1986, p. 10. (Review of *The Bridge.*)

Poole, Steven. "Gigadeathcrimes." *Times Literary Supplement,* June 14, 1996, p. 23. (Review of *Excession.*)

———. "It's All in the Initial." *Guardian,* September 14, 2002, p. 29. (Review of *Dead Air.*)

Schoene-Harwood, Berthold. "Dams Burst: Devolving Gender in Iain Banks's *The Wasp Factory.*" *Ariel* 30, no. 1:131–148 (January 1999).

FILMS AND TELEVISION PRODUCTIONS BASED ON THE WORKS OF IAIN (M.) BANKS

The Crow Road. Screenplay by Brian Elsley and Gavin Millar. Directed by Gavin Millar. BBC TV, 1996.

Complicity. Screenplay by Brian Elsley. Directed by Gavin Millar. Talisman Films, 2000.

THOMAS LOVELL BEDDOES

(1803–1849)

Peter Scupham

THOMAS LOVELL BEDDOES oversaw the publication of only two books in his lifetime: *The Improvisatore* (1821), which he soon made a point of destroying whenever he found a copy, and *The Brides' Tragedy* (1822). After age nineteen his only publications were occasional and appeared for the most part in German periodicals. The first great wave of Romanticism was over, and John Keats, Percy Shelley, and Lord Byron were all dead by the time Beddoes left Oxford and England for Germany in 1825 and cut himself adrift from English literary circles. However, the lack of widespread critical attention to his work is balanced by an almost fanatical devotion from his admirers. This devotion was demonstrated in his lifetime when his friend, correspondent, and biographer Thomas Forbes Kelsall made sure the poet would not be entirely forgotten. After Beddoes' suicide in Basel, Switzerland, at the age of forty-five in 1850, Kelsall published the poet's major work, *Death's Jest-Book,* and followed this a year later by an edition of the poems together with a memoir of the poet.

Sardonic, cultivated, at home in the sciences and the arts, skilled in many languages, Beddoes was a difficult, humorous, depressive man, a citizen of Europe and a gifted anatomist. *Death's Jest-Book,* the unwieldy drama he could never complete to his own satisfaction, became his life's companion. Often tinkered with late at night in his self-imposed exile, it is itself a creature of the night, of death, of the search for a meaning behind the shadow show of existence. Beddoes' own work as an anatomist, his capacity for exact dissection, is applied in his work to the shadowy, incorporeal figure of Death himself. The result is work of a quite remarkable individuality. The fashion for churchyard and castellated horror that had its seeds in German literature and that had woven its way through Horace Walpole's *The Castle of Otranto,* the novels of Ann Radcliffe, Mary Shelley's *Frankenstein,* and the satirical deflation of the genre in Jane Austen's *Northanger Abbey* has its part to play in Beddoes' imaginative world, but the intellectual passion, the incision, the gift for image and extended metaphor he displays in *Death's Jest-Book* is quite out of the reach of the earlier exponents of Gothic frissons. Caught between the egotistical and Napoleonic sublime of the Shelley and Byron era and the less disturbing serenities suitable for Victorian drawing rooms, Beddoes, under the spell of his loved Elizabethan and Jacobean dramatists, offers his readers the alternative vision: the despair and death-longing that comes from realizing the limits set to all human ambition and pride in beauty or achievement. The universe is determined to keep its final secret from poet or anatomist, the living and the dead become interchangeable, and bones speak ambivalently of resurrection.

Devotion to the work of Thomas Lovell Beddoes was exemplified in the nineteenth century not only by Thomas Kelsall but also by James Dykes Campbell who, in another labor of love, transcribed the Beddoes papers Kelsall left to Robert Browning; these papers, known as "The Browning Box," disappeared after the death of Browning's son Pen. Edmund Gosse, in another labor of love, re-edited the poems and edited the letters in 1890 and 1894, but the definitive edition of the poetry and prose was prepared by Dr. H. W. Donner and published in 1935. Where quotations in the present essay have been taken from this edition, the citation is prefixed "Works." Dr. Donner also published a companion volume in the same year: *Thomas Lovell Beddoes: The Making of a Poet.* The citations for this are prefixed "Life." It seems appropriate to Beddoes' shifting and uncertain reputation that these two books, the foundation works for any serious study of Beddoes, are out of print, and the most accessible text is Donner's selection for the Muses' Library edition, *Plays and Poems of Thomas Lovell Beddoes* (1950). Citations from this edition are prefixed by "ML." Finally, while this essay was in preparation, a new edition of the 1829 text of *Death's Jest-Book* was published, edited by Michael Bradshaw (2003). All references to *Death's Jest Book* use this edition, and citations are prefaced by "Bradshaw." It is a pleasant irony that the editions of this specialist in anatomical and philosophical dissection, who left both his life and works as a puzzling series of uncompleted episodes, are themselves either out of reach or tantalizingly incomplete.

Beddoes has often been dismissively treated as a poet of fragments. Recent developments in criticism have tended to view the nature of fragments rather differently. Dispersed and incomplete pieces carry their own powers of suggesting completions. They mirror the process of anatomical dissection, which was the main theme of the poet's working life. They form a quarry whose brilliance, though limited, is stimulating in something of the same way in which Coleridge's *Notebooks* are stimulating. They deserve better than to be thought of as merely the records of that failure Beddoes thought himself. He was wrong.

EARLY LIFE AND BACKGROUND

Thomas Lovell Beddoes was born at Clifton, Bristol, on June 30, 1803. His parents provided him with an environment and a genetic inheritance that combined the waywardly eccentric and genuinely distinguished in full measure. His father, Thomas Beddoes, who died when the poet was only five years old, was a celebrity physician and polymath whose reputation made him a hard act to follow. Dr. Beddoes' accomplishments were varied, curious, and substantial. A good classicist, he also became proficient in German, Italian, French, and Spanish. After studying medicine in London and Edinburgh he became university reader in chemistry at Oxford, a post from which he had to resign in 1792 for making

too plain his radical views and sympathy with the French revolutionaries. Active as a translator, poet, scientific theorist, and rather less-than-effective practical investigator, he collaborated with James Watt and founded the Pneumatic Institution for research into the uses of gases for medical purposes. The doctor took the young Humphry Davy into his house to assist at this Pneumatic Institute and so became the patron of one of the most distinguished scientists of the nineteenth century. His own three-volume work *Hygeia* (1802–1803) is a monument to his scientific passion for the moral and physical improvement of society; his human and literary sympathies enabled him to number Robert Southey, William Wordsworth, and Samuel Taylor Coleridge among his patients and friends. The affection Dr. Beddoes called out may be judged from the letter Coleridge wrote to Thomas Poole on February 3, 1809: "O dear Poole! Beddoes's Departure has taken more hope out of my Life than any former Event except perhaps T. Wedgewoods—" (*Collected Letters of Samuel Taylor Coleridge,* vol. 3, 1959, p. 743).

Like father, like son. Both men shared the same impetuous, eccentric devotion to scientific knowledge, the same cool but affectionate temperaments, fitful brilliance, linguistic ability, and imaginative poetic impetus. Both, at the end of their lives, felt themselves failures. In a letter to Humphry Davy, written on his deathbed, Dr. Beddoes felt that from all his knowledge "neither branch nor blossom, nor fruit has resulted" (*Life,* p. 45); his son's farewell letter to Revell Phillips mordantly states "I am food for *what I am good for*—worms" and adds "I ought to have been among other things a good poet" (*Works,* p. 683).

The poet's mother brought an equivalent distinction, but her more equable temperament was not inherited by her son. Dr. Beddoes had met and become friendly with Richard Lovell Edgeworth and his family while they were staying at Clifton in 1793. Richard Edgeworth was, with his daughter Maria, to write seminal works on education: *Practical Education* (1798) and *Professional Education* (1809). Both men shared an inventive restlessness of mind, which in Richard Edgeworth's case resulted in a string of curious schemes and inventions that Lewis Carroll's White Knight might have appropriated: a plan for diverting the course of the river Rhône, ideas for sailing carriages, a one-wheeled chaise, a wind-driven train, an umbrella for covering haystacks, and most ingeniously "an early variant of the bicycle, a large cylinder holding a barrel six feet in diameter inside. The outer cylinder travelled five feet while the pedestrian walked thirty inches inside the barrel. Unfortunately the machine worked best down hill . . ." (Snow, p. 10). The dramatic climax of this contraption can best be left to the imagination. No one was killed. Dr. Beddoes fell in love with Edgeworth's daughter Anna Maria, and they were married in Edgeworthtown, Ireland, in 1794, Anna Maria's cheerful and straightforward manner forming a welcome marital contrast to the temperament of the gruff, absorbed, but affectionate doctor. After his father's death, young Thomas made frequent childhood visits to Edgeworthtown, overrun by the rackety, good-humored extended family that Richard Edgeworth's four wives and twenty-two children had created, a little world presided over by the benevolent despot himself.

With such marked individuality in his immediate background, it is not surprising that that course was already set which was to lead Thomas Lovell Beddoes into being the early-nineteenth-century equivalent of a medieval wandering scholar. His education was first conducted, if that is the word, at Charterhouse School in London, where his acting skills, literary talents, and capacity for creating mayhem made him prominent. Despite tormenting his elders and leading the contemporary equivalent of student riots, a kind of authoritarian charm seems to have won over both masters and pupils. His schoolfellow, Charles Dacre Bevan, left an engaging account of life with Beddoes at Charterhouse. Once, when the school locksmith did incompetent work on the boy's bookcase, Beddoes got up "a dramatic interlude representing [the locksmith's] last moments, disturbed by horror and remorse for his sins in the matter of the lock, his death, and funeral procession, which was interrupted by fiends who bore the body off to accompany the soul to eternal torments" (Snow, p. 13, quoting

an appendix to Kelsall.) It was some days before the locksmith could be persuaded to return to work. Clearly the mordant, satirical, corpse-haunted themes that were to become Beddoes' stock-in-trade were early in evidence, as was his fascination with drama and its mirror-self, melodrama. In 1820 Beddoes went to Pembroke, Oxford, where he seems to have cultivated a laconic disdain for his tutors, a radical approach to the issues of the day, and a love of the Elizabethan and Jacobean dramatists. In 1821 he made his literary debut with *The Improvisatore, in Three Fyttes, with Other Poems*—which he may well have started while he was still a schoolboy at Charterhouse.

THE IMPROVISATORE *AND* THE BRIDES' TRAGEDY

The archaic "fytte," used for a section of a poem, is essentially a medieval term borrowed by Thomas Chatterton in the eighteenth century for his pastiches of medieval verse. Beddoes is immediately placing his three horrific tales in a mock-medieval setting, Walter Scott's land of make-believe, where minstrels wander with their harps or lyres, knights are bold and ladies fair, and goblets pass from hand to hand in torch-lit banqueting halls. Behind these agreeable trappings, Beddoes' imagination is at an adolescent full-stretch, goaded on by his pressing desire to make the reader's flesh creep. The first fytte, "Albert and Emily," in skillful eight-line stanzas, a pair of rhymed couplets followed by an alternately rhymed quatrain, already carries a Beddoes trademark signature: the contrast between charnel-house events and a smiling pastoral landscape. The landscape is sugared by a soporific romantic imagery whose ancestry runs from Edmund Spenser through Keats, as when:

Quickly the moon, in virgin lustre dight,
Amongst the brilliant swarm cast forth her light,
Sailing along the waveless lake of blue,
Smiling with pallid light, a bright canoe.

(*Works*, p. 19)

Rather unfortunately, Albert is struck dead by lightning while embracing his Emily. She is found embracing the "loathsome lump" (p. 25) and, a parodic Ophelia, finds her recourse in "useless wailings and fantastic play" (p. 26). Eventually, united in the grave, the lovers' bodies metamorphose into a "thornless rose and lily" (p. 27), while the fragrance of their love lives on, as a "downy perfume whispers in the air" (p. 27). The other fyttes, "Rodolph the Wild" and "Leopold," pile on the horrors with a liberal hand. Rodolph, a young shepherd, is enticed by fiery and smoky phantasms, a mysterious beckoning hand, and the siren-like seductions of a mysterious song to a "low-browed cave" (p. 35). There Rodolph is enchanted by a supernatural beauty, whose mouth is a

> coral cave,
> Prison of fluttering sighs, cradle and grave
> Of noiseless kisses. . . .

(p. 36)

Her amorous invitations follow the usual pattern of such events. As soon as Rodolph attempts a kiss, the scene dissolves in laughter, blood, and dust, and he finds himself in "a body-jammed vault" (p. 37). His remaining years are spent as a frantic madman, the companion of toads and tombs, nightshade and hemlock. Here Beddoes echoes and intensifies the traditional fates of those caught in the loves of the faerie world: the knight-at-arms in Keats's "La Belle Dame sans Merci," forever wandering the silent, withered lakeside; the ambivalent, disturbing love episodes between queens of Faerie and mortals in the old Scottish border ballads of Thomas the Rhymer and Tam Lin.

In the final fytte the protagonist has hardly any redeeming features. In irregular iambic couplets, densely packed with sticky, physical imagery, we follow the fortunes of Leopold, the orphan who even as baby had an eye "leaden, motionless and cold" (p. 43). He grows to be a child of storm and night, murders his protector, the hermit Friar Hubert, and, annihilating space and time, becomes an elemental force, a kind of discarnate entity, at home with lightnings, phantoms, fogs, and blight. Returning to earth after several centuries, Leopold falls in love with a mortal girl, but his love brings about her immediate death. In a flurry of torment and curses the poem ends, or rather stops, unfinished. It is difficult,

reading the few poems added to *The Improvisatore,* to agree with Beddoes when he opens his hybrid sonnet *Thoughts* with the line: "Sweet are the thoughts that haunt the poet's brain" (p. 52).

This, then, is the only book of poems that Beddoes saw through the press. What is bad about it is obvious, but there is ambition, a sense of form and patterning, a tumultuous and fervid energy, and an unharnessed imagination that cannot help overloading the text with a whole Gothic wardrobe of rather fusty stage properties. Beddoes will never, though, cease exploring the relationship between flowers and the grave, love and death, the world of flesh on its way to becoming spirit, the world of spirit taking on its dress of flesh again. The concern expressed in these lines of Leopold's will intensify:

> What is this life, that spins so strangely on
> That, ere we grasp and feel it, it is gone?
> Is it a vision? Are we sleeping now
> In the sweet sunshine of another world?
> Is all that seems but a sleep-conjured ghost,
> And are our blind-fold senses closely curled,
> Our powerful minds pent up in this frail brow
> But by our truant fancy?

(p. 45)

In November 1822 Beddoes, at the age of nineteen, published *The Brides' Tragedy.* This was a quite different affair from *The Improvisatore.* In a burst of youthful energy and under the spell of the Elizabethan dramatists, Beddoes actually brought his play to a conclusion. In his dedicatory preface to the Reverend Henry Card, after an attack on the current state of the theater and the sight of "our countrymen barely enduring the poetry of Shakespeare" (*Works,* p. 528), Beddoes outlines his plot, based loosely on an Oxford legend that may have some truth behind it, in which an aristocratic student secretly married the daughter of a college servant, although he was already courting a dazzling young noblewoman approved by his parents. The student returned to Oxford, enticed his wife to a lonely spot, ironically called Divinity Walk, and murdered and buried her. Only much later, after a successful worldly career, did his deathbed confession reveal the story.

THOMAS LOVELL BEDDOES

Conceived by Beddoes as a closet drama, without thought of a stage production, the original story is teased out into complications and a parade of deaths. Young Hesperus loves Floribel. Floribel is also loved by Orlando. Orlando has a sister, Olivia, and plans to force Hesperus into marrying her, an act that will release Lord Ernest, Hesperus's father, from imprisonment. Hesperus falls in love with Olivia, murders his Floribel, is seen, and is arrested at his wedding to Olivia. In a dismal climax of death and madness, Floribel's mother, Lenora, poisons herself and Hesperus, thereby saving Hesperus from the executioner. The events take place in a kind of airy nowhere; the dramatis personae—Lords, Guards and Citizens, Floribel, Violetta, Mordred, Hesperus, Olivia, Lord Ernest—fit a kind of all-purpose landscape: city-state and pastoral, Italian and English, now and then. This cool, fantasticated, remote world carries strong reminders of Beaumont and Fletcher. As Royall Snow points out, comparing *The Brides' Tragedy* to their play *Phylaster,* there is a "soft tint of romanticism, distracted lovers in a forest, jealousies and pretty boys, which obscures the central callousness of both" (p. 46). Though we can hardly be concerned with the fate of the characters, the quality of the poetry they are compounded of shows a huge advance on *The Improvisatore.* Beddoes' pastoral imagery is still inclined to such elaborate and frigid conceits as the play's opening lines: "Now Eve has strewn the sun's wide billowy couch / With rosered feathers moulted from her wing" (*ML,* p. 3). But there are images that make a sudden leap into those imaginative perceptions that cannot be contrived to order, as when Floribel offers Hesperus flowers: "Here's the blue violet, like Pandora's eye, / When first it darkened with immortal life" (p. 4).

Hesperus himself does not share the worldly cynicism of his model in the Oxford story. He does not toy with his two loves simultaneously; his love for Olivia is the renewal of a former affection, and when his father reminds him of this, Hesperus is torn between his secret marriage and the new one that must be made to ensure his father's release. There is a grave beauty in Hesperus' address to Olivia that carries conviction:

We will be music, spring, and all fair things
The while our spirits make a sweeter union
Than melody and perfume in the air.

(p. 27)

Beddoes wishes us to share in the agony of the split self felt by his tragic hero, even if Hesperus' self-loathing falls at times into linguistic bluster and melodrama. The romantic sensibilities appropriate to Beddoes' own period are much in evidence, and Hesperus is seen as much the victim as the master of his circumstances. The murderer-hero cannot be judged too harshly; he must retain the reader's sympathies. Lord Ernest's account of his son's childhood shows that he was given a childhood experience of inexplicable terror, one that absolves him from final responsibility for his actions. While cradled in his nurse's arms, a "viewless bolt" struck and grotesquely killed her:

And as the months bring round that black remembrance,
His brain unsettles, bloody thoughts oppress
And call him from his bed.

(p. 33)

Before committing the murder, in a scene that carries a genuine frisson of spiritual danger, Hesperus, at the grave of a parricide-turned-suicide, makes an invocation to the infernal agencies reminiscent of Lady Macbeth. As he prays, he feels his own identity to be subsumed in that of the suicide:

'Tis here. A wind
Is rushing through my veins, and I become
As a running water.
I see a shadowy image of myself,
Yet not my perfect self, a brother self
That steps into my bosom.

(pp. 35–36)

At the close of a scene where the verse is almost Shelleyan in its yearning musicality, Hesperus, led by an ignis fatuus, or will-o'-the-wisp, one of those marsh lanterns of methane gas so useful as a Gothic trapping, leaves us with an image that is pure Beddoes in its memorable physicality, as he invites the snakes to participation in the coming murder:

Ye lovely fanged monsters of the woods,
We'll grovel in the dust and ye shall hiss
Your tunes of murder to me.

(p. 36)

The Brides' Tragedy is full of announcements that will be fulfilled in *Death's Jest-Book*. The melancholy passivity of the female characters (except Floribel's mother, Lenora), the interspersed songs that turn carousal into dirge and back again, the sudden, almost galvanic leaps from action to action and mood to mood, the varied and fluent handling of blank verse, the swoop into universal imprecations and aspirations, the return again to a sharp fascination with the sensuous details of mortality—together these will become Beddoes' dramatic signature. In maturity, though, he was to leave behind much of that sentimental and playful pastoral element that gives freshness to *The Brides' Tragedy*. Natural, easy dialogue, the individuality of created character that finds expression in appropriate speech—these would never be part of his armory. The thinking, observing animal, so firmly a part of Beddoes, was to grow stronger; his work would gain a biting edge, a philosophical insistence on first and last questions that is no part of the emotional theater of *The Brides' Tragedy*. Though the critics were enthusiastic, particularly the poets George Darley and Bryan Waller Procter (Barry Cornwall), who was to become a lifelong friend and supporter, there was to be no further volume from Beddoes in his lifetime. He was to attempt two further dramas that he could not bring to completion and that remain possibilities and fragments, *Torrismond* and *The Second Brother*. Then came the years spent in medical researches on the Continent and the isolated labors on *Death's Jest-Book*.

TORRISMOND *AND* THE SECOND BROTHER

In 1823 Beddoes spent the summer in Southampton, where he met Thomas Kelsall, who was to prove not only a most steadfast friend but the preserver of Beddoes' unpublished papers. One of his most important services was in preserving and giving titles to those fragments that so fascinate the poet's admirers. Paradoxically, the scattered images and perceptions Beddoes could fashion into radiant nuggets of suggestion but could never integrate into finished works are now seen as a record of success, not failure. These lyrical poems and fragments, however, deserve a section to themselves. In 1824 Beddoes' mother died in Florence; in 1825, the master of an independent income that allowed him to follow his own star, Beddoes started his linguistic and medical studies at the University of Göttingen. His life in England, which would only be revisited in brief forays, was over.

Torrismond is no more than the almost-completed first act of a tragedy, its theme the emotional collision between the Duke of Ferrara and his son Torrismond. The first scene drives the Duke's anger and contempt along at a furious pace, as he berates his courtiers for being his willful son's "echo-birds, the mirrors of his tongue" (*ML*, p. 124). The second scene introduces Torrismond himself, whose tumultuous behavior masks an essential seriousness, the hunger for a reciprocated love by one "not at home / In this December world, with men of ice, / Cold sirs and madams" (p. 129). In the third scene Torismond finds his echoed love in Veronica, and the scene interlaces their love with the natural world, the moonlit garden of their encounter holding together a cluster of images drawn from dream, imagination, and observation. The haunting song "How many times do I love thee, dear?" sets the untroubled tone for a scene in which Beddoes is at his most enticing, offering such simplicities as the "snoring wasps" (p. 132) and Veronica's blush, which is "the faint ghost of some dishevelled rose" (p. 131), or more elaborate conceits, as when Torrismond, gazing at the sleeping girl, sees:

How threads of blue, wound off yon thorny stars
That grow upon the wall of hollow night,
Flow o'er each sister-circle of her bosom . . .

(p. 131)

Scene 4 brings to a climax the Duke's rejection and banishment of his son, under the advice of treacherous councillors, and Torrismond welcomes a future that can only bring death in lines of convincing simplicity: "For winter is the season of the tomb, / And that's my country now" (p. 142). It is hard to see how the intensity could be maintained or where further development of the play could lead.

The Second Brother is more substantial, but Beddoes only managed three completed acts before losing the impetus to carry his theme further. The conflict this time is between two brothers. The Duke of Ferrara will soon die, and his brother Marcello, thought to be abroad, will inherit. The third brother, Orazio, desires the dukedom for himself. Orazio is a kind of walking extravaganza, whose first torch-lit and panther-skinned entry as the self-styled son of Bacchus is counterpointed by a meeting with his elder brother Marcello, who has returned to his native country as a beggar, a creature who seems to have "Burst from the grave in a stolen cloak of flesh" (*ML,* p. 146). He confronts Orazio, who does not recognize him, as a kind of living memento mori:

> I tell thee, brother skeleton,
> We're but a pair of puddings for the dinner
> Of Lady Worm; you served in silks and gems,
> I garnished with plain rags.
>
> (p. 149)

When Orazio rejects him and discloses his desire for the dukedom, Marcello, in one of those impossible psychological leaps Beddoes is expert in, embraces evil and isolation as his choice and doom. Invocations and curses are a Beddoes specialty, and Marcello, opening his soul to the forces of evil, expresses his desire to make "A staircase of the frightened breasts of men, / And climb into a lonely happinesss!" (p. 151).

The Second Brother has many of the qualities that mark Beddoes' other early dramatic experiments. The love scene between Orazio and his wife, Valeria, who approaches him dressed as a nun, displays Beddoes' penchant for both sentimentality and disguise. The blank verse struts magniloquently, as if Christopher Marlowe had been given a Romantic sensibility, and is studded with startling and violent images. Bed-

does' ability to produce astonishing developments of metaphor is well shown in Valeria's exchange with her young Attendant in the second act. The girl expresses her innocent sense of being loved with simple beauty: "I walk / Within the brilliance of another's thought, / As in a glory" (p. 165). Valeria sees the girl as a daisy closing in welcome on the first drop of evening rain, but that rain becomes "The shower of oceans, in whose billowy drops / Tritons and lions of the sea were warring," until the climax of her apocalyptic vision: "And every sea of every ruined star / Was but a drop in the world-melting flood" (p. 165). There are violent oscillations between riches and poverty, success and failure, as when Orazio is suddenly told that he is financially ruined and his wife is forced from him by her irate father. The final scenes have a Gothic air, set in such places as "A dungeon of Cyclopean architecture" and "The Campo Santo."

The play breaks off at the point where Marcello is to persuade Orazio that he can call back his vanished wife from the dead—a trick, since she is very much alive. Donner suggests that Beddoes could not reconcile mere conjuring with the true diabolism of Marcello's nature (*Life,* p. 157) and so was unable to end the play to his satisfaction. What the early dramatic pieces cannot do is jump to the future and demonstrate Beddoes' profound and doomed search for clues to a verifiable afterlife through both experiential science and poetry. There are glimpses, but glimpses only, of the cut and bite of an analytical mind at work on issues of substance, the quality that was to make Beddoes simultaneously a mordant and humorous commentator and a richly poetic creator. To see some of those qualities in action, we can turn to the letters.

CONTINENTAL LIFE AND LETTERS

Since Beddoes left no account of his own life, the letters his correspondents preserved are our best way of coming close to his multifaceted personality. They reveal an engagingly witty and quick-witted nature; the bursts of wild humor are counterpointed by moods of doubt and depression. The letters are also a guide to Beddoes' literary and scientific ambitions and demonstrate how those two obsessions constantly converge and part. Kelsall and Proctor were his chief, but not his only, correspondents in the twenty-four years of continental wanderings left to him after he left England to pursue his medical studies at Göttingen in the summer of 1825.

The external events of those years may be briefly summarized. Though Beddoes was an excellent student, a drunken and rowdy foray in which he "fatally injured a turkey" (*ML,* p. xliii) resulted in his expulsion from Göttingen and a move to Würzburg, where he took his doctorate in medicine. Following the bent of his radical father, Beddoes became involved in student agitation. Though English, he threw himself into the Bavarian world of speeches, articles, and secret-society politics. In July 1832 the government, unable to tolerate his anti-aristocratic and anti-monarchical activities any longer, expelled him from Bavaria. (How eagerly he would have participated in the university tumults of 1968!) Beddoes did not go quietly. His final exit, escorted from Würzburg by his admirers, was inevitable but triumphal. He then settled as a kind of perpetual student in Zurich, cushioned by his private income from the harsher realities of earning a living. Beddoes wrote some of his finest lyric poetry while at Zurich, and his innate egalitarian instincts seem to have been kept in enough check to save him from political trouble until 1840. The liberal government fell in 1839, and Beddoes left Zurich, possibly to avoid arrest, though the circumstances seem uncertain. A brief return to England failed to endear his native land to him, and he wandered among Zurich, Baden, Frankfort, and England. For the last five years of his life his close and intermittent companion was a young actor, Konrad Degen. Beddoes had always been a man of few friendships, his temperament being reserved and ironic, and those friendships had all been with men, apart from an easy relationship with his cousin Zoë King. It seems likely that his temperament was homosexual. In July 1848, after slow recuperation from blood poisoning occasioned by a cut finger while dissecting, Beddoes purposely slashed open an artery in his leg. Gangrene

supervened, and the leg was amputated in Basel Hospital. Though he recovered, the recovery was only a stay of self-execution, and in January 1849 Beddoes took poison, leaving a typically mordant note for his friend Revell Phillips: "I ought to have been among other things a good poet; Life was too great a bore on one peg & that a bad one." His final request was that Phillips should buy his physician, Dr. Ecklin, "Reade's best stomach pump" (*Works,* p. 683).

The fascination of Beddoes' temperament can be sensed by looking at the range of subjects covered in such a letter as the one to Kelsall of October 5, 1826 (*Works,* pp. 620–623). We have the opening in German, and then we glance from botanical expeditions to an aside on *Death's Jest-Book,* "my unhappy devil of a tragedy, which is done and done for: its limbs being as scattered and unconnected as those of the old gentleman whom Medea minced and boiled young." Then come a thumbnail sketch of a professor with a "toothless earthquake of a mouth," firecracker witticisms at the expense of German tragedians such as Friedrich Schiller, whose galvanic experiments made people think the Muse of Tragedy was alive "when she was only kicking," a description of the salamanders to be found in the crevices of the nearby castle ruins with a digression on their supposed immunity to fire, and an anecdote of the foundation of a local hermitage. This tale, which involves a despairing yet constant lover, leads Beddoes into an attack on his own age of "hard-heartedness & worldly prudence," where "we fellows who cannot weep without the grace of onions or hartshorn, who take terror by the nose, light our matches with lightning" are unlikely to create great literature. Beddoes ends the letter with his translation of a churchyard, robber, and murder poem by Dr. Ernst Solomon Raupach. The enticing blend of humor, passionate distaste, defensive pride, vivid observation, and learning worn lightly demonstrates well why Kelsall was so faithful a friend and admirer.

As the sequence of letters progresses we can chart something of the course Beddoes set as he balanced his interests between literary and medical activities. His own literary idol was Shelley, and his views of most of his contemporaries were, with some reason, disdainful. The letter to Kelsall from Clifton on January 11, 1825, contains Beddoes' often-quoted remark that "the man who is to awaken the drama must be a bold, trampling fellow—no creeper into worm-holes" (*Works*, p. 595), a remark sometimes held against him by earlier critics who saw Beddoes as essentially a pasticheur, an Elizabethan born out of his time. On December 4, 1825, after giving Kelsall a rundown of his grueling daily timetable at Göttingen, Beddoes claims that the exact sciences can help give the dramatist a proper basis for the construction of plausible characters, and so "the studies then of the dramatist & physician are closely, almost inseparably, allied" (*Works*, p. 609). He adds that *Death's Jest-Book* will be "entertaining, very unamiable, & utterly unpopular" (*Works*, p. 610). Comments on the progress of *Death's Jest-Book* intersperse the letters. Kelsall was told on April 1, 1826, that it "lies like a snowball and I give it a kick every now & then out of mere scorn and ill-humour" (*Works*, p. 616). In the same letter Beddoes claimed that dissection and anatomy, not poetry, would prove his true vocation, but the choice was never finally decided. It is clear that he felt cut off from the English literary world and consequently contemptuous of the current poetical favorites; he despaired of the state of dramatic literature both in England and Germany. His naturally sardonic and critical temperament found few effective models or admirations, and reading his admired near-contemporary Shelley only intensified his self-criticism.

In 1829 Beddoes nerved himself to send *Death's Jest-Book* in manuscript to three friends in England, but the reaction of two of them, John Bourne and Bryan Waller Procter, both of whom advised against publication, was disastrous for Beddoes. He made no further attempt to publish his tragedy, and for the rest of his life it grew more and more unwieldy and proof against any possible publication or production as it was tinkered with, expanded, and modified. The quest that increasingly obsessed Beddoes was the search, through anatomical dissection, for some assurance that man had a spiritual afterlife and was not merely a developed animal. "I search with avidity for every shadow of a proof or probability of an after-existence, both in the material & immaterial nature of man" (*Works*, p. 630), he tells Kelsall on April 20, 1827. *Death's Jest-Book*, among other things, is a kind of medical textbook, a *Gray's Anatomy* to Death, who himself suffers dissection and bobs about in various guises, sometimes imitating life, sometimes imitating himself. It is also the record of Beddoes' failure to find that proof which so obsessed him. His own life seems to have ended in weariness, depression, and a lack of concern as to what would become of his writings. An undated 1847 letter to Kelsall shows only too clearly the state of mind Beddoes settled into. His life, he says, is "monotonous, dull and obscure," his literary endeavors have failed, and he might have better succeeded "as a retailer of small coal" (*Works*, p. 679). His final dismissive words on *Death's Jest-Book* are "the unhappy Jest book" (*Works*, p. 630). On the contrary, it is now increasingly seen as one of the most remarkable productions of the Romantic movement.

DEATH'S JEST-BOOK

The most enticing account of *Death's Jest-Book; or, The Fool's Tragedy*, as Beddoes subtitled the original version of his drama, is to be found in a verse letter to Procter postmarked May 7, 1826. In easy, urbane couplets Beddoes sets out his thoughts on the work he has been engaged on as a respite from his anatomical studies:

> In it Despair has married wildest Mirth
> And to their wedding-banquet all the earth
> Is bade to bring its enmities and loves
> Triumphs and horrors: you shall see the doves
> Billing with quiet joy and all the while
> Their nest's the scull of some old King of Nile.

The "fool o' the feast" is to be Death himself, and Beddoes intends:

> of his night,
> His moony ghostliness and silent might

To rob him, to un-cypress him i'the light
To unmask all his secrets . . .

(*Works*, pp. 614–615)

The textual history of the drama is complex. The original manuscripts have disappeared, and Michael Bradshaw's informative note on the text (*Bradshaw*, pp. xxvii–xxviii) explains how he has followed the 1829 version—which was the one Beddoes prepared for publication—rather than the later conflations. Donner's huge variorum edition in the *Works* is unwieldy and inaccessible, and in his selection for the Muses' Library *Thomas Lovell Beddoes* he himself printed the 1829 version as the one closest to Beddoes' own intention. Though much richness was eventually added, particularly in the interspersal of lyrics to the blank verse text, the early version has the merits of a firmness of structure and a sense of youthful energy as the young anatomist's energies move quickly from scalpel to pen and back again. Plot is hardly Beddoes's strongest suit, but it is necessary to gain some hold on what happens, or seems to happen, before assessing the qualities of the whole.

The time of the action of *Death's Jest-Book* is supposed to be the thirteenth century, but the medieval trappings are external. The libertarian sentiments reflect Beddoes' own; the feelings that inform the play make no pretense of being other than the Romantic sensibilities of Beddoes' own period. Duke Melveric, captured in Africa, has left his dukedom of Münsterburg in the hands of a governor, Torwald. Two brothers, Wolfram and Isbrand, have made a pact to take revenge on the Duke for "a father slain and plundered" (*Bradshaw*, p. 14), but Wolfram, whose nature is seen as noble and forgiving, sets sail to rescue the Duke, while Isbrand, who is in masquerade as court jester, stays in Münsterburg to plot revenge. Wolfram, though, is murdered by Melveric as they become rivals for Sibylla. His body is shipped home and cunningly slipped by Isbrand into the grave of the Duke's wife, where he is designed to become a displeasing surprise at the Day of Judgment. The Duke himself returns, disguised as a pilgrim, and observes the machinations of his two plotting sons, Adalmar

and Athulf. The role of ironic commentator on events in Münsterburg is played by the madcap Homunculus Mandrake, a self-styled "amateur goblin" (p. 38), who also slips into the vault where Wolfram is buried. In a climactic piece of Gothic grotesquerie, the Duke's African servant and magus, Ziba, offers to raise Melveric's wife from the dead. The Duke promises to follow such raised spirit as appears back to its incorporeal home, but after the incantation, first Mandrake appears, followed by Wolfram, whose ghostly but corporeal presence is to be a controlling one in the latter part of the play. His remote and loving blandishments entice Sibylla toward death:

I am a ghost. Tremble not; fear not me.
The dead are ever good and innocent,
And love the living. They are cheerful creatures,
And quiet as the sunbeams . . .

(p. 88)

Isbrand foments rebellion, but his revenge motive and the justice of the republican cause are subservient to his personal ambition:

A sceptre is smooth handling, it is true,
And one grows fat and jolly in a chair
That has a kingdom crouching under it,
With one's name on its collar, like a dog
To fetch and carry. But the heart I have
Is a strange little snake.

(p. 51)

The Duke's rebellious sons quarrel over the girl Amala, a quarrel that results in the murder of Adalmar by Athulf. The closing moments of the play, set in a ruined cathedral, are announced by Wolfram's invitation to the painted skeletons on the walls: "Come forth and dance a little: 'tis the season / When you may celebrate Death's Harvest-Home" (p. 120). Isbrand is assassinated by Mario, a conspirator and "Roman in unroman times" (p. 63), whose watchwords are "Freedom" and "Liberty." As he dies, Wolfram re-crowns Isbrand with the jester's cap he had discarded for ambition's sake: "Meantime Death sends you back this cap of office / At his court you're elected to the post: / Go, and enjoy it" (p. 119). The masque of death leads to the suicide of

Athulf, the death of Amala, the announcement of Sibylla's death, and Wolfram's remorseless invitation to the Duke to accompany him back into the tomb. Torwald is left as Melveric's successor.

This bald statement of impossible events can only act as a very simplified map of the territory, but inside this revenge-tragedy framework is embedded a complex world of philosophical insight and jesting, conducted in language that is derivative of Elizabethan and Jacobean sources yet can hold its own in nervous intensity and power of metaphor without descending into pastiche. Though much early comment on *Death's Jest-Book* placed great emphasis on the derivative nature of Beddoes' blank verse, it must be remembered that the long, fustian doldrums of the eighteenth century's attempts at creating a tragic drama had left the writers of the Romantic period no later models on which to build. Shakespeare himself had been adapted, bowdlerized, and given endings that did not offend Enlightenment sensibilities. Beddoes was not alone in falling under the spell of the power and passion of the Jacobean tragedians, and it is better to see him in relation to the earlier dramatists as a brilliant successor rather than as a misguided imitator. To chase specific sources for events in *Death's Jest-Book* can be an intriguing academic labor, but the rich strangeness of Beddoes' blank verse is very much his own, despite such obvious debts as to the prose badinage of Shakespeare's fools, the cruel darknesses of John Webster, and the savage, twisted satirical edge of John Marston. Beddoes' own brief preface gives us a clear indication of his intentions and takes the form of a defense of the indigenous English dramatic tradition, placing against the direct clarities of Greek drama the layered and elaborate structures exemplified by Shakespeare. An Elizabethan play, Beddoes suggests, is analogous to a Gothic cathedral. There are two groups of words he uses to indicate the qualities both possess and which he admires: "Intricate, vast, and gloomy" (*Bradshaw*, p. 5) and "satirical, grotesque, or ludicrous" (p. 6). These adjectival trios apply with some exactness to the effects Beddoes achieves in *Death's Jest-Book,* which he offers as a specimen of the "florid Gothic" (p. 6) and which contains a host of brilliant, suggestive details lit against overarching clouds and shadows.

No one has ever suggested that Beddoes had a flair for characterization. The multifarious action proceeds by sharp twists and turns of melodramatic intensity. The most substantial figure is Isbrand, who combines the qualities of introspective philosopher, man of action, and jester. The other character who engages the reader's imagination most actively is Homunculus Mandrake, the witty and ironic parodist of the themes of life, death, and resurrection that are deeply woven into the play's texture. The name "Homunculus Mandrake" suggests both the strange folklore of the shrieking mandrake, the forked plant fostered by droppings from the gallows; and the homunculus, or little man supposedly created by the alchemical philosopher Paracelsus. Mandrake disappears from the action after the third act, having spent the first half of the play believing in his own invisibility. He had accompanied Wolfram to Egypt and there created a "bewitching butter" (p. 34), which sadly spilled over him on the return voyage. Mandrake's high comedy brings an agreeably prosaic gaiety into the general gruesome carnival: "Good folks, don't pretend any more that you don't see me. O Lord, I am half frightened already into the belief that I am vanished. Reasonable folks! I stand here in the corner, by the rack of plates" (p. 34). In the traditional dramatic division into plot and subplot, Mandrake is the hero of the subplot—that aping of the concerns of the makers and shakers of the world by their inferiors. He is irrepressible. His supposed invisibility apes death, his mock resurrection apes Wolfram's actual resurrection, and his final disappearance is ironically a kind of disappearance into life, as nearly every other character is bound for the grave.

The multifarious quality of *Death's Jest-Book* can be illustrated by looking at one climactic scene. The third scene of the third act is set in the ruins of a Gothic cathedral, appropriately lit by moonlight. We are at the family sepulchre of the dukes of Münsterburg, and a painted death dance looks down from the walls. Mandrake, who has hidden there, undercuts the scene with his opening remarks to the audience: "After all, being dead's not so uncomfortable when one's got into the knack of it" (p. 59). Isbrand, present with his henchmen, tells the disguised Duke Melveric, whom he takes to be a fellow conspirator, how completely he can read his enemies' thoughts: "each dark crack in which a reptile purpose / Hangs in its chrysalis unripe for birth" (p. 62), but the Duke ironically warns him that he can never learn that alphabet "In which the hieroglyphic human soul / More changeably is painted than the rainbow . . ." (p. 62). Mario, Isbrand's nemesis, appears and is enlisted as a conspirator. Plotters and pseudo-plotters leave, and Duke Melveric sets about the exhumation of his wife's urn, which he intends to take with him out of Germany, while the mysterious Ziba hints that he is the inheritor of an ancestral magic that can raise the dead.

Isbrand reenters with his companion Siegfried for a parodic festivity of wine and song and sings one of Beddoes' most extraordinary lyrics, a song of birth and monstrosity, a chant he claims he made "a-strewing poison for the rats / In the kitchen corner" (p. 68). The opening lines prefigure the extraordinary resurrections about to take place:

Squats on a toad-stool under a tree
    bodiless childful of life in the gloom,
Crying with frog voice, "What shall I be?
Poor, unborn ghost, for my mother killed me
    Scarcely alive in her wicked womb.

                (p. 69)

Ziba then introduces Isbrand to the concept of a human bone, "Luz," which Beddoes noted (p. 122) is supposed to possess the property of surviving the body's dissolution and then acting as a kind of seed for the resurrected body. On Isbrand's exit, the Duke, in a fine piece of Gothic drama, offers Ziba the blood bond he had made with Wolfram to burn and illuminate the scene and swears to follow to the grave the spirit Ziba raises, believing it will be his wife. Ziba's incantation—"Marrow fill bone, and vine-like veins run round them . . ." (p. 75) results first of all in footsteps, the grating of iron hinges, and

the comic emergence of Mandrake, who tells the Duke and Ziba to "look into the old lumber room of a vault again. Someone seems to be putting himself together there . . ." (p. 77). Mandrake makes a jaunty exit, and the Duke, fearful that Wolfram may appear, implores his wife to be the first to rise from the grave. Wolfram appears, refuses the Duke's attempt to order him back again, and with laconic certainty explains that when eventually he does decide to return to the grave he will take Melveric with him. Meanwhile he announces that he "will stay awhile / To see how the world goes, feast, and be merry . . ." (p. 79). The Duke and Wolfram go off together, the Duke helping Wolfram to accustom his eyes to the sunlight! The scene, like *Death's Jest-Book* itself, is full of convincing impossibilities and remarkable images; the balance between genuine frissons and stage frights is finely drawn, and Beddoes' alarming capacity for combining high imagination with biting intelligence is fully demonstrated. Though the 1829 text is the one used for this article, Alan Halsey's 2003 edition of the later and fuller text now gives the reader a welcome opportunity to delve further into the intricacies of the play.

POEMS AND POETIC FRAGMENTS

The general disorder in which Beddoes left his works has presented all editors with considerable difficulties in making selections from his poems and in deciding where to place the dramatic fragments and scattered fragments and lyrics designed for *Death's Jest-Book*. Contemporary practice is less interested in making the traditional distinctions between kinds, or in creating canons that assign secondary status to the tentative and fragmentary. Donner's classification in the *Works* has, for the most part, been accepted as authoritative. *The Improvisatore* and its appended poems have already been discussed. *Outidana, or Effusions, Amorous, Pathetic and Fantastical,* consists of poems written between 1821 and 1825. "Outidana," which means "valueless" in Greek, was Beddoes' disarmingly laconic title or the book with which he planned to follow the success of *The Brides' Tragedy* and the title under which Donner gathered together the poems written in the last years of Beddoes' life in England. Beddoes showed justice as well as accuracy in his choice of epithets. The poems are indeed amorous, pathetic, and fantastical, and their quality is uneven. "The Romance of the Lily" (*ML*, pp. 83–91) is an uneasy blend of sentiment and melodrama, technically varied and adroit but with a young poet's tendency to make cloudy abstractions a correlative for feeling. "Pygmalion" (*ML*, pp. 98–104) lacks vitality, and the author's consciously noble intention is not helped by the stately but soporific iambics. The "Sonnet" to the terrier Tartar shows a warmhearted affection and a nice sense of observation when the dog is observed at "Long scrutiny o'er some dark-veined stone" (*ML*, p. 95), but the most attractive poem in *Outidana* is the poem written shortly after the death of Beddoes' mother, "Lines: Written at Geneva, July 16 {1824}." It is a poem of longing and dissolve, a night-piece in which Beddoes explores the nature of silence, that haunting after-silence as the sounds of the day die away and yet leave no ghosts. The thought of the poem swings away from the natural sleep of grass and flowers—"They have drunk sunshine and the linnet's song, / Till every leaf's soft sleep is dark and strong" (*ML*, p. 92)—to the sleep of the ancient dead, who now "have no body but the beauteous air, / No body but their minds" (p. 93). The poem ends with a visionary image of the spirits of children at play among the ruin and decay of the recently dead. The poems' mood is in-turned, floating, but the strangeness is both remote and homely rather than grotesque.

The early plays Beddoes planned but failed to execute exist now in the form of scattered passages that were collected, numbered, and titled by Donner as *Dramatic Fragments {Composed 1823–5}*. These range from aphoristic singletons or pairs of blank-verse lines to more complex passages that extend and elaborate a concept or sensation into dramatic passion and metaphor. Such a tiny fragment as "XL. A Lake" is not easy to forget: "A lake / Is a river curled and

asleep like a snake" (*Works*, p. 245), and "XXXVIII. Rain" is in itself a small Imagist poem:

The blue, between yon star-nailed cloud,
The double-mountain and this narrow valley,
Is strung with rain, like a fantastic lyre.

(*Works*, p. 245)

The fragments are a rich quarry of suggestive plunder: small, unearthly visitations. Their planned context now lost, they float out of darkness into darkness with an air of menace and possibility. "XXII. Life a Glass Window" can be taken as a brilliant example of this power to haunt.

Let him lean
Against his life, that glassy interval
'Twixt us and nothing; and upon the ground
Of his own slippery breath, draw hueless dreams,
And gaze on frost-work hopes. Uncourteous Death
Knuckles the pane, and—

(*ML*, p. 110)

The mysterious persona of the poem, so easy to identify with as a correlative for our own sense of loss or failure; the strangeness and fragility of the opening image, the "glassy interval" (a phrase that gave Walter de la Mare the title for one of the sections in his distinguished 1939 anthology of sleep, death, and dream, *Behold, This Dreamer*); the physicality of glass and frost; the subtle "Uncourteous"; the final dash leading the reader to step blindly into nowhere—all these make the word "fragment" one that works toward diminishing the piece's status.

Donner's arrangement of the remainder of Beddoes' poetry is in three sections: *Poems Composed 1826–9*, the *Songs and Fragments from the Revisions of Death's Jest-Book*, which Beddoes had continued to revise from 1829 to his death, and poems from *The Ivory Gate*, which was planned for 1836 as a "dramatic Keepsake"—a jibe at the gift annuals of the time. This was to be a kind of Beddoes compendium including *Death's Jest-Book*, some prose tales, and some lyrical pieces. The ivory gate is in itself an undercutting title, since the ivory gate is distinguished in classical mythology from the gate of horn as the gate through which false dreams enter. A further level of irony was provided by Beddoes' choice of pseudonym, the splendid anagram of his name—Theobald Vesselldoom. Beddoes' mock-grisly style, his forays into the sentimental macabre, are much in evidence in "The Ghost's Moonshine," an intertwining of love and murder, with its insistent refrain:

Is that the wind? No, no;
Only two devils, that blow
Through the murderer's ribs to and fro
In the ghost's moonshine.

(*ML*, p 192)

Beddoes has a strong line in Death-and-the-Maiden wares, pouncing over his heroines with knives and blandishments. This poem, though, takes a new and more dramatic form when given in *Death's Jest-Book* to Wolfram, who heard "snaky mermaids" sing it "In Phlegethon, that hydrophobic river, / One May-morning in Hell" (*ML*, p. 324). The human lovers disappear, and a fierce, eldritch quality is added by exchanging them for a pair of Egyptian carrion crows, nesting in Cleopatra's skull. The refrain is the same, but "the" murderer is distanced to "a" murderer, and the song gathers to itself a strange independence, as if its cast lives beyond and as a commentary on human time but is not enclosed by it.

It is important to emphasize Beddoes' talent for melody and beauty. They become in his hands a pair of sirens luring the reader away from death's terrors to a world where his enticements are irresistible. Beddoes' capacity for making longing and dissatisfaction with mortal existence memorable is well demonstrated by such poems as the dirge for Wolfram, "Song from the Waters" (*ML*, p. 354), "Dream-Pedlary" (*ML*, p. 372), and "The Phantom-Wooer" (*ML*, pp. 397–398), with its extraordinary Frostian pre-echo:

Our bed is lovely, dark, and sweet;
The earth will swing us, as she goes,
Beneath our coverlid of snows,
And the warm leaden sheet.

(*ML*, p. 398).

It is good to end with something complete, even if it is a complete fragment. The poem titled by Donner "An Unfinished Draft" holds i microcosm those qualities of longing and sa questioning that make Beddoes at his best so fin a poet, the poet for whom the unfulfilled become fulfillment:

An Unfinished Draft

The snow falls by thousands into the sea;
  A thousand flowers are shedding
    Their leaves all dead and dry;
  A thousand birds are threading
    Their passage through the sky;
  A thousand mourners treading
    The tearful churchyard way
  In funeral array:
Birds, whither fly ye?—whither, dead, pass ye?
The snow falls by thousands into the sea.

(*ML*, pp. 391–392)

CONCLUSION

The search that concerned Beddoes so closely, the search for some proof of the survival of the human psyche beyond death, could not be solved through anatomical dissection or imaginative creation, and in that sense Beddoes died in weariness and dissatisfaction. It must be remembered, though, that his personality as it appeared in his social relationships was the antithesis of the lean, brooding, hermetic scholar. Witty, selectively social, and sardonic, his nature displayed the undercutting Homunculus Mandrake, partnered by the towering ambition of an Isbrand to solve the insoluble. Though critics will continue to be fascinated by the variant ways in which the text can be approached, the unacademic reader will still probably find the approach by Lytton Strachey in his essay on Beddoes, *The Last Elizabethan*, enticing: "One must wander with him through the pages of *Death's Jest-Book,* one must grow accustomed to the dissolution of reality, and the opening of the nettled lips of graves; one must learn that 'the dead are most and merriest,' one must ask—'Are the ghosts eavesdropping?'—one must realise that 'murder is full of holes'" (p. 262).

Death's Jest-Book, while infinitely richer than its possible counterparts, suggests certain simplified visual correspondences. The earliest is the emblematic Dance of Death itself, a medieval image, though Hans Holbein's suite of woodcuts made in about 1525 is the most widely known example. Another is the extraordinary set of tableaux made from dissections by the Dutch anatomist Fredrik Ruysch (1638–1731) and exhibited in his museum at Amsterdam. (Three plates from engravings of these exhibits can be found in Ruthven Todd's *Tracks in the Snow,* 1946.) In such tableaux, skeletons posture about a landscape made of *disjecta membra,* one plays a violin made of human arteries, another holds a mourning position for his or her mortality. In our own day, Dr. Gunther von Hagens has arranged his "plastinated" bodies of human beings and creatures in simulacra of life and bared death to the public in his "Body Worlds" exhibitions in Europe. Do these false resurrections, in the words of Beddoes already quoted, "uncypress" death? Beddoes moves far beyond such simple and grisly fascinations. As Strachey suggests, perhaps for Beddoes, death and love are ultimately interchangeable.

Selected Bibliography

WORKS OF THOMAS LOVELL BEDDOES

WORKS PUBLISHED IN THE AUTHOR'S LIFETIME

The Improvisatore, in Three Fyttes, with Other Poems by Thomas Lovell Beddoes. Oxford: Vincent and Whittaker, 1821.

The Brides' Tragedy. By Thomas Lovell Beddoes, of Pembroke College, Oxford. London: Rivington, 1822.

COLLECTED WORKS

Death's Jest-Book; or, The Fool's Tragedy. London: William Pickering, 1850. (This edition, published anonymously, was edited by Thomas Forbes Kelsall, who amended the text to taste.)

The Poems Posthumous and Collected of Thomas Lovell Beddoes, with a Memoir. 2 vols. Edited by T. F. Kelsall. London: William Pickering, 1851. (The memoir by Kelsall is the primary source for future biographical studies.)

The Poetical Works of Thomas Lovell Beddoes. 2 vols. Edited with a memoir by Edmund Gosse. London: Dent, 1890.

The Poems of Thomas Lovell Beddoes. Edited with an introduction by Ramsay Colles. London: The Muses' Library, Routledge, 1907. (This was the first popular edition of any of Beddoes' works.)

The Complete Works of Thomas Lovell Beddoes. 2 vols. Edited with a memoir by Sir Edmund Gosse and decorated by the *Dance of Death* of Hans Holbein. London: Fanfrolico Press, 1928. (This was a luxury edition, limited to 825 copies.)

The Works of Thomas Lovell Beddoes. Edited with an introduction by H. W. Donner. London: Oxford University Press, 1935. Reprint, New York: AMS Press, 1978. (This definitive edition includes letters, poems, miscellaneous prose, and a complete variorum text of *Death's Jest-Book.*)

The Browning Box; or, The Life and Works of Thomas Lovell Beddoes as Reflected in Letters by His Friends and Admirers. Edited with an introduction by H. W. Donner. London: Oxford University Press, 1935.

Plays and Poems of Thomas Lovell Beddoes. Edited with an introduction by H. W. Donner. London: Muses' Library, Routledge and Kegan Paul, 1950. (This supplants Colles as a reasonably accessible text.)

Selected Poems. Edited by Judith Higgins. Manchester, U.K.: Carcanet, 1976. Revised as *Thomas Lovell Beddoes: Selected Poetry.* Edited with an introduction by Judith Higgens and Michael Bradshaw. Manchester, U.K.: Fyfield Books/Carcanet, 1999.

Thomas Lovell Beddoes: Death's Jest-Book, the 1829 text. Edited with an introduction by Michael Bradshaw. Manchester: Fyfield Books/Carcanet in association with the Thomas Lovell Beddoes Society, 2003.

Thomas Lovell Beddoes: Death's Jest-Book: or, The Day Will Come. A new edition of the [gamma] text established by H. W. Donner. Edited and introduced by Alan Halsey. Sheffield, U.K.: West House Books, 2003.

CRITICAL AND BIOGRAPHICAL STUDIES

Bradshaw, Michael. *Scattered Limbs: The Making and Unmaking of "Death's Jest-Book."* Belper, U.K.: Thomas Lovell Beddoes Society, 1996.

———. *Resurrection Songs: The Poetry of Thomas Lovell Beddoes.* Aldershot, U.K.: Ashgate, 2001.

Donner, H. W. *Thomas Lovell Beddoes: The Making of a Poet.* Oxford: Blackwell, 1935.

Frye, Northrop. "Yorick, the Romantic Macabre." In his *A Study of English Romanticism.* New York: Random House, 1968. Pp. 51–85.

Halsey, Alan. *A Skeleton Key to "Death's Jest-Book."* Belper, U.K.: Thomas Lovell Beddoes Society, 1995.

———. *Homage to Homunculus Mandrake: A New Reading of "Death's Jest-Book."* Belper, U.K.: Thomas Lovell Beddoes Society, 1996.

Levinson, Marjorie. *The Romantic Fragment Poem: A Critique of a Form.* Chapel Hill and London: University of North Carolina Press, 1986.

Ricks, Christopher. "Thomas Lovell Beddoes: 'A Dying Start.'" *Grand Street* 1:32–48 (1982) and 3:90–102 (1984). Reprinted in *The Force of Poetry.* Oxford: Clarendon, 1984. Pp. 135–162.

Snow, Royall Henderson. *Thomas Lovell Beddoes: Eccentric and Poet.* New York: Covici-Friede, 1928.

Strachey, Lytton. "The Last Elizabethan" (1907). In *Books and Characters, French and English.* New York: Harcourt Brace and Company, 1922. Pp. 237–265.

Thompson, James R. *Thomas Lovell Beddoes.* Boston: Twayne, 1985.

SOCIETIES

The Thomas Lovell Beddoes Society publishes an enthusiastic and informative newsletter, with scholarly and general reviews and articles relating to Beddoes' life and work. Details can be obtained from John Lovell Beddoes, 11 Laund Nook, Belper, Derbyshire DE56 1GY or online (http://www.nortexinfo.net/McDaniel/tlb.htm).

EDMUND BLUNDEN

1896–1974

Peter Scupham

EDMUND CHARLES BLUNDEN will always be associated with that group of poets whose lives and works were tempered by their experiences in the Great War of 1914 to 1918. Of the three young infantry officer poets who also wrote prose accounts of their experiences—Robert Graves, Siegfried Sassoon, and Edmund Blunden—it is Blunden's *Undertones of War* (1928) that has most deeply moved subsequent generations. Graves held the war at bay with a grim jocularity and attempted to spit it out of his system in *Good-Bye to All That* (1929); Sassoon's semifictional self-examination placed the experiences recounted in his *Memoirs of an Infantry Officer* (1930) as one particular stage in a personal political and spiritual odyssey. Blunden, with a self-effacing and bitterly won wisdom that still astonishes, created a sustained and very human elegy, a book whose theme is love.

War is the figure in the carpet of Blunden's work. His frontline service was a long one, and there is no time in his life when that service and its accompanying pities, terrors, and loves was not a living presence to him, a theme constantly faced directly or glanced at in his prodigious output in poetry and prose. Although the last eight self-descriptive words of *Undertones of War*—"a harmless young shepherd in a soldier's coat" (p. 266)—have created an unforgettable image of him, this "harmless young shepherd," with a Military Cross to his credit, was made of steel, and his life was to pick its way through paradoxes. He worked much in academe but wrote for the common reader, not the scholar. Though his poetry was to celebrate his deep attachment to locality and the homelier intimacies of country scenes and habits, he spent substantial periods of his working life in Japan and Hong Kong. The ghosts of the Somme and Ypres could not be charmed away, but their insistencies could

retreat if hard, remorseless literary work and a passionate care for doing his best for his students were deployed against them. While the discursive prose Blunden wrote displays a bookish contemplative, his life seems that of a man of decisions and affairs, and though all writers are of necessity cats that walk by themselves, Blunden was a team player, a passionate cricketer, a man of great and sustaining loyalties—to his school, to those dead poets whose work he was assiduous in rescuing from oblivion, to his friends, his regiment, his college, his family, and the academic institutions he served. His poetry, with its care for the slight, the unregarded, the overlooked, and its sidestepping away from the urban world most of us live in, is not academically fashionable, but it has never lacked sympathetic readers who recognize the deep humanity and the qualities of sensuous perception possessed by this man who, in "November 1, 1931," ruefully admitted his habit:

Of being always on the bivouac,
Here and elsewhere, for ever changing ground,
Finding and straightway losing what I found,
Baffled in time, fumbling each sequent date...

> (*Poems of Many Years,* 1957, p. 184;
> hereafter cited by page number only)

In his poems and his idiosyncratic, humane criticism, Blunden worked with indefatigable persistence to share his deepest attachments. These returned again and again to England and its countryside, to the men of all ranks with whom he served in the Royal Sussex, to those older writers such as John Clare and Henry Vaughan. Samuel Taylor Coleridge, Leigh Hunt, and Charles Lamb, that constellation of talent associated with his own school, Christ's Hospital, he treated as familiars, friends talking in the next room. Time was a puzzle to him; the dead were the fabric of his imaginative life, often more vividly present than the living. His affections and loyalties were not a passing show; it was natural to him to admire, and where he gave his love and admiration, whether to an author, an institution, or his old commanding officer, Colonel Harrison, that gift was unconditional. It is possible to see Blunden as disabled by the strength of these loyalties. His poetry reaches no accommodation with the giant figures of the modern movement: Ezra Pound, T. S. Eliot, and W. H. Auden have no hold on him. In his reliance on varied but traditional verse structures and his refusal to modify a sometimes circuitous and thickly worked diction that draws its vocabulary from romantic antecedents, Blunden, like Walter de la Mare, remained unifluenced by the practice of his contemporaries. On his tombstone in Long Melford Church, Suffolk, are inscribed the opening lines from one of his late poems, "Seers":

I live still, to love still
   Things quiet and unconcerned...
            (*A Hong Kong House,* 1962, p. 70)

The integrity of this vision, the faith he keeps with what his heart best knows, should ensure that Blunden's poetry is resilient enough to find and move new generations.

LIFE AND WORK

Edmund Blunden was born on November 1, 1896, in Tottenham Court Road, London. His father, Charles Edmund, was a teacher by profession and a countryman by background and inclination. His mother, Georgina Margaret Tyler, also trained as a teacher and met her future husband when she joined the staff of the London primary school where Charles was headmaster. The brief London years ended in 1900 when the Blundens moved to Yalding, a Sussex village that was to become Edmund's great good place, a paradigm for the values of rooted and slow-paced neighborliness that meant so much to him. The family grew, and a sustained evocation of those

childhood years comes in "Old Homes," where a guided tour of his childhood world closes with the lines:

My day still breaks beyond your poplared East
And in your pastoral still my life has rest.
            (p. 97)

Here Blunden's father was church organist, schoolmaster, cricketer, fisherman, and hop-field manager when the season for hop-picking came around and the fields filled with casual labor from London. The family played a full part in a village life poised on the edge of dissolution as England's old preindustrial horse-led agricultural economy prepared to succumb to the forces of mechanization and mobility, though the Blunden family situation was often financially precarious—a not unlikely scenario with nine children and a loving but impractical father. In 1904 the family moved to a rambling old farmhouse on the edge of the village, Congelow, whose complex warren of rooms and sense of encapsulating a mysterious history gave Edmund's imagination a lasting and fruitful image.

Blunden was talent-spotted at Cleave's Grammar School, and it was suggested that he might apply for a place at Christ's Hospital. To gain such a place, talent was the only criterion. The school had recently moved to Sussex from London, where it had educated without charge poor but able boys since 1552, and was newly modeled on the English public schools of the day—"public schools," of course, meaning private boarding schools for the country's governing class. Christ's Hospital had its idiosyncratic traditions, one of which was the Writing School, which had trained generations in the clear and elegant calligraphy that commercial employers valued. Blunden's beautiful italic variation makes his own holograph one of the most recognizable and distinctive of all English poets. Christ's was commonly known as the "Bluecoat School" after its most obvious peculiarity to the outside world, the students' distinctive traditional uniform of a blue gown, or cassock, worn with yellow stockings. The school's past scholars are known as Old Blues, and the title was a source of lifelong pride and gratitude to Blunden, who

.eft the school in 1915, having distinguished himself on the classical side, gained a scholarship to Oxford, and had collections of his poetic juvenilia and translations from the French privately printed by a Horsham printer. Blunden's love for his school found expression in an act of *pietas:* the publication of his historical sketch *Christ's Hospital: A Retrospect* in 1923, with its coda praising "the ceremony and order of every day," "the sterling good will and constant, judicious word of the masters," and the "happiness hoarded up in memory, to be told over and over again in the days to come" (p. 194). Blunden owed the school too much to temper his attachment with critical reservations. In August 1915 he joined the Royal Sussex as a second lieutenant and spent the next six months in England and Ireland writing poetry when his duties allowed. In 1916 he went to join the Eleventh Royal Sussex Regiment, variously known as the "First Southdowns," "Lowther's Lambs," and the "Iron Regiment" in France. Blunden's biographer, Barry Webb, points out that, of the writers who fought, it is likely that "only David Jones's twenty-two months could compete with Edmund's two years in the firing-line" (*Webb*, p. 51). An infantry officer's life expectancy in the trenches could often be measured in weeks rather than months, so it is not surprising that Blunden, who gave his regiment an equivalent love to that he felt for Christ's Hospital, always felt that a part of himself should be lying out in France with his companions. "War Cemetery" takes him back in spirit to that old parade ground where

Dressed by the right, fallen in with perfect order,
The dead contingents in gray stone are seen.

(p. 223)

Blunden gave a brief, factual account of the vicissitudes of his service in "A Battalion History," written in 1933 and published in his volume of essays *The Mind's Eye* (1934, pp. 58–85). The account is virtually a litany of village and trench names that recall some of the fiercest fighting of the war: Beaumont Hamel, Thiepval, Jacob's Ladder, Stuff Trench. The battalion's part in the Somme offensive of 1916 was summed up by Blunden as a three-month ordeal of heavy

losses, when the men "had become accustomed to two views of the universe: the glue-like formless mortifying wilderness of the crater zone above, and below, fusty, clay-smeared, candle-lit wooden galleries, where the dead lay decomposing under knocked-in entrances" (pp. 69–70). He also wrote in 1918 a vivid and unfinished account of these early war experiences, *De Bello Germanico,* which his brother Gilbert printed in 1930. After France came Belgium and the Ypres salient, where 1917 was marked by "the apparent futility of the British effort, and the shattering of all unity by casualties beyond our counting" (p. 82). The last year of the war found the battalion back in France, where spring fighting along the Somme cost "20 officers, 300 other ranks killed, wounded and missing" (p. 83), but by then Blunden was back in England, posted to a training center. It is typical of the man that he never felt easy at having missed his battalion's last engagement. The cost of these war experiences was a terrible one; it is Blunden's triumph to have turned that cost into a tribute to and celebration of lives he considered more valuable than his own.

On June 1, 1918, Blunden married Mary Daines, a blacksmith's daughter. This wartime union was ill-starred. There was no community of intellectual interests, and their first child, a daughter they named Joy, died when only five weeks old. It was a loss that Blunden returned to many times in poetry but could never become reconciled to. Six years later, in "A 'First Impression' (Tokyo)" he finds her small presence still inescapable:

No sooner was I come to this strange roof,
Beyond broad seas, half round the swaying world,
Than came the pretty ghost, the sudden sweet
And most sad spirit of my vanished child...

(p. 117)

In 1919 Blunden took up his scholarship at Queen's College, but his stay there was a comparatively brief one. He moved out of college to Boar's Hill, forged literary friendships with the poets Robert Nichols, Robert Graves, and Sassoon, and became a visitor to nearby

EDMUND BLUNDEN

Garsington Manor, where Lady Ottoline Morrell continued to preside over her mixed bag of visiting artists and writers. Blunden took no degree but started his literary career most auspiciously when, in 1920, with his friend Alan Porter, he was instrumental in rediscovering the cache of the poet John Clare's manuscripts in the Peterborough Museum. The first fruits of this lifelong passion came when he and Porter coedited the publication of *John Clare: Poems, Chiefly from Manuscript* (1920), a landmark in Clare studies. The year 1920 also saw Blunden publish his first mature collection of poems, *The Waggoner,* and leave Oxford for the life of a hardworking literary journalist in London, when he took up a post on the *Athenaeum* at the invitation of John Middleton Murry, the editor. Life seemed to be set fair for him, especially with the birth of a second daughter, Clare, but his marriage slowly began to unravel. It is impossible now to estimate the scale of neurasthenic disturbance suffered by fighting soldiers in adjusting to domesticities and life among those civilians who had been shielded from the brutal knowledge of war at the sharp end. In 1921 the Blundens moved to a Suffolk village, Stansfield, where Edmund played cricket and football, set himself a punishing workload of literary articles and journalism, and prepared his second book, *The Shepherd, and Other Poems of Peace and War* (1922) for publication. Work might exorcise some demons; a three-month getaway-from-it-all expedition on a tramp steamer taking coal to South America did little. Blunden wrote his account of this foray in *The Bonadventure: A Random Journal of an Atlantic Holiday* (1922), but sandbags in coal yards, stew and lime juice, night fears and bad dreams all took him back to the trenches.

Asthma, the financial pressures of a growing family—a son, John, was born in 1922—and an inherent restlessness now led to a decisive change of direction. In 1924 Blunden sailed for Japan, without Mary, to take up a post as professor of English at Tokyo University. The contract was for three years, during which he forged a new and lasting loyalty. A later visit to Japan was made in 1947, when he undertook a two-year stint as cultural Liaison Officer to the British Mission. It is a tribute to the effect Blunden's English vision and quick sympathies had on Japanese cultural life that Alec M. Hardie, in his brief monograph *Edmund Blunden* (1971, p. 20) could say of his impact on Japanese hearts and minds: "It transcends trivialities and attains the dignity of a moral embassy." Blunden's bewildering combination of an informality that cut through the formal hierarchies of Japanese society and a huge care for his students proved irresistible, and though the post was an academic one, his approach to literature was broad and humane rather than prescriptive and specialized. The effect on Blunden himself, in such a poem as "The Visitor," was to deepen and enlarge his vision of how humanity and the natural world are intertwined; how the differences between East and West and how love and premonition—Blunden had felt a childhood affinity with the idea of Japan—make differences into new familiarities:

We moved within the wings of some ten words
Into a most familiar country air,
And like spring showers received it from the hills
That stood from our old hills ten thousand miles—
Or none; we paused along the yellow plains,
And kissed the child that ran from shyer friends
To take our hand...

(pp. 155–156)

In 1927 Blunden returned to England with Aki Hayashi, a Japanese teacher with whom he had formed a close relationship. She was to remain in England, and though love became friendship, she became his devoted London-based pensioner and research assistant for the rest of her life. His own career continued to be one of frenetic literary activity. The year 1928 saw the publication of *Undertones of War,* which he had begun writing in Japan, then in 1930 came *Poems 1914–1930.* In 1931 he published *Votive Tablets,* a collection of articles that, as the title suggests, were literary tributes to his favorite authors. In the same year his marriage ended by divorce, and Blunden became a fellow and tutor in English at Merton College, Oxford. It seemed, in his thirties, that Blunden's life was about take the settled shape of a stately academic progress. He never quite saw himself as a true Oxford academic, though in 1936 he published the work that he himself regarded as his most scholarly achievement, *Keats's Publisher: A Memoir of John Taylor, 1781–1864.* As his Japanese students had already found, his gift for unconventional and stimulating teaching won him many new friends, but literary affairs in universities are a battlefield for which Blunden's frontline experiences had not prepared him. The poet and critic Geoffrey Grigson, writing in his autobiography *The Crest on the Silver* (1950) of his own time at Oxford in the late 1920s, describes the opposed forces with his usual acidity, setting against Blunden, Humbert Wolfe, and Walter de la Mare "the 'experimental' modernism of Eliot and Joyce and Ezra Pound and Virginia Woolf and Laura Riding. All of us, that was the truth, were being weaned sharply from the last thin drops of the milk of a devitalized fairyland" (p. 122). Grigson's acidulous comment shows how fiercely and intolerantly literary distinctions could be made. Blunden's relationship to the modernists was always a wary one, and his reputation as a poet was always going to suffer from his stubborn way of swimming, if not against the tide, at a very personal angle to it. In 1933 he married Sylva Norman, a marriage that ended in 1945 with an agreed divorce and Blunden's happy remarriage to Claire Poynting; Sylva remained a friend and correspondent for the rest of her life.

As the war clouds gathered in the 1930s Blunden's reputation suffered from what was taken to be a sympathy with Hitler's Germany. In 1935 and 1937 he made lecture tours to German universities; in 1939 he attended a literary congress at Klosterhaus. There was certainly an element of naïveté in Blunden's inability to see the true face of Nazi power, but he was not a political animal. His frontline experience had given him a conviction that another war would be an unthinkable catastrophe, and so he did not allow himself to see its growing inevitability. In *Cricket Country* (1944) he vividly describes his emotions when war came: "During this new war, I have felt like one of the willows by the terrible Yser Canal, which stood unwrenched, unannihilated, though the iron pierced deep into it, while the surrounding world was in a furnace. I have been capriciously spared" (p. 193). He was hardly alone in such feelings. He found himself in uniform again as a part-time map-reading instructor for the Oxford Officers' Training Corps, but one of his most important services was to encourage and befriend his pupil Keith Douglas, another Old Blue, who was to become one of the finest fighting poets and was killed serving as a tank commander in Normandy in 1944. As for Blunden's own books, the war years opened with *Poems, 1930–1940* (1940) and continued with *English Villages* and *Thomas Hardy,* both published in 1941. In 1944, along with *Cricket Country,* a digressive and literary ramble (Edmund himself was a passionate lover and player of the game), he published a new book of poems with a deeply ambivalent title, *Shells by a Stream.*

The postwar years brought a cementing of his relationship with Japan and the forging of a new bond in the Far East when Blunden accepted a professorship in English at the University of Hong Kong. Horrified by the atomic bombing of Hiroshima and Nagasaki, he knew that he had to reestablish such cultural and human links with the Japanese as lay in his power, so for two years Blunden became a member of the United Kingdom Liaison Mission, traveling the country, lecturing, meeting old friends, helping literary aspirants, and attending functions at which he inadvertently and easily upstaged the attendant British professionals. The contacts with Japan continued for the rest of Blunden's life, and it is clear that his gifts in fostering understanding and affection between such different cultures were unmatchable. The Hong Kong years, which lasted from 1953 to 1964, were a rather different story. Blunden was established in Hong Kong with a happy marriage, a house and servants, and, eventually, four daughters. The close relationships with students, the customary hectic business of tours and visits, friends and colleagues, lectures and articles, continued as ever, but the cost was increasingly frail health, physically and mentally. Uncertain as to whether his own gifts as a poet could be recovered, troubled by trench-thoughts, tempestuous, prone to dependence on alcohol, and unhappy about the way English studies were moving away from literature to a limiting concern with linguistics, Blunden was happy to return to Suffolk and settle there with his family in 1964. The poetic fruits of his professorship were slight, gathered in *A Hong Kong House: Poems 1951–1961* (1962), effectively his last book of poems.

The last years were broken by one last foray into academic life, when Blunden was approached to stand for the professorship of poetry at Oxford. Associated with cloistered comedy, lobbying, and intrigue, the candidates could then only be voted for by Oxford MAs. The 1966 contest, following the retirement of Robert Graves, was between two poets who could not have divided the voters into clearer factions: Edmund Blunden and Robert Lowell. The expected walkover for Lowell turned into a huge majority for Blunden, but ill health and the attendant anxieties it brought when he was faced with the post's academic and social duties was too much for him. He retired in 1967, and his last years brought a retreat into silence and memory. Blunden died in 1974 and was buried in Long Melford churchyard. The final sentence of Barry Webb's biography is appropriate. Private Beeney, who had been Lieutenant Blunden's runner, or messenger, at Ypres and Passchendaele, was present: "Stepping forward he let fall from his hand a wreath of Flanders poppies which fluttered down on to the coffin in fond and final salute." In Blunden's later years, as for so many of his contemporaries, the presence of the war in which he had served had grown in intensity, pressing on his dreaming and waking lives. A friend of the present writer's once told him how his father, dying in his eighties, had asked at the end: "How did you get me back from France?" It is appropriate, then, to look first at the two prose versions in which Blunden cast his war experiences.

DE BELLO GERMANICO

De Bello Germanico: A Fragment of Trench History (1930), remains unfinished. Blunden himself felt that its immediacy and clutter of local detail was unsatisfactory, and it was only because his brother Gilbert, setting up as a printer, wanted copy that Blunden gave it to him. Its most accessible form now is as an appendix to the Folio Society's edition of *Undertones of War* (1989), which is the edition cited here. (For *Undertones of War* itself, the edition cited is the 1928 edition.) *De Bello Germanico* is a jaunty performance—Blunden called it "noisy with a depressing forced gaiety then the rage" in his "Preliminary" to *Undertones of War* (p. viii)—but it has a vivacity and immediacy that Blunden later calmed down, feeling that its journalistic tone was unsuited to the meditative, elegiac tapestry of *Undertones of War.* That immediacy is conjured up by the insistence on small detail, the "smell of linseed oil about new bales of sandbags" (p. 220) or the "hut built largely of biscuit-tins, and displaying gorgeously wrapped Chocolat Poulain, silk cards, Venus pencils, Maryland cigarettes" (p. 215). Blunden being Blunden, though, literary suggestions are present, if not dominant. The title itself ironically links Blunden's sketch with Caesar's *De Bello Gallico;* the chapter heading "Drowsed with the Fume of Poppies" is another ironic juxtaposition, recalling Keats's "To Autumn" ode (*Poetical Works,* 1956, p. 219), when autumn personified is seen "on a half-reap'd furrow sound asleep, / Drows'd with the fume of poppies." Already, in this account by a twenty-two-year-old, there are indications that his inclinations will eventually be to place frontline experience in a context of, for him, more enduring literary and pastoral landscapes, as in his recall of the battalion's billets at Festubert: "the evening tramp up communication trenches full of the 'dead man smell' of that marshland, suggesting a ferment of church lilies; and starry midnight dreaming a majesty on those humble lath-and-plaster ruins, the whooping owls by the church corner, the groaning stretcher-cases borne along the street, past my fairy rosebush blossomed silvery beyond belief; all these things and many more still make Festubert for me what it was then, a 'tale, a dream,' the village beyond the world" (p. 225). Already Blunden is writing as if a far greater gap exists between events and their recall than the actual two years that separates them, and Festubert is transposed into a composite image where human suffering, timeless night effects, the ruined houses, and the natural world interlock and recompose themselves.

Blunden's habits of indirection are also present in the stance he adopts for seeing his own callow self all those two years ago. *De Bello Germanico* is the story of a forced transition from innocence to experience. The new officer-arrivals at the battalion are announced under the ironical chapter heading "Entry of the Gladiators," with its portentous echo of Bizet. The young gladiator himself, though, is seen as "a humble Don Quixote facing war with beautiful idiocy" (p. 223), a dreamer learning slowly from wiser and older soldiers than himself, and the reader is made to feel that he himself is as naive as the writer, though the naïveté can sometimes seem a rather stagy comic turn, as when he is told his sector is holding the "islands": "Was this a maritime sector, I wondered? The mention of islands certainly implied aquatic surroundings, and further allusions to the 'duckboards' led me to imagine a kind of archipelago with enclosures for ducks, no doubt piously preserved by the troops until the return of their owners" (p. 215). In *Undertones of War* we learn that Blunden's battalion nickname was "Rabbit," then "Bunny," and he is happy to accept the implications of this affectionate sobriquet, the more so as it is apparent he was in practice effective and courageous. *De Bello Germanico* can be read as a simplified prologue to *Undertones of War,* just as the appended "Supplement of Poetical Interpretations and Variations" forms a coda to it.

UNDERTONES OF WAR

Paul Fussell, in *The Great War and Modern Memory* (1975), offers a possible subtitle for his study of the iconography and impact of the war on its more educated combatant-interpreters and consequently on the response to it of later generations: "An Inquiry into the Curious Literariness of Real Life." Edmund Blunden was steeped as a young man in traditional poetic forms and at the age of eighteen was already deeply responsive to the ways in which English landscape has gathered into itself layers of visionary and arcadian meaning. He had in fact acquired and confirmed for himself an imaginative landscape to which he was never slow to proclaim his allegiance. It was a worked landscape of traditional crafts, a horse-and-cart landscape, a southern England where character still seemed to grow and ripen slowly and where the impact of the huge industrialization that had transformed the cities and landscapes of the north had no apparent hold on the life of villages and market towns. Of course this landscape, transposed into images and certifying memories, was in part a fiction, but if it was a fiction, it held enough truth to be at the bedrock of Blunden's imagination when faced with an equivalent French landscape that was to become an image of his own imagination laid desolate. With understatement and irony—two of Blunden's most reached-for weapons—his "Report on Experience" laments this desolation:

I have seen a green country, useful to the race,
Knocked silly with guns and mines, its villages
  vanished,
Even the last rat and last kestrel banished—
    God bless us all, this was peculiar grace.

                              (p. 166)

The "Undertones" of the title itself announces an emphasis on the minor rather than the major key, just as Blunden himself sidesteps major authors in his expressed affections for minor names, particularly William Collins, whose "Ode to Evening" was an early and lasting part of his mental furniture, with its apparatus of personification, precision, and invitation to a calmed, mysteriously receding landscape of "hamlets brown and dim-discovered spires" (*The New Book of Eighteenth Century Verse,* 1984, p. 382). Sometimes Blunden in France seems a visitor from another century rather than another country, describing his grandfather's walking stick, quickly stolen in France, as "my pilgrim's staff" (p. 3), or conscripting Collins to be his alter ego in the early experience of watching a horizon lit by shells and flares: "On the blue and lulling mist of evening, proper to the nightingale, the sheepbell and falling waters, the strangest phenomena of fire inflicted themselves" (p. 14). *Undertones of War* is a tour de force of uniting the contemplative and the man of action, a constant exercise in multiple vision, where the literary, the pastoral, and mechanized violence have to learn to live with one another. While in Japan, Blunden worked on his book with nothing much except some trench maps and memory to help him, and this must have helped to create such distanced but uncluttered intensity as the memory of Richebourg-St. Vaast and "the sunny terror which dwelt in every dust-grain on the road, in every leaf on the currant bushes near that churchyard; the clatter of guns, the co-existent extraordinary silence, the summer ripeness, the futility of it, the absence of farmyard and cottage-doorway voices which yet you could hear" (p. 50). This disturbing and disturbed pastoral is a constant and haunting commentary on the overt violence of the battalion's experiences, and the undertones Blunden is so alert to are vividly expressed by the sensuous collection of floating images that haunt him as he imagines himself back in bed at Béthune before moving off to the Somme battlefield: "the bullets leaping angrily from old rafters shining in greenish flare-light; an old pump and a tiled floor in the moon; bedsteads and broken mattresses hanging over cracked and scarred walls; Germans seen as momentary shadows among wire hedges; tallowy, blood-dashed faces—but put back the blanket; a garden gate, opening into a battlefield." Such passages move the prose into poetry. The sheer brutality of events is never ducked, but the passages in which the reader is made savagely aware of the physical nature of the carnage are few and, because they are few, are the more effective, suddenly stilling the reader into a new dimension of awareness, as when Blunden, one summer afternoon, passes a young lance corporal brewing up some tea. A shell bursts: "For him, how could the gobbets of blackening flesh, the earth-wall sotted with blood, with flesh, the eye under the duckboard, the pulpy bone be the only answer?" (p. 63).

If the Somme gave Blunden a summer countryside as his backdrop, the battalion's move in the winter of 1916 to Flanders provided an opposing imagery. For the next year the battalion fought in the desolate and waterlogged Ypres salient. Blunden was never a poet of the city, but ruined Ypres, with its ghostly reminders of "the flush and abundance of antique life and memorial and achievement" (p. 177) became his deep city of the imagination. Again, he expresses his sense of the "sepulchral, catacombed city" (p. 176) in one of his floating image-trails: "the noble fragment of a gateway to Saint Martin's cathedral, interior walls with paintings of swans on green ponds, the rusty mass of ironware belonging to some small factory with an undestroyed chimney, ancient church music nobly inscribed on noble parchment, wicker chairs in the roadway outside St. Jacques" (p. 177). Blunden's tone grows darker as the changing nature of the battalion's composition, the return of his much-admired commanding officer to England, the incessant casualties, all create an overwhelming sense of confusion and endurance. It is typical that his literary companion was the eighteenth-century poet Edward Young, whose *Night-Thoughts on Life, Death, and Immortality* he carried with him, finding lines that could be ironically applied to present circumstances. In one of his own finest war poems, "On Reading That the Rebuilding of Ypres Approached Completion," included in the supplementary poems to *Undertones of War* (p. 310), Blunden speaks for himself and all those who fought there with no saving irony at all:

> but I
> Am in the soil and sap, and in the becks and conduits
> My blood is flowing, and my sigh of consummation
> Is the wind in the rampart trees.

Blunden's bedrock memory is of the qualities shown by the common soldier, "ruddy-cheeked under your squat chin-strapped iron helmet, sturdy under your leather jerkin" (p. 177). "It is time," Blunden says, "to hint to a new age what your value, what your love was; your Ypres is gone, and you are gone; we were lucky to see you 'in the pink' against white-ribbed and socket-eyed despair" (p. 178).

At the heart of the book lies this sense of shared humanity, this conscious elegy for a period and a generation from a man only in his late twenties when he started writing it. The "Preliminary" to *Undertones of War* is closed by a passage in which Blunden sees a visionary reuniting in death of himself with "companions like E. W. T., and W. J. C., and A. G. V., in whose recaptured gentleness no sign of death's astonishment or time's separation will be imaginable" (p. viii). Of these fellow Old Blues and officers in the Sussex, Tice and Collyer were killed in the Ypres salient on the same day in the battle of Passchendaele; Vidler survived the war, but in depression shot himself in 1924. A photograph reproduced in Barry Webb's biography (number 7) shows their reunion with Blunden and another Old Blue, Horace Amon, at St. Omer in 1917, when they "roamed the streets, the cathedral, the cafés and the shops with such exhilarations of wit and irony that we felt no other feast like this could ever come again; nor was the feeling wrong" (p. 203). Blunden's admiration for his commanding officer Colonel Harrison, "with his gift of being friend and commander alike to all his legion" (p. 178), is a constant, and his historical imagination delights in the fact that one of Harrison's ancestors served in the Hampshire militia with the great historian Edward Gibbon. Their military relationship turned into a sustained friendship after the war, as did Blunden's relationship with one of his sergeants, Frank Worley, loved by him for an undaunted kindliness, as he went about his business "for ever comforting those youngsters who were so numerous among us; even as the shrapnel burst over the fire-bay he would be saying without altered tone, 'don't fret, lay still,' and such things" (p. 62).

We are conditioned by our knowledge that the armistice of 1918 only heralded a brief cessation of violence, and the world was to be even more comprehensively at war again twenty years later. Since 1945, further wars and the threat of nuclear catastrophe have been the accompaniment to the way we live, and so we find it hard to imagine the impact of the Great War on the European comity. The stalemate of the Western Front, where the defensive power of the machine gun and the trench system proved stronger than assault, provided an iconography and a killing ground that seemed a foretaste of Armageddon and that decisively separated the experiences of the fighting-men from those of civilians. Blunden's imagination constantly homed in on the immemorial and literary consolations of a worked pastoral landscape, which he felt continually present or waiting to reassert itself when the mechanized assault on its existence had passed by. The knowledge that the desolation could only be a temporary one sustained him, as he was sustained by knowing and understanding the soldiers of the Sussex Regiment as countrymen in disguise. The irony was, of course, that that immemorial pastoral was itself passing into history. As he leaves the Western Front for the last time on a six-month posting to England, he moves into the continuous present tense, taking the reader into the yet-unravaged valley of the Ancre, balancing his two worlds, as "while we prowl inspectingly in the way of the fighting man round huts and possibly useful stores, the willows and waters in the hollow make up a picture so silvery and unsubstantial that one would spend a lifetime to paint it" (p. 265). *Undertones of War* is a book with a strange spell cast over it. It speaks with the voice of experience armed by the strength of innocence. The handful of poems Blunden included in the supplement are a patchwork of pastoral ironies, moments of intense actuality, and elegies, not only for his fellow soldiers but for that part of himself doomed to go on a young officer's trench rounds for the rest of his life. In "Their Very Memory" (p. 149), he is already conscious, ten years after hostilities had ceased, of the impossibility of doing more than the sketchiest justice to the unique, substantial lives of the dead:

Now my mind
Faint and few records their showings,
  Brave, strong, kind—
I'd unlock you all their doings
  But the keys are lost and twisted.

POETRY: THE INHABITED LANDSCAPE

Though Blunden's poetry was to celebrate love, historical continuities, the multifarious suggestions of the English landscape, and the shifts of perception given him by his experiences in Japan and Hong Kong, the constant need to set about finding and straightening those lost keys is never far away, and the poignancy of the attempt subtly informs his most memorable poems whatever their superficial theme. Blunden was not made into a poet by his war experiences; that vocation he had already chosen. It was his gift and his curse that the two years he spent in the front line turned him from being a respected poet whose limitations place him securely in the English tradition as a celebrant of romantic landscape into something more: a poet whose pain and privilege it was to be a voice for the early dead. The war added a huge dimension to Blunden's intuitive backward look, and though he has never been placed among the English mystics, his poetry gathered a numinous quality, a delicate sense that the veils between seen and unseen worlds could tremble and lift. After all, a part of him was always with the dead.

Critical and discursive works by poets are ostensibly for general edification, but in part they are self-prescriptive, praising by deflection the qualities the poets value or would like to exemplify in their own creative work. In 1929 Leonard and Virginia Woolf published at their Hogarth Press a little book by Blunden, *Nature in English Literature,* which gives a series of clues as to what we may look for in his own poetry of the natural world. Conscious that an older England is disappearing, he launches into a lament that gives hostages to fortune, talking of "the usurpation of old solitudes by despicable modern kraals" and of "rusticity depraved into new urbanism" (p. 10). The intemperateness of the language is not so much a hatred of the new as a longing and love for the known of his prewar childhood in rural Sussex. The book is a tribute to two approaches to landscape that Blunden knows his own work must unite. There are the empiricists of the physical world, men like Gilbert White or the eighteenth-century farmer William Ellis, of whom he says: "When his dogs howl in the moonlight, they do so with all their muscles; when he takes up a handful of soil, his speech answers the weight, colour and touch of

it" (p. 13). Then there are poets such as John Clare, who animates nature by his love, or Henry Vaughan, who binds the physicality of the world to a power and presence beyond its apparent sufficiency. For Vaughan, Blunden says, there is "a Being remoter than the stars, and nearer than the stones on his Welsh Journey" (p. 63).

Blunden's earlier poems are often uneasily poised between the substance of the world and the suggestions latent in that substance. His evocation of landscape is substantial enough, but it is blunted rather than sharpened by such occasional epithets and inversions as "goblin willows brown" in "To Teise, a Stream in Kent" (p. 233) or such a phrase in "Leisure" as "elvish gossamers go dance" (p. 50). A Georgian sentimentality can easily cloy, nature is overcataloged, and the images cluster so thickly that the impetus of the poems is lost in meander and drowse. "Almswomen," from his 1920 volume *The Waggoner,* can serve as an example of the kind of poem that had to be outgrown, with its pair of old ladies who "kiss and cry and pray / That both be summoned in the selfsame day" (p. 33) and its catalog of "Bee's balsams, feathery southernwood and stocks, / Fiery dragon's mouths, great mallow leaves" (p. 32). There are slacknesses in observation, an unfortunate reaching for the abstract, insubstantial word that evokes nothing, as in "The Pike," where the martins "Come with wild mirth to dip their magical wings" (p. 33). There is a reliance upon the antique vigor of dialect words that have outworn their use and that can only lend quaintness rather than vitality, as in the opening lines of his 1918 poem "A Country God": "When groping farms are lanterned up / And stolchy ploughlands hid in grief"—a poem that unfortunately contains a "moanish brook" and the oddity words "whirry" and "brished" (pp. 36–37). Blunden always had some problems with his diction.

In much of his best work, Blunden was to let his melodic line and versatility in structuring carry the poem forward more sparely and allow suggestion the space to breathe. Some of the earlier poems come triumphantly clean, as does the deservedly well-known anthology piece "Forefathers," from Blunden's second book, *The*

Shepherd, of 1922. It is perhaps extraordinary that he did not take immediately to heart some of the technical lessons "Forefathers" teaches. The poem, strongly rhymed, built exactly with its four-stressed lines and mercifully bared of Blunden's armory of adjectives, is a moving commemoration of rural continuities and the vivid life of the unrecorded dead, those who "Scarce could read or hold a quill, / Built the barn, the forge, the mill" (p. 60). In the little sketch of Thomas Hardy's life and works Blunden published in 1941, he quotes an influential antecedent to "Forefathers." This is "Our Father's Works," written in four-stressed lines and the Dorsetshire dialect by the poet and scholar William Barnes, celebrating the men who cleared the land:

An' built the mill, where still the wheel
Do grind our meal, below the hill;
An' turn'd the bridge, wi' arch aspread
Below a road, vor us to tread.

(Thomas Hardy, p. 5)

"Forefathers" (pp. 60–61) is a poem built lightly, but carrying the full weight of a working past, and its closing image lifts the whole landscape into another dimension, as Blunden suddenly identifies himself with a summer bee whose existential life is part of an essentially unknowable fabric of other lives:

Like the bee that now is blown
Honey-heavy on my hand,
From his topling tansy-throne
In the green tempestuous land—
I'm in clover now, nor know
Who made honey long ago.

One element in Blunden's poetry, particularly his earlier work, presents some difficulty to a harsher age. In writing of his touchstone poem, Collins' "Ode to Evening," he shows a deep affection for the associations that place natural phenomena in clusters of literary, mythological, and fanciful form: "Evening, as she appears in this Ode, is a country girl, a Fairy Queen, a priestess, a goddess, a ghost in the sky" (*Nature in English Literature,* p. 43). Later, in the same book, he talks of "that enchanted ground which lies for ever a stone's throw from the inns and yards of the villages in this country" (pp. 95–96). Blunden's habit of peopling the landscape with the ghosts of bookish and invisible entities, the dryad and the elf, is hardly an American habit, but late-Victorian and Edwardian England was a host for such presences, making their last stand when besieged by the imaginative powers inherent in urban, mechanized life. They are there in the cult of the god Pan, the children's stories of Rudyard Kipling, the illustrations of Arthur Rackham, the fairy books edited by Andrew Lang, the cult of the ghost story. In this Blunden is of his period, and the reader has to make an affectionate allowance for a vanished zeitgeist. And, of course, Blunden knew when he was playing with the fancy, rather than working with the imagination, as in his wry transference of Shakespeare's Titania from a wood near Athens to the Western Front, in "Premature Rejoicing":

What's that over there?
             Thiepval Wood.
Take a steady look at it; it'll do you good.
Here, these glasses will help you. See any flowers?
There sleeps Titania (correct—the Wood is ours):
There sleeps Titania in a deep dug-out,
Waking, she wonders what all the din's about.

(p. 176)

When Blunden's imagination chooses an English landscape to be at home in, it is a landscape without abrasion, without wide spaces or sharp winds. Thick with trees, the "shadows of rich oaks" in "The Pike" (p. 33) or "apple-boughs as knarred as old toad's backs" (p. 74), the atmosphere is usually dense, sunstruck, alive with flowers and insects. The characters—the mole-catcher, miller, or shepherd—move through such landscapes, earthbound and minor deities of place. And, for Blunden, never far off is the presence of water from river, mill-pool, brook, or sluice-gate. In "The Unchangeable" they are those "Waters whose lazy continual flow / Learns at the drizzling weir the tongue of sleep" (p. 35); in "The Running Stream" he considers, watching its course, how:

my life that has loved so many
Wildbrooks flowing, never had answer from any
To question of mine.

(p. 280)

Blunden pulls the "cobwebbed apple-loft, / And the sweet smell of Blenheims lapped in straw" of "Old Homes" (p. 95) and the "dishevelled eaves; unwieldy doors, / Cracked rusty pump, and oaken floors" of the "The Barn" (p. 41) out of decay. They become features in a celebration of what is half lost, unregarded, passing away as the graves themselves in "Pride of the Village":

Old ones are not so noticed; low they lie
And lower till the equal grass forgets
The bones beneath.

(p. 101)

It is when landscape is suddenly informed and lit by Blunden's experience of war that the poems can take off into quite another dimension. The drowsily picturesque is left far behind in a poem, such as "At Rugmer" given here in its entirety:

Among sequestered farms and where brown orchards
Weave in the thin and coiling wind, and where
The pale cold river ripples still as moorhens
Work their restless crossing,
Among such places, when October warnings
Sound from each kex and thorn and shifting leaf,
We well might wander, and renew some stories
Of a dim time when we were kex and thorn,
Sere leaf, ready to hear a hissing wind
Whip down and wipe us out; our season seemed
At any second closing.
So, we were wrong. But we have lived this landscape
And have an understanding with these shades.

(*Poems, 1930–1940,* pp. 104–105)

The tone is perfectly poised, grave, and understated. It is one of those poems where a deceptively lucid, ambivalent tone links Blunden's poetry with that of Edward Thomas, whom he admired. The landscape is suddenly opened up to an autumnal chill, a seasonal death appropriate to the soldiers' deaths now inextricably part of it. Kex is dried-up plant stem; the identification of the poet with his former companions and with a natural turn-of-season desolation

is complete. He writes as revenant, a kind of shade himself. It is a poem about a great violence with nothing of that violence in its texture. Its elegiac tone is not a simple gift of mourning for the dead; the poem is an elegy for a landscape, a season, a time, and for himself.

BLUNDEN AND THE POETRY OF ELEGY

The elegiac note has always been recognized as a dominating element in English poetry, an integral part of England's mild and rainy landscape, itself a palimpsest written on and overwritten by successive generations. Lament and celebration, though, are the two sides of the same coin, and Blunden is very much in the tradition that finds this mode natural to his gift as a poet. His own poems are often gifts brought to the gravesides of those poets he always had a particular sympathy with: the minor, the dispossessed, the overlooked. It is appropriate that the nineteenth-century "peasant poet" John Clare should be one of his first loves and great discoveries. He is closely sympathetic to the physical richness of Clare's poetic landscape, shares Clare's grief as that landscape disappears with the Enclosure Acts that destroy the commons and heaths, understands Clare's vanished loves, his madness. Clare is more than an admiration; he is a presence for Blunden, as in "Clare's Ghost" (p. 53) or "The Death-Mask of John Clare" (p. 115), in which Blunden responds imaginatively to the mask's "rich, sweet serious gaze" and the certifying example Clare gives him of keeping the springs of imaginative life alive through loss and madness. Blunden's quick fellow feeling for those who act as exemplars, picking courage from kinds of desolation, finds another literary hero in Charles Lamb, the essayist whose sister Mary murdered their mother in a fit of madness. Lamb's acceptance of responsibility for Mary, while keeping his sympathetic attractions of character, particularly endears him to Blunden, who, in "At Christ Church, Greyfriars," sees him before the shades fell on his life "with numberless, nameless blue-coat boys" holding "his boyish world for ever" (p. 206).

This need to pay personal tribute to character and the uniqueness of a human life, wherever he finds it, is a constant in Blunden's poetry. The sense of his lost daughter is never far from him, movingly expressed in "Achronos":

Think, in that churchyard lies fruit of our loins—
The child who bright as pearl shone into breath
With the Egyptian's first-born shares coeveal death.

(p. 111)

In "C. E. B." (pp. 290–291) his own father, with his "monastic face," is wonderingly defined by the objects once so necessary and familiar to him—pipe, shoes, stick, or cricket bag—all poised together momentarily before the inevitable dispersal and the slow metamorphosis of a life into "village clay." "A. G. A.V." is a tribute to Vidler, whose early death moved Blunden so profoundly:

If one cause I have for pride, it is to have been your
  friend,
To have lain in shell-holes by your side, with you to
  have seen impend

The meteors of the hour of fire, to have talked where
  speech was love,
Where through fanged woods and maw-grey mire the
  rain and murder drove.

Blunden's elegies are specific and personal; they are also filled with a huge "alas" for the suffering and courage of unrecorded lives. The poems of war experience often give the sense of being at an immeasurable distance from the events they record, but the sudden silence of the Western Front in November 1918 had its own disorienting immediacy as the physical and mental wars were immediately disconnected. In "1916 Seen from 1922" (p. 82), Blunden's major theme is summed up perfectly: "Passionate I look for their dumb story still, / And the charred stub outspeaks the living tree." In his 1937 publication *An Elegy and Other Poems,* Blunden's "Can You Remember?" (pp. 209–210) shows how the passage of fifteen years has re-created the war as a puzzling, difficult dream. The past becomes a sudden fragmentary immediacy, brought back into being by a quick shift or twist of living circumstance: "Edge and exactitude / Depend on the day," and the "prodigious scene," with its

ambivalent gifts of nightmare or sudden joy, lies for the most part shrouded in mists: "Those mists are spiritual / And luminous-obscure," clearing a little when "sound, smell, change and stir" make sudden temporary clearings. Then comes identification with the past, not simple memory, as when Blunden prepared to speak at a battalion reunion and sensed the dead gathered there with the living: "Will there be chairs enough for all of us...Are we not all in the same boat? Fall in, ghosts" ("Fall in Ghosts," in *Edmund Blunden: A Selection of His Poetry and Prose,* p. 257).

The elegiac undertone and the presence of war lurks in unexpected places. "The Midnight Skaters" (pp. 101–101) is one of Blunden's best-known poems and a twentieth-century anthology piece. Like "Forefathers," it is uncluttered and strongly rhymed, with a tense melodic flow. Its capacity to haunt the reader's imagination lies in that double twisting of the celebration and the lament. On one level, the scene, with its cones of hop-poles, is the Yalding of his childhood; the midnight skaters are village revelers. They are, though, a larger congregation of "Earth's heedless sons and daughters," skating, as we all do, on the thinnest of ice, while in the cold depths death waits: "With but a crystal parapet / Between, he has his engines set." Though the dancers "twirl, wheel and whip above him," the vitality of the dance is directly related to the strength of the underlying menace and despair. An additional historic layer is given by the use of the word "parapet." As Fussell points out, parapet is a trench word, and the enemy, death, is "like an unsleeping, malevolent sentry amply equipped with infernal machines" (p. 258). Always with Blunden after his battle experiences there is the dual interpretation, the sense of the tombstone in the arcadian setting, the rags of humanity calling to be remembered, as in "Illusions," where he sets against the deceptive beauty of trenches in the moonlight "Death's malkins dangling in the wire / For the moon's interpretation" (p. 137).

EPILOGUE

Edmund Blunden, who cared for the overlooked, the disregarded, stands in some danger of being overlooked himself. In part this could be seen as a self-inflicted wound. Though his poetry makes a very substantial body of work, he never became, or could have become, that contemporary phenomenon the professional poet, single-minded in attention to the craft, the public reading, the conference. There was always too much going on in life—students to teach, friends to keep in correspondence with, administrative tasks, the need for money to support his family, books to collect, articles to write, cricket to play. In Blunden's care for his students, his editing of neglected names in the English tradition, his tributary essays, he exhausted himself carrying a torch for good writing and civilized values. He would have agreed with Samuel Johnson's famous remark in his review of Soame Jenyns's *Free Enquiry into the Nature and Origin of Evil* (*Johnson: Prose and Poetry,* 1950): "The only end of writing is to enable the readers better to enjoy life, or better to endure it." Though he took his poetry immensely seriously, there is an occasional element to much of it, and telling the world how good he was not Blunden's style. The lighter poems have a crispness, a sharp elegance that makes the reader wish Blunden had visited that territory more often. "Incident in Hyde Park, 1803," from his 1932 volume *Halfway House,* the dramatic account of a duel, has a spring and bite that exactly suits its cool, aristocratic setting:

Montgomery, Macnamara—both speaking together
In nitre and lead, the style is incisive,
Montgomery fallen, Macnamara half-falling,
The surgeon exploring the work of the evening—
And the Newfoundland dogs stretched at home in the
  firelight.

(p. 179)

The central problem that Blunden's poetry presents is that pull of the diction into the romantic-antique which seems to keep him in the pre-Prufrock period, safely at home in his late-Victorian and Georgian world. But Blunden is not safely at home. After 1916 he is never safe, and the diction that derives from Collins, Keats, Shelley, or Clare is set off against powerful destructive factors as war, loss, and restless change invade his psyche. We are now accustomed to a poetry—Sylvia Plath, Lowell, John Berryman, Anne Sexton—that rides the nerve ends, that enters the labyrinth and feeds the minotaur. Blunden was not like that. In her article "The Lost Selves: Edmund Blunden's Connection to Ivor Gurney," published in *The Ivor Gurney Society Journal* (no. 9, 2003), Margi Blunden, his eldest daughter by his third wife, Claire, writes with sympathetic firsthand knowledge of the demons her father had to face but points out "how he kept himself firmly in control of any tendency to allow his writing to undermine him, by writing in a careful, well-constructed and, at times, literary fashion" (p. 50). Blunden, though he could reenter the worst the war threw at him in such a poem as "Third Ypres" and ask "But who with what command can now relieve / The dead men from that chaos, or my soul?" (p. 88), has a duty as a half-recalcitrant survivor to tell the story the dead cannot tell. Even in that poem, it is an undertone which keeps him sane:

Look, from the wreck a score of field-mice nimble,
And tame and curious look about them; (these
Calmed me, on these depended my salvation).

It is a way of looking that Blunden kept faith with, expressed definitively in the opening lines of "Values" (p. 169).

Till darkness lays a hand on these gray eyes
And out of man my ghost is sent alone,
It is my chance to know that force and size
Are nothing but by answered undertone.

Though Edward Thomas, Wilfred Owen, Siegfried Sassoon, Isaac Rosenberg, and, more recently, Ivor Gurney have commanded more attention as the poetic voices of the Great War, Edmund Blunden's work should be seen as carrying an equal weight and depth. In the poetry where the impact of his Western Front experiences is invisible or less obviously apparent, it is possible to move behind the screen of consolatory beauties, personifications, and abstractions and find in the best work a wisdom that had, in all senses, to be fought for, and an undefeated love for humanity and the living kingdoms. The opening of "Lonely Love" (p. 212) is an example of this constant habit in Blunden of reaching out to the other rather than elaborating on his own self-regard:

I love to see those loving and beloved
Whom nature seems to have spited; unattractive,
Unnoticeable people, whose dry track
No honey-drop of praise, or understanding,
Or bare acknowledgment that they existed,
Perhaps yet moistened. Still, they make their world.

In *Undertones of War* he recalls seeing "a sentry crouching and peering one way and another like a birdboy in an October storm. He spoke, grinned and shivered; we passed; and duly the sentry was hit by a shell" (p. 123). It is natural to Blunden to draw his vignette from the old country life, where ragged children scared birds from the growing crops. Keeping faith with the unnoticeable was a task demanding an inclusive steadfastness and courage that did not stop in 1918. The closing lines of "The Cottage at Chigasaki" (p. 192), a cottage where a Japanese poet once lived who wrote a famous haiku about the well bucket so intertwined with flowers he drew his water elsewhere, will serve as one kind of epitaph: "Though comfort is not poetry's best friend, / We'll write a poem too, and sleep at the end." So will the close of "A Swan, A Man" of 1964, one of the last poems Blunden wrote and a very good poem, though Blunden's last years were not poetically productive. It is a river poem again, and the old poet stares into running water puzzling over whether he is watching birds or leaves on the far grass:

The rainstorm beats the pitiful stream
With battle-pictures I had hoped to miss,
But winter warfare would be worse than this;
Into the house, recall what dead friends say,
And like the Ancient Mariner, learn to pray.

Selected Bibliography

WORKS OF EDMUND BLUNDEN

Poetry

Blunden's poems appeared in numerous slim volumes. The bulk of those he wished to preserve up to the outbreak of World War II are to be found in the 1930 and 1940 collections published by Cobden-Sanderson and Macmillan.

The Waggoner and Other Poems. London: Sidwick & Jackson, ltd., 1920.

The Shepherd and Other Poems of Peace and War. New York: A. A. Knopf, 1922.

The Poems of Edmund Blunden. (Lettered on the spine, *Poems 1914–30.*) London: Cobden-Sanderson, 1930.

Halfway House, A Miscellany of New Poems. London: Cobden-Sanderson, 1932.

Poems, 1930–1940. London: Macmillan, 1940.

Shells by a Stream: New Poems. London: Macmillan, 1944.

After the Bombing, and Other Short Poems. London: Macmillan, 1949.

A Hong Kong House: Poems 1951–1961. London: Collins, 1962.

Eleven Poems. Edited by Francis Warner. Cambridge, U.K.: Golden Head Press, 1966.

CRITICAL AND BIOGRAPHICAL WORKS

Nature in English Literature. Hogarth Lectures on Literature Series no. 9. London: Hogarth Press, 1929.

Leigh Hunt: A Biography. London: Cobden-Sanderson, 1930.

Votive Tablets: Studies Chiefly Appreciative of English Authors and Books. London: Cobden-Sanderson, 1931. (This is Blunden's most substantial book of literary essays, for the most part drawn from his contributions to the *Times Literary Supplement.*)

The Mind's Eye. London: Jonathan Cape, 1934. (This volume of essays, divided into four sections, "Flanders," "Japan," "England," and "The World of Books" provides an excellent sampler of Blunden's major themes.)

Keats's Publisher: A Memoir of John Taylor (1781–1864). London: Jonathan Cape, 1936. Reprint, Clifton, N.J.: A. M. Kelly, 1975.

Thomas Hardy. London: Macmillan, 1941.

Shelley: A Life Story. London: Collins, 1946.

Other Prose Works

The Bonadventure: A Random Journal of an Atlantic Holiday. London: Cobden-Sanderson, 1922.

Christ's Hospital: A Retrospect. London: Christophers, 1923.

Undertones of War. London: Cobden-Sanderson, 1928. Edition of note: Folio Society, 1989. (This edition is important as containing the first trade publication of *De Bello Germanico,* first printed privately in 1930 in an edition of 275 copies by Blunden's brother G. A. Blunden.)

The Face of England. English Heritage Series. London: Longmans, Green, 1933.

English Villages. Britain in Pictures Series. London: Collins, 1941.

Cricket Country. London: Collins, 1944; Reprint Society/Collins, 1945.

<small>COLLECTIONS AND SELECTIONS</small>

Edmund Blunden: A Selection of His Poetry and Prose Made by Kenneth Hopkins. London: Rupert Hart-Davis, 1950.

Edmund Blunden: Poems of Many Years. Edited by Rupert Hart-Davis. London: Collins, 1957.

The Midnight Skaters. Poems for Young Readers Series. Edited by C. Day Lewis. Illustrated by David Gentleman. London: Bodley Head, 1968.

More Than a Brother: Correspondence Between Edmund Blunden and Hector Buck, 1917–1967. Edited by Hector Buck and Carol Zeman Rothkopf. London: Sexton, 1996.

Overtones of War. Edited with an introduction by Martin Taylor. London: Duckworth, 1996. (This collects all those poems of Blunden's which have war as their theme.)

<small>EDITIONS</small>

John Clare: Poems Chiefly from Manuscript. Edited by Edmund Blunden and Alan Porter. Introduction by Edmund Blunden. London: Cobden-Sanderson, 1920. (The first of three important editions that laid the groundwork for future Clare studies, along with *Madrigals and Chronicles* and *Sketches in the Life of John Clare*.)

Christopher Smart: A Song to David, with Other Poems. Chosen with Biographical and Critical Preface and Notes by Edmund Blunden. London: Cobden-Sanderson, 1924.

Madrigals and Chronicles. By John Clare. Edited by Edmund Blunden. London: Beaumont Press, 1924.

The Poems of William Collins. Edited with an introductory study by Edmund Blunden. London: Etchells & Macdonald, 1929. (An edition of five hundred numbered copies.)

The Poems of Wilfred Owen. A New Edition Including Many Pieces Now First Published and Notices of His Life and Work by Edmund Blunden. London: Chatto & Windus, 1931.

Sketches in the Life of John Clare, Written by Himself. Introduction by Edmund Blunden. London: Cobden-Sanderson, 1931.

Poems by Ivor Gurney. Principally Selected from Unpublished Manuscripts. With a memoir by Edmund Blunden. London: Hutchinson, 1954. (The first attempt to bring Gurney's war poems to a wider readership.)

<small>MANUSCRIPT MATERIAL</small>

There are considerable holdings, including the letters to and from Siegfried Sassoon and all Blunden's diaries, at the Harry Ransom Humanities Research Center, University of Texas at Austin. Letters to Takeshi Saito, his Japanese friend, are held at Meisei University Library, Tokyo. His letters to Hector Buck, his lifelong friend from Christ's Hospital days, are held at the Bodleian Library, Oxford.

CRITICAL AND BIOGRAPHICAL STUDIES

Fussell, Paul. *The Great War and Modern Memory*. London and New York: Oxford University Press, 1975. (Fussell's study of the war and "some of the literary means by which it has been remembered, conventionalized, and mythologized" makes extensive reference to Blunden's prose and poetry. Fussell fought in the U.S. infantry in World War II.)

Hardie, Alec M. *Edmund Blunden*. Writers and Their Work Series. Longman Group, for the British Council, 1958. Rev. ed., 1971.

Kirkpatrick, Brownlee. *A Bibliography of Edmund Blunden*. Oxford: Clarendon Press, 1979.

Mallon, Thomas. *Edmund Blunden*. Twayne's English Authors Series. Boston: Twayne, 1983.

Webb, Barry. *Edmund Blunden: A Biography*. New Haven, Conn., and London: Yale University Press, 1990.

JOHN CLARE

(1793–1864)

Susan Balée

JOHN CLARE, BORN a peasant in Helpston, Northamptonshire, ranks among England's greatest poets of nature and rural life. Celebrated as a "peasant poet" when his first collection, *Poems, Descriptive of Rural Life and Scenery,* appeared in 1820, verses such as these from "Dawnings of Genius" introduced his poet persona:

Hence is that fondness from his soul sincere
That makes his native place so doubly dear.
In those low paths which poverty surrounds,
The rough rude ploughman off his fallow grounds—
That necessary tool of wealth and pride—
While moiled and sweating by some pasture's side,
Will often stoop inquisitive to trace
The opening beauties of a daisy's face....

Clare's next three collections did not receive the same flurry of public attention even though they were better books. Critical acclaim could not generate the readers necessary to make them profitable. Unfortunately for him, the best of Clare's work appeared during a period of changing literary tastes. By the 1820s and 1830s, the heyday of the Romantic poets was over and with it the dominance of poetry as a popular genre. As the era of poetry waned, the popularity of prose narratives burgeoned: the age of the novel had begun.

Clare's reputation in the nineteenth century suffered for two other reasons. The first was that his publishers marketed him to the public as a nearly illiterate peasant who nevertheless could write brilliant verse about the fields and woods where he worked and roamed. Certainly his spelling and grammar were egregious—he spoke and wrote in the vernacular of his region—but he was not the idiot savant that some critics made him out to be and that his publishers presented him as in the first book in order to stimulate sales. He had attended school until he was thirteen and he was always an avid reader of any books he could get his hands on, particularly the work of other poets (William Wordsworth, Robert Burns, and Lord Byron were favorites), Shakespeare, and other classic British writers. His autobiographical writings describe reading the Bible from the age of six on and his first encounter with a truly good book: Daniel Defoe's *Robinson Crusoe,* which he read at age seven. He read widely and astutely all his life and could mimic seventeenth-century poets so well that verses he wrote in the manner of Andrew Marvell or Christopher Marlowe and claimed he "found" could not be distinguished from the work of the actual authors.

Indeed, his ability to inhabit the styles and themes of other writers would haunt him later when he came to believe that he was Lord Byron and wrote reams of witty, often smutty, poetry in the voice of the deceased author of *Childe Harold.* This split in his identity is the second reason Clare's reputation suffered for decades among literary critics: he went mad in the mid-1830s and was committed to an insane asylum in 1837. Except for one brief period back home (when he escaped and walked over fifty miles home to his wife and children, arriving half-starved and "foot foundered"), he spent the rest of his life in two asylums. In 1864 he died at the Northampton General Lunatic Asylum in the town of the same name. He wrote a great deal of poetry during these decades, some of it his best, but the public knew nothing of it. Only the occasional poem, such as the brilliant "Lines: I Am" (1847) appeared in a local newspaper, and this was thanks to the intervention of an asylum steward who befriended Clare and wrote down his poems.

After Clare's death it was primarily poets who championed his work, but he has been renovated for the general public in recent years thanks to

JOHN CLARE

British and American schools' recognition of environmental writing as an important genre of literature. Clare's detailed and technically accurate poems about birds' nests and the other fauna and flora of his region have brought him belated attention as one of the premier poets of nature. A large biography and new edition of his poems brought forth in 2003 by the Shakespeare scholar Jonathan Bate seem certain to increase "Clare awareness" among twenty-first-century readers.

Clare's descriptions of rural life and landscapes before the enclosure of open fields and woods altered the countryside in the second decade of the nineteenth century offer a port of entry into that era that cannot be found elsewhere. Truly a peasant—Clare worked from the age of thirteen as a day laborer, a gardener, and a lime-burner— the poet understood simple people's lives in nature in a way that other Romantic poets did not. After all, Wordsworth, Samuel Taylor Coleridge, Percy Bysshe Shelley, and Byron were all upper-middle- to upper-class writers, but Clare was a manual laborer who worked the land. The closest poet to him in that respect is Robert Burns of Scotland (to whom he was often compared), but Burns was writing about a very different region of Britain in a period a quarter-century before Clare's first publications. John Keats, who shared the same publisher as Clare, was also a working-class poet, but he was an urban one. As Jonathan Bate points out in *John Clare: A Biography,* "The nightingale of Keats's ode is in a long tradition of poetic nightingales, going back to the ancient Greek myth of Philomel, whereas Clare's 'The Nightingale's Nest' is grounded in natural history" (p. 189).

As recent scholarship illustrates, Clare appeals to a wide variety of readers. Poets like Clare's gifts with rhyme and meter, particularly his unusual reworkings of the sonnet form. Poets also laud his creative use of language, as do folklorists and philologists: Clare's poetry preserves some of the ancient dialect of the English Midlands. Regional dialects began disappearing in the mid-nineteenth century as industry burgeoned in cities, drawing workers from rural areas, and railroads crisscrossed the country,

making everyplace accessible. The days when villagers lived isolated in their particular regions disappeared with the century. Marxist critics, such as E. P. Thompson, who write about the position of the poor and laboring classes in nineteenth-century England, are drawn to Clare because he embodies this segment of the population and can articulate the daily lives, desires, and experiences of poor and disenfranchised people in a rural setting. Clare also describes the effect on poor people caused by the enclosure (or privatization) of common lands on which they had once grazed their animals, farmed, and hunted. Enclosure, combined with the Industrial Revolution, altered in a handful of years landscapes that had been unchanged for centuries.

Finally, Clare's writings are intriguing to anyone interested in the history and treatment of madness. Bate and other critics diagnose Clare's condition as bipolar disorder, and they use Clare's own descriptions of his symptoms to corroborate this hypothesis. The steady, inexorable fragmentation of self-identity that a chronological study of his writings reveals is invaluable as a record of how mental illness progresses and the mind splinters. His poems show the progress of his malady, and his writings about the asylums he lived in for over twenty years provide an insider's view of the prevailing notions of mental health care in his era. Historians as well as literary critics can find much to write about John Clare, all of which is helping to elevate his reputation and make him accessible once again to the common reader.

EARLY LIFE AND EDUCATION

John Clare was born on July 13, 1793, the son of a thresher, Parker Clare, and a shepherd's daughter, Ann Stimson Clare. Parker was the bastard child of a traveling schoolteacher who skipped town as soon as he discovered he had gotten a local girl pregnant. In *Sketches in the Life of John Clare,* his autobiographical fragment (published in 1831), Clare wrote, "My father was one of fate's chancelings who drop into the world without the honour of matrimony—he took the surname of his mother, who to commemorate the memory of a worthless father with more tenderness of lovelorn feeling than he doubtless deserved, gave him his surname at his christening" (p. 45). John Donald Parker, the itinerant schoolteacher, was never heard from again, but it seems likely that he left some of his love of learning behind to blossom a generation later in his grandson.

The Clares were a poor family. Parker Clare worked as a day laborer in the fields but managed to marry above his station because Ann Stimson's parents calculated that their thirty-five-year-old daughter, eight years Parker's senior, was not likely to get any other offers. In the first year of their marriage she gave birth to John and his twin sister, Bessy, who died within a few weeks. Parker Clare enjoyed drinking ale and singing ballads, and John Clare's love of folk songs can be traced to his father. Ann Stimson believed her son was bright enough to warrant a good education, though she herself could not read.

To this end John began attending a village school at the age of five. His one surviving sibling, sister Sophy, born in 1798, also learned to read and write but did not attend school. School cost money, but the Clares kept John enrolled for a few months every year for as long as they could. If times were hard, however, Parker would pull his son out of school to help in the fields. Mrs. Bullimore, who ran the village school, inculcated the boy's lifelong love of reading. One of Clare's first poems pays homage to this kindly woman and her entertaining curriculum: "And by imbibing what she simply taught / My taste for reading there was surely caught" (*Early Poems*, pp. 197–199).

Later teachers, John Seaton and James Merrishaw, also encouraged Clare and praised his talents. Clare was forced to leave school for good at thirteen to help support his family, but he continued to teach himself. He bought textbooks on a variety of subjects and taught himself navigation, algebra, botany, natural history, shorthand, drawing, history, and many other topics. His downfall, as he noted himself in his autobiography, was grammar: "Grammer I never read a page of in my Life" (*John Clare by Himself*, p. 33). Clare's lack of ability—or sheer inventiveness—with grammar would come back to haunt him in his later dealings with publishers. It also has provided his biographers and posthumous editors with a watershed choice. Do they serve his work raw—with all its grammatical failings, lack of punctuation, and misspellings—or do they make it more palatable by correcting the grammar, adding the punctuation, and regularizing the spelling? The debate continues to rage, with scholars making compelling arguments on both sides. Most of the poems quoted in this essay are from *"I Am": The Selected Poetry of John Clare*, 2003, edited by Jonathan Bate. Bate gives credible evidence that Clare would have preferred his work edited and polished—but not substantially altered—to make it more accessible to readers.

In his biography, Bate wonders if Clare's later mental problems began in his teens when he first tried to master so many subjects by himself. Sitting at the cottage table after a day of manual labor, reading by the dim light of a burning rush, he would study "page by page, fancying he could master every detail. He felt physically sick when he came across something he could not understand" (p. 27). Clare himself noted that studying for long hours gave him terrible headaches, yet he was obsessed with learning. Later he would be similarly obsessed with writing poetry.

SOLITARY PURSUITS, IDEAL LOVE

Even as a teenager Clare craved books and solitude in nature. His preference for wandering alone or reading in the fields caused consternation in the village. In a place as small as Helpston, people noticed that he was different. They teased his mother that she was "qualifying an idiot for a workhouse" (*Sketches*, p. 50). Still, despite Ann's urgings that he be more sociable, Clare preferred his solitary pastimes: rambling in nature, fishing, collecting birds' nests. Roman ruins underlay the land around Helpston, and sometimes Clare found fragments of pottery. North of the town, Lolham Bridges' four ancient arches marked the remnants of the Roman Road. Occasionally people would turn up ancient coins or other strange artifacts in their plowing fields, all of which gave Clare a keen sense of the past—of the layers of history embedded in the landscape he loved. The past's continued presence and effect on the present is a concept that recurs often in Clare's poetry.

In his later teens Clare made two good friends with whom he hunted for nests and transplanted orchids from the forest. One of these, Richard Turnill, died of typhus when he was seventeen, and Clare felt the loss keenly. He also fell in love for the first time while still in school. At thirteen he became enamored of a classmate, Mary Joyce. His was an unspoken love, perhaps because the Joyce family, farmers, ranked far above the station of the day-laboring Clares. Still, whatever his feelings at the time, Mary Joyce came to symbolize ideal love in Clare's mind. He wrote numerous poems "to Mary" and even believed, years later in the insane asylum, that he was married to her in addition to his real wife, Patty. Childhood crystallized his emotions and idealized his relationships from that time. Mary symbolized perfect love, untainted by sexuality or adult cares.

ENCLOSURE

When Clare was sixteen Parliament passed the "Enclosure Act," and the common lands around Helpston were privatized. It took until 1820 to fence in all the open fields and assign them to their private owners, but it transformed the region of Clare's childhood. Poor people were no longer allowed to grow vegetables or graze their animals on the fields once shared by all, and Clare's beloved woods were chopped down to make room for fences and additional pastures.

Before enclosure, most old English villages sat in the center of a wheel of fields and woodlands accessible to all. As Bate describes it, "The countryside of Clare's childhood was in the most literal sense open, and many of his poems both describe and formally enact motions that are circular. But with the enclosure, the parish was divided into rectangular fields, which were further subdivided by their owners. The enclosure award

map of 1820 is ruled by a sense of the linear—and again in the most literal sense—*enclosed* space" (p. 48). Clare felt the enclosure personally and painfully. His friends the Turnills had to leave their farm when the land was given back to a large landowner. Gypsies who frequently camped on the waste grounds around Helpston were also forced out. Friends of Clare from whom he gathered folktales and songs, the gypsies were more than marginalized by enclosure: They were forced *off* the margins, to nowhere.

Clare saw his neighbors suffering as the fences went up—he even put some of them up, earning a laborer's wages to do so—and suffered personally by being cut off from his unrestricted rambling. Fields and forests he had once roamed were now private lands, and the old paths were closed to the public. The historian E. P. Thompson writes at length about the effect of enclosure on the working poor in general and Clare in particular in *Customs in Common*. Thompson sees Clare as a "poet of ecological protest" (p. 180) who realized that the equilibrium between the land and the people who lived on the land would be disrupted by enclosure. One of Clare's most powerful poems, "Remembrances," likens enclosure to the tyrant all England despised in the first half of the 1800s, Napoleon Bonaparte.

CHILDHOOD'S END, REMEMBRANCE

Many of Clare's poems celebrate the joys and innocence of childhood and lament their loss. Some poems, such as "Childhood," catalog the pastimes of working-class children in a rural area:

When we review that place of prime
That childhood's joys endow,
That seemed more green in winter time
Than summer grass does now,
Where oft the task of skill was put
For other boys to match,
To run along the churchyard wall
Or balls to cuck and catch

How oft we clomb the porch to cut
Our names upon the leads,
Though fame nor anything akin
Was never in our heads,

Where hands and feet were rudely drawn
And names we could not spell,
And thought no artist in the world
Could ever do as well.

This poem goes on to discuss the joys of spinning tops, throwing stones at weathervanes, playing hopscotch, making carriages of oyster shells and monarchs out of clay, chasing dogs, teasing cats, snapping switches from the willow row, tossing shuttlecocks, gathering acorns, making birds' nests, all out of doors. Nature weaves itself into the children's play:

Each noise that breathed round us then
Was magic all and song,
Wherever pastime found us then
Joy never led us wrong.
The wild bee in the blossom hung,
The coy bird's startled call
To find its home in danger—there
Was music in them all.

As the poet looks back, he would not wish to forget a moment of those childish pleasures— "Who can disdain the meanest weed / That shows its face in spring?" But his season of childhood is over, and it pains him to acknowledge that time destroys youth and joy.

The fairest summer sinks in shade,
The sweetest blossom dies,
And age finds every beauty fade
That youth esteemed a prize.
The play breaks up, the blossom fades
And childhood disappears;
For higher dooms ambition aims
And care grows into years.

Clare's adult ambitions—to be a published writer, to marry and father children—did lead him to care, sadness, and eventually the overthrow of his reason, but his childhood remained an unblemished memory that he called on often in his writing.

FROM MANUAL LABORER TO VERSE MAKER

John Clare had several different jobs in the course of his teenage years. He worked for a year as a busboy at a local pub; another year he hired on as a gardener at one of the local estates, Burghley House, home of the marquess of Exeter. When not formally employed he worked as a casual laborer in farmers' gardens or fields. As he records in his autobiography, by this time "poetry was a troublesome but pleasant companion, annoying and cheering me at my toils" (*The Prose of John Clare,* 1951, p. 30). Verses would occur to him as he worked, and he recorded them by writing on a scrap of paper braced on the crown of his hat. Of course he had to do this out of sight of his employers lest he be accused of shirking, hence his preference for fieldwork.

In August all the villagers worked together to bring in the harvest. During the harvest season when Clare was eighteen he saw a man named Thomas Drake fall off a hay wagon and break his neck. The scene affected him powerfully; as he wrote in his autobiography, "The ghastly paleness of death struck such a terror on me that I could not forget it for years and my dreams was constantly wandering in churchyards, digging graves, seeing spirits in charnel houses, etc., etc." (*Sketches,* pp. 70–71). Clare goes on to observe that after he saw Drake get killed he began to suffer from fainting fits himself and to dread death. Clare's biographers see the poet's later madness foreshadowed in this strong reaction to Drake's death. By the time Clare was first admitted to an asylum in July 1837, the spirits that terrified him had crept out of his dreaming mind and into his waking world.

In 1812, however, John Clare's melancholy thoughts were diverted by Napoleon's sudden return to power. The English feared a French invasion and began calling up soldiers. Clare joined the militia, though his service never extended to anything beyond a few weeks of training. By this time, however, Clare's family had become dependent on his earnings; his father's rheumatism had become so bad that Parker could no longer work and had to go on parish poor relief. John Clare, on whose shoulders the burden of supporting the family fell, could not seem to make enough from agricultural labor to get his parents off relief. In 1818, hoping to earn more, he became a lime-burner. As Bate describes it, "Lime-burning was choking work that required the heating of chalk or limestone in a kiln in order to make quicklime for mortar and fertilizer" (p. 83). During this time Clare lived in Casterton, near the limeworks. He boarded at a local house and saved his wages to pay his parents' back rent on the cottage in Helpston.

During his sojourn in Casterton, at the age of twenty-five, Clare met and fell in love with Martha "Patty" Turner, the woman he later wed and with whom he fathered seven surviving children. Like Mary Joyce, Patty was of a higher social class than Clare. If he was to have any hope of marrying her, he knew he had to improve his financial prospects. To this end he decided to try and publish some of his poetry.

POEMS, DESCRIPTIVE OF RURAL LIFE AND SCENERY (1820)

Clare spent two years trying to get his first book published. Talented though he was, he knew nothing about the publishing world and had no contacts there. Nevertheless he bought books often, and so he approached J. B. Henson, a trader in secondhand books who also had his own printing press. Henson liked the poems Clare showed him but said he would not print the book until a hundred subscribers had signed up to buy it. Next Henson asked for a ten-pound cash advance, and the poverty-stricken Clare began to balk. At this fortuitous moment a young printer named Ned Drury saw a prospectus of the planned book and decided to seek out the poet. Instead of asking Clare for money to publish his work, Drury agreed to pay Clare's expenses and also his debts.

Ned Drury gave Clare's poems to his cousin, John Taylor, a London publisher who had experience with poetry: he had just published John Keats's *Endymion* (1818). Taylor and his partner, James Hessey, were taken with Drury's description of the rustic poet and thought his verse had both merit and marketability. Drury was enthusiastic about Clare's gifts and envisioned him as a second Robert Burns. However, he also worried that Clare was too like Burns in his love of wine, women, and song. Taylor, for his part, was ready to commit to Clare in the same way he had committed himself to Keats (even though Keats's genius was not recognized by most readers until long after his death, and *Endymion*'s first critical reviews were mostly negative).

Throughout 1819, while Taylor edited his poems for inclusion in the first collection, Clare worked feverishly to create more. Fame was at last in reach, and Patty was pregnant with their first child (though Clare had not yet decided to marry her). Drury, though he irritated Taylor by claiming to have "discovered" Clare, nevertheless worried about the poet's working himself into a breakdown. He wrote Taylor, "It is to be greatly feared that the man will be afflicted with insanity if his talent continues to be forced as it has been these 4 months past; he has no other mode of easing the fever that oppresses him after a tremendous fit of rhyming except by getting tipsy.... Then he is melancholy and completely hypochondriac" (unpublished letter, quoted in Bate, p. 146).

Taylor and Hessey began publishing *London Magazine* in January 1820, and this periodical was their forum for introducing Clare and his work to the world. An article in the first edition described Clare, and two of his early poems were published as samples of his work. Two weeks after the article appeared Taylor and Hessey brought out *Poems, Descriptive of Rural Life and Scenery, by John Clare, A Northamptonshire Peasant.* Taylor wrote the introduction to the book, describing Clare's life of poverty and toil and then praising his use of the vernacular and regional dialect for their authenticity (and also providing a glossary at the back of the book for readers who couldn't puzzle out the meanings of the local words). Taylor presented Clare as a child of nature: "He loves the fields, the flowers, 'the common air, the sun, the skies;' and therefore he writes about them. He is happier in the presence of Nature than elsewhere."

The marketing campaign worked, and the book sold out its initial run of one thousand copies in two months. Two more print runs were needed by 1821. Reviews of the book were mostly good, with reviewers focusing on Clare's ability to write poems at all—much less compelling poems—with such an impoverished background.

JOHN CLARE

Like Taylor, critics praised Clare's affinity for describing nature, but the most popular poem in the book was one about mortality, "What Is Life?"

And what is life? An hourglass on the run,
A mist retreating from the morning sun,
A busy bustling still repeated dream.
Its length? A minute's pause, a moment's thought.
And happiness? A bubble on the stream
That in the act of seizing shrinks to naught.

The poem's catchy opener is followed by further descriptions of hope, trouble, and death. The last stanza ends with a Longfellow-like admonition to carry on despite all:

'Tis but a trial all must undergo,
To teach unthankful mortals how to prize
That happiness vain man's denied to know
Until he's called to claim it in the skies.

More important to Clare than the critics' positive reviews was the attention he received from the gentry in the neighborhood. Both the marquess of Exeter, in whose garden he had once worked, and the Fitzwilliam family—Lord Milton and his wife and children—all gave Clare money and worked with Taylor to set up a fund in their local poet's name.

In March, Clare visited London, where William Hilton painted his portrait and Taylor, Hessey, and *London Magazine* writers such as Thomas Hood attended parties in honor of "the peasant poet." The Hilton portrait now hangs in England's National Portrait Gallery and offers the only real likeness of the poet in his prime: A pale, angular face with a rather sharp nose, piercing light eyes, wavy blondish-red hair in need of combing, and full lips slightly parted as if about to speak. Clare stood barely five feet tall and resembled "a big boy who has never been used to company" according to Henry Cary, one of the *London Magazine* stable. On this visit Clare also met Eliza Emmerson, a middle-age patron of young artists who would become one of Clare's most enduring friends. When he got home Clare decided to "do the right thing" by Patty. Unlike his unknown grandfather, Clare married the girl he had impregnated.

FAME AND FATHERHOOD

Anna Maria Clare, John and Patty's first daughter, was born in June 1820. Clare had not been eager to marry Patty, but he adored their daughter. His "To an Infant Daughter," published in his second book, describes his feelings for Anna:

Lord knows my heart, it loves thee much;
And may my feelings, aches and such,
The pains I meet in folly's clutch
     Be never thine:
Child, it's a tender string to touch,
     That sounds "Thou'rt mine."

The same poem hopes that his daughter will be "unknown to rhyming bother" and that she won't have her "mad father's...feeling fears and jingling starts." At least Clare did not have to worry as much about money for a little while: His friends had set up an annuity in his name, and with gifts from the local gentry added to it he received about forty pounds annually, at that time considerably more than he could have earned from manual labor.

Clare had also become a celebrity, and many wealthy readers of his first collection drove out to Helpston to see the peasant poet in his rural cottage. For the most part the visitors irritated Clare, though some of them gave him books he wanted to read. And during these days he read avidly and was proud of his library, which included many volumes of poetry. Of his contemporary Wordsworth's "On Westminster Bridge," he wrote to a friend, "I think it (and woud say it to the teeth of the critic in spite of his rule and compass) that it owns no equal in the English language" (*The Letters of John Clare, 1985*, p. 87).

CLARE'S EDITORS... THEN AND NOW

An insightful critic of his contemporaries' work, Clare had more problems clearly seeing his own. As he worked on the poems that would comprise his second book, he often struggled with Taylor and Hessey's need to prune his abundant outpourings (when he began writing, rhyming became an obsession and he could not stop) and expunge the crudest of his country expressions. Clare wilted under criticism, but his poems would have been unpublishable without the intervention of his editors. Jonathan Bate expresses the central conundrum of Clare's relationship with Taylor and Hessey:

> Clare's country bluntness and lack of polish—his "own rude way"—had to be nurtured. These were the qualities that enabled them to market him as the peasant phenomenon.... At the same time, for Clare to make a national impact he had to be brought to London and introduced to influential figures.... There was a danger that a taste of this world would cut him off from the sources of his poetic power.
>
> (p. 204)

Besides introducing him to important social and literary figures, Taylor and Hessey also had to introduce Clare's poems to the average reader. To this end they had to edit. They had to normalize his spelling and grammar and provide glossaries of his local words and phrases. Occasionally they also had to interpret his manic effusions. Taylor in particular had to parse Clare's words out of texts that the poet had scribbled in execrable homemade ink on odd scraps of paper, replete with almost illegible cross-outs, amendments, and additions.

Ironically, in the twentieth century Clare scholars began to portray the poet as the victim of oppressive editors. A good deal of Taylor-bashing appeared in articles about Clare, resulting in Oxford University Press's decision to publish a multivolume edition of Clare's writings in their unpolished, pre-edited state. The editors (or rather, un-editors) of these volumes, Eric Robinson et al., offer a fascinating glimpse of Clare's "raw" work. For equally raw readers, however, unedited Clare is difficult to decode.

Robinson's laudable aim has been to restore the "authentic voice" of Clare, a voice ostensibly distorted by his editors. Bate and other critics, however, have reacted against the "raw Clare" on the grounds that he himself often said he needed editors to help him with grammar, spelling, and clear copies of his poems. A representative sample from Clare's numerous letters to Taylor on the subject runs, "Your assistance in such things I find very nesessary and I in fact will not

do without it.... I saw their defects and wondered I never saw them before you crossed them out" (*Letters*, p. 167).

The best discussion of what Clare scholars call "the myth of solitary genius" appears in a book published by the John Clare Society, *John Clare: New Approaches* (2000). Although the Oxford edition of Clare's poems is ubiquitous, it is also possible to find edited versions that are more reader-friendly, such as Bate's 2003 edition of selected poems.

THE VILLAGE MINSTREL, AND OTHER POEMS
(1821)

John Clare's second book of poetry appeared in late 1821. He had been under a great mental strain since early in the year. He called his intense, obsessive periods of writing being "in the fit." Yet he had to subject himself to these fits—and their consequent depressions—in order to give Taylor and Hessey the copy they needed. His fainting spells, first triggered by Drake's death in 1812, returned, and with them his fears of death and devils. He wrote Eliza Emmerson that he was "mentally afflicted," his imagination taken over by demons.

Meanwhile his father's rheumatism continued, keeping his parents and sister dependent on his income, and Patty was pregnant with their second child. This baby, a boy, born in May 1821, died within a day of his birth. Clare's depression worsened, and his faith in God was shaken by the loss of the baby. The second collection appeared in September, and Taylor and Hessey printed two thousand copies. The title poem describes the life of a thresher's son named Lubin. Lubin is obviously Clare's persona in this long poem. Like Clare, Lubin is a lover of nature whose solitary ramblings make him suspect among his fellow villagers: "With other boys he little cared to mix; / Joy left him lonely in his hawthorn bowers, / As haply binding up his knots of flowers, / Or list'ning unseen birds to hear them sing." Many stanzas of this poem also deal with enclosure and its ill effects on land and villagers. The birds that young Lubin loved to listen to have been driven from their nests: "The thorns are gone, the woodlark's song is hush, / Spring more resembles winter now than spring, / The shades are banished all—the birds have took to wing."

Most of the poems in *The Village Minstrel* describe the poet communing with nature in all its minute details. Clare's local knowledge of the area around Helpston invigorates the landscape descriptions. The poet also shows his awareness of the layers of history lying beneath the flora and fauna. A stanza of "The Last of March (Written at Lolham Brigs)" describes the bridge built by Romans to lift their road above the swampy ground.

These walls the work of Roman hands!
  How may conjecturing fancy pore,
As lonely here one calmly stands,
  On paths that age has trampled o'er.
  The builders' names are known no more;
No spot on earth their memory bears;
  And crowds reflecting thus before,
Have since found graves as dark as theirs.

Several important magazines reviewed the new collection. The *Literary Gazette* thought the poems were better than those in the first collection but that Clare needed to focus more on the craft of poetry than the art of description. The *Monthly Magazine* was not impressed; that reviewer thought the sonnets in particular were competent but not likely to "enrich...our stores of national poetry." In contrast the *Literary Chronicle* ranked Clare "with the best poets of the day, though a humble and untutored peasant," and the *New Monthly Magazine* praised the moral and social value of his poems (Bate, pp. 229–231).

Taken together, the reviews of *The Village Minstrel* were positive. Unfortunately the market for poetry continued to shrink, and John Clare was no longer a novelty. Only eight hundred of the two thousand copies sold in 1821. Meanwhile, Clare's fame had made him even more of a village oddity than he was before:

I live here among the ignorant like a lost man in fact like one whom the rest seems careless of having anything to do with—they hardly dare talk in my company for fear I should mention them in my writings and I find more pleasure in wandering the fields than in musing among my silent neighbours who are insensitive to every thing but toiling and talking of it and that to no purpose.

(*Letters*, p. 230)

BYRON, BOXERS, BABIES, AND "BLUE DEVILS"

John Clare's second surviving child, Eliza Louisa, named in honor of his London patron, Eliza Emmerson, was born in June 1822 while Clare was enjoying his second visit to London. He got home when the baby was three days old, but he hated leaving his friends in London and facing his justifiably annoyed Patty. His correspondence with Eliza Emmerson, always flirtatious, now began to describe Patty as faded and dull. He told Eliza that he was tormented by "blue devils" and had turned to drink to deal with his unhappiness. Soon he also turned to other women. To her credit, Eliza always urged him to work things out with Patty and to avoid drinking and womanizing. Eliza also frequently bought gifts for Clare's children and gave the family money for their education.

By the autumn of 1823 Clare had fallen into a deep depression, a state that revisited him seasonally for the rest of his life. The birth of his son Frederick in January 1824 did little to rouse him from misery. John Taylor, who suffered from depression himself, was worried enough about Clare to hire a Dr. Skrimshire to check up on him. The doctor's main concern was the poverty in which Clare lived. The cottage in Helpston, where Clare resided with his wife, three children, parents, and sister, had only four rooms and was, according to Skrimshire, "altogether unfit for a human habitation being dark, damp, and ill ventilated, with a space so circumscribed as to be worse than a prison for two families" (Martin, p. 173). Dr. Skrimshire was the first person to recommend that Clare needed a better place to live if his health was to improve.

By late spring of 1824 Clare was no better, and Hessey and Taylor paid for him to come to London and see a specialist. Clare stayed eleven weeks, boarding with both Hessey and Taylor and walking over to visit Mrs. Emmerson. He would never stay late, however, for he feared walking in the dark and meeting "thin death-like shadows and gobblings with sorcerer eyes...continually shaping in the darkness from my haunted imagination" (*Prose,* p. 94). During this visit Clare spent much of his free time with another protégé of Mrs. Emmerson, the painter Edward Villiers Rippingille. "Rip" had a wide circle of acquaintances, reputable and not, and he took Clare everywhere from the Royal Academy to the pre-Victorian equivalent of strip clubs.

Regency England was in the grip of "boximania," and Rip also introduced Clare to the popular spectacle of men battering each other insensible. Clare soon loved "the fancy"—as the world of prizefighting was called—even more than Rip. In this Clare resembled one of his idols, Lord Byron. Byron had even hired "Gentleman" John Jackson as a sparring partner. Nor was Byron the only cultured writer to embrace the sport. Poets wrote odes in honor of favorite boxers, and critics reviewed the fights as examples of poetry in motion.

During Clare's sojourn in London, word came that Byron had died in Greece. His death seemed to exemplify the end of an era—that of poetry. On July 12 Clare witnessed his funeral procession, and the common people's love of Byron touched him deeply. This reverence of the ordinary people was just the kind of fame Clare himself craved. The summer's events—his depression, boxing, the death of Byron, the death knell of the market for poetry—fused in his memory and infused his unconscious mind. Years later he would come to believe that he was both Lord Byron and a famous boxer, or as he called himself then, "Boxer Byron."

NATURAL HISTORY, FOLKLORE

John Clare returned to Helpston, but the depression had not lifted. Nevertheless he spent his time reading and making notes on the flora and fauna of his native region. It seems to have been a conscious attempt to redirect his mind from dark thoughts. With a new journal book that he had obtained in London, he daily recorded what he had seen on his walks, books he had read, the state of his family's health, and anything else that seemed relevant.

The journal became the raft he clung to as depression swirled around him. Sometimes he recorded suicidal thoughts, the observer of nature observing his own human nature as depression breached his mind's defenses:

A wet day, did nothing but nurse my illness—Coud not have walked out had it been fine—very disturbd in conscence about the troubles of being forcd to endure life and dye by inches and the anguish of leaving my children and the dark porch of eternity whence none returns to tell the tale of their reception.

(September 23, 1824)

His journal also records the recurrent illnesses of the rest of his family, the fevers and chills and agues brought on by poverty and their damp cottage.

Many of the entries in Clare's journal are detailed descriptions of birds' nests. These prose observations formed the basis for some of his best and most original poems. Clare also took pains to record the folk songs and customs of his region before they disappeared. Clare did for the oral tradition of his region of England what Burns had done for Scotland a quarter century earlier.

In June 1826 his son John was born. Financial strains added to mental anxieties; Clare spent the rest of that summer working in the fields to earn extra money. Meanwhile he was also working on a series of poems based on the months of a rural year. Taylor published these in monthly issues of the *London Magazine* and then decided they would add up to a new book. However, in the course of assembling the poems, Taylor and Hessey dissolved their partnership. This and Taylor's difficulties deciphering some of Clare's drafts of poems delayed the volume.

Clare also wrote poems for other magazines, including imitations of Andrew Marvell and other seventeenth-century poets. Some of these were published in the *Sheffield Iris,* a newspaper edited by James Montgomery, who summed up the literary culture of the mid-1820s in one of his letters to Clare: "Poetry has had its day in the present age and two more generations must go by before there is such another revival in its favour" (quoted in Bate, p. 309).

Finally, in April 1827, *The Shepherd's Calendar; with Village Stories, and Other Poems* was published. The book received favorable reviews but had almost no sales. Nevertheless this collection shows how much Clare had matured as a poet. His lyrical art is finally the equal of his descriptive powers, and well-turned verses breathe fresh life into village scenes.

Material from Clare's journal shows to good effect here too. Not only does he capture the landscape and the weather, he publishes accounts of the folk customs of his region. As the poet persona says in the last stanza of "December,"

Old customs! O I love the sound,
However simple they may be—
Whate'er with time hath sanction found
Is welcome and is dear to me—
    Pride grows above simplicity
And spurns them from her haughty mind,
    And soon the poet's song will be
The only refuge they can find.

THE RURAL MUSE, *LOST AT HOME*

Eight years went by before John Clare's fourth and final book of verse, *The Rural Muse,* was published in 1835. During those years Patty bore John three more children, William (1828), Sophie (1830), and Charles (1833). Illness, physical and mental, continued to dog Clare. In 1830, at a performance of *The Merchant of Venice,* Clare leaped out of his seat and began yelling at the actor playing Shylock, "You villain, you murderous villain!" (Martin, p. 266). Clare was asked to leave the theater, and the event confused and embarrassed him. Soon after this incident other friends of Clare began to notice him talking to invisible people. When asked about his behavior, the poet confessed that he was seeing evil spirits around him.

Money troubles intensified as his family grew. Interest rates had dropped, so he received less on the annuity. The only money he could make from writing came from occasional poems published in newspapers and magazines. In the summers, when his deep depressions relented, he worked in the fields to earn extra money. After Taylor and Hessey parted ways, Clare demanded an accounting of his book sales from Taylor. When he finally received it he found errors on both sides— the poet had never been paid for his contributions to *London Magazine,* but Taylor had never recovered his production costs on the poor-selling *Shepherd's Calendar.* This accounting marked the end of their business relationship, though they remained friends and Taylor continued to send Clare payments on the annuity he had set up for him.

In 1831 Lord Milton offered Clare a bigger, better-ventilated cottage with an acre of orchard and garden for thirteen pounds a year. This was more than double the rent of the Helpston cottage, but the new one, three miles away in Northborough, would be much healthier for Clare and his family. He accepted the offer, and the family moved in April 1832. The move had a monumental effect on Clare's already fragile mental state. As Bate observes, "The change in physical environment was a serious concern for a man who had derived his strongest sense of identity from his immediate surroundings" (p. 363). Clare's feelings are described best in a poem he wrote soon after the move, "On Leaving the Cottage of My Birth".

Even though the market for poetry had fallen flat, Clare could not give up his dream of publishing another collection. Thomas Pringle, who had published some of Clare's poems in a magazine called *Friendship's Offering,* tried to interest book publishers in a collection of Clare's latest poems. He had no luck and wrote Clare a letter describing what he had learned: "Poetry they say is quite unsaleable—and even Wordsworth and other well-known writers cannot find a purchaser for their MSS" (Bate, p. 370). Taylor, of course, had been out of the picture for years: he had become a publisher of university textbooks, and Hessey had a new career as an auctioneer.

The person who managed to get his final book of poems published was his old friend Eliza Emmerson. She culled the mass of poems he had entitled "The Midsummer Cushion" (the name villagers gave to a piece of sod filled with wildflowers placed decoratively in their cottages) to half their original number and assigned this selection the more accessible title of "The Rural Muse." With her husband Thomas's help, Eliza Emmerson persuaded a Peterborough publisher to bring out the new book with a one-time fee to Clare of forty pounds. In July 1835 *The Rural Muse* appeared, and everyone who read it agreed it was Clare's best work yet.

The collection's most distinctive poems, and those that are Clare's signature compositions, are the nesting poems. "The Nightingale's Nest" describes the poet searching for the songbird's nest in the woods: "There have I hunted like a very boy, / Creeping on hands and knees through matted thorn / To find her nest and see her feed her young." On the fern leaves beneath the hazel bush, he stops to hear her sing, "and her renown / Hath made me marvel that so famed a bird / Should have no better dress than russet brown." He tries not to move, for the least rustle will make the bird fly and take her beautiful song with her: "Lost in a wilderness of listening leaves, / Rich ecstasy would pour its luscious strain." At last the poet finds the nightingale's nest while she looks on from her perch on an oak limb, "Mute in her fears; our presence doth retard / Her joys, and doubt turns every rapture chill." The poet studies the nest but does not disturb it: "We will not plunder music of its dower / Nor turn this spot of happiness to thrall." Clare loves nature too much to alter it. He describes what materials the nightingale used to fashion her nest and what her eggs look like, but he limits himself to observing and admiring the bird's ingenuity. The poem ends with the five eggs intact in their nest:

And the old prickly thorn-bush guards them well.
So here we'll leave them, still unknown to wrong,
As the old woodland's legacy of song.

The sonnets contained in *The Rural Muse* are also striking. Critics have noted that Clare subverted the conventions of the form, often beginning with a rhyming couplet instead of ending with one, and focusing on his raptures in nature rather than his passion for a human lover, at that time the usual subject of sonnets.

Unfortunately, no matter how good the work it could not overcome the public's aversion to poetry. Clare's gifts were real, but they were out of season, and despite the excellent critical reviews, *The Rural Muse* dropped out of sight. Clare himself was out of his natural element after the move to the cottage in Northborough. The blue devils that had been trailing him for years finally brought him to bay. In 1837 he was certified insane and committed to a lunatic asylum.

DR. ALLEN'S ASYLUM, ESSEX

As stated earlier, John Clare's mental illness would probably be diagnosed nowadays as manic depression, or bipolar disorder. The manic phases enabled him to write reams of poetry, but they were inevitably followed by deep depressions. As the illness progressed, the manic uplifts grew shorter and less energizing and the depressions became deeper and longer. Clare also grew paranoid, believing demons were cursing him and his family.

The alienation caused by the move to Northborough made Clare feel like a victim of nature. In addition to the soaring birds with whom he usually identified, the poems in the Northborough years often featured ground-dwelling animals being driven from their homes, hunted, and killed. In a sonnet sequence about the pursuit and persecution of a badger, the last sonnet is pruned to twelve lines, ending abruptly with the animal's death:

He falls as dead and kicked by boys and men
Then starts and grins and drives the crowd agen
Till kicked and torn and beaten out he lies
And leaves his hold and cackles, groans and dies.

John Taylor visited Clare in December 1836 and the poet was muttering to himself, "God bless them all—Keep them from Evil." Taylor told his sister that a doctor he had consulted suggested that Clare needed to be confined in an asylum because he was becoming more than Patty Clare could handle and "very violent...occasionally" (John Taylor to Elizabeth Taylor, December 9, 1836).

In July 1837 John Clare was committed to Matthew Allen's private asylum in Essex, northeast of London. He was forty-four years old. Luckily for Clare, attitudes toward the treatment of mental illness had undergone a sea change since the madness of King George in 1788 first called attention to it. In Clare's time the new approach to treating insanity was "moral management." The deranged king had been bound, doused with cold water, and otherwise tormented in the eighteenth-century manner of treating lunatics as if they were possessed by demons, but by Clare's era doctors recognized that mental patients needed comfort and security, not torture, to get better.

In the two asylums where Clare spent most of the rest of his life, he was comfortably housed, allowed to stroll in the surrounding countryside, help in the garden, play chess or other games, and otherwise relax. He had a fireplace in his room and good food. In fact his diet was dramatically better than it had been at home: Drawings and photos of him from the asylum years show a ruddy, plump Clare, looking more like a prosperous farmer than the hungry poet he once had been.

At Allen's asylum Clare lived in Leopard's Hill Lodge, the building that housed male patients who were not violent. Another building for wealthy "guests," Fair Mead, was where Alfred Tennyson stayed for several visits and to which Jane Carlyle, Thomas' wife, said any sane person would be delighted to be admitted. Dr. Allen sent annual reports on Clare's condition to John Taylor, noting that though the poet's mind was not better, it was also not worse. Allen also observed that Clare wrote "beautiful poetic effusions" whenever he could obtain a pencil and paper but that, ironically, in conversation or writing prose he could not maintain "the appearance of sanity for two minutes or two lines together, and yet there is no indication whatever of any insanity in any of his poetry" (June 23, 1840).

During his time in Allen's asylum, Clare missed home terribly. Many of his letters sound this note, and they also begin to record a new

delusion: he thinks he is married to Mary Joyce as well as to Patty. He began to write letters "to my two wives" to save time. He also believes he is Lord Byron and has begun, he tells his correspondents, to write *Childe Harold* and *Don Juan*. A stanza from Clare's version of "Child Harold" (no "e") evokes the author's misery.

Other parts of these poems teem with lewd puns and sexual suggestions. He writes about the asylum, describing women patients getting raped and male patients sodomizing each other. Dr. Allen, who made a habit of checking his patients' urine for diagnostic reasons, is not a figure of respect in Clare's poems:

Theres Docter Bottle imp who deals in urine
A keeper of state prisons for the queen
As great a man as is the Doge of Turin
And save in London is but seldom seen
Yclept old A-ll-n—mad brained ladies curing
Some p-x-d like Flora and but seldom clean

John Clare felt himself a prisoner in Allen's asylum, and in the summer of 1841 he escaped and walked home to Northborough.

HOME AGAIN, BRIEFLY

Clare's account of his fifty-mile walk home, "Recollections of Journey from Essex," is a remarkable biographical fragment. The writer opens a window on his era's landscape and culture, while also giving an insight into his mental state. Clare believed he was walking home to Mary Joyce, though she had actually died— unmarried and childless—several years before in a fire. When someone showed Clare the newspaper report of her death, he "took no notice of the blarney, having seen her myself about a twelve-month ago alive and well and young as ever—so here I am homeless at home and half gratified to feel I can be happy anywhere" (*"I Am,"* p. 264).

Patty Clare agreed to let her husband live at home, but after a few months his behavior again grew violent. Lord Milton, who had since become Earl Fitzwilliam, was asked for his assistance, and the lord arranged for Clare to be committed to a public asylum closer to home, the Northampton General Lunatic Asylum. This is where John Clare spent the rest of his life.

JOHN CLARE

John Clare lived twenty-three more years after being committed to the second asylum. During this time he believed he was Lord Byron, a famous pugilist, and other figures of his imagination. He told the editor of a local newspaper who visited him in the 1850s,

> I'm John Clare now. I was Byron and Shakespeare formerly. At different times you know I'm different people—that is, the same person with different names.
>
> (G. J. De Wilde to J. W. Dalby, letter printed in the *Times Literary Supplement,* June 30, 1921)

Patty Clare never came to visit her husband in the asylum, but she had much to deal with at home. In 1843–1844, Clare's children Frederick and Anna Maria—his beloved first daughter—died of tuberculosis. His father died in 1846. In 1848 his son Johnny came to visit him, after which Clare wrote Patty: "Here I am in the Land of sodom where all the peoples brains are turned the wrong way—I was glad to see John yesterday and should like to have gone back with him for I am very weary of being here" (*Letters,* p. 657).

He continued to write reams of poetry, and William Knight, the house steward of the asylum, recognized their worth and began to collect them. Thanks to Knight's stewardship of his manuscripts, scholars have a copious record of Clare's writings during his Northampton years through 1859 (when Knight left the asylum).

As Clare's mind slowly shattered, he tried hard to hang onto a sense of self-identity (a term he coined in one of his asylum poems) in his writings. One of his most brilliant poems is "Lines: I Am," which Knight and another friend arranged to have published in the *Bedford Times* on January 1, 1848. The poem's opening stanza reads

I am—yet what I am none cares or knows;
  My friends forsake me like a memory lost:
I am the self-consumer of my woes—
  They rise and vanish in oblivion's host
Like shadows in love-frenzied stifled throes—
And yet I am, and live—like vapours tossed

Over the years, various people visited him, and he spent a great deal of his free time wandering in the woods and fields around Northampton or sitting in the porch of the church there to smoke his pipe and write poems. He would write poems on the spot for people willing to buy him a quid of tobacco or a pint of ale. His physical health remained robust, even as other members of his family were sick or dying at home. His most bookish child, Charles, died of tuberculosis in 1852; his daughter Sophie also predeceased him, in 1863. After a series of strokes, Clare himself died of apoplexy on May 20, 1864 (Patty Clare lived until 1871). Thanks to the intervention of a churchwarden in Helpston, Clare's remains were brought home for burial rather than being put in a pauper's grave in Northampton.

Ironically for such a prolific writer, Clare's grave was unmarked until 1867. In that year a stone was erected with inscriptions on both sides. One side says "Sacred to the Memory of John Clare The Northamptonshire Peasant Poet Born July 13 1793 Died May 20 1864." The other side says, "A poet is born not made."

CRITICAL ASSESSMENTS

In exchange for an annuity of ten pounds, Patty Clare sold her husband's literary remains to a publisher named Joseph Whitaker. Whitaker showed the manuscripts to a Berlin-born Jewish writer, Frederick Martin, who published the first biography in 1865. *The Life of John Clare* is lively and well written, though several people who had known Clare claimed it was embellished at the very least and in some places pure fiction. Since Martin paints John's ideal love of Mary Joyce as a central force in the poet's life, Patty Clare in particular hated the book.

In 1893—the centennial of Clare's birth—Whitaker sold the Peterborough Museum all of his Clare papers, and this is where the majority of them remain. Unfortunately, not until decades after his death did any critics bother to really look at them. That is why Leslie Stephens' entry on him in a Victorian edition of the *Dictionary of National Biography* says "his poetry does not rise to a really high level and...requires for its appreciation that the circumstances should be remembered" (1887 edition of the *DNB*).

The tide of opinion on Clare's poetry did not turn until one of the great symbolist poets and critics of the 1890s, Arthur Symons, decided to champion the peasant poet. Symons' *Poems by John Clare* published many of the asylum poems (poems that Leslie Stephen never saw) and many of the poems that Eliza Emmerson had cut from *The Rural Muse*. Symons' book, which came out in 1908, alerted modernist poets to this important forebear. The great English poets of World War I have Symons to thank for their discovery of Clare. One of these men, Edmund Blunden, carried the book with him to the Western Front. He survived the war and returned to immerse himself in the Clare manuscripts at the Peterborough Museum. The book that derived from this, *John Clare: Poems, Chiefly from Manuscript* (1920), revealed even more of the poet's unknown verses to the world.

After Blunden, the husband-and-wife scholars John and Anne Tibble devoted their lives to bringing Clare's manuscripts to the public. Between 1932 and 1951 they published a biography, new editions of the poems, the letters, and a selection of the prose. Most of the other champions of Clare through the 1960s were poets rather than academics. Perhaps because of that, Clare was praised among practicing writers but little taught in universities. Students learned about the other Romantic poets—Wordsworth, Coleridge, Keats, Shelley, Byron—but Clare, if he was mentioned at all, was relegated to the rank of "minor poet."

Famous poets continued to vibrate in sympathy to Clare's verses, however. Robert Graves wrote, "I know Clare. I know him well. We have often wept together" (*Clare: The Critical Heritage*, p. 415). John Ashbery, Theodore Roethke, and Patrick Kavanagh wrote poems in his honor, grateful for his inspiration.

Since the 1960s critics have focused on textual issues in his manuscripts (see "Clare's Editors...Then and Now," above), his madness (see Roy Porter's essay in *John Clare in Context*),

his politics (see E. P. Thompson, mentioned above, and various articles in the *John Clare Society Journal*), but especially on his relationship to nature. Two excellent books on this subject are John Barrell's *The Idea of Landscape and the Sense of Place 1730–1840: An Approach to the Poetry of John Clare* and Timothy Brownlow's *John Clare and Picturesque Landscape*.

Although scholars are reviving Clare for educated readers, it is the K–12 teachers who are bringing his work to the common reader. Schoolteachers have begun to use Clare's poems to teach their students about nature and the relationship of humans to the earth. For younger readers, Clare's blunt-spoken verses are often more accessible than those of other Romantic poets. His descriptions of nature are also far more accurate, since they are based on actual observation and experience. In the twenty-first century, when the environment seems more threatened and more fragile than ever, John Clare's poems seem especially relevant, and his reputation blossoms afresh on the literary landscape.

Selected Bibliography

WORKS OF JOHN CLARE

POETRY: ORIGINAL EDITIONS, PUBLISHED IN CLARE'S LIFETIME

Poems, Descriptive of Rural Life and Scenery. London: Taylor & Hessey, 1820.

The Village Minstrel, and Other Poems. 2 vols. London: Taylor & Hessey, 1821.

The Shepherd's Calendar; with Village Stories, and Other Poems. London: for John Taylor by James Duncan, 1827.

The Rural Muse: Poems. London and Peterborough: Whitaker, 1835.

POETRY: MODERN EDITIONS
The "Oxford Clare":

The Early Poems of John Clare, 1804–1822. 2 vols. Edited by Eric Robinson and David Powell. Oxford: Clarendon Press, 1989. (These two volumes include many poems that predate Clare's first published book. This and the Oxford editions that follow offer a comprehensive selection of all of Clare's poems, adhering exactly to what the poet wrote before his editors touched his manuscripts—hence, if Clare misspelled or didn't punctuate, so too the Oxford Clare.)

Poems of the Middle Period, 1822–1837. 5 vols. Edited by Eric Robinson, David Powell, and P. M. S. Dawson, 5 vols. Oxford: Clarendon Press, 1996–2003. (Clare wrote approximately 3,500 poems, only about a quarter of which were published in his lifetime. The Oxford Clare editions remedy that deficit by bringing to light every draft of every poem as Clare wrote them.)

OTHER IMPORTANT EDITIONS:

Poems by John Clare. Edited by Arthur Symons. London: Henry Frowde, and Oxford: Horace Hart, 1908. (Symons included previously unpublished poems from Clare's asylum years and many unpublished poems that Eliza Emmerson had cut from *The Rural Muse.* Further, Symons' introduction put Clare in context: his early poems were truly the work of a poet who had a lived sense of village life, and his later poems were brilliant evocations of memory and loss. Symons' assessment of the asylum verse claimed it was "of a rarer and finer quality than any of the verse written while he was at liberty and at home.")

John Clare: Poems, Chiefly from Manuscript. Edited by Edmund Blunden and Alan Porter. London: Cobden-Sanderson, 1920. (Blunden, the Great War poet who survived the Western Front, returned home and set to work deciphering the vast collection of Clare manuscripts in the Peterborough Museum. His collaborator, Porter, was the literary editor of the *Spectator.* They brought to public consciousness many previously unpublished poems, and Blunden wrote an in-depth biographical introduction of Clare based on the poet's autobiographical fragment "Sketches in the Life of John Clare, Written by Himself," which Blunden obtained from Frederick Martin's daughter.)

Both of the above editions, as well as those that followed by John and Anne Tibble, are examined, with selections of their introductions reprinted in:

Clare: The Critical Heritage. Edited by Mark Storey. London and Boston: Routledge & Kegan Paul, 1973.

John Clare: Selected Poetry. Edited by Geoffrey Summerfield. London and New York: Penguin, 1990.

"I Am": The Selected Poetry of John Clare. Edited by Jonathan Bate. New York: Farrar, Straus, & Giroux, 2003. (This is an excellent selection of Clare poetry that also includes a chronology of the poet's life and Clare's prose account of his "Journey from Essex"—when he walked home from Allen's asylum to his cottage in Northborough. Bate's edition is particularly accessible for student readers because he edits the poems for punctuation and spelling but does not alter the poet's distinctive voice or

dialect. Instead he includes a glossary that defines the local vocabulary that Clare used in his poems.)

PROSE AND LETTERS

Sketches in the Life of John Clare, Written by Himself. Edited by Edmund Blunden. London: Cobden-Sanderson, 1931.

The Prose of John Clare. Edited by J.w. and Anne Tibble. London: Routledge & Kegan Paul, 1951. (This volume includes Clare's "Sketches" and his larger autobiographical fragment. It also includes a selection of Clare's observations on natural history.)

The Natural History Prose Writings of John Clare. Edited by Margaret Grainger. Oxford: Clarendon Press, 1983.

The Letters of John Clare. Edited by Mark Storey. Oxford: Clarendon Press, 1985.

John Clare by Himself. Edited by Eric Robinson and David Powell. Manchester: Carcanet, 1996. (Supersedes Robinson's 1983 Oxford edition of *John Clare's Autobiographical Writings.*)

BIBLIOGRAPHIES

Estermann, Barbara H. *John Clare: An Annotated Primary and Secondary Bibliography.* New York: Garland, 1985.

Goodridge, John. "A Chronological Survey of Clare Criticism, 1970–2000." In *John Clare: New Approaches.* Edited by John Goodridge and Simon Kovesi. Helpston, U.K.: John Clare Society, 2000.

BIOGRAPHIES

Bate, Jonathan. *John Clare: A Biography.* New York: Farrar, Straus, & Giroux, 2003.

Martin, Frederick. *The Life of John Clare.* 1865. Reprint, edited with notes by Eric Robinson and Geoffrey Summerfield, London: Cass, 1964.

Sales, Roger. *John Clare: A Literary Life.* London: Macmillan, 2002. (This biography includes a discussion of Regency England's literary culture and boxing mania.)

Tibble, J. W. and Anne. *John Clare: A Life.* 1932. New ed., London: Michael Joseph, 1972.

CRITICAL STUDIES

Baker, Anne Elizabeth. *Glossary of Northamptonshire Words and Phrases.* 1854. 2 vols. Thetford, U.K.: Lark, 1995.

Barrell, John. *The Idea of Landscape and the Sense of Place 1730–1840: An Approach to the Poetry of John Clare.* Cambridge, U.K., and New York: Cambridge University Press, 1972.

Blackmore, Evan. "John Clare's Psychiatric Disorder and Its Influence on His Poetry." *Victorian Poetry* 24:209–228 (1986).

JOHN CLARE

Brownlow, Timothy. *John Clare and Picturesque Landscape.* Oxford: Clarendon Press, 1983.

Chilcott, Tim. *A Publisher and His Circle: The Life and Work of John Taylor, Keats's Publisher.* London and Boston: Routledge, 1972.

———. *"A Real World & Doubting Mind": A Critical Study of the Poetry of John Clare.* Pickering, U.K.: Hull University Press, 1985.

Clare, Johanne. *John Clare and the Bounds of Circumstance.* Kingston, Ont., and Montreal, Canada: McGill-Queens University Press, 1987.

Dawson, P. M. S., et al., eds. *John Clare, a Champion for the Poor: Political Verse and Prose.* Manchester: Carcanet, 2000.

Deacon, George. *John Clare and the Folk Tradition.* London: Sinclair Browne, 1983.

Haughton, Hugh, et al., eds. *John Clare in Context.* Cambridge, U.K., and New York: Cambridge University Press, 1994.

John Clare Society Journal. Annually since 1982.

Leader, Zachary. *Revision and Romantic Authorship.* Oxford and New York: Clarendon Press, 1996.

Nettle, Daniel. *Strong Imagination: Madness, Creativity, and Human Nature.* Oxford and New York: Oxford University Press, 2001.

Stillinger, Jack. *Multiple Authorship and the Myth of Solitary Genius.* Oxford and New York: Oxford University Press, 1991.

Storey, Mark. *The Poetry of John Clare: A Critical Introduction.* London: Macmillan, 1974.

Thompson, E. P. *Customs in Common.* London: Penguin, 1993.

Todd, Janet. *In Adam's Garden: A Study of John Clare's Pre-Asylum Poetry.* Gainesville: University of Florida Press, 1973.

ROBERT CRAWFORD

(1959–)

J. C. Bittenbender

ROBERT CRAWFORD MADE a dramatic entrance onto the British poetic scene in 1990 with the publication of three separate volumes of poetry. Although his work had found publication in periodicals prior to that year, including in *New Chatto Poets 2* (1989) where he was featured as one of six up-and-coming poets, his output in 1990 signified the wide range of poetic interests that have concerned him ever since. In *Sharawaggi: Poems in Scots (1990),* he and fellow poet W. N. Herbert explored the possibilities of writing poems in Scots and infusing them with a postmodern consciousness. In *A Scottish Assembly (1990),* written primarily in English, Crawford examined literary and historical themes of concern to Scotland and seemed to announce that a major theme in his work was to be the state of Scotland and Scottish culture in particular. Finally, in *Other Tongues: Young Scottish Poets in English, Scots, and Gaelic,* Crawford first exercised his considerable talent as an anthologist concerned with the preservation and celebration of the diversity of languages available to Scottish writers. Later volumes of his own poetry include *Talkies* (1992), *Masculinity* (1996), *Spirit Machines* (1999), and *The Tip of My Tongue* (2003). He has been anthologized in such works as the *Penguin Modern Poets 9* (1996) and *Dream State: The New Scottish Poets* (1994). He has come to represent one of the growing number of poetic voices who acknowledge and celebrate the many languages, literatures, and histories that comprise an open Scottish identity.

LIFE

Crawford was born in Bellshill, close to Glasgow, and he spent much of his youth in and around that city. He studied English at the University of Glasgow and later at Balliol College, Oxford, where he worked with the scholar and critic Richard Ellmann, who guided him through a dissertation on T. S. Eliot that would later find publication as *The Savage and the City in the Work of T. S. Eliot* (1987). After earning his Ph.D. from Oxford, Crawford returned to Scotland and lectured at the University of Glasgow before moving on to the University of St. Andrews, where he became in 1996 Professor of Modern Scottish literature and later chair of the School of English. In addition to publishing six volumes of his own verse, he has written or edited a number of books of criticism, served as cofounder and editor of the international poetry magazine *Verse,* and served as associate director of the St. Andrews Scottish Studies Institute (in this position he served as an editor of *Scotlands,* an interdisciplinary journal of Scottish studies). He has also won a number of prestigious literary awards including the Eric Gregory Award and two Scottish Arts Council Book Awards, and in 1994 he was selected as one of the Poetry Society's New Generation Poets. In addition to his many poetic, critical, and academic duties he also serves as a coeditor of *Scottish Studies Review,* a publication of the Association for Scottish Literary Studies.

SHARAWAGGI *AND POETRY IN SCOTS*

In 1990 Crawford and W. N. Herbert published *Sharawaggi,* a collection of poems in Scots that, as Jeffrey Skoblow (1998) has indicated, is unique in its treatment of Scots as a highly charged poetic language for the postmodern moment. (The first part of the book, *Sterts and Stobies,* was published as a pamphlet in 1985.)

The playful nature of the book is suggested on its back cover:

SHARAWAGGI—"Of unknown origin; Chinese scholars agree that it cannot belong to that language" (OED). The word denotes the beauty and studied irregularity in landscape or architecture—or poetry.

"For as to the hanging gardens of Babylon, the Paradise of Cyrus, and the Sharawaggi's of China, I have little or no Idea's of 'em"—Alexander Pope
"sharawaggi: the art of making urban landscape"—*Architectural Review*

This comic combination of definitions that may or may not have validity is reminiscent of the carnivalesque puffs and testimonials that grace the covers of many of Alasdair Gray's works and provide insight as to what the reader is about to encounter upon opening the book. The same effect is true with the Crawford-Herbert volume, in which the opening poems, by Crawford, contribute to the sense that the word "sharawaggi" may indeed be a modern Scots version of "irregular" poetic feng shui. In "Cock o' the North" and "Ghetto-Blastir," Crawford announces a demotic voice that makes use of all that Scottish culture, politics, and society have to offer. The subject of "Cock o' the North" appears as the stereotypical drunken Glaswegian football fan who has certain preconceived ideas of what it means to be Scottish, including a healthy dose of the old chip on the shoulder and a longing for the heroic days of the Scottish patriot William Wallace. It is a rambunctious poem that sets the tone for the rest of the volume. "Ghetto-Blastir" follows suit with its mixture of Scots with the sounds and subjects of Scotland in the late twentieth century. Later in the volume Crawford and Herbert suggest a form of cyber-Scots that makes use of the richness of the Scots language found in the *Scottish National Dictionary*. The poems include both traditional Scots words that have fallen into disuse and, in the best tradition of Hugh MacDiarmid, words that seem to have been coined by way of the many synthetic freedoms granted to the modern Scots poet. Indeed both Crawford and Herbert acknowledge their debt to MacDiarmid, though

they extend the range of his linguistic experimentation to include forays into the worlds of cyberspace, cinema, and other forms of popular culture. This volume is also unique in its willingness to bring together a variety of voices that are not fundamentally Scottish in nature. Translations of poems by Vietnamese writers into Scots are just some of the highlights in a volume that in turn pays rich tribute to a Scottish past, condemns current complacency with static political Scottish attitudes, and reflects on the rich interchanges that Scotland and the Scots language may have with a variety of other cultures and languages.

At the heart of *Sharawaggi* lies "The Flyting of Crawford and Herbert," in which the two poets re-create the famous "flyting," or witty poetic sparring match, of the late-medieval makars William Dunbar and Walter Kennedy. Here Crawford and Herbert resuscitate the ancient art of flyting in a unique fashion that, while reminiscent of poetry slams, maintains the integrity of the synthetic Scots with which the two do battle. In the opening stanza Crawford attacks Herbert in the following fashion:

Daft Herbert wi yir pigtail Scoats
A' vitriol agin Dundee,
Yir poetry's a crood o quotes
Ye jist tak in fur B & B

(p. 25)

The sparring is playful, and Herbert can give as good as he gets:

Caa me a precious pickthank wad yi,
Younkir in Scots o hoo mony months?
An think Eh'll bide easy an no scad yi
Whilst you gae sea-queasy owre
Whit?...

(p. 26)

("Pickthank" means "thief," "younkir" is "youth," and "scad" is "scald.")

The two trade good-natured satiric insults for six pages, and the sequence gains in momentum as the attacks become more vitriolic and the Scots more complex. In the final section, titled "Coup de Poing," the note translates the title as "the finishing stroke in Scottish ping pong, usually delivered with a neolithic hand-axe" (p. 30). Here Herbert seems to pull out all the stops when he says of Crawford, "yi Muir-in-MacDiarmid's socks" (p. 29), thereby suggesting a comical amalgamation of the two greatest modernist Scottish poets, who were often at odds with one another over the future of Scottish literature and the appropriate language in which it should be written. It is, however, an interesting designation for Crawford, as he does seem to inhabit a variety of worlds in his poetry that capture both the subtle English resonances of someone like Muir while also capitalizing on the richly linguistic and nationalistic offerings of MacDiarmid.

The remainder of *Sharawaggi* is divided between poems by Crawford and poems by Herbert. Crawford's highlight a number of themes that he will develop in his later work, such as the importance of history, Scottish identity, and the plurality of voices to be found not only in Scotland but throughout the world. Crawford's commitment to a polyphony of voices that can be tapped into at any moment is clearly represented in this early collection, as is his devotion to furthering the health of the Scots language.

In "Burns Ayont Auld Reekie/Burns Beyond Edinburgh," Crawford presents a monologue in which Robert Burns considers his (and Scotland's) current condition. The poem is printed in Scots on the left-hand page and translated into English on the right-hand page (as are many that follow by Crawford and Herbert). It is a tribute to Burns (to whom Crawford will pay tribute not only in his poetry but in a number of significant critical works as well) and an extended paean to the possibilities of a vibrant language wedded to the living landscape of Edinburgh and (by extension) Scotland. Here Burns is a vociferous time-traveler who is as much at home among the small towns of Ayr as along the "Mekong" and the "Mississippi," above which his verses soar like the "Concorde." Along the way Crawford takes aim at the misuses to which Burns has been put by the "Burns industry," such as the placing of his verses on tea towels and tea cozies, as opposed to the more legitimate power that lies in his language: "Either they caa ma

mou a midden-dub, / Oar a demanit thocht-bane, prettified / Fur printit towels" (Either they call my mouth a hole into which a dunghill's sap is collected, or a demeaned merrythought of a fowl, prettified for printed towels) (pp. 50–51). Burns muses on his legacy, on how he has been treated and mistreated by history and what he still has to offer:

Ah amnae cummin towards yi, Ah'm muivin awa
Doon thi lang perspective. Ah leave yous wi thi leid.
Ah'm stuck in Embro, tea-cosified, deid in Err—
But vivual acors thi hail gloab. Ah've sprang ma trap.
    Ma leid
's in thi spittle o thi livin an atween thi sheets o thi
    dictionars.
It's growin oan thi green screen an amang thi
    peeggirrin blasts,
Forthens an here. In Glesca an Embro, fae Dundee tae
    Rugglen, Oan thi Solway, in thi Boardirs,
  amang
too'ir bloacks an Japanese lairches,
Tongue it an dawt it, tak it an mak. Mak luive.
                 (pp. 52, 54)

(I am not coming towards you, I am moving away down the long perspective. I leave you with the language. I'm stuck in Edinburgh, turned into a tea-cosy, dead in Ayr—but alive across the whole globe. I've sprung my trap. My language is in the spittle of the living and between the sheets of the dictionaries. It's growing on the green screen and among the heavy stormshowers, far in the distance and here. In Glasgow and Edinburgh, from Dundee to Rutherglen, on the Solway, in the Borders, among tower blocks and Japanese larches, tongue it and fondle it, take it and create. Make love.)
                 (pp. 53, 55)

In "Scots Gamelan," Crawford presents a beautiful fusion of languages in which the speaker's tongue seems to merge with other voices to produce "the sky's language." Crawford plays with the image of the Indonesian gamelon (orchestra) as a variety of voices and instruments respond to the changing Scottish landscapes they survey. What is interesting about this poem is that the English translation of the Scots that appears on the right-hand page becomes mixed with Scots, while the Scots on the left becomes mixed with English. This technique reinforces Crawford's intention of producing a rich blend of languages that yet have not lost their individual identities. It is not a confusion of languages that is being communicated but rather a mutually enriching mixture. A number of words used in the poem, including gamelan and "tjak" ("incessantly repeated cry accompanying the chanting of the Balinese Ramayana epic in which the gamelan is also used," p. 69) indicate that Crawford is in many ways calling for the fusion of Scots with other world languages. "Fur thi Muse o'Synthesis" echoes this interest as Crawford celebrates the possibility of a Scots unleashed, "wildcat dotmatrixed forever from Jamieson's *Dictionary of the Scottish Language* like a delicate orchard or the epitaxy layering crystals with a perfect glitter of molecular beam" (p. 71). Crawford writes a self-conscious poetry that taps into the force of a living language and shows how it will only thrive through constant interplay with other languages. He wants Scots to reclaim its lost vitality through dialogic relationships with voices that are many and varied, from those of Scotland's past to those of other cultures and modes of inquiry. This internationalizing of Scots is a recurrent theme in Crawford's work and recalls to the reader MacDiarmid's crusades to place Scots in dialogue with languages of other cultures and disciplines. Crawford is a true inheritor of this cause, and poems throughout *Sharawaggi* and *A Scottish Assembly* in particular mirror this concern.

As might be seen already, Crawford's poetry can be considered political in a thematic as well as linguistic sense, with subjects that range from meditations on the significance of Scots as a fertile language to important Scottish contributors to world culture. In "The Unbuilders" he highlights those individuals from Scotland's past who have contributed to the history of world communication. These individuals are chosen for their particular ability to transcend the boundaries that language and nationality frequently erect to keep others out:

Hilldykes pluff. Drystanes ur lipper, shued aff
Lik Romans fae thi Antonine, stanes an peats an
                                                    sheuchs

Fit fur jist kludges, yiss anely tae raise
Yon Scoats unbiggars o waas, wir Calgacusses
O thi imaginashun. Nutting tynes I thi leid's sleep
                                                    scrieve
Yir nemms, wir world: Alexander Graham
Bell, John Logie Baird, Thomson Lord Kelvin,
An Hugh MacDiarmid. Eftir yous
Thi warld wiz raxed. Baurheid went tae Kuala Lumpur
Wi'oot ae loss. Thru transatlantic raips
Purall-leid gairfushed wi licht, ram-stam and unguten-
                                                    berged-
Thi wey yi speik ut.

                                                    (p. 72)

(Walls made of turf burn with quick whiffs of smoke. Unmortared stone walls are the fat, leprous foam on waves, scared away like Romans from the Antonine Wall, stones and peats and ditches fit only for toilers, used only to excite those Scottish unbuilders of walls, our Calgacusses of the imagination. Forked instruments for pulling nuts from trees write your names in the sleep of the language: Alexander Graham Bell, John Logie Baird, Thomson Lord Kelvin, and Hugh MacDiarmid. After you the world was stretched and brought nearer. Barrhead went to Kuala Lumpur without any loss. Through transatlantic cables the language of the common people porpoised with light, headlong and freed from the regimentation of print—the way you speak it.)

                                                    (p. 73)

Here Crawford joins those famous Scots inventors of modern communication Bell and Baird with the great communicator of Scots as a living language, MacDiarmid. Bell and Baird were not selective in what was to be communicated to the world through their discoveries, and in essence they helped to de-cement culture by opening avenues of dialogue that were not subject to the censoring hand of print. Crawford celebrates these breakers of barriers who set the stage for a greater understanding of how language is spoken before it is codified, edited, and manipulated into particularly and often politically sanctioned modes of discourse.

Crawford's contributions to *Sharawaggi* also offer some fine examples of the potential for Scots to embrace and enrich other literatures through translation. In his offering of four poems translated from the Vietnamese ("Nicht Flittin," "Winter-Saturday," "Spring," and "Mum") Crawford follows in the footsteps of other modern Scottish poet-translators, such as Edwin Morgan (see especially Morgan's translations of the Russian of Vladimir Mayakovsky into Scots in *Wi thi Haill Voice*), who attempt to bring literatures from other parts of the world into energizing contact with Scottish voices.

IDENTITY AND *A SCOTTISH ASSEMBLY*

Although Crawford's status as an up-and-coming Scottish poet had been announced in his contributions to *New Chatto Poets 2* and *Sharawaggi,* his unique contribution to contemporary Scottish poetry is made even more evident through his first full-length collection, *A Scottish Assembly* (1990), which was short-listed for MacVitie's Scottish Book of the Year in 1990. Though there are no poems in Scots in this collection, Crawford continues his interest in showcasing important Scottish figures from the past and retelling their stories from the perspective of the present. He exhibits an extensive knowledge of the contributions of Scotland to the larger international community in the fields of politics, science, philosophy, education, and industry. In poems such as "Scotland in the 1890s," "John Logie Baird," "Man of Vision," "Sir David Brewster Invents the Kaleidoscope," and "The Great McEwen, Scottish Hypnotist," Crawford highlights Scottish history and celebrates a multitude of famous and infamous individuals from all walks of life. In "Scotland in the 1890s" the anthropologist James George Frazer, the scholar Andrew Lang, the industrialist Andrew Carnegie, the lexicographer James Murray, and the author J. M. Barrie rub shoulders and carry on dialogic relationships. "'I came across these facts which, mixed with others...'" reads Crawford's opening line, and it is the rich mixture of all types of knowledge and history that give not only this poem but others in the collection a pluralistic charge that seems to suggest at a larger level Crawford's intentional identifying of Scotland as a geographical and cultural space that is variform and composed of many interacting identities. *A*

Scottish Assembly is primarily a collection of pieces that interrogate the concept of identity, whether on a personal or national level. An early poem in the collection titled "Robert Crawford" examines the reactions of the poet to hearing that his name has become the title of an opera. The speaker meditates on how identity is framed by the names we assign to people and places:

> Normality's strange—
> Always more of it gets delivered in cartons
>
> With the names washed off. Maybe next century
> We'll have extra labels: a noun for the sensation
>
> Of hearing Philip Glass while being driven in a Citroen
> Or of sitting down to eat a bag of chips
> With two historians of mesmerism near Inverkeithing.
> (p. 13)

Toward the end of the poem the speaker reflects on the freedoms that are offered by an escape from naming and the burdens that go along with fixed identity: "I'm grateful to slip out quietly / By the cellar door and leave myself sometimes / Being private in a deckchair in the garden" (p. 13). In "The Railway Library," Crawford turns his attention to shifting literary identities that are created by the environments in which we read texts. Here the speaker relates the experience of reading classic works of British literature on the train and thus identifying those works in part with the towns, villages, and viaducts that pass outside the windows of the railway carriages: "Rochester met Jane Eyre / At Falkirk High.... A suffragette / Sits in her first-class carriage in the cells of Monte-Cristo" (p. 20). Time and space are condensed by such interplay between what seems to be the interior text and the exterior world. The classic works of the poem are given greater dimension by their translatability into other contexts and settings. Crawford's fascination with the concept of identity can be clearly seen not only in his poetry but also in his criticism, in which he often invokes a Bakhtinian view of the self as one composed of many voices that are in constant dialogue with one another. Critical works such as his *Devolving English Literature* (1992) and *Identifying Poets:*

Self and Territory in Twentieth-Century Poetry (1993) seem to more directly address this abiding interest that first made itself known in Crawford's poetry and in his first critical book, *The Savage and the City in the Work of T. S. Eliot,* in which Eliot's literary self is read as a fluid construction that partakes of a variety of influences from anthropology, popular culture, and other sources.

At the very heart of *A Scottish Assembly* is a pair of poems printed back to back, both titled "Scotland," that speak to the vibrant, fluctuating identity of the country. Here Crawford's love for the land is poignantly expressed in what appear to be two very different love poems addressed to the "you" of Scotland. The first "Scotland" captures the natural beauty of the landscape and presents it as almost a type of impressionistic painting:

Glebe of water, country of thighs and watermelons
In seeded red slices, bitten by a firthline edged
With colonies of skypointing gannets,
You run like fresh paint under August rain.

(p. 41)

The speaker of the poem seems to inhabit the entire country at once, presenting "erotic Carnoustie / Edinburgh in helio," "pastoral Ayrshires, your glens / Gridded with light" (p. 41). A summer rain shower causes the watercolor portrait of the country to run so that "Intimate grasses blur with August rain" (p. 41). Scotland's identity is thus formed by blurring colors taken from a number of different Scottish palettes. As there are many "pastoral Ayrshires," so too are there a multitude of Scotlands, a point made more forceful by the second "Scotland" poem, a postmodern tribute to the country in which the language is charged with the contemporary moment:

Semiconductor country, land crammed with intimate
    expanses,
Your cities are superlattices, heterojunctive
Graphed from the air, your cropmarked farmlands
Are epitaxies of tweed.

(p. 42)

Here Crawford identifies and joins the varied identities of Scotland so that not only is it a "semiconductor country" but also as always a "land crammed with intimate expanses." The intersections of the past and a pluralized present continue through the poem and are augmented by another fruitful tension that is produced by the revelation of a multitudinous world that exists within the "boundless, chip of a nation" (p. 42).

In an interview with the present writer Crawford indicated the feelings that inspired him to compose the two "Scotland" poems:

They're both love poems addressed to my country. I find it hard to "explain" them. Certainly in the one beginning "Semiconductor country" I want to convey that sense of great diversity within a small area that is vital to my sense of Scotland. At present, for instance, I'm sitting opposite a medieval castle beside the sea in the small, historic university town of St. Andrews. If I travel ten miles north I'm in a large, working-class, industrial-cum-post-industrial conurbation, Dundee. Beyond that are glens and mountains. Dundonians speak differently from the people here in St. Andrews, and from the people in Edinburgh an hour to the south. From Edinburgh a short flight would take me to an island where I might be the only person in a hotel bar who wasn't a Gaelic speaker. I love that intimate variety, and the way it's combined with a sense of hugeness in the landscape of what is after all a very small country. Scotland itself is protean, and I think that's a source of strength. Probably in both these poems in different ways I was trying to hint at the infinitely rich, protean quality of modern Scotland. There's more going on than just that, though; I wanted the language to point in many directions, political, scientific, lyrical.

(pp. 7–8)

One might argue that the vast majority of poems in *A Scottish Assembly* are love poems addressed to the "Micro-nation. So small you cannot be forgotten, / Bible inscribed on a ricegrain" (p. 42), though one might also make a case that Crawford's humor, first evident in *Sharawaggi,* is present in this volume as well. In "Alba Einstein" he imagines Albert Einstein as having Scottish roots and considers how that might affect the Scottish tourist industry: "Scotland rose to its feet / At Albert Suppers where The Toast to the General Theory / Was given by footballers, panto-dames, or restaurateurs" (p. 53). *A Scottish Assembly* is a wonderfully inclusive volume that articulates a number of Crawford's abiding concerns.

THE *"VOICES"* OF TALKIES

Crawford's next collection, *Talkies,* was published in 1992 and helped to secure Crawford's designation as a New Generation Poet. This volume begins with a quotation from the Russian literary theorist and philosopher Mikhail Bakhtin: "one's own language is never a single language." By invoking Bakhtin, Crawford reveals an increasing interest in recording the polyphony that he finds in the world, particularly in Scotland. The collection continues to focus on some of the themes of *A Scottish Assembly,* particularly Crawford's interest in arresting figures from the past and giving the reader a brief moment of insight into their lives. He is adept at singling out a defining moment in the lives of his poetic characters and enlarging it to reveal the profoundly complex elements that constitute identity. The predominating focus of the collection is a concern for voices and how particular Scottish voices modulate over time and space.

The title poem, "Talkies," concerns the transition from the silent screen to the talking motion picture and attempts to imagine how that must have affected the actors: "Already there is talk in Hollywood / About something new. Even the stars will need tests" (p. 13). This seemingly misplaced poem about the profound effects of new technology on the entertainment industry in California serves to amplify a larger condition of communication. The silent screen stars of the poem will, in essence, ironically be rendered silent by the advent of talking motion pictures. The message of this cautionary poem is reflected as well in the poem "Chevalier," which opens the collection. Here the voice seems initially to be that of Bonnie Prince Charlie, who is fleeing the British forces after his defeat at Culloden in 1746. The voice takes refuge in caves guarded by "Silent / Despised men" (p. 11). It soon transforms into a symbol of Scottish identity, the Scots language and perhaps even Gaelic. The voice

struggles to survive in a world that seems intent on silencing it:

The voice is nearly inaudible on a tiny island. Sun beats
      down on its vowels.
People are burned out for the voice, which sheds

Enough clothes for many generations.
          (p. 11)

The tiny island becomes the enclave of the Hebridean culture that signifies the last holdout of the Gaelic language upon which the "sun" of British linguistic imperialism appears to beat. The historically defining moment of the Clearances and the removal of the Scottish people from their land is implicated in the line "People are burned out for the voice." The voice must find a new place to hide, so as the poem progresses it emigrates to other parts of the world, where it becomes tainted by the inflections of frustration, persecution, and a sense of obstinate pride:

    The voice escapes
To Argentina and Cape Breton Island, gets drunk,
Mouthing obscenities, toasting itself
Over and over. Silence doesn't chasten it.
         (p. 11)

Finally the voice "Loses consciousness, won't be betrayed" (p. 11), thus suggesting that the only chance of survival for this voice is through a collective loss of consciousness that may preserve at least the essence of the language for future use. The possibilities of avoiding such a situation are explored in poems that follow upon this one in *Talkies.* "Simultaneous Translation" considers the postmodern condition of voice as one that is richly pluralistic. "Gaels in Glasgow / Bangladeshis in Bradford" (p. 14) signify a linguistic richness that rubs off on everyone in Britain and makes them speakers of a vast diversity of languages. "This is where we all live now, / Wearing something like a Sony Walkman, / Hearing another voice every time we speak" (p. 14). To identify oneself by voice is not as certain as it might once have been. Now one's own voice is subject to change whenever the mouth is opened and the influence of different languages (be they national or technological or otherwise in character) makes everyone's language richly different and yet dialogically viable in a larger conversation. The necessity of crossing barriers of language and identity are implied in the closing lines of the poem: "Already her finger is starting to creep / Closer to the binding of a parallel text, / Between the lines, then crossing over" (p. 14).

In addition to poems that showcase voice, *Talkies* presents more examples of Crawford reimagining the past or using past identities in a unique way as a form of imaginative parodying that opens up individual identities and histories that might otherwise suffer from being too rigid. In the long poem "Customs" he takes Sir James Frazer and Lady Frazer as his subjects, and in "Mary Shelley on Broughty Ferry Beach" he constructs an image of the author of *Frankenstein* during her time in Dundee, walking along a beach strewn with the remains of a whale. In "Napier's Bones" he provides a succinct yet idiosyncratic biography of the sixteenth-century Scottish poet and mathematician John Napier.

GENDER IDENTITY AND MASCULINITY

In *Masculinity* (1996), Crawford turns to a consideration of identity from both a gender perspective and a personal vantage point. The volume is divided into four sections: "Masculinity," "Growing," "Scotch Broth," and "Many Happy Returns." The first, "Masculinity," considers male identity and the expectations of male identity encountered in society and in media images. The poem "Chaps" is aimed at capturing particular attitudes toward gender that have been created by British imperialism:

With his Bible, his Burns, his brose and his baps
Colonel John Buchan is one of the chaps,
With his mother, his mowser, his mauser, his maps,
Winston S. Churchill is one of the chaps.

(p. 2)

The refrain in the poem is constructed to convey the sound of soldiers marching on parade,

and the almost plodding repetition of the word "Chaps" lends a particularly regimented sense to the gender stereotypes being displayed:

Chaps chaps chaps chaps
Chaps chaps chaps chaps

(p. 2)

At the beginning of the volume Crawford offers the reader a note on how to read these lines: "I imagine the refrain in the poem 'Chaps' first of all yelled in an upper-class English voice—'CHEPS!'—then spoken in a Scottish voice in the middle of the poem, then falling to a whisper at the end." This movement from the strongly voiced expectations of a Victorian imperialistic ideal to that of a gradually silenced Scottish male voice that is "filling the gaps / In the Empire's red line that can never collapse" signifies the problematic nature of what is expected of Scottish males and of Scotland itself. Crawford is a great debunker of mythologies that deny the authentic voices of a people, and in this poem the myth of British/English maleness is exposed and deconstructed. While other poems in this opening section are not so overtly political, they yet bear the impression of a demythologizing process. The second section, "Growing," provides considered reflections on the poet's own childhood and his special identity as a "son" of a father. What is most interesting about these poems is how Crawford leads the reader back with him in time, then brings the contemporary moment into focus by the end of the poems. In "Us," Crawford gives the reader a glimpse into his early home life in which "Dad polished shoes, boiled kettles for hot-water bottles, / And mother made pancakes, casseroles, lentil soup / On her New World cooker..." (p. 19). At a certain point in the poem the reader is brought forward to the contemporary moment when that childhood house is being prepared for sale:

Now someone will bid for, then clear these rooms,
Stripping them of us. We were that floral wallpaper,

That stuck serving-hatch, radiograms polished and
  broken,

Dogeared carpet-tiles that understood us,

Our locked bureau, crammed with ourselves.

(p. 19)

Place and personal identity become inextricably interwoven in this poem, and this reflects Crawford's interest in showcasing the ways in which the past leaves imprints that only seem ineradicable. There is a danger of losing a sense of self through a too-thorough obliteration of the past. This destruction might be the result of the death of any number of cultural indicators, such as language, or the disruption of particular interpretations of community, one of those being represented by the displacing of a family identity. This theme is echoed in "The Move," where Crawford recounts the experience of moving his father and mother to a new house, one that has been previously occupied by the poet: "Gradually they unbox their other life / Into this house, the one Dad, speaking to me, / Calls 'your house,' although we've moved" (p. 27). These lines are fraught with questions of identity and possession that are related to the spaces we inhabit and how they become recognizable to us as part of who we are.

In "Scotch Broth," the third section of *Masculinity*, Crawford returns to a poetry that looks at Scotland and the images it projects to the larger world. In the poem "Scotch Broth" he imagines Scotland as a rich stew that has ingredients that are both nourishing and self-destructive. The soup is "so thick you could shake its hand / And stroll with it before dinner" (p. 31). He describes the "face rising to its surface" as "the pustular, eat-me face of a crofter, / Turnipocephalic, white-haired" (p. 31). The broth is that "other scotch made with mutton / That intoxicates only / With peas and potatoes, chewy uists of meat" (p. 31). An interesting contrast is made between the various ingredients in the broth and the worn and decrepit face that partakes of the food. Crawford offers Scotland as a wholesome meal that is open to all but identifies the one diner who feeds off of the broth as being less than healthy in appearance. This suggests perhaps a difference between the ways in which "outsiders" view

Scotland and the views that Scottish people have of themselves. In "Recall" and "The Elgin Marbles," Crawford writes of a new Scotland that will be constantly engaged in the process of rediscovering itself. "Recall" is a poem against complacency, where the potential recall of the Scottish parliament takes the form of the mundane activities that have distracted the Scottish people from a healthy vision of themselves. They now need to "relearn and slowly unlearn themselves" (p. 33) as they reinterpret their identity in a more positive and proactive manner. In "The Elgin Marbles," Crawford deconstructs the monolithic structure of the Greek friezes taken by Lord Elgin from Athens and installed in the British Museum. For Crawford the true Elgin Marbles represent images from the countryside surrounding Elgin in the northeast of Scotland. There is no mention of the Greek marbles; instead the museum pieces are slices of Scottish life that are preserved in the landscape and the people. In "The Gaelic Caribbean" he presents a fine example of cultures intersecting and mutually illuminating one another. Here the poet imagines a boat from the Caribbean nosing into the island of Barra, "Volleyed by the Atlantic, anachronistic" (p. 9). As the poem progresses the Caribbean cultures on the boat become mixed with the voices and images of the Hebrides. There is a sense of shared identity that is realized in the language of loss and silence with which the two cultures are all too familiar:

All night a woman cries

Something island, a Creole
Clearing word that dismisses the silence

Then whistles it back like a shepherd calling
His lost black dog from the seaweed.

(p. 39)

In the final section of *Masculinity*, "Many Happy Returns," Crawford returns to poems of a very personal nature. Here images of childbirth proliferate as the poet anticipates the birth of his son and shares reflections on the early days of his own fatherhood. In "Loganair" the speaker, aboard a small airplane, simultaneously reads the scan of his unborn child and the landscape of Fife, Scotland, that spreads out beneath him. The language of technology intersecting with personal perspective gives the reader of this poem a feel for the inevitably constant process of change that infuses all of human experience.

Masculinity also includes a few examples of poems written in Scots, something that Crawford had moved away from beginning with *A Scottish Assembly.* Here poems such as "Heepocondry," "Whisht," and "Babby" draw a more domestic voice into the collection, reflecting the poet's return to a language of the home indicative of his new status as father. In "Whisht" and "Babby" the speaker's Scots seems to stand for a language of intimacy that brings him closer to the process of birth and to rich prelingual possibilities of communication. In the concluding poem of the volume, "The Judge," Crawford's six-month-old son sits "On the High Chairage of Scotland" (p. 69) while his parents wait for a "sentence" to be handed down. The speaker captures a sense of anticipation as the parents of the poem wait for the baby's first words that "Will be reported wise, long-considered, / Irreproachably just" (p. 69). The possible harm of an articulation that might close off possibility is Crawford's larger message in *Masculinity.* He is concerned with tensions that exist between potential identities, be they gendered or otherwise, and those that inevitably become fixed by language in the process of interpretation.

SELF AND TECHNOLOGY IN SPIRIT MACHINES

Crawford's fourth collection of poetry, *Spirit Machines* (1999) continues his interest in bringing together a variety of experiences from his life, work, and the condition of Scotland. Very personal poems about love, illness, loss, and a growing sense of the impact of technology on Scottish life and culture jostle against one another in this volume.

In "Knowledge," Crawford imagines the figure of James Frederick Ferrier (1808–1864), chair of moral philosophy at the University of St. Andrews. This is in keeping with Crawford's scholarly interest in the history of education in Scotland and particularly how it informed not only the Scottish Enlightenment but also played a significant role in the development of the study of English literature in a university setting (see particularly his *Launch-Site for English Studies* and *The Scottish Invention of English Literature*). In "Columban" the poet brings together modern technology with images of a Celtic, pre-Christian Scotland that is on the verge of conversion by Columba and his followers at Iona:

Dawn's fractured bone
Windchills your channels,

Small, remote radio stations
Broadcasting Christ to the waves.

(p. 14)

Modern forms of communication are juxtaposed with those more ancient forms of translation. In the second section of the poem Crawford wonderfully transcends time as he describes a nuclear sub having a "Viking blush" as it "passes down the islands" (p. 14). The sub is a new type of threat, yet it is also one that brings another dimension to what it means to be Scottish. Scottish identity is composed of a host of "invaders" that include not only Columba and Vikings but contemporary intrusions by weapons of mass destruction that perhaps "belong" to other political identities. The nuclear sub seems entirely out of place, though, as it embarrasses "Harris, North Uist, Benbecula, / Humiliating their stones" (p. 14). The final lines of the poem offer the hope of reclaiming hope, a condition the poem locates in what seems to be the monastic community of Iona and its

...shepherd's crook of psalms,

Community's tough-minded holy grit
Round which an anchor transformed to pearl

Shines across so-called Dark Ages
Its sol-fa brecbennach of calm.

(p. 14)

The nuclear sub seems to suggest some form of ultimate destruction, whereas the conversionary efforts of Columba worked more intentionally with the building blocks of community and the promise of shared identity. Nevertheless, as

Crawford continually points out in his technologically aware poems, the ever-changing landscapes of modernity require adjustment to changing scientific identities that may include the nuclear as well as the cybernetic.

In "A Life-Exam," the speaker compiles a list of exam questions that, according to information on the jacket flap, resulted from the poet's hospitalization. Here the speaker in both a humorous and contemplative tone considers essential questions that one might be tempted to pose to oneself in the face of possible death. The questions are unanswerable and yet also represent just a sampling of the endless possible questions that might be asked. Toward the end the poet reflects on the arbitrariness of questioning itself and how questions and answers always defeat themselves when one is searching for any type of certainty: "68. What is the question you'd most like to have asked / and never dared to answer?" (p. 29). For the poet one form of truth arises from the recognition that the questions themselves will always take precedence over the subjective and transitory nature of answers. The final "question" and what follows serves as an open-ended invitation either to embrace or to reject the very concept of examining one's life according to a prescribed course of interrogation:

71. From here on you may add optional questions, and need not supply answers.
(Success or failure in the above paper will inevitably lead to riches or poverty; define these in your own terms.)

(p. 29)

The section of *Spirit Machines* titled "Highland Poems" provides an interesting assortment of pieces that redefine "highland" in contemporary terms. True to form, Crawford here playfully constructs a poetry that reveals that even in the most remote and "provincial" parts of Scotland there exists a language and lifestyle of technocracy that demands recognition. He increasingly exhibits in his work savvy observations of the ways in which time redefines not only how we configure the past but also our understanding of the present and future. In "Zero," the seemingly comic answering system that directs callers to a variety of forms of technological destruction is, more seriously, indicative of the dehumanized voice that offers a variety of apocalyptic scenarios. The initial telephone voice is inviting yet threatening: "Thank you for calling Heatheryhaugh Nuclear Arsenal" (p. 34). The conjunction of "Heatheryhaugh" and its suggestive pastoral simplicity is complicated by its alignment with "Nuclear Arsenal." The suggestiveness of "Heatheryhaugh" is displaced by the designation of a nuclear arsenal, which leaves nothing to the imagination. Here is a clearly defined and limited threat to the more open mythologies and stereotypes implied by Scottish heather and the wide meadow expanses represented by the Scots word "haugh." Yet the voice of the nuclear calling service seems to offer options: "On your touch-tone phone jab one for details / Of bombs that kill crofters but leave brochs and megaliths standing" (p. 34). Crofters are every bit as much of the past as brochs and megaliths, but the slightly more modern connotations of the term seems to make the human element more expendable than those structures that might remain to remind the future of past civilizations. Behind the ironic tone of this response is the unspoken knowledge that brochs and megaliths speak themselves of vast populations that contribute to the larger definition not only of Scotland but of humanity. A wide range of possible Armageddons is offered by the prerecorded phone message, and many of the possible selections comically redefine Scottish stereotypes, such as the "Arsenal's renowned in-house distillery." The cautionary "Do not press zero," which concludes the poem, suggests the increasing power the caller has to alter history and the landscape of the world through technological actions that might be initiated in a moment.

In "Impossibility," a 360-line poem, Crawford memorializes the prolific Scottish Victorian novelist Margaret Oliphant. In the poem Oliphant is placed "Under the North Sea, a mile off Elie" (p. 43) where she composes her work and suffers the pains of authorship, childbirth, and the loss of her children. Along the way Crawford allows

Oliphant to comment upon feminism, history, nationalism, Scottish identity, and a host of other topics. Primary among the concerns of the poem are the sounds of the lost voices, the neglected and subjected. "Is the sea Scottish? What are the oceans' flags? / Britannia is ash on the surface of the waves" (p. 45). From her position beneath the waves where she "perfects" her pearl, "my impossible, nuanced grit / Nacring its pregnant shell, its given /giving / 360°" (p. 55). Oliphant is in the perfect location from which to pass judgment on the Victorian British society that attempted to assign her an identity. In observing the world above the waves she gives voice to contemporary concerns about the pigeonholing tendencies of history and the solidifying and partitioning of gendered identities. This poem is yet another reminder of Crawford's ability to revise our view of the past by inhabiting a voice that has been neglected or overlooked in Scottish history.

The final poems in the section titled "Spirit Machines" are dedicated to the poet's father, who died in 1997. Here the poems are tributes as well as considerations of how postmodern technologies interact with tradition. The poems consider language, time, and place as contributing to identity in a very fluid fashion that must include dialogue with the innovations of the computer age. Though Crawford is not alone among contemporary Scottish poets in his treatment of Scottish themes from a postmodern perspective (e.g., Edwin Morgan), he is perhaps unique in the consistent work of "upgrading" his poetic vision of Scotland to include the very latest technologies. In "Liglag" (the Scots Crawford translates as "Sensation of Another Language") he presents a poem in Scots that considers the untranslatable significance of Scottish place names and what they stand for. He imagines the fruitless attempt to "program" place names into a computer to derive some contemporary meaning: "Torry–eaten databases / Yield scotch mist o an auld leid, / Bodwords, bodes, thin scraelike faces" (p. 63); "Databases that are like exhausted land give up the small but wetting rain of an old language, traditional sayings expressing the fate of a family, portents, thin faces like shrivelled

shoes" (p. 64). Here "Nemms o places haud thir secrets, / Leochel-Cushnie, Lochnagar, / Luvely even untranslatit" (p. 63). In the final lines the poet summons the spirit of his father and recalls the significance that place names had for him and how the poet who wishes to translate them into a new cyber-language will always be doomed to failure:

Pour a dram an tak it neat,

Neat as Cattens, Tibberchindy,
Tomintoul or Aiberdeen,

Mapped an scanned, a karaoke
O gangrel souns I ken hae been

Mapread and spoken by my faither
I mony a cowpissed bield, a Bank

O Scotlan, or a Baltic dawn.
Skourdaboggie, auld an lank,

I key them intae this computer's
Empire by a taskit wa.

Peterculter, Maryculter.
Tine heart, tine a'. Tine heart, tine a'.

(pp. 63–64)

(Pour a dram and take it neat, neat as Cattens, Tibberchindy, Tomintoul or Aberdeen, mapped and scanned, a karaoke of wandering sounds I know have been map-read and spoken by my father in many a shelter pissed on by cows, a Bank of Scotland, or a Baltic dawn. Like the last surviving member of a family, old and spare, I key them into this computer's empire beside a wall fatigued with hard work. Peterculter, Maryculter. If you let sorrow overcome you, you lose everything. If you let sorrow overcome you, you lose everything.)

(p. 64)

The theme of the prevalence of a new type of translation is continued in the next poem, "Deincarnation," in which the poet imagines Scotland being "downloaded" onto a computer and vanishing with a flick of the keys: "Each daybread laptops siphon off the glens" (p. 65). One is led to suspect that this laptop is the "spirit machine" that is simultaneously ushering in a new era of potential progress and silently robbing language of its rich identifying capabilities:

Skulking on Celtic Twilight shores,

Each loch beyond is cleared of itself,
Gaelic names, flora, rainfall

So close, the tangible spirited away,
Cybered in a world of light.

(p. 65)

By making a verb of "cyber" Crawford suggests both an image of imprisonment and access, the double-edged danger/potential of computer technology. Here Scotland, the "chip of a nation" from *A Scottish Assembly,* is further expanded and reduced by its cybernetic systematizing of place names and specific Highland images that will now travel via light and fiber optics. There is a dispersion of identity that potentially allows for greater access and understanding but also may relegate that very identity to a new form of obscurity in the vast stretches of cyberspace. In "Alford," the concluding poem of the collection, Crawford takes the reader on a visit to the Internet, where he comes upon a site "designed as an old harled manse" (p. 66). The windows of this house offer views "on many Scotlands." This seems to be a pluralistically welcome sign until the site becomes haunted by visions the poet has of rooms in other houses, and ghosts parade across his computer screen as they confront him with images from the past that bear little resemblance to "virtual reality." In a strange sense of reverse technology the website seems to have downloaded the poet's memories of his father, and he finds avenues of travel much richer and variegated in that seemingly outdated form of experience than the brief and "designed" journeys offered by the Internet.

LANGUAGE AND GEOGRAPHY IN THE TIP OF MY TONGUE

Crawford's next volume of poetry, *The Tip of My Tongue* (2003), is a collection that is intensely personal and yet addresses many of the universal themes found elsewhere in his earlier work. In the title poem, the poet seems to address language as something that is only ever partially comprehensible and yet rich in interpretive potential:

Some days I find, then throw my voice
Deep down the larynx of Glen Esk,

Ears cocked to catch what rumbles back,
English-Scots-Gaelic hailstones.

Other days the tip of my tongue
Is further off than Ayers Rock.

(p. 3)

The image of the tongue suggests that which allows us to communicate only in a tentative and partial way. The tongue is both a physical appendage that helps us to taste the world and a symbol for language itself. For Crawford the tip of the tongue represents what first encounters experience as well as suggesting that there is much more that the tongue/language has to offer that may remain obscured for any number of reasons. The concluding lines have been glossed by other critics as implying a personal sexual image: "Or of waking at a lover's angle / With you on the tip of my tongue" (p. 3). But the "you" who makes contact with the speaker's tongue might well be Scotland, since Crawford's poem represents, as do a healthy number of his poems, a message of love to his country in all her varied splendor. The greater possibilities of the tongue are suggested too by the poet's use of the image in other poems in this collection and in previous works. In the poem "Oral," the final poem in *Talkies,* Crawford invokes the image in the following lines:

You taste salt spray and the day changes,
A boiled sweet, licked
From grey to opal to another colour
You're trying to name. Impatient as champagne

You can't but you want to—on the tip of your tongue,
        like forgetting
The next verse at yon Burns Supper, confident

It still belonged to you, and would tomorrow
When you'd slept with the taste of the toasts...

(p. 79)

The problematic nature of "ownership" of one's tongue is made evident here and in many of the poems that constitute *The Tip of My Tongue*. In "Planetist," the speaker praises the world with all parts of a body that refuses to commit itself exclusively to one sense or one understanding of geography: "From the tip of my tongue to the pit of my stomach, / From my eyeballs to the balls of my heels / With my lanky body I thee worship, / Scotland, New Zealand, all national dots..." (p. 18). The strange union of something as large and unwieldy as nationality with the reductive notion of "dots" emphasizes a tension that exists within a reader who might insist on interpreting the world in a way that identifies locations purely by attached labels and the limited identities that may be connected to those labels.

Other poems in *The Tip of My Tongue* expand upon the theme of learning a new language with which to experience the larger world. In "Conjugation," Crawford presents a grammar of love that aligns the love he feels for his wife with his love for Scotland. He opens the poem with a wonderful image of marriage as something that might be a repeatable event with the same person/country: "I love the bigamy of it, the fling / Of marriage on top of marriage" (p. 4). One might marry different versions of the same "self," providing for a pluralism of selves. In this way marriage becomes an ongoing process of shared identity construction. Crawford also links this, though, to a marriage with one's sense of cultural/national identity: "I'll marry you and Iona and has-been, / Shall-be firths of slipways and dwammy kyles" (p. 4). Here too is the essential tension of the poem (and of Crawford's work in general) between the past, present, and future. This type of reconstituted marriage refuses to dwell simply in the past or present; it makes way for constructions and marriages that define a fruitful future. There is a sense here that Crawford's view of Scotland is that it is a state of mind that should be in a constant state of reinven-

tion in order to provide for a healthy self-identity (whether that self is individual or collective).

In "Developing Worlds," Scotland again appears as a state of mind whose definition is formed through the interchange with other geographies. Here Crawford "makes use" of landscapes and images from other parts of the globe to create a greater understanding of what it is to be of this world rather than "of" (or from) a particular locality. Another poem on this theme is "From the Top," which displays a rich panorama of international geographies that speak to one another and define themselves in relation to one another: "Bings, sunlit mesas of the Scottish Lowlands" (p. 37). The culmination of the poem moves the reader from a position of defining the world with the language of the terrestrial to a sense of identification that is more universal. The perspective of the reader relies, at the end of the poem, on his or her definition of the landscape of outer space as it may be described using a specific Scottish geographical vocabulary: "And everything I see here from the top / Is overlooked by bens and glens of stars" (p. 37).

In keeping with Crawford's interest in Scottish nationalism and how it is often defined in narrowly prescribed terms, *The Tip of My Tongue* contains a few poems that acknowledge in some way the regaining of an independent Scottish parliament in May 1999. In "The Opening" the speaker examines the newly reconstituted parliament by the history of loss and emigration that followed the initial dissolving of the parliament with the Union of Parliament in 1707:

We have a crown no queen or king can wear.
Kings used to wear it, till they wore it out.

Drop it. Leave it behind on that long road
Forking to India, Canada, the Cape—

Past Guy Fawkes bonfires dowsed with Burns Suppers—
We took to reach this Scottish Parliament.

(p. 19)

Crawford traces the vestiges of stereotypes of Scotland and the Scottish people that littered the path leading to movements for independence. The "Guy Fawkes bonfires dowsed with Burns Suppers" suggest what was perhaps a fruitless mythologizing of Scotland that was in no way a practical or useful contributor to the gains made in forging a new political Scottish identity. Nostalgia as something that holds one back is a frequent theme in Crawford's work, and it can be detected as well in the poem "The Auld Enemy," where the focus is upon a self-destructive streak that often runs through Scots, the "the chip on the shoulder" that does more harm than good and seems replicated in almost every generation: "There they are, bonny fechters, rank on tattery rank, / Murderer-saints, missionaries, call-centre workers, Tattoos, / Bunneted tartans weaving together / Darkest hours, blazes of glory..." (p. 17). By the end of the poem Crawford identifies the strongest and most intrepid antagonist to a healthy Scottish identity as "the undefeated / Canny Auld Enemy, us" (p. 17). One cannot help but recall Crawford's earlier designation of Scotland as "chip of a nation," in which he seems to rework the chip on the shoulder into an image of possibility (a microchip) and rich plurality within the seemingly limited geography of a "small" country. In poems such as "Scots and Off-Scots Words," Crawford shows his love of the language of Scots and how it is able to capture nuances that are not available in other languages. After defining the words "Rumgunshoch," "Patagium," and "Jiggits," the poet goes on to identify the language with a plane that is in a constant state of motion:

> ...each Scots word's
> Frail undercarriage lowers, each sound glides down
>
> On damp runways of grass, in hidden neuks
> Where fiddle tunes are hummed in an age of rock,
>
> Words just flown in, turned around without refuelling,
> Which, quickly, have already got to go.
>
> (p. 42)

Another fine "language" poem is "Croy. Ee. Gaw. Lonker. Pit." It explores the rich variety of Scots and even pre-Scots words that must contend with a linguistic present that often attempts to deny them validity. The poem builds in intensity as the speaker repeats the words and reveals increasing levels of complexity and definition. By the end the repetition becomes talismanic, and the four words spoken together seem to represent a vast hoard of meaning that can only be excavated through close consideration of what they signify in different Scottish (and other) contexts. Crawford, while unique in his treatment of the richness of Scots and the connection of that language with place, seems also to recognize the integral importance of a semiotic awareness of naming that can be seen in other poets such as Seamus Heaney. In "Workman," a sign painter carefully reinscribes the names of Fife villages on signs that seem as "whited over" as the winter countryside: "The roadman lies, breathily concentrating / Like a sniper or a mine-disposal expert..." (p. 34). The painter must be cautious with his job, for the security of identity seems to rest with his task. The final lines of the poem emphasize the fragility and impermanence of identity, with the painter "Holding a fine brush primed with outdoor gloss / To last five years, slow letter by black letter / All afternoon repainting the names" (p. 34). It is as if the brush he holds must retrace the outlines of history and everything that has contributed to defining the places whose names he must make new.

Crawford is a poet who cannily captures the feelings of specific places as well as more generalized images of the Scottish landscape. In "Uist" he brings together the seeming remoteness of this island in the Outer Hebrides with the modern technology that has infiltrated even this seemingly isolated place. Here "e-mails graze sand-covered villages" and "cross-bred Hebridean sheep / Scratch themselves on a satellite dish" (p. 48). Again the impermanence of place and identity is implicated, and the alignment of ancient Uist with the world of e-mails and satellite dishes has shown how those "postmodern" objects now inhabit landscapes that were once exclusively dominated by ancient megaliths. Another poem that works with this theme is "Windfarming." Here the images of the "propeller-driven crosses" of modern wind farms do not necessarily supplant but rather supplement the images of earlier stone crosses and even the

"Great ghosts of standing stones" that have preceded them in the landscape. These new monuments are "sleek metals" that are "Totem-poled into acceleration's / Ultimate source and resource" (p. 38). Crawford nicely draws together the fundamental contexts that connect and separate those structures that served earlier civilizations in agriculture, astronomy, and time calculation and those that serve the "agribusiness of air" in contemporary times. The concluding image, while offering a tone of current hope, also suggests the inevitability of even newer and stranger-looking monoliths that may populate the landscapes of the future: "a choir of angels / Towering above us, beating their wings, / Piloting the earth on its way" (p. 38).

Other highlights from *The Tip of My Tongue* include four translations or, as Crawford terms them, "reconventions" of Latin poems by Arthur Johnston (1587–1641), an Aberdeenshire poet; a translation of "Blue Song"—"made by Mary, daughter of Red Alasdair, soon after she was left in Scarba," Crawford parenthetically explains, "after the Gaelic of Mary MacLeod (c. 1615–1705)"—and a memorial tribute to Iain Crichton Smith titled "Ceud Mile Failte" ("A Hundred Thousand Welcomes") in Scots Gaelic.

One of the most beautiful and personal of the poems in the volume is "Mons Meg," in which the poet celebrates the image of his young daughter, "wee ballerina, pas-de-bas-ing in front of Mons Meg," one of the huge cannons that dominate the esplanade of Edinburgh Castle, commanding the surrounding landscape. Here centuries of strife seem represented by the cannon, with its monumental gravity and solidified identity that draws the "alien-looking" tourist "cyborgs" with musuem-style headsets that no doubt tell a very particular story over and over again. The tourists seem enslaved by a vision of Scotland that is openly defied by the youthful, innocent freedom of the poet's daughter, who dances the dance of a future promise that is truly liberating.

CRITICAL WORKS

In a review that appears on the back of Crawford's *The Savage and the City in the Work of T.* *S. Eliot* (1987), the Scottish poet Douglas Dunn states: "a new Scottish poet-critic is announced, and his contribution could be immense." This identification of Crawford as a "poet-critic," while accurate, does not fully explain the particular way in which Crawford's criticism informs his poetry or how his poetic creativity feeds the intellectual inquiry that has produced a large number of groundbreaking studies on Scottish literature and its intersections with the larger world.

The Savage and the City in the Work of T. S. Eliot, which grew out of his Ph.D. dissertation prepared at Oxford under the tutelage of the eminent scholar-critic Richard Ellmann, was Crawford's first significant critical contribution. In this work Crawford evaluates Eliot's work as a product of the poet's fascination with the "barbaric"/primitive as well as the urban and sophisticated. Crawford takes into account Eliot's upbringing in the U.S. Midwest, his education at Harvard, and his mature life in the London metropolis. He outlines the influence of both high and popular culture in works such as "The Love Song of J. Alfred Prufrock," *The Waste Land,* and *Four Quartets.* Along the way he highlights Eliot's interest in the anthropological underpinnings of culture and how Eliot was able to combine this interest with what he took from writers as diverse as the Scottish poets John Davidson and James Thomson and French Symbolist poets such as Baudelaire, all of whom contribute to a modern vision of the city as a point of convergence for a multitude of refined and corrupt voices.

In 1992 Crawford published his highly acclaimed second book of criticism, *Devolving English Literature,* in which he investigates the centralizing aspects of British literary history that tend to unify all literatures produced in the British Isles under the label "English literature." Crawford sees this totalizing movement as a form of cultural imperialism that does not recognize the unique and independent regional and national voices that make up the larger literary identity of Britain. The primary claim in the book is the need to "devolve" a sense of "English" literary identity so that it better reflects the rich and varied nature of the multitude of cultural and literary identities that constitute and contribute to literature written in English. The book highlights the importance of considering the university subject of English literature as one that was first undertaken in Scotland, where it was intricately bound up with studies in anthropology, rhetoric and belles-lettres, and other fields of intellectual inquiry. This is a theme that Crawford treats at length in *The Scottish Invention of English Literature* (1998) and *Launch-Site for English Studies* (1997). *Devolving English Literature* has garnered many accolades among literary academics as well as cultural historians; a second edition appeared in 2000 with a new concluding chapter devoted to changes since 1992, notably the 1999 reestablishment of an independent Scottish parliament. This chapter points toward Crawford's view that the poet and poetic identity should be considered in conjunction with an understanding of the role of academia in forming a notion of literary study. This is an argument Crawford develops in *The Modern Poet: Poetry, Academia, and Knowledge Since the 1750s* (2001), in which he redefines a modern poetic identity as being necessarily both creative and critical. Also in this final chapter is a plea for the process of literary devolution to be more international in nature—a process that redefines the identities of Scottish and English literatures not only in relation to each other but in dialogue with a host of world literatures.

In *The Modern Poet,* Crawford looks at the intersections of poetic creativity as represented by poets working within academia and those who come from outside an institutional structure. He is careful to maintain that the two areas are not mutually exclusive but rather depend upon one another to define poetry in the contemporary world. As in *Devolving English Literature* and *The Scottish Invention of English Literature,* Crawford presents an argument that is both literary and historical, tracing the strands of influence and inspiration that have guided poets from the middle of the eighteenth century to the present. He links the Enlightenment/Romantic sensibility of poets such as Robert Fergusson, Robert Burns, and Sir Walter Scott with increasing influences of the academy that were later borne out in Victorian

"Gypsy-Scholar" poet-critics such as Matthew Arnold and subsequent modernist poets like Eliot, Ezra Pound, and MacDiarmid, who sought to nourish poetic inspiration with healthy doses of intellectual inquiry. In later sections of the book Crawford identifies "barbarian" poets such as Seamus Heaney, Les Murray, and Douglas Dunn as inheritors of the richly rewarding hybridities of culture and personality that are enabled by the poet-critic's citizenship in the diverse worlds of academic inquiry and private contemplation. Here Crawford admits to his own struggles to identify himself as a working poet-critic who must negotiate each identity. It is within the careful analysis of the relationship between poetry and criticism since 1750 that Crawford locates a growing interdependence. He rejects the standard view of creativity and critical activity as separate and competing worlds; rather, he presents them as areas of experience that inform and cross-fertilize each other. This is in line with Crawford's poetic and critical projects that challenge notions of static identity. For him pluralistic understanding of any self, be it poetic or otherwise, is only fruitfully approached by recognizing the deeply variegated fabrics of identity that are composed of any number of elements: personality, nationality, cultural and historical background, and technological change, to name just a few.

Each of Crawford's works, from poetry volumes and criticism to the numerous anthologies he has edited, represent in one way or another his interest in identity construction and the liberating consequences of providing disparate voices a wide arena in which to interact. He continues to contribute to a body of writing that moves beyond factionalism and those stale forms of identification that prevent communities from developing a healthy sense of collective self.

Selected Bibliography

WORKS OF ROBERT CRAWFORD

POETRY
New Chatto Poets 2. (Contributor.) London: Chatto & Windus, 1989.

ROBERT CRAWFORD

A Scottish Assembly. London: Chatto & Windus, 1990.

Sharawaggi: Poems in Scots. With W. N. Herbert. Edinburgh: Polygon, 1990.

Talkies. London: Chatto &Windus, 1992.

Dream State: The New Scottish Poets. (Contributor.) Edited by Daniel O'Rourke. Edinburgh: Polygon, 1994.

Masculinity. London: Cape Poetry, 1996.

Penguin Modern Poets 9. (Contributor.) London: Penguin, 1996.

Spirit Machines. London: Jonathan Cape, 1999.

The Tip of My Tongue. London: Jonathan Cape, 2003.

CRITICISM

The Savage and the City in the Work of T. S. Eliot. Oxford and New York: Clarendon Press, 1987.

Devolving English Literature. Oxford: Clarendon Press, 1992. 2d ed., Edinburgh: Edinburgh University Press, 2000.

Identifying Poets: Self and Territory in Twentieth-Century Poetry. Edinburgh: Edinburgh University Press, 1993.

Literature in Twentieth-Century Scotland: A Select Bibliography. London: British Council, 1995.

The Modern Poet: Poetry, Academia, and Knowledge Since the 1750s. Oxford and New York: Oxford University Press, 2001.

EDITED VOLUMES AND ANTHOLOGIES

Other Tongues: Young Scottish Poets in English, Scots, and Gaelic. St. Andrews, Scotland: Verse, 1990.

About Edwin Morgan. Edited with Hamish Whyte. Modern Scottish Writers series. Edinburgh: Edinburgh University Press, 1990.

The Arts of Alasdair Gray. Edited with Thom Nairn. Modern Scottish Writers series. Edinburgh: Edinburgh University Press, 1991.

Reading Douglas Dunn. Edited with David Kinloch. Modern Scottish Writers series. Edinburgh: Edinburgh University Press, 1992.

Liz Lochhead's Voices. Edited with Anne Varty. Modern Scottish Writers series. Edinburgh: Edinburgh University Press, 1993.

Launch-Site for English Studies: Three Centuries of Literary Studies at the University of St. Andrews. St. Andrews, Scotland: Verse, 1997.

Robert Burns and Cultural Authority. Edinburgh: Edinburgh University Press, 1997; Iowa City: University of Iowa Press, 1997.

The Scottish Invention of English Literature. Cambridge and New York: Cambridge University Press, 1998.

The Penguin Book of Poetry from Britain and Ireland Since 1945. Edited with Simon Armitage. London: Penguin, 1998.

The New Penguin Book of Scottish Verse. Edited with Mick Imlah. London: Penguin, 2000.

Scottish Religious Poetry from the Sixth Century to the Present: An Anthology. Edited with Meg Bateman and James McGonigal. Edinburgh: St. Andrews Press, 2000.

"Heaven-Taught Fergusson": Robert Burns's Favourite Scottish Poet. East Linton, Scotland: Tuckwell Press, 2003.

CRITICAL AND BIOGRAPHICAL STUDIES

Abel, Richard. *"The Scottish Invention of English Literature."* Publishing Research Quarterly 16, no. 1: 80–89 (spring 2000). (Review.)

Bittenbender, J. C. "An Interview with Robert Crawford." *Janus* 3:3–12 (winter 1997–1998).

Chandler, James. "Devolutionary Criticism: Scotland, America, and Literary Modernity." *Modern Philology* 92, no. 2: 211–219 (1994).

Collini, Stefan. "The Influence of the Marginal." *Times Literary Supplement,* January 1, 1999, pp. 8–9. (Review of *The Scottish Invention of English Literature.*)

Fowler, Alastair. "Strong Accent of the Mind." *Times Literary Supplement,* December 29, 2000, pp. 5–6. (Review of *The New Penguin Book of Scottish Verse.*)

Johnson, Kevan. "Insert the Personal." *Times Literary Supplement,* October 22, 1999, p. 28. (Review of *Spirit Machines.*)

Mapstone, Sally. "Drinking and Spewing." *London Review of Books,* September 25, 2003, p. 23. (Review of *"Heaven-Taught Fergusson."*)

Murray, Nicholas. Review of *Talkies. Times Literary Supplement,* June 26, 1992, p. 9.

Nicholson, Colin. Review of *Identifying Poets. Modern Language Review* 90, no. 3: 739–740 (July 1995).

O'Brien, Sean. "Don Paterson, Kathleen Jamie, Robert Crawford, W. N. Herbert: *Scotland! Scotland! Actual/ Virtual."* In his *The Deregulated Muse.* Newcastle upon Tyne: Bloodaxe Books, 1998. Pp. 261–269.

O'Donoghue, Bernard. "Parish and Province." *Times Literary Supplement,* March 24, 1995, p. 22. (Review of *Identifying Poets.*)

O'Driscoll, Denis. "Who Have We Got Now?" *Times Literary Supplement,* November 13, 1998, pp. 27–28. (Review of *The Penguin Book of Poetry From Britain and Ireland Since 1945.*)

Perry, Seamus. Review of *The Modern Poet: Poetry, Academia, and Knowledge Since the 1750s. Romanticism* 9, no. 1:102–104 (2003).

Potts, Robert. "From Father to Son." *Times Literary Supplement,* May 31, 1996, p. 25. (Review of *Masculinity.*)

Skoblow, Jeffrey. *"Sharawaggi:* Crawford and Herbert Meet

the Incubus." *Scottish Literary Journal* 25, no. 2: 67–85 (November 1998).

Sorenson, Janet. *"Robert Burns and Cultural Authority." Modern Philology* 98, no. 4: 685–688 (May 2001). (Review.)

Stafford, Fiona. "Review of *Devolving English Literature.*" *Review of English Studies* 46, no. 181: 129–130 (February 1995).

Zawacki, Andrew. "Robert Crawford: An Interview." *Verse* 15, nos. 1 and 2: 38–54 (1998).

William H. Davies

(1871–1940)

Helena Nelson

THE POEMS OF W. H. Davies, though still often anthologized, do not feature widely on contemporary student reading lists. Yet in his day this poet was a key figure. His work was compared to that of Robert Herrick, Thomas Campion, William Blake, and William Wordsworth; some of his lyrics were widely regarded as timeless. But although critics over the decades have attempted with varying degrees of success to place him as a writer, no one has been able to categorize him as a man or successfully to compare his life with any poet in living memory: Davies was—and is—unique.

The annals of many poetic lives are characterized by disappointments, suicides, tragedies, and compromises. Davies may well be the only poet who achieved his heart's desire. In "Truly Great" (in *New Poems,* 1907), the poet evokes a dream house. Inside there will be books, outside "leafy nooks" and flowers. He will have "a little gold that's sure each week" and "a lovely wife" who will delight to live a "self-made prisoner" with him. Davies went through extraordinary hardship to attain his dream—but by 1923 he was living both literally and metaphorically in that house. The story of how he got there almost beggars belief.

EARLY YEARS

According to the official register of births, William Henry Davies was born in 1871 in the Welsh border town of Newport, South Wales, on the Severn estuary. At that time the port town was growing fast. The coal industry was booming; railways were spreading; new housing for the workers was eating into the countryside. Davies regarded his childhood as a happy one, but the family was not without difficulties. His father,

Francis Davies, a molder by trade, had poor health. He and his wife, Mary Ann (née Evans), lost three children in infancy. Their fourth, (known in the family as 'Frank') Francis, survived but was brain damaged. William, a healthy son, followed two years later; three years afterward came a sister, Matilda. In the same year that Matilda was born, the children's father died of tuberculosis at the age of only thirty-one.

Davies's mother quickly remarried. Her late husband's English parents were not pleased. Lydia Adams Davies, the poet's grandmother, was a staunch Baptist who hotly opposed the idea of a second union. She offered to bring up her son's three children as her own, and the offer was accepted: it seems that Davies's mother, financially struggling, had little alternative. The grandparents had a comfortable living and were able to support the three children and a maidservant. The poet's Cornish grandfather Francis Boase Davies, formerly a master mariner, was now a publican. The three children therefore grew up in a public house—the Church House Tavern—literally a stone's throw from the docks where trading ships were moored.

Rigorous religious belief was a powerful influence—Davies was brought up as a Baptist—but there were interesting anomalies. The Church House Tavern catered to drinking men, locals and sailors, although it was situated very near, as the name suggests, to a house of God. The Baptist faith regarded intemperance and loose living (also novels and the theater) as reprehensible—nevertheless the poet was introduced to alcohol when very young, by his own account "receiving sups of mulled beer at bed time, in lieu of cocoa or tea." Cultural influences, too, pulled in different directions: on his father's side Davies's relatives were English, and English was the language he spoke all his life, albeit with a marked Welsh accent. On his mother's side, however, the relatives were Welsh: they delighted in a good fistfight and praised the young poet for his toughness in pugilism. Davies himself said he was "of seafaring folk," suggesting he identified closely with his Cornish grandfather.

Nonetheless, the poet's female relatives were women of strength and determination. His grandmother, who prized education highly, told him how *her* mother had thrown out a drunken husband (who later drank himself to death) and set up her own private school. Davies's mother taught herself to read at the age of forty, and supported herself and the children of later marriages by training herself in her father's art—that of shoemaker and cobbler.

The young William Henry loved his grandmother but fought against her control. He was led "as a prisoner" to school by the maidservant, according to his autobiography, but in *Beggars* (1909) he records sustained and successful efforts to escape. He "not only knew the town well, being a truant, but the green country for many a mile around." His grandparents must have regarded the boy with a mixture of pride and despair. On the one hand he did well on school tests (despite absences) and was appointed captain of the school football team in his final year. On the other he became a key member of a "band of robbers" who successfully stole miscellaneous goods from local shops. They did this for six weeks before they were caught and birched. A year later, aged fourteen, Davies left school.

Despite the boy's resistance to education, he was interested in reading and writing from an early age. In *Beggars,* he recalls how profoundly moved he was to hear that a distant relative had written a book. "My feelings," he says, "will be understood by all those who remember what books were to them as children." This chance comment reveals much. In later life Davies would be regarded by literary men as an "innocent"—someone who had produced an unexpected gift from practically nowhere. George Bernard Shaw, in his preface to Davies's autobiography, wrote: "There was...no sign of his ever having read anything otherwise than as a child reads." However, Davies had never read "as a child

reads." "Even in those early days," he says in *Beggars,* "I had made up my mind to write a book." Davies read not just for pleasure but in order to emulate. And when he made up his mind to do something, he generally did it.

His grandmother was determined to keep the boy on the right track (she would never have approved the idea that he might write a novel). She got him to chapel twice every Sunday, to baptism classes in his teens, and even to full baptism at the age of fifteen. Davies must have been completely familiar with the long rolling phrases of the Bible and with the music and lyrics of hundreds of Victorian hymns. Not that he suffered too much. In *The Autobiography of a Super-Tramp* (1908) he recalls "playing kiss in the ring, singing and laughing, dancing with merriment" in the chapel's schoolroom.

Davies's friend Dave, a fellow member of the chapel community, also shared his interest in writing. Together they read Byron. Dave was fascinated by the poet's romantic personality; William found, for the first time, that he was reading poetry for pleasure. He mentions Shelley, Marlowe, and Shakespeare as interests. John Milton and Edward Young were also officially encouraged by his grandmother. But Davies wasn't just reading poetry; he was writing it. In *The True Traveller* (1912) he self-mockingly recalls the composition of an early poem. He had "taken days and days in going through a dictionary to find three and four syllable words for a poem on death." The manuscript, Davies suggests, was lost in spring-cleaning, but perhaps his grandmother simply disposed of it. Whatever happened, the young versifier remained undeterred.

His grandfather's death—in the spring before William was baptized—must have been a serious blow. Davies loved the old man without reservation. Francis Boase Davies was already sixty-five when his son's three children moved in. Always addressed as "Captain Davies," he ordered the home as though it was a ship. One of the main preoccupations of his life was with the prevailing wind—and references to the wind in Davies's poetry are never casual. The boy was alone at the bedside when his grandfather passed away: in terror he witnessed the old man's long slow breaths, culminating in the final death rattle.

In the same year, Lydia Davies apprenticed her grandson to a local picture-framer and gilder. Davies would serve his full five-year term, although this was neither the trade he wanted nor the one he finally practiced. He was reading long and late, to such an extent that it made him too tired to work properly. He was also sneaking off to the theater periodically, even though his indentures expressly forbade this. Soon he composed another poem about a storm (probably the anonymous "Stormscape" featured in the local paper), and he got Dave to read it aloud to one of the chapel "mutual improvement" classes, naming him as author. He was gratified by their warm response—already he knew something about audience manipulation.

The young poet had some female encouragement too. He met a young woman, "a great reader of fine literature" who, he says, saw the writer in him and told him so. Although she died suddenly, he remembered her decades later as his guiding star, even though "Drink, my first officer,...endeavored to founder me." Indeed, toward the end of his apprenticeship Davies was, by his own confession, "running a bit wild." When he finally completed his term, he was, as so often in years to come, pulled two ways. His master kept him on in a fully paid post for a few months; his grandmother must have hoped he would eventually settle down. But no—the young Davies was keen to "start for the new world." All that held him back was the fact that Lydia Davies refused to fund his trip. He took a job in Bristol and there drank enough "to wreck the brains and health of any man beyond recovery." He forgot about his writing ambitions. Then his grandmother died—and everything changed.

TRAVELS TO THE NEW WORLD

Lydia Davies left her estate in the hands of a trustee, the profits from the weekly rents of several cottages to be divided equally among her three grandchildren. Davies was the proud possessor of ten shillings a week—not a vast sum but enough to revive his dreams of travel. He persuaded the trustee to give him an advance of fifteen pounds and set off for America. He was twenty-two.

The next five years were spent in a hobo-type existence, mainly in various American states but periodically working cattle boats between Baltimore and Liverpool. Davies mixed with tramps, vagrants, casual workers—and learned what it meant to be a "true traveler." He acquired enormous admiration for many of his fellow itinerants, regarding their resourcefulness (especially with language) as remarkable and their begging skills as an art form. Sometimes he worked; often he indulged in what he called "luxurious loafing." Davies the would-be writer seemed to have disappeared. Yet not only was he consciously studying the characters he met on his travels, but according to Barbara Hooper in *Time to Stand and Stare* (2004) he kept "a note book with a few scraps of original poems" which "disappeared when he was sleeping in a barn full of hay in the wilds of Michigan." Equally, during his visits to Liverpool, he left his companions and sought out public libraries, where he read greedily. Back on the road, he was haunted by fears that he was wasting his life. In 1898, aged twenty-seven, he returned to Newport and picked up his accumulated legacy with a view to commencing a writing career. However, once again a convivial drinking life proved his downfall—and consumed most of his cash. Plans to open a bookshop in London proved futile.

In February 1899 he read about the gold rush in the Klondike. Deciding in his typically impulsive way that some of that gold could solve his cash crisis he set off for Canada. A few weeks later he fell while attempting to jump the express train to Winnipeg. His right foot was completely severed by the wheels of the train. Later, doctors carried out a second amputation above the knee. Lucky to escape with his life, Davies limped back to Newport. But the man had always been tough. Now his fighting spirit took over. He purchased an artificial leg from a London firm, traveled to London in August 1899, settled himself in cheap lodgings, and started to write with grim intensity. He was twenty-eight.

WILLIAM H. DAVIES

In the first year of his new life, he claims to have written a blank-verse tragedy, a long narrative poem, over a hundred sonnets, a neo-Elizabethan tragedy, a comedy, a volume of humorous essays, and a number of short lyrics. He even found a publisher who would publish a selection of his poems—at a price. Davies couldn't fund the publication. He came up with the idea of printing a broadsheet of poems to sell from door to door. The plan failed—nobody was interested. In frustration and despair Davies burned the poems.

Unable to cope financially, the aspiring poet moved to cheaper accommodations. He was miserably poor, mingling with down-and-outs. He sacrificed part of the income from his trust money to help one of his Welsh connections. For year after year, Davies planned literary successes that didn't happen. He had no useful contacts. He didn't even have an address respectable enough to allow him to join a public library. He was just a one legged ex-tramp with wild aspirations. Or apparently so.

Somehow he survived and kept on writing. By 1904, at the age of thirty-three, he was busily negotiating with a publisher who agreed to print his work if he could provide a nineteen-pound advance. Davies managed to scrape the cash together by foregoing all trust payments for six months, during which time he went back on the road, begging and hawking shoelaces, thus saving the money he would have paid out for lodgings. Returning finally to London, he borrowed a pound from a Canadian friend so he could live while he prepared his final manuscript. In early 1905 he received the accumulated trust money. He didn't hesitate. Nineteen pounds went straight to his publisher for 250 copies of *The Soul's Destroyer,* his first collection of poems. Perhaps he thought he had arrived. He hadn't—not yet.

BECOMING A POET

Thirty review copies of Davies's book elicited only two lukewarm write-ups. Terribly discouraged he started drinking heavily and once again approached destitution. Surely he would give up

his literary aspirations now. Not Davies. He came up with yet another idea. From a library copy of *Who's Who* he picked out a set of significant names. To each person on his list he sent a copy of *The Soul's Destroyer* with a request for a small payment if they liked it. A few people sent him money. Many didn't reply. Desperate for cash he sent out a second set of books. This time he hit lucky. One of the names on his list was St. John Adcock, then associated with the popular newspaper the *Daily Mail.* Adcock had the journalist's eye for a story. After meeting Davies in person he wrote about him—not just a review of the poems but an account of their author's bizarre background as tramp and down-and-out. There was a flurry of publicity and positive reviews. For years Davies would be known as the "tramp-poet." The sobriquet was distinctive and memorable. At the same time, other writers on Davies's mailing list proved helpful: the well-known dramatist George Bernard Shaw sent him a pound to fund the mailing of another eight copies. The book reached literary men Edward Garnett and Edward Thomas. Davies started working furiously on a second collection. He thought he had finally won through.

In one respect he was right: his literary career had begun, but impoverished reality fell dramatically short of his expectations. Without financial assistance from Edward Thomas and other new friends, it is hard to see how he could have coped. He couldn't even afford the stamps to reply to his fan mail. A bitter preoccupation with money and/or the lack of it would remain a theme in his life and work. A reprint of *The Soul's Destroyer* and the issue of *New Poems* in 1907 failed to secure riches. The novelty of the "tramp-poet" had waned. However, at the suggestion of his new literary friends, he completed a prose work, the preface written by George Bernard Shaw. *The Autobiography of a Super-Tramp,* published in 1908, brought in a steady income, which continued over the years. At last Davies was able to be self-supporting, if not comfortably so.

FRIENDSHIPS

Davies made good and lasting friends. The stocky Welshman with limping gait inspired affection in

WILLIAM H. DAVIES

unexpected places. Many literary folk (Edward Thomas, the Sitwells, Harold Monro, Edward Garnett, Ralph Hodgson, Edward Marsh—and later Robert Graves and Richard Church) were fond of him. He was close to leading artists such as Walter Sickert and William Nicholson. People swapped stories about his eccentricities, but not without respect. In February 1911 a petition of friends secured him a government pension of £50. This was raised to £100 in 1915 and £150 in 1920. The pension, together with income from his writing, allowed him to pursue his chosen trade—that of poet.

But it wasn't easy. Between 1914 and 1918, World War I struck down many, including Davies's friend Edward Thomas. Davies, unable to fight, took part in poetry readings to support the war effort. His lyrical Welsh voice and the accessibility of his poems made him a success with audiences. At the same time the war itself fueled an upsurge of interest in poetry. By 1923, when Davies married and moved out of London, he had published at least a dozen volumes of poetry, including a *Collected* in 1916. Not only that, he had turned his hand to a successful autobiography, three volumes of autobiographical essays, and a novel; he had edited an anthology of short lyrics and was even working on the script of a "tramp opera." He was also acclaimed as one of the front-runners in a new poetic movement. Davies was one of the "Georgians."

GEORGIAN POETRY

The Georgian movement in British poetry took its title from a series of anthologies edited by Edward Marsh (private secretary to Winston Churchill), the first of which was published in 1912. The group of poets featured in its pages represented what Marsh felt was a "Georgian era" in British poetry—something fresh, vital, and accessible. It was a new century: time to leave the Victorians behind.

The poets of *Georgian Poetry 1911–1912* included Lascelles Abercrombie, Gordon Bottomley, Rupert Brooke, G. K. Chesterton, W. H. Davies, Walter de la Mare, John Drinkwater, James Elroy Flecker, Wilfrid Wilson Gibson, D.

H. Lawrence, John Masefield, Harold Monro, T. Sturge Moore, James Stephens, and Robert Trevelyan. (A. E. Housman was approached but declined.) The anthology sold well. The following year Rupert Brooke, a close friend of Marsh, died while on active service overseas. Brooke's death, and the subsequent memoir published by Marsh attracted enormous attention. For a little while the poetry of the Georgians was on every reader's list.

There were five volumes in the *Georgian Poetry* series, the last of them appearing in 1922. The first sold 15,000 copies, the second 19,000 (the highpoint). The fifth and final volume sold only 8,000. The Georgians were initially praised for integrity, directness, simplicity, and natural diction. Within a decade, however, they were being upbraided for false innocence, sentimentality, and poor technique. Another poetic movement was starting to steal the limelight, for 1922 saw the first issue of T. S. Eliot's journal the *Criterion,* in which a new kind of poem featured: it was called "The Waste Land."

It was a parting of the ways. W. H. Davies, who had benefited both in cash and literary status from inclusion in all five *Georgian Poetry* volumes, continued to command a popular readership, as did Walter de la Mare, who told Marsh he had made more from his publication in *Georgian Poetry* than the joint sum of all his other verse writing. But now there were two camps: the "Moderns" quickly established a reputation for intellectual depth, exploring new and freer forms; by contrast, the "Georgians" were increasingly perceived as lightweight and simplistic.

Davies finally married at the age of fifty-one and moved to the country. The period of his unconventional courtship is recorded in *Young Emma,* which was completed in 1924 but not published until 1980, forty years after his death. The rest of his life seems to have been relatively content: he lived with his wife in a succession of pleasant houses in the country. In such settings, he maintained a loyal readership and continued to write verse, uninfluenced by modernist trends. Until 1933 he also produced prose works, his style distinctive and rich in irony. After a period

WILLIAM H. DAVIES

of frail health Davies died in his home on 26 September 1940. The Battle of Britain was raging in the skies: that day a Supermarine aircraft factory in Southampton was destroyed by bombing.

In his final years the poet's Christian faith was increasingly evident in his verse. Although he had rebelled against it, his Baptist upbringing should not be underestimated—it left him intensely and uncomfortably aware of sin and retribution. At the same time, he affirmed the humanitarian principles of New Testament Christianity throughout his poetic career.

It is perhaps helpful to remember that this very private, optimistic, ambitious, disabled poet remained in many ways psychologically isolated, not least as a result of his inner fears. On his travels as a young man he had experienced terrifying episodes apparently without turning a hair—near-death through malaria; amputation; a lynching; a bloodbath among black river workers; a corpse fed on by rats. But his unperturbed narrative was a mask. After his overseas travels he was terrified of rats. Fear also lead him to develop deep and unreasonable antipathy for those whom he called "coloured men": several passages in his prose writing are explicitly racist. Even when challenged by his friend and fellow-poet Ralph Hodgson, he confessed his "prejudice" as a matter of pride, rather than shame. He had a morbid terror of death and bodily decay: the idea of worms feeding on corpses haunts his later verse. In the early days in America he carried a gun for protection; much later, as told in *A Poet's Pilgrimage* (1918), he carried a stick that concealed "a strong, sharp toledo blade about three feet long."

AUTOBIOGRAPHICAL WORK

Davies tended to downplay his prose writing, mainly because he wrote it not from choice, but to make money. Nevertheless, *The Autobiography of a Super-Tramp* was successful in both the U.K. and the U.S., bringing its author a small but steady income for life. It is easily tracked down today and still appears on lists of literary classics. In his critical biography of Davies (1963),

Richard J. Stonesifer has suggested that Davies's position in literature will continue to rest as firmly on *Super-Tramp* as on the poems, and there are several reasons to suppose this may be true. First, Davies's personal story is captured here, and it is like no other. Secondly, the parts of the text dealing with tramps and beggars form a valuable document of social history. Lastly, the book has a remarkable and individual style, combining plainness of diction with tonal complexity and a fine ear for dialogue. There are marvelous pen portraits of people whom Davies loved and admired. His seafaring grandfather is just one of these:

> In the dark winter evenings I would sit with my grandfather, my brother and sister, painting ships or reading before a large fire that was never allowed to burn below its highest bar. My grandfather, with his old habits, would pace slowly up and down the half dark passage, shutting himself out in the cold. Every now and then he would open the front door to look at the stars or to inform himself from what latitude the wind blew. The wind never changed without his knowledge; for this wary mariner invariably surprised it in the act of doing so. Three or four times in the evening he would open the kitchen door to see that his family were comfortable, as though he had just made his way from the hurricane deck to enquire after the welfare of passengers in the cabin. When this was done, the old lady would sometimes say, rather peevishly, "Francis do sit down for a minute or two." Then he would answer gruffly, but not unkindly—"Avast there, Lydia," closing the door to begin again his steady pacing to and fro. (chapter 1)

This is a true picture of a real person. It is one of Davies's chief skills to recreate idiosyncratic personages with careful detail and a kind of tenderness not reserved just for his own family but equally applied to his traveling companions—characters like the "notorious beggar" Brum and Three Fingered Jack, the expert loafer whose slowness at climbing aboard a Canadian train cost Davies his foot.

Davies recounts events both trivial and momentous with a curious degree of understatement: he doesn't seem to exaggerate, nor does he manipulate stories to achieve a dramatic highpoint. Often the only connection between incidents is Davies himself, and yet he draws no real conclusions about his life: it goes past in a slightly disconnected sequence, like a road movie without a theme. Richard Stonesifer praises the prose for its "spare quality" but is quick to point out what Davies *doesn't* do: for example, no descriptions of scenery, little reflection on key events, sentences lacking complex structure. But it may be that these absences serve to demonstrate that Davies from the start was cultivating a style of his own. He was as idiosyncratic as that "wary mariner," his grandfather.

Over the next twenty-five years, the poet would continue to publish autobiographical writing as a way of supplementing his income. In 1909 he brought out a book of essays, *Beggars,* intending to cash in on popular interest in an unpublicized way of life. This volume provides excellent insight into the language of the road, life in the doss-house, tips and tricks of beggars, and the contempt of "true" beggars for the working life (which Davies certainly shared). It evokes real experiences and real people. Davies identifies closely with many of the characters he describes, yet at the same time keeps himself at a remove. He does not convey a sense of superiority; it is a more subtle distancing than that—perhaps a sense of himself as one of life's narrators, a privileged observer.

More autobiographical essays appeared in *The True Traveller* in 1912, this time including narratives about encounters with prostitutes, which Edward Thomas at one time thought "wonderful but unpublishable." (In 1926 *Beggars* and *The True Traveller* were partially combined in another volume, *The Adventures of Johnny Walker, Tramp.*) In 1914, *Nature* briefly recorded Davies's experiences living in the country cottage Edward Thomas had helped him to find—the first of his prose works to include poems inside the text.

In 1918, *A Poet's Pilgrimage* chronicled Davies's experiences of walking through South Wales, this time as a seasoned traveler who could afford to stay in comfortable inns. The book incorporates flashbacks and memories of Davies's early life, often telling ironic stories that expose his own failures. As with *Super-Tramp,* there is a certain disconnectedness about the narrative, as though the journey is only a thread on which to hang a sequence of essay-type diversions. The anecdotal voice, however, is confident and clear, with Davies the humorist never far away. *A Poet's Pilgrimage* also includes poems, often as chapter prefaces. The chapter "Wasting Time," for example, culminates in a detailed description of the experience that gave rise to the lyric "The Moon and a Cloud," which is quoted in full at the start. It is a little like reading extracts from Dorothy Wordsworth's diary, side by side with her brother's poems, a reminder of how firmly rooted in real experience Davies's verse is.

Davies's next published autobiographical work was *Later Days* (1925). Richard Stonesifer roundly disparages this volume and charges Davies with "a conscious attempt to be naïve." However, *Later Days* was not the book Davies had originally planned, and Stonesifer had no way of knowing that the book was in fact a patchwork: Davies had carefully incorporated and reworked parts of another book—one that he was advised not to publish and thought had been destroyed. *Young Emma,* finally published in 1980, was the book that Davies did want—very much—to write, the only one of his prose works not primarily driven by a need for cash.

Young Emma, of all Davies's prose works, most clearly tells a coherent story—the tale of his courtship and marriage. None of the content is likely to shock a modern reader, although the author had originally intended to publish anonymously. The account opens with Davies's unhappy situation in the early 1920s. Aged fifty, he had still not found the lifelong female companion he had hoped for. Meanwhile he had found sexual release with prostitutes or, as he frequently termed them, "courtesans." Deciding that literary women bored him "with their long, lifeless talk on books and art" he determined to find a mistress on the streets and make her his wife.

At first Davies's search for a loving mistress was unsuccessful; then he finally found "young Emma." Emma (a pseudonym for Helen Payne) struck him as innocent, a very young woman forced to immorality and "not a professional street-walker." Despite a disparity in age of nearly thirty years, it was a love match. But things were not to proceed straightforwardly. Davies quickly found himself dangerously ill with a venereal infection and assumed that he had acquired it from Emma. Meanwhile, as she did her best to nurse him, Emma herself fell ill. Unknown to Davies, she had been pregnant when they first met, and she suffered a traumatic miscarriage. Davies, too ill himself to help her, was fortunately able to pay for hospital treatment, otherwise the love story would have ended then and there.

The two clear themes of the book are purity and love: Davies assumed Emma had infected him—he was wrong. He subsequently assumed her only interest in him was as a potential father to her illegitimate baby—wrong again. He consistently underrated both her innocence and her purity, and the tale is a moral one, championing the cause of goodness and innocence against the false judgments of a shabby society. There is no excursus into unnecessary anecdote or nostalgic reverie. Davies writes well, consistently turning his ironies against himself. His viewpoint and narrative voice are unparalleled elsewhere in his writing—perhaps even in literature itself.

Careful reading of *Young Emma* also reveals that Davies was prepared to adjust reality to suit a story (or to preserve a secret). The remarkable character of Mrs. Larkins, for example, who appears in both *Later Days* and *Young Emma,* is one that Davies specially enjoyed. He called her "Old Raspberry Face" behind her back although she ruled him, as his housekeeper, with a rod of iron. Despairing one day of the cheap soap she had provided, the poet timidly suggested she should buy a more expensive brand, one that would produce a lather: "There's nothing at all the matter with the soap," answered Mrs. Larkins in a calm voice. "It's the way you use it." The anecdote has the ring of authenticity. However, the selfsame conversation takes place in *Young Emma* with a much more attractive housekeeper/mistress—Bella.

In his later years Davies published two other nonfiction books: *My Birds* and *My Garden* (1933). Though easily dismissed as of little significance, these volumes are actually a rich source of interest. They incorporate many poems, often with detailed commentary about the circumstances of their composition. Moreover, Davies the ironist is still soundly present. Even Stonesifer, who had little time for these later works, remarks on the wonderful tale of "William Blake, the cat's-meat man," in *My Birds.*

DAVIES THE NOVELIST

Although Davies's nonfiction writing has outstanding qualities, the same cannot be said of his novels. Both *A Weak Woman* (1912) and *Dancing Mad* (1927) draw on personal experience, too thinly connected with an inadequate plot to function as convincing fiction. Stonesifer has suggested that Davies did not have the "sophistication" to manage novel writing. However, this focuses on what Davies didn't do at the expense of what he did—and he did have certain strengths. For example, the novels allowed him satirical diversions, and he was good at these: there are sharp, effective passages about the literary world in both novels. The narratives also afford insights into their author that none of his other writing reveals. The extreme secretiveness of the male protagonists, for example—hard to credit in terms of characterization—tells us something about Davies himself.

A writer who publishes autobiographical work has a certain advantage over later biographers. His or her version of what happened tends to be quoted and requoted until it is accepted as fact. However, autobiography is selective: it shapes the truth—to some extent at least—by omission. The troubled story of Davies's only full sister, for example, is mentioned nowhere in his autobiographical work. Nonetheless, the sadly fallen character of the "weak woman" seems to draw on at least part of her life. The novels, therefore, serve to "leak" some of Davies's biographical secrets, although they are obviously an unreliable source of evidence.

OTHER PROSE WORK

In the early 1920s, Davies experimented in other areas. He edited four issues of a revived poetry magazine called *Form*. He also brought out a collection of twentieth-century lyrics (purporting to include only one of his own poems, but actually including a second pseudonymously). He embarked on *True Travellers: A Tramps Opera in Three Acts* which, though illustrated by William Nicholson and published by Jonathan Cape in 1923, was firmly rejected by theater managers as unsuitable for performance. Yet it stands as a testimony to Davies's readiness to try something new, even in his midfifties. In 1924 he wrote the preface to an edition of Daniel Defoe's *Moll Flanders* and the following year introduced an edition of Robert Burns's poetry. In 1930 he brought out a further anthology of short lyrics, *Jewels of Song,* from across the ages. But what he mainly worked on, and what he chiefly valued to the end of his days, was writing poetry.

DAVIES THE POET

W. H. Davies was prolific. He published twenty individual volumes of verse during his lifetime, more in collected editions and prose works. Nearly eight hundred poems survive. Robert Graves observed that although he wrote too much, the "necessary" poems would last. However, at the start of the twenty-first century Davies's poetic reputation is at low ebb—even the "necessary" poems are endangered. What has happened to put him so far out of favor?

Davies's performance is radically uneven, from start to end of his life. He can be very good—with a lyric purity few would challenge—and very bad, with a heavy banality few would celebrate. Philip Larkin, reviewing *The Complete Poems of W. H. Davies* (1963), remarked on the way Davies's poems perched "perpetually on the edge of formula, mannerism, routine" and yet continually achieved "unpredictable successes." This habit of veering unexpectedly from one extreme to another partly explains the critical difficulty in placing this poet. Richard Stonesifer, half of whose biographical volume offers a detailed critical study of Davies's writing, lays one very interesting (and in some ways crucial) charge at his door: in countering Edith Sitwell's praise of Davies's "masterful" use of assonance,

Stonesifer comments: "Undoubtedly, Davies did not know he was doing all this." Edward Thomas, in a letter to Gordon Bottomley in 1906, remarked not dissimilarly, "It seems likely that he will often attain simplicity unawares."

In this way the idea of a curiously ignorant "peasant" figure has grown. Critics have labored to account for the literary influences that must somehow explain Davies's instinctive ability to "get it right" some of the time. It has been suggested that Davies's schooling (one head teacher was a keen poetry lover) was partly responsible, but considering how often Davies was absent from school, this explanation is unconvincing. Davies was a mainly self-taught poet, a phenomenon that educated writers often find hard to credit. His early influence was in biblical rhetoric, the hymnal, John Bunyan, and Edward Young; he took to Byron in his teens; William Shakespeare, Christopher Marlowe, and Percy Bysshe Shelley followed. As life went on, even during his tramping period, Davies continued to read when he could. He studied the characters he met on the road (they were one part of his education), while gradually absorbing from books an idea of what might be achieved. He served his poetic apprenticeship by emulating what he admired, in particular Wordsworth, Blake, and the lyric poets of the sixteenth and early seventeenth centuries. What he did not learn was the language of literary criticism: it is perhaps this fact that led to the later assumption that his method was "instinctive" rather than learned.

THE SOUL'S DESTROYER AND OTHER POEMS

Davies's first book (1905) gives a good insight into his starting point, as well as illustrating his characteristic strengths and weaknesses. It includes forty poems, which he later whittled down to a mere fourteen in the second edition (1907). The title poem, a lengthy narrative in blank verse about the perils of alcohol, musters a weighty persona for the poet. He employs epic simile and complex verse paragraphs to build toward a final rhetorical appeal to the "judging God" to "have mercy on our frailties." It is not a good poem, but it is not terrible either; its style owes much to Wordsworth and Milton but still shows what Davies had learned. He could handle blank verse confidently. He could hold to a masterful—if slightly pompous—narrative voice. And here and there he could slip in lines that marked him as his own man: "The motor-car goes humming down the road, / Like some huge bee that warns us from its way."

In this poem, as in many others, Davies adopts the eighteenth-century habit of capitalizing significant nouns, as well as using stylized poetic inversions, exclamation marks, and archaisms such as "doth," "ere," "e'en," and "'twas." There is a clear sense that he is writing in the way he feels "a poet" should write and that his sense of appropriateness has been formed by specific reading. The central theme is the dangers of alcohol, and there are lines Davies's grandmother would have been proud of:

Such is this drink that fathers half our sins;
It makes a simple one responsible
For deeds which memory makes no count to save,
And proves man guilty in his innocence.

In this one poem "joy" is mentioned eight times, joy being a central theme for Davies—almost, indeed, an obsession. It was the countering influence that enabled him, both in this poem and in his personal life, to avoid the terrible risks of intemperance. He associates "joy" with the green countryside, with childhood and purity. Nearly two decades later in "One Token" he would refer to:

The power...given at birth to me
To stare at a rainbow, bird or tree,
Longer than any man alive.

From such trancelike staring, according to Davies, came his "songs of joy...one by one." He believed fervently that he had a poetic "gift," an ability that came from outside himself, and that this gift was directly associated with his joy in nature.

The Soul's Destroyer mingles weighty pieces with lighter love lyrics. There are also poems honestly depicting life in the lodging house. It was these poems, combined with the issuing ad-

dress (The Farmhouse), which caught St. John Adcock's eye and secured Davies the literary springboard he needed. No one had written poems like this before. In "Saints and Lodgers," Davies celebrates some of the characters he would return to in later prose, his colorful style closer to folk ballad than anything else. Interestingly, he makes unabashed use of slant rhymes from the start (consecrate / Billingsgate, lost / most, foul / soul, cadgers / lodgers). One of the criticisms commonly leveled at Davies—even by Stonesifer as late as 1963—was that his rhyming technique was inadequate. The same criticisms, of course, were not made of Wilfred Owen or Edward Thomas, educated writers who, it is assumed, could rhyme when they wanted to. In truth, when Davies was intent to move a story on, he swung ahead at the dictate of metrical assonance rather than a need for precise rhyme. Sometimes this method worked and sometimes it didn't, but his conscious intention is plain enough. In neither life nor art was he inclined to obey the rules.

The poem "The Lodging House Fire" is one of the strongest of the set, and it shows Davies's instinct for a form that could echo mood and thought. The poem has at its heart the poet's terrible fear of wasting his life, dozing beside the lodging house fire. Davies was convinced this coke stove actually shortened men's lives. The narrative moves through deliberately sluggish quatrains—three trimeter lines and then a dimeter. The fourth short line creates a lengthy pause from which each subsequent stanza drags itself reluctantly back into action. The poet creates a nightmare scene, born of reality:

For listen: it is death
To watch that fire's glow;
For, as it burns more red
Men paler grow.

This poem is not derivative: it is pure Davies, the language almost entirely free of the conscious poeticisms that encumber him elsewhere. He moves from an image of death to one of sinister guilt: he himself has "murdered" time, sitting in front of the fire. Self-recrimination doesn't save him though, and neither does an attempt at moralizing. The final stanza sinks into despair, the metrical movement throwing bitter emphasis onto the word "poison" in the last line:

But all my day is waste,
I live a lukewarm four
And make a red coke fire
Poison the score.

This first collection, then, serves to illustrate different aspects of Davies that would run side by side in years to come. One last poem demands close attention because it offers a unique insight into how Davies saw himself as poet and, at the same time, shows how aware he was of other people's perceptions of him. "A Poet's Epitaph" was one of the poems Davies chose to exclude from the trimmed-down version of his first collection, nor was it included in the *Complete* edition in 1963. Jonathan Barker, in his 1985 selection of Davies—much the best introduction to the man and his work—has happily rescued it. Davies almost certainly believed that "A Poet's Epitaph" would be deemed clumsy by literary critics—perhaps, indeed, it had already received unfavorable comment. All the same, the poem was doing something unusual, and doing it with wordplay, conscious irony, and sheer delight. To see Davies at work, it is necessary to read the poem in full:

Here lie the bones of Davies—William,
    Who always called the moon Phoebe,
And Phoebus always called the sun,
    And must, therefore, a poet be.

'Twas one to him to sing in heaven,
    Or howl with demons in hell's pits,
To make himself at home, for he
    Was homeless here by starts and fits.

The world cursed him, and he cursed it,
    Till Death with dirt his throat did fill;
If e'er he wakes, he'll curse again,
    And worse—this Davies—William, will.

His granny oft foretold his fate,
    How he a ne'er-do-well would be;
'Twas well, maybe, she never heard
    The rascal call the moon Phoebe.

His grandad said—"He is a rogue."
    "Not me, grandad," said William's brother.

"Why, thou art fool!" their grandad roared.
    "Nay, young and simple both," said mother.

The first stanza is a studied exercise in epigram, the deliberate but slightly awkward reversal in line three capturing the spirit of gravestone verse. At the same time the whole stanza presents a humorous assertion: anyone who calls the moon "Phoebe" must be a poet. Davies often turns his ironies on himself, and this is no exception. He is joking about the stylized diction of early twentieth-century verse; at the same time, the allegation is true. He *does* call the sun "Phoebus" in "Autumn" in this selfsame collection. As he continues his self-portrait, there's a sense that he is enjoying lambasting himself in the alliterative language of the pulpit. Repetitions abound, as well as internal rhyme and assonance ("world," "cursed," "dirt," "worse"). The first three stanzas form the "epitaph," concluding with neat wordplay on his own name.

The poem could have ended here, but instead the poet shifts into a domestic interaction. He records the likely response of his grandmother to such "poetic" language as "Phoebe"—it would have confirmed her opinion that he was a "rascal" and "ne'er-do-well." His grandfather's reaction is equally dismissive: "He is a rogue." At this point brother Frank (who of course really was mentally challenged) cheerily interposes and is dubbed a "fool" by the grandfather. The mother sums up: the two boys are both "young and simple." Frank was "simple" in the sense of mental disability; William was just a bit daft, from the point of view of his mother. But "simple" was not a casual word for Davies. It had direct application in terms of his work. It was his "simplicity" that Edward Thomas later admired. His verse was praised by Walter de la Mare as "simple only in the sense that an essence is simple." Richard Stonesifer would later discuss the "complexity of his simplicity."

There is interesting evidence here, at the start of his career, that Davies was aware not only of his own "simplicity" but also of competing voices in his work. In the single poem "A Poet's

Epitaph" he deliberately moves from stylized poetic language (albeit ironic) in the first three stanzas, to completely natural dialogue in his final four lines. That movement—from what he thought necessary to where he was comfortable—was connected with Davies's sense of readership. On the one hand he was intensely aware of a literary (and critical) audience; on the other he desired to win the "common reader," people from less educated walks of life. The tension created by playing to two audiences may explain some of his failures. At his best he resolves the problem (as he does at the end of "A Poet's Epitaph") by writing with an ear so finely attuned to natural speech cadence that any reader can enjoy and admire the result.

DAVIES AS "GENIUS"

By 1918, Davies had published eight individual volumes of poems, contributed to numerous anthologies and had brought out a *Collected Poems* in 1916. Although he did not always feel sanguine (*Farewell to Poesy* in 1910 records in its title poem a fear that his "singing days are done"), his poems mainly sold well. He had a popular following both on the page and—especially during the war years—at public readings. He had received some stinging criticism, it is true, but also high praise from leading writers. Early on the "tramp-poet" tag had given him a unique identity, and his odd but engaging character continued to affect the way his work was received. Osbert Sitwell observes in *Noble Essences* (1950) that it is not easy "to disentangle his personality from his work" and that this is truer of Davies than of most poets. Stories about his idiosyncrasies were swapped readily. It was alleged, for example, that on one occasion, annoyed by what he regarded as too much praise in the press for Walter de la Mare, he acquired a pistol and practiced shooting at a portrait of the rival poet. Some found his behavior delightfully eccentric; others found him irritatingly mannered. However, the main characteristic that has affected criticism of his writing was his perceived vanity.

Robert Frost, who met Davies through Edward Thomas, thought his "egotism" insufferable.

What he meant, of course, was Davies's egotism about poetry—in all other respects he was a modest man. There is little doubt that Davies's firm belief in his own poetic gift had been fueled by early praise in the press. In 1908, Edward Thomas, in the *Morning Post,* criticized syntax, rhyme, and rhythm in Davies's second volume, *New Poems.* Yet, he also referred to him as a "fascinating genius." The idea of "genius" very much appealed to Davies. However, such status can be dangerous. Davies's alleged (and frequently self-professed) "genius" has given rise to unbalanced readings of his work. In Brian Waters and Thomas Moult, both of whom believed in Davies's superior ability, it led to excessive praise. By contrast Richard Stonesifer's biography, which for its attention to detail stands unrivaled, betrays an irritation with Davies's vanity that impairs its critical judgment. Adverse comments on individual poetic lines and stanzas feel in places like attempts to bring him down.

If Davies is approached not as a genius but as a flawed poet, he immediately becomes a subject of fascination. His strengths and weaknesses make him a man of his time: they mark a change which was taking place in the early part of the twentieth century, a movement away from stylized and self-conscious diction toward a poetic idiom born of spoken English. In many ways, this was the legacy of Wordsworth, but in Davies at his best it combined with a lyrical purity which even his fiercest critics do not deny him.

"The Kingfisher" (in *Farewell to Poesy*) illustrates the curious nature of Davies's vanity. The poem was singled out by Davies himself for the first volume of *Georgian Poetry,* and he later included it as a flagship poem in the two anthologies he edited himself. He believed this was a poem critics would admire. In fact it illustrates both his strength and his weakness. The first stanza displays the Augustan capitalization and complex simile dear to Davies's heart:

It was the Rainbow gave thee birth,
    And left thee all her lovely hues;
And, as her mother's name was Tears,
    So runs it in thy blood to choose
For haunts the lonely pools....

WILLIAM H. DAVIES

Davies claimed the kingfisher was his favorite bird; it was also the bird with which he most closely identified (in a later printing of the poem "thy blood" is changed to "my blood"). He identified with the kingfisher for two reasons: in the first stanza its preference for "lonely" haunts and in the second its beauty and "kingly" associations.

The second stanza of the poem moves into exhortation. Instead of continuing to address the bird as "thee," the poet says, "Go you and, with such glorious hues, / Live with proud Peacocks in green parks." The "you" produces an internal rhyme with "hues," but it is weak in terms of consistency, and that weakness is compounded by the subsequent clumsy line "Get thee on boughs and clap thy wings." Then the third stanza changes once again: the first two lines still employ "poetic" diction ("Nay, lovely Bird, thou art not vain; / Thou hast no proud, ambitious mind"), but their negatives accomplish a sharp tonal change and, interestingly, renounce the vanity and ambition Davies himself has been charged with. Davies is not the kingfisher: the bird only represents what he would like to be. And then, at the end of the poem, the poet suddenly switches into personal statement, the word choice plainer and more musical:

I also love a quiet place
    That's green, away from all mankind;
A lonely pool, and let a tree
Sigh with her bosom over me.

The enjambment of the last two lines reenacts the "sigh"; the simplicity of the phrasing ("a quiet place / That's green") can appeal to any readership. The ending of the poem is above all what sticks in the mind. Both in meaning and in movement it achieves resolution. The first two stanzas would not have saved the poem for posterity—but in combination with the last, the lyric works. It is not an artless piece: each stanza is a single sentence. The "lonely pools" of the first stanza connect with the "lonely pool" of the last. The last two lines of each stanza are enjambed in repetitive pattern. Even the revision from "thy" to "my" serves to strengthen a set of consciously controlled parallels.

TOWARD SIMPLICITY

In his early poetry collections Davies tended to conclude each volume with a weighty piece. These often accomplished the opposite of what he intended and showed his tendency to doggerel or pomposity. In *New Poems* the final poem, "Hope Abandoned," runs to fifty-seven stanzas, many of which show Davies at his worst:

Had I not hopes to feed one fond Desire,
Till Dark Despair gave me a torch of fire—
Intoxication—bade me burn my brain
And body up, for joy to kill my pain?

Despite negative criticism of this poem in press reviews, Davies did not forego the temptation to conclude each collection loftily until *The Bird of Paradise and Other Poems* in 1914. Even the first poem in this volume seems to commit the poet to a smaller scope. He refers to his "little songs" which "to the world / Are puny mole-hills" and there is a sense that he has decided to please himself rather than "the world." If so, the change is a good one. The collection includes "The Best Friend," one of Davies's best "joy" poems, and one in which Joy is personified as a woman. The last two stanzas serve to illustrate the effectiveness of simple language combined with neat syntactical parallels:

Now shall I dance,
    Or sit for dreams?
"Sit," answers Joy;
    "Dance," Pleasure screams.

Which of ye two
    Will kindest be?
Pleasure laughed sweet,
    But Joy kissed me.

The metrical irregularity in the final line works beautifully. Davies can break rules disastrously, it is true, but also to excellent effect.

The Bird of Paradise concludes with two connected pieces, "Nell Barnes" and the title poem. These two are in familiar ballad form (alternating tetrameter/trimeter) and jointly tell a life story. Nell Barnes, the central character, has "led a wicked life"—and her errant husband is no better.

When he emigrates though, she dies "for love." In the second poem, Kate Summers, a prostitute, tells the story of Nell Barnes's death. Nell, she says, had been "Unclean, a thief as well" but the best friend she ever had. The ballads are extremely direct. Their diction is completely accessible and the emotional impact forceful. The theme was dear to Davies too: the idea that fine feeling could be found in unlikely places, that "bad" people were capable of singular kindness. The poet does not, at any point, intrude with self-conscious poeticism; in fact, what is interesting is the degree to which he effaces himself. The style is understated, powerful, and lean.

Lawrence Normand, in *W. H. Davies* (2003), has suggested that Davies learned "a spareness of style" from the posthumous publication in 1917 of Edward Thomas' *Poems,* a spareness which Thomas had acquired from the symbolists and imagists. In fact, such a style was evident from the start in Davies's writing, albeit sporadically. Normand even finds modernist attributes in Davies's 1918 publication *Forty New Poems* and suggests that had he taken these "tendencies" further "he would have become another sort of poet altogether." This brings into focus another central issue in reading Davies. If modernism is seen as progress and Georgianism is seen as its regressive corollary, then Davies's progression as a poet is obscured. The danger of attributing "modernist tendencies" to Davies is that they become associated with whatever is good in his verse, while what is clearly bad is labeled "Georgian." Such terms are unhelpful.

The general feeling that Davies's poetry became weaker as he acquired a public readership is shared by many critics. Nevertheless, Davies was continuing to develop according to his own lights, even though his development may not have matched supercritical expectations. In *Forty New Poems,* although the stylized voice is still there in poems like "Birds," there are small, self-effacing lyrics that combine form and feeling with a forcefulness out of all proportion to their size. "The Excuse," in only two four-line stanzas, is one of these:

"Why did you kill that harmless frog?
    Tell me, my little boy."

He hung his head for shame, and gone
    Was all his joy.

But now a thought comes to his mind,
    He lifts his head with pride:
"I only *half*-killed it," he said—
    "And then it died."

Little about this lyric is modernist, but much is worthy of note. The ballad-like opening, *in medias res,* exploits direct speech to evoke situation and character in only twenty-four words. Then a switch into historic present sharpens the impact of the second stanza. This is underpinned by the parallel structure of question and answer, shame and pride, hung head and lifted head. The metrical form (tetrameter, trimeter, tetrameter, dimeter) comes into full force with the very short final line, which is both amusing and painful. The whole poem seems slight, though authentic. The poet does not attempt to draw a wider application. Yet if we remember when the poem was published—in the fifth and final year of World War I—the understated comment on cruelty and its justifications is unmistakable. This is good writing, and it, rather than "Birds," represents what Davies was working toward.

In 1920, the same year that Davies's Civil List pension was increased to 150 pounds, he published *The Song of Life and Other Poems.* (A year later this collection and *Forty New Poems* were published in a single volume in the United States under the title *The Captive Lion and Other Poems.*) "The Song of Life," an unwieldy poem started many years earlier, is a lengthy attempt to sum up Davies's philosophy of life and poetry. It must have done him more harm than good since it is so clumsily flawed, although (like nearly all Davies's inferior poetry) it has some lovely lines. But at the same time as this obvious failure, Davies—uneven as ever—was publishing shorter lyrics of undeniable quality. One of these is "The Villain":

While joy gave clouds the light of stars,
    That beamed where'er they looked;
And calves and lambs had tottering knees,
    Excited, while they sucked;
While every bird enjoyed his song,
Without one thought of harm or wrong—
I turned my head and saw the wind,

Not far from where I stood,
Dragging the corn by her golden hair,
Into a dark and lonely wood.

It is with sudden surprise that the reader realizes the first four lines are intentionally clichéd. The archaic diction of "beamed where're they looked" sets up a blandly relaxed atmosphere. Nature is a lovely place. And then suddenly it is not. The villain of the piece is only the wind, and yet it seems more profound than that, as though the narrator himself is touched by the sudden evil. Most of the poem is regular iambic tetrameter/trimeter, but the key line, "Dragging the corn by her golden hair," is quite different. The first two feet are anapests (long-short-short), emphasizing the force of the wind and the reluctance of the corn. It is not an error of metrical pattern: it is deliberate use of meter to enhance effect.

The Hour of Magic and Other Poems, published in 1922, was decorated with line prints by Davies's friend William Nicholson. This gave the volume a certain charm (the final page, which shows the poet asleep underneath the ideas that dominate his poems—a cow, a bee, a star, and so forth—is particularly attractive), but it probably also conveyed the message the Davies's poems were somehow pretty and childish. (It is hard to imagine a modernist poem illustrated with line drawings.) Davies loved children and theirs was truly the childlike viewpoint he aspired to. Taking a different view of the matter, Stonesifer charges him with studied naïveté—deliberately cultivating false innocence and fake charm. This was certainly a significant risk in what he was trying to do, and the little line drawings in many of his later collections can contribute to an impression of cloying sweetness. At the same time, some of the poems in *The Hour of Magic* reverse this effect. For example, in "A Woman's History," Mary Price starts life innocently, singing "sad hymns for hours" when her pet bird dies. Then, in her teens she is "ruined by a man." The poem creates a pathetic victim, with snapshots of the suffering heroine aged 5, 15, 35, and finally 75. A saintly ending seems predictable. But no—at thirty-five, when her ruinous husband dies, Mary Price takes "a lover." In the final

stanza, while the reader is still surprised by the lover, Davies jumps forward forty years. He draws no conclusions:

Now, Mary Price is seventy-five,
And skinning eels alive:
She, active, strong, and full of breath,
Has caught the cat that stole an eel,
And beaten it to death.

This is the simple voice he was aiming for: uncompromising, easily understood, each word striking home with the force of fact.

POETRY 1922–1939

When Davies married in 1923, he believed that his marriage would act as an inspiration to what he called his "horse of wind and fire." Richard Stonesifer is not alone in concluding otherwise. He suggests that the poetry after marriage is "of less force" and classes it mainly as "domestic scribbling." It is true that as Davies got older his poems became shorter and simpler. Instead of playing to two audiences, he had chosen the one he preferred—and it was the common reader, not the literary one. He eschewed complex form and language in favor of what was simply and easily understood—and this was quite deliberate. He wanted to make poetry popular. At the same time, modernist poets were pursuing a very different form and practice which, although losing popular readership, was gaining academic and critical approval.

Davies's best poems appeal on many levels. When he fails in his later years, it is not because of his earlier mismatch between stylized and simple diction; it is because simple directness can easily slip into banality, especially in tandem with regular meter. It was the attendant risk of what he was trying to do. All the same, it is not true that the work of his last years is lesser. It is as uneven as ever, but there is much of interest in the final collections, especially (but not exclusively) in the love poems. Davies's joyful attitude to love was mixed with fear and inhibition. There are often undertones of power, cunning and deceit, although sexual power for

Davies is often expressed in unusually innocent terms. (Few poets express male mastery in terms of "a powerful bee" overwhelming a flower.) His sexual experience before marriage had been mainly with prostitutes, a service he paid for. He did not marry until his income would support a wife; even then his wife's origins were hardly what the world would think of as pure. He was aging, lame, and anxious. A lifetime of financial penury had made him painfully aware of money and the power it signified. In the later love poems, despite the fact that he had apparently achieved love and security, imagery of commerce insinuates itself. In "Love's Payment" (in *Secrets*, 1924) Davies approaches the subject humorously, but the idea is uneasy:

All fish and fowl, all fruit, and all you drink,
    Lie at the bottom of my purse, and I
Demand at will two kisses for my one;
    This is my certain charge....

Affirmatory poems mingle with others that are dark and troubling: the brooding tone of "Down Underground," in which Davies envisages "Beauty" destroyed by worms, is picked up again in "Uncertainty" (in *Ambition and Other Poems*, 1929) where the poet refuses to declare his love, finding power in secrecy:

So let the game go on,
    Which Love calls "Yes or No,"
Till Death says, "Come with me—
    Come to a quiet show,"
Where she, or I, alone,
    Inside the cold, black vault,
Train worms to skip a hair,
    And make the somersault.

Love is undoubtedly crucial to Davies, even when he tangles with jealousy, but in his married retreat there is also a feeling of lonliness. In "The Loneliest Mountain," the four-line title poem of his last collection (1939), Davies sets up a parallel between himself and an isolated landscape:

The loneliest mountain, with no house or tree,
    Still has its little flower so sweet and wild;
While I, a dreamer, strange and but half known,
    Can find no equal till I meet a child.

Simplicity of phrasing matches the childlike quality he is talking about here, but there is also a willing acceptance of isolation.

In *Love Poems* (1935), published five years before the poet's death, the theme of money recurs forcibly in "Love and Money," "Where We Agree," "This Green Orchard," "Fortunes," "The Tyrants," "To-night," and, most painfully, in "Love Me No More":

Since Love cries out for money, still,
    Where little is, or none—
Love me no more till I am dead,
    And every penny gone.

At the same time, references to worms recur. Disparity in age and outlook between the poet and his wife seems to have strengthened both a brooding sense of mortality and a craving for "joy."

Davies began his poetic career by dedicating himself to "joy," a joy often personified as female in his poems. At the end of his life, this dedication was no less profound. His love for his wife was not in question, but she had a rival—he seems to have felt a conscious tension between human love and the "joy" that inspired his work. "The Players," which is the deliberately placed last poem in *Love Poems,* has caused some disquiet with critics, who have alleged at worst pornographic innuendo, at best, bad taste. The poem illustrates the degree to which personalized reference in Davies's work can lead to misunderstanding in a wider cultural framework.

Almost everything Davies wrote was not abstract, but very particular—and personal. In a letter to Edward Thomas in 1910 he said, "I never write a love poem but that I have some real woman in my mind"; he might as well have added "and some real moment." "The Players" is an important poem to Davies. It recalls an incident mentioned in "The Soul's Destroyer" when he, and a little girl he remembered all his life, used to play together in the town park, a day he also recalls in "Child Lovers." They must surely both have been part of the Baptist church community. Only children brought up in strict Christian teaching would choose to play "Christ and Lazarus," as innocently as others play cops and robbers. However, in "The Players" the game is reenacted with "Joy"—not with his wife or any other woman. The poem is constructed in two parallel stanzas, illustrating a role reversal by day and night:

To-day I acted Christ,
　　While Joy played Lazarus;
I buried her in ferns
　　And heaps of gathered grass.
And when I cried "Come forth!"
　　Up from the grave she rose
And, with a peal of bells,
　　Threw off her burial clothes.

When Sleep this night has come,
　　With feathers for our grass,
Shall we reverse our parts
　　Of Christ and Lazarus?
When I—a buried man—
　　Hear "Lazarus, come forth!"
I'll rise and, with both hands,
　　Ring every bell on earth!

The words "Lazarus, come forth" echo Saint John's Gospel precisely. The potential reader error is in assuming the "we" of the second stanza to be Davies and his wife. He is talking about himself and "Joy," his first love and his last, his poetic muse. He needs the call of "Joy" to write poetry, to rescue him from metaphorical sleep. "Joy" for Davies was not sexual. It is clear from the Joy/Pleasure contrast in his earlier work that Joy was finer and purer than her fleshly counterpart. Besides, Davies (who had written at length about encounters with prostitutes) did not write pornographically. If there is a subtext in this poem (and there may not be one) it is in the adjective "buried"—he calls himself "a buried man" and there is an aural resonance here with "a married man"—who perhaps needs rescuing. Poetry was the single most important thing in Davies's life: it was the source of his faith, his spiritual nurture, and his personal isolation.

Edith Sitwell, in *Aspects of Modern Poetry* (1934), recalls an occasion when she complained to Davies about a poem she was having trouble writing. Davies gave her some advice: "You sit quietly, and it will come. A poem is like a bird in a wood." These words are true to the man himself: he associated poetry with song, song with birds, singing with inspiration. He did not, of course, always follow his own advice. Many of Davies's poems, especially the longer ones, are deliberate artifacts, put together as self-conscious statements to the world. Nonetheless, during his writing career he consciously moved away from formalized structure and diction toward a lyricism born of speech cadence.

In "One by One," for example, in *A Poet's Calendar* (1927) the poet in his midfifties demonstrated how far he had taken this conscious practice—perhaps, indeed, as far as it is possible to go. The poem is in four stanzas, the second and fourth lines of each stanza in four monosyllables. The monosyllables fall with a heaviness reinforced by the repeating line "One by one" which recurs four times:

Few are my friends,
　　But kind and true;
One by one,
　　I lose my few.

Again a friend
　　Must leave this world;
One by one,
　　His limbs go cold.

Before the Sun
　　Has left yon wall,
One by one
　　The blinds will fall.

My visits change
　　From house to tomb:
One by one
　　My friends leave home.

The poem is simple enough to read and understand instantly. Its emotive power is driven not only by word choice, but assonance, rhythm, and number. The plangent rhyme of "true/few" in the first four lines is echoed in "lose." "Few" sounds dolefully as both the first and last word of the opening stanza. Then "friends/kind" leads into "Again/friend" in the second stanza. In the third, there is internal rhyme between "Sun," "yon," and "one," as well as a sound echo in "blind," which also picks up the earlier "friend" and "kind." The word "visit" in the last stanza has two syllables (the only other disyllabic word in the poem is "again") and it sounds a change, a sudden briskness. Then "tomb" falls with gloomy ponderousness, half-rhyming with the earlier "limbs." The two stresses of each dimeter line fall heavily, that heaviness further reinforced by the opening spondee in each third line: "One by one." The poem is simple but certainly not artless.

Shortly before his death Davies told his friend Brian Waters that he had done what he "set out to do." The elderly poet believed he had consciously developed his art toward a specific end, and there is evidence in his work to support that assertion. He influenced others—not always favorably: many versifiers picked up his simple rhyming forms without his subtlety or spareness. But his influence was far-reaching in another way too. His command of a plain language that could "sing" appealed to many writers, especially as a counterbalance to the self-conscious complexity of much free verse published in the 1930s and 1940s. Moreover, his turn of phrase in both prose and verse was memorable, and so was his outlook on life. Philip Larkin's poem "Toads" (self-selected in *The Oxford Book of Twentieth-Century English Verse,* 1973) famously begins: "Why should I let the toad *work* / Squat on my life?" The sentiment was Davies's own: like the beggars of his early essays, he despised work in the ordinary sense. And even Larkin's word choice echoes one of the characters in Davies's little-known "tramp opera": "Are you aware, Sir, that you contaminate this pure well of life by introducing that toad called work?" It is easy to underestimate W. H. Davies, but not easy, once his best work is known, to forget him.

Selected Bibliography

WORKS OF W. H. DAVIES

POETRY

The Soul's Destroyer and Other Poems. London: The Farmhouse, 1905. (Contains 40 poems, private printing.) London: Alston Rivers, 1907. (Abridged edition contains 14 poems.)

New Poems. London: Elkin Mathews, 1907. Boston: Humphries, 1938.

Nature Poems and Others. London: Fifield, 1908. Boston: Humphries, 1937.

Farewell to Poesy. London: Fifield, 1910. Boston: Humphries, 1910.

Songs of Joy. London: Fifield, 1911. Boston: Humphries, 1911.

Foliage. London: Elkin Mathews, 1913.

The Bird of Paradise and Other Poems. London: Methuen, 1914.

Child Lovers and Other Poems. London: Fifield, 1916.

Collected Poems. London: Fifield, 1916. New York: Knopf, 1916. (U.S. publication entitled *The Collected Poems of William H. Davies.*)

Forty New Poems. London: Fifield, 1918.

Raptures, a Book of Poems. London: Beaumont, 1918.

The Song of Life and Other Poems. London: Fifield, 1920.

The Captive Lion and Other Poems. New Haven, Conn.: Yale University Press, 1921. (Includes the poems from *Forty New Poems* and *The Song of Life and Other Poems.*)

The Hour of Magic and Other Poems. Illustrated by William Nicholson. London: Jonathan Cape, 1922. New York: Harper, 1922.

Collected Poems: First Series. London: Jonathan Cape, 1923.

Collected Poems: Second Series. London: Jonathan Cape, 1923. New York: Harper, 1923.

True Travellers: A Tramps Opera in Three Acts. Illustrated by William Nicholson. London: Jonathan Cape, 1923. New York: Harcourt, Brace, 1923. (Dramatic script, never performed, includes poems/songs.)

Secrets. London: Jonathan Cape, 1924. New York: Harcourt, Brace, 1924.

A Poet's Alphabet. London: Jonathan Cape, 1925.

W. H. Davies. Augustan Books of Modern Poetry. London: Ernest Benn, 1925.

The Song of Love. London: Jonathan Cape, 1926.

A Poet's Calendar. London: Jonathan Cape, 1927.

The Collected Poems of W. H. Davies. London: Jonathan Cape, 1928. New York: Cape and Smith, 1929.

Forty-Nine Poems. Selected and illustrated by Jacynth Parsons, with an introduction by Davies. London: Medici Society, 1928. New York: Cape and Smith, 1929.

Selected Poems. Arranged by Edward Garnett, with an introduction by Davies. Newtown, Montgomeryshire: Gregynog Press, 1928.

Ambition and Other Poems. London: Jonathan Cape, 1929.

Poems, 1930–1931. London: Jonathan Cape, 1932.

The Lover's Song Book. Newtown, Montgomeryshire: Gregynog Press, 1933.

WILLIAM H. DAVIES

The Poems of W. H. Davies. London: Jonathan Cape, 1934. New York: Oxford University Press, 1935.

Love Poems. London: Jonathan Cape, 1935. New York: Oxford University Press, 1935.

The Birth of Song: Poems 1935–36. London: Jonathan Cape, 1936. New York: Oxford University Press, 1936.

The Loneliest Mountain. London: Jonathan Cape, 1939.

The Poems of W. H. Davies. London: Jonathan Cape, 1940.

COLLECTIONS

Common Joys and Other Poems. Sesame Books. London: Faber & Faber, 1941. (A selection of 62 poems.)

Collected Poems of W. H. Davies. London: Jonathan Cape 1942. (Includes an introduction by Osbert Sitwell; contents otherwise the same as the 1942 volume.)

The Essential W. H. Davies. Edited with an introduction by Brian Waters. London: Jonathan Cape 1951. (Selected poems and prose extracts.)

The Complete Poems of W. H. Davies. Introduction by Osbert Sitwell, foreword by Daniel George. London: Jonathan Cape, 1963. Middletown, Conn.: Wesleyan University Press, 1965. (Includes 113 poems omitted from the 1940 volume.)

Selected Poems. Edited with an introduction by Jonathan Barker. Oxford: Oxford University Press, 1985. (Includes a chronology of the poet's life and work; reprinted as part of Oxford Poets Series, 1992.)

AUTOBIOGRAPHICAL WORKS

The Autobiography of a Super-Tramp. Preface by George Bernard Shaw. London: Fifield, 1908. New York: Knopf, 1917.

Beggars. London: Duckworth, 1909.

The True Traveller. London: Duckworth, 1912.

Nature. London: Batsford, 1914.

A Poet's Pilgrimage. London: Melrose, 1918. New York: Cape and Smith, 1929.

Later Days. London: Jonathan Cape, 1925. New York: Doran, 1926.

The Adventures of Johnny Walker, Tramp. London: Jonathan Cape, 1926.

My Birds. London: Jonathan Cape, 1933.

My Garden. London: Jonathan Cape, 1933.

Young Emma. Foreword by C. V. Wedgwood. London: Jonathan Cape, 1980. New York: Braziller, 1981. (Completed in 1924 but not previously published.)

NOVELS

A Weak Woman. London: Duckworth, 1911.

Dancing Mad. London: Jonathan Cape, 1927.

AS EDITOR

Form. Edited by Davies and Austin O. Spare. Numbers 1, 2, 3 (October, November, December 1921), and 4 (January 1922). (A magazine of poetry.)

Shorter Lyrics of the Twentieth Century 1900–1922. Edited and introduced by Davies. London: The Poetry Bookshop, 1922.

Jewels of Song: An Anthology of Short Poems. Selected and introduced by Davies. London: Jonathan Cape, 1930.

CRITICAL AND BIOGRAPHICAL STUDIES

Church, Richard. "W. H. Davies: The Man and His Work." In his *Eight for Immortality.* London: J. M. Dent, 1941. Freeport, N.Y.: Books for Libraries, 1969.

Cooke, William. "Alms and the Supertramp: Nineteen Unpublished Letters of W. H. Davies to Edward Thomas." *Anglo-Welsh Review* 70:34–59 (1982). (Nineteen letters produced in full with an introduction by William Cooke)

Graves, Robert. *Collected Writings on Poetry.* Edited by Paul O'Prey. Manchester: Carcanet, 1995.

Hockey, Lawrence W. *W. H. Davies.* Cardiff: University of Wales Press, 1971.

Hooper, Barbara. *Time to Stand and Stare: A Life of W. H. Davies, the Tramp-poet.* (Includes a selection of 13 poems.) London: Peter Owen, 2004.

Larkin, Philip. "Freshly Scrubbed Potato." In his *Required Writing, Miscellaneous Pieces 1955–1982.* London: Faber & Faber, 1983. New York: Farrar Straus Giroux, 1984. (A review of *The Complete Poems of W. H. Davies* and of Richard J. Stonesifer's *W. H. Davies: A Critical Biography,* both published in 1963.)

De la Mare, Walter. "W. H. Davies." In his *Private View.* London: Faber & Faber, 1953.

Moult, Thomas. *W. H. Davies.* London: Thornton Butterworth, 1934.

Normand, Lawrence. *W. H. Davies.* Bridgend, Wales: Poetry Wales Press, 2003.

Poetry Wales 18, no. 2 (1983). (Entire issue devoted to W. H. Davies with six of his poems, articles by Jonathan Barker, Lawrence W. Hockey, Sybil Hollingdrake, Fiona Pearson, R. George Thomas, and a chronology of Davies's life.)

Sitwell, Edith. "William H. Davies." In her *Aspects of Modern Poetry.* London: Duckworth, 1934. Freeport, N.Y.: Books for Libraries, 1970.

Sitwell, Osbert. "W. H. Davies." In his *Noble Essences.* London: Macmillan, 1950. Boston: Little Brown, 1950.

Stonesifer, Richard J. *W. H. Davies: A Critical Biography.* London: Jonathan Cape, 1963. Middletown, Conn.: Wesleyan University Press, 1965.

Thomas, R. George. *Letters from Edward Thomas to Gordon Bottomley.* London: Oxford University Press, 1968.

FULKE GREVILLE

(1554–1628)

Neil Powell

"FULKE GREVILLE, SERVANT to Queen Elizabeth, Counsellor to King James, and Friend to Sir Philip Sidney. Trophaeum Peccati." Fulke Greville's modest epitaph, on his decidedly immodest tomb in St. Mary's Church, Warwick, is subtle and eloquent in its brevity. "Servant" here implies a service willingly given and properly appreciated, whereas the slightly more guarded "Counsellor" perhaps suggests that the counsel was not invariably well received; Greville's expression of unqualified intimacy is reserved for his childhood friend Sir Philip Sidney, who died in 1586, when both men were thirty-two years old. If that last name had a counterbalance, it might have been "Enemy to Sir Robert Cecil," though that would hardly be true to Greville's style; the addendum "Trophaeum Peccati"—"monument to a sinner"—is very much in character, however, and its piety is unfeigned. One of his modern editors, Thom Gunn, describes Greville's life as "that of a highly placed civil servant" (*Selected Poems, 1968,* p. 9), a phrase that may have us searching for the sixteenth-century equivalent of a smart suit and neatly furled umbrella; but a civil servant in the courts of Elizabeth I and James I was likely to have experienced extremes of favor and disfavor, wealth and poverty, unknown to his modern counterpart.

Greville's family was firmly rooted in the Vale of Evesham, on the borders of Warwickshire and Gloucestershire, where his fourteenth-century ancestor William Greville acquired Milcote House. The first Sir Fulke Greville, the poet's grandfather, was a younger son who consequently did not inherit Milcote, a disadvantage amply remedied by his marriage to Elizabeth, the granddaughter and heiress of Sir Robert Willoughby, Lord Brooke. Through this marriage, he acquired Beauchamp Court and other property, to which Henry VIII added, in recognition of Greville's

military service, the site of the monastery at Alcester; by the time of his death in 1559, he was among the most prosperous and extensive property owners in Warwickshire. His son, the second Sir Fulke Greville, was a justice of the peace, twice sheriff of Warwickshire, and from 1591 recorder of Warwick and of Stratford-upon-Avon; praised by the historian William Camden for "the sweetness of his temper," he was also "much given to hospitality," which greatly eroded the family fortune. His acquisition of the ruined Warwick Castle in 1604 added both to his position and to his debts; when he died two years later, his son would describe him as "a most worthy and kind father," adding: "The world, his debts, his will and executors shall bear witness with me that the ruins of his estate, which he has left behind him, will for divers reasons sink me lower than before" (Rees, 1971, p. 12). According to Sir William Dugdale's *The Antiquities of Warwickshire* (1656), his son was to spend the enormous sum of twenty thousand pounds on restoring and improving Warwick Castle.

This son—the third Fulke Greville and the subject of this essay—was born in 1554. At the age of ten he was sent to the recently founded Shrewsbury School, arriving there on the same day as Philip Sidney: "Fulke Greville is a good boy," wrote Sidney in his schoolbook, near the beginning of their friendship (Rees, 1971, p. 46). On leaving Shrewsbury, their paths temporarily diverged: Sidney went up to Christ Church, Oxford, in 1568, while Greville proceeded to Jesus College, Cambridge. In 1575 they were reunited at the court of Elizabeth I, where Greville quickly attracted the queen's favor: Sir Robert Naunton's *Fragmenta Regalia* (quoted in *Dictionary of National Biography*) says that he "had the longest lease and the smoothest time without rub of any of her favourites," a phrase that is subtly suggestive both of the court's turbulence and of Greville's diplomatic skills. He seems, nevertheless, to have pushed his luck: having in 1577 accompanied Sidney to Heidelberg, with Her Majesty's consent, the following year he went to Dover to embark for the Low Countries, without it; Sir Edward Dyer was sent from court to detain him. Undeterred, he set off with Sir Francis Walsingham for Flanders soon afterward and on his return "was forbidden the queen's presence for many months." But his favor was only glancingly eclipsed: in 1579 he went with Sidney's friend and tutor Hubert Languet to Germany and two years later was substantially responsible for organizing the grand pageant and tournament with which the queen entertained the French envoys sent to negotiate her proposed marriage with the duke of Anjou.

Sidney, Dyer, and Greville together formed an important focus of literary influence at court, and all three were members of the Areopagus, a literary society (named after the Athenian hill and the court that met there) founded by Gabriel Harvey in 1580. This society's main objective was to incorporate classical principles, including quantitative syllabic scansion, into English literature; the metrical precepts were soon abandoned, but other classical characteristics would continue to influence the work of these writers. When the scientist and philosopher Giordano Bruno visited England in 1583, Greville received him with enthusiasm, arranging a supper party in his honor at which the other guests included John Florio, Matthew Gwynne, and Sidney; Bruno's *Spaccio de la bestia trionfante* (1584), dedicated to Sidney, describes Greville as a "generous and humane spirit." Bruno's pantheism is another detectable influence in Greville's poetry and, although they cannot be dated with certainty, most of the earlier poems in Greville's major work, *Caelica,* probably date from this period of his life.

Two years later, persuaded against his own better judgment by "that ingenuous spirit of Sir Philip's," he prepared to embark with his friend at Plymouth on one of Sir Francis Drake's expeditions to the West Indies. This time, as he recounted in *The Life of the Renowned Sir Philip Sidney,* 1652, they were recalled by "a more imperial mandate, carefully conveyed and delivered to himself by a peer of this realm; carrying with it in the one hand grace, the other thunder" (*Selected Writings,* p. 141). It is characteristic of Greville that, while he had been drawn by friendship into a reckless adventure, he was nevertheless greatly relieved when prudence and obedience prevailed. Sidney's grudging acquiescence was rewarded—fatally, as it turned out—by the chance to serve under his uncle, Lord Leicester, in the Low Countries; he was killed at the Battle of Zutphen in 1586.

Although Sidney's death transformed Greville's inner life, turning him into the author of the darkly reflective poems that today command most admiration, the extent of this change would not have been evident to his contemporaries. They would have seen an occasionally reckless but well-liked young courtier softening into a successful middle age. He had been secretary for the Principality of Wales, a sinecure, since 1583; in 1592 he became member of Parliament for Warwickshire, a position he was to hold on three subsequent occasions; in 1597 he was appointed treasurer of the wars and the following year, treasurer of the navy. He had a more active naval role too, as rear admiral in command of the largest of the queen's ships, the *Triumph.* In return for his loyalty, Elizabeth presented him with the estate of Wedgnock Park in 1597; while he, devoted servant that he was, took part in the arrest for treason of his former friend and distant relation Robert Devereux, earl of Essex, in 1601. For as long as Queen Elizabeth—"this blessed and blessing lady, with a calm mind as well in quiet as stirring times," as he called her in the *Life of Sidney*—remained on the throne, his position seemed assured.

But the accession of James I in 1604, though it brought a knighthood for Greville, heralded a change in the court that was to keep him out of high office for a decade. This exclusion was largely the result of a distrust verging on paranoia on the part of Robert Cecil, now earl of Salisbury, the power behind the throne in the early Jacobean court: Greville's proposal to write a history of the preceding reign and Cecil's refusal to allow him access to the relevant state papers—apparently fearing an unfavorable comparison with James I's (and his own) management of state affairs—are clearly suggestive of a man and a regime chronically out of sympathy with each other. Yet the alteration in Greville's domestic circumstances after his father's death in 1606 also played a part: the focus of his life shifted firmly from London to Warwickshire, where he had the vast and costly restoration of Warwick Castle to contend with, and where he had extensive and sometime troublesome interests in other property. Moreover, in 1612 he adopted his four-year-old cousin and heir, Robert Greville, for whose subsequent upbringing and education he was to be responsible. Nothing would have been more natural than for Greville, who was by now in his late fifties, to spend his remaining years as a Warwickshire landowner and magistrate, nurturing both his estate and its inheritor. As Joan Rees puts it in her critical biography of Greville, "If to wish to have as much as possible of the land in one's own possession is a sign of affection—as Shakespeare's Henry V claimed to be a great lover of France because he would not willingly part with a village of it—then Greville was a devoted lover of Warwickshire" (p. 16).

Nevertheless, he was recalled to court in 1614 and appointed chancellor of the exchequer, an office he held for the following seven years; in 1618, he also became commissioner of the treasury. When he was ennobled in 1621, the title of his Willoughby ancestors was revived: he was created Baron Brooke of Warwick, taking his seat in the House of Lords on November 15. During the 1620s he continued to serve on important committees, including the council of war and the council to advise on foreign affairs. But his health was failing, and in 1628 he made a will leaving all his property to his cousin Robert; the witnesses included an elderly servant, Ralph Haywood. Although Greville later added a codicil granting annuities to many dependants, Haywood's name was apparently not among them. This aggrieved servant, while attending his master in the bedroom of his London house, complained of this omission and, on being rebuked by Greville, seized a sword and stabbed him before killing himself in an adjacent room. Greville, mortally wounded, lived long enough to make some further adjustments to his will, but he died on September 30; his body was carried to Warwick, where he was buried at St. Mary's Church on October 27, 1628.

LITERARY WORKS

Very little of Greville's work was published during his lifetime; but this does not mean, given the efficient literary bush-telegraph of the late-sixteenth-century court, that his poetry remained unknown. For instance, two pieces from the 109-poem sequence *Caelica* (5 and 29) were set by John Dowland in his *First Booke of Songs or Ayres* of 1597 and a third (52) in his *Second Booke of Songs or Ayres* of 1600 (*English Madrigal Verse,* pp. 454, 466, 475); this both provides evidence of the poems' currency within courtly circles (Dowland, interestingly, was a long-standing friend of Robert Cecil) and of course supplies a pair of dates by which much of *Caelica* had incontrovertibly been written. A setting by Michael Cavendish of the opening poem in the sequence, "Love, the delight of all well-thinking minds," was published in 1598, and several others were set by Martin Peerson, shortly after Greville's death, in 1630. But the complete text of *Caelica*, Greville's major achievement, was not to appear in print until the publication of *Certaine Learned and Elegant Workes of the Right Honourable Fulke, Lord Brooke,* in 1633.

This delay reflects Greville's own priorities. He did not think of himself as a poet but—as his epitaph accurately implies—firstly as a high-ranking servant to two very different monarchs and secondly as Sir Philip Sidney's friend; and when, after his friend's early death, he edited Sidney's *Arcadia* in 1590, he did so in precisely the same spirit. Choosing the later, longer and more morally instructive version of *Arcadia,* Greville viewed it as a philosophical treatise rather than as a work of literary imagination, just as in the *Life of Sidney* he was to focus on his subject's political achievements at the expense of his literary ones. Greville must have written the *Life of*

Sidney, which owes its misleading title to the editor who published it in 1652, during his politically fallow decade of 1604–1614: although it is partly a memorial to his friend, it is also a more general memoir of Greville's own life and times which would no doubt have been expanded to include his historical account of Elizabeth's court if Cecil had not denied him access to the relevant papers.

Besides *Caelica,* the 1633 edition of *Certaine Learned and Elegant Workes* includes three verse treatises (on human learning, on fame and honor, and on wars), *A Letter to an Honourable Lady, A Letter of Travell,* and two plays: *Alaham* and *Mustapha;* a pirated text of the latter had been published in 1609, but both works—closet dramas entirely innocent of stagecraft and unintended for the stage—are likely to have been written in the late 1580s, along with much of *Caelica.* Their interest is now confined to extracts such as the "Chorus Sacerdotum" from *Mustapha* which was for many years Greville's best-known single poem. Apart from *Alaham* and *Mustapha,* Greville was the author of a play, predating Shakespeare's, on the subject of Antony and Cleopatra, which he destroyed, fearing that it might be interpreted as a hostile commentary on the fall of Essex—a fear that was by no means fanciful, since when Samuel Daniel's *Philotas* was performed in 1605 its author "was promptly called before the Privy Council and charged with seditious comment on the trial and execution of Essex" (Rees, 1971, p. 30). Two further verse treatises, on monarchy and religion, appeared in *The Remains of Sir Fulke Grevill, Lord Brooke,* in 1670.

All this hardly constitutes an enormous oeuvre, and it is easy to see why Greville was not regarded until relatively recently as a major figure: when he was noticed at all, it was either as the author of two unactable (and barely readable) plays or as the author of a *Life of Sidney* that was substantially nothing of the sort. No wonder he was neglected. The transformation of his reputation can be dated, with unusual precision, to 1939, and to the publication in three issues of *Poetry* (Chicago) of Yvor Winters' essay "The Sixteenth-Century Lyric in England: A Critical and Historical Reinterpretation"; slightly revised, this essay forms the basis of the opening chapter in Winters' *Forms of Discovery* (1967). In typically robust and provocative fashion, it is noted that Greville became a great poet of the Renaissance, more so than his associates (including, of course, Sidney), and furthermore should be categorized a great master of the short poem, as is Jonson. The basis for this judgment, to which the present writer fully assents, is the extraordinary series of 109 poems called *Caelica.*

CAELICA: *EARLY POEMS*

Caelica, says Yvor Winters, "has the effect more of a book than of a casual collection" (p. 51). That may not seem to be an especially arresting remark, yet it holds a key to the way we should approach these poems: readers expecting to find a "sequence" (or even a "sonnet sequence": only 41 of the 109 poems are sonnets) are in for one sort of disappointment, while those who expect *Caelica* to be merely a random assortment of pieces are in for another. *Caelica* certainly has a shape, and it is the shape of its author's own inner development. To see what kind of book it really is, we might usefully borrow a formula from W. H. Auden and call it Greville's *Collected Shorter Poems;* but, whereas Auden famously arranged one of his collections in alphabetical order of first lines in order to disguise the poems' chronological order, it seems safe to assume that in *Caelica* we have at least an approximate chronology—a collection in which, although small groups of poems may well have been shuffled either randomly or for thematic effect, the overall progression is clear. We must therefore begin at the beginning.

At the start of *Caelica,* Greville is a young poet writing under the prevailing Italianate or "Petrarchan" influence of the time and in the shadow of his brilliant friend Sir Philip Sidney:

Love, the delight of all well-thinking minds;
Delight, the fruit of virtue dearly lov'd;
Virtue, the highest good, that reason finds;
Reason, the fire wherein men's thoughts be prov'd;

Are from the world by Nature's power bereft,
And in one creature, for her glory, left.

(1.1–6)

Though this may strike us as an entirely conventional opening—four qualities are delineated in turn, only to be subsumed in the "glory" of the idealized loved one—it nevertheless already hints at Greville's particular cast of mind. It is, after all, the least intuitive and emotional of the four qualities, Reason, that earns the most heartfelt and memorable definition ("the fire wherein men's thoughts be prov'd"), suggesting that the author may prove to be rather more passionate as a thinker than as a lover. Moreover, there is here, as there will often be later on, the hint of a theological echo in Greville's rhetoric. His comparison of four qualities followed, in the poem's final lines, by a recapitulation—"Delight, Love, Reason, Virtue let it be, / To set all women light, but only she"—recalls that famous passage in Saint Paul's First Epistle to the Corinthians, familiar to the sixteenth century in William Tyndale's translation, which ends: "Now abideth faith, hope, and love, even these three: but the chief of these is love."

To read late-sixteenth-century English poetry is to be continually aware of echoes; for, as Thom Gunn says, "the Elizabethans at their best as well as at their worst are always sounding like each other. They did not search much after uniqueness of voice" (*Selected Poems*, p. 20). Their work inhabits a community of poetry, reinforced by the fact that so many of the writers were personally known to each other; sometimes the ongoing conversation between poems narrows to a dialogue, as it does in the case of Christopher Marlowe's "The Passionate Shepherd to His Love" and Sir Walter Ralegh's reply, "If all the world and love were young." Greville engages in exactly this kind of dialogue with Sidney—for instance, *Caelica* 46 and 60 echo *Astrophil and Stella* 56 and 27—as well as with Sir Edward Dyer, whose punning conclusion to "A Fancy" ("*Dy er* thou let his name be known: his folly shows too much") is mirrored by the last line of *Caelica* 83: "For *Grieve-Ill*, pain, forlorn estate do best decipher me"). But even in Greville's

early poems, the attentive reader will be aware of a questioning, ruminative mind pulling away from conventional gestures: *Caelica* 4, for example, begins with a conceit that exemplifies the Petrarchan mode at its lightest and (one might even say) silliest—"You little stars that live in skies, / And glory in Apollo's glory..."—yet when the first-person author enters the poem he brings a typically disputatious edge to it. For this is how the poem concludes:

And thou O Love, which in these eyes
Hast married Reason with Affection,
And made them saints of beauty's skies,
Where joys are shadows of perfection,
Lend me thy wings that I may rise
Up not by worth but thy election;
    For I have vow'd in strangest fashion,
    To love, and never seek compassion.

(4.9–16)

If he is dedicating himself to the religion of love—as evidently he is, giving the word "saints" its due weight—he is doing so in the full knowledge that this goes against the grain of his thinking self, the analytical mind with which he sees himself behaving "in strangest fashion."

Still more impressive among the earliest poems in *Caelica,* as an instance of Greville's ability to enhance a conventional idea with his own knotty individuality, is 7:

The world, that all contains, is ever moving,
The stars within their spheres for ever turned,
Nature (the Queen of Change) to change is loving,
And form to matter new is still adjourned.

Fortune our fancy-god to very liketh,
Place is not bound to things within it placed,
The present time upon time passed striketh,
With Phoebus' wandering course the earth is graced.

The air still moves, and by its moving cleareth,
The fire up ascends, and planets feedeth,
The water passeth on, and all lets weareth,
The earth stands still, yet change of changes breedeth;

Her plants, which summer ripes, in winter fade,
Each creature in unconstant mother lieth,
Man made of earth, and for whom earth is made,
Still dying lives, and living ever dieth;

Only like fate sweet Myra never varies,
Yet in her eyes the doom of all change carries.

On one level, this merely reiterates one of the most common and least interesting ideas in Renaissance poetry—everything in the world alters apart from the loved one—and yet it seems too awkward, too insistently puzzled, for such a straightforward purpose. Part of our sense that the poet is more concerned with the perplexing processes of thought than with his unchanging Myra comes from the syntax. The poem is packed with verbs: every line ends with one, and the rhymes (mostly in -ed or -eth) take on a grating harshness that is unexpected in a poem about idealized love. The most remarkable (indeed, striking) image in the poem is that of the clock in line 7, where "striketh" combines the physical action of a bell being struck with the suggestion that the present may have a violently destructive effect on the past. If this seems an astonishingly complex and modern idea, it is also what we ordinarily call a "metaphysical" one, and the synthesis of abstraction and mechanical image will surely remind us of a poet in the generation after Greville, John Donne. Equally Donne-like is the syntactical trap of line 11, in which "lets" momentarily appears to be a verb meaning "permits" before resolving itself into a noun meaning "ways." Greville, in short, is already a poet to be read with some vigilance.

Yet he is by no means a charmless writer. In two adjacent sonnets, 12 and 13, Cupid is seen less as a deity of the religion of love than as a mischievous Puck, to be roundly scolded in both poems. He is a "naughty boy" who has clouded Greville's own eyes "with a seeing blindness" in 12, while 13 warns of the havoc he will cause to susceptible women: "Ladies, this blind boy that ran from his mother / Will ever play the wag with one or other." In several of the following poems, mostly in sonnet form, Greville describes Cupid's meddlesome attentions with mild complaints or grudging acceptance, addressing the "sweet boy" as if he were a spoilt child:

Cupid, my pretty boy, leave off thy crying,
Thou shalt have bells or apples; be not peevish;

Kiss me sweet lad; beshrew her for denying;
Such rude denials do make children thievish.

(25.1–4)

But this essentially lightweight sequence is interrupted by the far more substantial 22, which is understandably among the best known of Greville's early poems. After the predominantly abstract mode of the previous poems, the concreteness of these opening stanzas may come as a surprise:

I, with whose colours Myra dress'd her head,
I, that wore posies of her own hand-making,
I, that mine own name in the chimneys read
    By Myra finely wrought ere I was waking:
    Must I look on, in hope time coming may
    With change bring back my turn again to play?

I, that on Sunday at the church-stile found,
A garland sweet, with true-love knots in flowers,
Which I to wear about mine arm was bound,
That each of us might know that all was ours:
    Must I now lead an idle life in wishes?
    And follow Cupid for his loaves, and fishes?

(22.1–12)

Although this is not at all what we might expect after reading this preceding poems in *Caelica,* it is less astonishing in the context of its author's divided life: this is Greville momentarily forgetting he is a courtier and reverting instead to his Warwickshire origins. As the poet and critic Geoffrey Grigson memorably put it in a broadcast talk on Warwickshire writers, the poem "is unlike much Elizabethan verse in its indication of place and actuality; it is a love poem, you might say, of green Warwickshire and footpaths and stiles and large, lawn-like comfortable meadows and rook-haunted rectory or churchyard and elms, which Henry James found a little too much" (pp. 172–173). If the metaphysicality of *Caelica* 7 anticipates the next generation and John Donne, then the rural physicality of 22 anticipates the Romanticism of some two hundred years later—a kinship that, as we shall discover shortly, would not go unnoticed by Samuel Taylor Coleridge. The chimneys and the church-stile, the posies and the garland may be barely described, but they are indisputably *there,* and perhaps it is the churchyard scene that partly suggests the "loaves and fishes" of the last line, audaciously transforming waggish Cupid back into the Christ of love-as-religion and wryly implying—if the five thousand recipients of loaves and fishes in the parable are borne in mind—that Myra's affections are distributed widely indeed.

Three stanzas later, Greville moves to his conclusion:

> Was it for this that I might Myra see,
> Washing the water with her beauties, white?
> Yet would she never write her love to me;
> Thinks wit of change while thoughts are in delight?
>   Mad girls may safely love, as they may leave,
>   No man can print a kiss, lines may deceive.
>
> (22.25–30)

Nothing in the poem can have quite prepared us for the startlingly reversed image of the second line—an almost Shakespearean touch—nor indeed for its emphatic alliteration. But Greville is not content to end with the simple fact of the lover's betrayal; he has to add a piece of typically knotted and condensed introspection. "Thinks wit of change while thoughts are in delight" must mean "One doesn't think about inconsistency when one's thoughts are filled with pleasure"; yet the juxtaposition of "thoughts" and "delight" inescapably reminds us of Greville's own delight *in* thoughts. The final couplet is still more enigmatic, for it qualifies a fairly straightforward statement about Myra's fecklessness with the suggestion that his own lines (since he cannot "print a kiss") may also be deceptive: thus a poem that began by appearing to be so reassuringly local and straightforward ends with subtle distancing and self-qualification.

If the earlier poems in *Caelica* may be broadly described as "love poems," the affair or affairs to which they allude do not seem to have been very satisfactory. Poems such as 22, where the poet has been deserted by his mistress, greatly outnumber those (for example, 38: "Caelica, I overnight was finely used, / Lodged in the midst of paradise, your heart") that at least admit the possibility of a happier relationship. Moreover, it is impossible to avoid the sense—common

enough in Renaissance poetry but overwhelming in Greville—that love is being given an identity that is wholly independent of the (possibly nonexistent) loved one; and that *absence* is a far more powerful and pervasive state than *presence*. As early as 13, "Absence" is personified as Cupid's "foe"; but by the time we reach 45, he seems, at least for the opening stanza, to have become Greville's ally:

> Absence, the noble truce
> Of Cupid's war:
> Where though desires want use,
> They honoured are.
> Thou art the just protection
> Of prodigal affection,
> Have thou the praise;
> When bankrupt Cupid braveth,
> Thy mines his credit saveth,
> With sweet delays.
>
> (45.1–10)

This is highly accomplished writing, in a tone and form we may more readily associate with Sir Thomas Wyatt than with Greville; it is also subtly disingenuous, for we suspect, even as we read it, that the propositions it so elegantly and persuasively presents are to be proved false. There is of course a great tradition of poems that work by reversing their opening premises, from Wyatt's "They Flee from Me" to Gunn's "Tamer and Hawk," and this is one of them. Through four delicately shaped stanzas, Greville outlines the supposed advantages of absence, which "slakes" anguish, "cherisheth the spirits," and "shrouds" the "weak senses" ("like dainty clouds") from the "harming light" of his mistress's radiance:

> Absence maintains the treasure
> Of pleasure unto pleasure,
> Sparing with praise;
> Absence doth nurse the fire,
> Which starves and feeds desire
> With sweet delays.
>
> (45.26–30)

But Greville knows very well (and so do we) that, while maintaining the treasure and nursing the fire may be extremely admirable, this is hardly the point of passionate love. For the poem, as the reader will have gathered by now, is a kind of charm against absence, an attempt to make the best of an intolerable situation, and that is a project doomed to failure:

But thoughts be not so brave
With absent joy;
For you with that you have
Yourself destroy:
The absence which you glory
Is that which makes you sorry,
And burn in vain:
For thought is not the weapon,
Wherewith thought's ease men cheapen,
Absence is pain.

(45.41–50)

The reversal is now complete: from being "the noble truce" in line 1, absence has been transformed into the glumly monosyllabic "pain" in line 50. And if this has important consequences for Greville's thinking about love, it has even more momentous ones for his thinking about thought. *Caelica* 45 proves beyond doubt that, as a strategy for comforting the dejected lover, thought is impotent: it will not buy "thought's ease." For Greville the thinker this discovery, if hardly surprising, is nevertheless devastating; and the next group of poems can be seen as a battleground between earthly love and abstract thought.

CAELICA: *TRANSITIONAL POEMS*

In these poems—up to 84—Greville struggles to disengage himself from Cupid's clutches, employing modes that range from the introspective through the whimsical to the frankly ribald. There is, for instance, the tale of Scoggin's wife (50), who "by chance mistook her bed" and slept with a lord; Scoggin's remedy is to dress his wife's "breast and belly" in canvas, reserving "fine silk" for "her backside," "Joying to see it braver than the rest." To his puzzled neighbors, Scoggin explains:

That part of all his wife was only his:
The lord should deck the rest, to whom they are,
For he knew not what lordly fashion is.

If husbands now should only deck their own,
Silk would make many by their backs be known.

(50.26–30)

The rough humor and ludicrously named protagonist of this poem belong to a bed-hopping tradition, as familiar from Chaucer's tales as it is from eighteenth-century comic novels, that we may not readily associate with Greville; yet the underlying theme—the absurdity of sexual love and its consequences—is among his abiding preoccupations. "Many of the poems in *Caelica*," as Joan Rees says, "subject romantic love and the desires of the flesh to a sceptical and disenchanted commentary" (1971, p. 103), and it would be hard to find a more skeptical and disenchanted fable than Scoggin's.

Much more obviously in character is Greville's continuing series of fraught negotiations with the idea of absence. In 51 ("Caelica, because we now in absence live"), he looks back wistfully to the time when they "liv'd so long in free-born love as one," even though this sense of extended contentment is not readily conveyed by the earlier poems. But in 56, in bed with the lover here called Cynthia, he is troubled by the nightmares that will recur in the later poems: "Up I start believing well / To see if Cynthia were awake; / Wonders I saw, who can tell?" What follows is an extraordinary stream-of-consciousness portrayal of delirium, in which all sense of natural scale is confounded: he is in the sky, with "Jove and Venus" and "the Milken Way"; he thinks he is Mars, then Apollo; and when his thoughts return to Cynthia, she has become a geological feature of the earth, a river who "Runs away like silver streams." Despite the lovers' physical proximity in the bedroom, Greville's feeling of psychological absence is terrifyingly acute as he, coming back to earth, reaffirms in the following lines:

There stand I, like Arctic Pole,
Where Sol passeth o'er the line,
Mourning my benighted soul,
Which so loseth light divine.

(56.61–64)

He seems to envisage the Arctic Pole as an actual post, like a signpost, stuck in the ground;

yet this almost comical image enhances our sense of his helpless isolation, immediately contrasted with its geographical opposite, the equatorial sun that represents the heat of love. His soul is of course literally "benighted" because he is in darkness, as well as spiritually confounded by the lack of love's radiance: "absence" is here shading into "deprivation," and this is to become a crucial concept in Greville's subsequent forays into the dark night of the soul.

The very next poem (57) reinforces this movement. Caelica scolds him because "I suffer not / Absence with joy"—all pretense of that therapeutic use of absence posited in 45 having now evaporated—and she is once again compared to a free-flowing river: "You say that you do like fair Tagus' streams, / Swell over those that would your channels choke." The image clearly implies Caelica's oppressive, destructive quality (we may recall earlier hints of this, such as her "harming light" in 45) as well as Greville's own impossible predicament, for being released from this oppression is merely a different sort of death: "I like the fish bequeath'd to Neptune's bed, / No sooner taste of air, but I am dead." By the time we reach 64, this relationship, whether real or imagined, is recessed into the past ("when I did see you every day," "since my fall"), and in 65 Greville's retrospective tone becomes notably acerbic:

Your vows one way, with your desires did go,
Self-pity then in you did pity me,
Yea sex did scorn to be imprison'd so
But fire goes out for lack of vent, we see.

(65.5–8)

His period of happiness is not simply over, it has become almost historical, as 69 suggests: "My age is past, of woe begun, / Absence my presence is, strangeness my grace...." In poems such as 73–75, his detachment is further signaled by the fact that the male partner is no longer "I" but a third-person character, Myraphill or Philocell.

Yet Greville's bleakness about love has its counterbalance in his deepening immersion in abstract thought, which involves a withdrawal from worldly affairs: "I scorn the world, the

world scorns me, 'tis true" (60). Human love, he decides, is incomprehensible to the rational intellect, as is the unknowable "infinite":

The greatest pride of human kind is wit,
Which all art out, and into method draws,
Yet infinite is far exceeding it,
And so is chance, of unknown things the cause;
    The feet of men against our feet do move,
    No wit can comprehend the ways of love.

(63.1–6)

This is one of those stanzas, typical of the later poems in *Caelica,* in which pressure of thought bends and stretches Greville's syntax almost to the breaking point. By "wit" he seems to mean the rational intelligence that shapes all art and all systematic knowledge, yet even this is subject to the greater powers of the infinite and of chance; or, as Ecclesiastes has it, "the race is not to the swift, nor the battle to the strong, nor yet bread to the wise, nor yet riches to men of understanding, nor yet favour to men of skill; but time and chance happeneth to them all" (Eccl. 9:11). It is characteristic of Greville, however, to add a geographical image that is almost as eccentric as his Arctic Pole; for rational intelligence, he concludes, can no more understand love than it can understand how people on the other side of the earth walk "upside-down."

When finally he bids farewell to earthly love, he does so not in his sternest rational mode but in a poem of seductive, yearningly regretful cadences (84):

Farewell, sweet boy, complain not of my truth;
Thy mother lov'd thee not with more devotion;
For to thy boy's play I gave all my youth,

Young master, I did hope for your promotion.
While some sought honours, princes' thoughts observing,
Many woo'd fame, the child of pain and anguish,
Others judg'd inward good a chief deserving,
I in thy wanton visions joy'd to languish.

I bow'd not to thy image for succession,
Nor bound thy bow to shoot reformed kindness,
Thy plays of hope and fear were my confession,
The spectacles to my life was thy blindness:

But Cupid now farewell, I will go play me,
With thoughts that please me less, and less
    betray me.

The reader may have a disconcerting sense that this poem, like 22, has aspects of more than one period: that it wears a Romantic as well as a Renaissance face. Coleridge evidently felt the same when in 1806 he wrote "Farewell to Love," which his biographer Richard Holmes calls "a beautiful adaptation of a piece by Fulke Greville" (*Coleridge: Darker Reflections,* p. 69) but which, compared to the original, is little more than a piece of vulgarizing plagiarism. For the original is a remarkable poem, amply illustrating the supple variations of tone Greville can achieve within the limits of a sonnet. The first stanza's feeling of nostalgic regret is modified and transcended by its final line—"Young master, I did hope for your promotion"—where the tone, both sardonic and seductive, is complicated by the ambiguous hint of self-interest (for Cupid's promotion is also the lover's, and "your promotion" can mean equally promotion of and by Cupid). By contrast, the jangle of line 12—"The spectacles to my life was thy blindness"—is not merely paradoxical, for to see through Cupid's eyes is to see nothing at all, but jokily facetious: spectacles were not yet common, and late-sixteenth-century writers found the idea of them funny, as Shakespeare does in *Troilus and Cressida* when Pandarus greets the dejected lovers with the bathetic words, "What a pair of spectacles is here!" (4.4.13). The elegant farewell in the concluding couplet implies a causal relationship—the thoughts will betray less because they please less—and anticipates the wry version of Calvinism that informs the later poems in *Caelica*.

CAELICA: *LATER POEMS*

There is a sense in which relinquishing sexual love comes as an enormous relief to Greville, as if he recognizes that this, after all, is not the pursuit most suited to his talents. His writing becomes calmer, leaner; he dispenses with Pe-

trarchan trappings and adopts what is often called the "plain style" of the late Renaissance. In modifying both form and content, he follows his precept from stanza 113 of his "A Treaty of Human Learning": "Since if the matter be in nature vile, / How can it be made precious by a style?" Though we cannot tell for sure how seriously or realistically the love poems were intended, we may be fairly certain that these quasi-devotional late pieces are sincerely meant.

During the course of *Caelica,* Greville has grown increasingly fond of a six-line stanza in which the final two lines, often comprising a moral summary, are indented. This is perfectly suited to the calmly discursive voice he adopts in the late poems, and it now becomes his predominant form:

Man, dream no more of curious mysteries,
As what was here before the world was made,
The first man's life, the state of paradise,
Where heaven is, or hell's eternal shade,
    For God's works are like him, all infinite;
    And curious search, but crafty sin's delight.

(88.1–6)

That is, among other things, a self-reproach, for the younger Greville was often captivated by "curious mysteries," and it is also a step forward in literary time: the friend of Sidney now sounds like a contemporary of Donne and George Herbert, which in the course of his long life he also was. Yet to notice this is to be aware that he lacks on the one hand Donne's riddling complexity and on the other Herbert's devotional confidence: he remains an intellectual explorer, testing out his arguments and seeming modestly pleased when they click into place. The sonnet numbered 85, which follows his farewell to Cupid, is his version of Saint Paul's "The peace of God, which passeth all understanding" (Phil. 2:19):

Love is the peace, whereto all thoughts do strive,
Done and begun with all our powers in one:
The first and last in us that is alive,
End of the good, and therewith pleas'd alone.

Perfection's spirit, goddess of the mind,
Passed through hope, desire, grief and fear,

A simple goodness in the flesh refin'd,
Which of the joys to come doth witness bear.

Constant, because it sees no cause to vary,
A quintessence of passions overthrown,
Rais'd above all that change of objects carry,
A nature by no other nature known:
      For glory's of eternity a frame,
      That by all bodies else obscures her name.

Greville's style here is so plain, so Spartan, that we might want to borrow the phrase Donald Davie applied to the late Augustans, "purity of diction," and to add that here the diction is matched by purity of thought. Gunn calls 85 "a triumph of the plain style," but he is sufficiently candid to add that he finds Greville's position "at best sterile and at worst obnoxious" (*Selected Poems,* p. 34); when thought and language are both "refin'd" to such a "quintessence," they certainly run the risk of aridity. The other danger with this moral, abstract mode is sententiousness: 91 and 92, on nobility, fall into this trap, and the latter's repetition of "I think" may seem awkward and over-emphatic to modern readers.

Yet Greville is saved by his own uncertainty. The constant perfection of God's love does not eliminate anxiety from the sinful and inconstant mortal; rather, it makes him all the more aware of his own shortcomings, and this contrast—in which Greville's desolation is set in relief against God's magnanimity—is the subject of three astonishing poems, 98–100. This is the opening stanza of 98:

Wrapp'd up, O Lord, in man's degeneration;
The glories of thy truth, thy joys eternal,
Reflect upon my soul dark desolation,
And ugly prospects o'er the sprites infernal.
      Lord, I have sinn'd, and mine iniquity
      Deserves this hell; yet Lord deliver me.
                    (98.1–6)

The poem jolts us by beginning apparently in the middle of a sentence: "I am" has to be understood, although the pronoun "I" is unstated until line 5 (one might argue, not quite fancifully, that "I" has become invisible because so "Wrapp'd up"). The middle of the stanza is condensed and difficult: in the exemplary mirror of God's eternal truth are reflected both human despair and the prospect of Hell itself. However, "reflect" has not only the usual Elizabethan sense of "mirror" but also the newer meaning, first recorded by the *Oxford English Dictionary* in Ben Jonson, of "meditate," and this, together with the syntactical ambiguity of "Wrapp'd," permits an alternative reading: "I, wrapped up in man's degeneration, reflect upon my soul['s] dark desolation...." These ambiguities are fully intended, for the participial vagueness of "Wrapp'd" will be replicated by "Depriv'd" in 99, while the double meaning of "Reflect" recurs in 100; such effects are aptly characterized by Joan Rees as "a language of multiple reference by which [Greville] can present experience in its secular and its divine contexts simultaneously" (1971, p. 5). The summarizing couplet here and in the following poem becomes a refrain, repeated at the end of each stanza and modified at its final appearance. In the second stanza, clattering double rhymes such as "comprehended" / "extended" and "wounded" / "confounded" suggest Greville's psychological confusion, while the third holds out the possibility of redemption ("If from this depth of sin...") and ends with a conditionally modified refrain: "Lord, from this horror of iniquity, / And hellish grave, thou would'st deliver me."

Winters thought 99 "the greatest single poem in Greville":

Down in the depth of mine iniquity,
That ugly centre of infernal spirits;
Where each sin feels her own deformity,
In these peculiar torments she inherits,
      Depriv'd of human graces, and divine,
      Even there appears this saving God of mine.

And in this fatal mirror of transgression,
Shows man as fruit of his degeneration,
The error's ugly infinite impression,
Which bears the faithless down to desperation;
      Depriv'd of human graces and divine,
      Even there appears this saving God of mine.

In power and truth, almighty and eternal,
Which on the sin reflects strange desolation,
With glory scourging all the sprites infernal,

And uncreated hell with unprivation;
>>Depriv'd of human graces, not divine,
>>Even there appears this saving God of mine.

For on this sp'ritual cross condemned lying,
To pains infernal by eternal doom,
I see my Saviour for the same sins dying,
And from that hell I fear'd, to free me, come;
>>Depriv'd of human graces, not divine,
>>Thus hath his death rais'd up this soul of mine.

It seems strange to speak of a writer enriching his voice by curtailing his vocabulary, but that is what Greville does: a narrow range of morally weighted abstractions—words like "iniquity" and "deformity," "transgression" and "impression," "degeneration" and "desperation," "desolation" and (that menacing coinage) "unprivation"—bear the burden of the poem, and Greville stresses their importance by placing them at the ends of rhymed lines. This time, the ambiguously floating participle is "Depriv'd," in the refrain, and its implied subject "I" does not appear until the last stanza. A less remote though more puzzling syntactical wrench occurs in the second stanza, where the subject of "shows" is "impression"; Winters argues that this is not a result of an awkward structure, but rather allows Greville to organize by importance.

The poem begins from an even bleaker premise than its predecessor, for in the first five lines there seems to be no presence of God in this "depth," and when, in the sixth line, "Even there appears this saving God of mine," this is merely to make known the possibility of salvation through divine grace. For God is the "mirror" of the next stanza, in which man may see himself as the "fruit of his degeneration." In the startling fourth line of the third stanza, God, as Gunn says, "negates the negative" (*Selected Poems*, p. 39). And so Greville, recognizing God's "almighty and eternal" power, can feel himself to be, in a subtle modification of his refrain, no longer "depriv'd" of divine grace. By the end of the poem, enabled to comprehend the meaning of the crucifixion, he has at last been "rais'd up" from "the depth of mine iniquity." Thus he attains that rapturous sense of spiritual intimacy with Christ that so often characterizes the greatest English religious poems.

All Greville's modern selectors (Gunn, Rees, Powell, Astbury) and the editors of anthologies such as *English Renaissance Poetry* and *The New Oxford Book of Sixteenth Century Verse* include 98 and 99, but not all of them recognize that the sonnet that follows also belongs in this distinguished company:

In night, when colours all to black are cast,
Distinction lost, or gone down with the light;
The eye a watch to inward senses plac'd,
Not seeing, yet still having power of sight,

Gives vain alarums to the inward sense,
Where fear stirr'd up with witty tyranny,
Confounds all powers, and thorough self-offence,
Doth forge and raise impossibility:
Such as in thick depriving darknesses,
Proper reflections of the error be,
And images of self-confusednesses,
Which hurt imaginations only see;
>>And from this nothing seen, tells news of
>>>devils,
>>Which but expressions be of inward evils.

Where 98 and 99 both move toward concluding images of redemption, 100 offers a far more muted and ambiguous resolution: the description of an actual nightmare, which very gradually emerges as an image of Hell itself, is unfolded with multilayered precision and from a psychological perspective that is uncannily modern. The language, as so often in Greville's finest poems, enacts the stages of a mental process. The passive verb in the opening line implies both a surrender of human control and a sense that the colors themselves are being subjected to some unnatural deprivation; the qualifying "or" in the second line confirms that "distinction" has indeed been "lost" since it is no longer possible to decide whether it is indeed "lost" or merely "gone down with the light." The eye, whose job is of course to look outward—in fact, to apprehend the colors that are no longer visible—becomes "a watch to inward senses plac'd"; it finds itself in an intolerable and paradoxical state, "still having power of sight" and yet "Not seeing." In the second quatrain, nervously controlled language is replaced by open panic: the frustrated eye "Gives vain alarums to the inward sense," where instinct and intellect, "fear" and "witty tyranny," meet in confusion, and between them, they "forge and raise impossibility"—ghosts, visions, nightmares.

In eight lines, Greville has provided a compelling portrait of a disturbed night; but with the opening word of the sestet, he introduces a metaphysical dimension, for the "thick depriving darknesses" are now those of Hell itself. Accordingly, the language—"proper," "error," "evils"—becomes more explicitly moral, like that of the preceding two poems. The rhyme "confusednesses" / "self-confusednesses," discordant even by Greville's standards, reinforces the sense of moral crisis, while the idea that Hell is seen by those with "hurt imaginations" has an extraordinarily modern psychological air. The final couplet seems to offer the reassurance that the "devils" we may meet in dreams are nothing more than the "expressions" of "inward evils" but actually leaves us with the disquieting (and again oddly modern) conclusion that the devils are inescapably within us.

This hundredth poem of *Caelica*—which the editor of *English Renaissance Poetry,* John Williams, justly calls "one of the most remarkable short poems of the century" (p. xxi)—perfectly illustrates the extent of Greville's transformation from a talented imitator of his friend Sidney to a poet of astonishing power and great individuality. The remaining nine poems, all but one of them in Greville's trademark six-line stanza, continue to contrast man's degenerate state with God's perfection. Several, however, also contain reflections on statehood and governance that suggest they were probably composed during his years in the political wilderness. For example, 101 begins with a contrast between youth as "a field of large desires" and age "Dull'd with experience of unthankfulness," but this apparently personal idea unexpectedly modulates into a meditation on the health of nations:

But states grow old, when princes turn away
From honour, to take pleasure for their ends;
For that a large is, this a narrow way,
That wins a world, and this a few dark friends;

The one improving worthiness spreads far,
Under the other good things prisoners are.
(101.19–24)

This looks very like Greville's response to the early years of James I's court, from which he was excluded by "a few dark friends" such as Cecil and prevented from writing about the "good things" of the preceding reign.

The final poem in *Caelica,* "Sion lays waste...," has the air of an intended summation, especially in its highly compressed fourth stanza, where Greville provides his own parenthetical glosses for his divine paradigms:

Yet unto thee, Lord (mirror of transgression),
We, who for earthly idols, have forsaken
Thy heavenly image (sinless pure impression)
And so in nets of vanity lie taken,
   All desolate implore that to thine own,
   Lord, thou no longer live a God unknown.
(109.19–24)

THE POET AS THINKER

The finest poems in *Caelica* are so impressive that we may need to remind ourselves that Greville did not think of himself as a poet, still less as a literary figure: the priorities stated in his epitaph are those of the man. He viewed writing as a way of sorting out his ideas and recording, whether for himself or for posterity, matters that struck him as worth remembering. Recognizing this will enable us to understand (and to be less disappointed in understanding) why the verse treatises are so dull and the dramas so undramatic: they had no particular need to be interesting or actable, since that was not why Greville wrote them. "I have made those tragedies no plays for the stage," he said, in the *Life of Sidney,* adding: "But he that will behold these Acts upon their true stage, let him look on that stage wherein himself is an actor, even the state he lives in, and for every part he may perchance find a player, and for every line...an instance of life" (*Selected Writings,* p. 152).

The more readable of the two surviving plays—and the more accessible, since it appears in full in the *Selected Writings of Fulke Greville,* whereas *Alaham* has not been generally available since Bullough's edition of 1939—is *Mustapha.* Though it is tactfully distanced from sixteenth-century England by its Eastern setting (rather in the manner of Shakespeare's Roman plays), its themes of power and political intrigue have inescapable echoes in Greville's own world, and a contemporary reader would have had no difficulty in finding "an instance of life" for "every line." For the modern student of *Caelica,* its principal interest will be in the characteristic duality of the "Chorus Tartaorum" and "Chorus Sacerdotum" that close the play—although an authorial note describes the latter as "misplaced," as if Greville himself recognized that it is a different and separate kind of poem. The well-known opening lines of "Chorus Sacerdotum" restate the dichotomy between "Reason" and "Affection" that we have already noticed in *Caelica* 4:

Oh wearisome condition of humanity!
Born under one law, to another bound:
Vainly begot, and yet forbidden vanity,
Created sick, commanded to be sound:
What meaneth nature by these divers laws?
Passion and reason self-division cause:
Is it the mark or majesty of power
To make offences that it may forgive?

Yet even here, in the relatively concise form of a chorus, Greville's expression seems loose and unfocused compared with the intellectual and technical sharpness of *Caelica:* his "creeping genius," as he called it in the *Life of Sidney,* was best served by the shaping discipline of the short poem.

The traditional reading of Elizabethan poetry misunderstands Greville because it looks both for the wrong sort of poet and in the wrong place. C. S. Lewis, for example, in his volume of the *Oxford History of English Literature,* wants Greville to belong to his now somewhat quaint-sounding "Golden" period and so looks with approval on the early poems in *Caelica* but finds that the "later pieces, more often religious than erotic, are less Golden...we are sometimes tantalized by the spectacle of such an interesting writer failing so often, and only just failing, to bring off a success" (p. 524). Since Greville's poems cannot be precisely dated, he also appears in the next volume of the *Oxford History,* but he fares little better at the hands of Douglas Bush, who also attends to the Petrarchan early poems before merely noting that "towards the end they fade away altogether behind religious and philosophical reflection" (p. 98). In both cases, distinguished orthodox scholars find themselves unable to appreciate Greville's qualities because they are seeking a quite different sort of poetry. It is Yvor Winters who precisely identifies these special qualities by again comparing Greville's later poems to those songs and sonnets of Sidney, along with other poetic works of the Renaissance.

Fortunately for us, the essence of Greville's thought—or indeed, to borrow a favorite word from his own time, its quintessence—is to be found in his finest poems: in their rigorously honed language they represent the summit of the Elizabethan plain style, while in their fascination with abstract argument they look forward to the coming metaphysical age. On both counts, they should be ranked among the indispensable English poems of their period.

Selected Bibliography

WORKS OF FULKE GREVILLE

EARLY EDITIONS

Certaine Learned and Elegant Workes of the Right Honourable Fulke, Lord Brooke, Written in His Youth and Familiar Exercise with Sir Philip Sidney. London: E. P. for H. Seyle, 1633.

The Life of the Renowned Sir Philip Sidney. London: H. Seyle, 1652.

The Remains of Sir Fulke Grevill, Lord Brooke: Being Poems of Monarchy and Religion. London: H. Herriman, 1670.

Caelica. Edited by M.F. Crow. London: Trench, Trubner & Co., 1898.

MODERN EDITIONS

The Works of Fulke Greville. Edited by A. B. Grosart. Blackburn, 1870.

Sir Fulke Grevill's Life of Sir Philip Sidney. Edited by Nowell Smith. Oxford, 1907.

Poems and Dramas of Fulke Greville. 2 vols. Edited by Geoffrey Bullough. Edinburgh: Oliver & Boyd, 1939.

The Remains, Being Poems of Monarchy and Religion. Edited by G. A. Wilkes. London: Oxford University Press, 1965.

Selected Poems of Fulke Greville. Edited by Thom Gunn. London: Faber, 1968.

Selected Writings of Fulke Greville. Edited by Joan Rees. London: Athlone Press, 1973.

Fulke Greville· Poems. Edited by Anthony Astbury. Warwick: Greville, 1980.

Selected Poems of Fulke Greville. Edited by Neil Powell. Manchester: Fyfield, 1990.

ANTHOLOGIES

English Madrigal Verse, 1588–1632. 3d ed. Edited by E. H. Fellowes; revised and enlarged by Frederick W. Sternfield and David Greer. Oxford: Clarendon Press, 1967.

English Renaissance Poetry. Edited by John Williams. New York: Doubleday & Company Inc., 1963.

The New Oxford Book of Sixteenth Century Verse. Edited by Emrys Jones. Oxford: Oxford University Press, 1991.

CRITICAL AND BIOGRAPHICAL STUDIES

Bush, Douglas. *English Literature in the Earlier Seventeenth Century*. 2d ed. rev. Oxford: Clarendon Press, 1962.

Croll, Morris William. *The Works of Fulke Greville*. Philadelphia: J. B. Lippincott, 1903.

Frost, William. *Fulke Greville's "Caelica": An Evaluation*. New York, 1942.

Grigson, Geoffrey. "The Idea of the Centre." *Listener*, August 12, 1976, pp. 172–173.

Lee, Sidney. "Fulke Greville." In *Dictionary of National Biography*. London: Oxford University Press, 1949.

Lewis, C. S. *English Literature in the Sixteenth Century Excluding Drama*. Oxford: Clarendon Press, 1954.

Rebholz, Ronald A. *The Life of Fulke Greville*. Oxford: Clarendon Press, 1971.

Rees, Joan. *Fulke Greville: Lord Brooke, 1554–1628*. London: Routledge & Kegan Paul, 1971.

Ruoff, James E. *Handbook of Elizabethan and Stuart Literature*. London: Macmillan, 1975.

Winters, Yvor. *Forms of Discovery*. Denver, Colo.: Alan Swallow, 1967.

KEVIN HART

(1954–)

Jacques Khalip

IN THE CONTEMPORARY tradition of Australian poetry, Kevin Hart's eminence rests upon a striking combination in his work of the sounds and stories of his native country and the more difficult underpinnings of his visionary and spiritual aspirations. Professor of English as well as Director of the Program in Religion and Literature at the University of Notre Dame, Hart writes criticism and poetry that mutually inform one another, and they emphasize not only a Romantic attachment to place and memory but also provoke searching inquiries into the nature of poetic expression and human faith. In this sense, the aesthetic represents for Hart a category of knowledge as well as a deeply spiritual exercise in self-examination, one that does not simply collapse religiosity into poetry but rather takes art as the medium through which learning and personal discovery are to be attempted. Poetry, then, is indicative of a greater consciousness, at once human and divine, but Hart's writings do not simply "celebrate" this belief; rather, they test the limits of belief by soliciting and contemplating the kinds of possibilities that such a complex consciousness might or might not be responsible for.

Hart takes his place within a group of outstanding Australian poets who have emerged in the twentieth century: David Campbell, A. D. Hope, John Kinsella, Kenneth Slessor, Francis Webb, and Judith Wright. Although he has been praised by the likes of Harold Bloom, Charles Simic, and John Ashbery, Hart's reputation has developed slowly, in part perhaps because he deliberately eschews a kind of poetry that is extroverted, grandiose, and oratorical. The comparatively softer tones of his work can be said to have affinities with the meditative lyrics of George Herbert (1593–1633), Christopher Smart (1722–1771), and John Clare (1793–1864). Closer in time, he also bears similarities with the work of such contemporary masters as Giuseppe Ungaretti (whom Hart has translated in *The Buried Harbour*), Eugenio Montale (an early favorite), 1990, Philippe Jaccottet, and Roberto Juarroz. The many polarities of Hart's poetry—at once modernist and Romantic, locally Australian and globally cosmopolitan—position him at the intersection of different poetical traditions. His work in turn solicits and reflects these polarities with considerable intellectual analysis and emotional intimacy.

LIFE

Kevin Hart was born on July 5, 1954, in Ockendon in the country of Essex in England of working-class parents. His father, James Henry, was a boilermaker and his mother, Rosina Mary (whom he mourns in the opening poem of *Wicked Heat,* 2000), a dressmaker. At a young age, he moved with his family to Rowdowns Road, Dagenham, in Essex, where he attended primary school, but having failed the eleven-plus examinations he was sent to a comprehensive school that, in Hart's words, "had kept faith with all the brutality described by Dickens." In primary school Hart's painful shyness made teachers believe that he was mentally challenged—a situation that led to the suggestion that he be taken out of school and apprenticed to a butcher. When he was eleven years old, however, Hart's family immigrated to Brisbane, Queensland, Australia, where he attended Goodna Primary School while still living with his family at the Wacol Migrant Hostel. Soon after, his parents bought a house in Oxley, where he studied at Corinda Primary School and Oxley State High School. At the latter institution Hart achieved something of an about-face in his life: having all along been a poor student, he suddenly rose to the top of his class, excelling in mathematics and eventually winning a scholarship to the Australian National University in Canberra, where he pursued a double honors degree in English and philosophy between 1973 and 1976. The dryness of the ANU English department, however, stemming from what Hart has described (with a mix of distaste and humor) as its atmosphere of "moral seriousness" and "Shelley bashing," compelled him to take a philosophy honors only, specializing in philosophical theology. Hart graduated with a first-class honors degree, winning the Tillyard Award (given to the top student in the university each year), the Literature Board Fellowship, and then a Wallace Stegner Fellowship to Stanford University, where he spent the 1977–1978 academic year reading German theology and philosophy.

During his time at Stanford, Hart published his first collection of poems, *The Departure,* in 1978. *The Lines of the Hand* followed in 1981. Upon returning to Australia, Hart taught at the Geelong College from 1979 to 1984. In 1980 he experienced a pivotal moment in his life when he converted to Catholicism. Four years later he published his third collection, *Your Shadow.* In 1986 he completed his dissertation in the Department of Philosophy at the University of Melbourne, where he had already begun teaching while still a doctoral candidate. However, because of the department's hostility to European philosophy, Hart took up a lectureship in the Department of English. He gained his first tenure-track job at Deakin University, publishing several important works: the poetry collections *Peniel* (1991) and *New and Selected Poems* (1995); a philosophical study, *The Trespass of the Sign: Deconstruction, Theology, and Philosophy* (1989); and a critical study of the Australian poet A. D. Hope (1992). In 1995 he moved to Monash University, where he was elected to a personal chair at the end of his fortieth year. Hart has been a visiting professor at Georgetown University (1996–1997), Katholicke Universiteit in Leuven, Belgium (1999), and Villanova University (2001); in 2002 he and his family—

his wife, Rita Judith Hart, and two daughters, Sarah Rosina and Claire Shoshana—moved to South Bend, Indiana, where he is professor in the Department of English at the University of Notre Dame.

THE DEPARTURE (1978)

As the title of the collection suggests, Hart's first book is at once a leave-taking and an announcement of origins. Published while he was a student at Stanford, the book reveals in miniature many of the themes and styles cultivated by Hart throughout his career: personal loss, erotic love, social displacement, spiritual release, and aesthetic contemplation. Despite the difficulty posed by many of these themes, Hart's poetry is remarkably minimalist and pointed, never craving an excessive plenitude or reducing itself to terse, random speculations. The tautness of the writing signals both intensity and openness to experience, qualities captured in the collection's opening poem:

Sunset—and the harbour
reduces to one ship:

men in polo-necks
lash ropes round poles, pull

knots undone: the breeze
wraps itself up

in sails, lumpy, a girl
wriggling into her dress—

fills out, a face appears
is gone: ropes dangle,

the ship diminishes—
a final shout

unwinds towards me,
dissolves into the sea.

(p. 3)

Although the tone of emotional detachment sounds uppermost in this poem, "Departing Ship" evokes a speaker ambivalently poised between the possibilities of a new beginning and a solitary withdrawal. This ambivalence characterizes much of the volume, which is conscious of itself as an apprentice work poised on the brink of achieving a mature voice. In the three-part "The Convert," the speaker walks to the Missionary Baptist Church out of curiosity and encounters a diverse group of converts, singing hymns. Hart concludes "The Convert" with a brief description of a revival, witnessed when he was seventeen, which details the fire-and-brimstone speech of the Minister and frightens Hart with the possibility that the preacher somehow knows his deepest secrets. This tale of adolescent angst evokes a theme that recurs throughout Hart's poetry: the relationship between spirituality and sexuality. For the boy in "The Convert," religion at once attacks and summons erotic sensation.

For the most part, Hart experiments with tonal and thematic variety in the first section of *The Departure:* reveries on histories of war ("I Dreamt Gallipoli Beach," "A Dream of France") and brief aesthetic pieces ("Seated Woman," "The Departure," "Impasse," and "The Sea Voyage"). In the collection's second part, however, Hart's poetry is more expansive, both narratively and thematically: he details the errancies of intimate feelings ("Office Girl," "Visiting Julia") alongside lyrical improvisations on the philosophers Baruch Spinoza, Blaise Pascal, Friedrich Nietzsche, Martin Heidegger, and Dietrich Bonhoeffer ("The Gallery"). A poem such as "The Old" pays an unconscious tribute to Philip Larkin, echoing some of that poet's characteristically detached writing style and withering attentiveness:

You cannot forget the old.
They become part of you.
They take you for themselves.

I have watched them in the city.
They stack themselves up
against the walls like chairs.

(p. 37)

Such musings work as obvious contrasts to poems like "Spinoza," where the image of the philosopher moving "through the litter of half-scarped lenses" (p. 33) considers abstractions and

theories as of a piece with a deeply human depiction of philosophical contemplation. The final section of the book, entitled "Homecoming" begins with yet another poem on departure. The tone of this piece is more profound in that Hart links personal dislocation with a renewed sense of the ineluctability of history. As the speaker yawns and sinks back into his boyhood years, he comes to understand that he cannot escape aging, especially with the awareness that time is swiftly diminishing itself into the past. The lightness of the poem's simple rhyme scheme subtly evokes a formal necessity that compels Hart to listen to a past that he does not inhabit but which nevertheless implicates him. The rhyme thus pushes him out of the apparent solitude of fond farewells and into the rhythms of a more alert attentiveness, one that transforms the lyrical voice into a summoning of past, present, and future histories. "In Memoriam W. H. Auden" conveys something of this new austerity, as does the concluding three-part "Homages," where Hart revisits personal "spots of time" in Australia and England, thus bringing *The Departure*'s theme of departure and recovery full circle.

THE LINES OF THE HAND *(1981)*

In his second collection, Hart improves upon his first book by more deliberately exploring his intellectual preoccupations. Although he has often said that he finds little he would like to preserve in *The Departure* (he has in fact somewhat rewritten one or two of the poems—"The Convert," for example, being recast in "The Hall"), *The Lines of the Hand* displays an extraordinarily controlled and eloquent talent, one that is intellectually and sensuously nourished by sources at once obscure and seductive. Choosing quotes from Paul Valéry, Jakob Böhme, and A. N. Prior as epigraphs, *The Lines of the Hand* begins with a poem that echoes *The Departure* in terms of its evocation of a leave-taking, although here it is the privacy of poetry to which Hart bids farewell. After telling his book to go because "I have lived with you too long already / I have another now / whose each word I breathe in like mountain air,"

Hart humorously describes his collection as a former lover or child whom he beseeches to "return in fifty years, pause at my grave / and see where you were born." The closing tone of sadness infuses many of the poems in the book, including one of its better known pieces, "The Hand":

I have seen the hand
even now as it slowly winds the clock
leaving its fingerprints I know so well,
I have seen it
opening its palm to me saying Look, see
soon all this will be yours,

all my life I have seen it
always offering me its map useless without names
its five-pronged signpost
pointing me off to God knows where.

Yet it is my only country
and I must live here I have no choice
waking each day
hearing its tremendous roar, its great rivers
pouring and pouring into my small cup.

(p. 1)

Like George Herbert's poetry, which evokes in hushed, plangent tones the generality of a Godhead in relation to the particularity of personal faith, Hart's spiritual dynamic oscillates between sublime recognition and individual reflection, concentrating on the minutiae of life in order to expose a greater significance. Although certainly bizarre, "The Hand" is mesmerizing in its attempt to convey intellectual expansiveness within the small iconic image of the hand.

In "The Lines of the Hand," Hart speaks of following his future self "for years / trying to glimpse his face, trying to catch / any word he has to spare, trying / to judge him from his taste in clothes" (p. 13). Recalling some of Mark Strand's early poetry, which similarly identifies stylistic sparseness with the emptying out of egocentric concerns, Hart describes the bizarreness of being defamiliarized from oneself—an experience that is weirdly intense and hypnotic rather than despondent:

my body casts two shadows
yet always I choose the wrong one to follow home

where I find, as always,
blank paper, a pen, and the lines of my face.

(p. 13)

The image of the body casting "two shadows," with Hart claiming always to "choose the wrong one to follow home," suggests a theme of deliberate self-negation that comes to the fore in his later work but that is already evident in this early collection. Rather than simply taking the road less traveled, as Robert Frost would have it, Hart's descent into otherness nears a kind of personal and aesthetic vacancy: "where I find, as always, blank paper, a pen, and the lines of my face." He is brought to consider this strange blankness as a mode of being that crucially depends on desolation and loss.

One of the collection's strongest pieces is "Ten Ghazals," which refers to an Arabic form that proceeds according to a deceptively simple rhyme scheme: *aa ba ca da,* and so forth. Although Hart entirely eschews the rhyme scheme from his piece, he develops the ghazal's play of disjunction and unity which demands that there be no continuity from stanza to stanza. In this sense, each "unit" of two lines stands as a miniature philosophical reflection, one that follows the ghazal's dreamy, disruptive logic:

The forest does not need you to believe in it
but will watch you sleeping here, like an owl.

In a valley night comes suddenly, a slammed door;
here, on the summit, the sun must first cross an ocean.
"Stockyard Creek" (p. 16)

Hart's images flow with seeming naturalness, despite their cognitive difficulty. Some of the poems evoke puzzlelike phrases: "When the city of towers is destroyed / the city of broken glass begins its reign" ("The Jury," p. 16), while others are distinctly surrealist "The hours stretch off like lampposts. / Where they end, if ever, there is morning" ("Insomnia," p. 16).

While many of the poems in *The Lines of the Hand* are almost phenomenological in their concerns, a significant number of them are openly devotional, as in this prayer to God spoken by a stone:

KEVIN HART

Father, I praise you
for the wideness of this your Earth, and for the sky
arched forever over me,
or the sharp rain and the scraping wind
that have carved me from the mountain
and made me smooth as a child's face.

       …

Keep me, I pray, whole
unlike the terrible dust and pieces of bone
cast above in the wind's great breath, unlike men
who must suffer change,
their endless footprints deep as graves;

keep me in truth, in constancy,
until the day when you will burst into my heavy soul
and I will shout your Name.

                                (p. 23)

The stone's faith in God suggests, on the one hand, a pantheistic universe where all things are endowed with a soul. But Hart moves away from this easy celebration of anthropomorphism by emphasizing the stone's fixed attentiveness and controlled pleas, potentially unheard but nevertheless fully vibrating within its form. The stone's desire for constancy amid the contingencies of a mortal world throw into relief a kind of withdrawn consciousness that seeks to assert despite being subject to external flux and destruction—a High Romantic plea for the autonomy of the imagination and its immortality despite the limited life of humanity. But Hart's Romanticism is tempered here by his quiet lyricism, which is not self-aggrandizing and empowered but rather recessive and reluctantly affirming. The stone is not a symbol of stalwart power but rather of muted anguish. The patience of poetic thought reveals itself in several other poems: "Desire," for example, explicitly connects the reflective experience of waiting and openness to sexual revelation:

It will open slowly, a night flower:
the moon's long fingers stroking your bare arms.
the courtyard with its jasmine breath
and all the warmth of blood.

                                (p. 24)

Desire promises beauties and fulfillments that it can only offer as figures in the present. In the

searing "My Death," on the other hand, the speaker confronts his own potential demise with disinterested precision:

Like the sun
I cannot bear to face it—
I say that it has nothing to do with me,

exists outside of me, a silence
a darkness
where everything is done.

Yet even now
I feel it deep within me, closer
than my breathing,

moving within me, slow as my blood,
and measuring me
with all I care to do, a shadow

I follow
or that follows me
and leads me to my centre not my edge.

                                (p. 19)

Death lies at the center of being, not on its circumference. It exposes a vacancy in the self that rids it of all personal interests and properties. Paradoxically the mind is animated by its own pursuit of mortality, fully exposing it to a scene of annihilation that becomes ever more vivid.

YOUR SHADOW (1984)

What is striking about many of these early verses is their palpable emphases on inwardness, on deeply internalized experiences and impressions that convey a fully lyrical, albeit morally troubled, interiority. It would seem that despite his characteristically taut and articulate style, Hart gives up the external world for the more abstract, seemingly ahistorical and atemporal dimensions of meditative thought. The poems in *Your Shadow* provocatively address these questions by depicting consciousness as something that is not autonomously detached from the world but rather powerfully socialized by it. In other words, subjective contemplation for Hart dynamically registers and responds to a reality in which the individual is a committed intellectual participant. Aesthetic thought possesses a cognitive dimension that pushes the self to consider questions of identity, agency, and history. By depicting realms of consciousness and pungent landscapes that position the self in a variety of probing contexts, Hart suggests that the mind is extroverted and heterogeneous, avidly extending itself toward other persons, places, and things in order to better understand its relation to the world. The collection's title poem, which is "rewritten" differently four times, suggests a darkness that is cast by the self, haunting its stride like an otherness it cannot assimilate yet also cannot fail to notice and absorb as its own:

Fed by its eye, the falcon
Swims with the flooding wind, watching
Its shadow writhe
Like something left half-dead.

(pp. 64–70)

As the falcon concentrates its gaze on its shadow down below, its dying shadow reminds it that the heights to which it ascends are only escapist dreams. The speaker counsels us to follow our shadow as it appears in various places in our lives in the shape of different things: the darkness in the hand, "a gift, a birth right, your baby shawl / Now growing into a shroud"; a "trapdoor / Into the secret earth" where one meets "the child you were, covered with dirt." Although the shadow signals an ominous dimension to personality, Hart also reminds us that it represents a vanishing point or obscurity we must assimilate and learn to live with:

It will not hurt you, it simply shows
That you are not alone,
That what you fear is part of you,
That you are both the killer and the kill.

(p. 64–70)

In subsequent versions, Hart pares down the shadow to a series of brief, puzzling meditations:

You are a window
And everyone can see inside; your shadow
Means protection, a curtain

Whose darkness discloses
You live in a tight corner, out of the light,
While on this earth.

(p. 64–70)

The shadow protects the self by obscuring it: although others can apparently look inside, there is a certain opacity to each one of us that resists easy depiction. The self, for Hart, stands apart from itself. It is at once the purest expression of inner being and a performance or simulation that draws attention to our inner difference. One of the strongest pieces in the collection is "Your Shadow's Songs," which begins with the acknowledgment that "The angel of death is older now / And finds the pleasures of the flesh / Too tiring, closing dead men's eyes / A job he'd rather do without" (p. 76). Despite the sense that the angel is nearing a kind of retirement, he cannot help but see "the future, jammed in reverse, / Out of control; the cheating senses / Like a hand about each throat; / The field of blood within the heart" (p. 76). The angel's prescience is based upon a sense of the future being a citation of the past, which appears morbid and bleak: "A child is born and wrapped in lace, / A knife is placed upon its tongue; / You close both eyes and only find / A darker shadow cast inside" (p. 76). The series of songs orbits around a theme that links the mortifications of the soul with a deeply spiritual investment in negation: Hart calls into question not only our reliance on the tangible, everyday world but also our confidence in the power of words to redeem us.

Other poems in the volume offer quieter but no less compelling observations: in "The Storm" the speaker says, "But it is good to know, also, / That the soul is hail thrashing a stone wall / and not always a lake in moonlight, / And who in the world would show me that?" (p. 10; revised in *Flame Tree,* p. 51). Whether the soul is hail or a moonlit lake, Hart considers it as conceivable as a series of metaphoric substitutions: its apparent "essence" is premised upon the ability of language to convey a sense of its shifting tones, ever darting about us and never revealing the mysteries of its content. In fact it is precisely the soul's inaccessibility that makes the speaker relish the coming storm: "I need to learn that nothing lasts. / Lord knows, / I have to learn it fresh each year" (p. 10; revised in *Flame Tree*, p. 50). To be unsettled and troubled only further describes the tropological logic of "soul": it is defined according to a system of metaphoric substitutions, ever mobile and changing.

In many other pieces, Hart cultivates the lyric's capacity to generate a kind of phenomenology of the everyday. In "Sunlight in a Room," the invisible and seemingly unremarkable qualities of quotidian life are raised to the level of texture and depth: "The silence attending words, / The body firm as a plum / And the spirit now weightless / And willing as a needle" (p. 63). Similarly in "The Hammer," a poem that owes much to Heidegger's meditations on the materiality of a consciousness engaged in labor, Hart describes the interaction between individual and tool as a dense evocation of the "mind's energies" in relation to the act of striking: "This is the archer's erasure of himself from his tense / Matrix of forces, the moment of conditioned release / When the mind delights in its freedom to step outside / And adore the body, a perfected instrument of will" (p. 58). As mind sinks into the action of hammering, an action that signals the body's physical presence in the act of consciousness, it also stands apart from the body's activity, adoring it and contemplating its own distinct power. What is stunning about this poem is that it contemplates a moment that is almost insubstantial in daily life—a mute activity given vivid materiality by Hart. In "The Real World," the significance of the everyday is carried even farther. Hart begins by juxtaposing various quotidian scenes without any commentary or observation: "Ray of sunlight quietly fishing from tall trees; / A wrestler, smoking, his fingers fat as toes; / Old men in bars, with arms that end in glass; / A haloed moon tonight, a hole within a hole" (p. 68). What is unsettling about the poem is that it appears at first almost devoid of any consciousness—it is entirely external and freed of subjective commentary. However, this stark "realism" seems nevertheless to summon up a wild assortment of images that bespeak a stunning heterogeneity: "Steel factories like German

concentration camps"; "A discotheque bulging with mirrors and music"; "The child's black pupil with its coffin shine" (p. 68). On the surface, there does not seem to be any logical link between these images, but it is precisely their arbitrariness that brings them together as consequences of a speculative mind. As the mind contemplates the world as consisting of various objects, it can only do so by conferring personal meanings upon such objects, distorting their "thingness" through subjective thought. It is this tension between the personal and the acknowledged difference of other persons and things that surfaces in Hart's poem as both a philosophical and aesthetic problem: how to lyrically represent otherness without subsuming it entirely in personal intentions and perspectives.

Many of the poems in *Your Shadow* are also spiritual prayers that speak to the difficulties of faith: "To the Spirit" and "A Silver Crucifix on My Desk" are devotional, again recalling the metaphysical meditations of George Herbert. The latter poem addresses the crucifix as an object of adoration and obsession: "Each day you wait for me, / Your arms / Raised as if to dive into my element" (p. 87). The force of the poem lies in the speaker's relentless piling up of descriptions for the crucifix, which represents:

A simple cross
Where two worlds meet, a man
Caught there
And punished by the storm between two worlds,
A sword thrust into my desk
That tells me
With each new morning that the world
Will not escape
The world that we have made.

(p. 87)

Despite symbolizing transcendent faith, the crucifix embodies the very complexity of that faith by returning the speaker to the material world, compelling him to assume a devout attention to his environment. The speaker's devotion is nothing short of being a painful test: "How often / Have I tried to shrink you down / And wear you round my neck, / As safe / As any of the stars you made" (p. 87). The crucifix cannot be moved or altered and is as unshakable as the speaker's faith. But it is also a symbol of the persistence of doubt and mortification in spiritual thought.

PENIEL *(1991)*

Hart's fourth collection of poems was preceded by two other significant works, *The Trespass of the Sign,* which explores mystical theology, or the intertwining of negative and positive theologies, in relation to the deconstructionist philosophy of Jacques Derrida; and a translation of selected poems by the contemporary Italian master Giuseppe Ungaretti, *The Buried Harbour (1990).* The influence of these two books on *Peniel* is unmistakable: if Hart's work on Derrida theoretically approaches questions of spiritual negativity, *The Buried Harbour* addresses the same issues in terms of poetic theory and translation.

In his introduction to *The Buried Harbour,* Hart meditates on Ungaretti's "openness to negativity" as something that aesthetically and philosophically brings poetry into being rather than disrupts it: "Lyric poetry is not an affair of immediate engagement with present events or presentable objects; it is a belated meditation on the withdrawal of presence, one that insists on making another world which may or may not be closely related to ordinary experience" (p. xii). According to this definition, poetry cannot be ascribed to the will—it occurs precisely at the moment where consciousness withdraws, and the poetic "gift" is given over or transmitted involuntarily. Translation, then, partakes of this kind of withdrawal: it seeks to evoke the original while at the same time canceling any hint of the translator's own voice. It channels rather than simply transcribes poetry.

Hart's negative poetics, then, develops the modernist desire for impersonality a step farther: by questioning the contours of the lyrical self, one comes to confront the limits of personality and self-designation. In *Peniel,* which garnered praise from Harold Bloom, who included it in his 1994 book *The Western Canon,* Hart attends to these limits in a series of short poems, all of which conform to a single form: nine stanzas of unrhymed tercets. Although the strictness of the form might appear to prove limiting (visually it recalls the classical structure of terza rima and pays an oblique homage to Dante's famous use of the form in *The Divine Comedy*), Hart uses reduction and simplicity as a means for achieving an almost crystalline clarity in addressing the various subjects throughout the book: death and mourning, historical retrospection, and geographical dislocation. All of these are addressed as experiences that render the self less secure, less certain in its regard toward itself and others. The opening poem, "Gypsophilia," which refers to a flowery herb, depicts a still-life scene that is reminiscent of Wallace Stevens' philosophically inflected musings:

Another day with nothing to say for itself—
Gypsophilia on the table, a child's breath
When breath is all it has to name the world

And therefore has no world. It must be made:
Her shadow sleeping on the wall, the rain
That pins fat clouds to earth all afternoon,

Ariver playing down the piano's scales."

(p. 2)

Images of transparency and fluidity (a shadow, clouds, a river) are brought into sharper relief as concrete objects that the mind arranges and rearranges as material extensions of its own thought. The effect here is to suggest that thinking is less a matter of reverie and more a creatively constructive act: "the child will tune the world to her desire / and make another to keep in mind" (p. 3). The abstractions of thought actually contribute to making and unmaking the social reality that informs thinking in the first place. The child's innocence in this passage suggests an openness to conceiving the world as an object that is vulnerable to the mind's desire to change and transform it. Although such a world is described as "a world of things with nothing at all to say, / a margin that absorbs our silences," the child is instructed to take "the lightning from her eye / and place it in the sky, her shadow must be told to fall asleep" (p. 3). For Hart, creatively engaging with the world means projecting oneself infinitely throughout it. The imagination disperses the self amid its creations, testifying to an emptiness or "withdrawal of presence" that proves to be aesthetically and cognitively productive.

Hart's speculations throughout *Peniel* wrestle with the predicament of how the mind can engage with the world. In "Firm Views," Hart gives us another still-life scene whose composition depends upon the mind's perception of it:

Back to the things themselves: this empty glass
With no idea of water; sleeping cats
That dream of ancient Egypt in the sun;

And ivy on the porch. Now leave the mind
With its divisions training on the page
And walk out through a world untouched by thought
Where things exist as things, not otherwise.

(p. 6)

What would the world look like if it were "untouched by thought"? Does the world precede our thoughts of it? And can one approximate a kind of state of mind that can contain and appreciate the world in such a way as to resist imposing thought or function upon it, much like the "empty glass / with no idea of water"?

In "Facing the Pacific at Night," a drive east returns Hart to the world of the child—"the web of names is brushed aside from things. / The ocean's name is quietly washed away / revealing the thing itself, an energy, / an elemental life flashing in starlight" (p. 18). The ocean's loss of identity brings about a surge in "energy," suggesting that the "idea" of the ocean is distinct from our name for it. In "Dispute at Sunrise," however, this concentration on the mind signals a hallucinatory upheaval:

Pushed to one side the mind becomes extreme

And cultivates a glasshouse world. Strange things
Breed in the margins of your prayer books:
Tall knights afraid of snails, a grunting bull

That milks a naked woman, monkey dressed
In doctors' coats with glinting knives in paw.

(p. 23).

Mind's transformation into an object, a "glasshouse," suggests that it has become a container

for wild reveries that are at odds with the world outside. In fact the poem juxtaposes these lines with a series of italicized stanzas describing a contrasting world of almost indifferent plenitude: "*cities wild with heat / Cicadas shake maracas through the night / And make the sleeping sprawl beneath their sheets / Or walk in moonlight close as a lover's breath*" (p. 22). The poem thus offers at least two competing perspectives on the work of the imagination: that of a world independent from mind yet nevertheless receptive to it, and the world transformed according to the mind's vagaries. Hart's attention to creative thought thus disorients rather than replenishes the self. If lyric poetry is the site of the "withdrawal of presence," then selfhood is endlessly lost in the eddies of such dissolutions.

The collection's title poem, which refers to the location in the Bible where Jacob successfully wrestled the angel and changed his name, foregrounds the process through which the self is negated and rendered transparent, exchanging identity for another. "My mother is dead: I have no name, and so / she quietly sings to me all day all night, / a name I never heard till now, a name / she whispered months before I was born" (p. 46). The speaker's name is something that has been seemingly withheld from him and now returns as an alien thing, a linguistic distortion of the emptiness he feels. There is a restless poignancy in these lines, as the speaker seems lulled back into a childlike mood, almost easily giving himself up to the sense of evacuation that wrests all sense of identity away from him:

My name is quiet as a fingerprint—
It makes no trouble, it tells me who I am,
I've seen it often. And yet I don't know why,

These past few months I brood on Genesis,
Those stories like a rainbow at evening,
And find them all too true.

(p. 46)

If the name identifies the speaker like a fingerprint, it is also something he can leave as a mark or imprint on other persons and things. "Peniel" thus evokes what the French philosopher and writer Maurice Blanchot (a figure Hart has written about) would have called the "space of literature," or the strangely impersonal territory where the self is pushed to the very limits of recognition, confronting its otherness as an effect of the alien sonorities of language.

In other poems Hart momentarily relieves the intensities of his philosophical inquiries with more comical improvisations: "'This Stone Is Thinking of Vienna,'" "'The Present King of France Is Bald,'" and "'The Philosophy of Furniture'" all depart from *Peniel*'s brooding lyricism with their chattiness and mordant wit. Other poems such as "The Letter" or "The Map" are almost fabular in a Kafkaesque way, developing brief narratives about the ineluctability of death. A poem such as "Making a Rat" deliberately positions itself between morbidity and wicked absurdity: the speaker eerily describes his attempts at fashioning a rat, a sloppy process that recalls a Rube Goldberg machine. His obsession with assembling the rat turns him into a kind of psychotic, the opposite of the kind of ethically engaged persona of the thinker/poet who predominates in *Peniel*. Another such persona is described in one of the most striking poems in the volume, "The Historian of Silence," which might very well stand for Hart's own position as a poet fascinated with the simplicities of the everyday: "The historian of silence casts no vote. / The polling booth, he finds, is always closed; / his name not on the roll. He pays a fine, / and likes the feel of bank notes in his hands" (p. 52). Silence does not represent a dearth of meaning but rather a deliberate refusal or reticence regarding the ways in which meaning is subjectively generated. In remaining attentive to that which is most meaningless—"tart, thin smells / of boiling overalls on Sunday walks, / or how, last war, French country girls would keep / bright slabs of butter wrapped in cabbage leaves, / or how a word can sting you like a wasp" (p. 52)—the historian of silence intimates the intensity of his focus. What is interesting about his reflections in these poems is their cultivation of a political voice alongside, rather than in competition with, a more meditative one. The historian of silence, for example, provides a different record of everyday events, not one that is idealized but rather is more pensively restrained and panoptic, attentive to the minutiae that are potentially eradicated by more oppressive forms of institutional historiography. Hart's words do not offer or produce any kind of "actual" evidence, but they do seem to suspend thought in a state of contemplative vigilance. His focus thus remains simply trained, almost ritualistically, on the life of things without intruding into their interiorities.

WICKED HEAT *(2000)*

Although not utterly different in shape and style from his earlier work, *Wicked Heat* is a manifestly more ample and thematically varied collection than *Peniel*. In his fifth collection, Hart explores themes of family remembrance, death and mourning, eros and spiritual awakening, but instead of portraying the self as an alien entity corroded by its memories, personal identity is calmly evoked as free from debilitating anxieties. In other words, the kind of self that emerges in *Wicked Heat* is one that has accepted the world around it as the site of intellectual and emotional expectations and provocations rather than a source of pain and malaise. The calmness of Hart's voice, working almost at low volume, surfaces in the two moving elegies to his mother and maternal grandfather, "The Dressmaker" and "The Carpenter." Although one would expect a sentimentalized series of recollections, the starkness of Hart's aesthetic is intriguing because it evokes a mind that has almost accepted loss as a condition of its own contemporary peace. Recalling how his mother labored to sew dresses, Hart speaks in a voice that is hushed and concise:

I walk around her empty house—it's just the same—
And feel old February heat
That slobbers over you for hour on hour.
Nothing to do, I sit the evening out
On her verandah: wisps
Of grass smoke rising way above the power lines,
A car radio turned low somewhere near.

("The Dressmaker," p. 13)

Hart's peaceful withdrawal into his own surroundings at the conclusion signals a kind of non-traumatic registering of the loss of his mother:

her death is incorporated like a wonderfully textured image into everyday life, alive with small sounds, smells, and things. Speaking of his grandfather, however, Hart seems more urgent: "Don't go, old man, / Straight-backed in your forbidden shack / Built out of bits and pieces of leftover night, / Don't go now / You've come this far" ("The Carpenter," p. 14). Hart's appeal here is quite poignant. Other poems such as "Heat" and "Drawing Room, Annerley, 1996" recollect life in Australia, while "Brisbane" evokes the speaker's desire to move away from his native country by following the strangely beautiful orientation of his own impressions:

I sat and wrote my future in a daze:
And though the sun kept hammering my head
And though a *no* uncoiled within each *yes,*
I listened hard for what is left unsaid.

And while the sun kept hammering my head
The bright hours took my body, one by one.
I listened hard for what is left unsaid,
Convinced it called to me from far within.

(p. 33)

Listening to "what is left unsaid" conjures the "historian of silence" who attends to the meager aspects of life as small felicities and celebrations. Hart here employs the pantoum form (which Baudelaire develops in *The Flowers of Evil*), which requires that the first line of each stanza repeat the second line of the preceding one. Themes of motion and change are thus inseparable from the formal momentum of the pantoum. Indeed, "Brisbane" drives the speaker forward, buoyed by a power that seems utterly outside his control, "a strangeness I could trust."

"The Voice of Brisbane" similarly conveys a haunting recollection of Hart's home city:

Yet still I heard a murmur in the quiet,
Lying in bed those summer nights, as though
All Brisbane were a shell against my ear,

A distant roaring somehow caught in calm:
The Voice of Brisbane, I would tell myself,
Though sensing even then, that undertone

Was older than goanna and brown snake...

(p. 35)

Hart doesn't seek to convey empirical representations but rather affective, lyrical impressions that shimmer and haunt the mind like ghosts. This ghostly effect is compellingly conveyed in the spiritual poem "Soul Says," which is also rewritten several times in the book. The poem takes an almost classic form: a dialogue with the soul that raises questions about identity, agency, and belief. In the first version, Hart speaks to his soul as if it were an external entity or guide that instructs him on how to properly observe and judge himself in relation to the world:

Soul says well let us watch the old night sky
Until the darkness gazes back: your river murmurs as
  it turns
But will not break our tie

(p. 42)

The poem's spareness—there is virtually no punctuation—conjures a kind of pared down experience, a spiritual simplicity as the dialogue with the soul seeks to bring us down to bare essentials. Hart's concentration is on the crystalline and minute, "A hundred spiderlings are hanging from this leaf / Their world was silk / Now they await a small warm air to carry them away." The kind of instruction imparted by the soul ministers against any beliefs that would have the self fall into solipsism; it suggests that what we consider to be "subjective" actually describes a complex negotiation between the authenticity of personal revelation and social values: "The sound you heard above your head was me / Soul says / And for a moment I was almost free." This freedom, however, suspends thought indefinitely in a dynamic of call-and-response with the soul. It teaches a kind of contemplation that pushes the speaker to experience "the darkness gazing back" (p. 42). The speaker is ironically replenished by his own emptiness: the darkness that gazes back doesn't forestall thought but rather invites its endless circulation, refracting without any sense of end.

In "Those White, Ancient Birds" the speaker confronts the birds in the title as if they were

133

lingering traces of an idea that has yet to be developed: "I do not think they know much about longing, / Those white, ancient birds, / they know just where to go / And fly there, at their appointed time." The drift of thought here corresponds to the movement of the birds, and in this sense one could say that the poem suggests another form of attention that has no proper object. What is taught in these ascetic descriptions is a way of conceiving the world and oneself in such a way as to relinquish all sense of mastery:

There is a word that's set out from my death.
I know it has already left my lips
Although I don't know what on earth I'll say

When the time comes. It circles round the world,
And some dark nights I almost think I hear
The lemon tree out back repeating it.

("The Word," p. 52)

Like the name that is won and then lost in "Peniel," the last word before death exists in complete separation from the person it is meant to issue from. Hart's point is not to suggest that the world is determined but rather that our ability to express ourselves through language is unsettled by the experience of death, which rids us of our confidence in linguistic utterance. Death separates identity from the languages it uses to describe itself: Once the self dies, where does language go? In Hart's estimation, language persists as an alien thing that precedes and lies ahead of us.

In "No Easy Thing," this sense of the self standing apart from itself nears an especially beautiful lyricism:

Angels of summer live closest to the earth
And know the joys of late November days.
No easy thing, my friend, to sense the thrill
Of mouth on mouth and not to have it now;

To see a breeze, right off Deception Bay,
Amaze a man who's lived in afternoon
Abandoned to the heat.... If sunlit minds
Can gaze at earth and almost feel desire,

What hope for us?

(p. 19)

Angels, of course, cannot feel desire, and Hart takes the angels' predicament of knowing and perceiving life without truly participating in it as a thematic for exploring the self's dissociation from itself through spirituality and erotic desire, temptation, and fulfillment.

These elements are brought to the fore in the volume's longest poetic series, "Nineteen Songs," which detail the complexities of love and loss with exuberance and precise reflection. The formal precision of these brief songs seems to suggest a level of control that the speaker feels is slipping away from him despite his best attempts at emotional mastery:

Today I think that love
Is simply watching her
Peeling a mandarin
(As though an entire life
Could turn on fingertips)

I have not spared my eyes
Since I became a man
And yet I little thought
That I would feel desire
For fingers sprayed with juice

(p. 67)

The erotic inflection in the speaker's voice as he watches his beloved peel a mandarin suggests that his longing to depict her in his mind can never fully possess the object of his affection: "How little it will seem / Enclosed in memory, / Sharing that mandarin / (But two entire lives / Turned on her fingertips)" (p. 67). The pleasures of love depend upon its evasions—a theme that motors the overtly physical descriptions throughout the songs. The earthiness of love recalls the "wickedness" of the title—while "wicked" certainly implies malevolence, it also colloquially refers to something being exceptionally good. Hart's writing is thus never obsessive or sentimental. His sense of romance derives from a willingness to pursue the beloved despite her unwillingness to cede to his advances: "Men simply look at you and fall in love again: / I only want the world to turn / A little faster now so they fall off the globe / And a great turtle eats them up" (p. 70). The intelligence behind Hart's experience of love is fueled by a delight in the metaphoric plays that make such love possible:

thus when he declares that "I want to enter you / Like a young lion that strides / Into the Serengeti / While locusts chant nightfall" (p. 82), he calls upon a tradition of erotic poetry that depicts the call to the beloved as a deeply aesthetic plea on behalf of the imagination that is entangled with more earthy impulses. *Wicked Heat* returns to the theme of negation by suggesting that all such images are empty projections—empty not in the sense of being failures but in that they conceptually extend the self's own transparency into the world, forever mobile and interesting.

Selected Bibliography

WORKS OF KEVIN HART

POETRY
The Departure. Brisbane: University of Queensland Press, 1978.
The Lines of the Hand. Sydney: Angus & Robertson, 1981.
Your Shadow. Sydney: Angus & Robertson, 1984.
Peniel. Melbourne: Golvern Arts, 1991.
New and Selected Poems. Sydney: HarperCollins, 1995.
Wicked Heat. Sydney: Paper Bark Press, 2000.
Flame Tree: Selected Poems. Highgreen: Bloodaxe, 2002.

CHAPBOOKS/PAMPHLETS
Dark Angel. Dublin: Dedalus Press, 1996.
Nineteen Songs. Sydney: Vagabond Press, 1999.
Madonna. Sydney: Vagabond Press, 2000.
Night Music. Melbourne: Best Oven House, 2003.

CRITICISM
The Trespass of the Sign: Deconstruction, Theology, and Philosophy. Cambridge, U.K. and New York: Cambridge University Press, 1989. 2d ed., New York: Fordham University Press, 2000.
A. D. Hope. Melbourne and New York: Oxford University Press, 1992.
Samuel Johnson and the Culture of Property. Cambridge, U.K. and New York: Cambridge University Press, 1999.
The Dark Gaze: Maurice Blanchot and the Sacred. Chicago: Chicago University Press, 2004.
Postmodernism: A Beginner's Guide. Oxford: Oneworld, 2004.

CRITICAL BOOKLETS
Losing the Power to Say "I." Melbourne: Art School Press, 1996.

How to Read a Page of Boswell. Sydney: Vagabond Press, 2000.
The Impossible. Sydney: Vagabond Press, 2003.

COLLECTIONS AS EDITOR
The Buried Harbour: Selected Poems of Giuseppe Ungaretti. Canberra: Leros Press, 1990.
The Oxford Book of Australian Religious Verse. Melbourne and New York: Oxford University Press, 1994.
The Fifth Question and After: Poems for Tomaz Salamun. Sydney: Vagabond Press, 2001.
Nowhere Without No: In Memory of Maurice Blanchot. Sydney: Vagabond Press, 2003.
Derrida and Religions: Other Testaments. Edited with Yvonne Sherwood. New York: Routledge, 2004.
Experiencing God. Edited with Barbara Wall. New York: Fordham University Press, 2004.
The Power of Contestation: Perspectives on Maurice Blanchot. Edited with Geoffrey H. Hartman. Baltimore: Johns Hopkins University Press, 2004.

CRITICAL STUDIES
Brennan, Michael. "'What Bliss to Be Her Slave!': Discipline, Silence, and Death in the *Symboliste* Project." In *Masochism: Disciplines of Desire, Aesthetics of Cruelty, Politics of Danger.* Edited by Natalya Lusty and Ruth Walker. Sydney: PG ARC Publications, 1998. Pp. 79–88.
Catalano, Gary. "In the Mirror: On the Poetic Identity of Kevin Hart." *Imago* 10, no. 3:60–71 (1999).
Harrison, Martin. "Horizons of the Name." *Ulitarra* 10:69–81 (1996).
Kane, Paul. "Philosopher-Poets: John Koethe and Kevin Hart." *Raritan* 21, no. 1:94–113 (2001).
Khalip, Jacques. "A Difficult Attentiveness: Kevin Hart, *Flame Tree.*" *Antipodes,* December 2002, pp. 200–201.
Kinsella, John. "An Interview with Kevin Hart." *Salt* 10:256–275 (1997).
McCooey, David. " 'Secret Truths': The Poetry of Kevin Hart." *Southerly* 55, no. 4:109–121 (1995).
Mead, Philip. "Reading the Signs." *Adelaide Review* 25:109–119 (1986).
Pearson, Kevin F. "The Canberra Poets: The New Australian Poetry." In *Poetry of the Pacific Region.* Edited by Paul Sharrad. Adelaide: Centre for Research in the New Literatures in English. Pp. 109–119.
Spinks, Lee. "Sketching the Horizon: An Interview with Kevin Hart." *Journal of Commonwealth Literature* 71:5–14 (2000).
Watson, Stephen. "Interview." *Verse* 20, nos. 2–3 (2003). Pp. 49-73.

Elizabeth Jane Howard

(1923–)

Neil Powell

ACCORDING TO MARTIN Amis, who between 1965 and 1983 was her stepson, Elizabeth Jane Howard "is, with Iris Murdoch, the most interesting woman writer of her generation. An instinctivist, but an elegant one (like Muriel Spark), she has a freakish and poetic eye, and penetrating sanity" (*Experience,* 2000, p. 215). This is a subtle judgment, and the comparison with Iris Murdoch—whom, at first glance, Howard seems not to resemble at all—is an especially acute one. Yet Amis's careful choice of words such as "instinctivist" and "freakish" hints at a problem worth confronting at the outset. Upon first reading, Howard does not seem to be an intellectual writer in the same league as Murdoch or A. S. Byatt; indeed, some readers may suspect her of being an altogether more popular, middlebrow sort of novelist. She straddles a borderline which has existed since the novel's earliest days but which late-twentieth-century publishing and bookselling practices made conspicuous: a fact acknowledged by her current British paperback publisher, which produces her books in the larger format associated with their literary imprint, Picador, but under their mass-market label, Pan. If the practical consequence of this is that her books reach an audience undreamt of by most literary novelists, it is unlikely to trouble her; and it is also true to her eventful, varied, and blessedly nonacademic life.

Elizabeth Jane Howard was born on 26 March 1923, the eldest of three children. Alexander Howard, her paternal grandfather, perversely nicknamed "the Brig" because he had never been in the army, ran a successful family timber business and owned a country house in Sussex—a location that recurs in Howard's fiction. Her father, David, had been a major in the First World War before joining the family firm. As Howard observes in her autobiography, *Slipstream* (2002), at heart her father "remained a boy—a dashing, glamorous boy" (p. 14), and he is in several respects the model for Edward Cazalet. Her maternal grandfather was the composer Sir Arthur Somervell, and her mother, Katherine, had danced in Diaghilev's Ballets Russes. Her parents' marriage in 1921 thus represents the alliance of upper-middle-class prosperity and cultured eccentricity that figures so largely in her fiction. She grew up mostly in Kensington, educated by governesses at home and, not very successfully, at local schools.

In the summer before the Second World War she was sent, like her character and contemporary Louise Cazalet, to a domestic science school; she stayed only two terms before gaining admittance to the London Mask Theatre School. Meanwhile, she had met Peter Scott—having been invited to the family's country home by his mother, Kathleen Kennet—whom she would marry three years later in 1942, when she was nineteen and he thirty-two. Their daughter Nicola, Howard's only child, was born in February 1943. It was a disastrous marriage, about which both her autobiographical and her fictionalized accounts are unsparing. Scott's biographer, Elspeth Huxley, though naturally well disposed toward her own subject, is notably understanding of Howard in her treatment of the relationship. In the summer of 1947, writes Huxley, "she walked out of No 8 Edwardes Square with £10, a suitcase containing her half-written novel and some of her smart New York clothes" (*Peter Scott,* 1993, pp. 156–157). The novel was *The Beautiful Visit* (1950).

During the latter years of the war, Howard worked as a continuity announcer at the BBC and briefly as an actress. This was to be followed by a series of stints in publishing, as a reader and editor, notably at Chatto and Windus alongside Cecil Day Lewis; later she became a regular book reviewer for *Queen* magazine. In fact, during the 1950s she lived the typically precarious life of the literary freelancer, in which necessary part-time assignments continually jostled with her own writing. Her second marriage, to James Douglas-Henry in April 1959, was short-lived and (even in the candid terms of *Slipstream*) not easily explicable, but her appointment as director of the Cheltenham Festival of Literature four years later would lead to the most enduring, important, and difficult relationship of her life.

By the time Kingsley Amis made his appearance at Cheltenham in 1962, Elizabeth Jane Howard had published two more novels, *The Long View* (1956) and *The Sea Change* (1959), and was at work on *After Julius* (1965). Their mutual attraction was instantaneous, and they were to marry, after their respective divorces, in May 1965; but they were very different novelists, and an intriguing cross-fertilization of styles takes place in their subsequent work. Howard becomes both more darkly comic (as in *Something in Disguise,* 1969) and more playful (*Getting It Right,* 1982), and Amis more ready to experiment with narrative technique—in its method, his much-praised *The Old Devils* (1986) could be a novel by Howard. In 1968 the Amises moved out of London to a house at Hadley Common, Hertfordshire, but Kingsley's depression and heavy drinking were already putting a strain on their marriage. Howard, in *Slipstream,* is generous toward him, whereas Amis in his *Memoirs* (1991) does not mention by name the woman he calls simply his "second wife." She left him in 1980, and they were divorced in 1983.

The Amises had returned to Hampstead in 1978, and Howard was to remain in London until, in 1991 shortly after the publication of *The Light Years* (the first volume in the highly successful Cazalet Chronicle, 1990), she moved to Bungay, a market town in Suffolk, where she still lives. This brief introductory outline has not attempted to deal with her extraordinary range of friends and lovers, her travels, and many other aspects of her life which are described in her memoir, *Slip-stream,* for this essay must now concern itself with her twelve remarkable novels.

DAUGHTERS AND LOVERS

Almost all of Elizabeth Jane Howard's novels—the apparent exception is *Getting It Right*—draw clearly on her own character and experiences, yet none of them is a straightforward roman à clef. Even in the four Cazalet books, despite their deep and complex grounding in their author's early family life, the autobiographical elements are carefully shuffled and transposed. Her first three novels employ three distinct strategies designed to put some distance between author and subject; nevertheless, each deals with a young woman's leaving home and experiencing both happiness and loss as she tries to define her place in the world.

"I was born in Kensington. My father was a composer." Thus the unnamed narrator of *The Beautiful Visit* introduces herself, adding: "We had the usual childhood, with governesses, and interminable walks in Kensington Gardens" (p. 9). But of course this was hardly "usual" by 1950, when the book was published, and it was ceasing to be so even in Howard's own childhood in the 1920s and 1930s: the action has been pushed back to her parents' generation. When the story begins, in 1913, its narrator is sixteen, and when it ends some six years later, the First World War has taken place entirely off stage, just as it does in Virginia Woolf's *To the Lighthouse.* Despite its gentility, the family is short of money—they abide by "a code laid down by generations; and in a flash of understanding I realized how poverty must strengthen it" (p. 102)—and the novel follows the younger daughter's repeated attempts to break away from this stifling environment; the fact that most of her attempts turn out to be dead ends lends the book authenticity at the expense of shape. For instance, early in the novel she meets a boy, Michael Latham, flying a kite in Kensington Gardens. He has been expelled from his school—the first of several boys in Howard's fiction who quarrel with their education—and his example of intellectual independence is a significant one; yet, after listening appreciatively to her father playing the piano, he vanishes and does not reappear.

Like Fanny Price in Jane Austen's *Mansfield Park,* the narrator is packed off to visit her wealthier distant relations, the Lancings, at their country house. Her elder sister had refused to go, and the imperious telegram, which says merely "Send another daughter" (p. 28), strikes a note that Austen would surely have recognized. The scene in which the shy and terrified girl arrives and finds herself entering a drawing room "very full of people" (p. 35) is one which recurs in Howard's work, but the visit itself turns out to be both enjoyable and life-changing—if not quite in the ways we are at first led to expect. She is delighted by Lucy Lancing and her more accomplished (and more superficial) sister Deb; she thinks she falls in love with charming, rakish Rupert Laing; but here, especially in the Austen-like dance which concludes the visit (chapter 8), readers must be alert to the echoes of Fanny and Henry Crawford. It is the less glamorous characters we should attend to, especially Rupert's friend Ian and the awkward, bluntly intelligent Elspeth, whose virtues will be replicated in *The Sea Change*'s Alberta and the Cazalets' Clary. Howard is already a moralist, fiercely defending unflashy integrity, as well as a satirist: the visit contains a characteristic comic vignette in the portrait of Mrs. Druid, an apparent escapee from *Cold Comfort Farm,* and her infant son George, "a large baby with a grey face and pale curls" who is alternately convulsed and static: "George hung motionless like seaweed" (p. 63).

On returning to London the narrator expects "life to be different at home" (p. 93), not at first seeing that, in kite-flying Michael's prescient words, she has to "learn, listen, and find out, and then choose" (p. 22) how to change her own life. Her first attempt to do so, through reading, striking up a friendship with a librarian, and applying for a job in the library, is doubly disastrous: an evening out with Agnes and two male friends ends with her fighting off an unwelcome sexual advance, while working in a library is deemed unsuitable by her parents. Soon afterward her father, scanning the evening paper, notices that "some Archduke or other has been murdered at...at Sarajevo. That's it. Sarajevo" (p. 131); but two days after the declaration of war, he dies from a feverish cold, caught while walking home from a concert in a thunderstorm. The atmosphere of the narrator's home is made all the more unbearable by the temporary presence of her odious elder brothers, so she plans her escape, announcing that she is going to visit a friend (by implication, female) in Chelsea, whereas she actually intends to take up Rupert's invitation to stay with him. She is, inevitably, in for a shock.

When she arrives at Rupert's address, she is at once confronted with Maria, "almost the first person I had ever heard speak with a foreign accent" (p. 153), whom she discovers to be his mistress, a concept hitherto unfamiliar to her upper-middle-class sensibility. Rupert himself, having dabbled as a painter, is off to join the army the next day. There are both positive and negative lessons here: the Bohemian life offers an open, unmannered set of emotional responses (they will be more sturdily embodied in *After Julius*'s Daniel Brick) which are always denied to Howard's main characters; yet counterbalancing this is the gradual recognition that Rupert's apparent freedom is in fact self-centered fecklessness. On the rebound from all this, the narrator takes a job in the country as companion to an elderly lady who is a prolific and terrible painter, a tyrannical fantasist, and the owner of a deranged nocturnal parrot. The possible escape routes are steadily disappearing. Back in London again, however, the narrator re-encounters Ian Graham, from the Lancings' Christmas house party, falls in love, and finds her vocation as a writer. Love temporarily, and perhaps pardonably, turns the prose a rhapsodic purple—"They are the moments of life which continue it: the vindication of all the desolate hours and days and years that each one spends searching" (p. 254)— but the deeper significance of this moment, in a first-person first novel, will be clear. Ian at last enables her to follow Michael's advice from two hundred pages earlier:

"You should write," he said. "You observe things very well."

"Is that the most important thing about writing?"

"No, not really. But I think it is for women who write. Observation is their strong suit. They seldom write out of pure imagination." (p. 235)

Questionable though this generalization may be, it shows that the young novelist has a shrewd awareness of her own gifts and limitations.

But the book is not to have a neat or unequivocally happy ending. Ian is killed in action, and it is Rupert who returns, wounded, and attempts to reassemble the components of the earlier beautiful visit. The result is only a partial success: Deb, in particular, is now unhappily married to Aubrey, "someone who seemed so exactly designed to pair with her" (p. 297), an idea which usually strikes an ominous note in Howard's work, where the surprise of apparent incompatibility bodes better. They are overheard arguing, and here it is Deb who speaks for the young Elizabeth Jane Howard: "I thought marriage meant *more* freedom, not less. I didn't know it meant years of plans, and having children, and sitting by myself all day" (p. 309). For the narrator it is sufficient warning: she takes herself off to a bed-sitter, where she fills several notebooks with the novel which is *The Beautiful Visit;* this she shows to the independent, resourceful Elspeth—her true soulmate, had she known it, all along—with whom she sets off on a long sea voyage.

If Jane Austen is the shaping spirit, at least in its earlier pages, of *The Beautiful Visit,* the dominant voice in Howard's second novel, *The Long View,* is Virginia Woolf's. The book has an unusual structure—it comprises five sections in reverse chronological order, beginning in 1950 and ending in 1926—and a narrative tone that juxtaposes an almost stream-of-consciousness psychological inwardness with poised observation of the external world. The following passage, in which Conrad Fielding's ornate parenthetical ruminations as he bathes following an afternoon with his mistress are capped by a brisk, balanced single-sentence paragraph, might almost be Woolf herself:

Innumerable women had inquired why he had married his wife; and it had fascinated him to hear the varying degrees of curiosity, solicitude and spite, with which they contrived to put the damaging little question. It had fascinated him no less to reply (throwing contemptuously aside such repertorial excuses as youth or inexperience) with fantastic, and apparently circumstantial detail; in such a way as to defer their hopes, excite their interest, or disprove their theories: discovering, each time (and he never told the same story twice), that there was no limit or horizon to the human capacity of belief. He did it, he considered, in the best possible taste. He never deprecated his wife, even by implication. He simply added, as it were, another storey to the structure of his personality, and invited the lady in question to put herself temporarily in possession: there she might perch precariously, in what she could be easily persuaded was an isolated castle in a rich and strange air.

He was bathed; he was dressed.

(p. 18)

Shortly afterward we find Conrad's wife, Antonia, presiding over a dinner party, like an updated version of Mrs. Dalloway or Mrs. Ramsay. Here too the prose style, amused and slightly mannered, owes much to Woolf: "Deirdre unwisely attempted to introduce the Pyramids, but Mr. Fleming waved them gently aside as so many castle puddings" (p. 25).

In the first (which is chronologically the last) part of *The Long View,* the Flemings' marriage is breaking up; moreover, their son and daughter are both embarking on disastrous alliances of their own. Julian is about to marry June Stoker, arguably the stupidest character in all Howard's fiction, while Deirdre—always involved with two men, "one dull, devoted creature whose only distinction was his determination to marry her...the other, more attractive, but even more unsatisfactory" (p. 9)—is pregnant by the unmarrying Louis and destined to marry the unsatisfactory Miles. "Man hands on misery to man," as Philip Larkin said, and woman to woman too: the book proceeds to unpeel the successive layers of this process. In the next section, set in wartime, Antonia has to meet her husband at Euston: she has come up from their house in Kent, where Deirdre and an assortment of evacuees are parked (Julian is away at school), and they are to spend the night at their London home, which also contains a recuperating naval officer. It is an archetypal Howard scene: returning to an only partly inhabited house, somehow preparing a meal, and being emotionally knocked off balance by a third party. And it is clear that the marriage is already in serious difficulties.

Why this should be becomes much clearer in the pivotal third section, which takes place in 1937. The Flemings and their young children have gone on holiday with dull friends, the Talbots, to St. Tropez. In their hotel bedroom Conrad considers the question that we have already seen him touch on thirteen years later:

> Either one marries a woman who gradually sharpens, intensifies, exaggerates herself, to the essence of her original appearance—or a woman brimful of a kind of beauty that runs over and dissipates—that blurs and diffuses until there is no constant picture of her at any one time, but simply a vast series of impressions—even asleep, she is not a picture of herself, but of someone who *was* like her, asleep. The first is intellectually aesthetically desirable: her men can watch her becoming what at the beginning they hoped she would be; only that was at the beginning and in the end they no longer want it. The second is always elusive, always disappointing, fascinating because nothing is ever attained.
>
> (pp. 104–105)

Antonia is the first kind of woman: the pair are, like Deb and Aubrey in *The Beautiful Visit,* too well matched. He returns to his affair in London with Imogen, a scatty art student; she begins one in Marseilles with Thompson, an illiterate engineer. An almost unbearable tension springs from the reader's recognition that, although both Conrad and Antonia deserve better than this (they deserve each other), they need the stimulus of inequality; the moral point is nothing as simplistic as the corrosive effect of adultery, for the corrosion is built into the marriage. But both affairs are doomed too: "I can't talk with all this destruction going on," says Conrad (p. 160), as Imogen burns her work, but the remark has a wider resonance; while Antonia realizes that Thompson has no emotional interest in her whatsoever. They both break off their relationships and a reconciliation of sorts is achieved; yet Conrad, returning home, notices "how the paint on the door had discoloured round the brass" and reflects: "Cleaning up one thing dirtied another" (p. 193).

The book's two remaining parts take us back to the couple's Paris honeymoon in 1927—when the overprotective nature of Conrad's love for her first becomes evident to Antonia—and the country-house summer of 1926: here, she falls for a horsy Irish scoundrel called Geoffrey Curran, whom she eventually realizes is having an affair with her mother, a recurrent Howard motif. This is familiar territory: the sheltered teenage girl's headlong plunge into sexual confusion, which in this case is resolved when she meets a stranger on a staircase, who asks, "Were you looking for someone?" (p. 367).

The Sea Change borrows a Woolf-like method—its narrative viewpoint is shared among four main characters in short, named sections—but swiftly establishes a quite distinct territory. It is in some respects Howard's most ambitious and accomplished novel. The ambition is immediately apparent: those four characters embrace a more diverse range of background and experience than she has previously attempted, while the action takes us from England to New York and then on to Greece. Emmanuel is a successful playwright in his sixties, with whom susceptible younger women readily fall in love. Capable of unprompted generosity and goodness, he is nevertheless inclined to self-dramatize, as if he were indeed a character in a not especially good play. His wife, Lilian, is an invalid who has never ceased to grieve over the death of their daughter Sarah many years earlier. Lilian experiences her relationship with her own life as semidetached, a notion which will come to haunt Howard: "After that day [her fourteenth birthday], everything seemed to swoop and pounce and happen too fast; as though I was running breathlessly behind my life—shrieking with the need to choose—out of earshot—in a frantic slipstream of the events which rocketed on before me" (p. 14). Jimmy, Emmanuel's amanuensis and general fixer, is a younger American: he provides, at first, a fairly disengaged viewpoint, for it is he who opens the book in a cool first-person narrative tone, reminiscent of Nick Carraway in *The Great Gatsby*. Into this established trinity comes another Sarah, immediately renamed Alberta, a country vicar's daughter who combines innocence with robustness. We have moved from a kind of novel in which a central character's life unfolds against a background of people and events to one which provides interplay within a small group: it is the difference between a concerto and a string quartet.

The plot of *The Sea Change* is creaky—much depends on Alberta, Emmanuel's newly appointed secretary, turning out (after endless auditions of professional actresses) to be the ideal person to play a part in the New York production of his new play, an event both improbable and surely unacceptable to Equity, the actors' union— but this seems not to matter, for three reasons: the warm solidity of the characterization, the vivid scene-setting, and the richly comic vignettes. The heart of the novel is the evolving relationship between Emmanuel and Alberta, as they discover each other's capacity for goodness, a quality which at first we may more readily associate with her than with him. But Emmanuel's goodness is doubly, and discreetly, established. Firstly, there is his kindness toward his neurotic former secretary and her impoverished sister: "He was smiling at her now, and afterwards—for the rest of her life—this precise and delicate goodness was her secret blessing" (p. 42). Secondly, and just as secretly, there is his longer-term support of the Friedmanns and their violinist son. But it is Alberta who perfectly and intuitively understands Emmanuel, as he also recognizes:

There was a complete silence: he was looking at her, and he saw her so clearly that in her was his own reflection: he saw so much of himself that there were no words in his mind for it—the few seconds were filled so that they were round and unrecognizable drops of time. She knew something—or understood that there was something for him to know, because she did not break this moment; having furnished him, she was still, and when it was over she waited for him to resume, or assume what he would. It was much as though she had unerr-

ingly laid a finger on something he found it very difficult to find, and left him to count the beats.

(pp. 115–116)

Alberta is a fully rounded and immensely engaging character, worthy of Jane Austen or George Eliot; we shall meet her kind of goodness, and the profound love it can engender, again when we reach Clary and Archie in the later Cazalet books. Like Clary, too, she writes letters and keeps a diary, through which Howard provides us with a more inward view of her.

The atmospheres of both New York and Greece are finely conveyed, through four pairs of eyes ranging from the astonished to the world-weary. Alberta, for instance, is understandably starstruck by New York—"a bunch of upright needles glinting, and the newborn feeling went on when one looked at them" (p. 86)—whereas Jimmy, striking the true Scott Fitzgerald note at a fashionable party, has seen it all: "Debbie Westinghouse was one of those women you only see here—half doll, half little girl—she'd never had a thought in her head, and that went for the nasty ones too—she was crisp, and silly, and sweet and simple, and so clean you could have eaten off her" (p. 151). There is, moreover, a whole sequence of lively vignettes, mostly comic: a garrulous cabdriver, a porter tormented by an abandoned monkey, a weird wise child in Greece. Emmanuel, transfigured, will come "to see his life as though he was on some height, and it lay on a distant plain below him; occurring without chronology, but with amazing swiftness and certainty" (p. 314), and the extent to which the reader shares in his transformation is a measure of the novel's success.

In *After Julius,* Howard very clearly builds on the strengths of the three earlier books. The chamber-music structure of *The Sea Change* is further refined: it is arranged in three sections— the Friday, Saturday, and Sunday of a single weekend—in which a quintet of characters each has a chapter, followed by an authorial coda. The book's defining event has taken place twenty years earlier, when Julius Grace died in a quixotic attempt to assist at the evacuation of Dunkirk in

1940—an action prompted partly by his wife Esme's infidelity. Now she lives in Sussex, while her two grown-up daughters (Cressida, a widowed, professional pianist, and Emma, an editor in the family publishing house) share a flat in London. The predictable pattern of a weekend in the country is disrupted in three interlocking ways: Felix, Esme's former lover, now a doctor just back from an overseas posting, invites himself; Cressida's current lover, an unaccountably boring Sussex neighbor, is forced by his unwitting wife to make a social appearance; and Emma is accompanied by a novelty both in her life and in Howard's novels, a northern working-class poet called Daniel Brick.

Dan is the great innovation in *After Julius* as well as its major problem. He is a mass of paradoxes: gauche yet sensitive to nuance, puritanical yet unscrupulous. He steals scenes as well as hearts. His social ineptitude may be grotesquely comic—he picks blackberries off a flower arrangement, downs his sherry in one more gulp—but it also exposes the sillier aspects of polite convention. The difficulty lies partly in reconciling his utter naïveté in worldly matters with the fact that he has written, delivered, and had two books accepted by a leading publisher; and partly in the way that someone from so rough a background is so easily scandalized by others' sexual conduct. When he casually describes Cressida as a "tart" to her sister, the reader will be as appalled as Emma herself, yet (and this is the scene's skillful balancing touch) unable fully to endorse her own retreat into a different sort of primness: "It may be different on canals and wherever else you've been, but I assure you that nowadays people don't get all stuffy and call other people tarts because they go to bed with people without marrying them" (p. 135). In saying this, incidentally, she prefigures, and arguably invites, the violent consummation of her relationship with Dan later in the book.

Skillful balance is also the key to the novel's other interloper, Felix. Intelligent, resourceful, and kind, he has been guilty of one terrible moral misjudgment: on Julius's death he joined the army and vanished from Esme's life, feeling then that this was the right thing to do but recognizing

now that perhaps he "ought to have been married to her for the last twenty years" (p. 73). Cressida (who knew about her mother's infidelity at the time) devastatingly puts the case against Felix: "it's people like you who go around ruining other people's lives. And the funny thing is you're too selfish and *stupid* to see more than a fraction of the damage you do" (p. 150). But it is Felix who will rescue Cressida from her emotional chasm and help her to reconstruct her life, at the cost of Esme's at last discovering the extent of her own loneliness. Her moment of recognition is beautifully handled:

> A feeling of helpless terror, like the beginning of drowning, was succeeded by all the evidence edited, linked like film. He had gone to Battle with Cressy; had offered to go with her and Brian last night; had come back hours late; had tried to tell *her* something last night; but she, she had been too wrapped in the courage of her own convictions to listen, to have saved herself the final humiliation. Now that she could see nothing else, she felt she must have been mad not to see it. Her own daughter! Why not? Perhaps that, too, would be a splendid arrangement. A feeling of hatred for her daughter came—and went.
>
> (p. 253)

Readers who occasionally feel that Howard is more sympathetic to her women than to her men will note that, in *After Julius,* the two most complicated and surprising characters are Dan and Felix.

Apart from its subtle characterization and its careful delineation of emotional change, *After Julius* is interesting for the ways in which it intersects with Howard's life and work. The movement back and forth from London to country home in Sussex is part of her own past experience which also shapes the Cazalet quartet; the scene in which Cressida remembers accompanying her late husband to Cowes is closely based on Howard's visit there with Peter Scott (*Slipstream,* pp. 122–124); while the disastrous Saturday dinner party, which alters all the lives in the novel, was partly written, according to Howard, by Kingsley Amis (*Slipstream,* p. 347).

ELIZABETH JANE HOWARD

WRONGS AND RIGHTS

In her first four novels Howard had both drawn on her own experiences and experimented with a number of fictional structures; and if, in *After Julius,* she had found the one that suited her best, she was perhaps wise to put it aside for a while, saving it for her extended late work, and in the meantime writing four rather more orthodox-looking books: *Something in Disguise* (1969), *Odd Girl Out* (1972), *Mr. Wrong* (1975), and *Getting It Right* (1982).

The appearance of orthodoxy is, appropriately, deceptive in *Something in Disguise,* which for two of its three parts seems to be a fairly unthreatening social comedy. Almost all the main characters' lives are complicated by their own or their parents' remarriages: May, mother of Oliver and Elizabeth, is married to Colonel Herbert Browne-Lacey, father of Alice; when the novel opens, these five are temporarily under the same roof—the ugly, cold, and enormous Surrey house that Herbert has persuaded May to pay for. The children quickly make their escapes: Alice by marrying Leslie Mount, a dull property developer from Bristol; Oliver and Elizabeth by retreating to their London house. The plot then branches. Oliver, brilliant but aimless, dabbles with a series of absurd jobs and gets involved with beautifully brainless girls called Sukie and Ginny; Elizabeth, through a richly comical agency run by Lady Dione Havergal-Smythe and Mrs. Potts—"Lady Dione looked about fifteen—even in dark glasses—and Mrs Potts, who was the perfectly ordinary age of about fifty—old, anyway—turned out to be Hungarian" (p. 49)—cooks for private dinner parties. One of these engagements is an evening *à deux* for John Cole and his divorced alcoholic wife, on whose early departure John rather easily persuades Elizabeth into bed: later they travel to the South of France, a visit complicated by the arrival of John's daughter Jennifer and, after their marriage, to Jamaica. Alice's marriage, however, proves disastrous in every respect, from the appalling Mount family to the bungalow which Leslie is having built for them (along with forty-nine nearly identical others) to the obnoxious puppy, a present from Leslie's mother. Meanwhile, the colonel is conducting an affair with an aging yet increasingly expensive prostitute and pursuing Myrtle, owner of the Monkey Puzzle Hotel; and May joins a bogus spiritualist society whose Dr. Sedum persuades her to leave her house to them. Much is made of dreadful meals and hideously furnished rooms; there is an enormous cat, Claude, whose cumbersome obtuseness sets him apart from most of Howard's animals.

So far, so funny. But there is more than comedy to *Something in Disguise.* It is a book that both probes the nature of misalliances and is wary of overexplication; as Oliver asks Elizabeth, "Can you imagine what on earth made May marry Herbert? People are so keen on explaining every nuance of human behaviour that they fall back on the kind of invention that tells you more about *them* than it tells you about what they're explaining" (p. 149). It is also a book which darkens in its final part, set in an inhospitably wintry December. Oliver is abandoned by Ginny, who tells him (exactly reprising his earlier opinion of her) that he is "one of the dimmest people I've ever known" (p. 240), but that is the lightest of the conclusions. Alice, tripped by the wretched puppy on an icy path, has a miscarriage and develops pneumonia; John, driving to the airport to meet Jennifer, who has announced her intention of coming to Jamaica (changing her mind at the last minute), is killed in a car crash; Herbert, who has been slowly poisoning May so that he can inherit the house, discovers her will and poisons himself, as well as the unfortunate Claude. May, we may assume, would also have died if Alice, deserting her husband, had not discovered her trying to bury the dead cat in the snow: both May and Alice realize that Herbert was a serial poisoner who had murdered two previous wives, yet each protectively withholds this knowledge from the other. The book ends with Elizabeth, now pregnant, and Oliver tacitly acknowledging filial love as the only moderately reliable kind. This almost unremittingly bleak denouement is untypical of Howard's fiction, to be matched only in the chilling title story of *Mr. Wrong* and in the late novel *Falling* (1999).

Odd Girl Out revisits one strand from *After Julius,* although the disrupting force this time is neither a young poet nor a middle-aged physician but wayward, charismatic, Botticelli-like Arabella Darwick. Arabella, the daughter of Edmund Cornhill's ex-stepmother Clara (a typical Howard relationship), pays an extended visit to Edmund and his wife Anne, partly to convalesce after an abortion but mainly to evade Clara's plans to marry her off in a financially advantageous way. Accompanying Edmund, an estate agent, on a visit to what is recognizably Kingsley and Jane Amis's house at Hadley Common, Hertfordshire, she swiftly seduces him; and when Edmund has to go to Greece on business and Anne is confined to bed with glandular fever, Arabella seduces her too. This swinging sexuality is very much of its moment, but Howard's treatment of its consequences is characteristically serious and thoughtful. There is also, equally characteristically, a magnificent cat, Ariadne, who chooses to give birth to kittens on Arabella's bed and who becomes, not at all sentimentally, the image of a generous yet passionless love which mirrors Arabella's own.

Like Daniel Brick, whose eccentricities neatly counterpoint hers (for instance, she arranges runner-bean flowers and artichokes in Anne's Dresden and Edmund's Sung jar: Dan would have then eaten them), Arabella ought to be a monster but is nothing of the sort. She is one of Howard's truth-tellers, redeemed by the kind of honesty from which more emotionally engaged people shy away; a notable instance of this occurs when she explains to Edmund her inability to return his gushy feelings for her:

> Oh—that. I love you, I love Anne, I love Ariadne, I love this house and your and my life in it: I love the summer here, and the garden and the river. I love Scarlatti and being in one place and not being with Clara and having money and my good health. But in the sense you mean, no: I don't love you—I don't love anyone. I never have. Except the one, dead person I told you about. And as I don't love anyone, I'm a private menace.
>
> (p. 163)

That idea of a "private menace" is a recurring one in Howard: it is the charge Cressy levels at Felix in *After Julius,* and it reappears in similar terms when Anne's friend Len (for Leonora) visits and apprises the situation with an outsider's clear eye. When Arabella plausibly defends herself, saying, "I have never been in favour of subterfuge," Len replies, "Oh. Just in favour of messing up other people's lives" (p. 223). Arabella, who insists that she would not "do anything to hurt Anne—or him," is left contemplating the "gap between her conscience and her heart" and the troubling paradox that emotional honesty can be so much more damaging than deception.

While *Odd Girl Out* thus engages with serious moral questions, it also has the lightness typical of midcareer Howard: the wry attentiveness to domestic details and, indeed, domestic animals; the delighted enjoyment of food—for instance, the dinner prepared by Anne (pp. 75–83), the lunch at Prunier's (pp. 100–107), and in a different register, Arabella's comical shopping expedition (pp. 169–171). The influence of Kingsley Amis is detectable in the comic writing and, at one point, in a graceful allusion: when Anne asks Arabella, "Do you think we are much nicer than men?" (p. 197), she ironically echoes the lines in Amis's poem "A Bookshop Idyll": "Women are really much nicer than men: / No wonder we like them." Arabella decides that women are "kinder—and more gentle with people"; interestingly Anne balks at "more gentle."

Getting It Right—the "hairdresser novel" which she "hoped desperately…would be a breakthrough for me" (*Slipstream,* p. 432), a revealing anxiety for an established writer in her sixtieth year—is the oddity among her books, the one that scarcely engages the social milieus in which she is most at home. Its central character is Gavin, a virginal thirty-one-year-old hairdresser, who suffers from spots and dandruff and still lives with his dreary parents. He views experience in terms of a "Ladder of Fear" (p. 10) and is, as Minerva Munday tells him, "somebody who makes the least of everything that happens to you" (p. 108). Yet this, as Howard fully understands, may be a quiet kind of virtue, which will enable Gavin to behave with an honest decency unavailable to more confident and flamboyant characters. Like a figure in a morality fable, he is presented with a sequence of emotional possibilities, each of which has to be rejected in turn until he eventually chooses the "right" one.

First there is his friend Harry, with whom he shares a passion for music; but Gavin is fairly sure he isn't gay, and anyway Harry is devoted to the mercurial, deeply unreliable Winthrop. Then there is Joan, whom he meets at a strange, chaotic party and with whom (after a further, improbably coincidental meeting at Covent Garden) he has his first and only sexual encounter in the novel. Thirdly, and rather more complicatedly, there is anorexic Minerva Munday, "the thinnest person he'd ever seen in his life" (p. 75), who drives him home from the party and invites herself, accompanied by a parrot, to spend the night there. The scene in which Minerva meets Gavin's parents over breakfast the next morning is among the funniest (and most Amis-like) in Howard's work. Minerva subsequently appears at the salon, and Gavin finds himself obliged to take her home and to admire her infantile attempt at painting. Later he agrees, against his better judgment, to visit her parents, the grotesquely pompous Sir Gordon Munday and his alcoholic wife, in Weybridge. When it dawns on him, long after it has dawned on the reader, that he is being set up as a "respectable" husband for the daughter whom Sir Gordon believes to be pregnant, he makes a dash for it. In the meantime his friend Harry is distraught at the desertion of Winthrop who, not very probably, is going abroad with Joan. Much of this is played at the level of highly entertaining farce, in contrast with the developing relationship between Gavin and his junior Jenny, a single mother with "the most beautiful child—well, almost the most beautiful *person*—Gavin had ever seen in his life" (p. 178), to whom he becomes both friend and cultural mentor: it is she, in pages heavily indebted to Sir Thomas Wyatt's "They Flee from Me," who eventually shows him that "it was no dream" (p. 286).

The greatest pleasures of *Getting It Right* come from the exuberance of the set-piece writing and the cumulative comedy of Howard's descriptive satire, of which a single instance must suffice here—the tea tray Mrs. Lamb brings into the cultural haven of Gavin's attic in the family home:

> The tray was a round tin one with a cat crouching in some buttercups printed on it. The teapot was encased in a knitted cosy the alternating colours of a ripe banana. There were three cup cakes arranged on a paper doily on a plate. The milk jug was shaped like a yellow chick from whose beak the milk was supposed to pour (Marge had given it to his mother at Easter), the cup was one of her best square ones whose handle was too modern to have a hole in it. Even before he lifted the shrouded teapot he knew it would be the one with feet— amusing china boots upon it. The whole tray was crowded with her affection—never expressed in words but in countless domestic deeds of this nature.

> (pp. 58–59)

Nevertheless, the tension between Gavin's cultural aspirations and this resolutely lower-middle-class background presents a problem which the novel doesn't quite solve: like Leonard Bast in E. M. Forster's *Howards End,* Gavin runs the risk of seeming absurd when he ought to seem admirable. Moreover, the comic register brings to his passion for music and literature—not to mention his vocation as a hairdresser—an intrusive campness. Like Harry, we can hardly help wondering if Gavin is gay. And this question is made all the more legitimate since Howard tells us, in *Slipstream,* that he is based on a pair of cultured gay painters who worked on the Amises' house at Hadley Common. In pairing him off with the worthy but not terribly interesting Jenny, Howard seems to sell him short: the ending of *Getting It Right* might have had more resonance if Jenny had been both livelier and a man.

Howard returns to some of her earlier themes, viewed through a darker lens, in *Falling.* It is the story of Daisy Langrish (an echo of Richard Sheridan's Lydia Languish), who escapes from two failed marriages to a country cottage in North Oxfordshire; there she is befriended by Henry Kent, who lives on a moored cabin cruiser and offers his services as gardener and caretaker. She is sixty-one; he, sixty-five; the time is the late 1980s. The narrative is divided between them, more or less alternately; but, since Daisy's chapters are in the third person and Henry's in the first, he strikes the reader as the more confiding and trustworthy of the two. This is important, because he is a psychopathic fraud; much of what he tells the reader, and himself, is simply untrue. If he wins (and does not wholly forfeit) our sympathy, this is because his character is rooted in a deeply unhappy childhood and because he is a victim of his own self-deception. Recalling a film in which Daisy's second ex-husband had played "a Walter Mitty–like character living one day of his life simultaneously as his imagination dictated and as it really was" (p. 71), he detects no resemblance between this and his own life. Daisy, meanwhile, falls off a pyramid in Mexico; falls, during a wonderfully evoked storm, on the garden path that Henry has on his own initiative paved for her; and falls in love with Henry, whose caretaking modulates into taking care of her. The book is full of that sort of irony; when Daisy inspects the garden he has planted for her in her absence she reflects: "It was clear that Mr Kent has done his job well" (p. 208). He is, indeed, devoted to her.

His shady past is eventually exposed by Daisy's hitherto estranged daughter, Katya—"I'm better *about* her than I am *to* her," Katya presciently observes (p. 197)—and her clear-sighted agent Anna Blackstone, who resembles Leonara in *Odd Girl Out*. When he is told to pack his bags, Henry "couldn't understand it…looked the picture of shocked innocence" (p. 406). We leave him on a train bound for Edinburgh, seated opposite a solitary woman traveler and knowing—a chilling touch in the novel's final sentence—"that in the end she would be the first to speak" (p. 422).

FAMILY FORTUNES

The novels of the Cazalet tetralogy—*The Light Years* (1990), *Marking Time* (1991), *Confusion* (1993), and *Casting Off* (1995)—are an achievement of a different order from anything in Howard's previous fiction; yet that difference has an ambiguous quality. For while this huge work of almost two thousand pages is unquestionably

her most ambitious undertaking, there are crucial senses in which it is *less* ambitious than her earlier novels: it breaks no new ground technically—although it increasingly exploits the character-by-character narrative technique perfected in *After Julius*—and it reverts to subject matter which is close both to previous novels and to her own experiences. If the Cazalet books seem likely to be Howard's most enduringly popular work, that is partly because they most resemble what we usually mean by "popular fiction."

This is not to belittle them but, on the contrary, to suggest that the most remarkable aspect of these four novels is the way in which the framework of a conventional family saga becomes unexpectedly adventurous and involving. As is so often the case in the earlier novels, the sense of place is of huge importance: despite the use of several subsidiary locations, most of the action is shared between the various Cazalet homes in London and their family country retreat in Sussex. This simple fact provides one key to Howard's method: when characters leave the symbolically named Home Place and its satellite Mill Farm, they divide, misbehave, and sometimes fall apart; when they return, they regain coherence and reassume their positions in an extended family circle. Moreover, the close correlation between the fictional place and her grandfather's Sussex estate informs her deeply affectionate portrait of it. Her initial description of the house in *The Light Years* has both the prosaic exactitude and the autumnal mellowness of recollected childhood, which informs even such details as William Cazalet's desk, covered with an array of miscellaneous samples he enjoyed having around.

William Cazalet, called "the Brig" like Howard's actual grandfather, and his shrewd, capable wife Kitty, "the Duchy," are the presiding deities of Home Place. The next generation consists of their three sons—Hugh, Edward, and Rupert—their wives, lovers, and relations by marriage, together with their unmarried daughter, Rachel, and her lesbian partner Margot Sidney (Sid). The third Cazalet generation, consisting of the author's contemporaries, is inevitably more numerous and more complicated: Hugh and his terminally ill wife Sybil have three children, Polly, Simon, and Wills; Edward and Viola (Villy) have four, Louise, Teddy, Lydia, and Roland; while Rupert is the father of Clarissa (Clary) and Neville by his deceased first wife, Isobel, as well as Juliet by his second wife, Zoë. The oldest of these, Louise, was born, like her author, in 1923; the youngest—Wills, Roland, and Juliet—are born during the course of the four novels, which cover the years 1937 to 1947. During this time, too, Louise will unhappily marry Michael Hadleigh, whose close resemblance to Peter Scott will be evident to readers of *Slipstream,* and give birth to a son, Sebastian, in 1943. This rich cast of characters is supplemented by Villy's sister Jessica, her husband Raymond, and their children, Angela, Nora, Christopher, and Judy, four more cousins for the third generation; by Archie, an old family friend, once the hapless suitor of Rachel; and by numerous employees of the Cazalet family, including the morose chauffeur Tonbridge and the splendid governess Miss Milliment, a faithful recreation of Howard's own Miss Cobham (*Slipstream,* pp. 43–44). Since it would be impossible to do justice to them all in a short essay, my discussion will focus mainly on the fortunes of three cousins—Louise, Polly, and Clary—who are at the very heart of the Cazalet quartet.

They will remind us of young women in earlier Howard novels—such as the narrator in *The Beautiful Visit,* Alberta in *The Sea Change,* and Emma in *After Julius*—because they represent her most sustained attempt to answer a recurring question: how does a girl of her generation and background sort out her own life? One advantage of the four books' decade-long time span is that personalities can evolve in both predictable and unexpected ways. Louise, for instance, begins in error—she wants to be an actress and to marry John Gielgud—and is mercilessly burdened with her author's own youthful mistakes. Early on she affects a heartless superiority to mask her ignorance and insecurity, as when twelve-year-old Clary announces that she is writing a book about an Australian cat who goes to England for adventure. Louise informs Clary that she couldn't write such a story because the cat would have to be quarantined for six months.

This brittle, vindictive note will be only gradually softened by experience. A year later, having resisted her father's drunken sexual approaches, she has acquired at least some self-knowledge, as she finds herself criticizing her activities and questioning whether they are suitable for her age. As the likelihood of war first advances and then recedes in the late summer of 1938, Louise allows herself to be persuaded by her cousin Nora to enroll in "a sort of cookery finishing-school place next summer" (p. 254).

There she learns little about cooking but meets Stella Rose (based on Howard's friend Dosia Verney, to whom *Marking Time* is dedicated). Stella, who comes from an intellectual, cultured Jewish family (her father is a surgeon, her brother a pianist), will become the genuinely educative force in Louise's life. But Louise, meanwhile, has to make her own mistakes. She meets Michael Hadleigh, naval officer and painter, at "her very first really grown-up dinner party" (*Marking Time,* p. 261), and is soon persuaded to visit his mother, the terrifyingly possessive Zee, and stepfather. "Actually, I went to stay out of pure vanity," she tells Stella, who perceptively observes: "I knew that. It sometimes worries me that you are so unsure of yourself" (p. 279). This is not, as Stella could have told her, a sound basis for marriage, and the marriage is doomed in every respect. Michael is self-absorbed, insensitive, obsessed with fathering a son and heir before his own possible (and no doubt heroic) death on active service, and so devoted to Zee that when he has three nights' leave, he chooses "to spend the first with his mother and the third on a bombing raid over Germany" (*Confusion,* p. 130). Louise is obtusely ignorant about the war (when the aircraft carrier *Ark Royal* is sunk, she has no idea what it is), indifferent to her husband's ambitions, and a hopeless mother: "The core of the trouble was that while everybody at Hatton...adored baby Sebastian, she, his mother, who was supposed to be the most besotted was nothing of the kind" (p. 242).

She is, moreover, unfaithful to Michael—her lover, Hugo, is killed in action, like Ian in *The*

Beautiful Visit—and, increasingly, a social liability to him. Having attended an eccentric drama school in Devon, she pursues a spasmodic acting career, which includes an appearance as an extra at Ealing Studios; over dinner she repeats a bawdy anecdote told on set by the comedian Tommy Trinder to their guests:

> Patricia Cargill said, "Good gracious!", and her husband, to be Number One is Michael's destroyer, gave an uneasy smile and said, "How awfully funny," before he turned back to Michael, who said, "Take Patricia upstairs, darling, and leave the gentlemen to their port." There wasn't any port actually, it was just a way of getting rid of her—of them.
>
> (*Casting Off*, p. 87)

This failure to keep up appearances is, for Michael, the ultimate disgrace. Eventually it is Louise who decides to leave both husband and son: "An impoverished divorced woman of twenty-four (well, she would be even older before she was actually divorced), with no skills, no qualifications, it all sounded pretty frightening, but it was a challenge and she had to risk meeting it" (p. 501). She shares both her author's predicament at the same age and her courage.

Polly is quite different, and her robust straightforwardness is evident from the outset. She is honest and direct when stating her mind and never acts, unlike Louise. But her tendency to be indecisive is, as Howard understands, paradoxically a product of her moral strength, her ability to give due weight to opposing points of view. Of all the younger Cazalets, she is the only one who imaginatively grasps the appalling potential of the coming war, and when, later on, her pacifist cousin Christopher is living reclusively with his dog in a farm caravan, it is Polly who visits and empathizes with him. When Clary attempts to persuade her of their own safety in Sussex, she is undeceived: "Polly was silent, not from conviction, but from the hopeless sense that the more people tried to be reassuring, the less you could trust their views" (*Marking Time*, p. 71). Her instincts serve her well, and her tactlessness mellows with experience: the scene in which she and her father Hugh visit an antique shop,

during her mother's final illness (pp. 336–344), supporting each other without resorting to crass reassurance, is among the most touching in the entire quartet.

After Sybil's death Polly and Clary settle into a ramshackle London life, gently watched over by the benign Archie, with whom she falls briefly and mistakenly in love—an idea which takes both cousins by surprise as they discuss an imaginary man who gradually emerges as forty years old (like Mr. Rochester or Mr. Knightly, Polly insists defensively), uninterested in sport but keen on art. "You're beginning to make him sound like Archie!" Clary protests, "It sounds exactly like him." To which Polly, mildly disingenuous for once, replies: "Well, it wouldn't matter if it *was*, would it? I mean, it's all a made-up business" (*Confusion*, p. 408). However, when she recognizes her mistake, she informs Archie in her usual engagingly candid fashion:

> Just as he was beginning to wonder whether she no long thought she was in love with him, she said, "Archie. I feel I ought to tell you. I've got over you at last. Oh dear, it sounds rather rude, doesn't it. But I mean you needn't worry any more. Naturally, I'm extremely *fond* of you. But I do realize that the difference in our ages made the whole thing silly." She smiled charmingly.
>
> (*Casting Off*, p. 312)

Instead, through her work as an interior designer, she meets Gerald, a penniless aristocrat with a decaying Norfolk mansion. He looks "rather like a frog," she decides, but in his integrity, good humor, and unfussy manners she has found her match.

Clary is both the least changing (her literary ambitions are there from the start) and the most surprising of the three. We first see her through the eyes of Louise, who has to share a room with her as well as with Polly, but the reader will learn to distrust Louise's judgments and, conversely, to trust Miss Milliment's. Unlike Polly and Louise, Clary is rather ordinary in her looks, but Miss Milliment recognizes Clary's ability to notice things and write about them in an extraordinary way.

We have already met this emphasis on the writer as acutely sensitive observer in *The Beautiful Visit;* and Clary's sharp perceptions and wry verbal formulations are among the continuing pleasures of the Cazalet books (for instance in *Marking Time* she imagines the infant Miss Milliment as "a sort of pear, in pigtails," p. 345). When her father, last heard of serving aboard a destroyer, is reported missing in France after Dunkirk—news which she is the first to hear, accidentally taking a phone call intended for her stepmother—her talent is her salvation, for she begins a journal to give her father on his increasingly unlikely return, which in turn provides substantial passages of *Marking Time* and *Confusion.* It is in this journal that we first hear of Archie Lestrange: "One interesting thing. A friend of Dad's is coming to stay! He is on sick leave from the Army: he was at the Slade with Dad, and they went to France as students together" (*Marking Time,* p. 330). Soon Clary is wondering "with careful carelessness" "what Dad's friend will be like," but it is Polly who supplies the nicely poised description: "He was definitely Archie, Polly thought. He was immensely tall, with a domelike forehead and fine black hair receding from it. He had heavy lids to his eyes and an expression in them that looked as though he was either secretly amused, or wanted to be" (p. 347).

Archie, as has already been hinted, is the benevolent catalyst whose presence transforms Clary's and Polly's lives. After both girls—now seventeen—have spent a "thoroughly grown-up evening" with him in the summer of 1942, Clary decides he is "the most understanding person she had ever met" (*Confusion,* p. 74). (She also, almost in the same thought, characteristically observes: "Isn't it extraordinary how Grand Marnier gets on the outside of the glass? It's surprising there's any left inside at all.") It is crucially important that his understanding should be just, generous, and also, as Polly had noticed, "secretly amused": after Clary has told him how, recalling a moment in *The Light Years,* she had told her brother Neville that she wanted to be "kind and brave" (rather than "rich and pretty"), she finds him "looking at her in her thoughts again, but this time was not like the other: this time his eyes, which seemed to see and to tell so much, were fixed upon her with an expression that she could not bear":

> What she said was: "You look extremely soppy to me. What on earth are you thinking?"
>
> And he had answered at once, "I was trying not to laugh."
>
> She had been so grateful for this (people certainly weren't *pitying* somebody while they were trying not to laugh at them) that she was able to change the subject without confusion.
>
> (*Confusion,* p. 186)

It is a pivotal moment, after which Clary's troubled life gradually resolves itself. Her father does return from France, though burdened by his secret life there; and, during the course of *Casting Off*—beneath whose troubled surface runs a long slow resolution like the final movement of a Mahler symphony—she at last comes to understand her love for Archie and his for her. It is a notably upbeat conclusion, in which the good are rewarded with happiness more satisfyingly (because more ambitiously) than at the end of *Getting It Right.*

There is much more to the Cazalet Chronicle than the lives of these three cousins, but it is through them that Howard shapes her central moral argument; she is perhaps less successful with their male near-contemporaries, Teddy and Simon, who seem young for their age and whose vocabulary is overdependent on schoolboy slang which has worn badly. The Cazalets of their parents' generation lead lives fraught both with private complications and with the wider consequences of wartime; at one remove, the family of Villy's sister Jessica proves especially odd and unfortunate. And, beyond the human protagonists, there is a slow underlying narrative of time and place, often conveyed in sustained passages not susceptible to quotation.

In her passages—with their sure grasp of period detail, social context, and conversational register—Elizabeth Jane Howard takes her place among the great chroniclers of twentieth-century English life.

Selected Bibliography

WORKS OF ELIZABETH JANE HOWARD

NOVELS

The Penguin and Pan editions listed below are those from which the quotations in the essay are taken:

The Beautiful Visit. London: Jonathan Cape, 1950. New York: Random, 1950. London: Pan, 1993.

The Long View. London: Jonathan Cape, 1956. New York: Reynal, 1956. Harmondsworth, U.K.: Penguin, 1976.

The Sea Change. London: Jonathan Cape, 1959. New York: Harper, 1959. London: Pan, 1995.

After Julius. London: Jonathan Cape, 1965. New York: Viking, 1966. London: Pan, 1995.

Something in Disguise. London: Jonathan Cape, 1969. New York: Viking, 1970. Harmondsworth, U.K.: Penguin, 1971.

Odd Girl Out. London: Jonathan Cape, 1972. New York: Viking, 1972. Harmondsworth, U.K.: Penguin, 1975.

Getting It Right. London: Hamish Hamilton, 1982. New York: Viking, 1982. Harmondsworth, U.K.: Penguin, 1983.

The Light Years. London: Macmillan, 1990. New York: Pocket Books, 1990. London: Pan, 1993. (The Cazalet Chronicle, volume 1.)

Marking Time. London: Macmillan, 1991. New York: Pocket Books, 1992. London: Pan, 1993. (The Cazalet Chronicle, volume 2.)

Confusion. London: Macmillan, 1993. New York: Pocket Books, 1994. London: Pan, 1993. (The Cazalet Chronicle, volume 3.)

Casting Off. London: Macmillan, 1995. New York: Pocket Books, 1996. London: Pan, 1996. (The Cazalet Chronicle, volume 4.)

Falling. London: Macmillan, 1999. London: Pan, 2000.

OTHER WORKS

We Are for the Dark. London: Jonathan Cape, 1951. (Short stories; coauthored with Robert Aickman.)

Mr. Wrong. London: Jonathan Cape, 1975. New York: Viking, 1976. London: Pan, 1993. (Short stories.)

Peter Scott. Golden, Colo.: Fulcrum Pub., 1995.

Experience. New York: Talk Miramax Books, Hyperion, 2000.

Slipstream: A Memoir. London: Macmillan, 2002. London: Pan, 2003. (Autobiography.)

HANIF KUREISHI

(1954–)

Stefanie K. Dunning

HANIF KUREISHI'S NOVEL *The Black Album* (1995) satirizes and critiques one of the most defining moments in diasporic South Asian culture: namely, the book burning of *The Satanic Verses* (1988) and the subsequent *fatwa* issued against its author, Salman Rushdie. With his characteristic wit, Kureishi takes to task religious fundamentalism and the conformity that typically accompanies it, while linking the struggle of the "black" British—a category that in England includes South Asians as well as people of African descent—with the struggle of African Americans through the title of the book, which is an invocation of a Prince album by the same name. *The Black Album* is a defining literary moment for Kurieshi because, of all of his work, it most succinctly links a series of concerns that pervade his oeuvre. Though Kureishi also responded to the book burning and *fatwa* in political essays, *The Black Album* represents a full-scale rejection of a set of ideologies that contribute to, and make logical, acts like the burning of books.

It might seem odd to use the title of a highly erotic Prince album as the title of a book that ostensibly exposes fundamental Islam and censorship, but the use of the erotic in Kureishi's work is far more symbolic, metaphoric, and therefore important than the mere presentation of libidinal desire. The erotic in Kureishi's work functions as a path to self-knowledge, emphasizing the individual over the mob and enabling a kind of freedom for his characters that allows them to transgress boundaries that essentially serve the purpose of maintaining a racially and sexually rigid status quo. It is no coincidence, therefore, that the shadow or implied character in *The Black Album* is Prince himself, an artist who has purposely and skillfully traversed the interstices between black and white, male and female, straight and gay. In addition to being an extremely

talented musician, Prince is also a transgressor of rules—and Kureishi's novel invites the kind of personal (as political) insurgency represented by Prince in his music and persona.

What *The Black Album* suggests, though, not unlike Prince's album, is that at the center of controversy there is always love, however temporary or fleeting. And while it might seem that most of the significant "love" scenes in the novel occur between the protagonist, Shahid, and a professor at his school, Deedee, the most unsettling love occurs when the members of an Islamic fundamentalist group attempt to love Shahid. Kureishi, while ridiculing the group and also exposing their beliefs as extreme and dangerous, does not characterize them inhumanely; indeed, he does the opposite by portraying these fundamentalist characters as intensely human in their personal flaws and by highlighting their yearning for freedom and their intense confusion about how to obtain it.

The Black Album is the story of Shahid Hasan, an upper-middle-class Pakistani college student. Arriving at college, Shahid becomes simultaneously involved in an Islamic youth group and his white, radical and liberal former professor, Deedee Osgood. The narrative moves forward through a series of conflicts felt by Shahid, between his fundamentalist and South Asian comrades and his white lover. When he is with Deedee, he traverses London's club scene, doing drugs and attending raves and making wild, liberating love to Deedee. With the Islamic group, whose leader is named Riaz, he participates in planning community interventions and events— some of which are noble, others of which are ridiculous. One of these noble events is sitting up in the home of a Pakistani family being terrorized by white supremacists who want the family to get out of their neighborhood. Perhaps the most ridiculous event is an incident involving an eggplant, where a person claims to see a holy sign within the aubergine. It becomes old and shriveled, and yet the fundamentalist youths continue to revere it as a holy object.

The Black Album is in many respects a novel about the 1980s, summoning up the club scene, the music, and the racism of contemporary London. Kureishi connects all of these elements through the dynamic of power—each group, each scene, and each individual is vying for power and trying to figure out their own relationship to powerful forces. This power dynamic plays out between Riaz's "activist" Islamic group and the society in which they live, between Shahid and Deedee, and between Shahid and the group. The novel sets up a binary that seems to suggest that Shahid must choose between his Islamic comrades and his white lover; one represents—quite loosely speaking—his "culture," which is aligned with religious fundamentalism and religious asceticism, while the other represents hedonism, cosmopolitanism, and freedom. The most critical difference between them, however, is that in his relationship with Deedee, Shahid must be willing to experience both dominance and submission, while in his dealing with Riaz's group he is never empowered to make individual decisions, nor can he be heard in his attempts to disagree with many of the tactics of the group. Ultimately Shahid chooses the healthier relationship, which is with Deedee.

An unsophisticated reading of *The Black Album* might lead some readers to conclude that Shahid chooses "whiteness" over Asian-ness. However, Kureishi's novel insists upon a far more complicated relationship to identity and power. What Shahid actually chooses is himself and impermanence rather than any simple racial or ethnic categorization. The very title of the book metaphorically suggests this play on ambivalence through the invocation of Prince; but in and of itself, as a title it also suggests the proximity of what occurs in the novel—and ultimately Shahid's decision to be with Deedee—to blackness, which is the very "identity" that it might seem that Shahid disavows. In this way, Kureishi manages to symbolically rescue "blackness" as a

metaphor from the rigid fundamentalism it had come to represent through the burning of Salman Rushdie's now famous tome and instead relocates it to the site of the subversive, foregrounding the powerful possibilities of racial and sexual ambiguity.

Perhaps more importantly, the novel participates in a tradition that the literary critic and Kureishi's fellow Briton Paul Gilroy would later identify as "the Black Atlantic," an intellectual cosmopolitanism that links colonial communities throughout various diasporas in a kind of constant exchange and flower of cultural information. What is utterly revolutionary about Kureishi's deployment of the Black Atlantic is that he not only connects communities that have race in common, he links the black British community (which significantly also includes Asians) to the struggles of those of African descent in the Americas. Throughout *The Black Album,* Kureishi references African American writers, including W. E. B. Du Bois's *The Souls of Black Folk* as well as writers like Maya Angelou, Alice Walker, and Malcolm X. Closing the distance between those of Asian descent and those of African descent, Kureishi connects Shahid's struggles to a larger political context that includes both slavery and colonialism. This is a radical and subversive move because frequently Asian and African constituencies are seen in quite different ways, and the resultant differences in treatment have at times contributed to strife between these two communities. By linking Shahid to African and American struggles against oppression, Kureishi at once shows his awareness of the injustices suffered by those of African descent and also metaphorically aligns himself with *all* oppressed communities.

CHILDHOOD AND YOUTH

Perhaps one of the things that makes Hanif Kureishi's work so intriguing in its play with various dialectics—race, sexuality, and class—is the fact that he is biracial. He was born on December 5, 1954, in Bromley, England, to a Pakistani father and an English mother. He grew up in the suburbs and lived a very middle-class and in some ways idyllic childhood. He delivered papers and was a sports fan of both cricket and football (soccer). The young Kureishi was also obsessed with music—he loved the Beatles and the Rolling Stones as well as the African American music form of rhythm and blues. Kureishi's life was truly a bicultural and biracial one; while experiencing what some might call a "typical" English childhood, he was in significant ways outside of both English culture and Anglo-Asian culture. As far as his religious upbringing was concerned, his parents raised him neither as a Christian nor a Muslim, and he never learned to speak Urdu, the language spoken by many Pakistanis.

One aspect of his background that had a significant effect on Kureishi's upbringing was his father's unsuccessful attempts at being a published novelist. His father, before immigrating to England, was a journalist in India. When India and Pakistan divided in 1947, Kureishi's father immigrated to England rather than going to Pakistan—though he referred to himself throughout his life as Pakistani. Once in England, he worked as a civil servant and tried without success to get six novels published. Kureishi has said that his father, perhaps wanting to live through his son's success, strongly encouraged him to write, conveying to him that it was the best job one could have; at age fourteen Kureishi took his father's suggestion and decided that he wanted to become a writer. He says that this decision changed his life because it provided a coping mechanism for dealing with the racism he experienced in 1970s England. Kureishi has noted that writing functions as a guard against the despair that one can experience when confronted with racism. However, his biracial background does not allow him to simply withdraw—as his fundamentalist characters do in *The Black Album*—from London society in (an often well-justified) rage against "white" society. His fiction, therefore, has a sense of nuance that demonstrates the humanity of all parties involved—English, Asian, Black—in a way that speaks to his mixed heritage.

After studying philosophy at King's College in London, Kureishi quickly found himself immersed in the life of a writer. As the critic Kenneth Kaleta notes, Kureishi was attractive and brilliant, so he fit in quite easily with the scene of London's up-and-coming literati. He fleetingly supported himself by writing erotic fiction under the pseudonym "Antonia French." He also worked as an usher at the Royal Court Theatre, where eventually he would become the theater's writer-in-residence. In 1976 he saw a reading of his first (and unpublished) play, *Soaking The Heat,* take place at the Royal Court. His start at the theater was the beginning of a profound and prolific career that would see the publication of not only plays but also essays, short stories, novels, and screenplays.

PLAYS

Kureishi's first full-length play, *The King and Me,* was performed in January 1980 at the Soho Poly Theatre in London. In the play, a husband and wife are equally obsessed with Elvis Presley, so much so that the husband participates in Elvis impersonation contests and the apartment of the working-class couple is almost a shrine to the long-dead American pop icon. The wife, Marie, sees her husband Bill's chance to win an Elvis contest and a trip to America as an opportunity for them to transcend the difficult aspects of their working-class lives. Their lives are in chaos in a number of ways: Marie is fond of putting on Elvis records at full blast so that she can dance to the music; she neglects her children in pursuit of her Elvis obsession and forces Bill to a level of zeal about Elvis he might not achieve on his own. The play takes place over the course of one day, when Bill is to go to the contest. He almost wins, but he misses one question about Elvis history and so loses. When he returns home, he encourages his wife to give up Elvis so they can begin to live; he identifies the obsession for what it is, a kind of escapism. Marie and Bill have a confrontational conversation in which he tells her that her obsession with Elvis is almost certifiably insane. The play ends when Marie agrees to let Bill buy an Elton John record, but even as the last line is delivered, Marie has her eyes closed.

Kureishi was praised for his representation of the working class in this play, particularly for his ability to represent Bill and Marie sympathetically rather than ridiculing them as outlandish lower-class characters. The play was also significant because it demonstrated Kureishi's ability to write outside of his own ethnic identification; indeed, both Marie and Bill are white characters and there are no characters of color at all. It is striking that for Marie and Bill, their icon of escape is an American one. The figure of Elvis functions as more than parody; indeed, Elvis functions as a kind of symbolic reference to the "American dream," of the possibility of social mobility that is thought to be inherently American and not historically part of the British notion of class. Elvis, himself at one time a poor southern boy, eventually achieved the very pinnacle of wealth and status. This is an apt fantasy for the working poor, and the figure of the American hero, represented by Elvis, offers the kind of hope for transcendence of class oppression Marie and Bill long for. However, Kureishi's use of Elvis as a symbol of class uplift or possibility does not mean that he is simply valorizing an unexamined notion of how class can function in the American landscape. The fact that the Elvis fantasy does not better the lives of Bill and Marie—in fact, it causes problems—demonstrates that Kureishi is critiquing the possibilities of the Horatio Alger narrative. Elvis himself, despite his financial and artistic success, ultimately died a broken man, a fate from which no amount of wealth could save him. In this way he functions as a complicated symbol that embodies both the possibility of class mobility and the limits of it. Marie and Bill look outside of themselves, to a different shore and face, for the picture of success, and they must ultimately come to realize the emptiness of such enterprises. The fact that the play ends with a gesture toward a British pop icon, Elton John, does not mean that Kureishi's point here is that they should look to British icons rather than American ones. It suggests instead that pop icons are interchangeable to large degree and can be found on any shore, and that Marie and Bill cannot look to them as models for how to change their economic situation. Finding the trace of the human in characters so different from himself is

perhaps the most indelible mark of Kureishi's special imprint on any given work.

Kureishi would go on to write five more plays in his early career. His second play, *The Mother Country,* produced in 1980 as part of the Riverside Studios' "Plays Umbrella" series, was critically lauded and introduced an important character type that recurs in Kureishi's fiction—the Anglo-Asian immigrant. An artful play in some respects, it was noted for its satirical tone and lack of detachment, marking the beginning of what was to become Kureishi's ironic treatment of issues affecting Anglo-Asians. His third play, *Outskirts,* was produced at the Warehouse at the Soho Poly in 1981. Critics have noted that of all Kureishi's plays, *Outskirts* is perhaps the one most specifically constructed for the theater; in twelve scenes that take place over twelve years the play details the friendship of five characters and the sexual tensions among them.

The plays that followed, *Borderline* (first performed at the Royal Court Theatre in 1981) and *Birds of Passage* (Hampstead Theatre, 1983), received far more critical praise than his earlier efforts. In *Borderline,* Kureishi combined the lessons he had learned in *Outskirts* about writing for the stage with what he had learned in writing *The Mother Country* in terms of critical distance in his portraits of immigrant characters. Critics were impressed with both the theatricality of *Borderline* and with Kureishi's deft political analysis in his portrayal of the Asian community in Britain. The play stages the confrontation between two friends—Ravi, who has only recently come to England, and Anil, who has lived in England for a long time. Ravi lands on Anil's doorstep only to find that Anil is living with a white woman—something people back home had warned Ravi to avoid. Anil lies and tells Ravi that his lover is actually his social worker in order to make sure that Ravi does not tell anyone who could tell his wife back home that he has taken up with a white woman. The narrative of Anwar and Yasmin, two adolescents who have grown up in England, counterbalances the conflicted narrative between Ravi and Anil. The youths discuss their budding sexuality as well as the racism they experience in England and their conflicts with their parents, who want to inflict upon them the strictures of a different time and place. Yasmin's father arranges a marriage for her, and when she refuses to comply, he threatens to starve himself to death. Many of the themes explored in *Borderline* reappear in Kureishi's later work, such as *The Buddha of Suburbia* (1990). The importance of *Borderline* in his career is that it shows a young Kureishi beginning to find his voice in his discussion of Britain's Asian community, demonstrating his burgeoning ability to represent the racism experienced by Asians in England while at the same time critiquing the community from within. Rather than offering an uncritical valorization of the Asian community, he is able to critique stifling traditionalism and fundamentalism as well as racism with a perfectly balanced rendering of the conflicts experienced by his characters.

His next play, *Birds of Passage,* depicts a white family who takes in a Pakistani student, Asif, and chronicles Asif's encroachment of their home. Like *Borderline, Birds of Passage* deals with racial difference and generational issues but in a slightly different setting; placing the Pakistani student in an all-white setting allows Kureishi to deal with similar issues from a different perspective.

By the time *Birds of Passage* was staged, Kureishi had established himself as a dominant and important voice in the London theater scene. Theater, however, was simply the beginning of Kureishi's illustrious career, though he would return to it much later with another play, *Sleep with Me,* which was performed at the Royal National Theater in 1999.

FILM

Kureishi might be best known as a screenwriter, beginning with *My Beautiful Laundrette* (1985). His screenplay was nominated for an Academy Award in 1986, won the award for best screenplay from the New York Film Critics Circle, and brought Kureishi critical and popular acclaim. *My Beautiful Laundrette* tells the story of Omar, a Pakistani entrepreneur who opens a laundromat with his white lover, Johnny. We are first intro-

duced to Johnny, a longtime friend of Omar, when Omar is the victim of a hate crime by a group of neo-Nazis; Omar is shocked to see his friend Johnny among them. Ultimately Johnny leaves the neo-Nazi group and joins Omar in his laundry business. The film unfolds through a series of events that highlight the difficulty of being gay in the Pakistani community as well as the difficulties of interracial love. It also depicts aspects of Pakistani culture usually absent from film representations—Omar raises part of the money for his laundrette from a drug-dealing uncle, and his father is an alcoholic. Some members of the Pakistani community railed against these representations of members of their community, but Kureishi's vision is nuanced and indicative of his ability to represent people and communities complexly.

My Beautiful Laundrette confronts several issues and humanizes characters usually ostracized by mainstream society. Through its representation of a homosexual relationship, it specifically rejects homophobia. We follow Omar, the protagonist, which allows viewers to more intimately identify with him. The story is told from his point of view, and we therefore have no choice as viewers but to want what he wants. This is a powerful film device known as "subjective camera," and *My Beautiful Laundrette* masterfully shows us the interior life of a gay man of color. It also redeems a character that most communities of color find irredeemable—the white supremacist. Johnny is not simply a person who spews racist ideology; he is an active participant in a hate crime against Omar. As a figure, he could represent little more than terror in the minds of people of color. The fact that the film recuperates him as Omar's lover reveals its remarkable ability to recognize a range of human emotions in any given character. Furthermore, it demonstrates the complexity of racism—that it at once embodies disgust and desire, admiration as well as condemnation. The film is also self-consciously about the Anglo-Pakistani community; it is invested in showing the community in ways only an insider can see it. While on the surface members of the British Asian community might see this merely as "airing dirty laundry," the effect of this insider's point of view is to overturn mindless and shallow "positive" representations, which do little to connect viewers to the characters. By showing the audience only things someone from within the community can see, it ostensibly puts the viewer within the subject position of a member of the community, hence making objectified readings of the community more difficult.

Kureishi's second film, *Sammy and Rosie Get Laid* (1988), follows the relationship of a racially mixed couple in London during a race riot, a reference to the 1981 Brixton race riots. *Sammy and Rosie Get Laid* is a film that rejects all that is conventional about relationships—for example, although Sammy and Rosie are married, they are both free to explore their sexuality with others, and of course their relationship also represents a break from convention because it is interracial. This film, though equally masterful in its exploration of character and its critique of contemporary racism, was less critically acclaimed than *My Beautiful Laundrette*. Though some critics—such as the literary and cultural critic bell hooks—have criticized the film for its nihilism, the film is an apt critique of England under the conservative prime minister Margaret Thatcher, as seen through the eyes of a couple on the fringe of society. When Sammy's father arrives from Pakistan to visit the couple, he is depressed by the riotous state of England and the sexual licentiousness of his son's marriage as well as plagued by his own political indiscretions in Pakistan. He eventually commits suicide by hanging himself, and Sammy and Rosie reevaluate their relationship, paralleling the reevaluation the British nation must do in response to the riots, which were sparked by the murder of an innocent black woman. Like the novel *The Black Album*, *Sammy and Rosie Get Laid* connects the oppression suffered by a black woman in Britain to the struggles of people, like Sammy's father, living in the former colonies.

As in all of his previous work, Kureishi's treatment of these difficult topics is at once humorous and solemn. The seeming "craziness" of Sammy and Rosie's relationship—their cultural difference from one another as well as the open sexual nature of their union—is contrasted by the "real" insanity of London at the time. The film seems to suggest that while society would generally look down upon a relationship such as Sammy and Rosie's, the real crime and transgression that occurs is the policing of individuals and lifestyles that harm no one. That Sammy and Rosie's open relationship should be such a "scandal," while the killing of an innocent black woman is not, is the real madness the film highlights: people can die in the streets and conservative governments do little to prevent this, yet the moral imperative that disciplines sexuality remains strong. At the same time, however, *Sammy and Rosie Get Laid* is not simply a call to activism. It is, rather, a nuanced critique of the political climate during Thatcher's tenure as well as an exploration of individuals bearing up under the pressure of such a climate for those who are nonwhite and whose lifestyles put them at the margins of society rather than at the center. For this reason, *Sammy and Rosie Get Laid* manages to produce a scathing critique of Thatcher's England while resisting didacticism or a call for the institution of another kind of morality, albeit a liberal one.

Several more Kureishi screenplays would make it to the large and small screen. Venturing out on his own, in 1991 Kureishi wrote and directed the film *London Kills Me*. Set in contemporary London, the film is the story of a white character named Clint whose main goal in life is to escape the urban street life he leads in Notting Hill for the suburbs. Throughout the film Clint works to achieve his goal through a variety of nefarious and counterproductive occupations, such as selling drugs, conning his relatives, and having affairs. Clint's desire to get out of his "ghetto" is metaphorized in a pair of red cowboy boots—a clear reference to *The Wizard of Oz*—which he attains by robbing a person who will ultimately give him work. *London Kills Me* was roundly criticized and to date is the worst-received work of Kureishi's career. Compared in some reviews to a migraine headache, the film had limited distribution and consequently is one of the least analyzed works of Kureishi's oeuvre. Critics blamed Kureishi's directing, not his writing, so his reputation as a writer remained unscathed.

Still, the reviews were so poor that the clear metaphorical and symbolic genius evident in *London Kills Me* was lost, and the experience left Kureishi gun-shy about the prospect of directing any more films.

Because of the horrible response to *London Kills Me,* when Kureishi was approached about adapting *The Buddha of Suburbia,* his first novel, into a television miniseries for the BBC, he was at first hesitant. Ultimately, however, Kureishi joined the BBC team as a screenwriter, and the novel became a critically acclaimed four-part miniseries in 1993. In 1998 his short story "My Son the Fanatic" was also adapted into a film. Kureishi's next film project was an adaptation of his novel *Intimacy* (1998). It was released in Europe in early 2001 and in the United States in the fall of that year, earning the Golden Bear Award for best film at the Berlin Film Festival.

PROSE

Kureishi's prose is extensive; he has written four novels to date and scores of short stories. Some of his short stories were later developed into novels (this was the case with *The Buddha of Suburbia*) and films. *The Black Album* and *The Buddha of Suburbia* have received the most critical attention and both are brilliant novels.

As his first novel, *The Buddha of Suburbia* (1990) is often characterized as Kureishi's autobiographical novel. It follows the character Karim Amir, whose father ultimately becomes a "guru" of sorts, as he deals with the vicissitudes of late adolescence as well as the dissolution of his parents' marriage. As in his previous work, Kureishi manipulates and teasingly examines notions of culture, class, and gender while critiquing British racism. Generally recognized for its originality and genius, in 1990 *The Buddha of Suburbia* won the Whitbread Prize.

The Buddha of Suburbia not only indicts British racism; it also shows a "multicultural" England, highlighting the inheritances of colonialism on the indigenous British as well as the more recently British. The novel, however, should not be read as a representation only of multicultural England but rather as a representation of England

generally. Kureishi has famously said that he is English through and through. The character Karim echoes the author's sentiment when he states, "My name is Karim Amir and I am an Englishman, born and bred, almost." At stake in this claiming of English identity is something radical. It is not a disavowal of Asian identity; rather, for Karim (and Kureishi), to claim Englishness is to demand that English identity represent all of England—a postcolonial England that includes those who are not white. A subversive redefinition of English identity is at stake for Karim, and this refiguring of English identity is a central theme in *The Buddha of Suburbia.* The suggestion underlying the novel is that, like tea, which is read as particularly British and central to the construction of English cultural identity but which is only possible as an English commodity through colonialism (tea cannot grow in England; it can only grow in tropical countries like India and Sri Lanka), so too are people like Karim characteristically British in ways that racism in England refuses to confront.

Following *The Black Album,* discussed above, Kureishi published a collection of his short stories, *Love in a Blue Time,* in 1997. These stories highlight the sense of alienation Pakistani immigrants feel in England while at the same time focusing on ties among lovers and family members. Like the very apt title, these characters experience "love" amid a quagmire of overt and implied racism. Included in this series of short stories is "My Son the Fanatic," which was adapted into a film in 1998. The story deals with the growing religious fundamentalism of a son against the wishes of his father. Parvez, a Punjabi taxi driver, hopes his son, Ali, will become an accountant and has worked as a driver for twenty years to insure this. Ali, however, undergoes a radical change and becomes a religious Muslim, regarding his father with contempt, sitting in judgment of him for drinking alcohol and for his genuine friendship with a prostitute, Bettina. After Ali insults Bettina, who runs away from both of them, Parvez is unable to deal with his son's fundamentalism and ends up brutally beating him. The story ends with the son asking his father, with a bloodied face: "So who's the fanatic now?" This story enacts a conflict that contrasts Parvez's unconventional relationships (his friendship with Bettina) and more Westernized view of life with Ali's growing desire to align himself with oppressed people throughout the world, which takes the form of his religiosity. Most of the short stories in *Love in a Blue Time*—other notable ones include "In a Blue Time" and "With Your Tongue Down My Throat"—also deal with difficult issues of racism, intergenerational conflict, friendship, love, and sexuality. In 1999 Kureishi published another collection of short stories, *Midnight All Day*.

Kureishi published his third novel, *Intimacy,* in 1998. *Intimacy* takes place almost entirely in the mind of the protagonist, Jay. The central problem of the novel is that Jay wants to leave his wife, Susan. The entire novel unfolds as he builds up the courage to leave his wife and two children and as he fantasizes about and remembers an extramarital affair with a lover named Nina. Jay traces the history of his relationship with Susan, remembering their days of courtship. His remembrance of the beginning of his relationship with Susan is significant because it is not marked by the kind of excitement and passion that is usually expected; instead, it marked by ambivalence. It seems that Jay marries Susan because it is the next thing to do in their relationship and in his life, yet Susan bores him sexually and otherwise, and domestic life is for Jay a kind of protracted torture. Just when it seems that Jay will never leave Susan and will only talk endlessly about it, he finally does so. The novel ends with him attempting to talk with Susan and his sons in order to sort through the "mess" that the two of them living together had become. There is also a suggestion at the end that Nina, the woman he had had an affair with and who he thought about endlessly while screwing up his courage to leave Susan, attempts to contact him. And he finally makes contact with her, via the telephone. The last word of the novel is "love," suggesting it is this state Jay was attempting to reach all along.

Although it might at first seem that *Intimacy* is less politically charged than Kureishi's previous two novels, it is just as politically informed. It is simply that the terrain of critique has shifted to

the moment at which, we might argue, *The Black Album* ends: when Shahid decides to stay with Deedee "as long as it's fun." *Intimacy* opens with a domestic scene that is no longer "fun" and explores what happens when a relationship dies. The novel has been hailed as an honest portrait of a man in crisis; *Intimacy* takes the idea of the midlife crisis and divorces it from any possible stereotypical trivialization. Furthermore, the novel demonstrates the importance of sex and sexual play, which is quite absent in Jay and Susan's relationship. The exploration of sexuality so vital and integral to Kureishi's other work is figured in *Intimacy* as its absence; without sexual freedom, the novel seems to suggest, the individual stagnates. *Intimacy* caused quite a bit of controversy when it was published; it was speculated that Jay's story was autobiographical, and the novel's seeming endorsement of extramarital affairs drew some criticism. But to see this novel as merely endorsing extramarital affairs is to miss its larger critique of monogamy and marriage as an institution. It is an honest and brilliant portrait of a stifling domesticity that is devoid of passion, excitement, or genuine love and filled instead with objects and obligations. *Intimacy* is a critique of marriage and of bourgeois lifestyles; instead of finding redemption in the family unit, Jay can only find a kind of ennui that would inevitably lead him to self-destruction.

Kureishi's next novel, *Gabriel's Gift* (2001), is told from the perspective of a fifteen-year-old Londoner named Gabriel whose parents, Christine and Rex, are in the midst of a separation. It is a bildungsroman in which Gabriel must learn to accept his own burgeoning gifts as an artist as well as the decline of his father's as a musician. The novel opens with Gabriel being accompanied by his Russian nanny from school; even though he is fifteen, his mother feels the nanny is necessary since she must work, and Gabriel would otherwise spend much of his time alone. But for Gabriel, being with the nanny is the equivalent of (or worse than) being alone, and he finds himself thrust into a world of his own making, drawing pictures in his room that somehow magically come to life—hence the title, which refers to Gabriel's special gift. He also spends his time thinking about and talking to his twin brother, Archie, who dies when the boys are very young. The novel stages a kind of existential crisis around the two boys, as we learn later that Christine and Rex are not actually sure which child died, since the boys were identical twins— Gabriel realizes he could actually be Archie, and what follows is a kind of loop, like a Möbius strip in which the boundary between Archie and Gabriel becomes increasingly blurred.

Like many children who suffer their parents' separation, Gabriel wants Christine and Rex to get back together. This is especially the case when he sees the kind of squalor and turmoil Rex is living in. In addition to having lost his family, Rex is also a washed-up musician, and a greater part of the narrative is about his attempts to revive his musical career as well as stay afloat financially. At the same time that Rex struggles to make ends meet and use his talents, Gabriel finds himself in a world of rock stars, specifically his father's old friend Lester, who remains an icon in the music world. Through a series of incidents, Gabriel comes into possession of one of Lester's drawings (which he drew when Gabriel and Rex visited him), and Gabriel agrees to let this piece of art be shown in a local establishment. Not trusting the proprietor, he forges a very believable fake of Lester's piece and puts this on display instead. The conflict that revolves around Lester's painting and the forgery centers Gabriel as the master of this narrative, rendering him powerful—a most unlikely circumstance in the life of the child. This is significant because he begins the novel feeling relatively powerless. This novel ends happily; Rex gains employment teaching music, the conflict around the forged painting is ultimately resolved, and Christine and Rex reunite. Gabriel decides to become a filmmaker, which represents a way for him to continue to make his "pictures" come to life.

Gabriel's Gift is a departure for Kureishi in that it does not treat the themes of immigration, racism, and sexuality evident in his previous work. At the same time, it does offer the same nuanced portraits of people in flux and conflict.

And, unlike some of Kureishi's other work, it ends positively with Gabriel on his way to becoming an actualized artist, with his family unit intact.

ESSAYS AND OTHER WORK

In addition to writing short stories, plays, screenplays, and novels, Kureishi has also edited *The Faber Book of Pop* (1995) with Jon Savage and has written several important essays. Perhaps Kureishi's best-known essay is "The Rainbow Sign," which is included in the volume *London Kills Me: Three Screenplays and Four Essays* (1992). In it Kureishi explores a variety of issues related to his identity as an Anglo-Pakistani. Unlike his other work, a section of this essay is about his experiences in Pakistan and provides an interesting view into the writer's mind about both England and Pakistan. Although Kureishi clearly is not a nationalist in any sense, this essay represents his attempts to come to grips with two national sites, both of which claim him and both of which are vexed in various ways. He begins by describing aspects of his childhood— namely, his sense of isolation in an increasingly racist England. The isolated boy in *Gabriel's Gift* whose only refuge is art is recalled when reading "The Rainbow Sign," as Kureishi describes his youth as one where he "mooched" around libraries, looking for signs of another life. Tormented by the racism occurring around him, young Kureishi found inspiration in many of the figures prominent in the black power movement in the United States. He recalls plastering posters of the Black Panthers on his wall in place of white pop stars; he voraciously read James Baldwin and Richard Wright. James Baldwin is perhaps a phantom figure in Kureishi's essay, as his title most certainly invokes the Baldwin text *The Fire Next Time*. Like Baldwin in his attempt to make black and white Americans see how deeply they are connected to one another, Kureishi sets out in this essay to balance the dichotomy between white and black, British and Pakistani. His goal here is to indict racist England but also to demonstrate that some of the things that happen in Pakistan are no solution to the problem of oppression experienced during colonialism and afterward.

In Pakistan, Kureishi reports on the demise of a liberal Lahore society as the country begins to "Islamicize." Yet Kureishi's lamentations about the prohibitions in Pakistani society (dancing, for example, is illegal) are balanced by his recognition of the place of the sacred in the society. One morning he witnesses a woman praying. He writes: "Now, on the shabby prayer mat, she was tiny and around her the universe was endless, immense, but God was above her. I felt she was acknowledging that which was larger than her, humbling herself before the infinite, knowing and feeling her own insignificance. It was a truthful moment, not an empty ritual." Kureishi's criticism of various aspects of Pakistani society is not simply that of a semi-outsider who does not understand the country he visits. It is a careful and delicate treatment, replete with his obvious love for the country and his kinsmen. Yet, he notes, he must return to England. Kureishi confronts his difficulty in calling England "his country" because it is a place that rejects him and, as he indicates by quoting a well-known conservative and racist, Enoch Powell, it sees him merely as a problem to be solved rather than as a citizen within its borders.

Upon arriving back in England, Kureishi immediately experiences racism at a laundrette, where a woman refuses to touch the clothing of "foreigners." In this way, the essay demonstrates the frustration felt by Kureishi, who can see all too clearly how both the English world and the Pakistani world are unable to contain him. Comparing life in Pakistan with life in England, he notes that while people are distant and relationships are forced in England, in Pakistan the feeling of familial love and warmth is common, present, and real. Kureishi is recognized in Pakistan in ways he can never be in England; when he goes to the bank the clerk recognizes his family name and treats him with more respect than he might have before. The intimacy he experiences in Pakistan is not merely the class privilege afforded him by his family name (he has influential and wealthy relatives), but it also

contrasts with the "otherness" he experiences in England. Being a racial "other" in England, which is to be regarded as an anonymous person of color in the supposedly "white" Britain, there is no recognition of him as an individual or specificity in how he is seen. Exactly the opposite is true in Pakistan, where he is recognized and known—where he can quite literally be "read" for who he is. In short, in England he is a brown nobody to the white Britishers who see him more as a problem to the nation than as a citizen, whereas in Pakistan he is recognized not only as a member of the nation (as Pakistani) but also as a *particular* member of that nation, contextualized as he is against the backdrop of family.

He also discusses at length the contradictions in both the English working class and the Pakistani upper classes. He notes that the working-class British regularly insult Pakistanis, calling them filthy and lazy, in the same language the British upper class uses to describe the working-class. Likewise, upper-class Pakistanis do not understand that British racism does not just apply to lower-class Pakistanis—whom the upper-class Pakistanis despise as well, so much so that they sometimes even argue that poor Anglo-Asians deserve British racism—and that no matter what their class status, in England all Pakistanis are alike. Kureishi thus maps not only the cultural and class divides between these various and complicated groups but also the intellectual divide. He finds himself painfully in the middle.

This is not, however, a treatise of a tragic mulatto. In perhaps one of the most astute statements on being biracial and bicultural, Kureishi writes: "I wasn't a misfit; I could join the elements of myself together. It was the others, they wanted misfits; they wanted you to embody within yourself their ambivalence." Kureishi ends his essay by calling on England to truly become the "democratic" society it claims it is.

"The Rainbow Sign" is a powerful essay that is able to speak through the difficulties of race identification, racism, and national identity. Kureishi's politics and style in this essay are reminiscent of Baldwin, who, like Kureishi, found racism intolerable but also found separatism a flawed response to oppression. The quote that both Baldwin's book *The Fire Next Time* and Kureishi's "The Rainbow Sign" is taken from is biblical, recast through the words of an old Negro spiritual: "God gave Noah the rainbow sign, no more water, the fire next time." Baldwin's title takes the less optimistic section of this passage, prophetically summoning up the riots and civil unrest that surely await the oppressive nation. Kureishi's title suggests more hope—as does his final line in the essay, "The future is in our hands." By referencing Baldwin's title in his own, Kureishi connects the struggle he experienced as an Asian in England in the 1960s, 1970s, and 1980s to the struggle of African Americans. This move is political, to be sure, but it also importantly highlights the truly oppressive nature of Britain and connects it to global liberation struggles that are specifically about countering white supremacy.

Also included in *London Kills Me* are the essays "Some Time with Stephen: A Diary," which deals with the process of making the film *Sammy and Rosie Get Laid* with director Stephen Frears; "The Alchemy of Happiness," which discusses a drug-selling boy Kureishi meets and who eventually becomes the person who spawns the idea for the character of Clint in the screenplay *London Kills Me;* and the essay "Eight Arms to Hold You," which focuses on the liberating power of popular music in the face of stringent and stifling educational institutions. Kureishi opens this piece by describing a peculiar incident in his music class: his teacher, one Mr. Hogg, tells the class that the Beatles are not responsible for writing their own music or lyrics. Shocked, Kureishi is almost incapable of interpreting what Mr. Hogg is trying to convey about the Beatles, whom—like most people in his peer group—he loves dearly. Kureishi ultimately recognizes that Mr. Hogg cannot recognize the genius of the Beatles as their own because he cannot concede that boys like the ones he teaches could have anything productive to say.

Furthermore, Kureishi goes on to note that the Beatles represented freedom—even in their most genial period before their experimental drug phase—and that while this was a threatening prospect to the educational powers that be, for the youth their music was a welcome avenue for self-expression. "Eight Arms to Hold You" celebrates the power of popular music with Kureishi noting that:

> Music is simply to get into. And pop musicians never have to ask themselves...who is my audience, who am I writing for and what am I trying to say? It is art for their own sakes, an art which connects with a substantial audience hungry for a new product, an audience which is, by now, soaked in the history of pop music and is sophisticated, responsive and knowledgeable.

Pop music, for Kureishi, represents art by kids from "state schools, kids from whom little was expected" and is therefore a kind of art of rebellion. It is this spirit of rebellion that Kureishi so deftly captures in all of his own work, a body of work that is rich in commentary, humor, wit, and critique. Kureishi worked to become a writer, at his father's urging, and found that it could be an outlet for the frustration that he felt growing up in a racist society. He notes in "The Rainbow Sign" that if he had had the capacity for violence, he surely would have acted on it. Thankfully his capacity in letters rather than in violence allowed him to voice, in starkly honest terms, his view of an often unjust yet frequently beautiful world. His work clearly demonstrates an earnest grappling with all the complicated aspects of life—it disavows nothing and claims everything, it does not speak for but speaks *near,* which the postcolonial feminist critic Trinh Minh-ha notes is the only possibility for self-conscious and politically informed representation. As such, Kureishi's work is utterly germane in its personal and political take on contemporary life in London. It would not be overstatement to argue that Kureishi's voice, perhaps more than any other, exemplifies contemporary British literature. Hanif Kureishi regularly posts unpublished short stories and essays on his official website, and his latest novel, *The Body,* was published in 2004. He continues to write, work, live, and love in London.

Selected Bibliography

WORKS OF HANIF KUREISHI

NOVELS

The Buddha of Suburbia. London: Faber, 1990; New York: Viking, 1990.

The Black Album. London: Faber, 1995; New York: Scribners, 1995.

Intimacy. London: Faber, 1998; New York: Scribners, 1999.

Gabriel's Gift. London: Faber, 2001; New York: Scribners, 2001.

The Body. New York: Scribners, 2004.

SHORT STORIES, ESSAYS, AND PUBLISHED PLAYS AND SCREENPLAYS

Borderline. London: Methuen, in association with the Royal Court Theatre, 1981.

"Dirty Washing." *Time Out,* November 14–20, 1985, pp. 25–26.

"Erotic Politicians and Mullahs." *Granta* 17:139–151 (autumn 1985).

"Bradford." *Granta* 20:149–170 (winter 1986).

"Esther." *Atlantic Monthly,* May 1989, pp. 56–62.

London Kills Me: Three Screenplays and Four Essays. London: Penguin, 1992. (Contains the screenplays *My Beautiful Laundrette, Sammy and Rosie Get Laid,* and *London Kills Me* and the essays "Eight Arms to Hold Me," "The Rainbow Sign," "Some Time with Stephen: A Diary," and "The Alchemy of Happiness.")

The Faber Book of Pop. (As editor, with Jon Savage.) London and Boston: Faber, 1995.

"We're Not Jews." *London Review of Books,* March 23, 1995, pp. 34–36.

"D'Accord Baby." *Atlantic Monthly,* September 1996, pp. 68–73.

Love in a Blue Time. London: Faber, 1997; New York: Scribners, 1997.

Midnight All Day. London: Faber, 1999.

Outskirts and Other Plays. London: Faber, 1999.

Plays One. London: Faber, 1999.

Sleep With Me. London: Faber, 1999.

CRITICAL AND BIOGRAPHICAL STUDIES

Aldama, Frederick Luis. *Postethnic Narrative Criticism: Magicorealism in Oscar "Zeta" Acosta, Ana Castillo, Julie Dash, Hanif Kureishi, and Salman Rushdie.* Austin: University of Texas Press, 2002.

Ball, John. "The Semi-Detached Metropolis: Hanif Kureishi's London." *ARIEL* 27, no. 4:7–27 (October 1996).

Chatterjee, Ranita. "An Explosion of Difference: The Margins of Perception in *Sammy and Rosie Get Laid.*" In *Between the Lines: South Asians and Postcoloniality.* Edited by Deepika Bahri and Mary Vasudeva. Philadelphia: Temple University Press, 1996.

Hashmi, Alamgir. "Hanif Kureishi and the Tradition of the Novel." *Commonwealth Novel in English* 6, nos. 1–2:50–60 (spring-fall 1993).

Ilona, Anthony. "Hanif Kureishi's *The Buddha of Suburbia:* 'A New Way of Being British.'" In *Contemporary British Fiction.* Edited by Richard J. Lane et al. Cambridge, U.K.: Polity, 2003.

Kaleta, Kenneth C. *Hanif Kureishi: Postcolonial Storyteller.* Austin: University of Texas Press, 1998.

Mohanram, Radhika. "Postcolonial Spaces and Deterritorialized (Homo)Sexuality: The Films of Hanif Kureishi." In *Postcolonial Discourse and Changing Cultural Contexts: Theory and Criticism.* Edited by Gita Rajan and Radhika Mohanram. Westport, Conn: Greenwood Press, 1995.

Moore-Gilbert, Bart. "Justice and Morality in the Plays of Hanif Kureishi." *European Studies* 17:241–253 (2001).

Nasta, Susheila. "'Homing In': Opening Up 'Asian' Britain in Hanif Kureishi and Ravinder Randhawa." In her *Home Truths: Fictions of the South Asian Diaspora in Britain.* New York: Palgrave, 2002.

Oliva, Juan Ignacio. "Literary Identity and Social Criticism in Hanif Kureishi's *The Black Album.*" In *On Writing (and) Race in Contemporary Britain.* Edited by Fernando Galván et al. Spain: Universidad de Alcalá. 1999.

Ranasinha, Ruvani. *Hanif Kureishi.* Tavistock, U.K.: Northcote House in association with the British Council, 2002.

Ray, Sangeeta. "Rethinking Migrancy: Nationalism, Ethnicity, and Identity in *Jasmine* and *The Buddha of Suburbia.*" In *Reading the Shape of the World: Toward an International Cultural Studies.* Edited by Henry Schwartz and Richard Dienst. Boulder, Colo.: Westview, 1996.

Sampat-Patel, Niti. *Postcolonial Masquerades: Culture and Politics in Literature, Film, Video, and Photography.* New York: Garland, 2001.

Stein, Mark. "Posed Ethnicity and the Postethnic: Hanif Kureishi's Novels." In *English Literatures in International Contexts.* Edited by Heinz Antor and Klaus Stierstorfer. Heidelberg, Germany: Carl Winter Universitatsverlag, 2000.

Yousaf, Nahem. "Hanif Kureishi and 'The Brown Man's Burden.'" *Critical Survey* 8, no. 1 (1996).

SARA MAITLAND

(1950–)

Sandie Byrne

SARA LOUISE MAITLAND was born in London to Adam and Hope Fraser-Campbell Maitland on February 27, 1950 and was brought up in London and southwest Scotland. After attending a girls' boarding school in Wiltshire, she went up in 1968 to read English at St. Anne's College at Oxford, where she is said to have discovered the four guiding principles of her life and writing: feminism, Anglo-Catholic religion, socialism, and friendship. She received a BA in 1971, graduating with honors, and was married on 24 June 1972 to an American named Donald Hugh Thompson Lee. Her husband became an Anglican priest that year and Maitland converted to Anglicanism. The couple, who gave birth to a daughter and a son, were married for thirty years, divorcing in 2002.

Maitland began publishing as soon as she graduated from Oxford. As well as producing her own widely diverse writing, she has fostered talent in others by serving as a tutor coordinator and a mentor for the British Council's Crossing Borders project, which supports young African writers; a member of the advisory board of the City of London University; a tutor for Lancaster University's distance learning master's degree in creative writing; and a visiting fellow of St. Chad's College, Durham University.

During the 1970s, Maitland was part of a feminist writing group with Zoë Fairbairns, Valerie Miner, Michèle Roberts, and Michelene Wandor. The group published short stories in magazines such as *Spare Rib* and *Bananas,* and subsequently collected them in two anthologies: *Tales I Tell My Mother* (1978) and *More Tales I Tell My Mother* (1987). Three members of the group, including Maitland, later contributed to two collections of short stories by women writers edited by Alison Fell, *The Seven Deadly Sins* (1988) and *The Seven Cardinal Virtues* (1990).

Maitland has continued to collaborate with other writers and specialists throughout her career and to affirm her need for their support and companionship on the quest she envisages her work to be ("A Feminist Writer's Progress," *On Gender and Writing,* p. 20).

Maitland's first novel, *Daughter of Jerusalem,* published in 1978, won the Somerset Maugham Award in 1979. Since then she has published five novels: *Virgin Territory* (1984); *Arky Types* (1987, coauthored with Michelene Wandor); *Three Times Table* (1990); *Home Truths* (1993), which won for her the Scottish Writer of the Year Award; and *Brittle Joys* (1999). She has also contributed short stories to numerous magazines and anthologies and has published five collections of short stories, the fourth of which, *Angel Maker* (1996), collects thirty stories from the earlier three volumes. Her first radio play, *Other Voices,* broadcast in October 2001, won the Mental Health Media Award in 2002, and her second, *Heartbreak,* was broadcast in December of 2001. In 1995 Stanley Kubrick invited her to work on the screenplay for the film *AI: Artificial Intelligence,* although nothing came of the association, but she did write the screenplay for Ruth Lingford's prize-winning 1998 animated film *The Pleasures of War.* Her nonfiction writing includes numerous works of theology, children's books about ancient Greek and Egyptian mythology, and a book about the history of gardens.

Since 2001, Maitland has lived in northeast England on the moor above Weardale in County Durham, following what she describes in an article in *Mslexia* magazine as less a midlife crisis than the arrival of the question "well, what now?" as she turned fifty and her youngest child left home. "And 'what now' turned out to be Silence," she says, "a new way of living—particularly of seeing and hearing—and from that (hopefully) a new way of praying and writing." She continues, "Virginia Woolf famously taught us that every woman writer needs a room of her own. She didn't know the half of it, in my opinion. I need a moor of my own."

NONFICTIONAL WRITING

"A Feminist Writer's Progress" describes an early conflict between Maitland's artistic and political consciousnesses. The artistic held "that politics and great writing cannot go together" and that inspiration "will not be held captive to theory, to an isolated vision, to a message"; the political asserted that feminist fiction is usually poor feminism and poor fiction; that literary value and accessibility were sacrificed to the personal and polemical (p. 19). Working with the Feminist Writers' Group, which included Zoë Fairbairns and other writers who collaborated to publish short fiction, helped her to resolve the issue. Her essay on feminism and aesthetics in *Tales I Tell My Mother* reminds us that all art is political, and the personal is political, but some art forms are more overtly political than others. Art is a way of organizing and clarifying experience. The politicized art of the writing group is not "a private presentation of our individual experience" nor "a cry of anguish or a whimper at the disagreeableness of things in general and men in particular. It is becoming a struggle to express, render accessible and dynamic our interpretation, not of our experience alone, but of experience at large" (p. 114). By presenting the stories in an openly polemical way the group is stating that it is not ashamed of what Maitland describes as the "inevitable function" of art.

Maitland is not among those women writers whose work has been categorized as what feminist theorist Hélène Cixous calls *écriture féminine,* the representation of a specifically female language not subject to the rules dictated by the patriarchal discourse into which we enter when we enter the language system. Rejecting the need for logical ordering, linear time, and rational argument, *écriture féminine* embraced multiplicity and flowing rhythms. Rather than attempt to create a women's language, Maitland

prefers to write of a feminist discourse, and to set for herself a social agenda. She argues that literary texts should be "vehicles of social revolution" and should explore and explode constructions of gender that lead to the oppression of women ("Futures in Feminist Fiction," *From My Guy to Sci-Fi,* pp. 193–203). Maitland argues that the feminist writing of the 1980s and 1990s failed to fulfill the optimistic agendas of the 1970s women's movement for challenging essentialist views of the female and femininity and for celebrating both diversity and community among women. Her stated aim is to redress that failing.

For Maitland, Christianity is not incompatible with feminism, but her passionate and energetic affirmations of awe, wonder, and gratitude for God's works (in, for example, *Awesome God: Creation, Commitment and Joy,* 2002) do not preclude pungent criticism of actions taken in God's name. She has charted the history of women in the Christian religion and interrogated the myths of female sainthood but has also examined the history of women's oppression in the name of religion.

FICTIONAL WRITING

Maitland's fiction is often compared to that of Angela Carter, and less often to that of Emma Tennant, and is like theirs labeled "magic realist." The term was applied in the later 1920s by German art critic Franz Roh to a school of post-expressionist painting whose stated agenda was the revelation of the mysteries inherent in the everyday. It was later adopted by Latin American critics to describe a literary form, and has been applied to the work of authors such as Franz Kafka, Gabriel García Márquez, and Mario Vargas Llosa. A subgenre of feminist magic realism has been identified, associated with (among others) Isabel Allende and Laura Esquivel in Latin America and Angela Carter and Emma Tennant in the United Kingdom.

Literary magic realism brings one discourse, which could be called the fantastic or antirealist (that is, the magical, supernatural, or inexplicable), into another discourse, realism.

Whereas realism represents things and events that can be accounted for empirically, the discourse of magic allows the representation of things and events for which there cannot be empirical proof. This does not suggest that these things and events do not happen or are impossible but that empiricism has its limits. As a Christian, Maitland accepts that aspects of her faith cannot be proven empirically, but she asserts in *Awesome God* that this does not matter. As a scholar she is well acquainted with the myth-kitty of the Western world and beyond, with its fantastic elements of metamorphoses, mythical beasts, human flight, spells, supernatural powers, journeys to the underworld, and so on, but she does not simply import such elements into her writing as metaphors or allegories, nor does she create alternate worlds. Such stories, set in never-lands where things fantastic in the "real" world are normal, are not magic realism, which requires that the magical events must transgress the laws of the world in which they happen. Like all labels, "magic realism" is reductive, but together with "Christian" and "feminist", it is a useful starting point for readings of Maitland's work.

The cover of the British paperback edition of Maitland's first novel, *Daughter of Jerusalem*, shows an attractive, golden-skinned woman whose long blonde hair is pinned up to show an expanse of seemingly naked back. Although slender, the model is far from the novel's stick-thin, crop-haired central protagonist, Liz. The back cover copy suggests an attempt to market this as the kind of book that used to be found in bookstore displays labeled "writing by women for women": confessional stories of struggle by feisty heroines with upbeat endings. The character of Liz is presented as someone to whom women might aspire: "The complete woman. Modern... liberated...strong-willed...sexy!" She is described as fulfilled and independent, yet not so independent, career-minded, and autonomous as to have lost her "femininity," which is signified by her overpowering desire for motherhood. Readers of the novel might not recognise Liz in the description: "Likeable and intelligent, she's a strong-willed lady with a zest for living. Her career and her husband satisfy her needs and her longing for success. To the world she represents the image of the total woman...in every sense but one." This reduces a rounded and complex character to cartoon. Liz is a successful characterization precisely because she is not always likable, or strong, or intelligent in her choices. Her career as a literary agent is not entirely satisfying; her marriage to a younger gay man with a traumatic past as a "rent boy" is troubled, difficult, and sometimes violent; and her relationship with her father has led her to disparage and ignore her mother.

The main narrative strand of the novel, Liz's attempt to conceive a child, is intercut with a number of brief episodes from other stories. These are day-in-the-life glimpses of women from the Bible—Elizabeth, Sarah and Hagar, Delilah, Jael and Deborah, Mary Magdalen, Leah and Rachel, and the Virgin Mary—whose fertility, sexuality, and evident femininity are cruces of their stories. A number of the women are paired into fruitful and nonfruitful women, as Liz is with Alice, a member of the same women's group, who arrives at Liz's flat in labor. Blood is a motif in the subsidiary strands as it is in Liz's story, whether as a marker of fertility (for women who are not yet menopausal), failure (the menstruation that shows the absence of pregnancy), or success (the blood present at childbirth). It also signifies death, as when Delilah uses her sexuality to kill Samson, and Jael to kill Sisera. Liz has to reconcile the conflict she feels between her desire to become pregnant and her support for women's rights to terminate pregnancy. She has to understand that both are aspects of a woman's right to own her sexuality and fertility.

Liz's struggle against the patriarchal figures of her father, her boss, and the gynecologist who treats her for infertility might seem overfamiliar and oversimplified, as might the encounters between the members of the women's group that Liz attends, but the characterizations are neither demonized in the case of the men nor glorified in the case of the women. Maitland's acute and clear-eyed observation, occasional earthiness, and leavening humor make the novel more than a manifesto or a parable.

The form of *Daughter of Jerusalem* is straight-forwardly realist, using a third-person limited perspective narrative with an occasional free indirect style when the narrative voice takes on the voice style of a character whose thoughts are being represented indirectly. But the reader sees almost everything from Liz's point of view, and the motives and thoughts attributed indirectly to other characters are often her interpretation of them. For example, the gynecologist makes a remark, and we are told: "He liked that, and smiled at her encouragingly, thinking he was clever and funny. She did not think he was remotely amusing, but hypnotically smiled back" (p. 4). This is not privileged access to the gynecologist's thoughts, but to Liz's. Finding him arrogant and smugly self-satisfied, Liz attributes these thoughts to him. The next paragraph takes the narrative voice, speaking of Liz with the third-person pronouns "she" and "her," but the words clearly represent those that are going through Liz's mind: "What the hell did the rejection of femininity mean anyway? Beyond a biological rearrangement of facts. Of course she accepted her femininity: her own self as woman. Rôle Model Confusion, the doctor called it." The interwoven biblical stories appear without explanation or framing device and with no attempt to integrate them into the here-and-now of the main strand. Their function appears to be to parallel the main story and offer Liz alternative models of the female paragons which they are conventionally held to represent.

Religion in *Daughter of Jerusalem* is introduced only in the parallel Bible stories rather than as a vital part of the characters' lives or as an integral part of the plot. In *Virgin Territory,* published six years later, it is brought into the foreground as an active force. The novel begins with the rape of Sister Katherine Elizabeth, a nun working at a mission house in an unnamed South American country, but *Virgin Territory* is not the story of Sister Katherine Elizabeth but that of Sister Anna, a member of the same order, for whom the event precipitates a crisis. Anorexic and ill, Sister Anna leaves the mission house for London, where she stays for some months ostensibly researching a history of the Catholic faith in South America, but in fact in search of healing and restoration. *Virgin Territory* introduces elements which leave the reader in doubt as to whether they should be understood through a realist framework and interpreted as hallucination, or symbolically as standing for anxieties and pressures made manifest metaphorically, or through a magic realist framework as actually happening. Disembodied voices are heard, spirits are summoned, and when a nun loses her virginity through rape she sees a pure white unicorn disappearing into the stars.

In London, Anna is hounded by voices that torment and abuse her, undermining her confidence, her convictions, and even her identity. The voices, which Anna thinks of as "the Fathers," are represented in exactly the same terms as the "real" events and characters in the story, and the reader is at first unsure of whether to consider them metaphors for the oppression of women by a patriarchal church, projections from Anna's own subconscious, or actual manifestations of the Fathers of the early church. Anna also encounters another voice, that of Caro, a child of three who was so severely brain-damaged at birth that she has no control over her movements and apparently no awareness of her self or her surroundings. Caro's parents are attempting to help her brain to make new synaptic pathways by forcing her limbs through endless patterns of exercises and other sensory stimuli, hour after hour, day after day. Throughout it all Caro thrashes, struggles, and screams. From the outside she appears to be insensate, a lump of flesh without volition or consciousness; but as Anna grows closer to Caro through becoming a volunteer in the project, Caro's self emerges, at first through third-person narration and later through her own voice, which no one but Anna can hear.

Caro could be said to be speaking from what the feminist theorist Julia Kristeva calls the "chora." The chora is the early stage of an individual's psychosexual development. It is pre-linguistic and undissociated; that is, the individual cannot distinguish itself as an entity separate from the mother or the world; it knows no boundaries. It is controlled only by its subconscious drives (in Freudian terms its drive to life and drive to death), and it experiences sensory input as pleasure. The mirror stage, which follows this phase in usual development, represses the chora. In the chora the individual has not entered the symbolic order; it has not entered the world which language prearranges into significance-laden concepts. During the chora, the individual is in what Kristeva calls the semiotic, a preimaginary domain characterized by rhythmic babble, language not formulated by the rules of the symbolic. The semiotic is not innately female, though it can be seen as the place of a repressed femininity. It can remain to challenge and disrupt the symbolic, rupturing "meaningful" language by meaninglessness and silence. Since the semiotic is prelinguistic, conventional language can create only an impressionistic representation. That Caro apparently thinks in words could suggest that Anna is translating the impressions she is receiving into words her mind can process, or it could suggest that Anna is projecting onto Caro her own sense of frustration and anger.

At first Caro expresses little but rage, but later she calms. Anna then has two sets of voices tugging at her: the Fathers, who demand her abject submission and acceptance of their doctrine of the sinful and disgusting nature of women; and Caro, who wants Anna to join her in rejecting "the world of sunlight, logic and cleanliness" into which her parents have tried to force her (p. 225). Though either path is dreadful, each is a temptation: the Fathers offer relief from the burden of freedom of choice; Caro offers the refuge of the dark womblike place to which she is returning, a female place. Either way would lead to an end to the struggle of volition, action, and responsibility that is adult life.

Though she has come to love Caro, Anna rejects this way, choosing life, struggle, and if not absolute faith, a willingness to suspend her disbelief. Although she has left the order, she does not choose a secular life, nor does she choose the life of a loving relationship offered by Karen, whom she has met through her work with Caro. For a time the Fathers and Karen wage war over Anna, each representing one side of the hierarchized binaries male/female, language/

silence, body/spirit. In the end she chooses neither. Both sides deal in certainties, and she chooses the tentative and ambiguous, and adult. Though her war with the Fathers is not over, we see Anna achieving a victory that wins her time to regroup, to garner her mental resources and choose her own ground for the next battle.

Anna's story ends with her having stepped "freshly outside her own conditioning, out of her carefully constructed skin" and though frail and vulnerable, "ready to go travelling." She is armed with two new weapons: the Fathers' power of naming, the power of language which she will use against them (p. 215); and the discovery of a theology which does not envision God as a distant and wrathful patriarch but as possessing the supposedly feminine virtues of nurturing and gentleness (p. 230). Christ is envisaged in terms of his relationship with women as son, brother, and bridegroom (to nuns), and as on the side of all women (p. 214). The novel ends with Sister Katherine Elizabeth, having lost, along with her virginity, her protection and privilege, but reflecting that now she has something in common with women everywhere and with "her friend and brother on the cross" (p. 236). She muses that she would like to stay out late, to play with the unicorn that comes dancing down the trail of stars to her, but her sisters would worry if she were late for compline, so she continues trudging up the hill to the women's house.

Though Anna's visitations or assaults by the Fathers are horrific, they are a form of religious experience, mysticism. Caroline Guerin sees the visitations as an ordeal, a form of purgatory through which Anna travels in order to emerge purified ("A Comparative Study of Iris Murdoch's *Nuns and Soldiers* and Sara Maitland's *Virgin Territory*," (June, 1992 p. 159)). The experiences are mystical, an area of spiritual endeavour which feminist theorist Luce Irigaray describes as the only one in which women have excelled more often than men, and one of the only occasions in the history of the West that women have been able to speak and act publicly. Mysticism can grant the highest revelations to the most abject, and Irigaray points out that women are brought up in a condition of abjection and repression. The mystical experience involves the loss of selfhood and dissolves the subject/object opposition, so would be expected to appeal to women. It often involves an ecstatic sensation of oneness with God or the divine and is represented in imagery suggesting the orgasmic. The experience is often represented in discourses which disrupt the masculinist attributes of intelligibility and rationality.

The conversational tone and direct address of Maitland's "Particles of a Wave," her afterword to her first book of short stories, *A Book of Spells* (1987), give the impression of an author who makes little or no distinction between her life and her fiction, or who at least is happy to make her private life public, especially if it is to explain something to her readers about her writing.

> I rang the commissioning editor to discuss this essay....
>
> "You will put in something about being a vicar's wife, won't you?..."
>
> Appalled, writhing, I terminated the conversation cravenly. Then I felt depressed.
>
> Why? I mean, why so depressed? I am after all married to a vicar and people do find this interesting.... I cannot help feeling that it is perceived as suitably batty that I should be a Christian at all, for a feminist writer to be a vicar's wife is splendidly part of that way of perceiving writers.
>
> (p. 165)

But a cautionary footnote to "A Feminist Writer's Progress" warns: "Whether, and in what ways, you believe any of this is, of course, entirely up to you, but remember always that the writer is a writer of fictions and too literal or chronological a belief may prove dangerous to your health" (p. 23).

Exactly how Maitland and Michelene Wandor collaborated to produce *Arky Types,* an epistolary novel (that is, a story told through letters), is not explained, so it is possible that Maitland wrote some or all of the letters which appear over Wandor's name and vice-versa. At first the reader is likely to try to read the letters as fact, or rather as fiction ostensibly fact, tracing the process

through which a book is commissioned, its outline planned and its payment agreed. The tone is chatty and casual:

> Dear Sam
>
> Michelene is away so I can't get in touch with her, BUT I am reasonably certain that she would agree with me that this whole thing is ridiculous. We aren't going to write an outline or sample chapter because we're not working that way. And because Nicky initiated the whole project. I don't understand what is going on; if they wanted the book—and we showed you the invitatory letter—they must have thought about paying for it then (??) Next Nicky will be wanting to dictate the whole damn thing.... I can't help wondering if it's going to be worth it whatever the money.
>
> (p. 29)

It seems as though readers are getting a slice of Maitland's life. But as the various correspondents—editor, agent, authors, fans—show themselves to be devious, greedy, arrogant, vain, and duplicitous, the reader perhaps becomes suspicious. Then there are letters between Mrs. Noah (preparing for the coming flood) and "Mrs. Vicar," (her initially skeptical and conventional correspondent) and another element is introduced.

> Count us out of your Brave New World.... We repudiate pro-sun, anti-wet weatherism. Power to the antediluvian chelonian sisterhood. Power to all dykes with backbone—the more the better. Power to wimmin of all species.
>
> Yours disrespectfully you sold-out wifist,
> Amorelle and Gertrude
> (p. 49)

Amorelle and Gertrude are tortoises who write like caricatures of leftist feminist activists of the 1970s. *Arky Types* is not, then, autobiography, but it is an exploration of the prevailing concerns of Maitland's work: women's history and the possibilities of its re-envisaging, Christianity, myth, and sisterhood.

Three Times Table is perhaps Maitland's most engrossing and fully realized novel. The action is restricted largely to the activities of three women in one house in Bayswater, London, during twenty-four hours, but the backstory ranges over forty years, and the themes explored are far from mundane. Each of the three women—in a way the ancient triad of maiden, mother, and crone—has something known only to herself. Whether she shares the secret will determine her future and the nature of the relationship among them.

Rachel, a celebrated paleontologist and curator of a natural history museum, finds that the conviction on which she has founded her life's work is false. She has to decide whether to announce this to the world, sacrifice her reputation and standing, and reorder a fifty-year-old way of thought, or to cling stubbornly to her blinkered ways of seeing not only her professional but her family life. Rachel's daughter Phoebe, once a brilliant mathematical prodigy, has rejected mathematics as a cold and reactionary form of elitist thought and science as a produce of masculinist thinking, and she is now a gardener. Estranged from her mother for years, she has returned to share a house but, as far as possible, not a life with her. Having long concealed the knowledge that she has a tumor in an advanced state, she has to decide whether to share the knowledge with family and friends and thus become an officially ill person, a patient, subject to others' treatment, or to retain her carefully preserved autonomy and her long-nurtured secret intimate friend, death. Maggie, a bright and sensitive fifteen-year-old, is anorexic and alienated from the youth culture around her. She has created an alternative secret world to inhabit, but it threatens to engulf her. She must decide whether she is willing to share the secret of her difference and perhaps lose it, and whether she is ready to accept the development of her woman's body and enter the constrictions of the adult world and lose the unconfined soaring joys of her free imagination. Some of the most interesting passages in the novel describe Maggie's journey through an ordinary day, representing the exquisite anguish of the sensitive and self-conscious adolescent whose skins of self-protection are constantly being flayed by the notice of others.

The choices the women make not only shape their future but also reshape their past, as each has to strip away layers of illusion and misreading and learn about mothers and daughters, men and women, truth and love. Like most of Maitland's work, the novel could be said to have a feminist agenda in that it portrays women who sacrifice or downplay their own intellectual and professional attainments in order to maintain the approved relationship between husband and wife, and men who dismiss, belittle, or appropriate their wives' achievements to maintain their illusion of superiority. Also like most of Maitland's fiction, it depicts men who leave the women to whom they have been close (by death and by being asked to leave the commune in this case). More importantly, perhaps, the novel shows how women become complicit in this process, how "daddies' girls" learn early to flirt with and cajole father and despise and fight with mother. Resisting the easy feel-good ending of three women in a relationship of unconditional love and mutual admiration, however, Maitland depicts their coming to a new understanding which brings an invaluable respect.

The label "magic realist" is clearly appropriate to *Three Times Table*. Maggie's secret is her life as the friend of Fenna, a dragon. Fenna is the antithesis of the empirical scientific world that Rachel inhabits, and the no less rational world of the commonsense, down-to-earth pragmatism of Phoebe. Fenna comes into being as a story told to Maggie to console her for the loss of a small plastic toy, but the dragon assumes a solid form that can transport Maggie not only across the skies of the real world but also to a place magical beyond most imaginings. The price of the joy and delight of companionship, flight, magic, and power is high: Fenna does not want Maggie to menstruate, to become a woman, to learn desire. Maggie has to fight this powerful being alone. Her mother is too absorbed in her own conflicts, and her grandmother, though she has written about dragon legends having their source in dinosaur fossils, is resolutely blind to the possibility of irrational, unscientific truth.

Maggie has to fight and hurt her beloved; Phoebe has to fight her entrenched ways of thought, to sacrifice her detachment and self-containment and something of her pride; and Rachel has to fight her desire to be right and sacrifice her past, her sense of a life built on secure foundations. The victories the women achieve are each at a cost. Maggie begins to eat and to menstruate but has lost her uniqueness and power; Phoebe enters a new understanding of her mother and daughter and will have support for her illness but has to admit to herself the possible imminence of death; Rachel has to give way to a new generation of paleontologists but finally, at Maggie's command, enters the world of myth and imagination.

Fenna has some of the attributes accorded to unicorns elsewhere in Maitland's work. As do the unicorns in *Virgin Territory* and in the short story "Lady with Unicorn" (in *Women Fly When Men Aren't Watching,* hereafter *Women Fly*), Fenna loves a prepubescent virginal girl. As in many myths, the delicate beauty and freedom, or self-ownership, of the girl is mirrored by and attracts the mythic beauty of the fabulous creature. Their bond is powerful—the girl can summon the creature and will defend and be defended by it—but the bond is broken by the onset of sexual desire. Once the girl sleeps with a man, her body is no longer in her own keeping, and the creature, enraged or saddened, leaves her. Maitland suggests, however, that virginity is not a matter of a present or absent hymen but of self-ownership, and she makes an important distinction between virginity and chastity.

In Maitland's fiction older women, often postmenopausal or at least done with childbearing, may return to a magical state in which they again desire the companionship of the unicorn or dragon, and the creature returns to them. In *Three Times Table,* as Rachel leaves the museum following the announcement that ends her career, she sees a dragon waiting for her in a tree. In *Virgin Territory,* Sister Katherine Elizabeth can again play with the unicorn after losing her virginity. In "Lady with Unicorn," when Clare first sleeps with a man, the outraged unicorn comes, savagely bites and tramples her, and then deserts her forever, but in "Dragon Dreams" (in *Women Fly*), the princess, supposedly rescued by Saint George, writes to her dragon beseeching him to return to her. The princess knew that people hunt and slay "the darkness of the dragon, the unnamed, the fierce freedom" in the name of civilization, so she summoned George to keep her safe from her own desires (p. 182). The dragon allowed itself to be killed for her but clearly is still living or is capable of being resurrected, since, as a mature woman now free of George and other claims on her, she recalls the dragon, or the dragon part of herself. "There is no safety, but there is wildness and joy, there is love and life within the danger. I love you. I want to be with you. I want to reclaim my dragon soul and fly" (p. 183). "Rapunzel Revisited" (in *Women Fly*) is another internal monologue by a woman who has returned herself to her own keeping, who having performed the roles expected of women at different stages of their lives by wearing the costumes and masks of daughter, desirable lover, mother, now sheds them to uncover an unproscribed self.

Home Truths, published as *Ancestral Truths* in the U.S., presents questions it does not answer and ambiguities it does not resolve. It follows the story of Clare Kerslake as she travels to and joins a family gathering at a hunting lodge in Scotland. It also follows, in flashback, Clare's earlier journey to and within Zimbabwe with her partner, David, and her journey within her own mind as she painfully tries to recall events that she cannot or will not allow herself to remember. Clare has left three things in Zimbabwe, her camera, her right hand, and David, and she does not know where any of them are. A large segment of memory is also missing, from the moment she and David began the ascent of Mount Nyangani to the moment she was found, alone, concussed, and with her right hand crushed beyond repair, nearly twelve miles from the ordained path.

Nurses, doctors, police, insurance agents, family, and friends all interrogate Clare, demanding that she reconstruct the lost hours to clear up the mystery of what has happened to David. Did he fall? Was he captured by guerrillas? Did she kill him? As Clare tries to end the ambiguity of unanswered questions she uncovers others. She remembers David as overbearing and even sadistic, but did she project onto him her need for a father figure domineering enough to order and make safe her life? She has always been afraid of storms and has been warned about the sudden extreme changes of weather in the mountains. Was what she believed to be sensible caution actually a symptom of her neuroses? Was she right to see bandits behind every rock? Did she hear ancestral spirit voices and the singing of the beautiful naiad-like spirit Chirikudzi on the mountain, or was it all a product of her overactive imagination? Is the prosthetic hand she has been given following the amputation of her own really a miracle of modern science, better than the original, or is it a sinister and possibly malign entity with a life of its own?

The background to the main plot also presents the reader with ambiguities and puzzles which are resolved as the story develops: a family in which we are told two sisters are only four months apart in age; a Christian family whose ethos demands tolerance and charity but which celebrates a rite of slaughter; a loving family which seemingly encourages aggressive and even cruel "ragging." As the title suggests, each of the main characters of the story, brought home to Scotland, is also brought face to face with some home truths about his or her self and his or her relationship with the others and their home. Clare's accident is not the only crisis in the family; her sister Felicity and brother-in-law are faced with a dreadful decision to make about their only child, the profoundly deaf Alice; one of her brothers, Ben, an Anglican priest, has been "outed" as homosexual by a tabloid; a sister must confront decades of stored and seething resentment and anger; their parents must face the fact that this will be one of the last times the family will visit their old home and that their life of privilege is coming to an end. Only one in the family is unchanged by the holiday gathering and appears to be serenely unshakeable in her holiness and faith, but it transpires that Sister Cecilia's faith is not serene at all.

At the end of the novel, though people have faced the truth, not everything is neatly resolved, nor is everyone redeemed or reconciled. Ben has had to resign from his parish and doesn't know what he will do; Thomas, the younger son, has to accept that although he loves and understands the land, his cousin will inherit the family estate and will immediately sell it; Felicity realizes that her deaf daughter will never speak to her and that she will not have another child. Clare has not succeeded in conquering her amnesia, but in trying to retrieve recent memories has dredged up some old ones. A spectacular display from the Perseids (a meteor shower visible from the United Kingdom in late autumn) triggers the memory of her real parents' death in an explosion. She remembers what they (the sister and brother-in-law of the uncle who has adopted her) were like and how they died, and discovers that her desire for safety, for protection by someone stronger than herself, is not a character trait but a reaction to their love of danger and risk. Early in her life Clare has made a choice between taking a risk (a love affair with a tempestuous, passionate and unpredictable Italian woman) and taking the safe path (return to Britain, stability, and a predictable heterosexual relationship). She now decides to embrace danger, risk, the wild; Felicity learns to accept that Alice must be allowed to encounter it; and Ben must face the consequences of having embraced it. Cecilia has already embraced it in the form of her perception of God.

Home Truths is unusual in Maitland's work in that while the other magic realist stories draw on the lexicon of Western mythology and fairy tales (dragon, mermaid, broomsticks, gingerbread house), it goes to African sources. It does, however, return to a number of Maitland's themes. Alice resembles Caro from *Virgin Territory* in that she has no voice, can make no verbal utterances that others interpret as meaningful. She is an adept user of sign, which has become her first language; but though they doggedly learn some signs, the rest of the family members are largely locked out of her world, as she is from theirs. Like Clare, Alice has a prosthetic device, a hearing aid, and like Clare she hates it with a passion. Alice's parents' desire for her to talk to them and to interact with the "normal" world leads them to force this intrusion on her consciousness, to make her experience sound even though it is for her painfully loud noise which she cannot interpret as meaningful. The rejection of a loving sexual relationship with another woman also recurs, standing, as it partially does in *Virgin Territory,* for a failure of nerve, the failure to make a leap in the dark, and the turning away from of a whole possible alternative life.

The religious in the novel—Clare's adoptive father and brother, both priests in the Anglo-Catholic tradition; Cecilia, a Catholic nun; and the bishop who appears offstage as the voice of conventional middle Anglicanism—represent and debate different aspects of faith and religious practice in the twentieth century, while the lay but devout members of the family—Clare's adoptive mother, some of her siblings, and her brother-in-law—show how a secular life concerned with worldly things (raising a family, operating an estate) can be run on Christian principles. The Christian religion practiced by the family is not mystical (though Clare's mother has a clear vision of each of the patron saints she petitions for intercession) nor entirely spiritual, but strong, humorous, practical. In spite of its evident importance to the family and to the novel, Christianity is not allowed undisputed sway. Competing discourses are heard from Anni, the adoptive sister closest to Clare, from Joyful Masvingise, a Zimbabwean freedom fighter now working with traditional medicine and magic, and from Clare herself. Clare is eventually given absolution by her brother and achieves peace. She is aware that life will not be simple or easy, nor will all questions be answered, but she will continue to strive. She will dare, take risks, face danger, and sometimes fall.

The title of *Brittle Joys* is taken from Saint Augustine's Sermon III: "For in life we must struggle to hold on to brittle joys." The brittle joys in the novel are both metaphorical—the comforts of marriage, friendship, and material possessions, which can easily be lost—and literal—the beautiful glass objects which the protagonist creates and which can so easily be broken. At one point in the novel Ellie says that she wants joy. She is told: "Joy is a virtue.... You have to work on it." (p. 33). On the surface, from outside, Ellie Macauley has a wonderful life: acclaimed as an artist in glass; proprietor of a studio that nurtures new talent; married to the charming, successful psychiatrist Henry; mother of Stephanie, doing field research in an important project in Borneo; close friend of the endlessly supportive Judith and Hugo.

Below the visible surface, however, Ellie's joys and accomplishments are brittle: the glassblowing studio contains pressures and factions which might crack it apart; her young protégée seeks to oust her; the marriage is about to end; Stephanie has gone abroad primarily to get away from Ellie's overprotective control, and doesn't write; and Judith and Hugo are each about to need support that Ellie may not be able to give. Further beneath the surface is not Ellie, wife, mother, and friend; nor Héloïse Macauley, internationally acclaimed artist; but Helen, lonely, miserable, fish out of water in the cold desert of Presbyterian Scotland; and Nelly, unsatisfactory sister and unfilial daughter. Further still is the angel. Angel lurks somewhere in Ellie's spinal column, which she/he ascends to speak in Ellie's head.

> Then she felt the too familiar twitchy sensation just above her coccyx, followed by the odd warm glow up her spinal column and there was Angel manifesting somewhere in the region of her *corpus callosum.* Ellie found it slightly sinister that Angel located herself just there so that she could never be quite sure if she was dealing with a rational, objective, verbal perception, or an imaginative, fluid, musical one.
>
> (p. 32)

The location of Angel in Ellie's spinal column invites comparison with William Golding's *The Spire* (1964) in which Dean Jocelin, whose obsession brings the great spire of a medieval cathedral into being, feels the presence of an angel whom the text associates with his tuberculosis of the spine. Maitland's angel is nothing like Golding's however. She is not at all medieval, nor like the flowing robed, spiritual-looking, sentimental, lily-carrying handmaidens of nineteenth-century illustrations: "'You should have brought a woolly,' said Angel, in her slightly adenoidal accent" (p. 32). When Ellie protests that she wants sensible consolations, the present comfort of God or mystical visions or something, Angel replies, "Oh grow up, Ellie," and tartly remarks that Ellie has more consolations than most, but doesn't recognize them.

"What do you mean?"

"Well, there's me, who might well be described as a sensible consolation, and indeed whom your beloved Blake would have seen as a mystical vision...."

"You are not a mystical vision," said Ellie.

"Of course I am. Or if I'm not, you're psychotic...schizophrenic probably.... Diagnostically, you've only got two choices: I'm either a physical manifestation of the divine glory—that is to say a mystical experience —or you have a serious psychiatric illness."

(p. 33)

Sometimes Angel seems to bring small pockets of time with her, episodes from the lives of other of her "clients," which sometimes she drops to spill open in Ellie's mind. Ellie experiences as intense physical sensations the sights, sounds, scents, and feelings of long-dead people: a child caught in the wreck of a Phoenician ship carrying glass ingots from Sidon to Colchester; a young girl apprentice who has swum the lagoon to escape from Venice's Murano glassworks; the Saxon priest celebrating Mass with a glass chalice forbidden by the church; the Queen of Sheba presenting a rare green glass bowl to the House of Israel.

The story follows Ellie through a series of breakages and losses, of things and people. Beautiful artworks vanish, objects shatter, couples break up, and people crack up. Even Angel's wings, which would be glass if they were material, devitrify. The "time-pouncing" that has afflicted Ellie is a symptom of angelic confusion, and Angel has become confused too often. She has fallen in love with matter, with glass, with bodies, with physical sensation. She has become addicted, and the sickness is incurable.

Angel is recalled to the eternal, immaterial infinity of heaven, where she brings out from under her wings five beautiful objects from Ellie's studio that she has been unable to resist. "The courts of heaven Lurch; the adamantine

walls crack, refract, and crizzle.... For now there is matter in heaven. The material has penetrated the immaterial: mass and matter and time have crashed the perfectly constructed barrier between their own appointed spheres and the ever-ranging, spaceless, placeless zones of eternity" (pp. 234–235). In the resulting fear, the Everlasting Word comes and raises hands which each have a plug of black obsidian deep within a wound. All is well, and the immaterial heaven reiterates its love of the body and all its ways.

Ellie survives the loss of Henry, and finally posts one of the letters she has been writing to her daughter in her head throughout the novel. This one does not reproach, justify, or demand, but simply says that she is sorry for having behaved badly, and sends her daughter love. The friends have weathered their storms—the threat to Hugo's health and Judith's abandonment by her lover. Angel will remain Hugo's "fag-hag" and perhaps be "fairy godmother" to the child he and Ellie's lesbian assistant plan to have. (The novel was originally to be called "Hagiography"). She and Judith may live together. Nothing will get easier; some things will get harder. Angel says goodbye. Ellie has learned to inhabit the joys she has. The joys of mortal, bodily life may be brittle, but they are valid.

In *Brittle Joys,* Christianity is treated as factual reality and is handled on the same level and in the same terms as techniques of glassblowing or the treatment of HIV-positive patients. Ellie is a Christian, a Catholic. For her, faith is "a matter of mind and heart" (p. 77), but she lives in the real, secular rather than conventual world, and is no way evangelical or nunlike. She enjoys food, wine, clothes, jokes, and flirting, swears, and is happy in the company of her homosexual friends. Her Christianity requires no extreme holiness, self-denial, or martyrdom.

Just as Maitland returns to certain themes in her fiction, so she reproduces situations and even conversations, perhaps suggesting that some kinds of human intercourse are generic or cyclical, at least among certain types of people. In *Brittle Joys,* Henry discusses cerebral commissurotomy (severing of the *corpus callosum,* the bond of nerves between the right and left hemispheres of the brain, which eliminates normal integration of sensory information) as a discredited cure for epilepsy (p. 88). In "Cassandra" (in *Women Fly*) the Trojan prophetess who was cursed to be forever disbelieved is suffering from the aftereffects of a commissurotomy inflicted by the god Apollo in revenge for her rejection of his advances. The same kinds of dinner party are described in *Three Times Table,* where Phoebe's memories are described indirectly:

One of those dinner parties which she loved and mocked and almost equally, where people envy each other their success while feeling faintly guilty about their own. Friendship networks so old and intimate that the differences and difficulties could collapse into wild mirth at any instant, or could flare into fights which, however vicious at the time, would not actually change anything nor prevent her and all her friends coming together again soon after, at identical but different pine kitchen tables, scattered in a loose lop-sided circle around central London. The detached, amused part of Phoebe sometimes thought that her main feeling at these parties was a wish that she, and everyone else too, would dare to improve the quality of the wine, but they were all too self-consciously afraid of being mistaken for Yuppies.... Property prices and psychoanalysis were mentioned shyly, rather as Rachel might mention sex, but once in the air everyone turned out to be immensely knowledgeable about both.

(pp. 145–146)

Both *Brittle Joys*' Ellie and the unnamed narrator of "Fag Hags" (in *Women Fly*) have gay friends who are tested for HIV. In the hours between the taking of a blood sample and the test result, both walk on London's Hampstead Heath, passing the places where the men have picked up partners for casual sex and where the women lost their virginity years before. Both women have the same fantasy. Should her friend be confirmed HIV positive, she will care for him as he becomes ill, taking him into her home, bringing him breakfast in bed, and giving him gifts: a Japanese kimono and primrose-yellow silk pajamas.

Writers seeking a way to envisage a life for women more liberated and less cut off from their own and wider nature than is possible in recent times have sometimes turned to preindustrial eras and pre-Christian religions and learning. At worst this has resulted in a crude flipping of binary hierarchies: all Christians are imperialist patriarchal oppressors; all worshippers of the Mother-Goddess are good, wise, and farsighted. But at best it has produced stories of great power and grace. Magic realist fiction has sometimes juxtaposed a pagan past, often of matriarchal religion and matrilocal society, with modern-day city life. Maitland has written stories in this genre, but she does not represent this mythologized history as a lost Utopia of maternal, sisterly, and universal love. She notes that her stories have gotten darker and that now they frequently represent "the conniving, treacherous, unloving, unlovely things" that women do (*On Gender and Writing,* p. 21). In "The Burning Times" (in *Women Fly*) a girl jealous of her mother's beautiful lover Margaret sets the Inquisition on the two women and sees her mother burned. In "Witch-Woman" (in *On Becoming a Fairy Godmother,* (2003) hereafter *Fairy Godmother*) jealous villagers send Issobel Gowrie to the Inquisition and the stake.

In other stories Maitland explores the enduring archetype of the witch or wise woman, with respect but not undue reverence, and with humor. The witch in "Angel Maker" (in *Book of Spells*) lives deep in the forest in a house made of sweets, to which Hansel and Gretel come as children, and she rides a broomstick, but she has an oxygen-cooled thermos flask and a centrifuge, and she mentions a Channel 4 documentary. The Angel Maker gives women control over their fertility and teaches them that they have control over themselves but also must take responsibility for what they do. Issobel Gowrie has no real magical power but invents spells and conjurings to defy her accusers with laughter. A menopausal wife dumped for a younger model becomes an unexpected kind of wise woman after an encounter with a mermaid in an S-bend in the funny and poignant "Why I Became a Plumber" (in *Fairy Godmother*). The "fairy godmother" in the same collection of stories is a social worker who finds her advice is better heeded when she dresses up as a fortune-teller. The witches in "Let Us Now

Praise Unknown Women and Our Mothers Who Begat Us" (in *Book of Spells*) gently and unobtrusively help a troubled young girl to become more comfortable in her own skin, and pass on the knowledge that any woman can be a witch.

Like other feminist writers, Maitland has retold classical myths and fairy tales, "writing-back" to the originals in a way which makes the reader question the assumptions and archetypes (ugly old witch, dauntless hero, daring quest, imprisoning tower, and so forth) on which they are based. Maitland lightly mocks this convention in her story "The Wicked Stepmother's Lament" (in *Book of Spells*).

In "The Lady Artemis" (in *Women Fly*) the traditionally callous virgin-huntress goddess is entirely indifferent to the fate of Actaeon, who is destroyed not by her but by his fear of female power. The narrator of "Penelope" (in *Tales I Tell My Mother*)—who in Homer's *Odyssey* is a modest wife waiting patiently at home for her hero husband's return from the Trojan War, raising her son, fending off suitors, with little more than weaving to occupy her—is a practical and active woman who faces the difficult truth: "that I had done better, gone further than he [Odysseus]" (p. 147). In "Foreplay" (in *Fairy Godmother*) Guinevere desires Lancelot and exults in their rare adulterous meetings but is contemptuous of the delusion of courtly love he weaves about them.

A more complex treatment of this form occurs in the stories about two Christian martyrs, Felicity and Perpetua, who appear in "Requiem" (in *Weddings and Funerals*, 1984) in "Perpetua and Felicity" (in *Angel and Me*, 1985) and whose story is invoked in *Home Truths*. The process of rewriting or reimagining, usually one-way, becomes more interactive as Felicity and Perpetua resist the attempts of the author to produce them in her ahistorical image. The languages and therefore the concepts are different; the gap between third-century Roman and twentieth-century English women seems unbridgeable; and the attempt to cross it seems culpable, an act of cultural vandalism, yet in "Requiem" Maitland suggests that it can be bridged.

"Sailing the High Seas" (in *Fairy Godmother*) returns to the theme of women reclaiming their lives after they have done with childbirth and child rearing. In this story, on hearing that one of her daughters has gained a first-class degree and been awarded a scholarship to Yale University and the other is expecting a baby, a respectable retired schoolteacher says, "Now I can be off to be a pirate," and roars away in red biker leathers on a motorbike (p. 65). The motorbike and an unseen ship convey the woman away from the confinement of domestic life and responsibility and thus represent freedom, autonomy, and the power to escape and progress. The epitome of the stories' empowering forms of conveyance is the broomstick, which enables women to fly; but better still is the ability to fly without any conveyance, which suggests inherent power, magical power, and offers an exhilarating, exciting alternative to the domestic and mundane. Women who can fly unaided have come into themselves and their power. Paul Magrs reports Maitland as saying that the idea of flying "has a very particular reading for feminists at the imaginative level because it's what witches do. It's the magical space that belongs to women—the power to fly, and it's a power you can get burned for. It's a very potent, wonderful thing" ("A Planned Wilderness: Paul Magrs Talking with Sara Maitland," *Engendering Realism and Postmodernism*, p. 358).

Women's relationship with food is another important theme for Maitland. She illustrates the competing and conflicting pressures on women to be nurturers and providers of food and to deny themselves sensual pleasures in order to preserve an abstemious, ascetic image or a body that pleases men. Some of her female characters, such as Sister Anna, become anorexic, finding in refusal of food their only form of control. In Anna's case this has a parallel in the physical struggles of Caro, whose only power is resistance. In "Apple Picking" (in *Women Fly*) the main story is cut both with observations of the Superior of an order of nuns who proudly starve themselves in the pursuit of holiness and with recipes for dishes containing apples. The main story is an interview in which a mother describes in highly physical terms her adoration of her baby and her delight in bathing, cuddling, and feeding the infant, usually whilst also enjoying or imagining food. It transpires that the interview (conducted, we assume, by a social worker, police officer, or psychiatrist) follows the woman's having eaten her baby "à la tartare," that is, raw (p. 25). The mother lingeringly describes the pleasures of food and is in a constant state of desire; the Mother Superior disciplines herself to sacrifice the pleasures but cannot prevent the torment of want. The recipes provoke desire in the reader, and the story ends with the Mother Superior's vision of Eve in the Garden of Eden reaching for the apple, not from the sin of pride or to gain knowledge, but from simple greed.

In 1983 Maitland described her writing career as a quest "to re-tell the old stories again and fill in some bits that got left out" and her chosen form as "the intense and even constraining space of the short story, vibrating with the voices of tradition and memory, which could uniquely force the emotions she wanted to explore down into her own vulnerable places, and thence she hoped into the vulnerable places of other women" (*On Gender and Writing,* p. 20). She is almost dismissive of her other writing: "it developed her muscle and fed her face (and sometimes distracted and sometimes helped her)." Nonetheless her novels and nonfiction have met with both critical acclaim and popular success, and her published output has continued to be an eclectic mix of fiction, feminism, radical theology, criticism, and garden design. She has said, "They're all about the same things though; about sex and gender and risk and beauty and stories and language and power and glory" ("Sara Maitland: Novelist, Fabulist, Feminist," *Island Voices,* http://trace.ntu.ac.uk/voices/maitland.htm).

Selected Bibliography

WORKS OF SARA MAITLAND

Novels
Daughter of Jerusalem. London: Blond and Briggs, 1978. Published in the U.S. as: *Languages of Love.* Garden City, N.Y.: Doubleday, 1981.

Virgin Territory. London: Michael Joseph, 1984. New York: Beaufort Books, 1986.

Arky Types. London: Methuen, 1987. (Coauthored with Michelene Wandor.)

Three Times Table. London: Chatto and Windus, 1990. New York: Henry Holt, 1991.

Home Truths. London: Chatto and Windus, 1993. Published in the U.S. as: *Ancestral Truths.* New York: Henry Holt, 1993.

Brittle Joys. London: Virago, 1999.

Short Stories
Angel and Me: Short Stories for Holy Week. London: Mowbray, 1995. Harrisburg, Pa.: Morehouse, 1997. (The American edition is subtitled only *Stories.*)

Angel Maker: The Short Stories of Sara Maitland. New York: Henry Holt, 1996. (Thirty stories collected from the previous three volumes.)

On Becoming a Fairy Godmother. London: Maia Press, 2003.

Contributions to Anthologies
Tales I Tell My Mother: Feminist Short Stories. London: Journeyman, 1978. (Also includes stories by Zoë Fairbairns, Valerie Miner, Michèle Roberts, and Michelene Wandor.)

"Let Us Now Praise Unknown Women and Our Mothers Who Begat Us." In *Stepping Out: Short Stories on Friendships Between Women.* Edited by Ann Oosthuizen. London: Pandora, 1986.

More Tales I Tell My Mother: Feminist Short Stories. London: Journeyman, 1987. (Also includes stories by Zoë Fairbairns, Valerie Miner, Michèle Roberts, and Michelene Wandor.)

"Gluttony." In *The Seven Deadly Sins.* Edited by Alison Fell. London: Serpent's Tail, 1988.

"Justice." In *The Seven Cardinal Virtues.* Edited by Alison Fell. London: Serpent's Tail, 1990.

"Fall from Grace." In *The Penguin Book of Modern Women's Short Stories.* Edited by Susan Hill. London: Penguin, 1991.

"An Edwardian Tableau." In *The Oxford Book of Historical Stories.* Edited by Michael Cox and Jack Adrian. Oxford: Oxford University Press, 1994.

Nonfiction
A Map of the New Country: Women and Christianity. London: Routledge and Kegan Paul, 1983.

Walking on the Water: Women Talk About Spirituality. Edited by Maitland and Jo Garcia. London: Virago, 1983.

Vesta Tilley. London: Virago, 1986.

Very Heaven: Looking Back at the 1960s. Edited by Maitland. London: Virago, 1988.

The Rushdie File. Edited by Maitland and Lisa Appignanesi. London: Fourth Estate, 1989; Syracuse, N.Y.: Syracuse University Press, 1989.

A Big-Enough God: Artful Theology. London: Mowbray, 1994. New York: Henry Holt, 1995. (The American edition is subtitled *A Feminist's Search for a Joyful Theology.*)

Pandora's Box: A Three-Dimensional Celebration of Greek Mythology. Illustrated by Christos Kondeatis. Boston: Little, Brown, 1995.

The Ancient Egypt Pack: A Three-Dimensional Celebration of Egyptian Mythology, Culture, Art, Life, and Afterlife. Illustrated by Christos Kondeatis. Boston: Little, Brown, 1996.

Virtuous Magic: Women Saints and Their Meanings. London: Mowbray, 1998. New York: Continuum, 1998. (Coauthored with Wendy Mulford.)

Gardens of Illusion: Places of Wit and Enchantment. London: Cassell, 2000. (Coauthored with Peter Matthews.)

Awesome God: Creation, Commitment and Joy. London: SPCK, 2002. Published in the U.S. as: *A Joyful Theology: Creation, Commitment, and an Awesome God.* Minneapolis: Augsburg, 2002.

ESSAYS AND ARTICLES

"Abortion and the Sanctity of Life." In *Catholicism and Conflict.* Edited by Terry Drummond. London: Jubilee Group, 1982.

"A Feminist Writer's Progress." In *On Gender and Writing.* Edited by Michelene Wandor. London: Pandora, 1983.

"Two for the Price of One." In *Fathers, Reflections by Daughters.* Edited by Ursula Owen. London: Virago, 1983. New York: Pantheon, 1985.

"Margaret Laurence's *The Stone Angel.*" *Canadian Woman Studies/Les Cahiers de la Femme* 8, no. 3:43–45 (fall 1987).

"Passionate Prayer: Masochistic Images in Women's Experience." In *Sex and God: Some Varieties of Women's Religious Experience.* Edited by Linda Hurcombe. London: Routledge and Kegan Paul, 1987.

"Futures in Feminist Fiction." In *From My Guy to Sci-Fi: Genre and Women's Writing in the Postmodern World.* Edited by Helen Carr. London: Pandora, 1989.

"For the Menopausal Woman." In *A Certain Age: Reflecting on the Menopause.* Edited by Joanna Goldsworthy. London: Virago, 1993. New York: Columbia University Press, 1994.

"The Secular Saint." In *After Diana: Irreverent Elegies.* Edited by Mandy Merck. London: Verso, 1998.

"Religious Experience and the Novel: A Problem of Genre and Culture." In *The Novel, Spirituality and Modern Culture: Eight Novelists Write About Their Craft and Their Context.* Edited by Paul S. Fiddes. Cardiff: University of Wales Press, 2000.

"Finding Out." In *The Creative Writing Coursebook: Forty Authors Share Advice and Exercises for Poetry and Prose.* Edited by Julia Bell and Paul Magrs. London: Macmillan, 2001.

"The Sound of Silence." *Mslexia* 21:20–21 (April–June 2004).

CRITICAL STUDIES

Alexander, Flora, *Contemporary Women Novelists.* London: Edward Arnold, 1989. (Maitland is not dealt with extensively, but several passages address her work.)

———, "Contemporary Fiction III: The Anglo-Scots." In *A History of Scottish Women's Writing.* Edited by Douglas Gifford and Dorothy McMillan. Edinburgh: Edinburgh University Press, 1997, pp. 630–640.

Guerin, Caroline, "Iris Murdoch—A Revisionist Theology? A Comparative Study of Iris Murdoch's *Nuns and Soldiers* and Sara Maitland's *Virgin Territory.*" *Literature and Theology: An International Journal of Theory, Criticism and Culture* 6, no. 2:153–170 (June 1992).

Gutenberg, Andrea, "Thresholds and Boundaries: Limit Plots in Eva Figes, Penelope Lively and Sara Maitland." In *Engendering Realism and Postmodernism: Contemporary Women Writers in Britain.* Edited by Beate Neumeier. Amsterdam: Rodopi, 2001, pp. 191–205.

Leonardi, Susan J., "The Long-Distance Runner (the Loneliness, Loveliness, Nunliness of)." *Tulsa Studies in Women's Literature* 13, no. 1:57–85 (spring 1994).

Magrs, Paul, "A Planned Wilderness: Paul Magrs Talking with Sara Maitland." In *Engendering Realism and Postmodernism: Contemporary Women Writers in Britain.* Edited by Beate Neumeier. Amsterdam: Rodopi, 2001, pp. 353–365.

Muchnick, Laurie, "Bewitched: Sara Maitland Stirs it Up." *Village Voice Literary Supplement* 123:28–29 (March 1994).

Palmer, Paulina, *Contemporary Women's Fiction: Narrative Practice and Feminist Theory.* New York: Harvester Wheatsheaf, 1989.

PHILIP MASSINGER

(1583–1640)

Dan Brayton

PHILIP MASSINGER BELONGS to the great age of English drama that began during the reign of Queen Elizabeth I (r. 1558–1603) and ended with the suppression of the London theaters in 1642, in the early days of the English Civil War. His immediate theatrical predecessors were some of the greatest dramatists of the English language, including the likes of Robert Greene, Thomas Kyd, Christopher Marlowe, and William Shakespeare, while his contemporaries, almost equally renowned, were John Fletcher, Francis Beaumont, Thomas Middleton, John Webster, John Ford, and Thomas Dekker. Massinger collaborated in writing plays with several of his peers, including Fletcher, Dekker, and Middleton; he also wrote a number of good plays on his own. To earn a living as a dramatist in an era so full of great playwrights required a great deal of ability and tenacity. Massinger had both, but he never had the fame or financial success of playwrights like Shakespeare and Fletcher. A protean writer who created comical, villainous, heroic, exalted, and debased characters, Massinger rarely attracts the same kind of attention as his peers. Nonetheless Massinger was a playwright of great talent and skill who learned from his more celebrated predecessors and created some memorable characters, engaging scenes, and delightful plays. His achievement as a playwright and poet puts him among the handful of leading playwrights of Stuart (1603–1642) drama.

In addition to being connected with many of the greatest writers of his own age, Massinger has been written about by a number of celebrated writers since his death, several of whom considered him one of the great figures of English drama. Others considered him a lesser light. Many writers were conflicted between these two positions, finding Massinger at once an impressive craftsman and an uninspired workhorse. The list of his admirers and critics includes the celebrated diarist Samuel Pepys, the essayist Charles Lamb, the poets Samuel Taylor Coleridge, John Keats, and Lord Byron, the poet and novelist Walter Scott, and the poet Algernon Charles Swinburne, to name only the most prominent. Such an extensive list would seem to suggest that Massinger's reputation lies beyond dispute, but this is not the case. As Swinburne claimed, "the fame of no English poet can ever have passed through more alternate variations of notice and neglect" than that of Massinger (Garrett, p. xiii). It is indeed remarkable that a writer as well known in his own day as Massinger unquestionably was should have to be resurrected, as it were, by successive generations of poets. Part of any overview of Massinger's life and works, therefore, must be an account of his perpetually waxing and waning reputation.

What, exactly, are the merits and limits of Massinger's dramaturgy? For one thing, the best of his plays seem particularly modern in comparison with other plays from the same era. In their clarity, symmetry of plot and structure, and characterization they anticipate the drama of the Restoration: they are well crafted and written in a flexible, balanced language that often appears more modern than the generally more bombastic writing of Massinger's contemporaries. He rarely attempts to juggle multiple strands of plot as, for instance, Shakespeare does in plays like *King Lear.* This makes them generally easy to follow and unified in theatrical effect. His style too tends toward clarity and elegance rather than intensity or singularity. Admirers comment on his masterful use of blank verse. Indeed his plays contain line after line of easy, unforced poetry. Detractors, on the other hand, complain that his metaphors are labored compared to those of

Shakespeare and that his characters too often speak of themselves as if they were their own audience. Coleridge opined that "Massinger's characters have no character," and others have concurred (Cruikshank, p. 71).

Massinger's writings tend to draw out the extremes in critics. Those who prefer well-crafted plays that subordinate character to plot appreciate him, while those who savor the grandeur and rhetorical complexity of Shakespeare often find Massinger's simpler plot structures and more mundane characters to be meager fare. Criticism generally tends to allow him some strength as a playwright but less as a poet. Based on this distinction, the twentieth-century poet T. S. Eliot dedicated an essay to putting Massinger in his place in literary history. Eliot criticizes Massinger for his failings as a poet and compares him unfavorably with Shakespeare, all the while concentrating on the ephemeral criterion of "moral fibre," which he never adequately defines but evidently (along with various Victorian readers) perceived Massinger to lack. While Eliot's concern for a writer's moral fiber today seems pompous and a bit silly, it is undeniable that Massinger's willingness to depict social vices vividly and directly made his works seem somewhat vulgar to moralists.

A quality that seemed a weakness to some appears a strength to many modern readers, for the plays vividly depict many of the most pressing social and cultural issues from the era in which they were produced. The villain Sir Giles Overreach of *A New Way to Pay Old Debts*, for instance, is a wonderful version of a crafty, unscrupulous usurer who ensnares debtors financially and takes their land. The consummate social climber and man of resentment, Overreach stands for many of the vices and social problems rife in Stuart England: usury, disenfranchisement, rapacious greed, and the abuse of power. His greed for wealth and status comes across in lines full of predatory imagery. Unlike Shakespeare's Shylock, a similar character, who is safely located in Venice and, as a Jew, safely categorized as the cultural "Other," Massinger's Overreach is both English through and through and a consummate villain. The nature of his villainy can be said to

betray an impulse toward social realism on Massinger's part that is well ahead of his time. Massinger's penchant for such a quasi-realism has largely contributed to his failure to achieve the fame of some of his contemporaries. Yet he has not disappeared from view and seems poised to reemerge as a favorite for readers less interested in the splendors of lengthy soliloquies than in well-crafted, highly readable plays. Norton's 2002 anthology *English Renaissance Drama*, for example, includes his excellent play *A New Way to Pay Old Debts*.

Scholarship since the 1980s has largely, but not entirely, neglected Massinger. At a time when Shakespeare scholarship has burgeoned into an immense and ever-growing industry, many of the Bard's contemporaries have fallen into a kind of critical limbo, Massinger included. The most insightful recent work on Massinger is largely historicist in nature, concerned with the social, cultural, and political conditions in which plays were produced. Thus, for instance, in his important study *James I and the Politics of Literature* (1983), Jonathan Goldberg sees *The Roman Actor* as a statement about the spectacular nature of Jacobean politics. For James I, kingship was a kind of performance, and playwrights who worked under his rather watchful eye mediated the problems and necessities of absolutism in complex ways. By relocating questions of sovereignty from contemporary England to imperial Rome, Massinger encodes a timely statement about theatricality and power that obliquely criticizes the king.

In an article that assesses Goldberg's account of *The Roman Actor* alongside a competing reading by Annabel Patterson (1984), Andrew James Hartley (2001) suggests that Patterson takes an overly textual approach to the play, one that neglects theater history. Instead, he argues, any account of the ways in which a play comments on the political context of its own era should remain sensitive to questions of performance:

Simply put, Massinger the *play*wright...supplies an important corrective to a body of critical scholarship that, while embracing historical contextualization of the original performances' social and political milieu, remains largely text-centered in the most conservative sense. Massinger's approach to censorship in *The Roman Actor* grounds the issue squarely in a dramatic realm where meaning is not carefully calibrated to enact a kind of semantic guerrilla warfare against the censors, striking indirectly and then vanishing into the cover of apparent orthodoxy, but is deeply unstable, and the very effort expended in the regulation of dramatic meaning could be dangerously counterproductive.

(p. 2)

Hartley's argument grants the playwright a place in the history of dramatic interpretation as well as production, for he sees Massinger rehearsing an argument about the political status of plays that scholars will later take up with varying success. By this account, *The Roman Actor* attests to Massinger's sophisticated understanding of theater as an unstable cultural artifact determined as much by performance as by textual conditions. As Hartley's essay demonstrates, the shift from interpreting early modern drama as texts to an emphasis on performance significantly alters our understanding of their contextual meanings. Indeed scholarly attention to the specificity of theater history that characterizes much recent scholarship on the literature of the Stuart period opens up new possibilities for understanding and appreciating Massinger's plays.

BIOGRAPHY

Piecing together the life of any playwright from Tudor or Stuart England requires some speculation, as relatively little biographical information tends to be available. Much of what is known of Massinger derives from his ongoing familial association with the wealthy Herberts and from the writings—not always completely reliable—of his literary colleagues. The second of five children to Anne and Arthur Massinger, Philip Massinger grew up in rural, southern England in relatively privileged circumstances. His early days in Wiltshire undoubtedly colored his portraits of rural characters arriving in London ignorant of city ways, and his regional upbringing clearly contributed to his later characterizations of servants in

his plays. No playwright except perhaps Richard Brome so fully depicts the speech, habits, and perspectives of servants. The son of a steward entrusted with the management of the estate of a wealthy, aristocratic family, Philip Massinger began life with an intimate understanding of the ways of a great household, an aristocratic family, and its servants. He was also surrounded by literate people at a time when literacy was not nearly as widespread as it is today. His father, Arthur Massinger, was educated at Oxford, having taken a B.A. degree at St. Alban Hall, becoming a fellow of Merton College and taking M.A. degrees from both Oxford and Cambridge.

As the steward of Sir Henry Herbert, the second earl of Pembroke, the elder Massinger interacted with powerful people, and his important position in the Herbert household garnered the patronage of his employer's family for his son. Upon the death of Sir Henry in 1601, his son William succeeded to the title, and it was he who paid the expenses for Philip Massinger to follow his father's footsteps to St. Alban Hall, Oxford, which he entered on May 14, 1602. We know little of Massinger's life at Oxford, but it seems that his interests tended toward literature rather than the more pragmatic study of law, a tendency that may have angered his wealthy patron. Leaving Oxford without having taken a degree (not at all unusual at the time), Massinger arrived in London in 1606. From that point we know nothing of his life for several years, but in 1613 Philip Henslowe, a theatrical entrepreneur and diarist, mentions Philip Massinger by name in his diary. An association with Henslowe is a good sign of a career in theater, and several documents indicate that Massinger was on close terms with him. At this point in his career our playwright collaborated with a number of other writers but made little money.

Massinger's evolution as an independent and prominent playwright was a slow and, by all indications, impoverished one. In the early part of his career he collaborated with such playwrights as Fletcher, Middleton, Rowley, and Dekker, all successful and established dramatists. With Middleton and Rowley he wrote *The Old Law,* and with Nathan Field *The Fatal Dowry.*

With Dekker he wrote *The Virgin Martyr.* His association with Fletcher is especially notable, as many lines in the collected works of Beaumont and Fletcher have been plausibly attributed to Massinger. How far this collaboration in fact went can only be a matter of speculation, but Massinger clearly spent a good deal of his career in the shadow of Fletcher, who had become the leading playwright for the King's Men, the premier playing company in London, after the death of Shakespeare. Fletcher was also highly successful in his collaboration with Francis Beaumont; their collected works, well liked in their own day and widely read even today, form an important part of Stuart drama. When Beaumont married and retired from writing for the stage in 1613, Massinger filled the vacuum and began working regularly with Fletcher. This was not, however, a ticket to immediate fame and fortune.

By this time his circumstances were not of the best. In that year, in debtor's prison along with the writers Nathaniel Field and Robert Daborne, Massinger wrote to Henslowe begging for a loan to be repaid by the proceeds from a play being written in collaboration with Fletcher. There were other, similar appeals: Massinger also wrote to Sir William Herbert, his patron from university days and now lord chamberlain, for financial support. In an era when the patronage of wealthy aristocrats was often critical in launching and sustaining a writer's career, such an appeal was not necessarily an act of desperation but part of being a writer. It is not known whether Massinger's attempts to curry favor with wealthy patrons paid off, and several letters to Henslowe attest to Massinger's ongoing poverty. The London stage was a commercial venture that could, and sometimes did, pay quite well (Shakespeare, for instance, made enough money to purchase a coat of arms for his family). But several appeals for money written by Massinger attest to the financial insecurity of a writer who, in his own lifetime, never managed to become an especially popular playwright.

By 1620 Massinger had begun writing plays on his own in addition to continuing to collaborate. He is mentioned along with some of his colleagues as a good writer by John Taylor in a work called "The Praise of Hemp-Seed." Before long, however, he seems to have switched his allegiance to the Queen's Men, writing three plays for this venue—*The Bondman, The Parliament of Love,* and *The Renegado.* But with Fletcher's death in 1625 he returned to the King's Men and became its principal playwright, with many of his plays performed at the Globe, an open-air theater, and the Blackfriars, an indoor theater. As the successor of Shakespeare and Fletcher in writing for these renowned theaters, Massinger at least achieved a measure of success and was well known to London audiences, players, and playwrights alike. He continued to write for the King's Men between 1630 and 1636, although some of these plays have been lost. *The City Madam* (1632), which reveals a great deal about Caroline culture, is generally considered to be one of the best plays that have survived from among his late works.

Many Elizabethan and Jacobean writers have been the subject of legend and mythology. Misinformation based on the suppositions of subsequent editors and readers frequently contribute to the pseudo-biography of a writer. The life of Shakespeare, for instance, has been mythologized according to the requirements of nationalism, racism, imperialism, and a number of other ideological formations. Massinger is no exception to this tendency. The main myth about his life derives from three of his plays that sympathetically depict Catholic figures. This fact gave rise to the widespread belief that Massinger himself converted to Catholicism at some point in his career, as had the playwright Ben Jonson for a time. The only evidence, if it is, for Massinger's Catholicism is internal to the plays themselves: they portray Catholics in a favorable light. To argue that an author must belong to a group that he chooses to depict in a friendly fashion is hardly compelling at any time, and without any external evidence of Massinger's religious affinities such an argument is merely speculative at best. England during Massinger's lifetime was a staunchly and officially Protestant nation. The Church of England, with the monarch as its spiritual and secular leader, had separated from Rome a century earlier, and to be a Catholic in England was dangerous and unusual. Playwrights, subject to political censorship, could ill afford to publicize their own religious positions. It seems much more likely that Massinger chose the subject matter for his three so-called Catholic plays because of their sensationalism—martyred virgins and crafty Jesuits were objects of fascination for London audiences.

Myths abound where information is scarce, and what we know about Massinger comes from the work of scholars interpreting a small amount of data. But we do know that, for a very capable and at times brilliant playwright, Massinger has remained better known to poets and scholars than to popular audiences. He is often associated with the decline of the golden age of English drama, an art form that had seen its very best days come and go by the time Massinger rose to relative prominence. In part this is due to the fact that his life was immediately followed by the English Civil War, a historical crisis of immense significance. In the early 1640s the London theaters were shut down by the Puritans, a political and religious faction generally hostile to drama. Massinger never found out. He died suddenly some time during the night of March 18, 1640, having gone to bed in good health the night before. He is, appropriately, buried in St. Saviour's Church, Southwark. A suburb of London and a legally defined "liberty" where the laws of the city of London did not reach, Southwark was a major theater and entertainment district and notably the location of the Globe Theatre, home of the King's Men. Massinger lived in Southwark for most of his adult life, and his plays were acted there. His remains are said to be in the same grave as those of John Fletcher.

OVERVIEW OF THE PLAYS

Sixteen plays by Philip Massinger have survived. Two of these are tragedies, the rest comedies and tragicomedies. The list of Massinger's works, excluding those on which he collaborated with other writers (with the exception of two believed to be primarily his), and the theaters (playing companies frequently performed at more than one theater. Thus, the King's Men produced plays at both the Globe, an open-air theater, and the

Blackfriars, an indoor theater) and dates in which they appeared, are as follows:

The Virgin Martyr. (With Thomas Dekker.) King's Men, 1622.
The Duke of Millaine. King's Men, Blackfriars, 1623.
The Unnaturall Combat. King's Men, Globe, 1623.
The Bondman. Princess's Servants, Cockpit in Drury Lane, 1624.
The Parliament of Love. Cockpit, Drury Lane, 1624.
The Roman Actor. King's Men, Blackfriars, 1629.
The Picture. King's Men, Globe and Blackfriars, 1630.
The Renegado. Queen's Men, Phoenix, 1630.
Believe As You List. (Written 1631.)
The Emperour of the East. King's Men, Globe and Blackfriars, 1632.
The Fatal Dowry. (With Nathaniel Field.) King's Men, Blackfriars, 1632.
The Maid of Honour. Queen's Men, Phoenix, 1632.
The City Madam. King's Men, Blackfriars, 1632.
The Guardian. King's Men, Blackfriars, 1633.
A Very Woman. King's Men, Blackfriars, 1633.
A New Way to Pay Old Debts. Queen's Men, Phoenix, 1633.
The Bashful Lover. King's Men, Blackfriars, 1636.
The Great Duke of Florence. Queen's Men, Phoenix, 1636.

In perusing this list, one immediately notices the large number of plays that were performed at the Blackfriars, an indoor, so-called private theater with relatively high-paying audiences. This is significant for several reasons. The two main types of theater in Massinger's era were indoor and outdoor, or private and public, theaters. The Globe was an outdoor theater, as were the Rose, the Phoenix, and the Red Bull. Outdoor theaters were large, open amphitheaters in which audiences from all walks of life tended to mix and mingle. The groundlings immediately in front of the stage paid a penny for a ticket and stood for the entire performance. They often could be quite rowdy. The sheltered galleries behind the stage, where wealthy audience members could sit and be seen by the entire audience, cost more. Inclement weather could shut down a performance, and what we now call special effects were far less integral to the performance of a play than they are to movies today.

In contrast, at indoor theaters like the Blackfriars, an old monastery on the London side of the

Thames, smaller, seated, more educated audiences were the norm, the weather was not a factor, and effects of lighting, music, and machinery could be more heavily emphasized. Playwrights writing for these two types of theaters often crafted their work to fit the venue. Thus the theatrical venue of a play influenced the artistic choices a playwright made: goddesses being lowered from the heavens on chariots, low music playing to create an otherworldly mood, dim lighting to evoke a midnight scene—these were effects much more suitable for an indoor theater. Massinger's plays frequently reflect the taste and cultural knowledge of an educated gentleman, the same class of people who frequented the Blackfriars.

The great bombastic, declamatory tragedies of Christopher Marlowe, like the history plays of Shakespeare, were well suited to the outdoor theaters. Massinger's quieter plays to some extent reflect the popularity of the indoor theaters in the latter half of the Stuart period. They also reflect the predilections of a writer whose talents tended more toward comedy than tragedy. Not only did Massinger write a significantly greater number of comedies than tragedies, his best works are comedies. Perhaps this fact helps to account for Massinger's not being taken as seriously as other playwrights whose talents tended in the direction of tragedy; in the conventional hierarchy of genres, comedy has historically tended to be looked upon as the lesser of the two.

Few playwrights have an equal aptitude for both tragedy and comedy. Tragedy deals with the fortunes of the great and mighty, characters that are caught up by forces they think they can control but cannot. Comedy, in contrast, treats the familiar, the everyday, and the vulgar. Aristotle, in the *Poetics,* claims tragedy as the realm of characters who are above the common run of humanity and sees comedy as the realm of those who are beneath us because they are ridiculous in some way. The novelist Henry Fielding concurred, arguing that comedy deals with the ridiculous, and "the only source of the true ridiculous (as it appears to me) is affectation." By affectation Fielding meant pretending to be what one is not. In his famous preface to *Joseph Andrews* he goes on to argue,

> Now affectation proceeds from one of these two causes; Vanity, or Hypocrisy: for as Vanity puts us on affecting false Characters, in order to purchase Applause; so Hypocrisy sets us on an Endeavour to avoid Censure by concealing our Vices under an Appearance of their opposite Virtues.

Affectation, for Fielding, is the target of comedy, and good comedy must look to expose and ridicule it whenever possible. Fielding looked to Ben Jonson, one of the preeminent playwrights on the London stage at the time of Massinger's arrival there, as his master in the art of exposing affectation; so too did Massinger, whose work owes a good deal to Jonsonian comedy. Comedy has a didactic purpose, as great comedians like Plautus and Jonson well knew. For Jonson, the function of comedy was to expose vice to laughter and thereby chasten it.

To achieve its end, comedy, unlike tragedy, tends to portray commoners, or the vulgar, particularly those who ape their social superiors. Many of Massinger's characters accordingly seem excessively affected and self-deluded. At worst they become caricatures, stage versions of social stereotypes known to Elizabethan and Jacobean readers from the popular genre of "character literature," most famously written by Thomas Overbury. Overburian characters are static moral types, scarcely human in their extreme embodiment of a moral trait. In portraying such characters, Massinger tends to craft his plots as a corrective exercise. In the words of Philip Edwards, "Everyone who writes on Massinger recognizes him as a moralist, a sage and serious man determined to indicate what behavior was acceptable and what was not" ("Massinger the Censor," p. 1). Massinger's frequent depictions of social vices in conjunction with moralizing commentary can offend both puritanical and anti-puritanical sensibilities. For all his moralizing gestures, Massinger was not at heart a moralist. But the "serious" quality of Massinger's comedies is partly a function of comedy itself, which, in its drive to expose and ridicule, has an inherently didactic quality. At its best comedy makes us laugh in a serious—that is to say, a thoughtful, self-reflexive—way, and many of Massinger's works do precisely that.

Massinger's talent for comedy is evident in his best plays—*A New Way to Pay Old Debts, The City Madam*—which expose the vices and vulgarities of recognizable English types: the country gentleman eager to learn the ways of the city, the aging madam pretending to be still young, the fawning servant who imitates his master's manners. As Alfred Hamilton Cruikshank notes in his important study of Massinger (1920), "our poet had a keen eye for social evils, for the man who sells food at famine prices, the encloser of the commons, the usurer, the worker of iron, the cheating tradesman" (p. 12). Massinger's comedic works are marked by a sharp focus on the economic changes of the Stuart period in England and the corresponding destabilization of the social structure. Indeed Massinger's works seem driven by anxiety about the instability of the social order. The plays are particularly concerned with the new liquidity of wealth, often represented by the ease with which a gentlemen can eat up his own resources by profligate living and the malign aid of usurers. The liquidation of property, in particular, is a recurring theme in the plays. As the character Luke puts it in *The City Madam*, "Here lay / a mannor bound fast in a skin of parchment, / The wax continuing hard, the acres melting" (3.3. 35–40). In Massinger's world, there are gentlemen and there are servants; those who are "gentle" derive their status from family genealogy and the ownership of land. When the land is lost, so too is the stability of the world that Massinger portrays.

It is fair to say that Massinger pokes fun at, and frequently punishes, characters who do not know their place or refuse to stay in it. Social climbers (to use a modern idiom), especially ones whose behavior threatens the stability of the traditional English soical structure, fare poorly in Massinger's comedies. Massinger's comedy has a normative force: the representatives of social and cultural change are punished, rendered laughable by their own mutability and triviality. At a time when all kinds of social transformation were occurring throughout England, but particularly in London, it is not surprising that writers of comedy, such as Jonson and Massinger, would find sympathetic audiences among a populace threatened by plague, famine, financial disaster, and change of all varieties. Theatergoers included lawyers, prostitutes, con men, apprentices, petty thieves, brawlers, actors, and poets. The spectacle of characters with glaring moral weaknesses, whose fortunes change suddenly for the better or the worse, appealed to a large part of the London populace. Part of Massinger's interest for modern readers is the detail with which he portrays the language, behavior, anxieties, and antagonisms of characters drawn from a nation on the brink of revolution. Even if his plays tend to suggest a conservative, even reactionary, moral vision, Massinger faced the social world he inhabited with clear eyes and a remarkable ability to convert everyday types and their problems into engaging and often memorable plays.

Instead of attempting an overview of everything Massinger wrote, the remainder of this essay will be devoted to extended interpretive readings of two of Massinger's plays—*A New Way to Pay Old Debts* and *The City Madam*—which are most likely to be read today and which typify his best work. Following these two readings are very brief summaries of several other plays by Massinger that are worthy of special notice.

A NEW WAY TO PAY OLD DEBTS

A carefully crafted comedy of intergenerational and class conflict, *A New Way to Pay Old Debts* has long been Massinger's most popular play. Its villain, Sir Giles Overreach, is one of the great roles of Stuart drama and was performed to great acclaim throughout the Restoration and eighteenth century. Published in a carefully prepared quarto edition in 1632 but written and performed in late 1625 or early 1626, the play does not seem to have been an immediate hit, but it certainly became one before long. Its theatrical success in subsequent generations is rivaled only by the plays of Shakespeare, a fact that gives it a special place in theater history. The renowned actor David Garrick revived the play in 1748, and it subsequently became something of a staple in

PHILIP MASSINGER

English theater. One reason for this remarkable success story is immediately apparent on reading the play: written in clear, relatively simple English, it contains vividly drawn characters, an easily followed plot, and requires no elaborate machinery to produce. The plot is based on an earlier play by Thomas Middleton titled *A Trick to Catch the Old One*, but Massinger transforms his material into something entirely different. Massinger's reputation depends on *A New Way to Pay Old Debts* more than on any other play.

The title reveals much about the major themes of the play—the new, the old, debt, and the ways and means of payment. At a time when social antagonisms—between the rich and the poor, church reformers and religious conservatives, Royalists and Parliamentarians, country and city, monarchy and landed gentry, finance capital and landed interests—were at an all-time high in England, these themes were particularly pressing in everyday English life. Less than a decade after the play's publication, the nation would move into civil war, with drastic results. By writing a play that deals directly with the profligacy of the aristocracy and the rapaciousness of capitalists, Massinger did what Marlowe, Shakespeare, and Webster would not: he engaged in a form of dramatic social realism. In addition to being an entertaining comedy in which the villain is punished and the hero rewarded, *A New Way to Pay Old Debts* is a telling examination of the allegiances that bond the social order. As Katherine Eisaman Maus has pointed out, "the language of indebtedness, credit, and redemption that runs so insistently throughout *A New Way to Pay Old Debts* refers not just to financial transactions but to the more general way past obligations and promises reach into the future, binding people to fulfill them" (*English Renaissance Drama*, p. 1836). Indeed, the play is a meditation on the forms of obligation that create antagonisms as well as alliances by means of business, marriage, and inheritance.

The main thrust of the story is the redemption of a debauched aristocrat and the corresponding downfall of the rapacious villain who has deviously defrauded him of his inheritance. The tension between intra-aristocratic bonds and inter-class antagonism forms the thematic basis of the play, with the characters Frank Wellborn and Sir Giles Overreach as hero and villain. While Overreach bears the title of "Sir," it is only because he has risen in rank socially by means of his acquisitiveness; he is a new man, not a member of the traditional aristocracy. At one point he notes that there has "ever been / More than a feud, a strange antipathy / Between us and true gentry" (2.1.87–89). Wellborn, in contrast, belongs to the traditional, landed (or "true") gentry, a class that was, at the time of the play's creation, experiencing a financial crisis. The specific nature of this crisis is the growth of a market economy and a corresponding unsettling of traditional social bonds. At the start of the play, Wellborn has lost his land and Overreach has acquired it. We encounter both men in starkly contrasting conditions, with Wellborn introduced as a filthy ragamuffin whose only signs of aristocracy are his speech and his martial demeanor, while his antagonist is a successful businessman making the most of his wealth and influence.

The action begins in the countryside in the middle of an argument between Wellborn and the appropriately named alehouse-keeper Tapwell, along with his wife, Froth. Wellborn, in tattered clothes and general disarray, has worn out his welcome, and the tapster will no longer provide for him on credit.

WELLBORN: No booze? Nor no tobacco?

TAPWELL: Not a suck, sir,
    Nor the remainder of a single can
    Left by a drunken porter, all night palled too.

FROTH: Not the dropping of the tap for your
        morning's draft, sire.
    'Tis verity, I assure you.

WELLBORN: Verity, you brach!
    The devil turned precisian? Rogue, what am I?

TAPWELL: Troth, durst I trust you with a look-
        ing glass
    To let you see your trim shape, you would quit
        me
    And take the name [of "rogue"] yourself.

PHILIP MASSINGER

WELLBORN: How, dog?

(1.1.1–9)

We are immediately thrown into an argument between a member of the hereditary aristocracy and a "menial," or servant. The aristocratic Wellborn owes too much at the alehouse where he eats, drinks, and carouses, and when he threatens the tapster with violence he is himself threatened with the law. The spectacle of a social subordinate talking back to an angry but down-at-heels superior is both comical and serious.

We go on to learn, as the argument becomes more heated, of Wellborn's family history and his fall from grace—or wealth, to be more precise. He asks the Tapster, "Am not I he / Whose riots fed and clothed thee? Wert thou not / Born on my father's land, and proud to be / a drudge of his house?" (1.1.26–29). Clearly times have changed and, from Wellborn's perspective, not for the better. The tapster answers him in an interesting way: "What I was, sir, it skills [matters] not. / What you are is apparent" (1.1. 29–30). Whereas Wellborn insists on the acknowledgment of his own status based on familial wealth and the (former) ownership of property, Tapwell insists that the past does not matter, saying, in effect, "it does not matter what I was (a servant), while it is clear what you are (a pauper)." The rest of the play seems bent on proving Tapwell wrong and justifying Wellborn's values. In the scheme of the play, it turns out that the past does matter, as do family lineage and the traditional inheritance of lands and wealth.

Massinger uses this argument between the former master and his former man to lay out the major antagonism in the play, which is not between gentlemen and servants but between what we might call the traditional gentry—those who have inherited wealth and titles—and the upstarts, represented by Overreach. As Tapwell goes on to point out to Wellborn:

Your were then a lord of acres, the prime gallant,
And I your under-butler. Note the change now.
You had a merry time of't—hawks and hounds,
With choice of running horses, mistresses
Of all sorts and all sizes—yet so hot
As their embraces made your lordships [estates] melt.

Which your uncle, Sir Giles Overreach, observing,
Resolving not to lose a drop of 'em
On foolish mortgages, statutes and bonds,
For a while supplied your looseness, and then left you.

(1.1.42–51)

Once the proprietor of a great estate possessed of all the signs of wealth and status, Wellborn now has nothing, due, we believe at this point, to his profligacy. The signs of wealth and privilege—hawks, hounds, horses, and mistresses—formerly defined Wellborn's social standing, whereas now his wealth and property have "melt[ed]" away. In his book *The Crisis of the Aristocracy* (1965), the historian Lawrence Stone describes the prerevolutionary period in England as a time when the English nobility and gentry suffered the financial setbacks and corresponding diminution of social status that we can see in the characterization of Wellborn.

A more timely picture of a Stuart-era aristocrat could hardly have been painted: Wellborn's fallen condition, and Tapwell's relative affluence, reflect the kinds of economic and social change occurring all over England. As the historian Christopher Hill demonstrates in his book *The World Turned Upside Down* (1972), the motif of a wide-scale reversal of fortune, of a topsy-turvy world, was an extremely popular one in Stuart England, when traditional relationships were rapidly being transformed by market conditions and political tumult. Not only Wellborn's poverty but also Tapwell's willingness to talk back to a figure of authority was characteristic of the age. Massinger, of all playwrights, was particularly interested in the dramatic potential of a world turned upside down, for comedy functions by inverting conventional hierarchies and normative relations in order to mock, scrutinize, and reconfigure the image of social relations. In sketching such timely characters as Wellborn and Tapwell, Massinger engages theater with the most pressing issues of his times.

The social crisis of inversion that we see in the opening scene is in fact a situation that Massinger is bent on depicting and correcting in the plot. The opening antagonism between patron and servant contrasts starkly with the following scene, in which we are shown an idealized aristocratic household, that of Lady Allworth, in which the servants compete to do their best by their lady. The son of a steward, Massinger knew a great deal about the lives and household roles of servants, which knowledge is reflected in his depiction of Order the steward, Amble the usher, Furnace the cook, and Watchall the porter. While the comical first scene makes us laugh at a world turned upside down, the humor of the second scene derives from the caricatures of servants who perfectly embody their offices. Lady Allworth, a widow, enjoys all the benefits of wealth that Wellborn has lost; she also represents a principle of economy, of proper management, that contrasts with Wellborn's appearance.

Herein lies the major plot device. Wellborn, cursed and scorned by every servant, public and private, that he comes across, devises a scheme to get back into the good graces of his uncle-by-marriage, Overreach. In an eloquent appeal that lays out the ideology of hereditary aristocracy, Wellborn asks a favor of Lady Allworth.

WELLBORN: Scorn me not, good lady;

> But, as in form you are angelical,
> Imitate the heavenly natures and vouchsafe
> As the least awhile to hear me. You will grant
> The blood that runs in this arm is as noble
> As that which fills your veins; those costly
>   jewels,
> And those rich clothes you wear, your men's
>   observance
> And women's flattery are in you no virtues,
> Nor these rags, with my poverty, in me vices.
> You have a fair name, and, I know, deserve
>   it—
> Yet, lady, I must say, in nothing more
> Than in the pious sorrow you have shown
> For your late husband.

(1.3.88–97)

The gist of Wellborn's appeal is simple: you, lady, are no more noble than I, since we both come from well-born families, and it is your grief for your dead husband, not your wealth or household, that makes you virtuous. These lines are significant both because they articulate the ideology of hereditary aristocracy by locating nobility in blood and virtue, not wealth, and

because they are delivered in elegant iambic pentameter. Wellborn's measured speech in this scene contrasts strikingly with his language in the opening scene, and his mastery of language, as much as his claim of noble blood, establishes him as a man of gentle status. As such he demands a kind of class privilege in gaining Lady Allworth's attention. Particularly interesting is the fact that what he has to say to her works like a charm in winning her over to his side in the conflict with Overreach.

Wellborn goes on to establish a connection between himself and Lady Allworth's deceased husband:

WELLBORN: That husband, madam, was once in his fortune

> Almost as low as I. Want, debts, and quarrels
> Lay heavy on him. Let it not be thought
> A boast in me though I say I relieved him.
> 'Twas I that gave him fashion; mine the sword
> That did on all occasions second his;
> I brought him on and off with honor, lady
> And when in all men's judgments he was sunk,
> And in his own hopes not to be buoyed up,
> I stepped unto him, took him by the hand,
> And set him upright.

(1.3.100–110)

Here Wellborn points out that when Allworth, the lady's late husband, was himself in dire straits, he always found a friend in Wellborn, who acted as his second in duels and other matters of honor. Lady Allworth immediately acknowledges these claims and tells a servant to give Wellborn a hundred pounds, thereby offering to transform social capital (Wellborn's status as a gentleman) into economic capital, or money. But Wellborn refuses to accept it.

Wellborn asks not for money but the appearance of Lady Allworth's interest in him as a suitor. He is not yet ready to convert his social capital into money; instead, she will provide him with new clothes and the use of her household (and servants). Wellborn proceeds to invite Marall, one of Overreach's henchmen, to dine with him at Lady Allworth's. After the meal, during which Lady Allworth treats Wellborn with great respect and signs of affection, Marall reports to Overreach the change in Wellborn's fortunes, announcing that Lady Allworth intends to marry Wellborn. Overreach later invites Lady Allworth and Wellborn to dinner at his own house, hoping that they will be financial prey for him in the future. Wellborn's plot is hatched.

After many comical episodes and scenes in which Overreach betrays his own villainy time and again, Wellborn's scheme works so effectively that eventually he not only redeems himself by winning back his wealth and lands from Overreach but accomplishes much else that is good. He is instrumental in marrying off Overreach's daughter (who is not at all like her father) to the worthy young son of Lady Allworth, punishing Overreach's toadies for their crimes, and helping Lady Allworth herself to get over her widow's grief and wed anew.

The variety of villainy that characterizes Overreach makes him an unforgettable and perennially popular character. Several great Restoration and eighteenth-century actors were famous for playing him. One is tempted to call him Shakespearean, as he has something of Shylock about him and something of Richard III. He ruins honest landowners, bullies his subordinates, and gleefully entraps all comers in ruinous financial schemes. At one point he threatens his daughter with his sword. He is not merely a typical, if somewhat extreme, stage villain, however, since Massinger is careful to portray him as the representative of unscrupulous financial innovation and the will to radical social change. Overreach thus personifies the times. In fact, Massinger based his character on the career of Sir Giles Mompesson, a financial impresario and villain who was prosecuted for various kinds of fraud in the 1620s. Like his namesake in Massinger's play, the real-life Sir Giles made a fortune by ruining others in financial swindles of various kinds.

In addition to personifying the vices and villains of Caroline England, Overreach also has some deliciously evil lines, such as the following:

Methinks I hear already knights and ladies
Say, "Sir Giles Overreach, how is it with

Your honorable daughter? Has Her Honor
Slept well tonight?" Or, "Will Her Honor please
To accept this monkey? Dog? Or parakeet?"
(This is state in ladies), or "My eldest son
To be her page, and wait upon her trencher?"
My ends, my ends are compassed! Then for Wellborn
And the lands. Were he once married to the widow,
I have him here. I can scarce contain myself,
I am so full of joy, nay, joy all over!"

(5.1.131–141)

In reading these lines one can see why the role appealed to many actors. In imagining himself as a grandee, Overreach performs little skits that would permit virtuoso performances of self-involvement and ill will.

In the end, the topsy-turvy world of the opening scene is itself inverted, reestablishing the social world of the play as a traditional and hierarchical one of the kind that Stuart-era Britons looked back to with nostalgia. The hereditary wealth of blue bloods is returned to them (to Wellborn in particular), and the upstart Overreach is ruined and thereby returned to a position of powerlessness and lack of status. Lady Allworth marries the noble Lord Lovell, while young Allworth will marry Overreach's daughter Margaret, thereby redeeming her and all that she represents from the threatening position of interloper and assimilating her into the landed gentry. While the rest of the characters are bound together in the traditional reordering of society by marriage that ends most comedies of the era, Overreach goes mad and finds himself tied up and committed to Bedlam, the madhouse. There is a good deal about this ending to trouble the modern reader with regard to its imaginative undoing of the historical developments of the early seventeenth century and its profoundly traditional reordering of society. The neat and tidy wrapping-up of social antagonisms Massinger offers up in his play was in fact, historically speaking, an unraveling of social cohesion: the English Revolution, not a restructured traditional society, would end the Stuart period in England. But Massinger's play, in running against the historical grain, reveals much about the era in which it was created and in doing so offers a socially engaged and theatrically engaging spectacle.

PHILIP MASSINGER

THE CITY MADAM

Much like *A New Way,* a play that it resembles in several respects, *The City Madam* depicts a world of vanity and affectation, of changing fortunes and changing times. In both plays the curative effect of comedy is stressed: the plot is an elaborate structure in which the hypocrisy of characters is eventually exposed and disciplined. As one editor of the play has remarked, "vanity and hypocrisy are...the dual themes with which Massinger's play is concerned" (Hoy, p. xiii). The plot revolves around the home of Sir John Frugal, who has a wife, two daughters, one brother, and two apprentices attached to his household, but no male heir. His wife is hideously vain, convinced at fifty that she is still attractive and young and continually in need of reassurance from her two daughters and many attendants. Her daughters, because they have no brother, hope to inherit a great deal from their father and thus to marry someone of greater wealth and social rank than they. Because of Frugal's uxoriousness, his wife and daughters have taken control of the household and live like the upper aristocracy, denying themselves no luxury. Meanwhile Sir John works hard to maintain the wealth and standing of his family.

Sir John's younger brother Luke, having once been a "gallant" entirely given to entertainment— "No meeting at the horse race, cocking, hunting, / Shooting, or bowling, at which Master Luke / Was not principal gamester, and companion / For the nobility"—has since fallen on hard times (1.2.114–117). He has been redeemed from debtor's prison by his brother and now lives in the household as a kind of servant to the women of the house, who abuse him and constantly remind him that he should be grateful. In the course of the play he becomes villainous, and it is the spectacle of his transformation that holds most of the play's intrigue. Luke's villainy runs deep, and he is the perfect object for the rigors of comedy: a thoroughgoing hypocrite. He pretends to be what he is not, fooling those around him (except his knowing brother) into believing him honest, all the while deceiving and manipulating them, and in so doing he becomes the main target of Massinger's comedic critique.

The play is as interesting for its perspective on social antagonisms as it is for the well-crafted plot. When two characters, one a wealthy country bumpkin and the other an urban gentleman, begin a duel by insulting each other's class identity, their insults sketch a picture of two competing social classes, the nouveau riche and old money. Maurice, the representative of the latter class, accuses Plenty, the arriviste, of having been made by his tailor, as if there were no substance behind his appearance of being a gentleman. But Plenty replies with his own barbs directed at impecunious members of the old nobility:

> MAURICE: What a fine man
> Hath your tailor made you!
>
> PLENTY: 'Tis quite contrary,
>
> I have made my tailor, for my clothes are paid for
> As soon as put on, a sin your man of title
> Is seldom guilty of, but heaven forgive it.
> I have other faults, too, very incident
> To a plain gentleman. I eat my venison
> With my neighbors in the country, and present not
> My pheasants, partridges, and grouse to the usurer,
> Nor ever yet paid brokage to his scrivener.
> I flatter not my mercer's wife, nor feast her
> With the first cherries, or peascods, to prepare me
> Credit with her husband, when I come to London.
> The wool of my sheep, or a score or two of fat oxen
> In Smithfield, give me money for my expenses.
> I can make my wife a jointure of such lands too
> As are not encumber'd, no annuity
> Or statute lying on 'em. This I can do,
> An it please your future honor, and why therefore
> You should forbid my being a suitor with you
> My dullness apprehends not
>
> (1.2.44–64)

Country bumpkin (or "clown," as Maurice calls him) or not, Plenty proves well able to defend himself verbally in this exchange. He boasts of his own wealth and financial honesty, and in doing so directs several implied barbs at his seemingly more sophisticated adversary.

Maurice's reply is so directly insulting that we can be assured Plenty has struck home. He responds by insulting the Plenty family, calling them commoners and suggesting that they are not "gentle" at all.

I have heard you, sir, and in my patience shown
Too much of the stoic's. But to parley further,
Or answer your gross jeers, would write me coward.
This only: thy great grandfather was a butcher,
And his son a grazier; thy sire, constable
Of the hundred, and thou the first of your dunghill
Created gentleman

(1.2.65–71)

In these lines, Maurice points out in no uncertain terms that Plenty can hardly be considered a gentleman with such a family lineage. But his insults are so direct and crass that he threatens to demean himself, and in dueling at the gate of Sir John Frugal they are both threatening their own reputations. When Frugal intervenes and makes the adversaries shake hands, they part ways reconciled and free to court Frugal's daughters, Anne and Mary. This scene suggests a somewhat different perspective than that of *A New Way* for the scene suggests that two classes, old money and nouveau riche, can operate on the same level. One can readily imagine the reactions of an audience whose members must have included many such men.

Once reconciled, the two young men go together to court Anne and Mary. Unfortunately the two young women are completely under the sway of their egotistical mother, who is herself guided by a ridiculous astrologer. Maurice and Plenty must woo their women through the intermediary forces of mother and astrologer, who devise an intricate prenuptial list of requirements that would shift power utterly to the women and strip the men of any power over money or household management, reducing them to the status of servants. The wooers become enraged by these terms and, united in their anger, resolve to travel together for three years.

Meanwhile, Luke has begun to corrupt the apprentices, Young Goldwire and Tradewell, who work in his brother's house and have much of the management of the family fortune. Intelligently, Frugal decides, with the help of his friend Lord Lacy, to test his brother and to teach his wife and daughters a lesson. He pretends to run off to a monastery, dead to the world, and leave his brother his entire fortune. When Lord Lacy pretends to read his friend Frugal's will to Lady Frugal, Anne, Mary, and Luke, the female characters are horrified to learn that they have been completely disinherited. Everything goes to Luke who, Cinderella-like, exults in this sudden, drastic change of fortune. His brother's household and wealth, he believes, is now his.

Of course, this is only a ruse. Massinger employs the plot device, used by Shakespeare in *Measure for Measure,* of a feigned disappearance or death by a powerful figure who then dons a disguise to observe the behavior of those he has left in charge of his estate. Sir John has not gone to a monastery and, disguised as a Native American, proceeds to spy on his own household in order to observe the conduct of his family.

Ever the dissimulator, Luke responds to the news of his inheritance with saccharine assurances of his goodwill. His address to Lord Lacy and the Frugal women is worth quoting at length for its smooth language.

LUKE: [to Lady Frugal, Anne, Mary]   Pray you rise,
   And rise with this assurance, I am still,
   As I was of late, your creature; and if rais'd
   In any thing, 'tis in my power to serve you,
   My will is still the same.—[To Lord Lacy] O my lord!
   This heap of wealth which you possess me of,
   Which to a worldly man had been a blessing,
   And to the messenger might with justice challenge
   A kind of adoration, is to me
   A curse I cannot thank you for; and much less
   Rejoice in that tranquility of mind
   My brother's vows must purchase. I have made
   A dear exchange with him. He now enjoys
   My peace and poverty, the trouble of

PHILIP MASSINGER

His wealth conferr'd on me, and that a burden
Too heavy for my weak shoulders.

(3.2.107–122)

Such elegant protestations of a pure mind notwithstanding, Luke proceeds to embark on a binge of spending and crime that shows his true colors. Like Shakespeare's Edmund in *King Lear,* Luke represents an opportunistic form of ill will that the playwright does his best to expose and eradicate. The rest of the plot will be an exercise in giving Luke enough rope to hang himself, as Sir John and the audience watch him grow more and more monstrous in his dishonesty. The pleasure in watching or reading the play lies in the knowledge that both Sir John and the audience know what Luke is about, and that the generic structure of comedy demands his ultimate downfall.

THE VIRGIN MARTYR

One of the allegedly Catholic plays written by Massinger, *The Virgin Martyr* takes as its material the persecution of the Christians and the martyrdom of Dorothea, an early Christian killed during the reign of the emperor Diocletian. Written at a time when religious conflict on the European continent was at its height, this play deals with religious subjects in striking ways. First, it resembles the medieval miracle plays that formed part of the foundation for English Renaissance drama. As in any number of medieval plays, the Devil himself takes the stage, both in human form and with supernatural trappings. An angel also appears onstage, first in human disguise and then in the form of a supernatural being. Comic scenes illustrating the grossness and prominence of the Devil in matters of the flesh also evoke ancient traditions of liturgical drama. Massinger frequently betrays the influence of medieval dramatic practice in his plays, particularly in the naming of characters, which often seems nearly or fully allegorical. This play exhibits this tendency more than most.

The story of the martyrdom of Saint Dorothea in 303 AD would not immediately appear to lend itself to good theater. But Massinger makes the most of the traditional emblem of the saint, the roses and fruit that adorn her in most images. According to the legend Dorothea was mocked on her way to execution by a judge's secretary named Theophilus, who asked her to send him some fruit and roses from Paradise. After her death, an angel brings him the fruit and flowers, at which point he is immediately converted to Christianity. In choosing to dramatize what Catholics considered a miracle and Protestants, generally speaking, a legend, Massinger transgressed some of the most powerful conventional religious codes of his era and nation.

The Virgin Martyr is visually striking for a number of reasons. Emblems of holiness, such as a cross of flowers and a basket of fruit invested with heavenly nourishment, give it a Baroque feel. But the visual feast is not entirely pleasurable. While the play appears to have been popular with contemporary audiences, modern readers are not likely to enjoy the spectacle of Dorothea being tortured onstage, her hair pulled and her body kicked and hit with cudgels. Part of the theatrical appeal of such scenes lies in the heroine's miraculous preservation from harm, for her guardian angel (cleverly named Angelo) stays by her side and prevents her pain. Other forms of supernatural intervention include a tormentor's falling into a fit when attempting to sexually molest Dorothea and another's conversion from his diabolical ways upon eating of a magical basket of fruit. Dorothea dies at the end of the fourth act, but instead of an anticlimactic finish, the fifth act is a visual feast.

At the end of the play the transfiguration of the martyred virgins is represented by their taking the stage in white robes. It is worth considering the stage directions, which give a clue as to how much more viewable than readable this play must have been: "Enter Dorothea in a white robe, crownes upon her head, led in by Angels, Antoninus, Caliste, and Christeta, following, all in white, but lesse glorious, the Angell with a Crowne for him" (Cruikshank, p. 33). As Cruikshank summarizes the sensational ending, "at the sight of the glorious vision the persecutor dies, converted to the Christian faith, and the evil

194

spirit, which has prompted his cruel acts, sinks to his own place with thunder and lightning, while Diocletian and his court look on in amazement." In its aestheticization of religious history and its adaptation of religious emblems in visually striking ways, *The Virgin Martyr* is an undeniably powerful drama.

THE RENEGADO

Religious topics are also dealt with in striking and historically daring ways in *The Renegado*. The fact that its hero, Francisco, is a Jesuit priest is itself remarkable, as the Jesuits were widely considered to be a dangerous group of spies intent on undermining the Church of England. In the wake of the Gunpowder Plot of 1605, the memory of which was still quite fresh in English minds two decades later, such a hero seems a highly unlikely choice. The Gunpowder Plot, a Catholic conspiracy to blow up King James I along with the assembled Lords and Commons in the Houses of Parliament, was prevented with the timely capture of Guy Fawkes, who was to have lit the powder. Although the plot was nipped in the bud, such a theatrical production must have been both politically risky and scandalous enough to pull in large audiences, and *The Renegado* was indeed a popular play.

In addition to the religious identity of the protagonist, who could hardly have been more strongly identified as a Catholic, several incidents have provided fodder for the belief that the play reveals Massinger's own religious leanings. These include the immediate and total conversion of a character upon baptism, the magical power of an amulet in protecting the chastity of a lady in captivity, and the idealized portrayal of Francisco as a heroic, self-abnegating, and ultimately triumphant moral leader. As a foray into English notions of the Mediterranean world at a time when the Ottoman Empire was dominant and the Catholic countries on its shores perpetually beleaguered by powerful Muslim states, *The Renegado* is a historical document of note. It is also a well-crafted and entertaining play.

Selected Bibliography

WORKS OF PHILIP MASSINGER

INDIVIDUAL PLAYS IN PRINT

The City Madam. Edited by Cyrus Hoy. Lincoln: University of Nebraska Press, 1964.

Beggars Bush. With John Fletcher. Edited by John H. Dorenkamp. The Hague and Paris: Mouton, 1967.

The Fatal Dowry. With Nathan Field. Edited by Thomas Alexander Dunn. Berkeley: University of California Press, 1969.

The Old Law. With Thomas Middleton and William Rowley. Edited by Catherine M. Shaw. New York: Garland Publishing, 1982.

The Bondman: An Antient Storie. Edited by Benjamin Townley Spencer. Princeton, N.J.: Princeton University Press for the University of Cincinnati, 1990. (Edition originally published 1932.)

A New Way to Pay Old Debts. London: A. & C. Black, 1993.

The Custom of the Country. With John Fletcher. Edited by Nick De Somogyi. New York: Theatre Arts Books/ Routlege in association with Globe Education, 1999.

Three Turk Plays from Early Modern England: Selimus, A Christian Turned Turk, and The Renegado. Edited by Daniel J. Vitkus and Robert Daborne. New York: Columbia University Press, 2000.

A New Way to Pay Old Debts. In *English Renaissance Drama.* Edited by David Bevington et al. New York: Norton, 2002. Pp. 1833–1904.

The Roman Actor. London: Nick Hern, 2002.

COLLECTED WORKS

The Plays of Philip Massinger: In Four Volumes. Edited by William Gifford. New York: AMS Press, 1966. (Edition originally published in 1813.)

The Poems of Philip Massinger, with Critical Notes. Edited by Donald S. Lawless. Ball State Monograph 13. Muncie, Ind.: Ball State University, 1968.

The Plays and Poems of Philip Massinger. Edited by Philip Edwards and Colin Gibson. Oxford: Clarendon Press, 1976.

The Selected Plays of Philip Massinger. Edited by Colin Gibson. Cambridge, U.K. and New York: Cambridge University Press, 1978.

CRITICAL AND BIOGRAPHICAL STUDIES

Adler, Doris. *Philip Massinger.* Boston: Twayne, 1987.

Bamford, Karen. "Sexual Violence in *The Queen of*

Corinth." In *Other Voices, Other Views: Expanding the Canon in English Renaissance Studies.* Edited by Helen Ostovich, Mary V. Silcox, and Graham Roebuck. Newark: University of Delaware Press, 1999. Pp. 234-252.

Bentley, Gerald Eades. *The Jacobean and Caroline Stage.* 7 vols. Oxford: Oxford University Press, 1966–1967.

Bentley, Gerald Eades, ed. *The Seventeenth Century Stage.* Chicago: University of Chicago Press, 1968.

Clark, Ira. *Professional Playwrights: Massinger, Ford, Shirley, & Brome.* Lexington: University Press of Kentucky, 1992.

———. "The Power of Integrity in Massinger's Women." In *The Renaissance Englishwoman in Print: Counterbalancing the Canon.* Edited by Anne M. Haselkorn and Betty S. Travitsky. Amherst: University of Massachusetts Press, 1990.

Cruikshank, A. H. *Philip Massinger.* Oxford: Blackwell, 1920.

Dunn, T. A. *Philip Massinger: The Man and the Playwright.* Edinburgh: Thomas Nelson, 1957.

Elam, Keir. *The Semiotics of Theater and Drama.* London and New York: Routledge, 1980.

Eliot, T. S. *Elizabethan Essays.* London: Faber & Faber, 1934.

Fulton, Thomas C. "'The True and Naturall Constitution of that Mixed Government': Massinger's *The Bondman* and the Influence of Dutch Republicanism." *Studies in Philology* 99, no. 2:152–177 (spring 2002).

Garrett, Martin, ed. *Massinger: The Critical Heritage.* London and New York: Routledge, 1991.

Goldberg, Jonathan. *James I and the Politics of Literature.* Baltimore: Johns Hopkins University Press, 1983.

Gurr, Andrew. *Playgoing in Shakespeare's London.* Cambridge, U.K.: Cambridge University Press, 1987.

———. *The Shakespearean Stage.* 3d ed. Cambridge, U.K.: Cambridge University Press, 1992.

Hartley, Andrew James. "Philip Massinger's *The Roman Actor* and the Semiotics of Censored Theater." *English Literary History* 68, no. 2:359–376 (summer 2001).

Howard, Douglas, ed. *Philip Massinger: A Critical Reassessment.* Cambridge, U.K.: Cambridge University Press, 1985.

Huebert, Ronald. "'An Artificial Way to Grieve': The Forsaken Woman in Beaumont and Fletcher, Massinger, and Ford." *English Literary History* 44, no. 4:601–621 (winter 1977).

Lawless, Donald S. *Philip Massinger and His Associates.* Ball State Monograph 10. Muncie, IN: Ball State University Press, 1967.

Maxwell, Baldwin. *Studies in Beaumont, Fletcher, and Massinger.* Chapel Hill: University of North Carolina Press, 1939.

Nakayama, Randall. "Redressing Wrongs." *Renaissance Drama* 30:25–41 (1999–2001).

Otten, Elizabeth Spalding. "Massinger's Sexual Society." In *Comedy from Shakespeare to Sheridan: Change and Continuity in the English and European Dramatic Tradition.* Edited by A. R. Braunmuller and J. C. Bulman. Newark: University of Delaware Press, 1986. Pp. 188–189.

Paster, Gail Kern. "Quomodo, Sir Giles, and Triangular Desire: Social Aspiration in Middleton and Massinger." In *Comedy from Shakespeare to Sheridan: Change and Continuity in the English and European Dramatic Tradition.* Edited by A. R. Braunmuller and J. C. Bulman. Newark: University of Delaware Press, 1986. Pp. 165-178.

Patterson, Annabel. *Censorship and Interpretation: The Conditions of Writing and Reading in Early Modern England.* Madison: University of Wisconsin Press, 1984.

Worthen, William B. *The Idea of the Actor: Drama and the Ethics of Performance.* Princeton, N.J.: Princeton University Press, 1984.

REDMOND O'HANLON

(1947–)

James P. Austin

THE BRITISH NATURALIST, professor, and renowned travel writer Redmond Douglas O'Hanlon was born on June 5, 1947, in the rural town of Dorset, in Wiltshire, England, and raised in a vicarage. His father, William Douglas O'Hanlon, was a canon in the Church of England; his mother, Katherine Stenhouse O'Hanlon, was, by contrast, an actress. This parental duo may seem an unlikely pair to raise a child who grew up to become one of England's best-known modern naturalists and literary travel writers. But O'Hanlon's father, a former missionary in Abyssinia (today known as Ethiopia), kept a large collection of reference books in the vicarage. The young and curious O'Hanlon liked to sneak into his father's office for peeks at these reference books (entitled, among other things, *The Birds of Tropical West Africa*), and in this peeking was born O'Hanlon's future career as a Charles Darwin scholar, naturalist, travel writer, and traveler into unmapped, unknown, and potentially dangerous regions of the planet.

Redmond O'Hanlon began his academic career at Oxford University in 1965 intending to study English literature, but it was not until he was asked to leave the university in 1967 for working on a racy novel that his personal life and literary goals began to take more mature shape. On April 6, 1967, he married Belinda Margaret Ingham Harty, the director of her own fashion house. A year later, having focused his academic interests on Charles Darwin—a marked difference from his father's religious worldview, but seemingly influenced by the older man's curiosity about the natural world—he regained entrance into Oxford and earned his bachelor's degree from Merton College there in 1969. O'Hanlon pressed forward in his academic career, earning three more degrees from Oxford: a master of philosophy in 1971, a master of arts in 1974, and a doctor of philosophy in 1977. His dissertation, which studied Darwin's impact on Joseph Conrad's fiction, was published several years later as his first book, *Joseph Conrad and Charles Darwin: The Influence of Scientific Thought on Conrad's Fiction* (1984), and it subsequently received the Scottish Arts Council Award.

While earning his degrees from Oxford, O'Hanlon held a number of notable posts that enabled the completion of his education and augmented his course of study. He was a senior scholar at Oxford's St. Antony's College while completing his MA from 1971 to 1974, and an Alistair Horne Research Fellow in 1974, the first of three years he spent in doctoral studies at Oxford. From 1970 to 1974 O'Hanlon served on the literature panel of the Arts Council of Great Britain, and in 1971 he became the director of Annabelinda Ltd., his wife's fashion house, which was named after their daughter, Puffin Annabelinda.

Upon completing his Ph.D in 1977, O'Hanlon took a postdoctoral position teaching English literature at Oxford, but he found that his own interests did not correspond with the curriculum or the interests of his students, who were required to learn about more contemporary writers like T. S. Eliot rather than such O'Hanlon favorites as Charles Darwin and Joseph Conrad. When he was sacked, O'Hanlon turned to the London *Times Literary Supplement,* becoming its natural history editor in 1981. In 1982, O'Hanlon contributed to *Charles Darwin, 1809–1882: A Centennial Commemoration,* edited by Roger Chapman. And in 1983 he made the first of his rugged travels into dangerous and foreign territory—both geographically and culturally. What began as a snorkeling expedition to Borneo with his friend the poet James Fenton became the beginning of a new direction in O'Hanlon's career, which would combine his love of nature with his encyclopedic knowledge of and passion for the natural world.

Signaling a theme that resurfaces in his other travel books, O'Hanlon and Fenton were drawn in by the danger of Borneo, in particular by a region of jungle that had not been traveled by Westerners since 1926. The book *Into the Heart of Borneo* (1984) catalogs their journey in search of a rare and perhaps extinct Borneo rhinoceros, but it is not mere travelogue or anthropology. Unlike the narratives of many foregoing European travel writers, O'Hanlon's first-person account is not stilted or overly formal, even as it retains the reserve and sardonic humor that characterizes the British. The account is often humorous, delivered with candor, weaving O'Hanlon's considerable knowledge of the region with an outsider's unflappable curiosity and bearing recognizable traits of other British writers who have traveled into unknown and dangerous regions far from home. Distinct from the genre, however, is O'Hanlon's increasing willingness to be wonderstruck by the cultures and peoples he encounters; his narratives rely less on anthropological study as they progress and evolve. Indeed, O'Hanlon is no cold cultural analyst.

In 1985, O'Hanlon returned to St. Antony's College at Oxford as a senior visitor, a position he would hold for years to come. In the meantime he continued cementing his reputation as one of England's most prominent and adventurous travel writers. In 1988 he published *In Trouble Again: A Journey Between the Orinoco and the Amazon* in England, and it appeared in America a year later. His partner for this adventure is the ill-suited Simon Stockton, a casino manager in London who abandons the trip midway. For the journey he takes in 1989, which is recounted in *No Mercy: A Journey to the Heart of the Congo* (1997), O'Hanlon returns to the academic realm by asking an American colleague, Lary Shaffer, to march with him into unmapped forests in the middle of the Congo in search of a rare bird and a Loch Ness Monster–like creature—a journey that Shaffer also departs from early, and which has a strong spiritual, emotional, and cultural impact upon O'Hanlon. This book completes the triumvirate of travel narratives that find O'Hanlon in some faraway jungle, traveling largely wild and uninhabited lands. So, too, does this book represent the end of a startling change in O'Hanlon as a traveler—from observer to participant. O'Hanlon's fourth travel narrative, *Trawler: A Journey Through the North Atlantic,* was published by Knopf in 2005. The book is a departure of sorts, with O'Hanlon leaving behind dense jungles in favor of the frigid and choppy North Atlantic—but the danger to his life is no less.

Throughout his career O'Hanlon has been widely published in London's *Sunday Times,* the *New York Times,* the *Los Angeles Times, Granta, Essays in Criticism,* and *Tatler.* He is also a member and a fellow of the Royal Geographical Society and belongs to the Society for the Bibliography of Natural History. Writing about his work has appeared, among other places, in the *New York Review of Books* (1985), *Time* (1985), the *Times Literary Supplement* (1984), the *Washington Post* (1985), *The Sewanee Review* (1997), and *Sports Illustrated* (1998).

INTO THE HEART OF BORNEO

The first of O'Hanlon's adventuresome travel narratives establishes a structure and pattern the following two narratives, *In Trouble Again* and *No Mercy,* at once imitate and evolve from. He opens with what will become his traditional laying-down of the gauntlet, describing for readers various bacteria and animals of Borneo and the particular havoc they can wreak on a human body. There are "yellow and blackwater and dengue fevers, malaria, cholera, typhoid, rabies, hepatitis, tuberculosis" (p. 1), not to mention an abundance of leeches, parasitic worms that attack the human bloodstream, Wagler's pit viper, and wild-boar ticks that attach themselves to human genitalia.

Another recognizable trait established in the early going is O'Hanlon's cavalier sense of humor, an unwillingness to take seriously what he invites readers to take seriously. He suggests solving these problems by wearing a rubber suit and steel waders, until he counters himself by describing the heat of the Bornean jungles, "120°F in the shade, and the humidity is 98 per cent" (p. 1). O'Hanlon also invokes books on the region, listing them at length until he slyly comments that they "offered no immediate solution" to his quandary: how to prepare for the many hardships he will face in the jungle.

The purpose of this journey to Borneo is to attempt to find "a Borneo rhinoceros or two still about on the higher slopes" (p. 10), which even the security officer at their layover in Singapore finds ludicrous and unnecessarily dangerous. Nevertheless at the next airport, in Kuching, a city in Borneo on the South China Sea, O'Hanlon's handgun is confiscated; the security officer there promises it will be kept until O'Hanlon returns for it.

Because O'Hanlon and his sidekick, the renowned poet James Fenton, arrive in Borneo during the Chinese New Year, they are forced to remain in Kuching for two days before they can ferry into the interior along the Rajang River to Kapit, "the real starting-point for [their] journey proper" (p. 18). O'Hanlon wakes from a nap at the town of Sibu, noticing that the "now-wooded banks had edged to within a mile of each other" (p. 18); indeed, traveling into the interior means traveling into the jungle.

Once arrived in Kapit, O'Hanlon (who leaves Fenton relaxing in their hotel) visits "Immigration and The Police" (p. 21) carrying with him a letter from the Senior Proctor of Oxford University assuring the reader that O'Hanlon and Fenton are "travelling in Borneo for Scientific purposes" (p. 21). Asking permission to travel to Mount Tiban in search of the Borneo rhinoceros, O'Hanlon is initially rebuffed, but when he presents the letter from Oxford, his difficulties disappear, and the Bornean officials grant permission. Moreover, they arrange for their Tuai Rumah—a headman or chief—named Dana, to accompany O'Hanlon and Fenton; Dana in turn hires two young men named Leon and Inghai to assist in the journey. After these arrangements are made, the governmental executives invite the Westerners to meet the three guides and to "get drunk together." "Come and buy us lots of beer," they urge (p. 22).

A few days later the group waves farewell to "thirty or forty children…gathered on the bank" (p. 31) and sets off down the river where none of them, not even Dana, has ever been. O'Hanlon notes an intense change in the river: "The river itself began to turn and twist, too, the banks behind us appearing to merge together into one vast and impenetrable thicket, shutting us in from behind just as the trees ahead stepped aside a meagre pace or two to let the river swirl down ahead" (p. 31). The river's complicated path becomes a factor not long after O'Hanlon first observes its confusing, winding nature. When the group must avoid a waterfall by changing paths into a tributary, "the river-bed suddenly dip[s]" just as the rowers are assuming new positions, sending Fenton over the edge and into a powerful whirlpool and underwater rocks. Leon saves Fenton, who begins hyperventilating until Inghai reveals happily that he has also saved Fenton's hat, which had fallen off during his ordeal. It makes everybody laugh and breaks the tension, but for days afterward O'Hanlon is visited by nightmares of Fenton's sister Chotty coming after him as if Fenton actually had drowned. In one dream she comes at O'Hanlon with a knife; in another she approaches him holding a meat hammer in one hand and a thorny stick in the other.

Not long after Fenton's near drowning, the group encounters the Kenyah, a tribe Leon describes as "not our peoples" (p. 59). When the chief's son formally invites the group to disembark and set foot on their land, they gladly do so. This development excites O'Hanlon, who surmises that they must be approaching the dead center of Borneo, where the primitive Ukit live and where he might discover "whether or no the Borneo rhinoceros was still to be found" (p. 61).

At the same time, O'Hanlon, having been warned by a friend back in Britain that native tribes in Borneo expect their guests to drink heavily and to sing and dance for their entertainment, goes about attempting to trick Fenton into singing in front of the tribal celebration to be held in honor of their visit: "Look—don't tell James, because…he's so modest. But, in England, he's *very* famous. He is the poet of all the tribe, the chief poet in all England. His *whole life* is making songs. That's what he does all day…. He *sings songs.* And he dances. He knows *all* the dances" (p. 61).

That night at the celebration in the Kenyahs' longhouse O'Hanlon's innocent deception does not go as planned. A tribal warrior begins the festivities by dancing in front of the assembled crowd, imitating a hunt while wearing a huge mask supposedly made of "tufts of hair which, we were led to believe, had long ago been taken from the scalps of heads cut off in battle" (pp. 66–67). When the warrior finishes, the mask is handed to O'Hanlon, and much to his dismay he realizes that he is expected to dance. Moreover it seems that Fenton caught wind of O'Hanlon's scheme and turned the tables on him. "You'll be all right," the drunken Fenton assures him. "Just do your thing. Whatever it is" (p. 67).

O'Hanlon, forced to perform for the crowd wearing the mask worn by the previous dancer, attempts to imitate the same dance, with much less success. "There was an uproar in the longhouse" as he dances, cramps, and falls to the floor, and an old man in the audience "fell off his seat" (pp. 67–68). After O'Hanlon completes his hilarious display, Fenton takes to the stage, and "to the beat of the big string he launched into a rhyming ballad, a long spontaneous poem about our coming from a far country…and [about] the hospitality of the strongest, the most beautiful people in all the world, the Kenyah of Nanga Sinyut" (p. 69). After Fenton's improvisational performance the envious village clown takes to the stage, imitating Fenton by putting on "an imaginary hat and…fasten[ing] his imaginary shirt-cuffs. He looked about, unconcerned, like a great chief." The clown follows this mimetic performance by imitating O'Hanlon, becoming "a Neanderthaler, struggling in the river…unable to walk and push at the same time." Leon recognizes the performance: "It's Redmon! He very fats!" (p. 70).

After their visit to the Kenyah, the group begins marching through the jungle, away from the "dazzling sunlight of the river-side"; this heat had an "all-enclosing airless clamminess that radiated from the damp leaves, the slippery humus, the great boles of the trees" (p. 115).

Other difficulties also arise deep within the jungle. Their mosquito nets, which had provided ample nighttime protection throughout their journey, are penetrated by tiny black bugs. But the bugs wake only O'Hanlon and Fenton; the three natives remain "fast asleep, untroubled" (p. 105). Later the group—and in particular O'Hanlon and Fenton—is set upon by jungle leeches. O'Hanlon finds them "edging up [his] trousers, looping up towards [his] knees with alternate placements of their anterior and posterior suckers." He looks down at his boots and sees them "moving towards [him] across the jungle floor from every angle." (p. 117) He even notices leeches "rearing up and sniffing at [him] from the trees" (p. 118).

Compounding these natural dangers, the group finally enters the territory of the Ukit, known as the most savage people in all of Borneo, whose lands may also be home to the Borneo rhinoceros that O'Hanlon wants so much to find. In order to inform any passing Ukit that their presence is peaceful and temporary, Dana "cut a yard-length of sapling and carefully peeled back strips of bark from its centre. He then hacked down a branch, trimmed it altogether clean of bark, spliced its top, set it in the ground, and placed his rod of curlicues on top" (p. 119). Nonetheless the group begins traveling armed front and rear as a precaution in case the Ukit do not receive the messages Dana leaves for them.

The journey—and the book—ends when O'Hanlon and his group reach the Ukit and find a resolution, of sorts, regarding the Borneo rhinoceros. The Ukit turn out not to be savage or dangerous at all—their first request of O'Hanlon and Fenton is to be taught to dance like Westerners do in discos. O'Hanlon first asks the Ukit if they have seen any of the rare birds he has studied in *Mammals of Borneo,* a book which he produces for their inspection. While none of them have seen the birds, an old man does recognize the photograph of the Borneo rhinoceros, telling O'Hanlon that he had killed eight of them as a young man near the Tiban Mountain. The book ends bluntly with: "Our search had ended" (p. 183), a statement that is more complicated than it initially may seem. In the most literal respect the search had not ended, because O'Hanlon himself does not sight the rhinoceros with his own eyes. At the same time, the statement implies that a secondhand account of the rhinoceros may be the closest he will come to witnessing it himself; it further implies that he has received his answer, and the Borneo rhinoceros was eradicated long ago at the hands of hunters like the old Ukit man.

The closing statement opens itself and the entire book to further questions as well. If the search both has and has not ended, what was O'Hanlon searching for in the first place? How can you imply that your goals have been at once met and frustrated? *Into the Heart of Borneo* begs these questions, answering them that it was the search itself and not its ultimate goal that most mattered to O'Hanlon. The process of searching, the camaraderie among O'Hanlon and his companions were significant. The rigors of jungle travel, of inhabiting—if briefly—a foreign land: these too were important to O'Hanlon. *Into the Heart of Borneo* leaves these impressions, asking questions it does not answer. But O'Hanlon responds to his own questions in subsequent travel narratives. Taken together the three books represent a progression: *Into the Heart of Borneo* comprises the first chapter of a greater journey for Redmond O'Hanlon. In future travels he is less inclined to stick to his original plans, even as those plans become more ambitious and less structured. He also more thoroughly investigates his fascination with the cultures of the civilized natives he encounters, next in South America and finally in the Congo.

IN TROUBLE AGAIN

O'Hanlon begins the narrative of his journey to South America by recounting the many difficulties he faced in finding a suitable companion, and by cataloging the potential natural dangers the formidable South American jungle presents. He attempts to convince James Fenton to join him in South America, to which Fenton replies that he *"would not come with you to High Wycombe"* (p. 4), site of some of the most beautiful pastoral countryside in England. Undeterred, O'Hanlon approaches another friend—and an-

other poet—Craig Raine, but Raine also begs off. This leaves O'Hanlon with only one option, his old friend the casino manager Simon Stockton, whose primary qualification seems to be that he does not know what exactly he is getting into—despite his claim to have read *Into the Heart of Borneo*.

O'Hanlon visits Stockton at his London casino and later at his home, which was "dramatically distinguished from the row of look-alikes because Simon had painted it purple all over, and an enormous blown-up photograph of his head entirely blocked off the left upstairs window" (p. 9). Given also Simon's preference for fine liquor, fine food, and women, O'Hanlon arrives at an understandable apprehension once Simon officially signs on for the journey: "it gradually dawned on me that it was too late to change anything: I was not just going to the jungle, I was going to the jungle with Simon" (p. 13). Aside from this momentary pause, however, O'Hanlon never again mentions his choice to bring Simon along. He rather seems to enjoy being perpetually better prepared than Simon—a stark departure from *Into the Heart of Borneo*'s Fenton who not only holds his own under difficult circumstances but is openly admired by the guides and the Kenyah. The inclusion of Simon on this journey also indicates that O'Hanlon wants to take more chances.

Here at the start of his tale O'Hanlon predictably describes many potential dangers awaiting him and Simon in the South American jungles. O'Hanlon again lays down the gauntlet as he did in *Into the Heart of Borneo*. But he provides much more detail in *In Trouble Again*. Aside from the mundane varieties of malaria, typhoid, rabies, hepatitis, and tuberculosis awaiting him, O'Hanlon tells us of "one or two very special extras." These include Chagas' disease, "carried by various species of Assassin bugs which bite you on the face or neck and then, gorged, defecate next to the puncture. When you scratch the resulting itch you rub the droppings and their cargo of protozoa into your bloodstream; between one and twenty years later you begin to die from incurable damage to the heart and brain" (pp. 1–2).

REDMOND O'HANLON

There are other vile illnesses and microscopic predators. O'Hanlon tells us that onchocerciasis is an infestation of worms that migrate to the eyeballs, that leishmaniasis is carried by sandflies and eats away the warm extremities if not quickly treated. But O'Hanlon's greatest fear, "which swam most persistently into my dreams on troubled nights" (p. 2), was the toothpick-fish, which lives in the Amazons and will swim into the urethra of a male human should he decide to urinate while standing in the river. The toothpick fish will then "stick out a set of retrorse spines. Nothing can be done.... You must get to a hospital before your bladder bursts; you must ask a surgeon to cut off your penis" (p. 2).

It is facing these ominous conditions that O'Hanlon arrives with Simon in South America. Although the precise nature of his mission is not entirely settled, O'Hanlon has some ideas. He takes the advice of another friend, Charlie Brewer-Carias, a photographer who had also declined O'Hanlon's offer to come with him into the South American jungles. Charlie does, however, help supply O'Hanlon's journey with a vague shape while at the same time expressing his thoughts on the foolhardiness of the venture he proposes—which is that O'Hanlon and Simon begin their journey by traveling "north up the Rio Negro, turn east into the Casiquiare; and then swing south down the Pasimoni which narrows into the Baria.... And here...the river divides into a thousand tributaries. It disappears entirely beneath the red, the forest. You can say goodbye to sunlight" (p. 19). Later O'Hanlon informs Simon that they are attempting a journey that has confounded experts and not been successfully completed for hundreds of years. To make matters still more complicated, they will attempt to reach Neblina, the highest mountain in Brazil and the biggest mountain in South America. Simon understandably is not happy.

The prospective terminus of the journey is Brazil, and Charlie assures O'Hanlon that "there'll be plenty of water. You should be able to get through to Brazil" (p. 19). Perhaps even more daunting than the circuitous, dangerous route into Brazil is the Yanomami, one of the last uncivilized peoples on earth, known to anthropologists for their brutality and their use of a psychedelic drug called yoppo, which they "blast up each others' noses through a metre-long tube. It...produces severe shock in the ear, nose and throat system and the pain blows your head off" (p. 20). Not surprisingly O'Hanlon is intrigued and decides that he would like to find the Yanomami if possible. It is a possibility that becomes reality.

Once the journey is underway, almost nothing goes according to plan. Simon, of course, does not exactly take to hiking through the jungle or gliding through it on a dugout in the rivers. O'Hanlon notes that he looks thinner and has assumed an expression similar to that of his friend Douglas a few weeks before his suicide: "In the evenings he had taken to lying in his hammock, saying nothing, not moving, staring into the trees" (p. 111). There are more ominous harbingers of Simon's eventual departure. Shortly into the journey Simon is already oppressed by the changelessness of the jungle's geography. "I thought the jungle would *change* every day. You never told me it just went on and on the same forever.... Something terrible is going to happen" (p. 74). Simon reveals himself further unprepared for the rigors of jungle life when the group, on a search for food, kills a cayman and cracks open the bony plates protecting its stomach—only to find the intact corpse of a small monkey inside. Simon recoils in horror.

Further exacerbating Simon's alarm, the group manages to get lost in the complex network of river tributaries about which Charlie had warned O'Hanlon. At one point the group approaches an area where "the vegetation had been cleared right down the stream. Someone had come here before us. We had been forestalled. It was all too late. I felt cold down my back, dull and blank in the head, weary, old" (p. 113). In a darkly humorous turn, the inexperienced Simon is the first to recognize that they themselves had cleared the land away and that they are going in circles. And only Simon considers this a serious development. "We're lost...it'll take months. *We're lost.* ...You've got to let me go, Redmond. I don't trust myself. *I shall do something terrible*" (p. 113). That "something terrible" turns out to be a volcanic eruption over a bottle of ketchup, which Simon decides he simply must have to accompany his dinner one night:

> "Come on, Galvis," said Simon, banging his mess tin with his spoon, "it's the eighth day—where's my tomato ketchup?"
>
> Juan translated.
>
> "Galvis says it is in the boat," said Juan. "And it is only the seventh day. You divided the stores. It is your rule. You must stick to it."
>
> "It's the eighth day," said Simon, doggedly, still banging his tin, "and I want Galvis to get my tomato ketchup...."
>
> "It's only a bottle of tomato ketchup," I said.
>
> "*Precisely,*" said Simon.
>
> (p. 116)

The exchange ends when Simon screams into the forest, "Where's-my-tom-ato-ketch-up" (p. 117), and nothing and nobody replies.

For five days following Simon's outburst it rains without pause, forcing O'Hanlon to scrap his original plan to negotiate the intricate jungle tributaries and arrive finally in Brazil. As his guide Chimo assures him, "Reymono, don't you worry...we will find you other problems" (p. 120). The revised plan calls for the group to find a man who lives on the Siapa River, who is friends with a dangerous tribe called the Chloris, who are in turn friendly with the Yanomami—a prospect which excites O'Hanlon and frightens Simon enough that he departs for home as soon as they are no longer lost. The group manages to retrace its original steps, even though downpours have swollen the rivers and made it difficult for them to recognize landmarks.

After a series of intervening visits to other villages, the group finally departs in search of "the Fierce People" (p. 142), and O'Hanlon gets his opportunity to encounter the Yanomami. Along the way, however, O'Hanlon and company happen upon a tribe, based alongside a river, that copies many of the Yanomami's appearances and customs. The guide Juan informs O'Hanlon that these are not real Yanomami: "The Yanomami are not a river people.... [These people] copy everything.... You'll see" (p. 165). Nevertheless,

O'Hanlon is intrigued by the quasi-Yanomami, perhaps because they also use the mind-altering drug yoppo. O'Hanlon, of course, is interested in sampling the drug and does so one night with the natives and his group, despite the pleas of his guides, who urge him not to be a "fool" or "make more stupids" (p. 168). He watches Jarivanau, a native, administer the drug to other natives, realizing only after witnessing the violent reactions of the recipients that it is now his turn to ingest the drug: "Jarivanau blew the dust into my left nostril. Someone at once seemed to hit me just above the bridge of the nose with a small log.... Someone else eased a burning stick down my throat. My lungs filled with hot ash. There was no water, anywhere" (p. 169). After a blast up his right nostril, his "ear, nose and throat system went into shock.... And then suddenly I was gulping oxygen through a clogging goo of ejaculating sinuses; I mouthed for air as yoppo-stained snot and mucus from nasal recesses whose existence I had never suspected poured out of my nostrils and on down my chin and chest" (pp. 169–170).

After this crushing pain subsides, the drug begins taking effect. The Yanomami "seemed the most welcoming, the most peaceful people on earth," and O'Hanlon feels as though he "could sit on the mud floor, happily, for ever." His eyes finally alight on Jarivanau's wife, whom O'Hanlon calls the "matchstick girl." He "admired her, slowly. [He] stroked, in imagination, her cropped neck" (p. 170). He imagines kissing her and making love to her, and he imagines that her "most enormous, encouraging, kind smile" is an unspoken statement of her mutual feelings for him. O'Hanlon imagines talking to her, inviting her to slip outside together for a brief encounter. His drug-induced reverie is snapped when Chimo demands that they retire for the night. As they climb about their dugout, Chimo admonishes O'Hanlon, informing him that "you were staring at Jariavanu's woman for *several hours*" (p. 172).

The following day, despite growing protests and warnings from his more experienced guides, O'Hanlon and his group go in search of the "proper" Yanomami who live deep in the jungle, away from the rivers. In so doing O'Hanlon skirts a fine line between being adventurous and just plain foolish. As they advance further into the jungle, the guides and other hired help grow skittish. When they enter lands that are not of the guides, Chimo warns O'Hanlon, "Anything could happen. We are not welcome here. It is not our country" (p. 199). Uncertain but playing as if undaunted, O'Hanlon coaxes the group to come along, to proceed with him and Jarivanau, who had agreed to lead them into Yanomami territory.

When they finally arrive in a large opening representing the entrance to the Yanomami camp, an excited Jarivanau, eager to see his friends, races into the opening and fires his gun into the air in greeting. When the Yanomami emerge, O'Hanlon coaxes their acceptance by producing a Polaroid camera and snapping photographs of them. The fact of his acceptance among the Yanomami is confirmed when Jarivanau and the chief produce a yoppo pipe, and again O'Hanlon partakes.

O'Hanlon and his group return to their base camp after staying with the Yanomami for a few days. O'Hanlon thinks that "everything should have changed" (p. 239) after his visit with the Yanomami, but finds everything the same—in circumstances and in perception. Like his other travel narratives, *In Trouble Again* does not give its readers the comfort of a decompressing exit. The book ends with O'Hanlon still immersed in the foreign land—gazing at the egg of an African nighthawk, a find which should excite him because "very few...had been described." But O'Hanlon is still influenced by his mind-bending visit to the Yanomami, and like them, he is "ignorant momentarily...of the laws of science." Instead he just gapes, observing "that suddenly the world seemed freshly made and the future ceased to matter" (p. 258). In that respect everything has changed for O'Hanlon, even if momentarily, and evidence suggests that this is the real mission he had sought all along, whether he understood it or not. His narrative-length preoccupation with the Yanomami never falters; only the formal mission of sailing to Brazil is forgotten.

In Trouble Again represents a bridge between *Into the Heart of Borneo* and *No Mercy: A Journey to the Heart of the Congo*. In this second installment, O'Hanlon's goal is more ambitious and difficult—made more so by his selection of Simon as a travel mate. He also participates more freely and perhaps more recklessly with the foreign culture he visits. Not only that, but the Yanomami are much less "civilized" and familiar to a Westerner than the Kenyah and Ukit whom O'Hanlon encountered in Borneo. Indeed, the Yanomami have had almost no contact with the outside world. Their reputation is more brutal, as is their choice of drugs—the Kenyah prefer to drink heavily while the Yanomami ingest a violently mind-altering drug through long pipes into their noses. *Into the Heart of Borneo* ends when O'Hanlon achieves his purpose; *In Trouble Again* ends when O'Hanlon momentarily loses his scientific self, forgetting the daring mission at which he has not quite succeeded, and only in this forgetfulness does he achieve a sense of satisfaction. This forgetfulness of self will continue and reach its terminus in *No Mercy*.

NO MERCY

Originally published in Great Britain in a slightly different form under the title *Congo Journey* (1996), *No Mercy: A Journey to the Heart of the Congo* (1997) is O'Hanlon's own journey into a heart of darkness first evoked by one of his favorite writers, Joseph Conrad. This masterwork also represents a drastic departure from O'Hanlon's earlier travel narratives about Borneo and the Amazon River region of South America. Indeed, the journey into the Congo had a deep psychological impact upon O'Hanlon, a distinct and unanticipated difference from his earlier adventures, during which O'Hanlon never loses his candor or sense of self, despite the journeys' hardships. In this adventure, however, he is deeply affected by the vast, dense jungles and the culture of sorcery and mysticism prevalent in the Congo, and unlike his previous adventures, in which he always maintains a foreigner's distance even as he interacts within his surroundings, O'Hanlon finds himself drawn to the culture, inexplicitly believing in it even as his native guides have difficulty understanding or believing in this transformation, just as O'Hanlon has difficulty articulating it to his hosts.

The opening part of the book bears strong resemblance to O'Hanlon's earlier works. As in them *No Mercy* begins with a stated purpose: to travel into a largely unmapped and untraveled portion of the Congo, the final goal being to arrive at Lake Télé, which is known throughout the Congo as the residence of Mokélé-mbembé, a dinosaur-like creature resembling the Loch Ness monster. A secondary goal, which corresponds with O'Hanlon's interest in ornithology, is to observe the Pennant-winged nightjar, a rare bird of Africa that O'Hanlon had seen only in a bird book as a child. Also O'Hanlon wishes to visit a village of pygmies, and ultimately the expedition makes a lengthy detour to satisfy this desire.

Despite the warnings of government officials and his many guides (who ultimately do take him to the lake in order to profit from him), O'Hanlon is initially undaunted by the wilds of the African jungle. Indeed, the book opens like the others: the mortal danger of the journey is given first say. O'Hanlon and his companion Lary Shaffer are informed in the very first chapter that they will not survive their proposed six-month journey. As in O'Hanlon's earlier travel narratives, the dangers of the exotic land are narrated in dry, matter-of-fact fashion—and then readers watch as O'Hanlon and his companion barrel forward into unspeakable danger, emerging battered and scratched, but victorious and none the worse for wear.

Unique among his narratives, however, the danger in *No Mercy* is initially articulated by a *féticheuse*, a fortune-teller of the Congo. The threats she foresees are much different than those of the natural world with which O'Hanlon regales the reader at the beginning of his previous narratives. In those cases the risk, while exotic and violent, existed tangibly, as dangers of the natural world. Being an ardent and knowledgeable naturalist, O'Hanlon seems to revel in the threats of nature. To him these very real dangers are wondrous aspects of the foreign land, to be accounted for, surely, but also to be savored. But the first notice of danger in *No Mercy* is not of the temporal realm; it is a warning of unforeseen dangers that lurk beyond the reach of O'Hanlon's knowledge and comprehension. Of course, O'Hanlon is not dissuaded by the féticheuse's dire warning; it is his choice to open the narrative at this meeting that foreshadows the circumstances of his transformation within the jungles of the Congo.

His foil, the American Shaffer, is another story. Like James Fenton and Simon Stockton before him, Lary Shaffer serves a necessary function, for he not only gives O'Hanlon another English speaker with whom to banter, but he also stands diametrically opposite O'Hanlon's initially gleeful outlook on the journey into the jungles. Instead the professor of animal psychology from upstate New York is in constant conflict with both his surroundings and O'Hanlon himself; strangely enough, the conflicted nature of Shaffer's presence acts as the normalizing influence in the narrative. Initially it is through Shaffer's observations and interactions with the Congo that readers can see themselves in the book. Like O'Hanlon's previous foils, Shaffer has been brought on the trip with a number of legitimate reservations, and his resistance to the many dangers—caused by both a shady Communist government and the untamed jungle—not only approximates a reader's response to the Congo, but serves as a contrast to O'Hanlon's childlike enthusiasm. Moreover, the narrative gradually reveals Shaffer as the more sensible and cautious of the two—he is consistently prickly and resistant to his surroundings, untrusting of the people, as it could be argued he should be. This contrasting perspective not only deepens the degree to which the reader understands O'Hanlon's more cavalier approach to the journey, but also keeps the writer on an even keel as the two are guided more deeply into the jungles. That Shaffer's early departure from the journey corresponds with O'Hanlon's transformation is no accident.

Nonetheless, the narrative's early focus is on the completion of the intended mission. The difficulties of arranging their journey are most evident when, upon first arrival, O'Hanlon and Shaffer must negotiate with government officials in order to obtain the proper permission and guides. Shaffer is indignant and on guard; O'Hanlon plays the role of experienced traveler who enjoys even this transaction: for him it is all part of the journey. At this early juncture O'Hanlon also takes care to articulate some of the many dangers awaiting them in the jungle. As he and Shaffer make their formal requests for permission, the government officials warn them of "two very common and very dangerous snakes of the forest floor, the Forest cobra and the Gaboon viper," mentioning in passing the possibility of being attacked by packs of sea snakes. Shaffer, of course, is horrified by this revelation, while O'Hanlon jokes that he has morphine and so they at least will "die happy." Moreover, the government officials warn that "the northern province is not fully under the control of [the] Government. We have reports of bands of poachers, armed with automatic weapons from the Sudan, who hunt elephant in our forests, and they kill our people, too" (p. 30). Additional peril posed by the natural world is divulged by Marcellin, a government official and a leader of their expedition: swamp waters up to the waist, attacking bees, leopards stalking camp at night, leg ulcers, body fungus, and tsetse flies at riverbanks (p. 45).

Despite this long list of killer animals, violent poachers and guerrilla fighters, and other unpleasant hygiene issues awaiting them in the jungles, what separates the Congo from Borneo and South America is the recurring presence of the mystical realm, an area within which O'Hanlon increasingly finds himself participating, a harbinger of the true difficulties that lie ahead, beyond his immediate view. In response to O'Hanlon's declaration that he must find the pygmies, Marcellin tells him:

> They say there's a Frenchman in the north. He's sixty years old. He was a journalist in Paris. He came out here to write an article on the pygmies— all about the pygmies who live just like our early Stone Age ancestors lived 100,000, maybe 250,000, years ago. Well, so they do, but he fell in love with a pygmy girl and he married her and he stayed up there. He's their Chief…. So now the Frenchman is rich. But his money is no good to him. He thinks he's king of the pygmies. But really they have him

as a prisoner. When the moon is full he howls like a dog. All night.

(p. 39)

O'Hanlon offers no direct response to Marcellin's story, instead observing Shaffer as he stares at light reflected from his beer mug "as if it were some inner pointer, loaded with meaning" (p. 39). It is significant that O'Hanlon observes meaning after Marcellin's story but that he fails to understand it. He does not recognize the portent within a story of a Western journalist who loses his sense of self in the jungles of the Congo, but it is a danger he will have to face himself.

In O'Hanlon's other books the purpose of the mission corresponds closely with the book's conclusion. Not so in this case. As O'Hanlon and Shaffer travel through the jungle, fatigue sets in. Shaffer, in his role as foil to O'Hanlon's straight man, complains. O'Hanlon seems entertained by the difficulty—again a recognizable aspect of his travel work. Indeed he is drawn to the opportunity to witness firsthand what he teaches and studies back in England. The Congolese jungles, however, offer unanticipated difficulties for O'Hanlon that drastically alter the course of his mission and the book. Nevertheless he pursues and succeeds in his original missions, although Shaffer—perhaps sensing the difficulties ahead—opts out of the journey at the end of the second chapter, before they approach Lake Télé, choosing to return to America. "A million miles away," he says, "I dimly remember I have a job. I'm a professor, you know" (p. 274). The following chapter, entitled "Mokélé-Mbembé" after the mythical creature, narrates what should have been one of the book's ultimate moments. But it begins nearly two hundred pages before the end, indicating that the end O'Hanlon had originally anticipated is not the end at all.

Indeed Lake Télé, while impressive in its natural beauty, is most impressive to O'Hanlon because he begins to feel the influence of the Congolese culture within which he has been immersed. O'Hanlon believes that the legendary monster of the lake might actually exist—a bow, perhaps to his homeland's own Loch Ness monster—or at the very least that his guides may believe in the physical reality of the monster. The monster never appears, but their stay at the lake is uneasy nonetheless. Even after O'Hanlon is told by his guides that they had lied about having seen the monster—for the purposes of procuring a lucrative fee from O'Hanlon—Marcellin, one of the most experienced guides on the expedition, hides himself in his tent for the entirety of their stay at the lake. "*I hate this place*," he tells O'Hanlon. "I don't feel well. I've had enough" (p. 366). The aura and specter of the legendary monster are best articulated when O'Hanlon asks Doubla, another of the guides, if he has ever seen Mokélé-mbembé: "What a stupid question," says Doubla. "Mokélé-mbembé is not an animal like a gorilla or a python. And [it] is not a sacred animal. It doesn't appear to people. It is an animal of mystery. It exists because we imagine it. But to see it—never. You don't *see* it" (p. 372).

The meaning of Doubla's statement is illustrated by the apparent effect the lake has on O'Hanlon. It begins when the guide Manou claims he "can see the spirits in [O'Hanlon's] face" (p. 365) and continues when O'Hanlon finds himself relying on the magical "powers" of a fetish he acquired earlier in the book. According to the culture, a proper fetish (each person has one individually created) can protect a person from unforeseen danger. He begins "compulsively thrusting [his] right hand into [his] pocket, checking that the small bundle of fur and bone and string, the fetish, was still there.... I hate this nonsense...this is magical thinking" (p. 379). It is not until the end of the book that O'Hanlon comes to learn that his compulsiveness toward the fetish is not necessarily out of character for him at all. In the moment, however, O'Hanlon resists his inclination toward the fetish, perhaps feeling uncivilized.

His sense of what is civilized, however, grows increasingly blurry. His guides argue with him, critiquing O'Hanlon's Western worldview. For instance, they criticize Christianity as phony, claiming that it asks questions it refuses to answer: why would a god who supposedly loves everybody allow such suffering to exist in the world, particularly in the poor countries of Africa? O'Hanlon's guides accept that gods are

vengeful and unfair and that appeasement is the only way to protect oneself. Moreover Marcellin points out rather bluntly another significant contradiction: "Really, the whites are terrible. They brought the guns here and now they say don't kill your wildlife. They're cruel one minute, sentimental the next. And it makes me sick" (p. 387). These contradictions embodied by O'Hanlon take on heightened significance in the context of the Congo, and O'Hanlon feels himself drifting away from his home culture and sense of self. Even his discovery of the rare Pennant-winged nightjar, one of the primary reasons for making the journey in the first place, fails to grip him. It is a brief flash of excitement, barely a page in length.

The reason for O'Hanlon's lack of engagement with the rare bird is that another animal—a baby gorilla—grabs his interest and takes all his attention. Not coincidentally, just before O'Hanlon is introduced to the baby gorilla, one of his guides again notes that he's "gone crazy.... I've seen it before. White men like you—something happens out there in the forest. Every time. They get a kind of madness in there. They can't leave" (p. 384). Of course, O'Hanlon does not see his behavior as mad—though he resists and surprises himself—nor does he view it as entirely sensible either. Until the end of the book, O'Hanlon views his behavior as appropriate: not at all Congolese but not necessarily British.

O'Hanlon receives the baby gorilla as a gift from an injured man he helps. At first the creature is only a "bundle of black hard against [his] chest." Its "two little arms hugged [him] tight" (p. 384). The gorilla cowers against his chest as the others discuss eating it, and O'Hanlon announces that he's keeping the gorilla. The guides think he is crazy, and they attempt to change his mind, but O'Hanlon goes so far as to refuse to cage it, stating that the gorilla will be sleeping with him at night. The guides find this news disgusting, and warn O'Hanlon that the gorilla will not let him wash himself.

None of this is any matter to O'Hanlon, who refuses to bathe while the gorilla is in his care. As a result his body and clothes become moldy; nobody wants to be near him, including the cashier who sells him a bottle of whiskey. O'Hanlon observes these reactions but seems unconcerned by them. He is instead compelled by the complex relationship he has forged with the gorilla, which seems to have no one meaning attached to it. In one respect it is like the fetish, a thing to keep O'Hanlon safe from the arbitrary dangers of this foreign land, a shield of sorts. The gorilla also represents a stark departure from O'Hanlon's educated observations of the natural world. In this book and others, O'Hanlon's experience of the natural world is distilled by his educational preparation for the journey—he sights an animal and identifies it, sharing with the reader his considerable knowledge of it. In the case of the gorilla, it is precisely the opposite. He forges an intimate relationship with the gorilla—whose mother had to be killed for the baby to be captured—caring for it, protecting it from others. His keen observational eye now focuses on the particulars of his interaction with the gorilla. He does not seem to care that others find his behavior abhorrent, and it is a vast departure from the detached, gregarious O'Hanlon who first began his journeys in *Into the Heart of Borneo*.

Even before encountering the baby gorilla O'Hanlon was feeling the effects of his extended stay in the Congo. At the lake he envisions a conversation with Samale, a spirit of Congolese religion, who goads him:

> You're infected. You're marked forever…. My dear new friend, it's the language of fetish…It's like the language of marriage as Tolstoy describes it. Marriage of many years. A language that has no use for your logic, no need for your premises and deductions and conclusions. It's the language of dream, my friend, unreal and incoherent. It contradicts itself, all the time, and in everything except the emotion that underlies the dream—and that feeling is powerful, and clear, and true.
>
> (p. 379)

This conversation is a sign of things to come, particularly O'Hanlon's relationship with the baby gorilla. He is drawn to the gorilla for reasons he never attempts to understand—for which he is ridiculed by his Congolese guides. It matters only that he is compelled to protect and

ultimately rescue the animal from a certain and premature death.

More than any other thing—and certainly more than the stated mission of his Congo journey—*No Mercy* explores the disorienting experience of O'Hanlon in the African jungles. By the end of the book he does not seem even to recognize himself and yet does not seem bothered by it. What does bother him, however, is when the guide Manou "outs" O'Hanlon as a sorcerer back in Britain. Manou feels guilty about having cast a spell upon another guide, whose father subsequently dies. When O'Hanlon attempts to put Manou at ease by saying that nature does not work that way—in so doing returning to the educated, rational man who began the journey—Manou does not believe him. He references Shaffer, long since returned to America, who had shared with Manou the peculiar contents of O'Hanlon's home in Britain: the burnt foot of a dead friend. According to Manou, this led Shaffer to speculate about what other bizarre objects might be within the walls of O'Hanlon's home—leopards' teeth, gorilla skulls, and so on.

O'Hanlon, seemingly regaining his old self, is appalled, but Manou does not understand: "Why be ashamed? It's African! It's sensible! It's a fetish house!" Manou has been convinced that O'Hanlon "look[s] white—but you're an African…. And that is why you went crazy, and why you wanted to walk in the forest, with no food, for ever and ever, all the way to Ouesso" (p. 452). To the Congolese, O'Hanlon is a changed man—a change that cannot be undone, a change that alters the signification of everything about him, even his home in Britain and what he collects there. O'Hanlon gives the reader no comfort in this realization: the book comes to a rest with O'Hanlon still in the Congo, only beginning to wrestle with the implications of his journey.

TRAWLER

O'Hanlon's next travel narrative seems to represent both a change in direction and a continuing elevation of O'Hanlon's preoccupation with dangerous, other-cultural experiences.

In the book, O'Hanlon leaves behind the jungles of Borneo, South America, and Africa—perhaps because he has taken those experiences as far as he can, both in terms of literary achievement and in significantly risking his life and his sense of identity. Instead, O'Hanlon books passage on a trawler sailing from Stromness in the Orkney Islands to Greenland. Naturally there is tension involved in such a journey—not only are the waters dangerous, but the captain and crew are deeply in debt. This forces them to take risks they might not normally take, including steering the boat through a junior hurricane and making long journeys to find the fish they are not able to find in the North Sea or Icelandic waters.

Needless to say, O'Hanlon is safe in the water from the self-warping claustrophobia of the jungle. At the same time, the danger does not seem diminished; it has simply changed form and in some ways seems greater than in the jungles. In this way *Trawler* continues elevating the daring and tension of O'Hanlon's travel narratives. A journey through icy waters is probably not a journey the O'Hanlon of *Into the Heart of Borneo* would have completed—or even attempted in the first place. In that book, O'Hanlon's mission remains a prominent focus of the narrative, even as he grows curious about the cultures he encounters. It is not until *In Trouble Again* and, finally, *No Mercy* that O'Hanlon gives himself over to the cultures he visits; the line between traveler/anthropologist and participant becomes blurred, causing O'Hanlon to become perhaps a less objective narrator, but also a more engaging and involved one. *Trawler* seems a continuation of this progress.

SYNTHESIS

As we have seen, O'Hanlon's career as a travel writer, which marked a drastic departure from his previous work as an academic, begins with an account of his journey in 1983 to Borneo, continues in *In Trouble Again,* reaches a terminus in *No Mercy,* and strikes out in new directions in *Trawler.* O'Hanlon's Borneo journey remains relatively faithful to the original purpose of the trip—finding some trace of the Borneo rhinoceros deep within jungles relatively untraveled by Westerners. But O'Hanlon and Fenton's stay with the Kenyah, which forms a substantial bulk in the middle of the book, implies O'Hanlon's curiosity with the other cultures he encounters in his travels. But his contact with the Kenyah hardly represents integration within their culture. O'Hanlon is painfully reminded of his "otherness" in his embarrassing dance at the longhouse. Besides, their stay with the Kenyah occurs in the middle of the book, implying that it is only a stop in a greater journey that has its conclusion elsewhere. That conclusion comes only when O'Hanlon hears, finally, news of the Borneo rhinoceros that seems to indicate that it has indeed become extinct. Moreover, the journey's success is predicated upon O'Hanlon's association with Oxford, and proceeds for that reason through official channels; the government supplies O'Hanlon and Fenton with Dana and the other guides. It was, at the time, the most daring journey of O'Hanlon's life, but it made him curious for more perilous journeys, with fewer safety valves and less predictability.

In Trouble Again exhibits O'Hanlon's increasing interest in and preoccupation with jungle cultures. The mission of the journey is not as rigidly defined as in *Into the Heart of Borneo;* the actual mission is not determined until O'Hanlon and Simon arrive in South America. That the journey is difficult and dangerous only encourages O'Hanlon, who clearly wants to demand more from himself in South America than he did in Borneo. When the original mission is foiled, it does not discourage O'Hanlon so much as grant him further opportunity to locate a still more daring mission, that of finding the famously violent Yanomami. When he finally does encounter the Yanomami, O'Hanlon is eager to participate in their yoppo-ingesting tradition, despite the pleas of his more experienced guides not to do it. That he stared at Jarivanau's wife for several hours while under the influence of yoppo was also disconcerting to his guides, but O'Hanlon does not seem bothered. Again, he appears to enjoy this close, edgy contact with the Yanomami.

The choice of Simon as a companion for his South American journey also indicates that O'Hanlon was eager to take more risks. In Borneo, Fenton was as steady as they come, despite nearly losing his life by drowning. Fenton also proved to be an asset with the Kenyah, impressing them with an impromptu poem. Simon had none of these traits and was presented in the book as wholly unprepared for the rigors of the jungle, inadequate as a partner. Still, his horrified reactions to the jungle stand in stark contrast to O'Hanlon's and are more in line with how O'Hanlon's readers may react to what they face in the jungle. O'Hanlon's choice of foil, in this book and in others, seems to fit the nature of his immersion.

This is certainly the case in *No Mercy,* when Shaffer is so openly dubious about O'Hanlon's well-being—and thus his own safety—that he chooses to leave, even though he (unlike Simon) maintains his sanity. As he watches O'Hanlon gradually become immersed within Congolese culture, he comes to realize that his departure from the Congo is the only sane thing to do. Shaffer ultimately acts as the outside "eye," a role that had been filled by O'Hanlon in his earlier narratives when he was still something of an outsider. O'Hanlon never actually *becomes* Congolese, of course, but he becomes immersed within the culture like never before. He acquires a fetish—which he kept thereafter—and his "mission" becomes the preservation of a helpless gorilla. His original missions—to observe a famed dinosaur-like creature in Lake Télé and the Pennant-winged nightjar—are missions of an outsider, an anthropologist, distant and disengaged. When O'Hanlon finds himself deeply influenced by and deeply engaged within the Congolese culture, these detached missions lose their significance.

Taken together, these three travel narratives reveal a writer who is at once highly self-aware and also forgetful of himself. On the one hand, the recovering academic augments all his narratives with lengthy quotations from notable travelers and academics. The books bear the unmistakable imprint of an educated man who is able to place his travels within the greater context of travel narrative writing and colonialism. That such quotations disappear during moments of immersion also demonstrates that O'Hanlon is able—and willing—to forget what he has formally learned in favor of better understanding and of recording the culture within which he is immersed without seeing it through an educated lens. He is drawn in by his curiosity to these other cultures; the progression of the three books demonstrates this.

Selected Bibliography

WORKS OF REDMOND O'HANLON

Joseph Conrad and Charles Darwin: The Influence of Scientific Thought on Conrad's Fiction. Edinburgh: Salamander Press, 1984. Atlantic Highlands, N.J.: Humanities Press, 1984.

Into the Heart of Borneo: An Account of a Journey Made in 1983 to the Mountains of Batu Tiban with James Fenton. Edinburgh: Salamander Press, 1984. New York: Random House, 1984. (The American edition omits the subtitle.)

In Trouble Again: A Journey Between the Orinoco and the Amazon. London: Hamish Hamilton, 1988. New York: Atlantic Monthly Press, 1989.

No Mercy: A Journey to the Heart of the Congo. New York: Knopf, 1997. First published in a slightly different form as *Congo Journey* by Hamish Hamilton in 1996.

Trawler: A Journey Through the North Atlantic. London: Hamish Hamilton, 2003. New York: Knopf, 2005.

CRITICAL AND BIOGRAPHICAL STUDIES

Cockburn, Alexander. "Bwana Vistas: The Lost, Lamented World of the Imperial Travel Writer." *Harper's,* August 1984, 65–69.

Fox, Wade. "*In Trouble Again.*" *Whole Earth Review,* winter 1995, 28. (Review of *In Trouble Again.*)

Lidz, Franz. "He Did What to a Monkey? Oxford Naturalist Redmond O'Hanlon Writes Travelogues of Unknown and Odd Places." *Sports Illustrated,* 12 January 1998, 6–7.

Murphy, Richard McGill. "In the Sorcerer's Realm." *The New Leader,* 6–20 October 1997, 15–16. (Review of *No Mercy.*)

Taylor, John. "Elephant Nose and Bear Chops." *The Sewanee Review* 105 (fall 1997): 608–611. (Review of *No Mercy.*)

REDMOND O'HANLON

Tisdale, Sallie. "Never Let the Locals See Your Map: Why Most Travel Writers Should Stay Home." *Harper's,* September 1995, 66–74. (Review of *Into the Heart of Borneo* and *In Trouble Again.*)

WILLIAM PLOMER

(1903–1973)

Andrew van der Vlies

WILLIAM PLOMER DESCRIBED himself during a conference address—delivered during a return visit to his country of birth, South Africa, in 1956—as a "sort of doubly displaced person" who was "simultaneously a South African writer and an English reader, but also an English writer and a South African reader" ("South African Writers and English Readers," p. 55). This description highlights the complex and ambiguous affiliations of a man born of English parents in the northern part of South Africa who spent periods of his childhood in England, left South Africa as a young man to live in Japan, and finally established himself as an English man of letters in London in his late twenties. Plomer moved between sites of cultural identification and production; this was the case for many writers from British colonies and dominions who published in Britain or migrated to the "home" country to achieve there the recognition they felt was lacking at the margins of Empire. Many, including Jean Rhys, Katherine Mansfield, Christina Stead, Plomer's erstwhile collaborator and friend Roy Campbell, and Plomer himself, became members of a transnational, modernist literary scene in Britain; they were, as Plomer declared of himself in his conference address, "doubly involved and doubly detached" (p. 55).

Plomer's career as a writer falls into three distinct periods. During its early stage, primarily in South Africa, his work attacked the bourgeois complacency, racism, and chauvinist nationalism of colonial white society. He wrote his first novel, *Turbott Wolfe,* as a precocious young man while helping his father in a rural trading store in Zululand. It was published by Leonard and Virginia Woolf's Hogarth Press in 1926, caused a literary storm in South Africa, and was highly praised in Britain. After his permanent move to England in 1929 (with a three-year detour in Japan), Plomer's writing explored themes of alienation and disaffection, some of which were fed by anxiety about his homosexuality. After World War II, increasing domestic stability and public recognition contributed to a productive, three-decade-long career as a poet, editor, librettist, and man of letters. Plomer published five novels, six collections of short stories, fourteen volumes of poetry (including selections and collected editions), two volumes of memoirs (later amalgamated and edited into a single autobiography), two biographies, four libretti, and numerous reviews and introductions, including volumes he edited. This article is unable to discuss his oeuvre in detail and aims instead to balance an account of his most influential early work with discussion of severely neglected writing (particularly novels) from his "middle" period and to give a sense of the trajectory of the career of a prolific, prolix, and fascinating man.

LIFE

He was born William Charles Franklyn Plomer, of English parents, in Pietersburg, in the northern part of the Transvaal (which had only recently come under British rule), on December 10, 1903. His father, Charles, had arrived in the Cape Colony in 1889 with a letter of introduction to Cecil Rhodes, the mining magnate and later prime minister, served with a mounted regiment, and was later variously a farmer and forestry worker. At the time of William's birth Charles was employed by the Repatriation Commission, charged with resettling farmers in the Northern Transvaal in the wake of the Anglo-Boer War. The young William, his mother, and later his younger brother moved several times between South Africa and Britain: William was left with an aunt in Britain in 1908, returned to South Africa in 1911, and was sent back to England to school in Kent in 1914 and to Rugby School in 1917. He returned to South Africa in 1919 to attend St. John's College in Johannesburg and in June 1921 was apprenticed to a farmer in the Stormberg Mountains of the Eastern Cape. When a newly elected Afrikaner nationalist government of the self-governing Union of South Africa (formed in 1910 from the Cape and Natal colonies and the former Boer republics, the Orange Free State and the Transvaal) began to encourage the employment of Afrikaners rather than English-speakers and British expatriates in the civil service in the early 1920s, Plomer's father lost his job, and the family moved to Natal in 1922 to run a trading store at Entumeni, in rural Zululand.

SOUTH AFRICAN NOVELIST

One of the earliest publications in which Plomer's poems appeared was in John L. Dube's Zulu newspaper, *Ilanga Lase Natal*. "Three Folk Poems" were published on March 14, 1924, under a pseudonym, with an author's note expressing the hope:

> that these simple verses may help to serve an early movement towards our own literature. A national literature can only be built up of many parts, and with infinite pains, but if we can plainly express now some of the true feelings of our people, however simple, we may be able to lay a sure foundation.

> (Alexander, p. 77)

It becomes apparent that it is by no means easy to "situate" Plomer. In his early attempts at publication he played simultaneously on an incipient South African (perhaps even African nationalist) identity, but his early attempts to bring his work to a British audience demonstrate the extent to which he kept abreast of literary developments in London and desired metropolitan validation for his work. He wrote, for example, from Zululand, to Leonard Woolf in London, in praise of the Hogarth Press. Although small, the

Woolfs' press was making a name as a publisher of new and foreign writers and titles on important contemporary political, social, and economic issues (including racial prejudice and imperialism) and was introducing new continental European movements in science and psychology to a British audience. Plomer explained in his *Autobiography* (1975) that he sent the manuscript of his first novel (which he began age nineteen and completed at age twenty-one) to the Woolfs because he had "liked their own writings and (no wonder) had been impressed by some of the writers they had published" (p. 167). He claimed (in the first volume of his memoir *Double Lives, 1943*) that he had intended that it should "present, in a fictional form, partly satirical, partly lyrical, partly fantastic," his own "impressions of life in Africa and to externalize the turmoil of feelings they had aroused in me." He had no desire to present an autobiographical narrative or give "a naturalistic account of African life"; the novel was merely "a violent ejaculation, a protest, a nightmare, a phantasmagoria" (pp. 186–187). It was published in 1926 (although it bears the date 1925; there was a printers' strike).

The narrator (who we learn later is called "William Plomer") visits his old school friend, Turbott Wolfe, who is "about to die at no great age, of a fever he had caught in Africa" (p. 9), and hears Wolfe's deathbed account of his experiences in the fictitious Lembuland (modeled on Zululand). Like Cecil Rhodes, Wolfe had been ordered to Africa for his health. He set up a trading store in Lembuland, at Ovuzane (as the Plomers had done at Entumeni), with the help of a "remarkably steady 'civilized' native," Caleb Msomi (p. 12). A principled trader with an interest in folklore, painting, writing, music, sculpture, religion, and handicrafts, Wolfe befriends the natives and alienates the local white farmers. A sympathetic Englishman, Francis d'Elvadere, tells Wolfe that he should not believe that "because South Africa is painted red upon the map and has at present a white population of a million and a half, it is in consequence a white man's country"; in fact, he argues, it "can never be anything but a black, or at least a coloured man's country" (p.

118). This advice ironically echoes Marlow's belief in Joseph Conrad's "Heart of Darkness" that "real work," which "redeemed" colonialism, was done in British colonies (traditionally red on world political maps in the late nineteenth and early twentieth centuries).

During a visit to the provincial capital, Dunnsport (modeled on Durban), Wolfe encounters a multiracial crowd at a funfair and realizes "suddenly in that harsh polyglot gaiety that I was living in Africa; that there is a question of colour" (p. 13). He becomes obsessed with the question of how to live in a society in which race is the determining characteristic of social, economic, and political relationships and begins "to learn the hard lesson that in Lembuland it is considered a crime to regard the native as anything even so high as a mad wild animal" (p. 29). Wolfe realizes he will have to face the "the unavoidable question" of what his relationship to race and racial politics ought to be; he declares it "a question to which every man in Africa, black, white or yellow, must provide his own answer" (p. 26). Mabel van der Horst—who joins Wolfe, Caleb Msomi's cousin Zachary, and Rupert Friston, a new missionary who believes the world ought to become a mixed-race one, in forming the idealistic Young Africa Society—argues that there is no "native question":

> You take away the black man's country, and, shirking the future consequences of your actions, you blindly affix a label to what you know (and fear) the black man is thinking of you—"the native question." Native question, indeed! My good man, there is no native question. It isn't a question. It's an answer.
>
> (p. 65)

The society's manifesto proclaims the necessity of miscegenation; Mabel subsequently falls in love with Zachary Msomi, while Wolfe has himself become infatuated with a local black woman, Nhliziyombi, whom he idealizes as an "ambassadress of all that beauty...the intensity of the old wonderful unknown primitive African life—outside history, outside time, outside science" (p. 55). (This is another echo of "Heart of Darkness," of Kurtz's African lover.) Yet Wolfe finds himself committed to theory rather than practice. He is alarmed that Mabel wants to marry Zachary and concludes that they were "only feeling about for principles, after all" (p. 98). Principles transformed into action destroy the novel's naively idealistic characters. Friston, for one, goes mad—on account, it is later explained, of drugs and frustrated desire for Mabel—and runs away. News arrives later that he has been murdered in Swedish East Africa, which is loosely based on Portuguese East Africa (present-day Mozambique) in Plomer's fictitious but highly suggestive geography. Lembuland's provincial town, founded by Voortrekkers, is named "Aucampstroom" but is probably modeled on Pietermaritzburg (or any number of smaller Natal towns founded by the Dutch farmers who migrated from the Cape Colony in the 1830s and 1840s). Furthermore, the "Dukela" is the Tugela River, "Goldenville" is Johannesburg (built on the site of major gold reserves), "Bladesia" is Rhodesia (present-day Zimbabwe; similarly, the suggestively named "Blades" is modeled on Rhodes), and the "Dark Continent Exploration Company" is based loosely on Rhodes's British South Africa Company.

Wolfe decides to leave Africa even before he is summoned by the commissioner for Lembuland to the ironically named Department of Aboriginal Protection, presented with numerous letters of complaint from local white farmers, and told to leave. The final chapter is a present-tense account by Wolfe of his departure. The novel concludes with two appendices containing fragments of writing by Friston, discovered by Wolfe, and given by him to the narrator. The first contains three poems: one had been among the poems published by Plomer separately, under a pseudonym, in *Ilanga lase Natal;* another includes the line "HORROR was written on the sun," a deliberate echo of Kurtz's (in)famous exclamation in "Heart of Darkness." The other appendix purports to offer "notes for a diagram" that Friston had been preparing, sketching the manner in which an individual might balance the aesthetic and the political: "On the right hand he is politico, on the left aesthete. His left eyelid droops in languor, heavy and sallow over the brightest of eyes; his right eye is fastened on the main chance" (p. 118). The notes are comic but serve a serious purpose in reflecting Plomer's own perception of his dilemma as a writer in South Africa.

In their act of saving and publishing Friston's work, Wolfe and the narrator here assume, and reverse, Marlow's relation to Kurtz's papers in Conrad's novel. Plomer's use of a framing narrator for his novel echoes Conrad's use of the same to introduce Marlow's act of storytelling in "Heart of Darkness" (Cecily Lockett has written usefully about the connections). Plomer's novel is not an appropriation but rather a creative reworking of the same kind of conflict depicted by Conrad, with Wolfe acting both as Marlow to Friston's Kurtz and as Kurtz to the narrator's Marlow. The book's experimental narrative technique marks it as South Africa's first significant contribution to a transnational, modernist literature in English while simultaneously questioning the adequacy of a European aesthetic response to Africa.

Numerous critics have written perceptively on the significance of *Turbott Wolfe* for South African literary history, chief among them Stephen Gray, Peter Wilhelm, Michael Herbert, Cecily Lockett, and Michael Chapman. Wilhelm suggests intriguingly, and persuasively, that the nub of the novel is sex: Wolfe's reactions to Cossie von Honk (Aucampstroom's local woman of ill repute), Nhliziyombi, and Zachary and Mabel's marriage suggest a pathological fear of uncleanliness and contamination. At the novel's "theoretical core," Wilhelm claims, is "the desirability of effecting male-female miscegenation, and the impossibility of achieving it without becoming 'unclean'" ("Mask and Reality," p. 183). He wonders whether Friston desires Mabel or whether he actually desires Zachary and suggests that the "impossibility of the confession of inversion—the love of white male for black male"—leads, in the frustrated entanglements of Wolfe and Friston, to the fictional and metaphoric deaths of these latter two characters, who might both be read as embodying the author's own relation to Africa and to his own sexuality (p. 184).

Plomer was proud that many white South African critics called for his novel "to be burnt—a form of tribute which has been paid to greater writers for holding up a mirror to catch a society in attitudes which, when reflected, make nonsense of its self-esteem" (p. 188). Only three South African reviewers praised the novel; all others condemned it. Laurens van der Post's important introduction to the 1965 Hogarth reprint emphasizes its truly seminal status, claiming that *Turbott Wolfe* had "ended the age of European innocence in Africa" (p. 52). While vaguely melodramatic, the claim is not entirely without foundation: "Like *Max Havelaar*"—a seminal nineteenth-century Dutch anticolonial novel—"in Holland and Indonesia," van der Post concluded, "Plomer changed the course of our imagination in South Africa" (p. 53).

SOUTH AFRICAN POET

In June 1925, during a trip to Durban to buy provisions for the family store, Plomer met Roy Campbell, who had recently published a long poem, *The Flaming Terrapin* (1924), in London, to great acclaim. Campbell and his wife and daughters lived at Sezela, south of Durban, in a bungalow on the seaside estate of a young sugar baron, Lewis Reynolds, who would finance the publication of a small literary journal, *Voorslag* (Whiplash), which Campbell was to edit. Plomer joined the Campbells in May 1926 and collaborated on writing and editing the first two issues of the magazine, which launched an eloquently unforgiving attack on the pretensions and stuffiness of the colonial South African literary and artistic scene. Peter Alexander's exemplary biographies of Plomer and Campbell provide full accounts of the period, which supplement Plomer's own circumspect accounts in his memoirs and in an article, "*Voorslag* Days," written for *London* magazine forty years later.

After conflicts with the journal's backers Campbell resigned as editor in July 1926, and Plomer and the young Laurens van der Post, who had provided Afrikaans copy for *Voorslag,* left for Japan shortly after. Van der Post had befriended two Japanese journalists in South Africa and been invited to journey to Japan with a visiting Japanese merchant mariner. Plomer decided to accompany him and remained in Japan, teaching English in Tokyo and undertaking some editorial projects. While there Plomer readied for publication two essentially South African collections: a volume of poetry (*Notes for Poems*) and a collection of short stories and sketches (*I Speak of Africa),* both published in 1927. The former includes several slight poems drawing on Plomer's experiences in Johannesburg, the Stormberg, and Zululand. Many offer satirical sketches of colonial buffoonery, as in "The Explorer":

Romantic subject of the Great White Queen,
See him advancing, whiskered and serene,
With helmet, spectacles, and flask of brandy
(That useful stimulant, he always keeps it handy),
Unmoved by cannibals, indifferent to disease;
His black frock-coat rocks sadly in the tropic breeze.

(p. 41)

"A Passage to Africa" offers a satirical portrait of the various types who emigrate; "The Pioneers" describes lazy, indifferent colonials, not unlike those Plomer hated in Natal: "Old rotting whales ashore and thick with flies" (p. 42). Other poems, like "The Factory-Owner," attack exploitation—the factory is a "tin cathedral built to hypnotise wage-slaves," whose machines "Control and govern human hopes and fears" (p. 43). The three poems included in *Turbott Wolfe* are reprinted in this volume. When Plomer came to reorganize his poems for his 1973 revised volume of *Collected Poems,* he gathered his "African Poems" together, retaining six from *Notes for Poems* and including six from the 1932 collection *The Fivefold Screen* (which also includes poems based on experiences in Japan, Greece, and Britain), one from *Visiting the Caves* (1936), and four poems written after his return visit to South Africa in 1956, which were first included in the 1960 *Collected Poems* and are grouped under the title "After Thirty Years."

Plomer's third collection of poems, *The Fivefold Screen,* is significant because it was the last to include a substantial number of poems inspired by his South African experience. Grouped together in a section entitled "African Landscape

with Figures" and dedicated to Laurens van der Post, these include "The Ruined Farm" and "Namaqualand After Rain" as well as one of Plomer's most anthologized poems, "The Scorpion" (first published in the British *Nation and Athenaeum* in 1930), which offers a powerful response to the Africa Plomer had left behind:

Limpopo and Tugela churned
In flood for brown and angry miles
Melons, maize, domestic thatch,
The trunks of trees and crocodiles;

The swollen estuaries were thick
With flotsam, in the sun one saw
The corpse of a young negress bruised
By rocks, and rolling on the shore,

Pushed by the waves of morning, rolled
Impersonally among shells.
With lolling breasts and bleeding eyes,
And round her neck were beads and bells.

That was the Africa we knew,
Where, wandering alone,
We saw, heraldic in the heat,
A scorpion on a stone.

(p. 40)

Malvern van Wyk Smith suggests that the poem "reads like a South African rewrite of Wordsworth's 'A Slumber Did My Spirit Seal,'" but instead of receiving the dead girl "into a benign communion," he suggests, "the Africa presided over by the hostile deity of the scorpion spurns the 'young negress'" (p. 61). This Africa is an anti-pastoral space in contrast to the stereotyped, promising, vacant vastness of the Southern Hemisphere's British dominions. The speaker is not at home in the landscape but a mere observer "wandering alone," ill at ease and alienated from the generalized scene. The Africa "we knew" was in fact never known, the poem implies, its meaning bound up in unyielding and dangerous ciphers—a scorpion, a stone—that declare a heraldry and genealogy illegible to the Western imagination. It presents a space of fascination that invites involvement but is simultaneously unknowable. "The Scorpion" enacts Plomer's double attachment to and displacement from South Africa; it is as if his valediction to the country involves condemning it to the fate of the poisonous tail of the scorpion, having failed to whip the country to order with the sharp words of the whiplash *(Voorslag)*. The poem is important for its shattering of romantic illusions about Africa and its determination to hold the European imagination to account in its engagement with Africa and Africans—a topic to which Plomer returned in the carefully controlled and sharply satirical poem "The Devil-Dancers," included in *Visiting the Caves*.

Plomer's later poems on South Africa, written "After Thirty Years" (the title of the grouping in the 1973 collection), include a meditation on "A Transvaal Morning," which conveys the same muted apprehension of hostility encoded in "The Scorpion" and "The Devil-Dancers," and includes these stanzas:

The stranger started up to face
The sulphur sky of Africa, an infinite
False peace, the trees in that dry place
Like painted bones, their stillness like a threat.

Shoulders of quartz protruded from the hill
Like sculpture half unearthed; red dust,
Impalpable as cinnamon softly sifted, filled
With heaped-up silence rift and rut.

(*Collected Poems,* 1973, p. 34)

The long poem "Tugela River" records Plomer's emotions at revisiting Natal and reads both like his rewriting of Wordsworth's "Ode on Intimations of Immortality" and of his compatriot and erstwhile friend Roy Campbell's celebrated poem from the mid-1920s "The Serf." The poem's final lines draw an imaginative comparison between the Tugela in flood and the revolution Plomer imagined might answer South Africa's apartheid policies. These lines come closer to direct political critique than most of Plomer's verse:

When patience breaks, the sinews act,
Rage generates energy without end:
Tugela River, in the time of drums
And shouting of the war-dance flood
Will break a trance, as revolutions do,

Will promise order, and a future time
Of honey, beer, and milk.

(*Collected Poems,* 1973, p. 41)

Perhaps the most poignant and devastating of Plomer's South African–inspired poems is the last he wrote about the country, "The Taste of the Fruit," an elegy for two young radical South African writers, Ingrid Jonker and Nat Nakasa, both of whom committed suicide in 1965. It was published in (and a concluding line gave the name to) the collection *Taste and Remember* (1966).

LEAVING SOUTH AFRICA

The prose volume Plomer prepared in Japan is entitled *I Speak of Africa,* an ironic allusion to the line "I speak of Africa and golden joys" in Shakespeare's *Henry the Fourth, Part Two* (v.iii. 100). Published by the Hogarth Press in September 1927, it includes seven short stories, two "plays for puppets" (masque-like satires on South African racial policies), and three "short novels." One of these, "Ula Masondo," is an account (in the author's own words) "of the effect upon a primitive native of going to work in the gold mines" (*Double Lives, 1943,* p. 192). The other short novels are "Portraits in the Nude"—which reads like a modernist response to Olive Schreiner's *The Story of an African Farm* and involves domestic abuse, hypocrisy, repression, lynching, and religious fanaticism—and "Black Peril," in which a white woman appears to initiate a sexual encounter with a black servant but subsequently dies from what her husband and community regard as shock from rape. Both of these stories indict the pervasive fear of racial degeneration through miscegenation, which was reflected in much white South African writing of the period. Plomer's preface to the volume states intemperately his disgust at political, literary, and cultural values in white South Africa.

Plomer included several South African sketches in his 1933 volume *The Child of Queen Victoria and Other Stories,* which heralded his move from Hogarth Press to Jonathan Cape. Some of these may have been intended as part of a failed autobiographical novel, particularly the long short stories "Down on the Farm" and "The Child of Queen Victoria." The former evokes Plomer's time in the Stormberg, contrasting two farming families, and portrays positively the relationship between a white farmer (Stevens) and his black laborer (Willem). The second revisits some of the same material that formed the basis for *Turbott Wolfe* (Wolfe's love for Nhliziyombi is echoed in Frant's falling in love with Seraphina). Another, "When the Sardines Came," is based on aspects of life on the Natal south coast: in the story, a medical student seeks quiet with a family on the coast and observes a relationship develop between his cousin's wife and a young man injured on the beach.

Although consistently outspoken in his opposition to racial segregation, Plomer's early work came increasingly to be regarded as reflecting the inevitable inadequacy of European responses to Africa. By the 1990s his insights were described by younger, radicalized South African critics in ambivalent terms, as challenging his own "colonial hankerings after landscapes empty of the indigenous people, his own colonial fears about Africa as savage and atavistic" (Chapman, p. 182). This apparent negotiation of tensions between the aesthetic, cultural, and economic demands of periphery and center makes Plomer a fascinating subject for the study of the manner in which, while "settlers" were complicit with the colonial structures that marginalized indigenous peoples, they were also themselves colonial subjects, culturally and politically subordinated to London (Boehmer, p. 112).

WRITING JAPAN

The English writer Edmund Blunden helped Plomer to find work teaching English in Tokyo, where he set up house with a student, Sumida. When Sumida was married off by his parents, Plomer set up house with another companion, Fukuzawa Morito at Higashi Nakano (*Double Lives,* p. 229; *Autobiography,* pp. 201–221). Fukuzawa was the model for Sado Masaji in Plomer's largely autobiographical second novel, *Sado,* published by Hogarth in 1931, two years

after Plomer's arrival in Britain. He struggled to complete it, and it appears to be all that he thought fit to salvage from a much longer autobiographical novel. Its protagonist, Vincent Lucas, is a young English artist who, rather like Plomer, has arrived in Japan on a whim; in a street he encounters Sado, "a young Japanese in the uniform of a university student" (p. 14), and they become intrigued by each other. Vincent bears a letter of introduction to an Englishwoman, Iris Komatsu, and her husband, a Japanese engineer, and is offered the use of a house on their property. Sado comes to stay with Vincent, and the stage is set for a carefully balanced triangle: Iris is attracted to Vincent and jealous of the time he spends with Sado, whom she also dislikes for allegedly encouraging her husband to gamble and visit geishas; Sado is jealous of Iris's interest in Vincent.

Sado is the first novel in which Plomer hints directly at the subject of homosexuality; in the words of Plomer's biographer, it "may not be too fanciful to suppose that his struggles to finish *Sado* reflect his personal search for identity at this time" (Alexander, p. 161). As in later narratives, there is a gap in the text where a sexual encounter might be inferred. During a group picnic, Sado and Vincent go off together to swim: "Lucas wondered whether he should light a cigarette or not. Then he looked at Sado, and Sado looked at him, and he put his cigarettes back in his pocket. By the time they returned to the waterfall, the sky was completely overcast" (pp. 186–187). The narrative voice, focalized at times through Vincent, often comes dangerously close to appearing crudely misogynistic; Japanese women are "stunted" (p. 11), and in a letter to England, Vincent describes his disappointment with Japanese women "in the mass, but isn't that the same in most countries" (p. 74).

The novel is interesting chiefly for its exploration of national types—particularly its concern with Japanese national identity in the late 1920s—as well as of the imperatives of creativity and authoritarianism. Vincent claims to find Sado interesting as a representative Japanese, while Iris thinks he represents "a bad side of the national character" (p. 48). Everything Vincent sees about him is suggestive of the pervasive influence of the rising Japanese nationalism of the period: "Every activity one saw going on around one was for the nation or for some nation-within-the-nation" (p. 11). The sailors with whom Lucas sails to Japan represent twin aspects of Japanese nationalism: one (Moroi) believes in "culture" and "a mystic-scientific approach to life," while the other (Sakurai) praises "nationalism, efficiency, propaganda, and 'progress'" (p. 21). Vincent's Englishness is also interrogated. He is described as a "member of a certain decayed stratum of Western society" who "instinctively dread[s] the domination of the mass"; he is "a typical figure of the transition" (p. 156), of a postwar world palpably on the verge of change and dangerously in thrall to a desire for authority. As an educated, upper-middle-class aesthete, Vincent's fear of the masses is exemplary; he derides the "new, awkward, ugly, unwashed, red, screaming, raucous lie—as ugly as a new-born baby—that is coming into being all over the contemporary world" (pp. 156–157). When a friend of Vincent's arrives from Paris, and Vincent decides that it is time to leave Japan, both he and Sado realize that separation will be difficult but that their worlds are too different to admit of another outcome. Iris declares her love for Vincent, claims that he ought to outgrow his "sterile" attachment to men (p. 262), and has "got the categories confused" (p. 163), but the novel ends with an understanding between them. They attend a Chinese opera performance together: "No one remembered whether the actor was male or female; all that was revealed was the aspiration of soul and body towards joy and pleasure" (p. 271). Whether or not Vincent, or Sado, are meant to be entirely representative of supposed national types is debateable: both are out of place as they strive "to keep one's balance, to treat past and future with equal respect, committing oneself to neither but trying to seize the best from each" (p. 163).

Plomer published several short stories and poems that draw on his Japanese experiences. He was influenced both by contemporary Japanese writing, to which he was introduced by his companions and students, and also by French and Russian models. Many of his Japanese stories, collected in *Paper Houses* (1929), explore differences between East and West, especially with regard to codes of behavior and honor. In "Nakamura," a taxi driver is tempted to act to avenge himself on his onetime sweetheart, a geisha, and her new lover, who travel in his taxi. He decides not to drive off a cliff with his passengers but then suffers an accident. Several stories explore nationalism, emperor worship, honor, and suicide. In "The Portrait of an Emperor," a school principal contemplates suicide after the theft of a portrait of the emperor; the story explores the younger generation's growing skepticism about the divinity of the emperor. "A Brutal Sentimentalist" presents the thoughts of a Japanese diplomat in London, who remembers a relative nearly having to commit ritual suicide and being pardoned only when he reaches for the sword. "Yoka Nikki: An Eight-Day Diary" describes the customs and sights encountered on a Japanese tour. The collection ends with a story of almost satirically comic exaggeration, "Mother Kamchatka; or, Mr. Mainchance in Search of the Truth."

Twenty years later Plomer included three of his Japanese stories in a collection entitled *Four Countries* (1949), along with a fourth written in 1946. The volume, as its title suggests, also includes stories from three other countries, South Africa (drawn from *I Speak of Africa*), Greece (including "Nausicaa," which explores the exploitative relationship between an older tourist and a young Greek boy trying to find his sister), and England. *The Family Tree* (also 1929) includes much of Plomer's best poetry inspired by Japan, in a wide range of forms and styles, but as Robert Doyle observes, "none of the imaginative and passionate quality of the South African poetry appears in the Japanese period. It was the author's intellect which was being stimulated in Japan" (p. 124). Poems of the period feature Japanese flora and landscapes—Plomer grouped them in the volume under the title "Notes for a Japanese Landscape with Figures"—and most of them were retained in the 1973 *Collected Poems* under the title "Poems Written in Japan."

WILLIAM PLOMER

AN ENGLISH WRITER: MAKING A CAREER

Plomer left Japan in March 1929, as the country's nationalist, militaristic political culture reached ever more frightening levels. He traveled by Trans-Siberian railway, and when he arrived in Britain he moved in with his parents (who had, in the interim, returned to England). It was at this point that he changed the pronunciation of his name: having rhymed with "Homer," it was henceforth to rhyme with "bloomer." Peter Alexander notes that Plomer had it put about that he thought his name derived from "plume" even though he knew it derived from "plumber." Plomer himself quipped in his *Autobiography* that, "pronounced to rhyme with Rumour, one can plume oneself on having a light touch rather than a leaden one" (p. 12). The change marked a break from his family and a remodeling of his identity to fit the new life he was determined to make for himself in Britain (Alexander, p. 155). He met Leonard and Virginia Woolf (who had published all four of his books to date) for the first time in May 1929, and through them and other contacts he soon became part of the liberal-left artistic establishment in London, making friends with many of the leading writers and critics of the day, including E. M. Forster, who came to regard him as one of his two favorite poets, the other being W. H. Auden (Alexander, p. 159). Plomer met many of the leading younger writers and would appear in print in collections with Stephen Spender, Auden, and Christopher Isherwood. He published poetry and reviews in papers including the *New Statesman, Nation and Athenaeum, Criterion, Life & Letters, Saturday Review,* and *New Adelphi* (Alexander, p. 165).

Plomer moved into a boardinghouse in Bayswater in September 1929. That November his landlady, Sybil da Costa (who called herself Sybil Starr), was brutally murdered by her jealous husband, who then went looking for Plomer. (Luckily, he was away.) Plomer calls Starr "Beryl Fernandez" in his autobiography, also using the name for the character modeled on Starr in his novel based on the facts of the case: *The Case is Altered* (1932). It became Plomer's most commercially successful work, selling over eleven thousand copies in its first six months, and was recommended by the influential Book Club (Alexander, p. 182; Willis, pp. 202–204). It deals pointedly with residual class snobberies and intergenerational conflict—as suggested by an early description of the rooming house smelling "of the past, stale cooking, thwarted hopes, and all the horrors of life at its worst in the bourgeois backwaters of Victorian England" (p. 7). It is expressly "a time of transition," the narrator notes: "new ideas, new aspirations, and new kinds of people are beginning to live [in] and move" into the old houses, and naturally "between the old ideas and the new there is confusion" (p. 8). Beryl Fernandez supports an unemployed, semi-invalid husband, Paul, and their child, Rosy. Tenants include the Rudds, a working-class London couple who take lottery tickets, squabble, and have false teeth; Eric Alston, who has moved to London from the provinces; and Constantia Brixworth, who tries to maintain appearances despite dwindling resources. Brixworth, who takes to Alston and entertains him to tea, complains: "When I had more money I used to have an ordinary afternoon tea and late dinner, but now the case is rather altered" (p. 83). This complaint is repeated in connection with several institutions and establishments that appear to be in terminal decline.

The house is the site of numerous conflicts and intrigues. The manservant, Empringham, leaves to work for Miss Brixworth's wealthy friend Miss Haymer (an inveterate snob and formerly an intrepid explorer). His replacement, an Irishman named Carol, becomes yet another object of Paul's jealousy. Tensions mount, Paul's paranoid outbursts become increasingly violent, and the novel culminates with his brutal murder of his wife. This summary does not account for the novel's numerous subplots, most of which serve to develop Plomer's concern with the manner in which old class divisions are increasingly breaking down. The novel is perhaps most interesting, however, for aspects that may not have struck its contemporary readers as particularly noteworthy. Eric Alston is one of Plomer's most troubled and fascinating characters, appearing to the modern reader to be a barely disguised portrait of a repressed homosexual. Plomer's handling of the homosexual suggestions in the novel is, however, itself deeply ambivalent. The novel reads as if he was *not* intending for Alston to be homosexual, but in attempting to portray a character alienated from the expectations of his class and surroundings, Plomer could not help but to portray Alston in this way (although the novel's dedication to Bernard Bayes, Plomer's guardsman lover at the time, may suggest the characterization was more intentional). About Alston's tentative relationship with a local young woman the reader is told that "public opinion required him to pay attention to a girl," and "he began seeing Amy as if it was a duty" (pp. 46–47). Soon, however, Alston has developed a crush on Amy Pascall's absent brother, Willy, who "took in his mind a place that his father had once held—the place of a person who was wise, good and beautiful, and whom one's actions must please" (p. 143).

The causes of Alston's alienation are never explicitly stated, but the narrator gestures toward "tribal taboos" that inform "conscience" and "duty" (p. 199) and constrain his behavior. One night in a pub he meets Amy's brother, and they form a strong, clearly homoerotic attachment: Willy for instance has "an interest in muscle control, and the sight of his firm and supple body, with its movements so easy, confident and splendid, and its tattooed symbols of experience on the white skin, began to teach Alston to take pride in his own body, which, with Pascall's help, he began to exercise and develop" (pp. 235–236). Meanwhile Amy becomes increasingly alarmed that the two are monopolizing one another's company. Hearing about Paul Fernandez's threatening behavior, Willy even spends a night in bed with Alston, his "arm…affectionately round him," giving Alston "a feeling of comradeship and safety" (p. 275). Alston's veneration of strong leadership figures is paradigmatic and exemplary. Plomer appears to comment on the attraction authoritarianism holds for those who are for whatever reason marginal, alienated, or insecure. Alston adores machines, fast cars, and the idea of war. He admires the "enormous crowds of young men raising their right arms in salute" in Fascist films, "all vigorous, all believing in one thing, all enthusiastic, all living for the same purpose"—

they afford "glimpses of the possibility of an active life led by many people with a common aim and altogether outside his own petty, personal existence" (pp. 140–141). Plomer's narrator, in the year before Hitler's accession to the German chancellorship, claims, apparently without irony, that a "vigorous youth movement of the German kind might have helped [Alston], but unfortunately he lived in a country which could offer him little but to join the Boy Scouts or the Y.M.C.A." (p. 200).

This apparently sympathetic portrayal of the attraction of authoritarianism reads problematically today. So too does the preoccupation of various of the novel's characters with the fact that Beryl Fernandez is Jewish. Miss Haymer utters what appear to be anti-Semitic sentiments: "The Jews usually look after each other" (p. 58); "When you can't understand her behaviour say to yourself, 'Well, she's a Jewess'" (p. 110). However, she also claims that Beryl is "likely to be much more human than the average landlady" (p. 39) because she is Jewish. It is difficult to establish whether these comments merely reflect the kind of casual but not necessarily overtly antagonistic attitudes toward Jews common in the 1920s or whether Plomer intends something more. That the narrator offers a lengthy discussion of Jewishness, in a digression in chapter 7, suggests that he might. The reader is told that "Mrs. Fernandez was typical of the spirit of modern life, which is Jewish, feminine, and paradoxical" (p. 110) and that the paradox of her loving her brutal husband is "a tiny illustration of the paradoxical nature of her race…. Half-way between East and West, they may be somewhere near the truth, if the truth really lies in paradox" (p. 111). The narrator also exclaims: "How rich are the ideas, and movement of ideas, with which the Jews have been associated! And how meaningless the individual without the race of which he is the epitome!" (p. 112). Whether this is merely pseudo-anthropological supposition is debatable, but Beryl appears, finally, to be offered as an example of how an individual embodies supposedly racial traits, as some of the English characters—Alston, Haymer, Brixworth—embody conflicting and often unattractive characteristics of a hypothetical Englishness. Such discussions of race are difficult for the modern reader to stomach, but if the novel is seen as a study of outsiders, Plomer may merely have intended both to add Jews to the list and to have a Jew serve as an ill-fated representative of the alienated and put upon. Furthermore, the Jew as migrant and cosmopolitan embodies the novel's attack on nationalism. Miss Haymer voices what we know to be Plomer's opinion, formed by observing English and Afrikaans-speaking white South Africans and increasingly nationalistic Japanese: "What on earth is the point of nationalism? Some day it will seem as ridiculous as the narrow-mindedness of colonials or provincials. To be a nationalist today is to be definitely provincial" (p. 246).

Miss Haymer's voice is frequently the closest to the novelist's. Elsewhere she expostulates on the dangers of love, praising the Greeks for understanding "that love, whether between lovers, or brothers and sisters, or children and parents, or people of the same sex, or husbands and wives, is a thing absolutely beyond human control, a thing which can easily land you in a mess" (p. 113). The novel concludes with Eric Alston and Willy Pascall together, "for an instant of time and for ever, an image of courage, beauty and love" (p. 341). They are held up as "one little sign among many of approaching changes," specifically, of the end of "the long Gothic ages of chivalry and Mariolatry—individualistic, commercial, 'Christian' and bankrupt," and of the arrival of a more "communistic" society in which all might be "good citizens, temperate, unselfish and resourceful" (p. 341). Why these two characters should embody such ideals is never made explicit but is clear if we view *The Case is Altered* both as an exploration of class politics in the early 1930s and Plomer's desire for a society in which his sexuality would be more easily accepted.

INVADER AT HOME: PLOMER AS OUTSIDER

Between May and November 1930, Plomer traveled in Germany, Italy, and Greece with his friend Anthony Butts. His Greek sojourn in particular provided him with material for short fiction and poetry. Plomer wrote in the second volume of his memoirs, *At Home* (1958), about his feelings of displacement in England after his arrival from Japan. He felt himself British, or at least he was keen to claim a British identity, but he was aware that his strongest formative experiences had been "abroad." His homosexuality too caused him to feel something of an outsider. With his third volume of short stories published and three books of poems in print, he set about writing his fourth novel, one whose title declares its theme. *The Invaders* (1934) is ostensibly an exercise in imagining what might happen to a young woman and young man (siblings Mavis and Chick Steel) arriving in London from the fictitious Midlands town of Crotchester (in *Turbott Wolfe,* Rupert Friston's father is bishop of the town, and it is Eric Alston's former home in *The Case is Altered*). In fact the novel is another extended exploration of the alienation at the heart of a class-bound, patriarchal, homophobic society— the homosexual subtext is even stronger in this novel than in the previous three.

Mavis is employed as a servant by Colonel Maurice Presteign, whose home is run by his daughter, Frances, and shared with his nephew, Nigel Edge—Plomer's alter ego and the real protagonist of the novel. The colonel is neither "thoughtless nor...irreligious" yet misses "the consolations both of philosophy and religion" (p. 31); he reads novels about cowboys, finding "the activities of the Wild West an astringent antidote to the respectability and quietness of his surroundings" (p. 63). He is preoccupied with thoughts of another war, longs for "a *man,* a leader" (p. 31), and while he concedes that he wants peace, he detests the pacifism of his nephew. Nigel "had returned from the [First World] War a nervous wreck, and had never really recovered" (p. 32). Born into "a narrow world of accepted ideas" (p. 44), Nigel is sensitive, damaged, and lonely: "he belonged to a damaged generation—they needed another war, but they were all pacifists; they needed a cause and had none; they needed something to look forward to, and found nothing" (p. 45).

Nigel befriends Tony Hart, a working-class young man from Lancashire, for whom he finds employment cleaning Presteign's windows. The colonel disapproves of Nigel's friendship with someone from the working classes. Meanwhile, Mavis's brother, Chick (Sidney), arrives in London to join the army. He becomes a guardsman and, visiting his sister at the Presteign house, meets Nigel, who is immediately attracted to him. That Nigel is a homosexual is hinted at in the strongest terms permissible at the time. There is no shortage of contemporary euphemism: he "suffers" from "self-centredness," "vulnerability," and "'defeatism' (as the colonel called it)," all "symptoms of a condition of not being able to find an order to adapt himself to" (p. 301), a condition that "could also be ascribed to a sort of infantilism or arrested development" but which did not call "for any assumption of moral superiority on the part of other people, or even of greater maturity" (p. 302). His cousin reminds him that it is remembered by his family that he spent all his time "with the gardener's boy. And once when he promised to take you out fishing and then never turned up you were absolutely heart-broken" (p. 115). Nigel and Tony meet regularly at a pub, and the barman is "curious as to the nature of the bond between them—the well-dressed City 'gentleman' and his much younger and clearly by no means prosperous acquaintance" (p. 116).

Nigel embarks on what appears to be a relationship with Chick—one that is modeled very clearly on Plomer's own frustrated relationship with Bernard Bayes, who had exploited his attentions and his wallet. Nigel keeps a photograph of Chick in the flat to which he moves; his cousin, Frances, comments that "it's the only photograph in the room, and that makes it so conspicuous" (p. 150). Colonel Presteign is concerned at the likely gossip: "why doesn't he get to know some nice steady girl of his own position in life instead of going and wasting his time and money and distracting his attention from his business and everything else with some lout out of a cavalry barracks?" (pp. 154–155). The narrator describes them, daringly (for 1934), as not unlike "many pairs of lovers" (p. 160). As Bernard Bayes did,

Chick plays Nigel off against a girlfriend, getting money from the former to spend on the latter. He grows careless, and Nigel, devastated, calls off the relationship: "Once trust's gone, everything's gone," he despairs (p. 255). The narrator (and it is difficult not to read this as Plomer writing about his own failed relationship) writes:

> In certain circumstances, it is not his blindness to the faults of the beloved that does most damage to the lover, but his unwillingness to accept the implications of what he can plainly see. And where one person would provoke a scene, a climax, would "have things out," another may have a kind of humility which causes him to await the pleasure of the person he loves: it is true that such humility is found more in women than in men, but its origin is not so much in femininity as in gentleness.
>
> (p. 203)

Retreating on holiday to France, Nigel toys with the idea of suicide. A strong swimmer, he ventures farther and farther out to sea, testing his limits. He tries going out with a young woman, but there is no spark, and he begins frequenting a café in Nice where he consorts with fishermen—to the horror of his host, who discovers him there: "Two women were dancing together, and so were two men. One of them was Nigel, the other a working man in a blue shirt" (p. 274).

Much else happens in the novel. Mavis leaves the Presteign house to work for crudely sketched Jewish dressmakers (the equally crudely named Goldapfels), is badly treated there, and leaves. Meanwhile Tony's petty-criminal brother arrives in London and steals from a Belgian jeweler, Olminus. Plomer's carefully circumscribed narrative suggests that Tony prostitutes himself on first coming to London and is later solicited by Olminus. While his friendship with Nigel appears largely platonic, there is a clear suggestion of a sexual encounter (pp. 284–285). Plomer's portrayal of Tony might strike the contemporary reader as patronizing—he attempts, for example, to convey his Lancashire accent; Tony asks: "Do you often coom oop this way?" (p. 15) and helps Nigel up after a "nasty toomble" (p. 17). But Plomer is good at portraying the marginal status Tony's class forces him to occupy. His life is "like a phrase in brackets somewhere in the vast volume of society" (p. 19), and that he is from the north of England is meant to suggest that he has been untouched by the corruption of the city (several echoes of William Blake suggest both the corruption of the city and of love by jealousy; see pp. 12, 146, 246). It is Nigel's relationship with Tony that proves the most sincere and meaningful. His war wound no longer hurts by the end of the novel, apparently healed by the sympathetic attachment he has formed to Tony. And while the invaders—Mavis, Chick, and sundry others—all flee the capital permanently, Tony merely embarks on a visit home with fare lent by Nigel; it is inferred that he will return to London and presumably to Nigel.

Plomer wrote only one further novel, *Museum Pieces* (1952), based on the life of his friend Anthony Butts, whose memoir he had edited and substantially rewritten as *Curious Relations* in 1945. The novel is narrated by Jane Valance, in many ways a female version of Plomer himself, who meets and tells the story of Toby d'Arfey, modeled closely on Butts. Valance, an archivist, is engaged by d'Arfey's mother, Susannah Mountfaucon, to sort through family papers. She observes the pair at close hand and reports on the family's stories, its present strained financial situation, and the succession of fascinating characters with whom d'Arfey becomes involved (before and after his brief flirtation with Jane). Toby says to his mother: "The trouble with us, my dear mother,…is that we're museum pieces. You're a museum piece; both your husbands were museum pieces, particularly your unaccountable second choice; *I'm* a museum piece" (p. 83). Their financial adviser swindles them, and mother and son, unable to adjust to their straitened circumstances, attempt a series of enterprises to raise capital (trying to sell a Rembrandt in their possession; Toby opens a hat shop), each of which eats farther into their capital. Jane asks herself on the first page: "Am I setting out to write a memoir in the form of a novel, or a novel in the form of a memoir?" (p. 7). *Museum Pieces* is both; an entertaining description of a certain social class in the run-up to World War II, it is also a tribute to Butts and an attempt to make sense of his eccentricities and alienation. Valance

asks "where, in this constant renewal of energy, this change of direction, this gathering momentum, was the central truth about him?…From later experience and wider knowledge of people, I should say that there are persons whose appetite for life and whose temperament are such that they must throw themselves again and again into some new enterprise foredoomed to incompletion by their very restlessness" (pp. 160–161). D'Arfey—Butts—was one of these.

MAN OF LETTERS: READER, EDITOR, LIBRETTIST, BALLADEER

Plomer had been asked to write a short biography of the imperialist mining magnate and onetime premier of the Cape Colony, Cecil Rhodes, for a series of short studies published by Peter Davies. *Cecil Rhodes* (1933) is more an anecdotal essay than biography; in Peter Alexander's words, it is "more interesting for what it says about Plomer's attitude to Rhodes than for any new light it sheds on its subject" (p. 184). Plomer's introduction makes clear his desire to tarnish the unjustly burnished image of Rhodes in the British popular imagination: "Are we not justified in assuming that a lofty idealism which is shamelessly cynical in its expression is not a lofty idealism at all?" he asks (p. 8). Of Rhodes's establishment of a kind of secret society—of "best souls"—to promote the global extension of British and Anglo-Saxon civilization, Plomer wonders:

> It doesn't seem to have occurred to him that many of the "best souls" at any given moment might not be of the English-speaking race and might not be especially keen on the advancement of that race, not that many of the "best souls" of our own race might have little interest in trying to dominate mankind by means of a sort of glorified Ku-Klux Klan.
>
> (p. 27)

Having enjoyed the exercise of writing one biography, Plomer embarked on another, of Ali of Tebeleni, the pasha of Jannina, an eighteenth-century Albanian warlord. It was published in 1936 as *Ali the Lion* (reprinted in 1970 as *The Diamond of Jannina*).

In 1937 Plomer began working as a publisher's reader for Jonathan Cape, the London firm that had become his own publishers after Hogarth. He succeeded the distinguished Victorian and Edwardian literary agent and promoter Edward Garnett and in time came to be no less influential: among the authors whose work Plomer recommended and consequently "discovered" for Cape were Ted Hughes, Derek Walcott, John Fowles, Stevie Smith, and Ian Fleming (with whom Plomer worked in naval intelligence during World War II and who authored the James Bond series). During the course of his work for Cape, Plomer came across the unpublished diaries of a provincial Victorian clergyman, Robert Francis Kilvert (1840–1879), which he undertook to edit. Kilvert's diaries cover the period between January 1870 and March 1879 and appeared in three sensitively edited volumes between 1938 and 1940 (and in a condensed one-volume edition in 1944), soon securing Kilvert a reputation as among the best of English diarists. Plomer himself described the work as painting "a unique picture of country life in mid-Victorian times" and "a minor classic"; "its author," he wrote, might be "compared to Dorothy Wordsworth, whom he admired, and even to Pepys" (introduction to the 1944 edition, p. 5).

Plomer's short-story collection *Four Countries* (1949) includes a group of stories set in England that are slight but nonetheless demonstrate Plomer's facility with issues of class pretension (in "No Ghosts," an upstart woman novelist has her romantic expectations disabused by the plainspoken owner of a minor stately home), personal and national crisis ("The Night Before the War" explores, through a minor crisis in the life of an individual, the tensions of a city on the verge of World War II), and sexual politics (in "A Wedding Guest," an elderly woman tells of how a strapping butler happily and discreetly fathered children for two aristocratic women whose husbands were infertile). He had become an acute observer of English class manners, and much of his writing for the remaining quarter century of his life was to exploit this interest and facility. He became known in particular for his English ballads, many of which take their subjects from apparently unpromising material (murders, the aftermath of bombing raids, affairs) and are darkly humorous, slightly callous or gruesome, and absurd (which Plomer felt reflected the brutality and absurdity of his age). These poems range from the faintly tragic ("A Shot in the Park") to the horrifying ("The Heart of a King"). In "The Dorking Thigh," for example, Stan and June, on a trip to Surrey to look at a new housing development, come across the thigh of a murdered woman; "The Flying Bum" recounts the unexpected arrival on a table of a piece of roasted horse meat, debris from a bombing raid in wartime London. There are also moving elegies like "In a Bombed House: An Elegy in Memory of Anthony Butts," "The Bungalows," and "Bamboo: A Ballad for Two Voices." Plomer's many collections of poems include *The Dorking Thigh and Other Satires* (1945), *A Shot in the Park* (1955) (a larger collection was published as *Borderline Ballads* in the United States in 1955), *A Choice of Ballads* (1960), *Taste and Remember* (1966), *The Planes of Bedford Square* (1971), and *Celebrations* (1972). A volume of *Collected Poems* appeared in 1960 and an expanded and revised version in 1973.

Plomer met the composer Benjamin Britten in 1937 and collaborated with him during the 1950s and 1960s, writing the libretti for Britten's coronation opera *Gloriana* (1953) and three "parables for church performance" (for which Plomer drew on the ancient Japanese Noh tradition): *Curlew River* (1965), *The Burning Fiery Furnace* (1966), and *The Prodigal Son* (1968). He published a second volume of his memoirs, *At Home,* (1958) won numerous awards, and was invited to read his work all over Britain. Plomer was awarded the Queen's Gold Medal for Poetry in 1963, became a Companion of the Order of the British Empire (CBE) in 1968, and served as president of the Poetry Society between 1968 and 1971. He lived with his companion, Charles Erdmann, from 1944 until his death on September 20, 1973.

CONCLUSION

The Hogarth Press reprinted *Turbott Wolfe* in 1965 with an important introduction by Laurens van der Post, but it was only with a revival of interest in Plomer's writing in the late 1970s that the other novels and Plomer's short stories, mostly out of print, were reissued, and then mostly in South Africa. Stephen Gray launched Plomer's reappearance there with a critical edition of *Turbott Wolfe* in 1980. There followed a volume of *Selected Stories* (1984), one of *Selected Poems* (1985), and a reprint of that part of Plomer's autobiography dealing with his youth in the country as *The South African Autobiography* (1984). Meanwhile, in Britain, Oxford University Press reproduced Hogarth's 1965 edition of *Turbott Wolfe* in the Twentieth Century Classics series in 1985 and published Peter Alexander's critical biography in 1989.

Plomer has featured prominently in South African descriptions of the development of a self-aware, indigenous, English-language, proto-national literature. Yet for most of his professional life in England he sought to minimize the importance of his colonial origins. He was fond of remarking (as he does in *Double Lives*) that "since...if a cat happens to have kittens in an oven" no one "regards them as biscuits," he would "be no more justified in pretending to be a South African than in declaring [him]self" a black African (p. 9). Other remarks suggest differently, however, and South African critics tend to characterize his denials as defensive and misleading; Peter Wilhelm is exemplary of the school that views him as "an African, of Africa, always" ("Mask and Reality," p. 25). Plomer consistently took a personal interest in South African writers abroad and acted as a kind of literary godfather (or midwife) to many, not least in his role as long-serving reader for Jonathan Cape.

In 1963, in a short piece published as *Conversation with My Younger Self*, Plomer has his youthful and aged personas engage in a discourse on the nature of belonging. The older asks the younger, yet to arrive in England (in 1929), how he will adjust, and he replies:

Perhaps I shall be able to look at England and the English with something of the detachment of an alien, and see them as they really are. I hope that in time I shall find myself reassimilated. I am not a specially envious person, but I do rather envy you your obvious feeling of being at home. And I like to think that I may look forward to enjoying it myself.

(p. 27)

Plomer did come to feel at home in England, as the title of his second memoir asserts, but it is a function of his never having lost his feeling of alienation that his English novels were able to evoke, and his poetry to celebrate and gently mock, aspects of life on the margins of English society in the third quarter of the twentieth century. In many ways an "alien" in Britain—a colonial, a homosexual, an intellectual—Plomer had also been an English alien in colonial South Africa and in nationalist Japan. His keenly attuned sense of his own marginality and his ability to turn observation into art has ensured a fascinating and often overlooked transnational oeuvre embodying and exploring many of the issues—hybridity, diaspora, exile, marginality—so popular as themes in examinations of contemporary, and no less interesting, international writers in English.

Selected Bibliography

WORKS OF WILLIAM PLOMER

NOVELS

Turbott Wolfe. London: Leonard and Virginia Woolf, 1925. Later editions include London: Hogarth, 1965; New York: Morrow, 1965; Johannesburg: Ad. Donker, 1980 (all quotations in the essay are from this edition); and Oxford: Oxford University Press, 1985.

Sado. London: Hogarth, 1931. Published in the United States as *They Never Come Back*. New York: Coward-McCann, 1932.

The Case is Altered. London: Hogarth, 1932; New York: Farrar & Rinehart, 1932.

The Invaders. London: Cape, 1934.

Museum Pieces. London: Cape, 1952; New York: Noonday, 1954.

SHORT STORIES

I Speak of Africa. London: Hogarth, 1927.

Paper Houses. London: Hogarth, 1929; New York: Coward-McCann, 1929.

The Child of Queen Victoria and Other Stories. London: Cape, 1933.

Four Countries. London: Cape, 1949.

Selected Stories. Edited by Stephen Gray. Cape Town: David Philip, 1984.

POETRY

Notes for Poems. London: Hogarth, 1927.

The Family Tree. London: Hogarth, 1929.

The Fivefold Screen. London: Hogarth, 1932.

Visiting the Caves. London: Cape, 1936.

Selected Poems. London: Hogarth, 1940.

In a Bombed House, 1941: An Elegy in Memory of Anthony Butts. London: Curwen, 1942.

The Dorking Thigh and Other Satires. London: Cape, 1945.

A Shot in the Park. London: Cape, 1955.

Borderline Ballads. New York: Noonday, 1955.

A Choice of Ballads. London: Cape, 1960.

Collected Poems. London: Cape, 1960.

Taste and Remember. London: Cape, 1966.

The Planes of Bedford Square. London: Bookbang, 1971.

Celebrations. London: Cape, 1972.

Collected Poems. New ed. London: Cape, 1973.

Selected Poems. Johannesburg: Ad. Donker, 1985.

BIOGRAPHY

Cecil Rhodes. London: Peter Davies, 1933.

Ali the Lion: Ali of Tebeleni, Pasha of Jannina, 1741–1822. London: Cape, 1936. Reprinted as *The Diamond of Jannina.* London: Cape, 1970; New York: Taplinger, 1970.

AUTOBIOGRAPHY

Double Lives: An Autobiography. London: Cape, 1943; Freeport, N.Y.: Books for Libraries, 1971.

At Home: Memoirs. London: Cape, 1958; New York: Noonday, 1958.

Conversation with My Younger Self. London: Stellar, 1963.

The Autobiography of William Plomer. London: Cape, 1975; New York: Taplinger, 1976.

The South African Autobiography. Cape Town: David Philip, 1984.

LIBRETTI (MUSIC BY BENJAMIN BRITTEN)

Gloriana: Opera in Three Acts. London and New York: Boosey & Hawkes, 1953.

Curlew River: A Parable for Church Performance. London: Faber & Faber, 1965.

The Burning Fiery Furnace: Second Parable for Church Performance. London: Faber & Faber, 1966.

The Prodigal Son: Third Parable for Church Performance. London: Faber & Faber, 1968.

OTHER WORKS

Various articles and poems. *Voorslag.* Durban, South Africa: A. C. Braby, 1926–1927.

"South African Writers and English Readers." *Proceedings of a Conference of Writers, Publishers, Editors and University Teachers of English.* Johannesburg: Witwatersrand University Press, 1957. Pp. 54–72.

"Coming to London." In *Coming to London.* Edited by John Lehmann. London: Phoenix House, 1957. Pp. 13–35.

"*Voorslag* Days." *London,* July 1959, pp. 46–52.

Electric Delights. (Posthumous.) Edited by Rupert Hart-Davis. London: Cape, 1978.

EDITED WORKS

Kilvert, Francis. *Kilvert's Diary.* 3 vols. London: Cape, 1938–1940. Abridged in 1 vol., London: Cape, 1944.

D'Arfey, William. *Curious Relations.* London: Cape, 1945; New York: William Sloane, 1947. Reprinted under William Plomer, London: Sphere, 1968.

CRITICAL AND BIOGRAPHICAL STUDIES

Alexander, Peter. F. *Roy Campbell: A Critical Biography.* Oxford: Oxford University Press, 1982.

———. *William Plomer: A Biography.* Oxford: Oxford University Press, 1989.

Boehmer, Elleke. *Colonial and Postcolonial Literature: Migrant Metaphors.* Oxford: Oxford University Press, 1995.

Brown, David. "Africa Through European Eyes: The 1920s and *Turbott Wolfe*" (1979). In *Turbott Wolfe.* Edited by Stephen Gray. Johannesburg: Ad. Donker, 1980. Pp. 186–191.

Chapman, Michael. *Southern African Literatures.* London: Longman, 1996.

Cunningham, Valentine. *British Writers of the Thirties.* Oxford: Oxford University Press, 1988.

Davis, Geoffrey W. "'Look Elsewhere for Your Bedtime Story': William Plomer and the Politics of Love." *Matatu* 2, nos. 3–4:255–275 (1988).

Doyle, John Robert. *William Plomer.* New York: Twayne, 1969.

Gray, Stephen. "*Turbott Wolfe* in Context." In *Turbott Wolfe.* Edited by Stephen Gray. Johannesburg: Ad. Donker, 1980. Pp. 192–203. (Gray's edition includes several excellent essays, excerpts from Plomer's letters, and a selection of important reviews and responses.)

———. "William Plomer's Stories: The South African Origins of New Literature Modes." *Journal of Commonwealth Literature* 21, no. 1:53–61 (1986).

———. "'Doubly Involved and Doubly Detached': William Plomer's Use of the Colonial-Motherland Bond." *Commonwealth Essays and Studies* 11, no. 1:46–54 (autumn 1988).

Herbert, Michael. "*Turbott Wolfe* and the Critics." In *Turbott Wolfe*. Edited by Stephen Gray. Johannesburg: Ad. Donker, 1980. Pp. 169–179.

Hynes, Samuel. *The Auden Generation: Literature and Politics in England in the 1930s.* London: Pimlico, 1976.

Lockett, Cecily. "*Turbott Wolfe*: A Failed Novel or a Failure of Criticism?" *UNISA English Studies* 25, no. 1:29–34 (May 1987).

Rabkin, David. "Race and Fiction: God's Stepchildren and Turbott Wolfe." In *The South African Novel in English: Essays in Criticism and Society.* Edited by Kenneth Parker. London: Macmillan, 1978. Pp. 77–94.

Van der Post, Laurens. "The *Turbott Wolfe* Affair." In William Plomer, *Turbott Wolfe.* London: Hogarth, 1965. Pp. 9–53. Reprinted in *Turbott Wolfe*. Edited by Stephen Gray. Johannesburg: Ad. Donker, 1980. Pp. 132–164.

Van Wyk Smith, Malvern. *Grounds of Contest: A Survey of South African English Literature.* Cape Town: Jutalit, 1990.

Wade, Michael. "William Plomer, English Liberalism, and the South African Novel." *Journal of Commonwealth Literature* 8, no. 1:20–32 (June 1973).

Walder, Dennis. *Post-Colonial Literatures in English: History, Language, Theory.* Oxford: Blackwell, 1998.

Wilhelm, Peter. "The Single Dreamer: The African Poetry of William Plomer." *Poetry South Africa: Selected Papers from Poetry '74.* Edited by Peter Wilhelm and James A. Polley. Johannesburg: Ad. Donker, 1976. Pp. 23–34.

———. "Mask and Reality in *Turbott Wolfe.*" (1978). In *Turbott Wolfe.* Edited by Stephen Gray. Johannesburg: Ad. Donker, 1980. Pp. 180–185.

Willis, J. H., Jr. *Leonard and Virginia Woolf As Publishers: The Hogarth Press, 1917–1941.* Charlottesville and London: University Press of Virginia, 1992.

JONATHAN RABAN

(1942–)

Fred Bilson

JONATHAN RABAN IS a travel writer whose work is marked by three features. He has a freshness of approach and originality of analysis that shows particularly in his writing about the United States, where he now lives; he is perceptive in his treatment of the visual and of the relationship between the landscape caught in words and the landscape caught in photographs or graphic art; and he is almost painfully confessional about his personal experience. He has also written a major and innovative novel, *Waxwings* (2003).

TRAVEL LITERATURE

Travel writing must be more than compiling a guidebook; its minimum agenda must be to convey a sense of what it is like to "be there." Raban is probably one of the most experienced sailors alive, and he is unmatched at conveying the sailor's reading of texture in the surface of the water or in the sky cover, his responsiveness to changes in the weather, his acceptance of the sheer unpredictability of things. When he comes to describe a journey on land in *Bad Land* (1996), he tells us that he visualizes the dry plain of Montana as a kind of sea. He has the ability to seek out the striking in both places and people, for instance, his description in *Old Glory* (1981) of the individual quality of life in Vicksburg, Mississippi, and his portrayal of Otis Higgs, a Democrat candidate for mayor of Memphis. He offers a profusion of well-managed detail. He regularly takes with him on his journeys charts and books by earlier explorers who have followed the same trail; accounts of art, animal and bird life; and folklore. These enrich his reading of each area, heightening his sense of change and stability over time; they also are integrated into his text so that the reader is able to have an enhanced view.

His work is always contextualized in time in two senses. Each of the journeys is undertaken at a unique historical time, which shapes his appreciation of the experience. For example, *Coasting* (1986) describes a journey around Britain in 1982 as the Falklands War begins and is marked by that event. The other contextualization is the placing of the journey in terms of his life and the rites of passage that this implies. For travel writing is confessional. Ever since Mark Twain detailed in *Life on the Mississippi* (1883) what he felt to be the shameful circumstances in which he took on the pen name previously used by another man, readers have expected travel writers to be as honest and open about themselves as they are about the country through which they travel, and Raban accepts this responsibility. From the dates given above it will be seen that writing the book takes a number of years after the journey is completed because it is only much later that the details can be seen in their true scale and can assume their true priority. This for Raban is part of the craft that every writer needs—in both senses, of course: the fitting out of the boat is the start of the journey; the crafting of the book is its conclusion.

LIFE

Jonathan Raban was born on June 14, 1942, the first son of Peter and Monica Raban (neé Sandison). At the time his father was on active duty in World War II as an artillery officer, and Raban was at that time an only child; he describes himself as very close to his mother and in poor health.

JONATHAN RABAN

From 1953 to 1958 he attended the King's School, Worcester, where he was not happy; he transferred to a sixth-form college to complete his schooling. He went on to Hull University to read English and American studies and went out of his way to develop a friendship with the reclusive poet Philip Larkin, then librarian at the university. Raban became a university lecturer, first at Aberystwyth, later at the University of East Anglia in Norwich. He had already begun writing and in 1969 decided to leave teaching and live entirely by writing and journalism—a change of course that paralleled the change in direction his father had taken some twenty years earlier. He now lives in the United States; in 1990 he settled in Seattle, which he finds congenial for its liberal atmosphere and its nearness to the sea, a proximity that has enabled him to indulge a major passion, single-handed sailing. Since 1996 he has been divorced and lives with his daughter Julia, to whom both *Passage to Juneau* (1999) and *Waxwings* are dedicated.

THE END OF ENGLAND: COASTING (1986)

Raban has described in detail how he came to cut the ties with England, though he remains English in tastes and temperament. For their style, he reads and rereads the work of P. G. Wodehouse and Evelyn Waugh (a distant cousin). His accent is unchanged, despite the mockery and even hatred it occasionally arouses. The reason for the cutting of the ties is connected to the end of Englishness, the loss of a sense of the distinctively English approach to life that dominated Raban's childhood. His description of that end of Englishness is found particularly in *Coasting* and in *For Love & Money* (1987), a collection of his journalism and autobiographical essays.

When Peter Raban returned from the war, Jonathan resented this boisterous, rather frightening figure that moved in to take up room in his and his mother's life. Peter Raban had not been able to find a place at university before the war and had trained as a teacher. He had not been happy or successful. Now he determined on a change of career and became a minister in the established Anglican (Protestant Episcopalian) Church. Politically a Conservative and in the conservative wing of the church, he was a man obsessed with membership in his social caste. Wider than simply class, caste dictated what jobs one could take, what friends and associates one could make, what standards one lived by. He was a keen historian of his family, making out genealogies and keeping souvenirs of generations of clergymen and colonial soldiers, which crowded the long succession of houses young Jonathan grew up in, each with its tight hedge designed to keep out the eyes of the world. The family lived in comparative poverty, but Peter made sacrifices to send his son to private school. It was a world that Jane Austen, the Brontës, or Anthony Trollope would have recognized at once. Raban writes in *Coasting,* "The cassock my father wore had belonged to my grandfather before him.... It looked as old as the Church of England itself...and this old cassock made my father himself seem like a very old man to me, a tall and shaggy Abraham.... He was thirty-six." Both at home and at school Jonathan never lived up to expectations, never managed to live by the dreary standards of the social order of England in the 1950s and adapt to his father's political and social conservatism. His writing constitutes an acute analysis of why in the end it had to give way to the liberalism of the 1960s. Until that change arrived, Raban simply "coasted," to quote his school reports (*Coasting,* pp. 16–22).

Coasting contains a graphic account of how Raban was shaped by his family and education and is a densely packed book full of sharp and intelligent observations of English people— fishermen, coal miners, hairdressers, trying to cope with the greatest economic depression in thirty years and losing the sense of what had once defined them as English. It is about England in crisis, written by someone who still feels committed to it but is not sure why. The fishermen feel that the government has betrayed them by giving away traditional fishing areas to foreign competitors. The miners, engaged in a major strike, are being broken by a Conservative government that wants to destroy their union. Raban joins their picket lines and in the course of this encounters a miner who hears his middle-class accent and instantly responds not with mockery but with aggressive hate. There is a deep defeatism and surliness in England, as people adjust to what Raban calls the "merrying" of England, the drive to dress up to give interest to the photographs of the tourists, increasingly the only real source of income for many of them. Those who drive public relations for the tourist industry package the country for individual markets. Raban has an eye for the lies the graphics represent: "for Saudi Arabia [the poster] shows what looks like an intricate mosque... actually a picture of Brighton's Royal Pavilion. Below...two twinned images; one of a Daimler illegally parked in Knightsbridge outside Harrods, the other of a woman bargaining with a smiling shopkeeper.... Britain is a Moslem country with a famously well-stocked souk." For Europe and the United States the posters show a party in the garden of a thatched and timbered pub, where guests are drinking from tankards, playing skittles, and helping themselves to cheese. "A space has been left...for the tourist to perch on the dry-stone wall and join in this rustic fun" (p. 212). The tourists are encouraged to read Britain in a particular—false—way, and the English are encouraged to read themselves into the script. But they won't do it.

Structurally the book is an account of a solo trip in a yacht around the coast of Britain undertaken in 1982, the year of Raban's fortieth birthday. He has chosen the single-handed voyage because, as he shows in discussing the work of earlier solo yachtsmen making similar voyages, there is no other way to be alone in England anymore and to reflect on it, and he is not happy with England. "It's no wonder that England seen from the sea looks so withdrawn, preoccupied and inward—a gloomy house, its shutters drawn" (p. 12). The country is full of change and innovation, but the sea around it remains the same. Raban will make a series of landfalls as the journey progresses, but he is traveling one of the most dangerous seas in the world: "England's message to every ship that gets near to her coast [is]: DANGER–KEEP OUT" (p. 13). Once again, as at school, he is "coasting," but "coasting," as the

nautical literature tells us, implies the need to "observe the time and direction of the tide, to know the reigning winds" (p. 21). Raban quotes Hilaire Belloc: "'the whole rigmarole [of cruising] leads us along no whither, and yet is alive with discovery, emotion, adventure peril and repose,'" (p. 31). And of course England is coasting too.

Raban has with him *Great Britain's Coastal Pilot* by Captain Grenville Collins. A book of descriptions of the coastline first published in 1693, it remains accurate. On his progress round the coast (slow, of course, six knots, twelve land miles an hour, bicycle speed) Raban is able to observe how much of England is still recognizable two hundred years after Collins and how much of the cheerful, suburban world of shops and houses can also be seen. Sometimes he has the experience of seeing a place he had known as a child, when it was different. He remembers a hotel in Lymington as it had been when his great-aunt dined there in the 1940s, quiet, stiff, rather dull. Now it is bright and full of people with plastic money eating more expensive, probably better food; they are people his great-aunt would have despised. There is no trace of nostalgia in Raban; he welcomes the social changes, yet he is "not quite at ease in the new dispensation," to slightly misquote T. S. Eliot's *Journey of the Magi*.

When the *Gosfield Maid* was first launched after a refit, Raban had never in his life taken charge of a boat at sea, but he found a retired naval officer to teach him the basics, taught himself navigation, and set off. This is, by the way, a brave or foolhardy thing to do, and what he does at the start of his voyage down the Mississippi is even more dangerous, as will be seen later.

One landfall on the 1982 cruise is at Douglas in the Isle of Man; Raban is driven into harbor by bad weather, while a Royal Air Force plane searches the seas for a lost trawler. Man is a parochial place—thirty miles from north to south, yet the people in the south don't trust the people from the north, and the parochial atmosphere means that the English settlers ("overcomers" as they are called) instantly take to the island, for the English are a parochial people. "We're thirty years behind the times here," an overcomer landlord tells Raban. "And we mean to keep it that way." The chips in the casino are still marked with values in the pre-decimal currency of fifteen years before. "The landscape was full of things I couldn't remember seeing since my childhood—steam trains, old cars, squads of butterflies, deep tangled hedgerows full of wild flowers" (p. 59).

Raban buys a copy of the poems of T. E. Brown, the poet laureate of Man, who wrote long dialect poems about the crofters and fishermen of the 1890s—a celebration of insularity and a voice protesting the colonialism of England, which is destroying Manx life (and Scottish, Welsh, and Irish life). Yet something doesn't ring true to Raban. Brown was a Manxman by birth but was educated at Oxford and taught all his life at an English public school where "my own grandfather must have been one of his pupils.... Who was [Brown] to shove my Englishness in my face and make me feel guilty for not being a weasel-browed Manx fisherman?" (p. 66).

The Isle of Man does not ring true either. Long a center of smuggling, it is now a tax haven. A semi-independent state, it sets its own income tax levels and sets them low (it does not bear any of the costs of the United Kingdom's armed forces, for example). So it attracts tax exiles from England, who pay lower taxes in return for residing there. The island is awash with funny money, large amounts of capital raised from insubstantial sources by millionaires and by "Englishmen with company pensions and tidy nest-eggs who wanted to hang on to as much as they could." It was a "gimcrack cultural superstructure.... The trouble was that for the exiles there was not a great deal to do" (pp. 70–71). Man is in this respect a microcosm of England; Man used to trap lobsters, now it traps tax-exiles, just as England puts itself out to trap tourists. Raban escapes through foul weather; like all lone yachtsmen sometimes do, he hallucinates that someone else is on the boat. He thinks he sees the old naval officer who taught him to sail going down to check the bilges.

Chapter 3, "An Insular War," begins with what Raban thinks is a hallucination, as a fleet of enormous warships steam past him in the channel.

It is only when he lands that he learns that, indeed, "I was pointing east by north for the Dover Straits; England was heading west and south for the Falkland Islands" (p. 92). Argentina had invaded and occupied this British possession, and a task force of British warships was off to drive the Argentines away. It is England that is suffering the hallucination. Following the war on radio and TV, he describes his reaction—cool, yet caught up during the broadcast of the expedition sailing from Portsmouth by the "insidious British genius for impromptu ceremonial [which] could dissolve a scepticism like mine in a few moments" (p. 115). A visit to the training college for officers of the Royal Navy reminds Raban of his time in the Cadet Corps at his school, where he had shown an aptitude for playing at war on "field days" when the whole school turned out for training. Now "the whole country was out on a field day" (p. 135). It is at this stage that he receives a postcard from an American friend. On the reverse of a photo of the Colonel Shaw memorial in Boston, she writes "Maybe you'd better emigrate—people here think your country has lost its wits" (p. 141).

In chapter 4, "Hunting for Fossils," which describes how different it is for Raban to hunt fossils at Lyme Regis now compared with his schooldays, he calls to see his parents. "I found [them]...in the red-light district of Southampton." Retired from the church, his father had bought a large old house, without a hedge. "'Hullo, old boy.' But the *old boy* was the only surviving component of the father I remembered.... He wore a CND [Campaign for Nuclear Disarmament] badge and his pipe, like mine, was couched in the left hand corner of his mouth.... Father and son, definitely. But an outsider might have found it difficult to tell who was which.... 'You've gone a bit thin on top', he said" (pp. 169–171). Peter Raban and his wife are now radicals, voting Labour, loathing Prime Minister Margaret Thatcher and planning a holiday in the still Communist Eastern bloc. "*Extraordinary.* But it was not really so extraordinary. My father was only keeping in tune with his Church and his times" (p. 174). For the church has been dispossessed of its old power and influence and has become in turn one of the voices of the dispossessed; Peter Raban is being vilified in the national press because he plans to sell a redundant church to the Sikh community in Southampton so that they can have the temple they need.

There follows a genuinely comic incident where Jonathan decides to take his parents out on the boat so that they will admire him and his management of the "hazards and enchantments of my new life." "It is a mistake to let a priest go on a boat.... Prepared for a slice of heroic adventure, they found themselves in the middle of a floating vicarage fete. The sun shone. The salt in the air glittered like tinsel."

His father, who has done a little sailing, is anxious to help, but Raban cannot communicate his instructions clearly. He has not bothered to learn the names of the ropes, for example:

> "No, not that rope. The other one...that's tied to that cleat thing."
>
> "The topping lift," my father said.... In his white cricket sweater, grey flannels and plimsolls, still as long and lean as he had been in his twenties, he looked comfortably in control of the occasion.
>
> (p. 180)

This episode is balanced by another moment of contact. Visiting one of his father's old churches a day or two later, Raban tells his parents he can remember his father's first sermon.

> "It was on Scott's last expedition.... It was Festival of Britain year [1951]. Captain Oates represented the spirit of British self-sacrifice."
>
> "It sounds *Thatcherite,*" my mother said.
>
> "Oh, it was."
>
> (p. 184)

Later in the book, he puts in to Hull, where the old fishing docks that once handled millions of tons of fish are now empty and about to be turned into marinas. Here he meets up with Philip Larkin and takes him to dinner in a Lebanese restaurant.

> "What sort of food would one get in a Lebanese restaurant?
> Would it be—*mushy*?"
>
> Fiercely defending my decision to escape the Royal Station

Hotel, I said, "No..."
> "But I *like* mushy food."
>
> (p. 261)

Told he can have *houmus* or *taramasalata,* Larkin, "suddenly skittish," drives to the restaurant as though "Hull was a city as foreign as Beirut itself."

> (p. 261)

There is an account of their conversation that is better than an interview because it is based on Raban actually understanding Larkin and knowing his tastes and interests. He tells us: "Larkin died...in 1985. Until his death I hadn't grasped how much he was loved in England.... His poems are heartbreakingly exact. If poems can teach one anything, Larkin's teach that there is no desolation so bleak that it cannot be made habitable by style. If we live inside a bad joke, it is up to us to learn...to tell it well." Yet despite all this positive appreciation, there lurks inside the same paragraph a contrary feeling. Larkin's life was typically English in that it was isolated and lonely behind the "separating glass of windows," and it was "a life from which most people would shrink in panic" (p. 268). Raban puts that last phrase in parentheses, as if to say it is something to think about again later.

The book ends with an envoi. In a new relationship, Jonathan Raban has settled in a cottage in Essex while refitting *Gosfield Maid* (he has anagrammatized it earlier (p. 48) to *Die, Dismal Fog,* a sort of prayer for mariners and for observers of England). This is a rich, prosperous community. Everybody has a sign in the front drive advertising some pin-money sideline: EGGS LAID WHILE YOU WAIT...HAIRCUT, SIR? ...CREAM TEAS, WELDING & RESPRAYS. "It seemed the right place for me...there had to be a space for my shingle BOOKS WRITTEN WHILE YOU WAIT" (p. 295). And all this wealth—the crops, the American combine harvesters—contradicts the picture of England that he has built up on his journey and must now set down in the book, which ends on a bitterly cold day, so cold he and his partner cannot yet set off again.

"The cold's insane.... How's it going?"

"Slowly...." Her coat at my ear is radiating a winter of its own.

"Where have you got to?"

"Not far. Only here where we are now, before we go—"

(p. 301)

One of the solo yachtsmen Raban describes earlier, R. T. McMullen, had died of a heart attack at the wheel. "Two days later, *Perseus* was spotted by a fishing boat off Cherbourg. It was maintaining a steady westward course.... The dead man, his limbs locked in rigor mortis, was keeping a firm grip on the tiller. If a member of the French lower orders (a category that had given McMullen no end of trouble during his life) had not unsportingly intervened, he might well be still be sailing today" (p. 29). It makes a complex multiple metaphor. To Raban it represents his determination to sail until he dies. But it is also a metaphor of England, rigidly locked in on the journey to the Falklands to settle the trouble caused by another set of foreign lower orders.

THE UNITED STATES

Raban has written extensively on the United States. *Old Glory* is an account of a journey by powerboat down the Mississippi, *Bad Land: An American Romance* reports an investigation of east Montana, and *Passage to Juneau* describes a journey up the strait between the mainland and Vancouver Island from Seattle to Juneau. *Old Glory* is included here to show how it fits into the pattern of the American work, though it was written before *Coasting* and describes a journey made in 1979, three years earlier than the journey in the other book.

Raban depicts the United States as much more varied, both geographically and socially, than European countries and shows that Americans are consequently more varied in character. In *Bad Land* he makes it clear that even if they now have it easy (though many of them do not) this is because in the past they have had it hard.

Earlier English writers on America (Charles Dickens, Frances Trollope, and her son Anthony Trollope) had tended to treat America with disdain. They particularly disliked the democracy and communality, reserving special venom for the lodging house and its meals served for all at one table. Raban has to break through a similar disdain at the start of *Old Glory*. It is part of a disorientation that expresses itself in several small observations in these books. Though he has no trouble with American liquor, he cannot finish a serving of catfish and french fries on the Mississippi because (as we learn later) he dislikes the sweet taste of the grilled fish; when he reaches Canada on the way to Juneau, he rejoices that he can again buy a distinctive English yeast-based spread called Marmite. (Other exiles show the same pattern: Elizabeth Asquith, who left Wales in the 1950s for Bowling Green, Kentucky, is totally at home; she has learned American as a foreign language by keeping vocabulary lists. But she still cooks every so often a traditional English Sunday lunch of roast lamb and mint sauce.)

Raban intensely dislikes the American drive to fake heritage features. The nineteenth-century buildings erected in riverside towns in imitation of Venice or Paris, now crumbling into decay, and the modern motel bedrooms that imitate Mississippi steamers are alike pernicious, he believes, in that they persuade local people to admire the tawdry. But he seeks out and praises the paintings of George Caleb Bingham (*Old Glory*), the photographs of Evelyn Cameron (*Bad Land*) and Native American art (*Passage to Juneau*).

OLD GLORY *(1981)*

Raban precedes Old Glory with three epigraphs. From T. S. Eliot's "Dry Salvages" (a section of *Four Quartets*) he quotes "the river is a strong brown god...keeping his seasons and rages, destroyer, reminder / Of what men chose to forget." From the French painter Jean-François Millet (1814–1875) he has a passage, of central importance in his thinking, that suggests that a painting drawn from the memory of a brief but strong impression may succeed better than a careful drawing made on the spot, "though all the details may be wrong." From Thoreau he has "travelling is no pastime, but it is as serious as the grave, and it requires a long probation." These epigraphs are a program for the book. A journey must be individual—the particular quality of the Mississippi will dominate this book and shape it in a particular way, and the Mississippi (the river of Eliot's own boyhood in St. Louis) can be a particularly violent river. Getting down it depends on chance; again and again Raban hears tales of sudden drowning. It is not "the heart of darkness," but it is both a light and a darkness at the heart of American life. Millett expresses the principle that it may well be that the journey can be shaped completely into art only after it is over, and Thoreau expresses the principle that a journey must be prepared for.

Old Glory is the flag of the United States, and the book is set at a time when the American embassy in Tehran has been taken over by Iranian activists who are holding the staff hostage. One of the themes of the book is that the response to this incident disturbs the average American emotionally in a way the Falklands crisis did not touch the average Englishman during the Falklands War, and this response centers on the flag. Old Glory too is the keynote of the communities on the Mississippi; in Mark Twain's day the wealth and commerce of America depended on the river, and each town had some share in them. Now once again traffic on the river is thriving, but on a new pattern. Huge tows, where a single boat tugs several enormous barges, bring immense wealth to a few communities and nothing to the rest. Finally, there are the cities—Minneapolis, St. Louis, Memphis, Vicksburg, New Orleans—born of the river. But Minneapolis, at the head of navigation for the river, has turned its back on the Mississippi; it has bridged it and hidden it. The city lives on the road, not on the river. St. Louis and Memphis are wastelands and New Orleans a tourist ghetto. Only Vicksburg has made the adjustment and kept its old glory.

The book starts on Twain's river. "It is as big and as depthless as the sky itself. You can see the curve of the earth on its surface as it stretches away for miles to the far shore. Sunset has turned the water to the colour of unripe peaches" (p. 11). The river of *Life on the Mississippi* and *Huckleberry Finn* is still there, and Raban details his boyhood love of Twain's world. "I found the Mississippi in the family atlas.... North Africa and Italy had come loose from the binding, from my mother's attempts to keep up with my father's campaigns.... North America, though, was virgin territory" (p. 12). The Mississippi, then, is where Raban will measure himself, "my best invention; a dream which was always there" (p. 14). On Labor Day 1979 he finds himself in Minneapolis caught on the expressway in the flow of traffic to the state fair and is swept along. He is not in sympathy with this vast concourse celebrating the last of summer before the coming of the North Plains winter; it is a vast, hot crowd full of grotesque and obese people in a stink of cooking meat. He finds some relief talking vaguely to a man hiding from his shrewish wife in the tent where the livestock is displayed—quiet, dignified beef cattle. But Raban will be at ease only with those who live on the river, or with the large number of those (especially women) who live by the river but never venture on it.

His boat (a twelve-foot Mirrorcraft) is on loan from the manufacturers, and he has a fifteen-horsepower outboard motor. It is fitted out by Herb Heichert at Minneapolis and re-christened by him *Raban's Nest*. ("Just came to me.") Herb shows him the gadgets: "Electronic fish-locator...all you got to do is put your pole over the side and catch it." "Will [it] tell you what bait to use as well?" "They must be working on that I guess" (p. 48).

That is a characteristic response by Herb; Americans often disconcert Englishmen by listening to what they say and responding to throwaway lines. Raban learns how to pilot the boat and begins to pick up the lore. Yet there is one strange feature in this briefing process. No one appears to suggest to Raban that he is taking his life in his hands by starting off with no radio, and he has immense trouble with the tows without one. It was a mistake he did not repeat three years later coasting around Britain.

Accompanied by Cramer's *The Navigator* (1814), the popular nineteenth-century guide to the river, and by the Reverend Timothy Flint's *Recollections* (1826), he casts off, remembering too late that he has left his *Huckleberry Finn* in the motel. "Damn, damn, damn. Slowing on the current, I thought that perhaps my loss wasn't such a bad augury after all. This was a voyage I was going to have to make alone" (p. 66).

Herb has told him, "Remember you don't have to do nothing fast. Think about it. Do it slow" (p. 57), and there is an easy pace about this long book with its many interests. Raban has the facility for making quick acquaintance. Some of the people he meets he loathes, some he admires, and the point of contact is always the river. He comes across an old man hiding from the game warden while he angles for catfish. The old man is eating cheap corned beef in his sandwiches, but his bait is prime steak; the river always has its price. The river can make for loneliness; there is a carpenter who spends each weekend away from his family in the old family place by the river. There are several millionaires and an old lady who lives on Social Security and a few odd dollars made by catching fish. There is generosity. He is finally persuaded to get a radio by a total stranger he meets near Cape Girardeau, Missouri, who insists on paying for one if Raban cannot afford the money; in fact he can afford it, and the radio makes him a member of the world of the captains—everyone in charge of a boat is "Cap." The river shapes the lives of them all.

Some of the relationships are longer and indicate an underlying turbulence in his life that is like the turbulence of the river. In St. Louis he moves in with Shirley, the daughter of a millionaire. For a while he is a househusband. Eventually he buys the charts for the lower Mississippi and hides them in the flat. He is going to leave; she tells him he is a coward.

At Memphis he stays awhile to join in the campaign of the Democrat candidate for mayor, Otis Higgs. Memphis, like St. Louis, has been severely hit economically because the middle class has moved out "to the county," leaving the city without a tax base to meet its needs. Higgs, who is black, is attempting to build an interracial coalition to revive the city. Raban depicts the strains of the project; in the end Higgs fails, probably because he cannot convey to white audi-

ences the vigor and charisma he projects to black audiences. After the election, Raban visits Higgs's church and hears him preach. Higgs concludes

> "We got a visitor in church this morning…he's from England. He's white…. I got to thinking…to-day when you preach you got to be so so-phist-icated…. And now look! I done preach just like I am!…"
>
> "Halleluia!…"
>
> I couldn't echo that halleluia…. I should have said… My whiteness doesn't mean logic, sophistication, self-control. And your blackness surely shouldn't just mean spontaneity, warmth, the "feeling within."…Otis Higgs told Memphis to *wake up* …you were fast asleep when you were talking about me.
>
> (pp. 444–445)

Raban cannot yet say to Americans the things that only an insider can say.

Perhaps nowhere expresses the independence of local communities better than Vicksburg, where Raban notices a Confederate cannon sighted on the river that is not "an empty historical symbol…it was more complicated than that." The city held out for forty-seven days in 1863 against Grant's Union Army until finally surrendering on the Fourth of July. It has never forgiven Natchez for surrendering without a fight and preserves a "scowling independence." Raban quotes from the memoirs of the siege written by the Confederate Colonel J. H. Jones of the Thirty-eighth Mississippi:

> Our friends of the [Union] 17th Illinois fraternized with the 38th and aided us greatly by many acts of kindness. They would go to their sutler's tent with the greenbacks we had borrowed from their dead comrades and purchase food from us, and doubtless many a starving "Reb" felt that his life was thus saved.

Raban comments: *"Friends? kindness? borrowed? dead? life?"* and tells us that on July 2 they had to dine off the quartermaster's mule (pp. 458–460). Vicksburg did not celebrate the Fourth for nearly a century, and when, on July 4, 1876, the Mississippi shifted its course and left the town high and dry, the citizens were determined that Vicksburg remain a river port and diverted the Yazoo into the old Mississippi channel.

Raban describes meeting the wealthy of Vicksburg as well as members of the local black community; the encounters are described with perception and detail. (There are black shoe stores in Jackson but not in Vicksburg, because in Jackson the white owners would not let black customers try on the shoes before they bought them, while in Vicksburg they would). But the most consoling encounter is with the "Director of Boils, Eddies, Cut-offs and Fast Currents" of the Corps of Engineers at the Experiment Station south of Vicksburg. (The river has been the responsibility of the U.S. Army since 1917).

> "When you come off the river at the end of the day, do you feel kind of shaky?" [asks the director].
>
> "Every time...I can't keep my hands steady."
>
> "Me neither...." I was delighted. [The director continues] "You take the disrespectingest man... Put him on the river. Just for one day. It'd change him."
>
> (p. 477)

Finally, below New Orleans in Cajun country Raban puts his hand into the water, and it tastes salt. He has made the trip from head of navigation to the sea. Only at the last has he felt in any danger, when, in a nowhere place, he is threatened by a drug addict. He is a "Cap."

There never was a more American Dream than Sam Clemens wanting to be a river pilot, making it, and then turning the experience into *Life on the Mississippi*. Raban set off with the same dream, with a smaller boat though with modern technology (army charts and radio in particular). The problem is the need to return. In Louisiana there are armadillos that have crossed over from Mexico and moved up the coast. Every so often they simply fall off a bank and drown. Yet they move on. Raban's discontent and lack of resolution is palpable. He ends thus: "[I] let the boat drift out on the tide for a while, then pointed the prow back, in the same, dumb, urban direction that the armadillos set their noses" (p. 527).

BAD LAND: AN AMERICAN ROMANCE *(1996)*

Bad Land is a detailed and thoroughly researched document covering an episode in American social history. It describes how, about 1910, the last of the Homestead acts enabled the railroad companies to persuade people to buy farmsteads in eastern Montana, the way most of these settlers met with disaster, and how those who stuck it out succeeded in creating viable farms, as a result of which they have become comparatively rich. It links this experience to the political views of those who now live there and tells what happened to some who moved on. At the same time, it derives the impulse of the first settlers from a version of the American Dream as they then saw it in the fiction of the times (even if they were not at that time Americans) and places the graphic art of Montana, especially the photographs of Evelyn Cameron, in context. These settlers were the generation of Raban's great-grandfather, and he tells us that, like many Englishmen, he has wondered at times what his life would have been had he been descended from such emigrants. The ancestors of one of the families Raban meets, the Wollastons, in fact came from the same English village as his own ancestors, but in that village at that time barriers of caste would have divided the two families, putting the Rabans lower down the scale.

Raban begins eating lunch in his car parked by the roadside in the endless dry plains of eastern Montana. "The ocean was hardly more solitary than this empty country, where in forty miles or so I hadn't seen another vehicle.... The surface of the land was as busy as a rough sea...ragged bluffs, hollow combers of bleached clay...waterless creek beds, ash-white" (p. 1). The air is full of the noise of "birds, the crooning wind, the urgent fiddling of the crickets." A Montanan passes in his truck, stops to visit. He farms eleven sections, his wife's folks' old place. His folks lost theirs in the Dirty Thirties.

> A section is a square mile. "That's quite a chunk of Montana. What do you farm?"
>
> "Mostly cattle. We grow hay. And a section and a half is wheat, some years, when we get the moisture for it."
>
> "And it pays?"

"One year we make quite a profit and the next we go twice as deep as that into the hole. That's about the way it goes round here."

(p. 3)

All around are relics of human occupation, now disappearing into the prairie—machinery, graveyards. Raban goes into an abandoned home where he finds traces of old pride. "This house had been built to last. Its frames were stout, its cedar floor laid like a yacht's deck. It had been meant for the grandchildren...and it must have seemed—in what, 1915? 1920?—a rock solid investment" (p. 8). The family had finally left, putting what they could carry in the pickup or the Model T and leaving behind a mess of papers, with figuring that shows how debt was piling up, and a book called *Campbell's Soil Management Culture.*

As Raban eats in the diner that night, it begins to rain, and the rain continues. It is "an astonishing gift. It falls like money" (p. 15). Montana is an arid region, and in 1910 Hardy W. Campbell was the expert on soil cultivation in arid areas. Like ex-President Theodore Roosevelt he was a Jeffersonian at heart. Roosevelt had a vision of an America carpeted with small communities of independent farmers, more productive then they had been in the past, "conservationist," to use a favorite word of his, and enjoying the benefits of electric lights and railroads, schools and churches. As in the previous century, the railroads wanted settlers to take up the land through which their tracks ran and generate freight. But eastern Montana? Dry—well, *dryish.* It has half the rainfall of eastern England, but mostly the rain falls in the growing season, so there is more sunlight. Additionally Campbell had written a popular book on scientific farming, and his theory was that if farmers compacted the subsoil, moisture would be drawn up by capillary action. Farming would be sustainable, even in arid areas, and "conservationist." Boastful statistics hold out hope of enormous fertility.

Raban says of his copy of the book that "its spine was broken between page 240 and 241 when someone trod on it.... The imprint...looks like a deliberate verdict" (p. 34). He places the work in the context of the fiction of the time including such million-copy best-sellers as Owen Wister's *The Virginian* (1902) and Gene Stratton-Porter's *A Girl of the Limberlost* (1909). These books, read by many of the settlers who came to Montana, have at their center a desire to escape from the city and find or re-create the wilderness in the West, and this desire finds its theoretical expression in Charles Wagner's *The Simple Life* (1901). Whatever else happened, the settlers did not go into this project blind. They had read up on the seemingly scientific literature, including that put out by the railroad companies.

What it is that they saw? "The new arrivals found themselves in country that defeated the best efforts of the eye to get it in sharp focus" (p. 49). It stretches out forever and has very few features—military roads, railroad tracks, survey pegs. Raban finds the country impossible to photograph in any way that conveys the scale. Even graphic art is defeated by the scale; Albert Bierstadt in 1859 had caught the landscape by reading it as a sea, and Frederic Remington had reduced it to a bare wash against which his cowboys stand out like giant, landscape-eclipsing figures. The most successful photographs are those of one of the settlers, Evelyn Cameron, which convey the emptiness and distance. "Nearly all of her people looked as if their presence in Eastern Montana came as a bewildering surprise to them, and they were photographed in surroundings that were either much too big, like the open prairie, or much too small like the dog kennel interiors of their claim shacks" (p. 62).

Raban describes the settling in, the building of homes, the hope. Fences are built, shacks erected, deeds obtained. It was a condition of the grant that the settlers take out citizenship; win or lose, they were now Americans. Of course it went wrong; crops were poor, rains failed, the soil eroded, and mortgages and loans for machinery advanced by optimistic banks in the first years became a liability. Campbell was a fraud. One by one, most of the families failed and moved away. Some achieved nothing. Worsell, so friendless that no one remembered his given name, was an English Boer War veteran and a widower with a son, Arthur. He was so lacking in common sense that he always had to rely on his neighbors to survive. Arthur became a bum. It was not quite as bad for the rest of them perhaps. They had the American way out—move on farther west. First they became fruit pickers in western Montana, and then perhaps they moved on to the West Coast and later did well in the aerospace industries.

If that were all, we would only have a more analytical version of John Steinbeck's *Grapes of Wrath* (1939). But Raban goes farther and details the next stage; how those who stayed survived and who survived.

The problem had been, as a Kansas congressman had pointed out in the debate on the bill, that the land allocations were too small. At a section they had seemed immense, especially to those settlers who were immigrants—half the size of Hyde Park in London. But a Montana farm needed to be several sections in size to sustain both cropping and livestock rearing. As the first to go moved out, their sections could be bought up dirt cheap; Raban meets a man who bought seven sections in the 1930s at $1.50 each. The abandoned homes could be dragged to new sites; Montana ranch houses are often several original houses put together. Machinery could be bought cheap too.

Who survived? Often, Raban points out, it was the religious families. First, they tended to be more frugal. Having read Exodus they knew that drought comes in cycles, and they resisted the loans from the banks. Second, they tended to blame themselves for the failures, and this was a strength; if you believe you are to blame for failure, you believe that greater effort can bring success. So they hung in there.

Nowadays, while those who moved out tend to show New Deal Democrat leanings, those who stayed tend to be politically conservative, but this is not because the government let them down at the first settlement. The reason finds expression in the collective memory; they remember the federal experts, for instance, well paid on the farmers' tax dollars, who held seminars to persuade them to plant trees to act as windbreaks and stop soil erosion. Of course the farmers knew that was the solution; they also knew the time scale, and in time the windbreaks have appeared (the older the ranch, the thicker the tree belts, Raban observes). So they have contempt for big government.

English reviewers have tended, mistakenly, to see *Bad Land* as a tale of the American Dream gone sour or turned to dust, but the American Dream has never been a promise; it is a hope. The Woolastons were disappointed in that hope. Then another hope came along like Scott Fitzgerald's green light seen across the water and persuaded them to move on. The book contains a dynamic tension between the success of those who stayed and the loss of those who moved on, between the various successes and failures of those who moved on, between the deceit practiced on those who read the railroad propaganda and those who turned the deception into a better, more sustainable reality. The book documents the way in which America may exact a higher price than Europe but has better rewards to give.

PASSAGE TO JUNEAU: A SEA AND ITS MEANINGS *(1999)*

What does the sea mean? To the young man Raban meets on the wharf at Seattle where the fishing boats are preparing for their trip to the Alaskan fishing grounds the answer is a job where he can earn good money and set himself up in life. But the flush times are over, the days of $1,000 earned every day (or so rumor had it); the salmon are almost played out, and jobs aboard the fishing boats are now kept for the family. And the cost was always high, as a service at the Fisherman's Memorial reminds Raban.

Raban sets off north along the interior passage from Seattle to Juneau in Alaska, retracing the eighteenth-century voyage of Captain Vancouver, sent by the British Admiralty to prove once and for all that there was no northwest passage, no route around America to the north. Failure to find the passage will be success. Though Vancouver has two ships under his command, he is a lonely man, cut off by his lowly social class from the other officers, especially the aristocratic midshipmen; cut off too by his personality from ease in command, he inflicts fierce punishments on the crewmen. Yet at the same time, he is a brilliant navigator; he has learned his trade under Captain Cook, the great explorer of the Pacific, and can fix the position of his ship within a third of a mile by observation of the relative position of sun and moon, without recourse to a chronometer. He is exploring what will be British Columbia. The sea is simply the medium through which he sails; the land on either shore is the object of his attention. He visualizes it cleared and laid out like an English estate described by Alexander Pope; his midshipmen see it as "sublime," terrifying in its awesome ruggedness.

The Native Americans Vancouver encounters have a different perspective. They live on and read the sea; they turn their backs on the land, needing only a narrow strip of coast to make their camps on. It is harder to find the meaning they once saw because their verbal tradition has been edited by generations of missionaries. But Raban finds in their visual art the domination of images that make sense because they are symmetrical, each side the mirror image of the other. Looking at photographs of logs floating on the water turned end up, he describes them as resembling totem poles. The Native Americans live their lives dominated by legend and myth; the myths are often of sudden and violent attacks by spirits like Komogwa who live deep in the water and bring sudden destruction. The woods too are full of violent spirits, especially bears; the rite of passage is for a young man to spend time on his own in the woods, facing out these dangers, acquiring his own guiding spirit. In itself the voyage itself ends on a note of hope. Raban learns of a theory that the drop in the number of salmon is due to a natural climatic cycle and is not due to over-fishing.

But there are two losses that Raban must endure during this period. The first is when he must break off the journey to travel to England with his wife, Jean, and his daughter, Julia, to be present as his father dies. The second is the end of his marriage to Jean. There had been clues all along of strain in the family; Julia's reluctance to let him go at the start of the journey; the coolness of their telephone conversations while Jean makes light of the difficulty she has developing her own career without his being there for her;

the symbolism of the frequent failures to get through on the phone at all. Early in the voyage he had given the name of his boat just once— Penelope. "I had intended to suppress that"; the aptness of the reference to the faithful Penelope waiting at home for Odysseus' return is too painful. Now, as the Native Americans would say, Komogwa has come up out of the depths and the boat is overwhelmed.

WAXWINGS *(2003)*

The central character in Raban's novel *Waxwings,* Tom Janeaway, lectures at Seattle University, having gotten the job on the basis of a novel called *Tunnels* that visualizes meetings between characters from different nineteenth-century novels. Critics have regularly suggested that, if we need a nineteenth-century parallel, *Waxwings* is like Dickens in that it brings together members of different social classes. But it lacks the urge toward the grotesque that we find in Dickens, which has the curious effect of making the villains less frightening (and there are villains in *Waxwings*). It is possibly more like one of Trollope's social satires such as *The Way We Live Now* (1875), which also crosses social barriers. Trollope was always careful to set his novels in a particular time, and this means that within a few years they came to be seen as historical novels. Raban sets *Waxwings* in November 1999 at the height of the dotcom boom, and the passing of only a few years between that year and the date of its writing has led Raban to claim that *Waxwings* is in some sense a historical novel.

Tom Janeaway (born Tamás Szany in Budapest in 1954 but taken to England at the age of two) is married to Beth, who works "24/7" (twenty-four hours a day, seven days a week) for a dotcom company developing virtual reality sites to sell real estate. They have a son, Finn. (The origin of the name is not Mark Twain's Huckleberry Finn—Beth is Irish.)

The central strand in the book is the portrayal of the partner-partner and parent-child relationships within a family. Finn is bound to his father partly through his father's tales about a character called Mr. Wicked, who dresses entirely in black and has an accomplice, a witch called Moira. The stories involve plotlines such as Mr. Wicked getting hold of a whole truckload of superglue, and all begin "As was his wont, Mr. Wicked...." Beth's friend Debra finds these tales sinister. Finn is pure id and hyperactive. It is an impressive piece of characterization.

One night Beth tells Tom she wants a separation. From upstairs, Finn listens to their conversation where each cries in turn and concludes that this is what his friend Spencer describes as making a baby. When they tell him they have some news, he is expecting the announcement of a baby brother or sister; subsequently his reactions are carefully charted, as he assimilates the new way of life into a child's frame of reference.

But children are at risk, and we see two instances of this. The book opens on a ship coming into Seattle; the relief pilot announces that the regular pilot is on leave because his granddaughter has been killed by a cougar that came down from the woods and raided her playschool as casually as it might raid a garbage can. Later Tom goes for a hike along a woodland trail. He is spotted behaving strangely by local people, who report him to the police when a little girl is abducted; she will later be found dead.

This tragedy leads to a carefully worked-out relationship with the investigating police officer Detective Paul Nagel, who is a balance of courtesy and drive. He and Tom ought to be friends; Nagel is a writer but Tom fears that Paul will ask him to read his scripts. Paul's principal aim is to eliminate Tom from the enquiry, but Tom cannot help himself. Locked in his misery, he had observed nothing on his hike. Nagel forces him finally to remember seeing a camper van with out-of-state plates from Alaska. No, says Nagel; Washington state plates, but the make was an Alaskan. This tiny incident marks a beginning for Tom's escape from his self-absorption.

News of the suspicion that has fallen on Tom leaks out; he is vilified, suspended from duty, and lampooned on the Internet. Tom complains that the police department should have done more to make clear he was not a suspect.

"How am I supposed to *live* with this? ...my whole *reputation?*"

"A little girl has gone missing.... Probably...a homicide investigation. And you seriously think, pardon my French, that this department gives a rat's arse about your personal self-esteem?"

(p. 241)

Paradoxically Tom is also genuinely perceptive. He gives a creative writing seminar in which his analysis of Henry James's technique in designing the opening of *Portrait of a Lady* represents a genuinely helpful encounter for his students. Raban actually succeeds in portraying the classroom side of teaching as well as the committee work. Tom's analysis of the great houses in James's novel also enables him to see that what he has done in Seattle is to buy a gloomy old house like that his parents had in England and stuff it with junk, like they did. It is a dark old timber house, rotting away in the damp, settling on foundations that rest on the fault line along which the Big One (the next major earthquake) will come. Beth's condo, on the other hand, is bright with huge windows over which no one ever draws the blinds (except Finn in his bedroom), full of IKEA packages of erect-it-yourself and then throw-it-away furniture.

It is because of the old house that Tom meets Jin Peng. A Chinese illegal immigrant, Jin arrives in a container on the ship we saw at the start. The description of the container is massive in its squalor; as they open the door of the container, the INS men hear a man calling "Today! Today!" What he actually means is "Two of us have died!" Jin is the only man in the container to escape the immigration service. He forages in garbage cans to eat and steals clothes from the dryer in a laundromat (having checked the customer's size first). How Jin gradually comes to find work, food, a place to sleep, and enough English to get by is told with graphic detail; he finally makes $300,000 in an elaborate deal fixed by the Dickensian lawyer McTurk.

Jin (now called "Chick," from "Chink") has been appalled at the waste in American society. He turns up on Tom's doorstep offering to fix the roof and porch for $5,000 in a city where, as Beth has found, "You could get a venture capitalist on the line in five minutes but trying to find a plumber or carpenter was about as hopeless as locating a reliable daguerrotypist" (p. 9).

Of course he is a thief, but the line between theft and recycling is blurred, and he does a lot of recycling. He renovates Beth's bike as a goodwill gesture and laughs as Tom tries to ride it. On the other hand, one of the jobs he has had is with a gang chopping out asbestos, working in thick, white clouds of it. The gang then bags up the asbestos and leaves it, a bag at a time, in dumpsters around the city. There are neat intersecting paradoxes in Chick; he is both friendly and rigidly businesslike, both a preserver and a destroyer of the environment.

Tom and Chick strike up a relationship of genuine friendship that includes Chick's openness toward Finn. This is epitomized when they watch Jack Lemmon and Tony Curtis in *Some Like It Hot* over Christmas lunch. Chick adopts as his own the final line of the film, "Nobody perfect." Elsewhere, Beth and her new date watch Woody Allen's *Sweet and Lowdown*.

Around them, the dotcom boom and other illusions are coming to an end. There are rumors at Beth's company. Tom has spent most of his time lately dealing with a mysterious Indian millionaire who has offered the university $4 million and wants them to hire Nobel Prize winners as writers in residence (William Golding is one of his suggestions). But Shiva Ray only seems to call from airplanes. One night Tom clearly hears the sound of a fire-engine siren during one of Shiva's calls and realizes the university has been the target of a hoax.

One of the many pleasures of reading this novel is spotting the cross-references. Shiva is the god of creation and destruction, as Chick is the agent of both. The film *Sleepless in Seattle*, in which a boy engineers a new relationship for his father, is named in the text, and Tom—like Frasier Crane of the TV sitcom *Frasier*, also set in Seattle—has a radio program. The name of the captain in *Voyager*, a *Star Trek* spinoff, is Janeaway (which doesn't, in fact, sound at all like Szany, which doesn't, in turn, seem to be a Hungarian word.) The waxwing features in the poem that opens Vladimir Nabokov's novel *Pale*

Fire (1962). There are at least seven points of similarity between Tom's history and personal characteristics and those of the playwright Tom Stoppard. Are all these coincidences in the best tradition of nineteenth-century novels, or are they clues? In any case, they tempt the reader to over-interpret, to follow Tom into intellectualizing his experience.

To do this is possibly to miss the point of the ending. Tom looks up from his computer and sees a flock of birds hovering around the holly tree. He calls his son, using his full name, Finbow. "The birds were brighter than their pictures—trim dandies, the sheen of their plumage bright beyond reason":

"Try counting them. How many do you think they are?"
"Millions."
"What are they doing?"
"I dunno. Nothing. Playing…. Can I go get a cookie now?"

So Tom watches till they disappear, and all he has left to look at is a container ship arriving to unload. "But as his eyes grew used to the darkness of the leaves, he could see…the waxwings had stripped every berry off the tree" (pp. 309–311).

There is a double structural purpose to this incident that we miss if we pass straight to assigning it a metaphoric value (it "means" that capitalist society is acquisitive, it "means" that natural resources are being used up). It marks an epiphany for Tom—a growing emergence of his new ability simply to observe and remember, which Detective Nagel has brought out. Additionally it marks a very American moment. Since the first settlement on the James River, Americans have encountered life (birds, fish, bison) in full teem, in "millions" as Finn puts it. And for a moment, in modern Seattle, Tom and Finn share that experience.

REPUTATION

Raban's writing as a travel writer is well regarded, and he has won several prizes for his work in this field. *Waxwings* has been insufficiently appreciated for the perceptive and well-worked complexity that it exhibits. It is planned as the first of a series, and Raban's reputation as a novelist is sure to grow with time.

Select Bibliography

WORKS OF JONATHAN RABAN

NOVELS

Foreign Land. London: Collins Harvill, 1985; New York: Viking, 1985.

Waxwings. London: Picador, 2003; New York: Pantheon, 2003.

TRAVEL

Soft City. London: Hamilton, 1974; New York: Dutton, 1974.

Arabia Through the Looking Glass. London: Collins, 1979. As *Arabia: A Journey Through the Labyrinth,* New York: Simon & Schuster, 1979.

Old Glory: An American Voyage. London: Collins, 1981; New York: Simon & Schuster, 1981.

Coasting. London: Collins Harvill, 1986; New York: Simon & Schuster, 1987.

Hunting Mister Heartbreak. London: Collins, 1990. (As *Hunting Mister Heartbreak: A Discovery of America,* New York: Edward Burlingame, 1991.)

Bad Land: An American Romance. London: Picador, 1996; New York: Pantheon, 1996.

Passage to Juneau: A Sea and Its Meanings. London: Picador, 1999; New York: Pantheon, 1999.

CRITICISM, SHORT FICTION, AND JOURNALISM

Mark Twain: "Huckleberry Finn." Studies in English Literature no. 36. London: Edward Arnold, 1968.

The Technique of Modern Fiction: Essays in Practical Criticism. London: Edward Arnold, 1968; Notre Dame, Ind.: University of Notre Dame Press, 1969.

The Society of the Poem. London: Harrap, 1971.

For Love & Money: Writing, Reading, Travelling, 1967–1987. London: Collins Harvill, 1987. As *For Love & Money: A Writing Life, 1969–1989.* New York: Harper & Row, 1989.

God, Man, & Mrs. Thatcher. London: Chatto & Windus, 1989.

AS EDITOR

Robert Lowell's Poems: A Selection. London: Faber, 1974.

The Oxford Book of the Sea. Oxford and New York: Oxford University Press, 1992.

Homesteading: A Montana Family Album. With N. Wollaston and P. Wollaston. New York: Lyons and Burford, 1988; Harmondsworth, U.K.: Penguin, 1999.

CRITICAL STUDIES

Greenland, Colin. "Humane Geography." *Guardian,* August 23, 2003. (Review of *Waxwings.*)

C. H. SISSON

(1914–2003)

E. M. Knottenbelt

IN THE *Contemporary Authors Autobiographical Series* (1987; hereafter *CAAS*), C. H. Sisson says with characteristic wryness: "The life of a poet—all that really matters to the rest of the world—is contained in his poems" (p. 307). Nothing could be truer. Long before he would have called himself a poet, Sisson was an established writer of prose, including autobiographical pieces—the essays "Autobiographical Reflections on Politics" (1954) and "Natural History" (1961), collected in *The Avoidance of Literature: Collected Essays* (*CE*, 1978), and a three-part memoir (1947 and 1956–64), later glossed with verse throughout, *On the Look-out: A Partial Autobiography* (*PA*, 1989).

The life of this poet was taken up with much else besides writing verse or thinking about being a poet: he was "primarily a civil servant—like Chaucer" (*CE*, p. 158). As the younger poet and novelist Robert Nye noted in his *Times Literary Supplement* review of *In the Trojan Ditch*: "The most throwaway of Mr. Sisson's remarks, fully grasped, turn out to have barbed edges." Like Swift, Sisson is a satirist at heart. But his spiky, if not savage, observations of most things, including himself, have no trace of either bad humor or self-defensiveness. The two-line "Epitaph" (1939) has the same clarity, acerbity, and unsparing wit charging Sisson's humor:

Here lies a civil servant. He was civil
To everyone, and servant to the devil.
        (*Collected Poems*, 1998, hereafter *CP* p. 34)

The brevity of the epigram, or moral aphorism, prose-like but with a final knife-edged twist, is typical of someone with other preoccupations. But the scornful rejection mixed with defiance also has something of the bitter nonchalance or proud contempt of another man of public affairs, Sir Walter Ralegh.

Such was Sisson's life, so tellingly contained in the rough dignity and assuredness of his poems—in the first place one of public service; if this has made for writing with a difference, it must lie in the perspectives such a life might offer. It explains, moreover, Sisson's own critical procedure. No matter the writer, poet, politician, political theorist, philosopher, he begins by giving a sense of the social and intellectual milieu and sketches in the native landscape and antecedents in order then to explore what he has made of them. Diffident, reticent, or ironic, Sisson is always illuminating:

To know when one has some truth to tell is in a way the whole tact of the poet—a sort of slyness he has to use within his own mind. Rilke talks about "Tausende von Liebesnächten" [thousands of nights of love-making] going to the making of a single line, and the poet's choice of a subject is no doubt related to his physiology and to the succession of his outward circumstances.

        (*CE*, p. 163)

EARLY YEARS

Charles Hubert Sisson was born in a poor district of Bristol on the eve of the Great War, on April 22, 1914, above the shop owned by his father. A suburban jeweler and watchmaker who later took up optics, Richard Percy Sisson had emigrated from Kendal in Westmorland after the closure of a comb mill, which had been in the Sisson family since the eighteenth century. Sisson's mother, Ellen Minnie Worlock, descended from a long line of West Country farmers going back at least to the seventeenth century. Sisson was the third of four children. He had a six-year-older brother, who became a successful chemist and industrialist, and a three-year-older sister, who died in her early forties. There was also a much-loved younger sister, invalided from birth. Her death at the age of eleven, when Sisson was fourteen, caused him acute suffering.

Sisson's own family was not well off, but with both more and less well-to-do relatives on either side, this was seen as a matter of circumstances. It meant that Sisson's schooling was "plebian" rather than "patrician," and, on entering the local Greenbank Elementary School, this still-illiterate six-year-old encountered for the first time a meanness and obtuseness altogether foreign to him. "This place was hell," he recalls. "I can remember no master who did not maintain a stance of menace. All this must be much exaggerated in recollection, but I do not think I had a happy moment in that school." He has also said, "I must have been a passive, wondering child" (CAAS, pp. 296, 295). Nonetheless, at age eleven he took the city junior examination. He did so well (on the strength of his English essay, the "History of a Piece of Paper," he imagines), that he could have chosen any secondary school. The best that could be afforded was the middling Fairfield Secondary School a couple of miles from home.

From Sisson we learn that mediocrity of the grimmer sort and its attendant poverty typified the establishments to which the Sisson children were exposed. Instead of the Anglican parish church of St. Thomas, more in line with family customs and habits of previous generations, they frequented the Eastville United Methodist Chapel with its Sunday school. This stood in shrill contrast to home life, where the children were expected to follow their own interests (the eight-year-old Sisson wrote his first poem at the kitchen table while his mother baked the Christmas cake). There were books. A wall lined with them appears in an early photograph taken in the dining room at Heath House, to which the family had moved when Sisson was six. And there was much visiting to and from relatives for tea, happy holidaying at Ellick Farm in the Mendip hills and endless roaming about, including fishing excursions, in the neighborhood and farther afield. In the final analysis, Sisson would say that, although

financial duress marked his formative years, he considered himself to have been fortunate.

As yet not a single pupil had gone from Fairfield to Cambridge or Oxford. Although "mixed," the boys and girls each had their own courtyard. But whatever the other boys' interests, mostly sports, at which he was no good, they were not Sisson's. Although Fairfield was more benign than his primary school, he says, "I was never at home in the place." The early years were especially dreary and unhappy for this boy, who still "must have been a pupil of unusual passivity" (PA, p. 206).

During this time, three long-lasting habits had their beginnings. With the little pocket money he had, Sisson took to scouring secondhand bookshops. (The book for tuppence numbered "17" in his private library containing extracts from Malory he had bought at fourteen; *Essays of Elia* was another.) The book-buying saw to ever more independent reading. And that reading, especially of poetry, sent Sisson to the writing of poems, the first of which appeared in the Children's Corner of the *Bristol Observer.*

> By the time I was thirteen my poems began to appear in the school magazine; at fourteen I won competitions in *Time and Tide,* put up to it by the English mistress, for I should never have heard of such a journal. A poem about Moses in the wilderness won a guinea; a little later, when I began to be influenced by the Sitwells [George and Edith], it was the second prize of half a guinea. By the time I was in the sixth form, or it may have been in the fifth, the French master thought fit to ask me to translate a poem...
>
> (PA, p. 206)

Naturally, the poets he successively read affected the sort of poems he was writing. Before the Sitwells, it had been John Drinkwater, who quickly gave way to Rupert Brooke, then James Elroy Flecker, and so on. The school library also provided Sisson with new discoveries, as did the special period of study in the sixth form devoted to Romanticism. That was at fifteen, when amidst his reading of Andrew Marvell, Ben Jonson, and much else, Sisson had a "passionate affair with Dante Gabriel Rossetti," of which "the hottest point of the obsession became the *House of Life.*"

C. H. SISSON

Sisson's comments on the couplet "Between the hands, between the brows, / Between the lips of Love-Lily" give an impression of what he was undergoing then:

This contains I know not exactly what of adolescent mystery; in those years it was beauty to the point of pain. The sonnet became the vehicle of my own hopeless love and I wrote a series, for all the world like Rossetti. It must have been at the emergence from this obsession—the literary one, for from the hopeless love I did not emerge— that my mind began to fix on Song VIII, the "Woodspurge," surely some of the best lines Rossetti wrote, with the *purest* line, so to speak:

> From perfect grief there need not be
> Wisdom or even memory:
> One thing then learnt remains with me—
> The woodspurge has a cup of three.

(*PA,* p. 202)

And, in his last year at school, T. S. Eliot, Ezra Pound, and James Joyce had done their work, to Sisson's further desolation.

FORMAL EDUCATION

Only in the first of his two sixth-form years did Sisson begin to do well in English, French, and Latin, his chosen subjects. Although it was clear that he should go to university, less so to him was that he should get the two distinctions necessary to win a state scholarship for a place at Oxford or Cambridge. This, as Sisson records, was "a possibility I had never even considered. My negligence made the choice for me" (*CAAS,* p. 296).

At seventeen, with his one distinction in English, Sisson had a scholarship to the University of Bristol and signed up for the course in philosophy and English literature. It included as a joint special subject the literature and philosophy of the seventeenth century, which would mark him indelibly. "An early introduction to the fissiparous political idealists of the Commonwealth is something an Englishman may be grateful for; and there is no eccentricity of idealistic socialism that will astonish him thereafter" (*CE,*

p. 135). No doubt if this serious young reader and writer of poems needed any further sobering up, these university years in the depth of the Depression saw to it that the last remnants of a "Romantic" inclination were eradicated for good. In addition to Eliot's and Pound's corrective work, the "public schoolboys," W. H. Auden and Stephen Spender, had "invited me to admire the working classes." And then "I had my *Weltanschauung* adjusted by T. E. Hulme."

From all this I never recovered. At intervals for the next year or two I wrote poems which "showed awareness"—that would have been the expression. For about a year (*circa* 1932) I must have been contemporary. How I got over this is mysterious, but it was not all done by literature. I was struck down by an appalling adolescent grief, as is not uncommon. René Béhaine identifies the very moment when he left behind him "le sens du bonheur et le pouvoir d'être heureux." ['the sense of joy and capacity for being happy']

(*CE,* p. 157)

So, at twenty, he determined he should write "with precision," but with more modest aims— prose, therefore, not verse.

His studies completed, in the summer of 1934 Sisson went in search of a job, for that was what was needed. He found that for whatever he applied, during these years of the Depression no jobs were to be had for people from provincial universities. But his double first-class degree in philosophy and English literature did qualify him for a small, if not meager, overseas scholarship. He chose the cheapest place, Germany, and spent a year at the universities of Berlin and Freiburg. In a café on the Potsdamerplatz that winter, Sisson wrote what for the time being would be his last poem. (It was published, like others, in the university magazine, *Nonesuch,* of which he had been an editor in his last year.)

Back from Germany, jobs were still not to be had. Thus, on the basis of what he was good at, Sisson decided to try for the civil service. (In those days a candidate who passed the highly competitive and elaborate examination for a position in the Administrative Class would have to be taken on.) He had begun to prepare for the examination when another grant came his way, this time for six months in Paris.

For Sisson, as he has said in *World Authors,* his stay on the Continent was "a profitable time not least because I did not write the thesis [on translation] which was the pretext for these excursions" (*WA,* p. 759). Certainly it is well documented, for there are unpublished notebooks recording what this serious young student, having become "a complete rubber-neck," saw, heard, and read. The refrain of the Nazi song, the *Horst Wessel Lied,* beginning with that all too memorable phrase, "Die Fähne hoch" ['Up with the flag'] is one such entry. (This Sisson would sing with the appropriate stridency and gestures, notwithstanding an ironic look in his eye, when in conversation about this time.) Another relates his first encounter with the Nazi world—in the form of two German toughs on the same boat to Germany—concluding, "I was beginning to know that I was English" (*CE,* p. 136). No doubt, whatever his education in politics before his departure for abroad, his time there did the rest. "If it was in Germany that I first learned to see Europe's nationalisms as plainly as my hand before my face, it was in France that the subject first acquired theoretical importance and the pattern of my future thinking about politics was determined" (*CE,* p. 138). Among others, he read Pierre-Joseph Proudhon, Léon Daudet, Charles Sorel, Charles Maurras, and Franz Kafka—perfect antidotes to Marxism or any other ideology, and the more extreme forms of logical positivism, characterizing the polemical 1930s.

CIVIL SERVICE BEFORE THE WAR

Back in England in 1936, Sisson began his career in the Administrative Class of the civil service only because he had passed the written examination with distinction. He had not been at the "right" university and was altogether ignorant of that world and of what would be required once in the service. It was out of naïveté that "I elected to go into the Ministry of Labour, where I thought crucial domestic events would be reflected" (*WA,* p. 759). When asked in the interview about why he had chosen the profession, he replied, "because

it was remote from anything that interested me" (*PA,* p. 158). Nonetheless, notwithstanding ever-increasing disillusion, he performed his duties impeccably, first as assistant principal with the Ministry of Labour (1936–1942), as the Department of Employment was then called. On from there he was principal (1945–1953), assistant secretary (1953–1962), and finally undersecretary, in his role as director of establishments (1962–1968) and director of occupational safety and health (1968–1973), before retirement at not yet fifty-nine.

With a full-time job, Sisson continued his habit of voracious reading and took to writing with a vengeance as he had earlier promised himself. Thus he was on the lookout for a place to publish. While browsing in the secondhand bookshops around Charing Cross Road, his usual lunchtime diversion, he found Philip Mairet's *New English Weekly.* To this most uncommercial and undogmatic of papers, with such contributors as Montgomery Belgion and Eliot on the committee, he immediately sent an essay. "Charles Maurras and the Idea of the Patriot King" of 1937 was the first of a host of pieces and reviews, mostly on politics, sociology, and the imminent war, that Sisson would write for the paper.

It was also in August 1937 that Sisson married Nora Gilbertson ("a girl I had known at school but who had then rejected my inept suit"); she had gone on to read history at Oxford and become a teacher. (*WA,* p. 759). According to a family anecdote, from the first moment he saw her in the doorway adjoining the girls' and boys' playgrounds, Sisson had determined that she was the girl he would marry. He was thirteen.

War having broken out, his wife's school was evacuated to Dorking in Surrey, while Sisson's department went to Southport, north of Liverpool. Just over twenty-five years old, he did voluntary war work such as keeping watch on a church tower; at this age people in his occupation were reserved. That changed as the war dragged on. In January 1942, after a serious bout of meningitis, Sisson enlisted and joined the Royal Irish Fusiliers at their depot in Omagh, Northern Ireland. He never applied for a commission. But on the strength of his reading and spoken knowledge of

C. H. SISSON

German and French, he was recruited for the Intelligence Corps and underwent further training deemed useful, including a course in Japanese. With Heinrich Heine's poems, Herbert Read's *The Knapsack,* and Dante's *Inferno* in his kitbag, Sisson went overseas again. This time he left behind a pregnant wife, who would give birth to their first daughter as his troopship left Durban, South Africa.

WORLD WAR II AND IMMEDIATELY AFTER

Sisson has written extensively about his two-and-a-half years of soldiering, first as a private and then a sergeant, in India, as it turned out, much of which has remained unpublished. Certainly they were important years for Sisson as appears from the second of the three-part memoir *On the Look-out*—"One Eye on India." In contrast to parts 1 and 3, which flank it on either side and tell Sisson's life story in the first person and backwards, this second part is in the third person and time moves forwards. Thus, as the preface to the memoir says about this chronologically forward-moving narrative, "the story of my life would have its true middle in the war which for me, as in one way or another for most people of my generation, is the Great Divide" (p. 8).

It was also the "Great Divide" in Sisson's writing. While sailing out to Asia, he wrote "On a Troopship," his first poem after ten years of silence, and his first verse translation, "Versions and Perversions of Heine." More poems followed in India. Otherwise, from 1942 to 1946, he wrote and published nothing. All in all, we learn from Sisson, what especially marked soldiering in India was the utter uselessness of one's existence amidst the most appalling mental and physical destitution. If this was a time "of extreme boredom and idleness," at least his habit of keenly looking about him, first developed on his European visits, was put to good use. Undoubtedly it did provide Sisson with additional perspectives and sharpened those he already had. Among these, as he had begun to learn in Nazi Germany, was that he was "English." On the first page of "One Eye on India," on the eve of his departure for the war, with both eyes still focused on England, the yet unnamed protagonist looks about and muses: "'Remember that we are English, that we are Christian.' The air above the little town was heavy with Christianity. The soldier shook his limbs, and the weight of his boots rippled the muscles to his shoulder blades. He was at least English" (p. 73).

On his way to England for leave, the war was declared over. Sisson returned to work in the altogether changed world of the civil service in an equally changed and much disfigured London. This and his encounter with India are reflected in the fictional prose effortlessly written during the early morning hours before work, including "One Eye on India" (1946–1947) and the novel *An Asiatic Romance* (1948–1949). And Sisson took up writing again for the *New English Weekly.* Whatever his interests, old or new, they were primarily focused on the conduct of affairs, with an eye for the local and particular as well as what was practicable in matters concerning the *res publica* in England. So the early self-imposed training of observing things closely at hand had become a method, "a technique of ignorance," for administrator and writer alike. After the *New English Weekly* ceased publication in 1949, Sisson found other places for his critical prose and was becoming an established man of letters. However, during the eight years after the war, apart from his translation of four of Jules Supervielle's short stories on Philip Mairet's suggestion, no publisher had shown interest in any of the fiction or the Heine translation, and no poems were written.

"NEL MEZZO DEL CAMMIN DI NOSTRA VITA" OR "THE RETURN JOURNEY"

The year 1953 was crucial for Sisson. Unlike his siblings he had for one reason or another not been baptized. In the shortest, most laconically pointed chapter of *On the Look-out,* in itself an indication of Sisson's way with matters of greatest significance to him, he narrates how at thirty-nine he became a member of the church to which his wife and by then two daughters belonged. The verse-lines preceding this chapter say as much: "His head has gone inside a volume / And he is no more than a margin" (p. 52).

At this time Sisson was writing a "novel to end all novels," *Christopher Homm* (1965). It relates the purposeless life of the most ordinary of lower-class figures. Beginning with Homm's death in the yard of his nondescript house and ending with his birth, it concludes: "Christopher crouched in his blindness. He was about to set out on the road to Torrington Street, and if he had known how bitter the journey was to be he would not have come" (p. 239). According to the poet and critic Martin Seymour-Smith: "It was found a depressing book but also a comic and extremely skillful one, an autopsy executed 'with grim precision and an attention to quotidian detail which sets his unlikely subject in an almost painfully literal light'" (*WA*, p. 760). Now considered a minor classic, for years it was rejected by publishers, including T. S. Eliot. (Faber, Sisson was told, was not interested in fiction.)

And, in 1953, while writing that novel, at last the poems once more began to surface. As somber and anguished as *Christopher Homm* and described as "thin in every sense of the term," they are similarly driven in their merciless cutting away of artifice and any other self-protective mechanisms that would obstruct this craftsman's need to speak sparingly, as befits a contemporary Christian everyman (*CAAS*, p. 302). The same incisiveness, with which the protagonist of *Christopher Homm* is reduced to man's essential nothingness, would also inform the procedure of reverse chronology of that novel's backward-moving narrative (of course, the title's initials are C. H. Sisson's own).

This would likewise explain the reverse chronology of the poems in *In the Trojan Ditch*, Sisson's first *Collected*, published in 1974, when he was already sixty. It begins with the most recent and ends with his first "real" poem, "On a Troopship." In the foreword to these poems, Sisson explains the gaps before the break to the surface occurred and how the bulk of the volume is the work of "a man going onwards from thirty-five—poems of the return journey, therefore. My beginnings were altogether without facility, and when I was forced into verse it was through having something not altogether easy to say" (p. 13). His "Selected Translations," included in this first *Collected*, tells the same story. Chronologically, both "On a Troopship" and the Heine translation written during the war, the "Great Divide" in his life, stand next to each other at the heart of the volume. From then on, whether in perspective or style, most "new beginnings" in Sisson's poetry were intimately connected with the poet he was then translating (or reading in depth). Of interest is that the first or most recent poems of *In the Trojan Ditch* carry the mark of yet another new beginning or one more leg on the "return journey." At this time, *circa* 1972, he had come back to Dante, who had accompanied him on that troopship.

To return to 1953, when the poems were also coming again at last, it was Dante, apart from Saint Augustine, who was telling the recently converted thirty-nine-year-old Sisson what he was hungering after most. Indeed, like "In a Dark Wood," the epigraph to that scatalogical satire *Christopher Homm,* the first lines of the *Inferno* could stand as an epigraph for this time: "Nel mezzo del cammin di nostra vita / mi ritrovai per una selva oscura …"

There is no credit in a long defection
And defect and defection are the same
I have no person fit for resurrection
Destroy then rather my half-eaten frame.

But that you will not do, for that were pardon
The bodies that you pardon you replace
And that you keep for those whom you will harden
To suffer in the hard rule of your Grace.

Christians on earth may have their bodies mended
By premonition of a heavenly state
But I, by grosser flesh from Grace defended,
Can never see, never communicate.

(*CP*, p. 7)

MIDDLE AND LATER YEARS BEFORE RETIREMENT

Onwards from 1953, while commuting to and from his office in St. James's Square, a stone's throw from Whitehall, Sisson was becoming an expert in the conduct of governing. In 1956, a Senior Simon Research Fellowship from the

University of Manchester allowed him to travel and examine the administrations of West Germany, Austria, Spain, Sweden, and France. His findings produced *The Spirit of British Administration and Some European Comparisons* (1959), ostensibly an instructive defense of British "intelligent amateurism," which, for its merits as independent political analysis, has been said to have had a lasting impact on developing thought about the civil service. However, most of its readers have agreed with Seymour-Smith that "it can be read as a Swiftean satire on incompetence and gobbledy-gook." As with all Sisson's discursive writing, notably on the *res publica*, the work can be read in two ways, in Nye's words—"with pleasure and for instruction either as a study of the workings of government or as an exercise in wit" (*WA*, pp. 759–760).

Something of Sisson's busy day-to-day life appears in the poems scribbled in pencil in the notebook he carried with him. It is striking how little has been altered in their printed versions. In one sense they are merely the jottings of a perceptive man, whose thought, however deeply intellectual, is inextricably connected with what he observes and with what happens in practice. They are not abstractions, therefore. But as notes on everyday contemporary life they are unique for this mind—discerning, un-self-sparing, joyless—which enters them, that of a man with a job to be done, whose real interests lie elsewhere. "Of course my thoughts turned frequently to getting out, though with no higher motive than to give myself more time for writing, which I conceived as being the proper business of my life" (*CAAS*, p. 303). (Among the jobs offered were the chair of government at the University of Bristol and the secretaryship of the Arts Council of Great Britain; before that he had been nominated to take over the editorship of the *New English Weekly* from Philip Mairet.) Frustration also marked these years with unsuccessful attempts to find a publisher. So in 1960 Sisson had *Twenty-One Poems* privately printed.

The change in his fortunes came when, thanks to his habit of browsing in secondhand bookshops, Sisson found *X*, the brilliant, short-lived quarterly of the day edited by the deaf poet David Wright and the painter Patrick Swift. On the appearance of part of *Christopher Homm* there in 1960, Sisson first came to the notice of genuine artists with an eye for the best. Thus, on a Friday, if time permitted after a day's work at the ministry, this man of public affairs met the editors of *X* and other artists in Soho, where Sisson's education in the ways of an altogether different world began. More importantly, Sisson had the sort of conversation he had always wanted. As the unpublished letters likewise attest, it was the beginning of lifelong friendships, with Wright in particular.

In 1961 Abelard-Schuman printed Sisson's first volume of poems, *The London Zoo*. In subsequent issues, *X* published more work and Seymour-Smith's essay "C. H. Sisson" (1962), the first to attend seriously to Sisson's writing. But the real breakthrough came in 1965. Methuen brought out his second volume of poems, *Numbers*, a book of essays, *Art and Action*, and *Christopher Homm*.

However demanding the job of an undersecretary, Sisson was remarkably productive. After Catullus (1964–1965) he translated, among others, Martial (1966), Virgil (1967), Ovid (1968), and Horace (1970–1971). Their influences are noticeable in the poetry, in *Numbers, The Discarnation* (1967), *Roman Poems* (1968), and *Metamorphoses* (1968), and in the critical prose, perhaps nowhere more classically astringent than in the *Sevenoaks Essays* (1967). *English Poetry 1900–1950: An Assessment* (1971) is a seminal work because it is a practising poet's critical redrawing of the map of modern English verse dominated by Yeats, Pound, Eliot, Auden, and Spender. As such it redirects attention to what has survived of the oldest of native traditions in English poetry, through the return of prose rhythms into verse. This is the often undervalued, unpretentious verse of, among others, A. H. Bullen, Lionel Johnson, and John Davidson; Ford Madox Ford and Walter de la Mare; F. S. Flint, Richard Aldington, and T. E. Hulme; Edward Thomas; and George Barker, Patrick Kavanagh, and David Gascoyne.

If this book—*English Poetry 1900–1950*—by a high-ranking civil servant did not reveal enough of his general independence of mind, the reviews and critical essays of this time dealing with the bogus in the conduct of affairs dispersed any doubt on that score. Especially notorious were the three essays in successive issues of the *Spectator* (February–March) of 1971. But so devastating was Sisson's criticism of the reorganization of the civil service and the training of civil servants that it cost him further promotion. Then came *The Case of Walter Bagehot* (1972), not taken seriously by a single reviewer except Nye in *The Scotsman.* He wrote that Bagehot had been "the revered subject of a minor politico-literary cult for far too long, vaguely adored by literary bankers and stockbroker critics." Of Sisson's book on this economist, critic, and constitutional commentator, Nye says: "Bagehot is now debagged, without heat, ever so gently and professionally, [in this] short but beautifully written critical study that looks not only at the man and his work but at what lies behind. The book's clinical title is apt, for Sisson sees Bagehot as a symptom of a disease which has afflicted middle-class Anglo-Saxondom for some while" (p. 20).

RETIREMENT

All this was after 1968, when the Sissons had sold their weekend cottage at Milton Abbas in Dorset and bought Moorfield Cottage in Bagehot's hometown, Langport, Somerset. After Sisson's retirement at the beginning of 1973, he and his wife went to live there for good, and the years of immense productivity began in which Sisson's reputation as translator of the classics, prolific essayist, editor, critic, and poet was formally established. In 1980, the year of his magnificent translation *The Divine Comedy,* even if Sisson maintains that "the range of my discursive writing has been such as an academic would consider a disgrace," he was made an Hon. Litterarum Doctor of the University of Bristol (*WA,* p. 759).

Happily for Sisson, in the year before his retirement his long relationship with Michael Schmidt, the young publisher of Carcanet New Press, had begun. From then on, following *In the Trojan Ditch* (1974), not only would most of his work initially appear with Carcanet, but Carcanet would also provide an outlet for all kinds of literary projects, such as the editorship of authors either long out of print or unfashionable. Through Carcanet, moreover, *Poetry Nation* (1974–1975), a magazine approximating the undogmatic excellence of the *New English Weekly,* was in the making. When, in 1976, it took the name *PN Review,* Sisson, the poet and critic Donald Davie, and Schmidt became joint editors and took turns writing the editorials for almost a decade. Their editorship ended in 1984, when Sisson's second *Collected Poems* was published to coincide with his seventieth birthday. Specifically, according to Sisson, "I could not decently leave my name on the magazine while Schmidt produced a number (*PN Review* 39) devoted to my work" (also in honor of Sisson's birthday) (*CAAS,* p. 307). In the preceding number Schmidt himself says that neither Sisson nor Davie "was ever entirely happy with *PN Review*":

> It has not lived up to their hopes, though it is perhaps better than they expected. I have been unable to locate the select, articulate readership C. H. Sisson had in mind or the broad responsive congregation Donald Davie hoped we could address. My own view is that the prose pages of a magazine of this nature must in the 1980s inform as well as criticize. For both Donald Davie and C. H. Sisson there has maybe been too much information, too much familiar ground covered again, and an unevenness in the criticism, an over-inclusive policy in the selection of poems.
>
> (p. 1)

Sisson continued to write commentaries and reviews for *PN Review,* as well as contribute poems, while there were plenty of other places for whatever he wished to have published—the *Times Literary Supplement,* the *Spectator,* the *London Review of Books, Agenda.* With David Martin, he was one of the most outspoken opponents of the relegation of the Book of Common Prayer to its alternative status in 1979 as he had been of the meddling with the Authorized Version of the Bible in the early 1970s. But it was as an active member in the parish of the church to which he belonged that Sisson spoke out on these and many other issues concerning the place, function, and purpose of Anglicanism.

C. H. SISSON

Witness some of these pieces collected in *Anglican Essays* (1983) and *Is There a Church of England?* (1993).

OLD AGE

The poems, after those of his second *Collected* of 1984, were starting to tell a different story, however. What had once been a public life had begun to be reduced to one lived on the margins, a life of involuntary exile, marked ever increasingly by isolation and, at times, desolation. A year earlier, Sisson's much loved brother, John, had died. (The last poem of the 1984 *Collected* commemorates him and their shared inheritance from a nation that for centuries had lived close to the ground. In tune with this plainest and most quiet-spoken of elegies is a line from Gower, with which the volume ends: "O gentile Engleterre, a toi j'escrits" ['Oh, sweet England, 'tis thee I address'] (p. 346). And there had been his departure from the editorship of *PN Review* in 1984 which he had also justified by saying: "At the age of seventy one should, properly, die, according to the Psalmist, who promises nothing but 'labour and sorrow' from then on" (*CAAS*, p. 307). But, like most of his self-ironic remarks, this one is no less barbed with edges. Sisson is quoting from Psalm 90 (*Domine, refugium* [Lord, thou hast been our refuge]), the first in the "Order for the Burial of the Dead" of the Book of Common Prayer of 1662. Since no Anglican rite is more centered on personal economy with respect to when one should and should not venture to speak, maybe its second Psalm 39 (*Dixi, custodiam* [I said, I will take heed to my ways]), was also in Sisson's mind:

I said, I will take heed to my ways: that I offend not
  in my tongue.
I will keep my mouth as it were with a bridle: while
  the ungodly is in my sight.
I held my tongue, and spake nothing: I kept silence,
  yea, even from good words; but it
was pain and grief to me.
My heart was hot within me, and while I was thus
  musing the fire was kindled: and at
last I spake with my tongue....

For at this same time, Sisson's *Anglican Essays* (1983) had been provoking questions about his "Anglicanism," also in *PN Review* 40, from Richard Harries, then dean of King's College, London (pp. 44–45). "Where does C. H. Sisson stand?" "Why does he so distance himself [from the Church]? First, because of the changing role of Anglicanism in the life of the nation. Secondly, because of the Alternative Service Book." As with "other literati pleading for the centrality of the BCP and the AV in the church," whose "concern for language," Harries says, he shares, Sisson's attitude to liturgical reform is highmindedly literary, out of touch with the changing role of Anglicanism. In the following *PN Review* Sisson's answer is summed up in a line he quotes from an early poem, "The Nature of Man": "If we have reasons, they lie deep." But no question irked Sisson more than Harries' concluding one, recalling "Why spit on your luck?," Auden's reply by way of declining the invitation of the Episcopal Church of the United States to help them write a new liturgy: "Now that C. H. Sisson is retiring from the editorship of *PN Review* perhaps he might take up the offer that Auden spurned?" Sisson replied: "Such fantasies reduce one to despair. What hope is there for a church in which a distinguished cleric can entertain such a dream, even half-jokingly?" (pp. 38–39).

No doubt the poems of this time in *God Bless Karl Marx!* (1987) are undisguisedly bound up with Sisson taking a "stand," as is their desolation. The volume's first poem, "Vigil and Ode for St. George's Day," is a poignant example of what he had already said about his involvement in politics in *Anglican Essays*:

I have nothing directly to offer. The concern which has permeated so much of my writing, and given it such political content as it has, is for something different. It is a long-standing obsession with the *res publica*. What attitudes towards it promise least damage to the things I most care for? If that seems too personal a question, in relation to so large a subject, one can only ask what other question can anyone ask.

(p. 136)

Dixi, custodiam. In all this there is a strong sense of Sisson having been fated. He was born

C. H. SISSON

on the eve of St. George's Day, a fact full of the sort of irony that amused no one more than himself.

At this time Sisson was translating the *Aeneid,* in Eliot's terms "the only one classic in Europe." Virgil's vision of human destiny worked out through his hero, at once historical and prophetic, would be absorbed into Christianity. In short, the *Aeneid* is a monument to that most rigorous and ancient of all civic virtues, *pietas.* Witness Sisson's unheroic and modest translation of Virgil's opening words, the first ever to dispense with the first person. Perhaps in tribute to that master-poet, it might likewise be a warning against the hubris of our own age. "Arma virumque cano..."; "This poem is about battles and the man...." (p. 1). Anyhow, like Virgil, every English translator of his epic, beginning with Gavin Douglas up to and including John Dryden, was also in the service of the *res publica,* often at great cost. It may be part of the same trajectory that Sisson went on from Virgil to translate Racine, another civil servant.

Sisson was made a Companion of Honour in 1993, not for his work in the civil service but for his "services to literature." Is this one more instance of incalculable irony? No doubt if the civil servant should have been honored, his own criticism of the service in the *Spectator* of early 1971 would have put an end to that.

From the age of seventy, the subject of Sisson's poetry remained life's commonplaces, exactly as Nye had said about *In the Trojan Ditch:* "Ringing true is all-important to a poet of his kind—impelled to find a personal rhythm for some more-than-personal truth which it has been given him to utter, belonging somewhere in the company of those who have used common speech to say things not commonly said." Whatever the commonplace, then, it is always viewed from within a perspective naturally in accordance with Sisson's own predicament at a given time. From now on it would be the perspective of an old man on the periphery of life—in short, that last, most ordinary of commonplaces, old age. Very few poets manage to speak of this condition; Ovid is one, Robert Frost another. For this alone Sisson is one of the most remarkable of poets.

LAST YEARS

The successes continued; his *Collected Translations* saw publication in 1996, and so on. And for those who knew him, Sisson remained his generous and altogether genial, quiet-spoken, self, for which he had been much loved, even if, as he also had reason to observe, "old age has not been friendly to me." In 1997 he had a stroke. Although he still managed the proofreading of his third *Collected* of 1998, no more poems followed. The last time anything "new" appeared in print was not under his own name—the beautifully produced Greville Press pamphlet of 2001, *C. H. Sisson* selected by Nora Sisson.

The Sissons remained at Moorfield Cottage, Langport, where Nora, a few weeks older than her husband, died on February 4, 2003, at almost eighty-nine. With a mind still capable of great lucidity and himself as always, but, as in all respects, worn out by old age, Sisson awaited his own demise up there on The Hill. At the back, the drawing room and Sisson's study one story up look out southward over their garden onto the River Parrett and the land stretching as far as one can see, on a clear day, to the Dorset hills. Arthurian country lies northward. Nearby at Althelney, King Alfred is said to have burned his cakes and at Aller Guthrum was baptized. More recently, Fairfax fought one of his battles there. One of the oldest parts of his beloved England made memorable in countless poems, this, Sisson has said, is "my penultimate resting-place" (*CAAS,* p. 307).

Sisson died on September 5, 2003. The retired bishop of Gloucester performed the service without a sermon or eulogies, according to the 1662 Anglican rite. This was in All Saints, Langport, Sisson's beloved parish church (redundant, against his powerful protestations, for some years), next door but one to Moorfield Cottage. After the service, in a procession led by the white-mitered and crimson-robed bishop, Sisson was taken to the graveyard of St. Mary of Huish Episcopi and buried next to his wife, not more than a five-minute walk down the road from their home.

C. H. SISSON

THE WORK

Opinions on Sisson's poetry are divided. For some, it is unnecessarily reticent, diffident, or self-ironic. In a review of *Anchises* (1976), Peter Porter saw "no marks of greatness other than a vein of aristocratic misanthropy.... I should be happy to welcome his late recognition, but I can find no emotional core to him than disappointment" (*WA*, p. 760). However, for his admirers, including a good number of poets of distinction, Sisson may be the finest poet of our time. And for a very diverse readership he is among the most profound and perceptive of twentieth-century thinkers.

Admired or not, who has read Sisson? First-rate publishers declare that he was the least marketable of major writers and is that more than ever. Indeed, after *In the Trojan Ditch* (1974), outside the usual reviews that came on each new publication and a handful of shortish pieces, including those in the *PN Review* anniversary issue (1984), attention to Sisson's work has been less rather than more. Perhaps with this in mind, his publisher's obituary in the *Independent* begins:

> Among twentieth-century English poets, C. H. Sisson was a magnificent anachronism: a hard-working civil servant and a radical modernist, an Anglican and a savage critic of the contemporary church, a committed Englishman without a trace of atavism, a Johnsonian Tory remote from the economic priorities of the current Tory party, a major scholar and translator distrustful of the academy. In short, he ploughed a lonely furrow.

Is this all the more reason to read him or the reverse? Naturally, the proof is in the eating of the pudding. Peter Mullen is of this persuasion: Sisson "always says exactly what he means. So if you want to know what he means, read him."

At the very least, Sisson provides an education, unless one only wants to read what one already knows. One may know Samuel Johnson's definition of a Tory, to which Sisson subscribes, as cited in "A Four Letter Word": "'One who adheres to the ancient constitution of the state, and the apostolic hierarchy of the church of England.' The term was 'opposed to a *whig*', and

Whig was 'The name of a faction.'" But does one know what Sisson means and his purpose for the reference? "If these notions, and the history which lies behind them, are not directly usable in a party programme, they at least provide the elements of a possible criticism of contemporary political manners" (*CE*, p. 533). Such statements have a historical point of reference: the critical period for the definition of English identity when, following out of the Elizabethan Settlement, England's institutions, which had seemed natural and given—in particular, the monarchy—were established. Sisson's knowledge of sixteenth- and seventeenth-century literature, notably of the origins of England's institutions in the controversies at that time, is far greater than that of most others, including specialist scholars. But profound and unique as his knowledge is, it is also radical in the sense "that it sees through to the roots of things" (as Fraser Steel observed in his obituary of Sisson in the *Church Times*). Hence Sisson's contempt for the relegation of the Anglican liturgy of 1662 or for the reform of the civil service, "the products of committees," of "this or that ideology" or "the ever-changing repertoire of bright ideas." His is a highly conservative position based on the duty to conserve with vigilance what was hard won by others, whatever their creed, a position all the more radical because substantiated by his being in the know about important public affairs from within the inner councils of government. Also, according to Schmidt in his *PN Review* obituary: "Sisson is rare among contemporaries in his belief that a writer serves best as a man engaged with the social machine, guarding the integrity of institutions even as he criticises and perfects them."

"Autres temps, autres moeurs," ['other times, other customs'] Sisson was wont to say. We are no longer accustomed to a considerable writer, let alone a poet, standing at the heart of contemporary national politics, for whom, circumstantially, literature and politics are of necessity inseparable. "My preoccupation with politics was never far from a preoccupation with words": "Bad writing is writing which expresses the politically manoeuverable sentiments and is therefore part of the system of force which is government. Good writing may be described as independent of government; and one has intellectual liberty just so far as one can distinguish between valid work and invalid" (*PA*, pp. 166, 140).

For something approaching this one has to go back to before the end of the seventeenth century, when it was usual that every writer worth his salt participated in the great affairs of the day—Sir Thomas Wyatt, Thomas Cranmer, Henry Howard, Earl of Surrey, George Gascoigne, Edmund Spenser, Sir Philip Sidney, Richard Hooker, Sir Walter Ralegh, Francis Bacon, John Milton, Andrew Marvell, Jonathan Swift and indeed the father of English poets, Geoffrey Chaucer, who preceded them (or farther afield, those Sisson has translated—Horace, Virgil, Catullus, Ovid, Dante, Joachim du Bellay, Luc de Clapiers de Vauvenargues, Andreas Gryphius, Jean Racine). The effects of their participation in politics are not measurable. But judging by the effects of the separation of politics and literature since the Restoration upon the language of political argument (to look no farther), the world is no better off.

Not that Sisson with his practical bent and experience pretends that the separation of literature and politics is not the reality it is—hence the pressure of Sisson's writing, his saying things as they are in search of what can be commonly held to be real or negligible. The no-nonsense attitude, one imagines, typifies a man primarily concerned with performing his duties in the service of the commonweal: "But probably it makes sense to say that these authors sound real because they are telling the truth, as it seems to them, which is the only form of truth anyone can tell, except inadvertently" (*CE*, p. 163). Sisson's observation refers to Lord Herbert of Cherbury's prose and Ralegh's poem "The Lie," which reflect thought bound up with a life of action in the world as they found it, instead of philosophizing about the self or anything else abstracted from it. No doubt Sisson's thinking that originality lies not in singularity of voice but in the ability to touch upon general truths would derive not from his not having known the world, but because he had.

From the start, as with the radical modernists, originality equated with singularity or novelty was not what Sisson was after:

> It is an absurdity to try to be original. You might as well try to be beautiful or intelligent. But the complementary process of ridding yourself of obsessive influences can possibly be assisted by some conscious effort. A young man, however, cannot shrink back at the first touch of an alien hand. He has to live through his Eliot, his Yeats or whatever it may be. For a time he must wear fashionable clothes. Then he must discard them, and be prepared to find, not merely that he is naked, but that under those clothes he simply was not there at all. Those who are simply not there at all do not hesitate to fill the poetry pages of respected journals, or even whole volumes, but silence is best.
>
> (*CE*, p. 162)

It took ten years' silence before "On a Troopship" was given:

> They are already made
> Why should they go
> Into boring society
> Among the soldiery?
> But I, whose imperfection
> Is evident and admitted
> Must year-long be pitted
> Against fool and trooper
> Practising my integrity
> In awkward places,
> Walking till I walk easily
> Among uncomprehended faces
> Extracting the root
> Of the matter from the diverse engines
> That in an oath, a gesture or a song
> Inadequately approximate to the human norm.
>
> (*CP*, p. 3)

The prose rhythms held within each line with their backward reach; the sober clarity and succinctness of statement; the absence of smoothness, imagery and color; the rough poise, as the subject requires, will remain hallmarks of Sisson's poetry. Obviously both style and subject have been determined by those previous choices, to write prose rather than poetry, to enter the civil service and to enlist, altogether different from those of Sisson's "obsessive influences," the radical modernists, Eliot, Joyce, and Pound, as well as Yeats, Auden, and Spender—those who were "already made." Like Milton, they had deliberatively set out to be great poets—a vocation best served by foreigners in exile from the philistinism of their countries of origin (America, Ireland, or England). This sort of ratiocination, or high-mindedness, also in their interest in political ideas, not the facts of government, is the opposite of what has gone into Sisson's poetry, which early on he thought of as that which he had no alternative but to write—"the reluctant deposit at the bottom of the mind" (*CE*, p. 160). It is hard to think of another poet who began and went on to write more plainly about common experience, more personally, with the authenticity and integrity the ordinary informed reader of poetry of any age demands.

Sisson "is one of the least self-protective of poets," Geoffrey Hill wrote in *PN Review* 39; he "distrusts artifice precisely because he is a craftsman," befitting the sobriety and innate modesty of his artisan-farming roots (p. 11). Hence the directness and the obliqueness. Both reflect that drive forwards and the backwards reach of Sisson's mind, one of great intellectual power at the same time that it temperamentally distrusts ratiocination and admits the irrational.

Some regard the reductive logic, the bleakness and the plain, emphatic language, typical of Sisson's verse at any time, a rhetorical trick. Then there are the poems some find too embarrassingly scatalogical. In both cases, however, the satirical approach, as ancient as its topos, the infinite absurdity of man's clothed bestial carnality, is intrinsic to the primacy of Sisson's subject:

It is the nature of man that puzzles me
As I walk from Saint James's Square to Charing
  Cross;
The polite mechanicals are going home,
I understand their condition and their loss.

Ape-like in that their box of wires
Is shut behind a face of human resemblance,
They favour a comic hat between their ears
And their monkey's tube is tucked inside their pants.

Language which is all our lies has us on a skewer,
Inept, weak, the grinning devil of comprehension; but
  sleep
Knows us for plants or undiscovered worlds;
If we have reasons, they lie deep.

(CP, p. 48)

The austere reticence of this and other poems can be similarly off-putting. It is the result of a rigorous mind, "patient of the truth...to the point of being disconcerting," without an iota of evasiveness or holding back. What disturbs *is* the emotion in a poem's thrust—its passionate intelligence. Tempered, as in a poem's wryness, it is always there, in the idiosyncratic but convincing rhythm, spat out with force or, as in "Virgini Senescens."

Sisson's distrust of reason is a constitutionally driven distrust of, and impatience with, what reasoning foolishly makes of those troublesome irrational forces—greed, lust, rage, anxiety—in what we are, do, or say. This is the real stuff of his poems—"The Theology of Fitness," the long "Discarnation," "A Letter to John Donne."

These are the issues of Christian belief for Sisson, if one's premise is the Cartesian "Cogito ergo sum," where the first issue is "whether there is any 'I' such that God could be incarnate as an individual human being." Some would agree with Fraser Steel that in this matter of incarnational theology, "No more profound question has been asked since St Augustine"; it is *the* question pervading Sisson's work, nowhere more finely argued than in the *Sevenoaks Essays:*

There is a trick in the abstraction of language which could deceive us either way. Because there is nothing of us but our bodies and their manifestations, the language which reminds us least of them seems most promising of a truth beyond them. But in fact what we say is said in words which have their start in the operations of the body. Words are not ours but the words of a myriad, having point only because of their history, ultimately of their prehistory.... We speak as historical persons—well, to say persons is to beg the question, but we do not speak as ourselves. If we are selves, it is by virtue of other selves that we are so. And our speaking is that of a race, of a tribe, of a time. There is no speech which is not of a here and now and it is nothing except in terms of other times and elsewhere. That is why the historical church is so apt to our needs and meaning. It is a congregation of meaning and there is no meaning without congregation....

The individual is nowhere in this. And what did God become, in Christian history? He became Man, one for all. The meaning of the first Adam was Man, and so with the second. His incarnation was like the descent of a Platonic form into physical shape. It was a reaffirmation of the kind. Every bit of the kind was important. In the end the bits thought they were important as "individuals." The claim is ill-founded.

(*CE*, pp. 205, 208).

Hence the need for "passive obedience," the choice of the "I" or "subject" to submit itself to something larger than itself—an application of personal economy only acquired through discipline, as once embodied in the Anglican liturgy of *the* Catholic Church *in* and *of* England. This is why for Sisson government is both indispensable and an act of force, "with limited powers," meaning powers validated constitutionally, and the art of administration lies in ensuring the peaceable compliance of the governed. Such governing arrangements must be based on the general acceptance of their legitimacy, as the product of history and tradition. If still operative in England, they are the means of tempering individuals who singly or collectively believe in puffed-up fashion that, never mind the feeling for ways of living and speaking that have meant something, we are here "to do our own thing."

Civil servant, essayist, translator, poet, Sisson is a constitutionalist in every respect, to wit, his procedure—a "return journey," as explained in the foreword to the poems of *In the Trojan Ditch:*

In a manner this defines the nature of the poet's problem. There is no question, as it has come to me, of filling note-books with what one knows already. Indeed as the inevitable facility comes, the conscious task becomes the rejection of whatever appears with the face of familiarity. The writing of poetry is, in a sense, the opposite of writing what one wants to write.

Here, in reference to "the embarrassing growth of the area of consciousness" and its accompanying willfulness, from which, temperamentally, he was not spared, Sisson has "recourse to the conscious manipulation of translation, as it were, to distract one while the unwanted impulses free themselves under the provocation of another's thought." This is similarly the application of the "technique of ignorance," plainly revealed in Sisson's comment on Dryden's "pride in being able to do a translation better than any of them": "He was glad, I imagine, to be able to release the energies of poetry without passing for having said anything of his own." Such is the modesty of Sisson's austere reticence as a human being: "The most satisfying literary activity is translation" (p. 13).

The sixty-line "The Usk" is exemplary for the sort of poetry resulting from the method of discovering not what one already knows—the essentially undeliberative or unwillful nature of Sisson's "return journey." Its epigraph reads:

Christ is the language which we speak to God
And also God, so that we speak in truth;
He in us, we in him, speaking
To one another, to him, the City of God.

(*CP*, p. 165)

In Nye's estimation: technically this, as other poems of the time, are "of much interest in that in their appetite to be 'crystalline' their thinking becomes so intense and their rhythm so subtle that a fluid syntax of pure intuition emerges":

Nothing is in my own voice because I have not
Any. Nothing is in my own name
Here inscribed on water, nothing but flow
A ripple, outwards. Standing beside the Usk
You flow like truth, river, I will get in
Over me, through me perhaps, river let me be crystalline
As I shall not be, shivering upon the bank.

(*CP* p. 165)

About rhythm Sisson has had a lot to say himself: "But is rhythm a part of the truth? It seems odd to say so. One feels for the subject, and if one finds it one finds the words. But the rhythm? The fact is that you cannot find the words without the rhythm" (*CE*, p. 163). In *English Poetry 1900–1950*, "The rhythm of [Hardy's] verse, with its hesitations, sudden speeds, and pauses which are almost silences, is the very rhythm of thought" (p. 30). His foreword to the poems of *In the Trojan Ditch* concludes: "The proof of the poem—any poem—is in its rhythm and that is why critical determination has in the end to await that unarguable perception" (p. 13). For Sisson, the rhythm of words in natural spoken speech *is* the incarnation of thought, a re-enactment of the Word made flesh in all its imperfections. Nye observes:

> Mr. Sisson is not just insisting that the greater part of our mental possessions lie below the surface of consciousness. His beatitudes and negations rehearse a scepticism of consciousness existing in any individual sense at all—other than the Incarnation, in which God as it were consented once more to be broken up again into man, His own image.

Donald Davie, with his Unitarian background and Augustan sympathies, might not have put it as Nye, but he did also claim in his review of *In the Trojan Ditch* that "The Usk" is "one of the greatest poems of our time," "an extraordinary triumph of the plain style in poetry precisely because, even as it deploys that style it convicts it of dishonesty."

What I had hoped for, the clear line
Tremulous like water but
Clear also to the stones underneath
Has not come my way, for my truth
Was not public enough, nor perhaps true.
Holy Father, Almighty God
Stop me before I speak

              —per Christum.

Lies on my tongue. Get up and bolt the door
For I am coming not to be believed
The messenger of anything I say.
So I am come, stand in the cold tonight

The servant of the grain upon my tongue,
Beware, I am the man, and let me in.

              (*CP*, p. 166)

"The Usk," in its need to be "crystalline" and anxiety that "I speak too plainly / Yet not so plain as to be understood" (p. 166), came a year after Sisson had first burst out with undisguised anger against the reforms of the civil service in the *Spectator*, which would cost him further promotion. Sisson had already completed his critical assessments of Eliot, Pound, and Yeats, in Geoffrey Hill's view, "brilliant, necessary, prejudiced." Following on from Edward Thomas, William Barnes, and Thomas Hardy, he had turned to Henry Vaughan—another quiet, modest, and intuitive poet. Vaughan's presence can indeed be felt in "The Usk," as well as in "In Insula Avalonia," "Burrington Combe," and "The Corridor," not merely because, as Sisson says, "the images of water are frequent—from the Usk, which [his brother scientist] Thomas Vaughan also celebrated in a poem, or some deeper stream." Sisson had his own river, the Parrett:

Dark wind, dark wind that makes the river black
—Two swans upon it are the serpent's eyes—
Wind through the meadows as you twist my heart.

              (*CP*, p. 22)

To these three lines from "In Insula Avalonia," Sisson's comments on Vaughan may be equally well applied: "The root of the matter for Vaughan was telling the truth, and having some truth to tell."

> The best poems of *Silex Scintillans* are well known, but it is necessary to read the book as a whole to understand the temper from which they come. If the prejudice which most people now have against a devotional subject-matter is set aside, it will be seen that the reader is in the presence of a mind of unusual integrity attempting to communicate experiences which are most often of an untraceable privacy.

              (*CE*, pp. 344–345)

Sisson would return to tighter, more traditional forms, and his rhythms, with their highly individual and authoritative cadences, would be touched by his subsequent submission to Dante, Virgil, and Racine. But under the auspices of these master-poets he only speaks as he must—in the plain style akin to both the prose and poetry of those brought up with the Book of Common Prayer, as the twenty-fourth of the *Thirty-nine Articles* (1662) says:

> It is a thing plainly repugnant to the Word of God, and the custom of the Primitive Church, to have publick prayer in the Church, or to minister the Sacraments in a tongue not *understanded of the people* (italics added).

The crucial phrase occurs throughout Sisson's writings and appropriately in *British Administration:* "this country retains enough of the fruits of the reformation to prefer to be governed in a language 'understanded of the people'" (p. 16). The plain Anglican style drew on the vernacular as it must have been more or less there to be tapped by Cranmer, and by William Tyndale, whose translation was then absorbed into the Authorized Version. It was also the style considered to be closest to the rhythms of English natural-spoken speech to which the first early modern poets commonly aspired and as stated in the first manuals, among them George Gascoigne's *Certayne Notes of Instruction*. Here life's commonplaces were at one with the sobriety of what was deemed a common style, the language of Sisson's origins. In one of his first postwar pieces for the *New English Weekly*, Sisson wrote of Charles Péguy:

> Laborious and frugal,—and these are adjectives that sound harsh in the England of today—the years served merely to expose the stamps of his beginnings: is not every sincere life, in a sense, a journey to the first years?
>
> (*CE*, p. 44)

The six poems of "On the Departure" (*Antidotes,* 1991) are in this plain style and also follow formal procedures. However, they are focused on what can be seen in present-day England if one cares to look ("The Turf," "The Sow's Ear," "Muchelney Abbey," "The Geese"), and they are not in a language that is merely an update of that other time, if one cares to hear. Moreover, like many of his poems, early, middle, or late, they set Sisson apart from what any of the radical modernists or many another contemporary poet has done with the "Book of Nature":

The turmoil of the geese,
Plodding across the sky with heavy wing
Is in the heart—not theirs, but yours and mine.
We see them pass, and by their flight divine
Our going too: and their diminishing
Tells us our own decrease.

Westward they go,
And where they vanish, there they will be fed.
But we? One tale, if true, would feed us too.
Yet we look backward on the way we grew:
Those who engendered us were left for dead
And we must follow.

Fly with the geese
Who grow without the prick of consciousness.
Knowledge is out of place, and speech betrays
The very thought it forms. Then end your days
In the security of nothingness,
And so fly loose.

(*CP* p. 429)

The poems that came in old age still contain any number of surprises technically. But, as in the ten elegiac epigrams of Sisson's last major sequence, "Tristia," they will always be driven by what is left after we have finished with thinking about who we are (instead of what we are: "nothing")—the bleakest but perhaps the most naked and truthful of truths to be had. The ninth states:

Speech cannot be betrayed, for speech betrays,
And what we say reveals the men we are.
But, once come to a land where no-one is,
We long for conversation, and a voice
Which answers what we say when we succeed
In saying for a moment that which is.
O careless world, which covers what is there
With what it hopes, or what best cheats and pays,
But speech with others needs another tongue.
For a to speak to b, and b to a,
A stream of commonalty must be found,

Rippling at times, at times in even flow,
And yet it turns to Lethe in the end.

(*CP*, p. 491)

Selected Bibliography

WORKS OF C. H. SISSON

POETRY

Twenty-One Poems. Privately printed. Sevenoaks, 1960.

Poems. London: Peter Russell. (Dated 1959 but not in fact available until 1961.)

The London Zoo. London and New York: Abelard-Schuman, 1961.

Numbers. London: Methuen, 1965.

The Discarnation. Privately printed. Sevenoaks, 1967.

Metamorphoses. London: Methuen, 1968.

Roman Poems. Privately printed. Sevenoaks, 1968.

The Corridor. London: Mandeville Press, 1975.

Anchises: Poems. Manchester: Carcanet New Press, 1976.

Exactions. Manchester: Carcanet New Press, 1980.

Night Thoughts and Other Poems. With lino cuts by Annie Newnham. London: Inky Parrot Press, 1984.

Moon-Rise and Other Poems. London: Snake River Press, 1984. (Finely printed edition.)

God Bless Karl Marx! Manchester: Carcanet New Press, 1987.

16 Sonnets. Privately printed. London: H. C. Laserprint, 1990.

Antidotes. Manchester: Carcanet New Press, 1991.

Nine Sonnets. London: Greville Press, 1991.

Ghosts in the Corridor. With Andrew Crozier and Donald Davie. Paladin Re/Active Anthology no. 2. London: Paladin, 1992.

The Pattern. London: Enitharmon Press, 1993.

What and Who. Manchester: Carcanet New Press, 1994.

C. H. Sisson. Selected by Nora Sisson. London: Greville Press, 2001.

FICTION

An Asiatic Romance. London: Gaberbocchus, 1953.

Christopher Homm. London: Metheun, 1965. Manchester: Carcanet New Press, 1975, 1984.

NONFICTION

The Curious Democrat. London: Peter Russell, 1950.

The Spirit of British Administration and Some European Comparisons. London: Faber, 1959, 1966; New York: Praeger, 1959.

Art and Action. London: Methuen, 1965.

Sevenoaks Essays. Privately printed. Knole Park Press, 1967.

English Poetry 1900–1950: An Assessment. London: Hart-Davis, 1971. Manchester: Carcanet New Press, 1981; New York: Methuen, 1981.

The Case of Walter Bagehot. London: Faber, 1972.

David Hume. Edinburgh: Ramsay Head Press, 1976.

Anglican Essays. Manchester: Carcanet New Press, 1983.

"Fourteen Letters." *PN Review* 39:33–39 (1984). (Letters to David Wright.)

The Poet and the Translator. Jackson Knight Memorial Lecture. Exeter: University of Exeter, 1985.

Letters to an Editor. Edited by Mark Fischer. Manchester: Carcanet New Press, 1989. (Letters to Michael Schmidt.)

In Two Minds: Guesses at Other Writers. Manchester: Carcanet New Press, 1990.

English Perspectives: Essays on Liberty and Government. Manchester: Carcanet New Press, 1991.

Is There a Church of England? Manchester: Carcanet New Press, 1993.

TRANSLATIONS

Angels and Beasts. By Jules Supervielle. London: Westhouse, 1947.

Versions and Perversions of Heine. London: Gaberbocchus, 1955.

The Poetry of Catullus. London: MacGibbon & Kee, 1966; New York: Orion Press, 1967; New York: Viking, 1969.

The Poetic Art: A Translation of Horace's "Ars Poetica." Cheadle, U.K.: Carcanet New Press, 1975.

De Rerum Natura: The Poem on Nature. By Lucretius. Manchester: Carcanet New Press, 1976.

Some Tales of La Fontaine. Manchester: Carcanet New Press, 1979.

The Divine Comedy. By Dante Alighieri. Manchester: Carcanet New Press, 1980; Pan, 1981; Chicago: Regnery Gateway, 1981; World Classics, Oxford: Oxford University Press, 1993.

The Song of Roland. Manchester: Carcanet New Press, 1983.

The Regrets. By Joachim du Bellay. Manchester: Carcanet New Press, 1983.

The Aeneid of Virgil. Manchester: Carcanet New Press, 1986; London: Everyman, 1990.

Britannicus, Phaedra, Athaliah. By Jean Racine. Oxford: Oxford University Press, 1987; World Classics, Oxford: Oxford University Press, 2001.

EDITIONS

Enemy Salvoes. By Wyndham Lewis. Edited by C. J. Fox with an introduction by C. H. Sisson. Plymouth: Vision Press, 1975.

The English Sermon: An Anthology. Vol. 2, *1650–1750.* Manchester: Carcanet New Press, 1976.

Selected Poems of Jonathan Swift. Manchester: Carcanet New Press, 1977.

Collected Poems and Plays. By Wyndham Lewis. Edited by Alan Munton with an introduction by C. H. Sisson. Manchester: Carcanet New Press, 1979.

Philip Mairet: Autobiographical and Other Papers. Manchester: Carcanet New Press, 1981.

The Rash Act. By Ford Madox Ford. Manchester: Carcanet New Press, 1982.

The English Novel. By Ford Madox Ford. Manchester: Carcanet New Press, 1983.

A Call: The Tale of Two Passions. By Ford Madox Ford. Manchester: Carcanet New Press, 1984.

Christina Rossetti: Selected Poems. Manchester: Carcanet New Press, 1984.

Ladies Whose Bright Eyes. By Ford Madox Ford. Manchester: Carcanet New Press, 1988.

Selected Writings of Jeremy Taylor. Manchester: Carcanet New Press, 1990.

Poems and Essays on Poetry by Edgar Allan Poe. Manchester: Carcanet New Press, 1995.

AUTOBIOGRAPHY

World Authors: 1970–1975. Edited by John Wakeman. New York: H. W. Wilson, 1980.

Contemporary Poets. Edited by James Vinson and D. L. Kirkpatrick. London and Chicago: St. James Press, 1985.

Contemporary Authors Autobiographical Series. Vol. 3. Detroit: Gale, 1987. Pp. 293–309. (Contains photographs.)

On the Look-out: A Partial Autobiography. Manchester: Carcanet New Press, 1989.

COLLECTED WORKS

In the Trojan Ditch: Collected Poems and Selected Translations. Cheadle, U.K.: Carcanet New Press, 1974.

The Avoidance of Literature: Collected Essays. Edited with an introduction and bibliography by Michael Schmidt. Manchester: Carcanet New Press, 1978.

Selected Poems. Manchester: Carcanet New Press, 1981.

Collected Poems. Manchester: Carcanet New Press, 1984.

Poems: Selected. Manchester: Carcanet New Press, 1995.

Collected Translations. Manchester: Carcanet New Press, 1996.

Selected Poems. New York: New Directions, 1996.

Collected Poems. Manchester: Carcanet New Press, 1998. (Includes a bibliography of works.)

MANUSCRIPT PAPERS

Special Collections Library of the University of Bristol.
John Rylands University Library of Manchester.

CRITICAL AND BIOGRAPHICAL STUDIES

Adcock, Fleur. "Rustic Jollity." *PN Review* 39:65–66 (1984).

———. "Lines of Enquiry." *Sunday Times,* March 10, 1991. *(Antidotes.)*

Alexander, Michael. "The Politics of Form." *Poetry Nation* 1:49–53 (1973).

———. "C. H. Sisson." *Agenda* 29, nos. 1–2:133–135 (1991).

Ashby, Cliff. "A Tribute." *PN Review* 39:63 (1984).

Attwell, Canon A. H. *"The English Sermon 1650–1750."* *PN Review* 3:63–64 (1977).

Barker, Jonathan. "'Cerne Abbas Is a Name I Like': C. H. Sisson and Place." *PN Review* 39:44–46 (1984).

Bedient, Calvin. "Coming Out: C. H. Sisson's Poetry." *Poetry Nation* 5:51–62 (1974). *(In the Trojan Ditch.)*

Caldwell, Roger. "Nec in Arcadia unquam." *Times Literary Supplement,* February 5, 1999. (*Collected Poems,* 1998.)

Cayley, Michael. "Lucretius Redivivus." *PN Review* 1:63 (1976). (*De Rerum Natura.*)

———. "Nothing Missing." *PN Review* 16:56–57 (1980). *(Exactions.)*

———. "Clerks and Tories: Sisson's Essays on Aspects of Government." *PN Review* 39:29–32 (1984).

Cox, Kenneth. "The Poetry of C. H. Sisson." *Agenda* 12, no. 3:45–49 (1974). *(In the Trojan Ditch.)*

Cullup, Michael. "C. H. Sisson's Du Bellay." *PN Review* 39:50–51 (1984).

Davie, Donald. "An Appeal to Dryden." *Listener,* May 9, 1974, p. 16 (*In the Trojan Ditch*).

——— "The Politics of an English Poet." *Poetry Nation* 6:86–91 (1976).

———. "Exacting Poetry." *PN Review* 20:26–29 (1981). *(Exactions.)*

———. "Two Modern Masters: Sisson and Milosz." *PN Review* 39:2–11 (1984).

———. "C. H. Sisson." *Guardian,* September 9, 2003, 44. (Obituary.)

Davis, Dick. "Sisson and the Acerb Florentine." *PN Review* 39:51–54 (1984).

Fisher, Mark. *Letters to an Editor.* Manchester: Carcanet New Press, 1989. (With references to C. H. Sisson.)

Fox, C. J. "The Sapper." *PN Review* 39:67–68 (1984).

Gifford, Henry. "A Latin Head and an English Heart." *PN Review* 39:20–23 (1984).

Gould, Rachel. "Sisson's Poetry and His Essays." *PN Review* 39:17–18 (1984).

Hall, Donald. *"Anchises." New York Times Book Review,* December 18, 1977, 16–17.

Harries, Richard. "C. H. Sisson's Anglicanism." *PN Review* 40:44–45 (1984). *(Anglican Essays.)*

Hibbert, Dominic. "Tough Measures." *Times Literary Supplement,* January 8, 1988, p. 17. (*God Bless Karl Marx!*)

C. H. SISSON

Hill, Geoffrey. "C. H. Sisson." *PN Review* 39:11–16 (1984).

Holmes, Richard. *"Christopher Homm." Times Literary Supplement,* January 2, 1966, p. 23.

Kart, Larry. "The Inferno of Dante." *Chicago Tribune,* September 6, 1996, p. 26.

Kavanagh, P. J. "Orthodoxies." *PN Review* 39:63–65 (1984).

Keene, Dennis. "Not of an Age." *PN Review* 39:67–68 (1984).

Knottenbelt, E. M. "Time's Workings: The Stringent Art of C. H. Sisson." *Black and Gold: Contiguous Traditions in Post-War British and Irish Poetry. DQR Studies in Literature* 13: 255–276 (1994).

———. "C. H. Sisson." *Post-war Literatures in English,* No. 26, Wolters-Noordhoff, Groningan, December 1994, pp. 1–26. (With bibliography.)

———. "A Tribute to Charles Sisson." *Agenda* 34, no. 2:159–162 (1996).

———. "C. H. Sisson's Translations." *Agenda* 35, no. 3:166–181 (1997).

———. *"Is There a Church of England? by C. H. Sisson." Heythrop Journal* 38, no. 3:353–355 (1997).

———. "Coming to the End: C. H. Sisson." *The London Magazine,* February/March, 39, nos. 11–12:43–54 (2000). (*Collected Poems,* 1998).

———. "C. H. Sisson on Ford Madox Ford and the Native Tradition in English Verse." *Modernism and the Individual Talent.* Edited by Jörg W. Rademacher. Münster: *Lit Verlag*: 2002. Pp. 156–163, 209–210.

———. "Romantic Residues? Virgil's *Aeneid* 'in Such a Tongue as the People Understandeth' or in a 'Language Really Spoken by Men.'" *Configuring Romanticism. Costerus New Series* 147: 235–257 (2003).

———. "'Change is my Subject': Translations of Ovid's *Metamorphoses," Agenda,* 40 no. 4: 75–100 (Autumn/Winter 2004).

Levy, David J. "A Kind of Civil Service." *PN Review* 39:27–29 (1984).

Manganiello, Dominic. "C. H. Sisson's Purgatorial Dark Wood." *PN Review* 137:15–19 (2001).

Martin, David. "The Avoidance of Literature." *PN Review* 12:57 (1979).

———. "Polity and Religion in C. H. Sisson." *PN Review* 39:23–26 (1984).

Massey, Alan. "Poet, Sergeant, Under Secretary." *Agenda* 37, no. 1:67–76 (1999). (*Collected Poems,* 1998).

McCarthy, Patricia. "Not Afraid of the Beautiful." *Agenda* 32, nos. 3–4:263–270 (1994–1995). *(What and Who.)*

McCarthy, Shaun. "The Poetry of C. H. Sisson." *Agenda* 22, no. 2:57–63. *(Collected Poems,* 1984).

McCully, C. B. "A Mine of Mind." *PN Review* 39:48–50 (1984).

Medcalf, Stephen. "The Authenticity of 'I.'" *Times Literary Supplement,* April 23, 1982, p. 15.

Morton, Brian. "Rights and Duties." *PN Review* 39:26–27 (1984).

Mullen, Peter. "A Poet Who Was Persuaded by the Creed." *Church Times,* October 1989, p. 26.

———. "Reputations: C. H. Sisson CH (1914–2003)." *Salisbury Review,* p. 32. Forthcoming.

Nye, Robert. "The Art of Money, or Walter Bagehot Debagged." *The Scotsman,* February 12, 1972, p. 23. *(The Case of Walter Bagehot.)*

———. "Into the River of Truth." *Times Literary Supplement,* November 29, 1974, p. 18. *(In the Trojan Ditch)*

———. "The Good and the Great." *The Times,* April 20, 1978, p. 21. *(Ghosts in the Corridor)*

———. "Blue Wreaths for Walter Bagehot." *Weekend Scotsman,* May 15, 1998, p. 31. *(The Case of Walter Bagehot)*

O'Brien, Sean. "Rosemary for Remembrance." *Sunday Times,* December 17, 1995, p. 35. *(Poems: Selected,* 1995)

Palmer, Penelope. "C. H. Sisson." *Agenda* 15, nos. 2–3:137–141 (1977). *(Anchises)*

Pilling, John. "The Strict Temperature of Classicism: C. H. Sisson." In *British Poetry Since 1970: A Critical Survey.* Edited by Peter Jones and Michael Schmidt. Manchester: Carcanet New Press, 1980. Pp. 14–21.

Poole, Richard. "The Poetry of C. H. Sisson." *Agenda* 22, no. 2:32–56 (1984).

———. "Unaccommodated Man." *PN Review* 39:61 (1984).

Schmidt, Michael. *An Introduction to 50 Modern British Poets.* London: Pan, 1979. Pp. 266–277.

———. *Eleven British Poets: An Anthology.* London: Methuen, 1980, 1987; London and New York: Routledge, 1988, 1990. Pp. 25–46.

———. *The Lives of the Poets.* London: Vintage, 2000, pp. 168-77.

———. "C. H. Sisson." *Independent,* September 9, 2003, p. 26. (Obituary.)

———. "C. H. Sisson 1914–2003." *PN Review* 154:3–4 (2003). (Obituary.)

Scruton, Roger. "Homm Insapiens." *PN Review* 39:59–61 (1984).

———. "C. H. Sisson." *Times,* April 19, 1984, p. 36. (*Collected Poems,* 1984.)

———. "The Verse Thing About Old Age." *Times,* August 13, 1998, p. 38. (*Collected Poems,* 1998).

Seymour-Smith, Martin. "C. H. Sisson." *X* 2, no. 3:189–197 (1962).

———. "Some Notes on the Poetry of C. H. Sisson." *Agenda* 3–4:207–214 (1970). *(Metamorphoses, Numbers.)*

———. "C. H. Sisson." *Who's Who in Twentieth-Century Literature.* New York: MacMillan, 1976. Pp. 339–340.

———. "Sisson, C. H." *The New Guide to Modern World Literature.* New York: MacMillan, 1985. Pp. 341–342.

———. "C. H. Sisson." *Times,* September 9, 2003, p. 36. (Obituary.)

Steel, Fraser. "Sisson in the Studio." *PN Review* 39:65 (1984).

———. "Charles Hubert Sisson." *Church Times,* October 17, 2003, p. 27. (Obituary.)

Tinkler-Villani, V. *Visions of Dante in English Poetry.* Amsterdam: Rodopi, 1989.

Wells, Robert. *"Anchises." PN Review* 2:49–52 (1977).

———. "C. H. Sisson." *PN Review* 39:39–41 (1984).

Wilmer, Clive. "Rhythm in Sisson's Poetry." *PN Review* 39:41–44 (1984).

———. "Dante Made Plain." *Times Literary Supplement,* September 6, 1996, p. 20.

Wright, David. "The Poetry of C. H. Sisson." *Agenda* 13, no. 3:5–17 (1975).

———. "A Letter to C. H. Sisson." *PN Review* 39:33 (1984).

INTERVIEWS

BBC's Poet of the Month for October 1989.

"C. H. Sisson in Conversation with Michael Schmidt." *PN Review* 39:54–59 (1984).

"C. H. Sisson Talks to Frances Welsh." *Telegraph,* October 25, 1997, pp. 23–4.

THOMAS TRAHERNE

(1637–1674)

Andrew Zawacki

THOMAS TRAHERNE ONCE referred to himself as "a Philosophical Poet," a writer committed to marrying divine love with reason (*Christian Ethicks,* p. 84). For a long time he was, however, all but unknown. Traherne published only one book during his lifetime, and that volume appeared anonymously. Following his death, Traherne's manuscripts changed hands numerous times, suffered from misattribution and neglect, and otherwise got lost in the shuffle of archives and authorial uncertainty. No sooner did his poems and theological tracts begin emerging from two centuries of obscurity, than Traherne was deemed a rather minor writer. The last of the "metaphysical" poets, until recently he has been widely considered less accomplished than his precursors John Donne, George Herbert, Henry Vaughan, and Richard Crashaw. These poets, the received critical response has wagered, demonstrate an intellectual sophistication and artistic acumen lacking in Traherne's corpus. This is no longer a unanimous position and, to the contrary, Traherne is starting to make his way forward to the center of debates about seventeenth-century poetry and poetics.

LIFE

Relatively little is known about the life of Thomas Traherne. He was born shortly before October 20, 1673, probably in Hereford, England, near the border of Wales. His father, also named Thomas, was a shoemaker from Lugwardine (Ridler, ed., 1966, p. xi). The family was apparently not well off, for years later, in the third division of his *Centuries of Meditations,* Traherne would recall his "little Obscure Room in my Fathers poor House," claiming he had possessed "so Scanty and Narrow a fortune, enjoying few

and Obscure Comforts" (Ridler, ed., p. 271). The Trahernes were likely related to an older innkeeper named Philip Traherne, twice mayor of the town. Along with his brother Philip, Thomas may have been put in the care of this elder Philip Traherne for several years in the early 1640s; the children seem to have received a private education, and their father might have died when they were little. Thomas may also have glimpsed the sufferings of the civil wars that thrice reached royalist Hereford during his youth (Day, 1982, p. 1).

Traherne matriculated at Brasenose College, Oxford, as a commoner on March 1, 1652. Under the direction of the Puritan principal Dr. Greenwood, Brasenose was among the strictest colleges in an Oxford becoming increasingly soberminded after the Civil War (Salter, 1964, p. 10). Ideologically Oxford was immersed in the traditional, logical systems of Aristotle and Aquinas. Traherne's first year there saw the publication of Thomas Hobbes's *Leviathan,* which contributed to an erosion of theology and spiritual existence that had begun with the partition between faith and reason established by Sir Thomas Browne and Sir Francis Bacon (Salter, pp. 4–6). It was also the era of John Locke, scientific objectivity, the Copernican universe, and the overtures to deism, all of which diluted God's significance. In his Third Century, Traherne would characterize his adolescent education: "I saw that there were Things in this World of which I never Dreamed, Glorious Secrets, and Glorious Persons past Imagination. There I saw that Logick, Ethicks, Physicks, Metaphysicks, Geometry, Astronomy, Poesie, Medicine, Grammar, Musick, Rhetorick, all kinds of Arts Trades and Mechanicismes that Adorned the World pertained to felicity" (Ridler, ed., p. 282).

If that passage declares one of Traherne's crucial themes—felicity—and puts it in positive relation to reason, the following section criticizes the impartiality of his formal studies:

> Som things were Defectiv too. There was never a Tutor that did professely Teach Felicity: tho that be the Mistress of all other Sciences. Nor did any of us Study these things but as *Aliena,* which we ought to have studied as our own Enjoyments. We Studied to inform our Knowledg, but knew not for what End we so Studied. And for lack of aiming at a Certain End, we Erred in the Maner
>
> (Ridler, ed., p. 283)

This belief in happiness as the highest purpose informed Traherne's desire to resist his century's efforts to pry religion and science apart. He was enamored of the "new philosophy" emerging from the other realm of Oxbridge, known as Cambridge Platonism. The Cambridge philosophers, among them Henry More, Benjamin Whichcote, Ralph Cudworth, and John Smith, claimed that Right Reason permitted one to see the truth intuitively, unmediated by inductive processes (Day, pp. 9–11). This Neoplatonism desired to preserve a Christian spirituality without, however, abandoning rational procedures. A latter-day speculative mysticism à la Meister Eckehart and Nicholas of Cusa, which asserted that the soul could unite with God by following his traces expressed in the material world, it served as enthusiastic counterpoint to Traherne's empirical Oxford training (Day, pp. 14–16).

Having received his bachelor of arts degree on October 13, 1656, Traherne probably spent the following year in religious instruction, also making preliminary entries in his "Early Notebook." On December 30, 1657, he was admitted to the rectory of Credenhill, five miles northeast of Hereford, a position he held until his death. He was sponsored by a group of Puritans who would soon be cast out during the Restoration. As the legal age for assuming rectorship of the tiny parish was twenty-three, Traherne may have continued studying at Oxford before being ordained as deacon and priest at Launton by Bishop Skinner of the English Church on October 20, 1660. "It does not seem possible to arrive at any positive conclusion on a point which may well call for comment," K. W. Salter argues, "that here we see a man who was vouched for by Puritan clergy before the Restoration and ordained by an Anglican bishop afterwards" (p. 13). It is not clear whether Traherne bent his principles or whether he simply benefited from a tolerance toward intending clergy exercised by the Commission for Approbation of Public Preachers under the Commonwealth.

Traherne received an M.A. by decree from Brasenose on November 6, 1661, and may have returned to Oxford for further study. During the succeeding two years he began writing earnestly, including the "Select Meditations." His first residence at Credenhill probably began in 1664, and most of the *Centuries* were likely written there between 1666 and 1668, along with the "Ficino Notebook," copied in Latin from Marsilio Ficino's commentary on Plato. Traherne took a bachelor of divinity degree from Brasenose on December 11, 1669.

Before the year was out, Sir Orlando Bridgeman, lord keeper of the seal, employed Traherne as his domestic chaplain. Traherne may have met his benefactor, who claimed some interest in Cambridge Platonism, through the former's close friend Susanna Hopton, née Harvey. She was the aunt of Traherne's sister-in-law, and the Harveys were an influential family. Prior to marrying, under the Commonwealth, Susanna Harvey had protested Puritanism by becoming Catholic, while after her marriage and the Restoration she returned to the Anglican Church (Salter, p. 16). She and her husband, Richard, lived mainly at Kington, fifteen miles from Credenhill, in a small, quasi-cloistered religious community in which Traherne may have been a participant.

The Bridgemans lived in a town house on the Strand in London, and Traherne must have found his new setting conducive. During the five years after becoming Bridgeman's chaplain Traherne finished his *Centuries* and composed nearly all his extant work: "Church's Year Book," the *Hexameron* and the "Thanksgivings," nearly a hundred lyrics, *Roman Forgeries,* and *Christian Ethicks.* In 1672, following his removal from the king's service for refusing to put his seal on the Declaration of Indulgence, the anti-Catholic Bridgeman relocated to Teddington in Middlesex, his family seat. Traherne became minister of Teddington Church, while undertaking research at Oxford. Bridgeman died in June 1674; Traherne was a signatory of his employer's will.

By late September of that same year, Traherne was himself unwell enough to draw up his own will, although he had few material possessions. He died the first week of October 1674 and was buried on the 10th beneath the lectern in Teddington Church. Thomas Good, master of Balliol College, had described Traherne as "one of the most pious ingenious men that ever I was acquainted with" (Day, p. 4), while the author of the preface to the first edition of his "Thanksgivings"—another contemporary, possibly Hopton—called him "a man of a cheerful and sprightly Temper...very affable in his Conversation, ready to do all good Offices to his Friends, and Charitable to the Poor almost beyond his ability" (Ridler, ed., p. xii). Five cottages that Traherne had owned were bequeathed to the parish of All Saints, Hereford, three years later, as almshouses for the poor (Salter, pp. 19–21). To his brother he left "All my books" and his "best Hatt."

THE MANUSCRIPTS

The staggered discoveries and publication of Traherne's works follow an itinerary spanning three centuries. Propelled by misattribution and namelessness, by death and deferral and disappearance, the stop-and-false-start narrative mimes the trajectory of Edgar Allen Poe's purloined letter, Jacques Derrida's *carte postale,* or a detective novel. Yet it is likewise a testimonial to friendship, one of Traherne's central concerns. The only volume published in Traherne's lifetime was *Roman Forgeries,* which appeared anonymously in November 1673. *Christian Ethicks,* which Traherne wrote and prepared for print during his final months, appeared posthumously in 1675. From there, matters become complicated.

Upon departing Credenhill in 1669, Traherne had entrusted some of his manuscripts to Susanna Hopton. She had the "Thanksgivings"

printed, anonymously, in 1699, though neither she nor Philip succeeded in publishing the other works. When Hopton died a decade later, the papers passed to her friend the Reverend George Hickes. And when Hickes died, the material went to their mutual friend Nathaniel Spinckes. He published the *Hexameron* in 1717 as the first part of *A Collection of Meditations and Devotions*— but listed Hopton as its author (Salter, pp. 16–17).

Nearly two centuries of erasure passed before W. T. Brooke bought, from a secondhand London bookstall, sometime between 1895 and 1897, a folio and an octavo. Both were anonymous, in good condition, and cheap. Brooke believed the poems in the former to be by Vaughan, as did editor Alexander B. Grosart, who intended to publish an edition of all the work, including the prose passages in the octavo. Grosart died in 1899 before the project could be realized, however, and his library was purchased by Charles Higham, a well-known bookseller. Word of the "Vaughan" manuscripts had spread, until another bookseller, Bertram Dobell, deciding to study the texts himself, bought the folio and octavo both from his friend Higham (Salter, p. 136).

Dobell suspected that Vaughan was not in fact the author of these poems and prose. Meanwhile, in an effort to help Dobell ascribe the works, Brooke copied out parts of the anonymous 1699 volume containing the "Thanksgivings" held at the British Museum. Dobell believed that whoever was responsible for the rhymed portions of the "Thanksgivings" had also composed the manuscripts in his keeping. Further, the address "To the Reader" in the former volume claimed that its author had served as Bridgeman's chaplain; Dobell consulted Anthony à Wood's *Athenae Oxonienses* to identify this chaplain as Thomas Traherne, author of *Roman Forgeries* and *Christian Ethicks.* Finally, in reading the *Ethicks,* Dobell found a verse excerpt beginning, "As in a Clock..." which was basically identical with a passage in one of the manuscripts he owned. He concluded, of course, that Traherne had authored both the prose *Centuries of Meditations* and the poems in what is now known as the

Dobell folio (Salter, pp. 136–137). Dobell published the first edition of Traherne's poems in 1903, complete with modernized spellings, and five years later he brought out the *Centuries*.

In 1910 Sir H. Idris Bell published a collection titled *Poems of Felicity* bearing Traherne's name, which he had stumbled across in the British Museum while hunting something else. The manuscript, handwritten by Thomas' brother, had been sitting around unremarked since 1818, when it had been acquired as part of the Burney manuscripts. Philip Traherne, who died in 1723, had transcribed most of the poems in the Dobell folio, altering the texts in many places, generally for the worse according to H. M. Margoliouth. Philip evidently also consulted, however, some other, still-to-be-discovered manuscript. Apparently he had been readying the Burney manuscript for publication, but as it was labeled "Vol I" he presumably intended to print at least a second collection of his late brother's work (Ridler, ed., pp. xiii–xiv).

Dobell landed two more Traherne manuscripts, which included several original poems. Margoliouth's two-volume "definitive" edition of Traherne, *Centuries, Poems, and Thanksgivings,* was published by the Clarendon Press in 1958. Six years later Dr. James Osborn announced in the *Times Literary Supplement* (October 8, 1964) his discovery of yet another manuscript in Traherne's handwriting. It contained 376 meditations apparently like, but not identical with, the *Centuries*. These are the "Select Meditations."

THE LYRICS

Traherne's earliest poetic ventures concern his earliest experiences: unmediated communication with God, unmitigated happiness, immunity from sin. This trio answers to the name "Infancy." There was a time, say Traherne's poems, when he lived in a blessed condition to parallel "Adam in his first Estate" (p. 9), when the world was offered for his felicity. (Unless otherwise noted, all page citations to Traherne's works refer to Anne Ridler, ed., *Poems, Centuries, and Three Thanksgivings,* 1966.) His poems devoted to commemorating that moment form the greater part of

Traherne's lyric oeuvre, and their titles are revealing: "Wonder," "Eden," "Innocence," "The Rapture," "Blisse." Traherne's state of "Original Simplicitie" meant that "My virgin-thoughts in Childhood were / Full of Content, / And innocent, / Without disturbance, free and clear" (p. 84). While certain poems testify to his poverty, both material and (in moments of doubt, melancholy, distraction, fear) spiritual, a single theme nonetheless predominates: "A Joyfull Sence and Puritie / Is all I can remember."

The poems of Traherne's idyllic youth, when "I nothing in the World did know, / But 'twas Divine" (p. 7) are expressed in tones oscillating between exhilaration and sadness. The first testifies to the amazement that continues in recollection to engulf Traherne years later, the latter bespeaking his remorse over the vanishing of childhood. He swivels almost obsessively from ebullience ("Sweet Infancy!") to longing ("I must becom a Child again"), from hopeful resolution ("To Infancy, O Lord, again I com") to self-critical analysis ("I never can complain / Enough, till I am purged from my Sin / And made an Infant once again") (pp. 17, 12, 79, 78). His theological and literary exemplars are Saint Augustine, John Milton, and the Book of Genesis, though his own experience leads. If as Christian apologist Traherne is not the systematic thinker his predecessors were, as a poet focused on early innocence and the desire to rekindle it, he is an elegist for paradises lost—but an elegist of a peculiar kind. For beyond lamenting what is gone, he seeks to lose that which will, only by losing, restore him to his remembered felicity. "O dy!" he implores, "dy unto all that draws thine Ey / From its first Objects" (p. 78).

Vision, Traherne's most recurrent trope, provides him with the means to happiness. His privileging of the phenomenal is reflected in titles such as "The Vision," "Sight," "An Infant-Ey," and the triad "The Apprehension," "Right Apprehension," and "Misapprehension." Traherne reports having felt inward joy toward "All Objects that do feed the Eye," admitting that "Their Constant Daily presence I / Rejoycing at, did see" (p. 11). God has provided all humanity with the luster of things to look at, as well as the faculty of enjoying them: "all his Works in their varietie, / Even scattered abroad *delight* the Eye," Traherne proposes in "The Improvement," adding, "Had he not made an *Ey* to be the Sphere / Of all Things, none of these would e're appear" (p. 18). Traherne in fact conceives himself as a principle of unobstructed vision capable of assimilating the creation, in a posture critics have deemed mystical, transcendental. "An Object, if it were before / My Ey," his poem "The Spirit" says, "Was all at once within me; all her Treasures / Were my Immediat and Internal Pleasures" (p. 28). In short, "My Essence was Capacitie," and "This Apprehension set / In me / Was all my whole Felicitie" (pp. 27, 31).

If humanity has a spiritual task, it is to readjust its perception, since "Felicitie / Appears to none but them that purely see" (p. 14). To take pleasure in the world God devised for them—and, in doing so, to enjoy the maker himself—people must relinquish their limited, earthly view and adopt instead a perspective framed by eternity. Equipped with "A Disentangled and a Naked Sence / A Mind that's unpossest" (p. 14), humanity will fit itself to receive the world as God has given it. So transformative is this faculty that, as "The Vision" announces, whatever is "seen in Celestial Light"—even ugliness, sin, and woe—are "Bright" (pp. 15–17). To miss this is to condemn oneself to blindness, while those who empty themselves will be granted an inward, infinite, "Infant-Ey," and "This Ey alone, / (That peer hath none)," Traherne promises, punning on the word "peer," "can pry / Into the End / To which things tend" (pp. 121–123). What he celebrates as "O Living Orb of Sight" pierces the material universe to arrive at "pure Things we find / In his Great Mind / Who made the World" (p. 30).

What constituted infant felicity, Traherne's poems are urgent to declare, is indeed still possible. It comes about through an activity of reciprocal relation between God and man, what Traherne names "The Circulation." A series of conceits, drawn especially from nature, characterize this exchange: the earth and trees each absorb rain, the former issuing in streams, the latter in flowers, while the "Air" one exhales is always

more "vital" than breath "suckt in." The moon earns its identity by accepting light lent by the sun— "and som men say," relates Traherne, even "The very Sun no Ray / Nor Influence could hav, did it / No forrein Aids…admit." Traherne wishes to indicate how, properly oriented, "The Soul a Vessel is," containing what it has been granted by God, while in the same movement, "all it doth receiv returns again." This traffic between heaven and the human—gift followed by gratitude, possession followed by praise—is what Traherne means by the verb "communicat." The procedure allows humanity to be human by participating in "the Mysteries of Blessedness," but it demonstrates God in the mutual act of fulfilling himself as well, for he is the alpha of everything and the working out of his own end. Mankind is a "Spotless Mirror," Traherne's opening metaphor runs, whose beauty is precisely a reflection of "fair Ideas from the Skie."

This equation of appearance with existence, of what is perceived with what *is*, recurs throughout Traherne's texts. "All things were made that they might be seen," he avows in *Christian Ethicks*, "For not to *be*, and not to *appear*, are the same thing to the understanding" (pp. 72, 28). In §53 of the First Century, Traherne posits that God "willed the Creation not only that He might Appear but be" (Ridler, ed., p. 187). Traherne even insinuates the rapport between visibility and being by constructing a compact palindrome—a verbal mirror—comprising *saw* and *was*: "What ere it saw," he says of the mind, "'twas ever wholly there" (p. 29). Identifying a pervasive ontological thrust to Traherne's writing, A. Leigh DeNeef, in his study *Traherne in Dialogue: Heidegger, Lacan, and Derrida* (1988), has positioned Traherne alongside Martin Heidegger in an effort to think Traherne's work according to the German philosopher's engagement with the relation between Being and being. The "clear strains of a Christian paradigm" in Heidegger, argues DeNeef, represent a fruitful opening onto Traherne (p. 289, note 50). So statements like those in §24 and §19 of the Second Century, that "By Things that are seen the Invisible things of GOD are manifested" and that "being invisible, He leaveth Room for, and Effecteth all Things," can be treated in light of Heidegger's concern with concealment, disclosure, and thingness (pp. 226, 221). "Traherne does not, of course, use Heidegger's unique terminology," DeNeef observes, "but his poetry is nonetheless an attempt to think Being-in-the-World" (p. 20). DeNeef conjectures many "lines" between the seventeenth-century poet and the twentieth-century thinker, interpreting Traherne through the lens of Heidegger's "poetic Saying of Being," considering Traherne's notion of existence as a gift in terms of Heidegger's conception of Being as given, and reading Traherne's fervent study of felicity via Heidegger's "reformative urgency" known as "authenticity" (pp. 39, 43). Even Traherne's style, DeNeef ventures, might be weighed against Heidegger's similar penchant for playing upon different grammatical forms of key words (p. 291, note 74).

However, Traherne's nostalgia for childhood, his desire to reclaim the uncluttered moment when he had communicated directly with God and enjoyed the world, has traditionally prompted critics to insist upon his sheltered puerility. In her 1944 biography *Thomas Traherne,* to take an early example, Gladys I. Wade describes her subject as "one of the most radically, most infectiously happy mortals this earth has known" (p. 3), a sentimentalism also brandished by Sharon Cadmon Seelig's *The Shadow of Eternity* (1981). Douglas Bush, in *English Literature in the Earlier Seventeenth Century* (1960), likewise observes, "Neither as Christian nor as philosopher does Traherne seem quite mature" (p. 158), and other scholars have put down Traherne by considering him the cheery avatar of a bygone, bucolic era that looks silly amid our tumultuous, supposedly more knowing contemporaneity. "There is a certain naivete about all this; it is too simple," avers Carol Marks in her essay "Traherne's Church's Year Book" (1966). "Opposed in his own day by the theology of Original Sin," she claims, "Traherne's joyful optimism crashes today against the Berlin Wall, the Vietnamese war" (pp. 71–72).

Marks's charge of "sincere but facile" hardly characterizes Traherne's complex accounts of the human body. The unequivocal directive opening

"The Instruction" follows Augustinian thought regarding the flesh: "Spue out thy filth, thy flesh abjure" (Ridler, ed., pp. 14–15). Its sixteen lines about purifying one's vision of "Contingents" and "Transients" contain no fewer than six negatives: "not," "impure," "Unfelt, unseen," "unknown," and "unaccurst." Despite the acute, reiterated abhorrence toward the physical here, however, other poems are pronounced encomiums for the body. Abstractly, "Fullnesse" speaks of "An Univers enclosd in Skin," while "The Enquirie," increasing the corporeality of imagery and language alike, constructs a somatic catalogue: "Their Eys the Thrones, their Hearts the Heavnly Rooms, / Their Souls the Diadems, / Their Tongues the Organs which they lov to hear" (pp. 31, 44). To the extent that this litany is metaphorical, it demonstrates, as A. L. Clements maintains in *The Mystical Poetry of Thomas Traherne* (1969), how "To redeemed men and 'Holy Angels,' all perception is a form of tasting and eating, spiritual nourishment" (p. 146).

That poem achieves philosophical significance, though, at the expense of emphasizing physique itself. A certain excitement accompanies Traherne's realization elsewhere that his body is just that, his own, and these seven jarring iambs from "The Person" are saturated with possession: "My Tongue, my Eys, / My Cheeks, my Lips, my Ears, my Hands, my Feet..." (p. 41). Traherne's wondrous discovery of his body is recounted in "The Salutation," in terms suggesting his flesh had before now merely been withdrawn from sight. "Where have ye been?" he asks his anatomical parts, claiming they are "wherewith my Life begins," an assertion that defies a Christian orthodoxy tending to mistrust the flesh. Traherne claims to be now "awake," understanding his body as "A Gift from GOD," and the poem's concluding repetition of "strange," six times in as many lines, enforces his realization that he is himself among the "Strange Treasures lodg'd in this fair World" (pp. 5–6)

Traherne is not squeamish about autopsy, either. Indeed, the contours and worth of the human form, he asserts, in syntax as sinewy as its subject, "best are Blazond when we see / The Anatomie, / Survey the Skin, cut up the Flesh, the Veins / Unfold" (p. 40). Yet his eye, however surgical, never strays too far from spiritual ends: "The Glory there remains," these lines continue, "The Muscles, Fibres, Arteries and Bones / Are better far then Crowns and precious Stones," because God fashioned them. Similarly, in "The Odour," Traherne contemplates his body according to the "Uses" from which it derives its divine value, advising, "Liv to thy Self; thy Limbs esteem: / From Hev'n they came" (p. 110). Still another poem qualifies that bodily features ought to be "the Pipes, / And Conduits of thy Prais" (p. 42). Traherne thus declares an imperative of utility and praise, ardor and art.

But the body is not only incomplete without the mind, it is also inferior, and Traherne's lyrics adhere to the Neoplatonic trust in Right Reason. If his infant perceptions were "unperceived, yet did appear: / Not by Reflexion" (p. 20), Traherne also maintains a commitment to thinking, as that which assists the soul's effort to restore its initial clarity. "Right Apprehension" argues that "What Newness once suggested to, / Now clearer Reason doth improv, my View," as Traherne supplements his early instruction by "Sense / Experience" with "Reason and Intelligence" (p. 113). Similarly "Shadows in the Water" claims that infancy imparts "Secrets" which "afterwards we com to know" (p. 116). Traherne conceives thought as a form of limitlessness, the divinely bestowed capacity to roam anywhere, across any time, in imitation of God's omniscient, ubiquitous nature. Traherne's apology for thinking is most concisely located in the quartet "Thoughts" I–IV, where he claims that, unlike the limbs—and even unlike the eye—the mind can be present anywhere. He qualifies his poems about the efficacy of sight by admitting, "Tis Strange that Things unseen should be Supreme," that thoughts incite all our earthly actions "tho they them selvs do not appear" (pp. 63, 68). Thoughts are "Joy Conceived," Traherne declares, adding that they are "the highest Things" and that they "bear the Image of their father's face"; they precede the soul's arrival in heaven, constitute a "Conversation" with God, and, unlike everything else, never fade (pp. 65–74). Traherne's praise for thought, however, is not without its caveats, for he does

not wish to devolve into abstraction or betray the material world by idealizing it. In "The Review," while asserting that proper thinking will found a paradise, he cautions himself against "misemploy[ing] / That Faculty," asking himself whether the movement "from *Things* to *Thoughts*" constitutes prosperous growth or static decay: "Did I flourish or diminish, / When I so in *Thoughts* did finish / What I had in *Things* begun…? (pp. 138–139).

An early wave of critical review argued the inferiority of Traherne's poetic capabilities, contending he "is a mystic before he is a poet" who does not approach Donne or Herbert in sophistication or complexity of verse (Salter, p. 113). New Criticism, otherwise interested in the metaphysicals, basically ignored him. These slights have been replaced by a diversified backlash proclaiming Traherne's accomplishment, from DeNeef's attempt to exhibit Traherne as a "serious" and "original thinker" whose work can be productively read in conversation with fundamental ontology, Lacanian psychoanalysis, and deconstruction (p. 19), to David Hawkes's inclusion of Traherne within the broader discourse of political economy and use value. On the level of poetic craft, A. L. Clements discerns that "The man who took such care as never to repeat a stanzaic form in a second poem in the Dobell Folio nor, with one exception…in his total poetic work indeed must have had a love for his medium" (p. 160).

Often overlooked is that, whatever his degree of giftedness, Traherne maintains serious reservations about writing poetry. He is a writer for whom the domain, resources, and purpose of poetry is always in question. If, on one hand, he believes it sinful to neglect thanking God—one "must, all his Days, / Return the Sacrifice of *Endless Prais*" (p. 20)—on the other, Traherne levels suspicion at speaking. In the *Centuries* he remarks how Picus Mirandula "permitteth his fancy to wander a little Wantonly after the maner of a Poet." This derogation of poetry—leveled in prose—is only secured by what Traherne says to redeem its content: "but most deep and serious things are secretly hidden under his free and luxuriant Language" (p. 353). Traherne's circumspection is clearly articulated: in serving no purpose, poetry, like any human endeavor failing to pursue its divine end, behaves ostentatiously.

"Dumnesse" and "Silence" establish theological grounds for Traherne's mistrust of words. Made to meditate, mankind was "therfore Speechless made at first, that he / Might in himself profoundly Busied be: / And not vent out, before he hath t'ane in / Those Antidots that guard his Soul from Sin" (pp. 22–24). Traherne believes mankind was originally protected from errancy by listening to a natural world that did the speaking: "evry Stone, and evry Star a Tongue." In Traherne's own youth too, "All things did com / With Voices and Instructions; but," he interrupts gravely, "when I / Had gaind a Tongue, their Power began to die." What followed this *"break"* in silence was a rupture in *"Bliss,"* a "Nois Disturbing," as Traherne became "infected" by "Errors and the Wrongs / That *Mortal Words* convey." In Traherne's view, "Sin and Death / Are most influenced by accursed Breath," and only the "first Words mine Infancy did hear" are worthy of "the Heart, if not the Ear." This notion of direct, nascent, preverbal communication with God is reaffirmed in "Silence," which posits, "The Inward Work is the Supreme" (pp. 25–27).

Traherne's reproofs of "an Empty Voice" do not cause him to renounce poetry, obviously, though he does stipulate what it should be, what sort of poems he will write. "The Person" may be read as an *ars poetica:* "I do not mean to bring / New Robes," Traherne declares, "but to Display the Thing: / Nor Paint, nor Cloath, nor Crown, nor add a Ray, / But Glorify by taking all away" (p. 40). Traherne offers poetry not as a means of embellishment but as a humble method of stripping away the superfluous. Poetry, by disappearing, allows things to appear, on the conviction that "Naked Things / Are most Sublime, and Brightest Show." Or, as he says in "The Demonstration," in terms that will achieve their twentieth-century philosophical framework in Edmund Husserl's phenomenology, "Those Things that are most Bright / Sun-like appear in their own Light" (p. 50).

Traherne's claims for and against poetry are even clearer in "The Author to the Critical Peruser." Conceiving "naked Truth" as hidden in the world *as* the world, hence legible, he names *"Felicity"* as the human "aim" and explains how to achieve it. "No curling Metaphors that gild the Sence," he dictates, "nor painted Eloquence," nothing that would obscure the world's self-revelation. It is "reall Kings" Traherne is after, "Not verbal Ones," and he is concerned that language assist, not obstruct, the movement that would discover and enjoy that mode of being. "Letting Poëtick Strains and Shadows go," then, he prescribes "An easy Stile drawn from a native vein, / A clearer Stream than that which Poets feign," once again pronouncing his difference from conventional poetry, claiming for the poetic act a new provenance, new privileges, more rigorous responsibilities. Foremost is the need for poets to express "God's Works," not to magnify "their *own,"* and to do that they must eschew the "Cloaths" in favor of "the Man they fence / Against the Cold" (pp. 3–4).

To the critical peruser, what is striking about this poem's attempt to avoid "Words, / (Like gilded Scabbards hiding Rusty Swords)" is its author's blatant recourse to exactly what he alleges to shun. Though Traherne promises to refrain from figurative language, this lyric pitched against traditional tools of lyricism nonetheless indulges simile and metaphor. He fails to evict "florid," "Superficial," "vulgar" expressions and arrive at "transparent Words," the "Poëtick Strains" he wants to repress returning when he least expects them.

THE CENTURIES

Perhaps Traherne's ambivalence toward verse is what caused him to turn to prose in his *Centuries of Meditations*—though the series is hardly less "poetic" for not being lineated, end-rhymed, or measured in feet. The "full power of Traherne's symbolic use of Paradise and Infancy is not displayed within his poetry," asserts Louis Martz in *The Paradise Within* (1964), since the "power of Traherne's mind seems hampered by the necessity of making ends meet in verse." Instead, "his peculiar combination of visual imagery and subtle, repetitive analysis finds its best medium in the flexible forms of the tightly-wrought prose paragraph" (p. 80). The genre of the devotional paragraph would have been familiar to Traherne through Joseph Hall's 1606 *The Art of Divine Meditation*, while improvisational prose meditations organized in series of a hundred included Hall's *Centuries of Meditations and Vows: Divine and Moral* (1605–1606) and Alexander Ross's 1646 *A Centurie of Divine Meditations upon Predestination, and Its Adjuncts: Wherein are Shared the Comfortable Uses of This Doctrine* (Day, p. 106). Martz suggests that Traherne's sequence also bears stylistic affinities to Augustine's *Confessions* and *De Trinitate*, "through the concatenation of repeated words and phrases, repeated always in a slightly different context, with a gradual increment of meaning, as the mind explores the central issues represented by these repeated words and phrases" (p. 43).

The arrangement of Traherne's work has elicited numerous, often competing theories, products of the structuralist moment in Anglo-American literary criticism. The best known belongs to Martz, who argues in fastidious detail the adherence of the *Centuries* to Saint Bonaventure's 1259 treatise *Itinerarium mentis in Deum*, itself informed by the stages and symbolism of Augustine's *De quantitate animae*. According to Martz, Traherne superimposes on his *Centuries* Bonaventure's threefold paradigm of "contemplation" as well as the seven-chapter journey that Bonaventure patterned after Augustine's seven steps of the soul's ascent (pp. 56–57). Richard Douglas Jordan's *The Temple of Eternity* (1972) perceives a scaffold based on Traherne's four estates of innocence, misery, grace, and glory, while Gerard Cox (1971) finds a "Platonic structure." Malcolm Day dismisses all these positions as overdetermined and outside Traherne's theological, stylistic spirit of circularity, before offering his own "outline" showing how "enjoyment forms the whole structural basis of the *Centuries*" (pp. 105–109).

The word "Century" does not appear in Traherne's manuscripts until after the first one hundred meditations, and the work's full title was apparently added later, by someone else (Ridler, ed., p. 165). However, the "Select Meditations," generally agreed to have been composed between 1662 and 1665, before the *Centuries*, are indeed titled as such on the originals. In part because the first eighty are missing, though, it is in turn uncertain whether the "Select Meditations" are draft versions of the *Centuries* or additional pieces of a larger whole comprising both together—albeit incomplete, for the Fifth Century is abruptly truncated after ten meditations. Whatever the case, a passage from "Select Meditations" demonstrates that Traherne did not limit his qualms about speaking to verse alone: "Profound Introspection, Reservation and Silence; are my Desires," he confesses. "O that I could attain them: Too much openness and proneness to speak are my Diseas…. Speaking too much and too Long in the Best Things" (Ridler, ed., pp. xii–xiii).

Based on the dedication of the *Centuries*, Traherne is ostensibly speaking to "the friend of my best friend," and as this addressee is "she," it is presumed Traherne meant Susanna Hopton, the "best friend" being God (Ridler, ed., pp. 166, xvi). Friendship surfaces throughout the First Century, from Traherne's amiable act of explicitly offering his book as a spiritual guide, to his belief that Jesus, who laid down his life for man's redemption, is a "faithfull Friend," even "my Sovereign Friend" (pp. 207, 192). More radical is Traherne's conviction that, through God's sacrifice of his only son on the cross, there even exists "Eternal Friendship" between the individual soul and God, a "Divine Friendship" whereby "His" life is "yours" and yours His (pp. 195, 187). Though he frequently refers to God as Father, Creator, Maker, Lover—traditional monikers—Traherne often evokes Friend, as if reminding himself of the privilege of being on familiar terms with the deity. God loves "evry one" in the world is "thy Peculiar Friend" (p. 212), the distinction between singular and plural effaced by his love.

The First Century is an homage to the appropriateness of desire. "An Empty Book is like an Infant Soul, in which any Thing may be Written" (p. 167), the meditations open, themselves a blank space Traherne resolves to fill with truths he does not yet know. Engaging Augustine's conundrum about whether it is possible to love what is not yet known, Traherne claims, "Things unknown have a Secret Influence on the Soul.... We lov we know not what: and therfore evry Thing allures us" (p. 167). Gravity and magnetism become conceits to describe desire and its "Invisible Ways of Conveyance." Desire is to be embraced, if directed properly: *The End for which you were Created is that by Prizing all that God hath don, you may Enjoy your self and Him in Blessedness* (p. 170). Deploring ingratitude, Traherne nevertheless elevates covetousness, declaring, *It is of the Nobility of Mans Soul that He is Insatiable* (p. 174). Traherne considers desire the "Parent of Celestial Treasure," for only "Infinit Wants Satisfied" can produce infinite joy (pp. 181, 183). Moreover, in wanting and needing, humans are linked to God, and §40–§51 examine the paradox of God's own desire: he wants what he already possesses, because such wants "put a Lustre upon His Enjoyments" (p. 184). God's desires and their satisfaction are both always present, though, so he is neither afflicted by desire nor corrupted by its fulfillment.

Love is another ligature between God and humankind. The soul "attain[s] it self" by loving, Traherne argues in the Second Century, while admonishing also "By Lov alone to attain another Self" (pp. 237–238). The statements are not as contradictory as they seem. By loving, the soul realizes the specific end for which God created it. Since love is endless and infinite, however, "By Loving a Soul does Propagat," becomes "Spiritualy Multiplied" in order to "liv again in other Persons" (pp. 240, 246). Hence to love is to realize one's own blessedness while in the very same moment sharing in existence with everyone else. While Traherne cautions a "well orderd Lov...guided to Divine and Celestial Ends," it is likewise the case that, once those divine ends have been determined, "no Man can be in Danger of loving others too much, that loveth GOD as He ought," for with love, "Excess is its True Moderation" (pp. 245, 239). In this entire dynamic that collapses boundaries between self and other, rendering metaphysics an ethics, love is not only the source and means but also,

as §46 celebrates, "the End of it self" (p. 236). Love "doth all things for its Objects sake," Traherne declaims, "yet it is the most self Ended thing in the Whole World" (p. 239). Hence God, the beginning of love, "by Lov wholy Ministereth to others," and at the same time, as love's end, he "yet wholly ministereth to Himself."

The few available firsthand accounts of Traherne's life and spiritual progress are mainly found in the Third Century, containing some of his most lyrically beautiful writing. Traherne traces his itinerary from infancy to adulthood, from innocent clarity and learned ignorance, through corruption that "Ecclypsed" this "first Light," into the maturity where he "unlearn'ed what had sidetracked his journey" (pp. 267, 264). Privileging the revelations of experience, he hopes his personal narrative will be instructive. "When I came into the Country, and being seated among silent Trees, had all my Time in my own Hands," he says in §46, "I resolved to Spend it all, whatever it cost me, in Search of Happiness" (p. 287). Traherne's decision to live in material poverty is an exchange for the "Study of Felicity," which alone renders him rich, free, divinely provided for. In §52 he explains why:

> I saw my self like som Traveller, that had Destined his life to journeys, and was resolvd to spend his Days in visiting Strange Places: who might wander in vain, unless his Undertakings were guided by som certain Rule; and that innumerable Millions of Objects were presented before me.... I made it my Prayer to GOD Almighty, that He, whose Eys are open upon all Things, would guid me to the fairest and Divinest.
>
> (pp. 290–291)

Concerned with purpose and the "Proper Places" of things, the Century concludes by citing, reciting, and examining the Psalms and Traherne's own songs of praise to God (p. 295).

In the Fourth Century, Traherne shifts from first-person to third, seeking to grasp the essential "principles"—a word he repeats some fifty times—of Christian existence. However, he is careful to qualify that contemplation, even the study of felicity and virtue, must always be accompanied by "Blessed Operations" and "continual exercise" (p. 316) for the soul is not meant to know God so much as to act in accordance with his eternal activity. Happiness is not to be merely comprehended but enjoyed, here and now, since love is participatory and it is against the nature of love to defer. There are two pragmatic ways of practicing such happiness, one oriented within the self, the other premised on self-effacement and outwardness. In §40 and §41, Traherne arrives at a "Maxime of notable concernment" (p. 332), that while God reserves all things for himself, he has nonetheless left each person in custody of his or her own heart. Traherne resolves of himself, then, "he had but one thing to do, and that was to order and keep his Heart • which alone being well guided, would order all other things Blessedly and Successfully." There is an obligation and a challenge issued to the self in this first principle, to be sure, but it does not come unaccompanied by a consolation: "If any thing were amiss," Traherne assures himself, "he still would have recours to his own heart" (p. 333). In addition, all people should "love one another as their own selvs," he implores, "tho they had never seen each other before" (p. 326). Aligning himself to this second tenet, Traherne determines that he has a duty to live so that "evry man approaching him, would be as welcom as an Angel, and the coming of a Stranger as Delightfull as the Sun." What Traherne had earlier named friendship finds its corollary here, in the love one bears toward one's neighbor, which is stronger than one's love for oneself. Such friendship is in imitation of God, whose "lov with violence" is so powerful "it will break in evry where" (pp. 347, 344).

HEXAMERON

"This vile World, which Sin has made an Hell": This phrase and others like it, alongside allusions to "Vice" and "Temptations," should challenge readers quick to claim that Traherne's anthropology is overly optimistic, squeamish about sin, and insufficiently freighted by evil and doubt (pp. 153–154). While his *Hexameron; or, Meditations on the Six Days of the Creation* is a celebration of "sacred Light," water, earth, "th' Eternal Sun" (pp. 148, 151) and humankind, ebullient and

faithful to the narrative in Genesis, it is not without dark, cautionary undertones. Thought *sub specie aeternitatis (or "under the aspect of eternity"),* from the vantage of God's creative act the world and its inhabitants are "Completely good, and naught in them to blame " (p. 153). But in the "Sixth Day," no sooner does Traherne conjure Adam, who was "proclaim'd / The King of Earth, and God's Vicegerent," than he turns urgently to his own degradation in the fallout from the Fall: "For shame, then, O my guilty Soul, begin / To weep, lament, and wash away thy Sin. / Begin before it be too late; / Beg pardon for thy Faults so great; / Repent" (p. 154). Traherne is even capable of detecting, in the natural order that *Hexameron* glorifies, signs of God's sadness at human folly. "But when from Clouds a watry Torrent spins," he admits, "Methinks Heav'n weeps for our unwept-for Sins" (p. 149).

Fortunately worldly wrong can be righted by God. If, as Traherne stipulates in his poem "Adam," "Sin is a Deviation from the Way / Of God: 'Tis that wherin a Man doth stray / From the first Path," then in its similar concern with Eden's inception out of chaos, sinful decay, and eventual recovery from sin, *Hexameron* is rife with images of straightness as a corrective (p. 82). "He gave the Word, and Day did straight appear," the First Day announces, and later, "Th' Almighty Word then spake, and streight was heard…" (pp. 148, 150). Similarly on the Sixth Day, "the Earth his Feet did touch, / The blooming Earth did streightway blush," just as, earlier, once "Th' Almighty Word has said…*Now let the Waters living be,"* the shoals are displayed (using a word repeated a fourth time) "streight" (pp. 153, 152).

In return for the riches God invested in the universe, and for the care with which he tends it, "O let not Man forget," Traherne reminds, "to raise / Both Heart and Voice to his great Maker's Praise." As usual, though, Traherne is wary of "the Danger" lurking in the language of "ancient Bards," hence also inhabiting his own words (p. 150). "Of thee how shall I sing? of thee how write?" he asks the sun, worried he might "the Way to miss." It is as if human utterance, faulty and idolatrous, would do best to imitate the divine Word and rest on the Seventh Day—the day to which Traherne precisely does not, of course, give voice.

Notwithstanding its author's suspicion regarding "Bards of old," the *Hexameron* participates in a long and once-popular tradition of commentaries on Genesis and the creation of the universe, beginning with Philo Judaeus in the earliest years anno Domini. The genre assumed the scriptural account of God's foundational works to provide scientific knowledge, not just theological and philosophical beliefs, spanning natural history, geology and geography, flora and fauna, legend and literature. Its instructive ends were pragmatic as well as spiritual. By the mid-seventeenth century the advent of rigorous, rational methods of experimentation meant that the Bible, still acceptable as a moral and religious authority, was certainly no longer a legitimate tool of scientific inquiry, and *hexamera* reflected this change (Day, pp. 58–59).

Traherne's exemplars are legion. Foremost is the Jesuit Father Luis de la Puente, whose *Meditations upon the Mysteries of our Holie Faith, with the Practice of Mental Prayer Touching the Same* (1619) provides Traherne with a meditative structure and an array of mystical meditations that Traherne copies verbatim. Puente encourages followers to adapt his method, offered as a guide for beginners, to their individual needs, and this generosity may account for Traherne's personal stylistic divergences from, elaboration on, and final relinquishing of his model (Day, pp. 56–57). Further, in starting all but the Second Day's meditations with Psalm 19, Traherne takes his cue from William Austin's 1635 *Devotionis Augustinianae flamma,* while the meditation for the Second is based on Sylvester's *Du Bartas* (Day, p. 61; Ridler, ed., p. 148). As Clements observes, Traherne even exploits the Petrarchan and Elizabethan convention of cataloguing the beauties of the human face, converting a secular standard into a personal, spiritual variation (pp. 141–142).

THE "THANKSGIVINGS"

No extant manuscript exists of what was published twenty-five years after Traherne's death as

A Serious and Pathetical Contemplation of the Mercies of God, in Several Most Devout and Sublime Thanksgivings for the Same. The nine "Thanksgivings," yet a third poetic sequence composed during the fruitful period 1670–1672, were likely conceived as a whole, though perhaps they represent only a fraction of Traherne's intention. The most celebrated is the first, "Thanksgivings for the Body," in which the body is called a "Treasury of Wonders," not despite but because of its internal "Precipices, Fractures, and Dislocations" (pp. 376, 389). While pitted against the "distracted, discomposed, confused, discontented Spirit," the body, descended from Adam's aboriginal flesh, is nonetheless "the Cabinet, or Case, of my Soul: / What then, O Lord, shall the Jewel be!" (pp. 389, 382). Thus the "understanding Eye" of the soul occupies the second poem, with subsequent subjects including "the Glory of God's Works," "the Beauty of his Providence," and "God's Attributes" (p. 390). The series exhibits a muscular formal architecture, while in its imagery, as Salter esteems, "Traherne writes of the senses as if they were spiritual and the spiritual as if it were sensuous" (p. 113).

Employing an Ignatian meditational schematic rather strictly throughout the first four, Traherne slackens the pattern thereafter. This dilation or dilution grants his verses and prose passages greater energy and expansiveness without totally relinquishing rational order to flexibility and flux. The ninth poem, "Thanksgiving and Prayer for the Nation," probably written a few years after its predecessors, during England's involvement in the Third Dutch War, is markedly different in style, content, procedure, tone. It is a continuous colloquy with God, compelled by lamentation and abruptly concluded, and this apparent departure has forced commentators to ask if Traherne had begun shifting from the theological abstract toward the political concrete, or even if his publishers had imposed emendations.

The "Thanksgivings" frequently, unabashedly quote the Psalms and to a lesser degree the Song of Solomon, Romans, Jeremiah, and other biblical books. "Traherne was perhaps of all the religious writers of the seventeenth century," suggests Harold Fisch in *Jerusalem and Albion*

THOMAS TRAHERNE

(1964), "the most deeply conscious of the *Psalms* as a model for writing and as a model for the good life" (p. 53). Occasionally noting sources within the body or margin of these texts, Traherne often neglects to signal their status as citation. The opening nine lines of the first poem, for instance, quote Psalms 103:1–5, while lines 20–30 are repeated from Psalms 139:14–18 (p. 375)—neither is attributed. Traherne also steals ideas and rhetorical strategies, consistently and covertly, from Augustine and Puente: *"O Infinite God...in thee I may take Rest, for thou didst make me for thee, and my heart's unquiet till it be united to thee"* (p. 388).

If such failures of acknowledgment are not wonderfully curious in a sequence expressly devoted to giving thanks, as a poetics they look somewhat ironic in light of the Catholic "forgeries" and falsified origins Traherne began condemning partway into composing this series. Moreover, that literary precursors are buried yet on display in these poems—linguistically "visible" but not marked *as such,* perfectly legible but not traceable to their sources because not indicated as hailing from anywhere foreign—is an inverse scriptural corollary to Traherne's scriptural belief that God, through his "Absent-Presence," is ascertainable within the creation he authored and that manifests him. "Thou hast hidden thy self / By an infinite miracle, / And made this World the Chamber of they presence," Traherne observes, thanking God "For all the art which thou hast hidden / In this little piece / Of red clay" (pp. 392, 379, 378).

More eccentric than his theological and thematic thievery, however, or his constant imitation of litany, parallelism, and other rhetorical structures used in biblical proverbs and prophecy, is Traherne's formal experimentation. Most explicitly he appropriates the device of bracketing words, phrases, and other syntactical units deployed earlier by, among other religious writers, Lancelot Andrewes. Traherne's brackets can harbor half a dozen words or clauses, sometimes split into two parallel columns and often staircased into subsets. They occur at the end of lines or even in the middle, the line closing up again behind. Noun and verb, subject and predicate,

adjective, synonym, object, exclamation—all find their way under Traherne's tipped umbrellas. Whereas Andrewes' *Private Devotions* (1648) had used brackets to economize time and trouble, as principles of efficiency, hierarchy, and mindfulness, Day proposes that Traherne piles up words and fragments to give the impression of divine plenitude and the soul's unbridled outpouring (pp. 80–81). Carl Selkin, in "The Language of Vision: Traherne's Cataloguing Style" (1976), considers Traherne's stacks as the typographical equivalents of the unity and simultaneity of God, in whom all multiplicity is one, all history eternally present (pp. 94–96).

Whatever grammatical "work" they do, the brackets are arrestingly visual, creating a sophisticated relation among form, content, and unusual formations. Brackets seem to testify, across the topology of the printed page, to God's interruption of the ordinary by the eruption of a strange sign. Premised on accumulation, the brackets focus attention on individual units while insinuating a further slew of unseen but possible alternatives. This resistance to exhaustiveness flirts with the endless and invisible, so that the logic and completion implied by a list is haunted by a sense of mystery, play, that which escapes. The brackets effect a movement "from the rigor of instrumental precision to the rigor of what is imprecise," as Maurice Blanchot (in "Man at Point Zero," 1971) says in a different context.

However, insofar as poetry is the flight from self-identity par excellence, Traherne's stylistics should not, as a matter of course, be piously considered as necessarily aligned with his theology. Combined with the longer, staggered lines in the "Thanksgivings," brackets can be thought to provoke a reversal, inaugurated by art, that Traherne himself would not have condoned: if God can straighten the crooked, the poet—or poetry itself—will make crooked the straight. And if brackets, being vertical, break the orthodox contract with horizontal linearity accepted by writer and reader alike, it must also be allowed that such punctuation introduces a puncture in what Traherne means to conceive theologically as an "eternal continuance," a seamless harmony "Expanded every where, / Yet indivisible" (pp.

279

393, 392). So while brackets, as a feature of syntax, bring different items and ideas into the fold as textual elements inscribed among words—outside language because capable of enclosing it—they refuse to conform to their surroundings or render themselves transparent. The bracket declares its distinction from the rest—indeed, as it appears in the "Thanksgivings," the bracket is *nothing but* a nonverbal declaration of difference. One may attempt to recuperate this difference via the theological tenet that mankind, though part of creation, is set apart; while God, in turn, "put[s] us at a distance," so "Thou mayest satisfie the Capacities / Of thy righteous Nature" (p. 379). Either way, Traherne's stylistics push his theology to the limit.

THE FORGERIES

Roman Forgeries; or, A True Account of False Records Discovering the Impostures and Counterfeit Antiquities of the Church of Rome was published anonymously in 1673, attributed to "A Faithful Son of the Church of England." The dedication to Bridgeman, however—to whom the "Author Devoteth his best Services and dedicateth the Use and Benefit of his Ensuing Labors"—would have rendered Traherne's identity obvious. Commentators such as Margoliouth detect in the treatise a hint of the dry, academic "thesis," and various passages of Traherne's book are indeed detached and patiently formulated, revealing an author capable of bringing rational lucidity to bear on matters passionately quarreled over in the seventeenth century. On the other hand, as Day contends, Traherne may have had an exigent political, social, intellectual, and even moral program in mind: the "Faithful Son" of the Anglican faith hoped to warn the king that no good could come of his recent leniency—if not leaning—toward Catholicism (p. 89).

On March 15, 1672, Charles II passed the Declaration of Indulgence, which eradicated laws leveling disadvantages on nonconformists. Bridgeman's refusal to fix his seal to the act ended in his dismissal, and Traherne, like many English citizens, was also angry. If the king were to become Roman Catholic, Traherne worried, he would be obliged to answer to a pope worshipped by his followers as infallible. Such obedience to a living embodiment of perfection is already a form of idolatry, Traherne admonishes in the *Forgeries,* but if the king were to submit, the Roman Church would have all it needs to justify the political treasons and other atrocities it is already attempting. The king's blind subjection to the pope's supremacy, as a principle of absolute inerrancy, would annihilate the foundation of all social organization—the rational capacity to judge right from wrong—and thus constitute tyranny (Day, p. 90).

Traherne mounts his argument by demonstrating that worship of the pope, hence the entire Catholic insurrection, is the direct result of the Roman Church's systematic creation, encouragement, and proliferation of false records and forgeries. In Traherne's mind, for Catholic authorities the Reformation simply marks the latest occasion, in a long lineage of lies going back to about 790, to increase the amount and intensity of its fraudulence (Day, pp. 99–100). Traherne seeks to illuminate—or, considering his self-righteous, ironic tone in places, to throw the harsh light of an interrogator's lamp upon—what he considers a dubious, contemptible ecclesiastical history. This invented heritage, Traherne believes, is premised on distortion and dissemination, convenience and inconsistency, the transmitting of what has been transmuted. Concordantly Traherne wants to expose the Church's "great company of forged Evidences, or feigned Records tending all to the advancement of the Popes Chair, in a very various, copious, and Elaborate manner" for the supreme fiction it is (*Roman Forgeries,* p. 29).

Traherne's species of historical criticism, Day expounds, is in keeping with the Renaissance emphases on textual analysis, the search for original documentation, and reassessment of old records (Day, pp. 91–92). Additionally Traherne represents a broader Reformationist impulse to shun dogma in favor of weighing tangible evidence, testing the validity of supposed facts, and arriving at a consensus of opinion on the truth. This need to address the case at hand, subjecting its elements to scrutiny and logical criteria, finds its justification in the ascent of rational science. However, the insistence on examining concrete, uncorrupted information can also be read as the culmination of a long-standing controversy between the English and Roman faiths, in which the former rejects the latter's unquestioning adherence to orthodox authority and its tendency to tamper with written doctrine in order to secure that power.

So Traherne's endeavor, by Day's account, is not original. The methods and unminced polemics of Thomas James, for example, author of the five-part *A Treatise of the Corruption of Scripture, Councels, and Fathers by the Prelates, Pastors, and Pillars of the Church of Rome, for Maintenance of Popery and Irreligion* (1611), clearly influenced Traherne (Day, pp. 95–96). Likewise, among the many targets of Traherne's critique is the *Index expurgatorius*, whereby the Roman Church altered texts before destroying the originals. However, William Crashaw, father of the poet Richard Crashaw, had already made the index the subject of his own attack in *Romish Forgeries and Falsifications* (1606). What Traherne adds is an urgency about recovering the original documents before they are forever lost, and he devotes the latter portion of the *Forgeries* to collating such documents, in chronological order.

Traherne initially associates Catholic forgery with "Adultery, Theft, Perjury, and Murder" (*Forgeries*, p. 1). Because the despicable rewritings invade holy Scripture, Traherne adds sacrilege, simony, blasphemy, and heresy to his list of accusations (Day, p. 97). The pope's imperious, irrational claim to infallibility— "nothing," Traherne proposes ominously, "can escape the Sublimity of his Cognizance"—is a monopoly that the Church has manipulated evidence to fashion and sustain (*Forgeries*, p. 109). As such it betrays and threatens the entire human order, from private conscience to public knowledge, from individual freedom to common justice, inquiry, and dissent.

THE ETHICKS

A paean to felicity, virtue, reason, variety in the universe, and the unity of God, *Christian Ethicks* is Traherne's last word. The book posits a world to be understood, acknowledged as a divine gift, praised for its beauty and usefulness, and most importantly, enjoyed. "Above all," Traherne advises, "pray to be sensible of the Excellency of the Creation, for upon the due sense of its Excellency the life of Felicity wholly dependeth" (*Christian Ethicks*, p. 6). Influenced by Plotinus and Origen no less than Neoplatonism, Traherne proclaims the infinite and eternal nature of God's presence. Hence if viewed properly, the finite, tangible world will lead one back to its maker. Traherne also asserts, following Giordano Bruno and Hermes Trismegistus, that because humanity alone is made in God's image, each person possesses unique access to God. Or, even more radically, the human mind shares an essential identity with the deity, such that the soul can participate in divine activity (Day, pp. 29–31).

Traherne sets out to anatomize the virtues, his purpose being to "elevate the *Soul,* and refine its Apprehensions" (*Ethicks*, p. 3). As frequently with Traherne, however, what aspires to systematic analysis quickly gets distracted as his excitement and associative capacity take over. The tract begins, according to Day, like most Renaissance studies of virtue, patterning itself after Aristotle's *Nichomachean Ethics* and Aquinas' *Summa theologica* (Day, p. 25). Defining virtue as "a Right and well order'd Habit of mind, which Facilitates the Soul in all its operations, in order to its Blessedness," Traherne outlines a detailed schemata of virtues: Theological, Intellectual, Moral, Divine (*Ethicks*, pp. 23–25). En route to examining each domain, though, Traherne's prose is swept away in anastomoses of language and idea, thematic and syntactic parallelisms, synonyms and similarities. The categories blur, inciting detours, crossings, crossings out. Some virtues, such as Repentance, are added without prior notice, while others—Obedience, Devotion, Godliness—are no sooner named than abandoned, without receiving explanation. Still others, like Justice, begin in one set (Moral) and end up in another (Divine), or else do double duty: Prudence is both Intellectual and Moral (Day, pp. 25–27).

Critics are divided on Traherne's methodology, or lack thereof. Either his divagations signal a careless lack of rigor and seriousness, or, to the contrary, his improvisational tendency demonstrates an appropriately zealous disregard for pedantry in matters verging on the ecstatic. A work purporting to classify virtuous behavior, especially one claiming that morality requires discipline, that *"Melody* is an effect of *Judgment and Order"* (Ridler, ed., p. 420), might have done well to follow its own advice. On the other hand, Traherne's stylistic penchant for concentric dispersal is very much to his theological point: that God is a principle of simultaneity, resolving all difference and contradiction, that "VERTUE," in short, "is a comprehensive Word" (*Ethicks,* p. 23). The music of Traherne's proposals and prescriptions—repetitive, consonantal, paradoxical, chiasmic—certainly facilitates, formally, his overwhelming mantra that happiness is the end for which mankind was made.

The passage where Traherne argues for the divine similitude of the human soul, for example, is melodiously arranged according to a barely restrained enthusiasm, revolving around the crucial word "like":

> Godliness is a kind of GOD-LIKENESS, a divine habit, or frame of Soul, that may fitly be accounted *The fullness of the stature of the Inward Man.* In its least degree, it is an Inclination to be Like GOD, to Please him, and to Enjoy him…. *GODLINESS,* or *GOD-LIKENESS* is the cement of Amity between *GOD* and *MAN.* Eternity and Immensity are the sphere of his Activity, and are often frequented, and filled with his Thoughts. Nothing less than the Wisdom of GOD will please the *GOD-LIKE Man:* Nothing less content him, than the Blessedness and Glory of his Great Creatour. He must enjoy GOD, or he cannot enjoy himself.
>
> (*Ethicks,* pp. 285–286)

Subtler wordplay is responsible for the excerpt's power. *"Inward,"* "In its least degree," and "Inclination" form a sonorous cluster of "in"-phrases that are in turn alliteratively seconded by "divine," "cement," *"MAN,"* "Immensity," "frequented," "content," and "enjoy." The suffix "-ness" is attached to four different roots, the implied *"fullness"* of each set against its thrice repeated contrary, "less" / "least." Hence linguistic (aural) similarities are enacted in a text about the theological (visual) similarity between God and man. Reaffirming this likeness between the divine and the human, Traherne's statement in one of several interpolated poems that "As in a Clock, 'tis hinder'd-Force doth bring / The Wheels to order'd Motion, by a Spring" applies equally to his own poetics (Ridler, ed., p. 141).

If the linguistic elaboration of such "Measures" does not seem "govern'd" enough, it should be remembered that, with Traherne, in spiritual arenas *"Lukewarmness* is Profane" (Ridler, ed., p. 141; *Ethicks,* p. 89). At the same time, however, "Humility is the basis," as he announces in one chapter title, "of all Vertue and Felicity." His audacious verbal style is not meant egotistically, as a distraction from the call to self-effacing service. Humility is "like a Mirror lying on the ground with its face upwards: All the height above increaseth the depth of its Beauty within, nay, turneth it into a new depth," Traherne writes of the individual soul (*Ethicks,* pp. 209. Elsewhere he broadens that principle to include others: "The best Principle whereby a man can stear his course in this World," he implores, "is to love every man in the whole World, as GOD doth. For this will make a man the Image of GOD, and fill him with the mind and spirit of Christ" (*Ethicks,* p. 253). The *Ethicks* is not so much an intellectual study of the virtues as a personal, impassioned attempt, by a dying man in full view of his death, to "guide" others "in the way of *Vertue"* (*Ethicks,* p. 3). More aggressively, Traherne seeks "to encourage them"—if not himself—"to Travel, to comfort them in the Journey, and so at last to lead them to true Felicity, both here and hereafter."

Selected Bibliography

WORKS OF THOMAS TRAHERNE

PUBLISHED WORKS
Roman Forgeries; or, A True Account of False Records Discovering the Impostures and Counterfeit Antiquities of

the Church of Rome. London: S. and B. Griffin for Jonathan Edwin, 1673. (The only book published in Traherne's lifetime, this was printed anonymously, its author referred to as "A Faithful Son of the Church of England.")

A Serious and Pathetical Contemplation of the Mercies of God, in several most Devout and Sublime Thanksgivings for the Same. London, 1699. (Published anonymously "by the Reverend Doctor Hickes at the request of a friend of the Author's.")

Poetical Works of Thomas Traherne, B.D., 1636?–1674. London, 1903. (Published by Dobell, from the Dobell folio.)

Centuries of Meditations. London, 1908. (Published by Dobell, from the untitled octavo Dobell manuscript.)

Traherne's Poems of Felicity. Oxford: Clarendon Press, 1910. (Edited by Dr. Bell, from the British Museum MS. Burney 392.)

The Poetical Works of Thomas Traherne. Edited by Gladys I. Wade. London: P. J. and A. E. Dobell, 1932; New York: Cooper Square, 1965.

Thomas Traherne: Centuries, Poems, and Thanksgivings. Edited by H. M. Margoliouth. 2 vols. Oxford: Clarendon Press, 1958. (Considered the definitive edition of Traherne's complete works. Preserves the irregularities of spelling, capitalization, and punctuation found in the author's original manuscripts. Includes detailed notes and, in order to demonstrate the degree to which Philip denigrated the originals, both versions of the twenty-two poems appearing in the Burney and Dobell manuscripts alike.)

Meditations on the Six Days of the Creation. Edited by George R. Guffey. Augustan Reprint Society, no. 119. Los Angeles: Clark Memorial Library, University of California, 1966. (Originally published in 1717 by Nathaniel Spinckes as *Hexameron; or, Meditations on the Six Days of Creation, and Meditations and Devotions on the Life of Christ,* with authorship attributed to Susanna Hopton.)

Poems, Centuries, and Three Thanksgivings. Edited by Anne Ridler. London and New York: Oxford University Press, 1966. (Shorter, less comprehensive than Margoliouth's edition, though based on his, not nearly as cumbersome, more easily accessible, and re-collated with the original manuscripts. Ridler has taken out five poems from the Margoliouth edition now thought not to be by Traherne.)

Christian Ethicks. Edited by Carol L. Marks and George R. Guffey. Ithaca, N.Y.: Cornell University Press, 1968. (Originally published in 1675, shortly after Traherne's death.)

UNPUBLISHED MANUSCRIPTS

"Church's Year Book." Bodleian Library, Oxford, MS. Eng. th. e. 51.

"Commonplace Book." Bodleian Library, Oxford, MS. Eng. poet. c. 42.

"Early Notebook." Bodleian Library, Oxford, MS. Lat. misc. f. 45.

"Ficino Notebook." British Museum, London, MS. Burney 126.

"Select Meditations." Osborn Collection, Beinecke Library, Yale University.

BIBLIOGRAPHIES AND CONCORDANCE

Clements, A. L. "Thomas Traherne: A Chronological Bibliography." *Library Chronicle* 35:36–51 (1969).

Dees, Jerome S. "Recent Studies in Traherne." *English Literary Renaissance* 4:189–196 (1974).

Guffey, George Robert, ed. *A Concordance to the Poetry of Thomas Traherne.* Berkeley: University of California Press, 1974.

CRITICAL AND BIOGRAPHICAL STUDIES

Barnstone, Willis. "Two Poets of Felicity: Thomas Traherne and Jorge Guillen." *Books Abroad* 42 (1968). Pp. 14–19.

Bottrall, Margaret. "Traherne's Praise of Creation." *Cambridge Quarterly* 1:126–133 (1959).

Bush, Douglas. *English Literature in the Earlier Seventeenth Century, 1600–1660.* 2d ed., rev. London: Oxford University Press, 1962.

Clements, A. L. *The Mystical Poetry of Thomas Traherne.* Cambridge, Mass.: Harvard University Press, 1969.

Colie, Rosalie L. "Thomas Traherne and the Infinite: The Ethical Compromise." *Huntington Library Quarterly* 21:69–82 (1957).

———. "Affirmations in the Negative Theology: The Infinite." In her *Paradoxia Epidemica: The Renaissance Tradition of Paradox.* Princeton, N.J.: Princeton University Press, 1966. Pp. 145–168.

Cox, Gerard H. "Traherne's *Centuries:* A Platonic Devotion of 'Divine Philosophy.'" *Modern Philology* 69:10–24 (1971).

Day, Malcolm M. *Thomas Traherne.* Boston: Twayne, 1982. (Concise, intelligent introduction to Traherne's life and work, beginning with a chronology and the few known biographical facts. Examines Traherne's texts individually, with a continuous attempt to frame his writing and thought in their historical, philosophical, and theological contexts, while taking relevant scholarship into account. Concludes with an annotated bibliography.)

DeNeef, A. Leigh. *Traherne in Dialogue: Heidegger, Lacan, and Derrida.* Durham, N.C.: Duke University Press, 1988.

Dickson, Donald R. *The Fountain of Living Waters: The Typology of the Waters of Life in Herbert, Vaughan, and Traherne.* Columbia: University of Missouri Press, 1987.

Dowell, Graham. *Enjoying the World: The Rediscovery of Thomas Traherne.* London: Morehouse, 1990.

Ellrodt, Robert. *L'Inspiration personnelle et l'esprit du temps chez les poètes métaphysiques anglais.* 2 parts. Paris: Librarie José Corti, 1960.

Fisch, Harold. *Jerusalem and Albion: The Hebraic Factor in Seventeenth-Century Literature.* New York, 1954.

Grant, Patrick. *The Transformation of Sin: Studies in Donne, Herbert, Vaughan, and Traherne.* Montreal: McGill-Queens University Press, 1974.

Hawkes, David. "Thomas Traherne: A Critique of Political Economy." *Huntington Library Quarterly* 62, nos. 3 and 4:369–388 (1999).

Hill, Christopher. "Thomas Traherne." In *The Collected Essays of Christopher Hill.* Vol. 1, *Writing and Revolution in 17th Century England.* Brighton: Harvester, 1985; Amherst: University of Massachusetts, 1985. Pp. 226–242.

Hodgson, Geraldine E. *English Mystics.* London: Mowbray, 1922.

Iredale, Q. *Thomas Traherne.* Oxford: Blackwell, 1935.

Jennings, Elizabeth. "The Accessible Art: A Study of Thomas Traherne's *Centuries of Meditations.*" *Twentieth Century* 167:140–151 (1960).

Jones, Rufus M. *Spiritual Reformers in the 16th and 17th Centuries.* London: Macmillan, 1914.

Jordan, Richard Douglas. *The Temple of Eternity: Thomas Traherne's Philosophy of Time.* Port Washington, N.Y.: Kennikat, 1972.

———. "Thomas Traherne and the Art of Meditation." *Journal of the History of Ideas* 46:381–403 (1985).

King, Francis. "Thomas Traherne: Intellect and Felicity." In *Restoration Literature: Critical Approaches.* Edited by Harold Love. London: Methuen, 1972. Pp. 121–143.

Leishman, James Blair. *The Metaphysical Poets: Donne, Herbert, Vaughan, Traherne.* Oxford: Clarendon Press, 1934.

Lewalski, Barbara Kiefer. *Protestant Poetics and the Seventeenth-Century Religious Lyric.* Princeton, N.J.: Princeton University Press, 1979.

Marks, Carol L. "Thomas Traherne and Cambridge Platonism." *Publications of the Modern Language Association* 81:521–534 (December 1966).

———. "Thomas Traherne and Hermes Trismegistus." *Renaissance News* 19:118–131 (1966).

———. "Traherne's Church's Year-Book." *Papers of the Bibliographical Society of America* 60:31–72 (1966).

Martz, Louis L. *The Paradise Within: Studies in Vaughan, Traherne, and Milton.* New Haven, Conn.: Yale University Press, 1964.

Matar, Nabil. "Thomas Traherne's Solar Mysticism." *Studia mystica* 7:52–63 (1984).

Nicolson, Marjorie Hope. *The Breaking of the Circle: Studies in the Effect of the "New Science" upon Seventeenth-Century Poetry.* New York: Columbia University Press, 1960.

Osborn, James M. "A New Traherne Manuscript." *Times Literary Supplement,* October 8, 1964, p. 928.

Osmond, Percy H. *The Mystical Poets of the English Church.* New York: Macmillan, 1919.

Quiller-Couch, Sir Arthur. *Felicities of Thomas Traherne.* London: P. J. and A. E. Dobell, 1934.

Ridlon, Harold G. "The Fraction of the 'Infant-Ey' in Traherne's Poetry." *Studies in Philology* 61:627–639 (1964).

Salter, K. W. *Thomas Traherne: Mystic and Poet.* London: Edward Arnold, 1964.

Sauls, Richard Lynn. "Traherne's Debt to Puente's *Meditations.*" *Philological Quarterly* 50:161–174 (1971).

Sayer, Dorothy L. "The Beatrician Vision in Dante and Other Poets." *Nottingham Medieval Studies* 2 (1958).

Seelig, Sharon Cadmon. *The Shadow of Eternity: Belief and Structure in Herbert, Vaughan, and Traherne.* Lexington: University of Kentucky Press, 1981.

Selkin, Carl M. "The Language of Vision: Traherne's Cataloguing Style." *English Literary Renaissance* 6:92–104 (1976).

Sherrington, Alison J. *Mystical Symbolism in the Poetry of Thomas Traherne.* St. Lucia, Australia: University of Queensland Press, 1970.

Stewart, Stanley. *The Expanded Voice: The Art of Thomas Traherne.* San Marino, Calif.: Huntington Library, 1970.

Wade, Gladys I. *Thomas Traherne: A Critical Biography.* Princeton, N.J.: Princeton University Press, 1944.

Wallace, John Malcolm. "Thomas Traherne and the Structure of Meditation." *English Literary History* 25:78–89 (1958).

Webber, Joan. *The Eloquent "I": Style and Self in Seventeenth-Century Prose.* Madison: University of Wisconsin Press, 1968.

ALAN WARNER

(1964–)

Andrew van der Vlies

ALAN WARNER WAS born on August 5, 1964, in Oban, a fishing port and ferry terminus in Argyll, on the west coast of Scotland. Warner's parents— his mother is from the Isle of Mull, his father from Yorkshire—ran a hotel in Connel, a nearby village. Oban appears, thinly disguised, as the anonymous port in each of Warner's novels. While he portrays the lives of many of the port's poorest inhabitants with some sympathy, in interview he has described Oban as a "philistine, patriarchal, sexist, violent," and "backwards" community, in which reading—let alone writing—had to be an "underground act" (Weissman, online). Warner recalls a great "sense of alienation" growing up in this society: "I can't express how completely I believed there was nobody alive in Scotland writing a book" (Redhead, p. 130). Encouraged by his English teacher at Oban High School, the distinguished writer Iain Crichton Smith, he began reading Scottish writing in his late teens, excited about reading literature that, if it did not always speak to his generation, was at least set in his homeland. The discovery was also "traumatic": "it drove me away from Oban, the more I read, the more I believed I had to leave to study literature" (Dale, p. 10). After leaving school, Warner worked on the railways, later attended evening classes, and went to university in London. He returned to Scotland to complete a postgraduate English degree at the University of Glasgow, where he wrote a thesis on Joseph Conrad.

For all their narrators' and characters' apparently poor education, Warner's novels are full of complex intertextual allusions. His familiarity with Conrad, for example, suggests a source for his interest in unreliable narration, although he also refers to *Wuthering Heights,* Herman Melville's *Benito Cereno,* and Samuel Beckett's trilogy as sources for this interest (Dale, p. 13).

He claims as his "masters" "Sam Beckett, Camus, William Faulkner and Juan Carlos Onetti" (Thomson, 1997); other writers he has cited as influences range from Miguel de Cervantes, Nikolay Gogol, André Gide, Jean-Paul Sartre, and James Joyce to contemporary novelists like Mark Richard, Annie Proulx, Elizabeth McCracken, Thomas McGuane, Cormac McCarthy, and Michael Ondaatje. Warner suggests that one ought not to attempt to understand writers "as personalities" but rather to consider the "complex influences other books have upon them" ("Paperback Writer").

Among earlier Scottish work that influenced Warner, Lewis Grassic Gibbon's 1930s *Scots Quair* trilogy offered a model with its rural and small-town settings, strong female protagonist, and use of dialect. Cairns Craig suggests that dialect in Gibbon's work "maintains the possibility of a community...in defiance of the hierarchies of the class system that are embodied in and through the voice of standard English" (p. 96). Dialect and colloquial Argyllshire English perform a similar function in all of Warner's writing. Among more recent Scottish writers, influences include James Kennaway, Tom Leonard, James Kelman, and Duncan McLean. Warner has spoken of gaining confidence to submit the manuscript of *Morvern Callar* (1995) after reading McLean's first collection of stories, *Bucket of Tongues,* (1992) which he calls "fantastic Scottish writing"; he was amazed that, although "set in the geographical peripheries," it was published (Dale, p. 9).

From all of these writers Warner draws the confidence to represent the lives of supposedly ordinary characters and communities using the "nonliterary" vernacular. Until the middle of the twentieth century, Scottish writing most often identified the nation with its rural Scots-speaking, and even occasionally with its shrinking Gaelic-speaking, areas. Since the 1970s it has been the urban centers, particularly Glasgow, that have come to dominate representations of "Scottish-ness" (Whyte, pp. 277–278). Warner's work is in part a reaction against this focus on urban metropolitan Scotland by many Scottish writers of the 1980s and 1990s, of whom the most prominent are undoubtedly James Kelman and Irvine Welsh. While Warner's work draws on this urban writing (indeed, some of his short stories are set in Glasgow or Edinburgh), his primary interest is in the lives of working-class and unemployed Scots in small towns dotting non-metropolitan Scotland.

Warner first began writing in his teens, but it was years before he had the confidence to seek publication. Early poems and short prose pieces appeared in small Scottish press anthologies. He is the author of four novels to date: *Morvern Callar* (1995) won a Somerset Maugham Award, was short-listed for the IMPAC Prize, and was filmed by Lynne Ramsay; *These Demented Lands* (1997) won an Encore Award; *The Sopranos* (1998) won the Saltire Award and is to be filmed (by Michael Caton-Jones); *The Man Who Walks* was published in 2002. In 2003 the magazine *Granta* included Warner in its list of the twenty best young British writers under the age of forty. Warner currently lives in Ireland.

A WRITER'S VOICE: MORVERN CALLAR

The eponymous working-class protaginist of Alan Warner's first published novel begins her first-person narrative with a description of the body of her writer boyfriend, referred to with capitalized third-person pronouns throughout, lying on the floor of their small house two days before Christmas:

> He'd cut His throat with the knife. He'd near chopped off His hand with the meat cleaver. He couldn't object so I lit a Silk Cut. A sort of wave of something was going across me. There was fright but I'd daydreamed how I'd be.
>
> He was bare and dead face-down on the scullery lino with blood round. The Christmas tree lights

were on then off. You could change the speed those ones flashed at. Over and over you saw Him stretched out then the pitch dark with His computer screen still on.

(p. 1)

The reader learns little about the late boyfriend: he is in his thirties, has traveled abroad, and was raised in a nearby village, which he has re-created in miniature in the loft of the house as the set for a model railway. Morvern takes no immediate action on discovering the body. She opens her presents, listens to music, clocks in for work in the local superstore as usual, attends a party with her best friend, Lanna (Allanah Phimister), and spends the following day in bed with a fever. She tells everyone that her boyfriend has gone away for good, without explanation. Apparently unwilling to mourn, she remains calm and relatively unemotional, winching his body up into the loft where he lies, a latter-day Gulliver, on the miniature landscape and village of the train set: "snow flakes twirling down on the summer land, coating the sides of the pass, layering the village roofs and the giant man" (p. 57).

When summer arrives Morvern dismembers the body and buries its parts across the slopes of a nearby mountain; a specially recorded soundtrack, the "happy sound of Salif Keita doing Nyanafin," accompanies her as she rounds "the great bank of Beinn Mheadhonach," where "The sun was hot on my hair and His chopped-off head bumped away against my back" (p. 93). Throughout the novel, music conveys or evokes emotions Morvern is unable or unwilling otherwise to enunciate. She blames "He Loved Him Madly offof Get Up With It" by Miles Davis, for example, for the fact that she does not report her boyfriend's death: "it was that bit where the trumpet comes in for the second time: I walked right past the phonebox. It was the feeling the music gave that made me" (p. 6). That much of the music is "His" is significant, offering, in some sense, the novel's only suggestions of the voice of the absent male writer figure: knowing, experimental, cosmopolitan.

Morvern's boyfriend leaves the manuscript of a novel on computer disk with a request that she submit it for publication. She does so, but only after substituting her name for his on the title page. The use by a male writer of a female character narrating her own story, literally over the dead body of a male writer character, gestures ironically to a number of literary historical and theoretical ideas, not least the "death of the author" (postulated polemically by Roland Barthes in 1968). Commenting on the symbolism of the novelist killing off his surrogate on the first page of his first novel, Jenny Turner, writing in the *London Review of Books,* called it "rhetorical self-slaughter." The boyfriend's suicide note asserts Morvern is "BETTER THAN US" (p. 87). Dominic Head reads this as a metafictional enactment of Warner's desire to "liberate the silenced Scottish underclass (for which Morvern stands) from the abuse of the neglectful novelistic imagination" (p. 150). The act of a female, poorly educated, working-class character, speaking in a regional vernacular, appropriating the role of the traditionally male, educated writer and narrating her own life, makes the novel an important challenge to class, gender, and literary stereotypes.

Morvern has worked in an exploitative superstore since the age of thirteen and, as her foster-father Red Hanna (nicknamed for his socialist views) explains, can look forward to little better than working "a forty-hour week on slave wages for the rest of [her] life" (p. 47). The port's pubs and nightclub, the Mantrap, offer the only escape for the novel's working-class characters. The money in her boyfriend's bank account and the small advance she receives for his novel (it is accepted by the first publishing company to which she submits it) offer Morvern an opportunity for a more dramatic, if just as provisional, escape from this life: she buys a two-week package holiday at a resort in Spain for herself and Lanna. (The Sopranos, in Warner's eponymous third novel, also save for just such a holiday). Warner acknowledges that his work is about "people trying to get a few joys with not much in their pocket" but also about "the moral vacuum when you have money" (Dale, p. 48). Red Hanna observes that "even with the fortnight in a resort theres no much room for poetry" in the kind of life Morvern seems destined to lead (p. 47). She finds little poetry in the resort either. The only

person with whom she has any sustained contact is a fellow holidaymaker who is distressed at news of his mother's death. Morvern comforts him and sleeps with him, but his sudden departure echoes her boyfriend's death, and once again she finds herself unable to articulate a response: "I lay on the bed then sat forward on the end with face in hands. I lay back again then starting greeting [crying] and dead quickly just stopped" (p. 155). She decides to leave the resort and, journeying north along the coast, finds a village where she is able to feel removed from her old life. She comments on its dissimilarity to the port: "Where you would expect a jumble of hills and a circular folly above a port: none. Where you would expect piers with a seawall between and an esplanade of hotels beyond: none." It "was really another place" (p. 160).

Returning to Britain a fortnight later than planned, Morvern spends a night in London, drinking and dancing with two executives from the firm publishing her (boyfriend's) novel. The gulf in class, income, and education results in a night of comic misunderstanding. Back in the port, Morvern discovers that Lanna is having an affair with Red Hanna (she has already discovered that Lanna had an affair with her late boyfriend). Finding too that her boyfriend has left her his inheritance of more than forty thousand pounds, she decides to return to the Mediterranean immediately. There is no indication of how long this absence will be, but at the end of the novel (during a conversation Morvern has with three people near the power station, some miles from the port, on her eventual return), it turns out that it has been at least three years (p. 222). All that Morvern reports of the intervening period is several detailed descriptions of her daily routine, a night swim, a typical night at a rave, and a walk through an orchard. The end of the novel finds her alone in the rain, perched on the mountainside above her boyfriend's childhood village (modeled on Lochawe), pregnant with a "child of the raves" (p. 242).

Money provides Morvern with the means to escape her life of routine and low aspirations. She chooses to spend it seeking a kind of physical oblivion: "You didn't really have your body as your own, it was part of the dance, the music, the rave" (p. 215). After the novel's success, Warner found himself promoted by some critics and anthologists (like Sarah Champion, editor of the 1997 volume *Disco Biscuits*) as one of a group of writers supposedly depicting rave and 1990s youth culture. He is wary of such categorization, preferring to place his work in the more serious "tradition" of the existentialism of Sartre and Beckett, whose work he had first read as a teenager (Dale, p. 48). Cairns Craig comments on the attraction of existentialism to many modern Scottish writers, citing, among others, Alexander Trocchi, Alan Sharp, and Allan Massie (pp. 106–107). Red Hanna is the clearest spokesman of an existentialist viewpoint in *Morvern Callar;* he observes that there is "no freedom, no liberty; theres just money…. We live off each other's necessities and fancy names for barefaced robbery" (p. 48). Warner is ultimately pessimistic about the extent to which it is possible for anyone to escape from his or her circumstances, even with unexpected wealth. Andrew Biswell observed in the *Times Literary Supplement* that Warner's depiction of the escapes that present themselves to Morvern in this novel—drink, drugs, raves—lays "bare an anti-culture" that Warner "apparently considers worthless." In the author's own words: "critics and some readers often confuse a reference to some aspects of 'popular culture' as an endorsement of support for it; they assume it's being celebrated" (Redhead, p. 131).

Several commentators have expressed discomfort at aspects of Warner's characterization of Morvern's sexuality and gendered activities, such as her bathing with Lanna and detailed descriptions of her application of makeup. For the Scottish writer Janice Galloway, although the novel is narrated by a female protagonist, it is always clear that "Alan's doing the observing" (in March, p. 68). Brian Morton, in the *New Statesman,* called Morvern "an unhappy, even misogynistic creation." Morvern's sensuality is, however, one of the few aspects of her life that is empowering and over which she has some control. Critics overlook the symbolic significance of the surrogate-author-boyfriend's death and the mythi-

cal resonances of Morvern's vitality and fertility. During her first trip abroad Morvern witnesses a festival procession in a coastal village that involves a burning effigy of the Virgin Mary being sent out to sea on a raft, and she later swims out, with the town's young women, to look at the effigy's face under the water (pp. 153–156). The echo of pagan fertility rituals is clear and not out of place in the novel: Warner told Sophy Dale that he had wanted "to tell a working class person's story as if it wasn't just realism, so that it had something of the quality of myth" (p. 66). In the film adaptation, director Lynne Ramsay and screenwriter Liana Dognini transformed this Marian rite into a small bull-running festival, and the film arguably suffers from the loss of the complex invocation of Catholic and pagan ritual in the novel. The story told by Couris Jean, Lanna's grandmother, about horses swimming ashore from the sunken transport ship also has the quality of myth and is likewise linked with fertility (as well as her regional, and Gaelic, identity). John LeBlanc suggests that Morvern is a latter-day embodiment of an ancient Celtic deity. Like her near-namesake, the goddess Morrighan, he argues, she "oversees the death of the dysfunctional patriarchal order and the rebirth of a matriarchal sensibility concomitant with her own emergence as an individual" (p. 146).

Morvern struggles to communicate with Tom and Susan, the London literary agents, who might just as well be speaking Spanish: "They talked so constant you found their blethers made less sense than locals back in the resort but you found you could get by with a Uh huh, a Mmm, giving the odd nod or coming out with a chuckle and that" (p. 169). "They didn't tell stories they just discussed" (p. 164), she says; theirs is a different kind of discourse, far removed from the mode of storytelling with which she is familiar from the port. Her own narration conveys a strong sense of traditional storytelling patterns. That these might not conform to conservative expectations is hinted at in the novel's epigraph, from Isak Dinesen's "The Immortal Story," which invites the reader to expect something out of the ordinary, or perhaps extraordinarily ordinary, an account "not of deals and bargains, but of other things which people at times had put down, and which other people did at times read."

The people of the port are lively storytellers, narrators of lives relived in the act of narration and fabrication. Their inventive nicknames attest to a different modality of naming and narrating. Morvern's hated supervisor is nicknamed "Creeping Jesus," and she works with "Smugslug" and "The Seacow" (p. 10). The bouncer at the Mantrap is "The Slab," and inside the club Morvern encounters, among others, "The Golden Binman, Overdose," "The Shroud, J the Harbour, Goldfinger, Big Apple, Shagger, Superchicken, Lorne the Gas, Spook, The King Prawn" (p. 16). Names are given for physical characteristics, occupations, places of origin, or memorable escapades and are not necessarily permanent: "Cheese" has, for example, been "called Suds since he started washing" (p. 16). Morvern's own name links her to the land and also, apparently, to her own character. An attendant in a Spanish hotel tells Morvern that Callar means "silence, to say nothing, maybe" (p. 132), and in *These Demented Lands,* in which she appears again, she explains that she is named after "the mountain range...on the opposite side of the Sound" (p. 49)—the mainland peninsula between Loch Linnhe, Loch Sunart, and the Sound of Mull (the narrow sea strait between Mull and the mainland) is known as Morvern.

Discussing his approach to language, Warner has described "correct usage" as "a mystifying obfuscation, held up as an ideal because it prevents whole worlds and experiences that would be uncomfortable to the artistic and political status quo from being rendered." It condemns, as "irrelevant and unsuitable as material for artistic expression," his own and many others' "lived experiences" (Dale, p. 46). Morvern's use of dialect and colloquial constructions conveys the flavor of a personal, unmediated record or reminiscence, something lost in Lynne Ramsay's film adaptation, which eschewed voice-over for suggestive but often inscrutable silence. From the very first page of the book the reader has to engage with Morvern's manner of internalizing external impressions and verbalizing responses in a distinctive, idiosyncratic language: "I stopped

the greeting cause I couldnt breathe and was perished cold" (p. 1); "I needed to boil the kettle to get the mess offof my face, what with the greeting and that" (p. 2); "All floor-blood had a sort of skin on" (p. 3); "Puddles were frozen and wee-ones off from school had burst all ice" (p. 6). Just as the dialect speech of Gibbon's characters conveyed the cadence of Scots in largely lexical English, so Morvern's speech makes use of west coast dialect and of more general 1990s Scottish colloquialisms in language accessible to readers from outside the region. The accent and intonation the reader is invited to hear in some of Warner's spellings appears much less marked than, for example, the approximated Glaswegian of James Kelman or the Leith accent of Irvine Welsh's *Trainspotting,* but it is an accurate representation of speech patterns in Argyll. Warner is keen to emphasize the regional particularity: Morvern is dismissive not only of English ("south") but also of metropolitan Scottish ("Central Belt") accents (p. 116).

Many of Morvern's descriptions and her idiosyncratically erratic punctuation convey the tentativeness of a relatively uneducated, youthful, but highly visually articulate character. Descriptions made during, or recollected from, her second Mediterranean sojourn are particularly vivid: "When you looked at the sky you saw how near the sun was paler diluted blueness but blueishness grew near the sea till both met at the horizon in a black thready line" (p. 209). Some critics regarded this language as artificial and unconvincing. For Frank Kermode, Morvern's detailed descriptions sounded neither demotic nor particularly Scots, while William Fiennes wrote in the *London Review of Books* that Morvern's prose was "a trick, an artful ventriloquism." He argued that "dropped articles, prepositions at the end of sentences, a child's quaint idiom and coinages" could not make Warner's "rhetorically self-conscious prose suggest the voice of a shelf-stacker in an Oban superstore" (p. 34). Morvern's letter to her publishers, it is true, appears to be written by someone with considerably less facility with language than later descriptive passages. The novel, however, suggests the growth of a writer's consciousness. Morvern observes initially that her boyfriend's "novel thing was page after page of words then a number then more pages of words and another number"; she is unable to "see the point in reading through all that just to get to an end" (p. 87). By the end of the novel, however, an older Morvern writes in a notebook, ostensibly composing the narrative presented to the reader in, and as, the novel (p. 228). She is finally the author of her own story.

Warner's first novel introduced readers to his fondness for including nonverbal, extra-textual signs in his work, as well as foregrounding its textuality. Numerous signs and texts are encountered by Morvern during the course of the novel, including written signs, text on computer screens, labels or buttons on electrical appliances, and texts written by Morvern herself: letters and cards, graffiti, a "list written on a torn bit of box" (p. 9), and playlists that may or may not be written down. Red Hanna draws Lanna a map. The people of the port may be portrayed in many cases as only barely literate, but Warner draws attention to the extent to which texts and signs are present in their daily lives and to which they register in Morvern's consciousness—after all, while she may initially pass herself off only as the author of another's work, she is a writer by the end of the novel. She has a strong affinity with nonlinguistic sign systems, professing affection for a road sign with a pictorial symbol for "Quayside or Riverbank," reproduced in the novel (p. 61). David Leishman reads this as evidence of "Morvern's admiration for a closed system of monosemic graphic symbols" in contrast to the ambiguity of language—as he notes, "the road sign is given not one but two names—*Quayside* or *Riverbank*" (p. 121). Morvern also renders the Caledonian Hotel the "Kale Onion Hotel," explaining that "the 'D' fell off the big sign and they never ever bothered to fix it" (p. 61). An ironic reference to the "kaleyard" tradition of nineteenth- and early twentieth-century Scottish writing about social conditions, it also draws attention to the nature of signs and their capacity to signify in the novel. Leishman cites Warner's claim that textual references and

typographic inventiveness "[take] the reader out of the delusion of the text into another delusion" (p. 113).

MAYHEM ON MULL: THESE DEMENTED LANDS

For all its darkness, *Morvern Callar* is also a comic novel. In Warner's own words (to the present writer): "Even I have an impression that *Morvern* is a moody, dark novel, but when I reread, I find it is full of jokes and humour. Even if it's gallows humour." The gallows humor continues in Warner's second novel, *These Demented Lands* (1997), which received a decidedly more mixed critical response than his first. For some it was an accomplished sequel to *Morvern Callar,* extending the author's impressive representation of a west coast vernacular voice and narrative mode. For others it was (paradoxically) too experimental, in a literary high-modernist manner, and wore its allusions too obviously on its sleeve. The novel is presented as a series of unreliable texts, pieced together, sometimes quite literally, by a series of editors (including Morvern Callar). Morvern is the narrator and putative author of the "First Text," which has two parts, forming the first and third sections of the novel. A "Second Manuscript," also in two parts, is narrated and apparently written by the mysterious Aircrash Investigator—also variously known, Morvern explains, as "the Failed Screenwriter, or the Man From The Department of Transport," or "Walnut or Warmer, though one night in The Heated Rooms when I pressed him he says his name was Houlihan," and also "The One Who Walked the Skylines of Dusk with Debris Held Aloft Above His Head," "the Aircrasher,…Monsieur Skyline" (pp. 16, 125, 137). This character's narrative forms the second and fourth sections. The novel concludes with the text of a letter from Morvern to her foster father, which includes a memorable explanation of her method: "Forgive my elliptical style: I want you to die in the maximum possible confusion" (p. 215).

The opening paragraphs of Morvern's narrative describe the sinking, by the wake of a large car ferry, of the small ferry on which she and several other passengers are crossing to an unnamed Hebridean island, clearly modeled on the Isle of Mull:

> I got near the island; Ferryman was about to ask me to see a ticket when the boat started to sink: "If it's the return tickets yous have got, best swim for it," Ferryman bawled then he jamp over the side into blackwater.
>
> It was neardark. Since Ferryman'd cut the outboard engine all was silent; could hear the loose, metal lampshade on the single bulb above the Boat Chandlers at Ferry Slipway. The lampshade was clattering in any gusts before they reached.
>
> (p. 3)

In *Morvern Callar* the reader learns that Morvern's beloved foster mother is buried on Mull, and she visits the grave toward the end of *These Demented Lands*, although the reader is never entirely sure whether Morvern actually reaches the shore. The Ferryman is more than a little reminiscent of Charon, ferrying souls across the Styx to the Underworld, and the reader is invited to wonder whether, as in William Golding's *Pincher Martin* (1956), the ensuing narration is a fabrication in the consciousness of a character at the moment of death. In Golding's novel the body of Christopher Hadley (Pincher) Martin washes ashore on a Hebridean island not unlike that in Warner's novel. Both begin with descriptions of the protagonists struggling in the water, and Morvern thinks about Golding's novel while making for the shore: "I was sorry for our death…. I'd heard around that the drowning could be not so bad but there was that book that had scared me: the *Pincher Martin* book; the book of drowning" (p. 11). She later tells the Aircrash Investigator that if one comes ashore in the dark, as she does, and as one of the pilots whose accident is being investigated did, "it crosses your mind you're back from the dead." She follows this with a question: "Ever read *Pincher Martin*?" (p. 89). The ambiguity is compounded by the explanation given for his investigations by the novel's second narrator. The Aircrash Investigator explains to Morvern that his project "frees you from causal-

ity: we're time travellers, obsessed with only a few seconds, minutes at most, of the past. All else becomes secondary and we live those moments again and again, until we've become part of the thing we investigate" (p. 78).

These Demented Lands, although published in 1997, culminates on Hogmanay on the eve of the new millennium, so its narrated action can be read as beginning in early 1999. Tantalizingly, in his fourth novel, *The Man Who Walks* (2002), Warner includes a reference to the fact that Red Hanna thinks Morvern drowned. As *The Man Who Walks* is set during the fuel shortages in Britain in early 2001 (pp. 4, 158, 256), the attentive rereader of the earlier *These Demented Lands* might well expect that, two years after Morvern's crossing, Red Hanna would have heard if she were alive. It only became clear with the publication of *These Demented Lands* that Warner also intended *Morvern Callar* (1995) to have been set in the future. Warner's third novel, *The Sopranos* (1998), is set on May 20 and 21, 1996 (pp. 266, 273), and reference is made to Morvern and her boyfriend still living in Oban at the time (p. 271). If the narrated action of *Morvern Callar* is read, therefore, as beginning before Christmas 1996 (more than a year after it was published), Morvern's absence in the Mediterranean can be assumed to have lasted from autumn 1997 to early 1999, more or less consistent with the passage of three years alluded to in its closing pages.

Morvern reaches, or appears to reach, the shore of the island, having saved a small blond girl on the same boat. She sets off to look for the legendary John Brotherhood's hotel, the Drome, a resort for honeymooners, where the young woman scientist she meets at the end of *Morvern Callar* suggested she look for work (p. 225). An epigraph from Robert Louis Stevenson's *Kidnapped* signals the novel's debt to the story of David Balfour. For Frank Kermode, with "its buried treasure and sunken wrecks," *These Demented Lands* is "a kind of surreal reprise of the Stevensonian adventure story." Balfour journeys across what Sophie Dale describes as "the strange moral landscape of Mull," meeting "blind catechists and other equally unhelpful guides as he goes" (p. 19). Morvern crosses the island, which she describes as "crazy" and "like a dream," meeting similarly fantastic characters who, in the words of the Devil's Advocate (a "sort of an investigative journalist for God," investigating claims of saints' miraculous works necessary for canonization), wander "these demented lands in days of the end" (pp. 52, 9, 59). She encounters a miniature-train driver (there *is* a miniature railway on Mull, near Craignure, the ferry terminus), a couple of brothers conveying their father's coffin across the island in order to throw it into the sea, a group of university students following old cattle-droving paths for an Arts Council–funded documentary, a contract logger, an itinerant knifegrinder, and a deranged Vietnam-veteran helicopter pilot.

The Devil's Advocate tries to dissuade Morvern from meeting Brotherhood. The Knifegrinder says of this Kurtz-like character (Morvern's approach resembles, in part, Marlow's approach to the inner station in Conrad's *Heart of Darkness*): "there's no rules binds that man to the earth" (p. 48). Known as the Sanctions Buster for once conducting illegal trade in Africa, Brotherhood is rumored to have caused the death of conjoined twins (with shared genitalia); he slept with them, and, driven mad with jealousy, they tried to hack themselves apart. Despite these warnings, Morvern is offered a room. She befriends the Aircrash Investigator, who is investigating a crash involving two airplanes and salvaging pieces of the wrecks from across the island. When both the Investigator and Morvern are unable to settle their accounts, Brotherhood installs them in caravans (trailers) and has them perform menial tasks for their keep. He exposes the Investigator as a fraud (in effect, a harmless delusionist) and causes him to be ridiculed by another shadowy figure, the Argonaut, a salvor who travels about in a kayak emblazoned with biblical verses. The novel culminates with a rave on the eve of the millennium, when Morvern enacts the dying wish of Brotherhood's embittered father and sets fire to the hotel, which burns as she is delivered of her child, a girl (pp. 196, 210–212). Liam McIlvanney called Warner's "deployment of religious symbolism"—Morvern refers to the birth as the Nativity and writes of a "flight into Egypt" (pp.

183, 215)— "heavy-handed." Religious imagery in *These Demented Lands* extends the use of myth in *Morvern Callar,* lending the characters the impression of archetypes (compounded by suggestive names and nicknames including that of the Argonaut, High-Pheer-Eeon, after the Greek Titan Hyperion) and rendering the landscape a dreamscape.

Some critics did not find the allusiveness of much of Morvern's dialogue believable. "Suddenly she seems to have read a lot of books," William Fiennes comments. "She refers to Joseph Conrad, William Golding's *Pincher Martin* and Walker Percy's *The Moviegoer*" (p. 34). Sophie Dale's defensive response is to argue that Fiennes either "thinks that working-class characters should not read poetry" or that "the mass culture of television and supermodels should not be allowed to violate the inner sanctum of Apollinaire and William Golding." "Both positions," she contends, "seem equally elitist, based on defending monolithic middle-class and particularly English culture" (pp. 33–34). It might also be ventured that the narrator of *Morvern Callar* has had three years to catch up on her reading; she is a more mature author consciousness in *These Demented Lands.* Clearly fascinated by language and modes of expression, she comments frequently on the Aircrash Investigator's turns of phrase in his reports. About a fragment of a report reproduced early in the first part of her "First Text" (the editor comments that it is glued into her manuscript), she notes: "I like that sentence: *where a provisions truck coming off the Slip must have clipped it one*" (p. 17). Later she recalls:

> As we walked up to the hotel, away from the ghost-sighting, in darkness now, One Who Walks the Skylines of Dusk says of how days had passed "as they do." He mentioned Chef Macbeth's buzzing remote-control aircraft "circling through these unbearable afternoons" and, the phrase I like best, "the couples who linger like graveyard statues in the pine plantation."
>
> (p. 128)

In the light of the later revelation that he is no longer employed by the Ministry of Transport (pp. 112–114), this explanation of his motivation acquires some poignancy.

Morvern's narrative runs out at the end of its first part with an "Editor's note" in boldface type noting "three words illegible; possibly *Villian once says* [sic]" (p. 59). The first part of the Aircrash Investigator's narrative likewise concludes with a boldface "Editor's note: poster inserted in manuscript" (p. 118). The novel—the manuscript (re)constructed from Morvern's texts and her reconstruction of the Investigator's texts—includes reproductions of road signs, posters, and even an "Argyll Archipelago Records press release glued into manuscript" (according to another boldface editor's note; pp. 119–121), which offers a schematic outline of DJ Cormorant's membership in a succession of failed bands. The reader learns very little else about this character and must interpret the chart alone. This textual and typographical playfulness extends an interest apparent in *Morvern Callar.* Warner explains that:

> there is something going on in the actual topography of my writing [that is] a direct attack on the "status" of written literary text, how middle class literary criticism normally would value certain texts above others; how the social positioning of one text is relevant to the "authority" of the other text on the page and indeed ALL texts…. I force what would normally be de-valued bits of text and graphics of toilet walls and wee scraps of paper INTO the prose so they take on narrative significance, become part of the art, so they cant be dismissed.
>
> (Dale, p. 42)

ACROSS THE FIFTH OR FOURTH BRIDGE:
THE SOPRANOS

Warner's third novel (1998) follows the members of the soprano section of the choir Our Lady of Perpetual Succour, the port's convent school, as they travel to "the capital" (Edinburgh) to perform in a national choir competition. During the course of one day and the early hours of the next, the girls quarrel, gossip, get drunk, and explore their developing sexual identities. A microcosm of their society, they have their own hierarchy—the reader is introduced to them in their "CHOIR ORDER ON LENGTH-OF-LEGS SCHOOL WALL" (p. 3)—and class divisions.

Each has her own problems and limited aspirations: Manda's father is poor; Chell has recurring nightmares about her father and brother, both missing at sea and presumed drowned; Orla has Hodgkin's disease and has to undergo chemotherapy, having already been taken by her religious family to Lourdes in hope of a miracle; Kylah is a member of a band, both of whose other members are in love with her.

Fionnula (the Cooler, to distinguish her from another Fionnula in the choir) is a Scottish nationalist with a social conscience. She explains to the fee-paying, middle-class Kay Clarke, whom the others think a snob, that only those with large houses can bear not to frequent pubs and nightclubs: "in a wee house yer sat looked at the four walls, or sat wi yer folks on the front room wi the telly blaring crap…it's a crippling feeling" (p. 67). On Manda's lack of aspiration Fionnula observes shrewdly, and not without pity: "all she really, really wants, is to get pregnant, soon as possible after leaving school, to a guy wi an okay job," to buy a "house up in the Complex, no far from her Dad," and end up with "a wee boy wi a skinhead an an earring, called Shane or something, an SKY TV" (p. 176). Charles Taylor wrote in the *New York Times* that Warner understood "that pop culture and consumer culture are predicated on a promise of freedom, of release from everything that's dutiful, drab and ordinary" while understanding too the illusory nature of the belief that consumption and gratification can bring satisfaction. Fionnula is the novel's voice of political conscience; she is outraged that people in Britain should live in poverty in the late twentieth century.

Despite warnings from Sister Condron, inevitably nicknamed Sister Condom, to be on their best behavior in the capital, the girls change out of their conservative uniforms into more suitable attire and embark on an afternoon of shopping and drinking, encountering a series of eccentric, entertaining, and threatening characters. These include a maudlin divorcé; his housemate, who, having spent much of the afternoon sticking himself to a Velcro-covered wall in a pub, strips naked, arouses himself by rubbing squid ink under his armpits, and is rushed to hospital with a gash to his foot; and a third man who makes off with the girls' school uniforms. Fionnula encounters Kay Clarke, and these two are soon exchanging intimate secrets. Kay shows concern for Fionnula, aware that her relative poverty excludes her from the kind of university education for which Kay seems destined. "What is there for you to do in the Port?" she asks (p. 167). Their mutual attraction becomes clear, and Kay's admission that she is bisexual prompts Fionnula to admit a curiosity about her own sexuality.

Warner's use of third-person narration, often focalized through different characters, sometimes adopts a vatic tone to comment on the characters' youth, as in this description: "Kylah has adolescent ears; impatient ears. Some might call this, in young people, narrow taste, or lack of experience, but it's exactly cause she tolerates so little that she still sings with her ears, no her head. You could call it brilliant taste" (p. 58). This narrative voice does not consistently use the colloquial tone but never entirely abandons it. The narrative voice also offers an affectionate, lyrical impression of the port. Describing their wanderings through the capital at one point, the narrator says of Fionnula and Kay:

> these girls who came from a town, hunched round a harbour like a classical amphitheatre, where the ocean grew still in a trapped bay an the mountains of the islands seemed to hang in the skies of summer nights and in November the sea turned black while salt gathered in the window corners of even the furthest-back houses. An even though Fionnula's family was hidden up the back, in the dip of land where history put council housing, away fro the Victorian resort villas, even there, was saving grace of the skies where clouds would always move faster than anywhere these girls would ever travel to and where the dying light of day would falter in the slow-moving coal-fire smoke above where owls an foxes moved in the grey-black woods of the sheltering hills, hundreds of feet above the bus-stops.
>
> (pp. 233–234)

The Sopranos is, like Warner's previous novels, very concerned with the imbrication of place and language. Several characters voice confusion about apparently ambiguous names: the Netherlands is known by several names; what, precisely, is "Britain"?; and, to the ears of the young and poorly educated, the Forth Bridge, the Firth of Forth (the stretch of sea the bridge crosses), and the region of Fife on the other side become the "the fourth bridge across the fifth or fourth to the Kingdom of Five!" (p. 104). The geographical speculation and verbal confusion revisit Warner's concern with the nature of language and signs. In the capital, the girls visit McDonald's, in which "signs were everywhere and language was vanishing"—signs designating the gender of toilet areas, indicating where trays should be deposited, warnings against the danger of slipping on wet floors: "all had no words (the sign of a stick figure, hopelessly in motion). Language was disappearing" (p. 98).

Needless to say, the choir performs that evening with a severely depleted soprano section, and the girls face possible dismissal from the convent the following morning. During the course of the night, back in the port, the likely outcome of the next day's interviews is debated, tensions simmer, and the novel's sexually charged subplots are resolved. Fionnula and Kay show open affection for each other, challenging the port's, and in some cases their friends', prejudices. William Fiennes interpreted Warner's representation of a lesbian relationship as a troubling fantasy on the part of the author, observing that he had "ventured into this girl-on-girl territory before" in his depiction of aspects of Morvern and Lanna's relationship in *Morvern Callar* (p. 34). Whatever demurs critics have expressed, the representation of a same-sex relationship in working-class, west coast Scotland, by a popular and marketable writer, is both bold and laudable. As the sun rises, the friends make plans to head out into the countryside, and despite looming crises—Kay has revealed she is pregnant, Orla's disease is no longer in remission, and they are all likely to be suspended—they are ready to confront whatever demands school, their parents, and the community make of them. Despite its portrayal of what some readers have viewed as a dysfunctional society beset by socioeconomic challenges, *The Sopranos* is finally a deeply affirmative, affectionate, and very funny portrait of adolescence.

ITINERANCY AND NATIONAL IDENTITY: THE MAN WHO WALKS

Undoubtedly the most ambitious of Warner's novels to date, *The Man Who Walks* (2002) divided critics even more than his previous work. Liz Jensen in the British *Independent* observed that "interesting things" can "happen when a brilliant, ambitious writer decides that he cares more passionately about language than about storytelling." When the author is James Joyce, the result is "the great stew of brain, heart and gut known as *Ulysses*. When Alan Warner...tries it," she noted dryly, "you get *The Man Who Walks*." However, for another British reviewer, Katie Owen, writing in the *New Statesman,* Warner's novel was a "picaresque mock-epic" that affirmed his reputation as "arguably the most mature and original" of a very talented generation of Scottish fiction writers who had generally "proved themselves more innovative and powerful as chroniclers of contemporary life [than] their counterparts in England, Ireland or Wales." The Scottish writer Ali Smith wondered admiringly in the *Guardian* whether there had ever been "a more urine-obsessed, blood-soaked, joyful/fearful explosion of a Scottish novel," but Theo Tait wrote in the *Guardian*'s Sunday sister paper, the *Observer,* that it suggested "promise and talent betrayed and the burnt-out ruins of a few ironic ideas" and was "trash without the conviction or passion of good trash." Reading it, he suggested uncharitably, was "comparable to an afternoon locked in a Portaloo with a wino."

A rambling narrative in eighteen unnumbered chapters (at times very funny, at times deeply unnerving), the novel employs three fonts to suggest different voices: short, untitled sections in italics offer third-person descriptions of the Man Who Walks and of his Nephew, in a Scottish landscape rendered both surreal and touchingly prosaic. The bulk of the novel is a third-person account, focalized through the Nephew, interspersed with short sections (in a different font) purporting to represent his reconstructions of the fanciful memoirs of his uncle, deciphered from discarded typewriter ribbons. While each of his previous novels featured flawed characters and unreliable narrators, in *The Man Who Walks*

Warner extends narrative unreliability in his invention of the Nephew, who is by turns comic, sinister, pathetic, and violent. Having returned from several years abroad, and casually employed as a rat baiter in an agricultural supply warehouse in the port, he is sent by the shadowy Foreman in pursuit of his mentally unstable uncle, who has allegedly made off across country with the Mantrap nightclub's World Cup kitty, some twenty-seven thousand pounds. As the Nephew explains: "He's no full shilling, the Unc, no right in the head, in *so* many ways"; "he sometimes does a wee runner.... They call him The Man Who Walks cause you'll see him, out in the most farthest of far places, stomped along vergesides in all weathers" (p. 9). The old man suffers too from an unusual affliction: when intoxicated, a "rare balance problem in his inner ear" prevents him from walking up hills (p. 232). Given his propensity to punctuate his cross-country ramblings with stops at local bars, the Nephew should be able to intercept him.

Inevitably, however, the Nephew gets sidetracked. He is offered lifts by a cattle transport driver and an elderly couple who all attempt to engage him in sexual acts. His narrative suggests he refuses politely (pp. 6–12), but it appears from newspaper headlines presented later in the text that he assaults them violently, as he does an Australian Buddhist snowboarder who gives him a ride (pp. 60–61, 69–77, 261). Rowing across Loch Etive, he is badly stung by wasps nesting in the canoe and fetches up at the home of an old girlfriend, Paulette, who allows him to recuperate there. Taking a shortcut through the grounds of a stately home, an opportunity for petty theft presents itself, but once inside the house he finds himself a guest at a decadent luncheon party where he meets Bill Wright, American location scout for a film based on Stevenson's *Kidnapped*. The Nephew later guides the American around local sites of historical interest before robbing him and leaving him bound in his car outside the Black Garrison (Fort William).

Warner uses both real and archaically descriptive geographical names (Ballachulish, Loch Etive, and Appin are real places, but instead of "Inverness" he uses a local name that was once the name of Inverness's railway stop, "Inversnecky"). Here he encounters a man who believes himself to be constantly on the air as a radio presenter, a couple of Irish mobile-telephone engineers, and a kleptomaniac railway stewardess. After a night's drinking the Nephew finds himself deposited on the roadside, where four thugs—members of what he terms, only half-jokingly, the "Argyll mafia" (p. 276)—find him and drive up the Great Glen, toward Culloden Moor, the site of the major battle of the 1745 Jacobite Uprising. These four, it appears, have abducted the Man Who Walks, whom they are attempting to blame for their theft of the Mantrap's World Cup kitty; one of the thugs is Paulette's husband, who extracts a terrible revenge on the Nephew for his indiscretions with his wife. The novel closes with the Nephew crawling, bloodied, across a field, in which he finds a mannequin, dressed somewhat ridiculously in tartan, on what is presumably the film set for Bill's movie.

A largely favorable review of *The Man Who Walks* by Paul Quinn in the *Times Literary Supplement* called it "an Odyssey with Telemachus as the hero" (Is there an echo of Telemachus in Machusla, the Nephew's family nickname?) and suggested it "works best in its evocation of the march of (post)modernity across the wild Scotland of Sir Walter Scott and Culloden." The Nephew comes in some ways to represent the best and worst of his nation: "a symbol of his nation, [he] shivered, stood square in the cow shit, musing under cloudy Scotch skies on better days ahead" (p. 87). The novel's climax in Glencoe (an early-eighteenth-century internecine massacre there has mythic anti-English resonances in the Scottish imagination) and the many allusions in chapter titles to events in Scottish history or to supposed Scottish cultural icons draw attention to the novel's concern both to explore Warner's own Scottish nationalist sympathies and to deflate the artificiality of the image of Scotland paraded for the entertainment of the country's tourists. Titles like "Bonnie Prince Charlie's Flight in the Heather," "Highland Clearance," "Queen Victoria's Highland Journal," "Donald, where's yur troosers?" (a song by Andy

Stewart, a popular entertainer), and "By the Bonnie, Bonnie Banks of Loch Lomond" (a traditional song, with the Jacobite risings as its subtext) invoke episodes or icons appropriate, sometimes ironically, to the narrative of the Nephew's journey.

During one of his putative interviews with the deranged DJ in the Black Garrison, it becomes clear that the Nephew is known for his past participation in pro-independence activities (which may have involved sabotage). He has changed his ways and is asked: "So you're not for independence then?" He replies:

> Sure! Imagine the joy of it all. Late parliament sittings to decide on the stewardesses' uniform for Scottish National Arlines.... The glory of it all, after centuries of struggle.... By the time you actually grasp it...freedom doesn't amount to much these days. It was packaged long ago.
>
> (p. 205)

The Nephew later describes the uniform of Tracey, the train stewardess, as being of "sleazy tartan to keep the tourists in fantasy land" (p. 224). He pokes fun at Scottish newspapers— "Scotia's swankiest newspapers"—for their middle-class nationalist posturing, casting it as patriarchal and violently masculine: among others, the *Scotsman* becomes "the *Scudsman*," and *Scotland on Sunday* becomes "*Scotland on Binday*" (p. 36). At the stately home,

> a great deal of luncheon conversation seemed to be directed over the bellies and towards the subject of the new Scottish Parliament, though the Nephew could not see, in any way whatsoever, how that venerable institution had affected or would ever affect the hegemony of this table. Doesn't change anything for the poor nor the rich, he thought.
>
> (p. 138)

Skeptical to the point of being cynical, the Nephew has an affinity with Karl Marx—he makes a mental note during dinner to reread the *Communist Manifesto*—that leads him to question whether the poor would gain anything from different political masters.

The Nephew is able to speak on behalf of the marginal and disenfranchised because he is not a member of what he calls the Settled Community. Inexplicably, no critics seem to have assessed the significance of the novel's exploration of notions of home and identity, of Warner's hints that the reader is to view the Nephew (and The Man Who Walks) as a Romany or Gypsy (a member of the Traveller, or Tinker, community, as it was known in the west of Scotland—see for example Couris Jean's use of the term in *Morvern Callar,* p. 32). The Nephew recalls being discriminated against as a child by other children because he was "swarthy" (p. 32); they would not swim with him in the same water and called him "Tinky" (p. 33). The mobsters refer to him as their "octoroon guest" (p. 248). He knows the land north of the port as his family's "old caravan pitch" (p. 25) and thinks about a game he played as a child "when the caravans moved from site to site" (p. 252). He tells the DJ that he was involved in fighting for the rights of "*Traditional* travellers" (p. 205), and he harbors a deep resentment of the "foul confident possessiveness" of the "Settled Community...round their secure little houses" (p. 56). He tells Roger, the American, that he knew of "gypsies moving up and round from Budapest to Spain for the festivals" (p. 189), and they discuss displaced peoples: Africans migrating to Europe, Russian Jews to Israel. Ali Smith observes that the novel explores "what it means to be settled, to live somewhere or to step out on its roads." While the Nephew stands to inherit the house of The Man Who Walks, he dreams too of what money could achieve—it could "get you somewhere *proper*" (p. 29).

Like other Warner novels, this one visits the theme of a crisis in representation: the Nephew "could read no meanings from resultant registration plates, nothing at all; no combination of number plates communicated to him usual informations.... That concatenation of letters and numerals seemed meaningless" (p. 55). Within the context of a novel that questions the legitimacy of supposed national symbols, the semiotic instability apprehended by a doubly marginalized character—a "tinky" *and* a member of a poor, nonmetropolitan, regional community (who notes that the fast cars of holidaymakers are not made for the winding roads of Argyll)—acquires a new

resonance. The Nephew's "tinker" connections also add another element to his celebration of observation or vision. This is the gaze not only of a novelist consciousness (like Morvern's) but of someone whose forebears lived in a more intimate and quasi-mystical relationship with the land (see the Nephew's knowledge of "an old tinker magic cure for the 'flu," p. 119). His gaze imbues even the most mundane agricultural landscape with significance: "The Nephew saw an ancient tractor in a field, chalky runs of bird droppings on the fenestrated seat back, where crows and buzzards had used the height to gain vantage point over the field, and hunt" (p. 251). He identifies with "the mountains," thinking that one ought to "return the gaze God gave us" (p. 249).

The Nephew is another surrogate novelist and editor, reconstructing the narrative of his uncle's fabulous memoirs from the typewriter ribbon on which it was ostensibly typed. He is proud of his reading—his own small library contains Greek and Latin authors (Aeschylus, Apuleius, Lucretius, Ovid, Seneca, Cicero, Flavius Josephus, etc.), contemporary popular fiction (Stephen King, Frank Herbert, Wilbur Smith), Beckett, occult writers (like Aleister Crowley), and Scottish writers (Sir Walter Scott, James Kennaway). He makes frequent mental notes to himself to reread a number of influential literary and sociological texts and frequently alludes, often self-deprecatingly, to literary example:

When things don't go well for him, the Nephew turns his mind to what is written in wry Suetonius: vain Caesar staring at a bust of Alexander the Great, thinking. By the time he was the age I am now, he'd conquered the world. Or old Art Schopenhauer, his steady gaze being returned for hours by the orange orang-utan in Dresden Zoo which the old cynic grew so fond of, towards the end.

(pp. 57–58)

Sam Phipps, writing in the *Spectator,* thought the many literary allusions suggested that "Warner is lost in a maze of his own erudition and frenzied imagination." It is sometimes difficult to decide whether the Nephew's reminders to himself to reread Marx or Eliot—"That reminds me, the Nephew thought. Must re-read

T. S. Eliot's *Notes Towards a Definition of Culture,* yacuntya, as he supped a gush more lager" (p. 199)—are meant ironically. The novel does, it is truc, wear its allusions on its sleeve; readers are invited (as elsewhere in Warner's work) to think of Jonathan Swift and Beckett.

IN EXPECTATION

Some early poems and prose pieces appeared in *Folk,* an anthology of work by young Scottish writers published by the independent Clocktower Press in 1993. Warner's contributions are all short, impressionistic pieces about drinking and poverty, involving characters very like those who appear in the novels. "A Spot of Night Fishing (for Kenny Crichton)," for example, prefigures a passage and character in *These Demented Lands.* A short story entitled "After the Vision" was included in Kevin Williamson's collection of young Scottish writers, *Children of Albion Rovers,* published by Canongate in 1996 and described as being "From a novel: *The Far Places,* 1991." Its protagonist, Scorgie, who describes himself as "a salvager" and a "diver" "in one of the far places" (p. 29), is a model for (or early description of) the Argonaut in *These Demented Lands.* Having made an arduous trip to what appears to be a remote location outside Edinburgh for an open-air rave (at a venue called the Vision), he fetches up in the capital and meets an old acquaintance, Duffles, who now works at a crematorium. While they watch bodies burning in the incinerator, Duffles comments on the changing demography of the west coast: "Its all fucking townies and new folk moving up; all the young Mullochs"—inhabitants of the Isle of Mull are properly Muilleachs— "are just reduced to caravans" (p. 32). Scorgie ends up in Glasgow, meets a cast of drugged or eccentric characters, and travels back to the Far Places by train, coming across the "Man Who Walks" at a station along the way (p. 61). Drunken, late-night wanderings around Glasgow recur in other of Warner's short writings. In *Disco Biscuits,* (1997) a collection by writers who are ostensibly members of a generation writing about dance and drug culture, his "Bitter Salvage" is an exercise

in extended tension and barely suppressed violence. It offers a short vignette of two men, Choker and The Lad Who Was Choked, stumbling through a city—recognizably Glasgow— and meeting up with two girls, at whose apartment they sleep.

Journeys feature in Warner's shorter writings as well as in his novels. Characters travel about Argyll, wander the streets of Glasgow, and journey to Edinburgh; as we have seen, Orla, in *The Sopranos,* has been on a pilgrimage to Lourdes, and Morvern spends time in Spain, which features in several of Warner's works. Two stories called "Costa Pool Bums" are set in or en route from Spain, and a 2003 extract ("That Hollywood Movie with the Big Shark!") from a novel in progress (*The Oscillator*) is set in Spain. The movie is *Jaws,* the protagonist (age fourteen in 1978, as was Warner) lives with his parents in a hotel in a village (as did Warner), and he has a tentative sexual encounter with two Japanese girls while watching the movie; Warner recalls elsewhere that his father read Peter Benchley's novel *Jaws* to him while on holiday in Spain when he was a child (Thomson, online). The novel will follow the protagonist's adult wanderings across Europe and feature a "Sancho Panchez-like sidekick, an economic refugee from sub-Saharan Africa, who has made a perilous and life-changing journey just to reach Spain in the first place" (Dale, p. 64). Another novel, based on Warner's experience on the railways, has been tentatively titled both *The Permanent Way* (according to Dale, p. 63) and *The Outlying Stations* (described by Warner in the Thomson interview as "a *Moby Dick* of railways").

James Kelman explained in a speech he did not quite deliver on accepting the Booker Prize for *How Late It Was, How Late* in 1994 (the speech was later published in a supplement to the *Scotsman on Sunday* newspaper) that his writing belonged to a postcolonial tradition, "a much wider process—or movement—toward decolonisation and self-determination." His writing assumed, and strove to represent and defend, "the validity of indigenous culture" and rejected "the cultural values of imperial or colonial authority" (Watson, p. 22). Warner's writing is engaged in a similar project, concerned as it is with the importance of producing a literature that is national but not nationalist, regional but not internationally inaccessible, and universal in its existentialist exploration of lives which, while ordinary, are always by definition extraordinary. His oeuvre thus far is, in Frank Kermode's slightly nonplussed definition, "sophisticated, bewildering and dismaying" (p. 29).

Selected Bibliography

WORKS OF ALAN WARNER

NOVELS

Morvern Callar. London: Cape, 1995; New York: Anchor, 1997.

These Demented Lands. London: Cape, 1997; New York: Anchor, 1998.

The Sopranos. London: Cape, 1998; New York: Farrar, Straus and Giroux, 1999.

The Man Who Walks. London: Cape, 2002.

POEMS, SHORT STORIES, EXTRACTS FROM NOVELS IN PROGRESS, JOURNALISM

"Yonder Cunt," "Blood of Eden," "A Spot of Night Fishing," "Smears 1," "Smears 2," "A Good Impression." In *Folk: More Zoomers by Jim Ferguson, Alison Kermack, Gordon Legge, Alan Warner, and Irvine Welsh.* Orkney, Scotland: Clocktower, 1993. Reprinted in Duncan McLean, ed., *Ahead of Its Time.* London: Vintage, 1998. Pp. 73–77.

"After the Vision." In *Children of Albion Rovers.* Edited by Kevin Williamson. Edinburgh: Canongate, 1996; reprinted, Edinburgh: Rebel Inc., 1997. Pp. 29–65.

"Bitter Salvage." In *Disco Biscuits.* Edited by Sarah Champion. London: Sceptre, 1997. Pp. 267–280.

"Costa Pool Bums." *Barcelona Review* (http://www.barcelonareview.com/arc/r2/eng/costabum.htm), 1997.

"Car Hung, Upside Down." In *Ahead of Its Time.* Edited by Duncan McLean. London: Vintage, 1998. Pp. 231–241.

"At a Fair Rate of Knots." In *Edinburgh Review Issue 100.* Edited by Sophy Dale. Edinburgh: Edinburgh University Press, 1999.

"Night Salient." *Northwords* (http://www.northwords.co.uk/sept2000.htm).

"Paperback Writer: Dream of the Perfect Novel." *The Guardian,* April 19, 2003, *Review,* p. 31

"The Costa Pool Bums." *Granta: The Magazine of New Writing* 81 (Best of Young British Novelists):107–124 (spring 2003). (Different from "Costa Pool Bums," published earlier, online.)

"That Hollywood Movie with the Big Shark!" *The Guardian,* August 2, 2003, *Weekend,* pp. 54–59. Available online (http://www.guardian.co.uk/weekend/story/0,3605,1009598,00.html).

INTERVIEWS

Thomson, Graham. "Interview with Alan Warner." *Barcelona Review* (http://www.barcelonareview.com/arc/r2/eng/warnerint.htm), 1997.

Weissman, Larry. "Interview: A Drink or Two with Alan Warner" (http://www.randomhouse.com/boldtype/0497/warner/interview.html).

FILMS BASED ON THE WORK OF ALAN WARNER

Morvern Callar. Screenplay by Lynne Ramsay and Liana Dognini. Directed by Lynne Ramsay. Produced by George Faber, Charles Pattinson and Robyn Slovo. Cowboy Pictures. 2002. Starring Samantha Morton and Kathleen McDermott. (See also: Gautier Deblonde, *Morvern Callar: Photographs.* Ipswich, U.K.: Screenpress, 2002.)

CRITICAL AND BIOGRAPHICAL STUDIES

Biswell, Andrew. "Mortal Remains." *Times Literary Supplement,* March 31, 1995, p. 22.

Craig, Cairns. *The Modern Scottish Novel: Narrative and the National Imagination.* Edinburgh: Edinburgh University Press, 1999.

Dale, Sophy. *Alan Warner's* Morvern Callar: *A Reader's Guide.* New York and London: Continuum, 2002.

Fiennes, William. "Mortal on Hooch." *London Review of Books,* July 30, 1998, pp. 34–35.

Head, Dominic. *The Cambridge Introduction to Modern British Fiction, 1950–2000.* Cambridge, U.K.: Cambridge University Press, 2002.

Hickling, Alfred. Review of *The Man Who Walks. The Guardian,* April 5, 2003.

Jensen, Liz. Review of *The Man Who Walks. Independent,* June 15, 2002. Available online (http://enjoyment.independent.co.uk/books/reviews/story.jsp?story=304958).

Kermode, Frank. "Lager and Pernod." *London Review of Books,* August 22, 2002, pp. 28–29.

Kornreich, Jennifer. "Books in Brief." *New York Times,* May 18, 1997, p. 21.

LeBlanc, John. "Return of the Goddess: Contemporary Music and Celtic Mythology in Alan Warner's *Morvern Caller*" [*sic*]. *Revista Canaria de Estudios Ingleses* 41:145–154 (November 2000).

Leishman, David. "Breaking Up the Language? Signs and Names in Alan Warner's Scotland." *Études Ecossaires* 8:113–129 (2002).

March, Cristie L. "The Islands of Alan Warner." In her *Rewriting Scotland: Welsh, McLean, Warner, Banks, Galloway, and Kennedy.* Manchester: Manchester University Press, 2002. Pp. 62–80.

Martin, Keith. "Significant Short." *New Statesman,* August 7, 1998, p. 48.

McIlvanney, Liam. "More of Morvern." *Times Literary Supplement,* April 4, 1997, p. 19.

Morton, Brian. "Scottish Literature and the Politics of Nationalism." *New Statesman & Society,* March 10, 1995, pp. 36–37.

Owen, Katie. "Novel of the Week." *New Statesman,* April 29, 2002, p. 51.

Phipps, Sam. "Slaughtered Budgerigar Territory." *Spectator,* June 1, 2002. Available online (http://www.spectator.co.uk/bookreview).

Quinn, Paul. "Highland Trails." *Times Literary Supplement,* June 14, 2002, p. 22.

Redhead, Steve, ed. "Celtic Trails: Alan Warner." *Repetitive Beat Generation.* Edinburgh: Rebel Inc., 2000.

San Roman, Gustavo. "Alan Warner: The Scottish Onetti." *Posdata* (Uruguay), August 1997. Republished in translation in *Barcelona Review* (http://www.barcelonareview.com/arc/r2/eng/artic5.htm), 1997.

Smith, Ali. "Scots Deaths." *Guardian,* June 8, 2002. Available online (http://books.guardian.co.uk/review/story/0,12084,728969,00.html).

Smout, Michael Gary. "Book Covers 2." *Barcelona Review* (http://www.barcelonareview.com/arc/r2/bookcovers/covers2.htm), 1997.

Tait, Theo. "Down the Pan." *Observer,* June 23, 2002. Available online (http://books.guardian.co.uk/reviews/generalfiction/0,6121,742132,00.html).

Taylor, Charles. "Choirgirls." *New York Times,* April 4, 1999, p. 18.

Turner, Jenny. "Fairy Lights." *London Review of Books,* November 2, 1995, p. 23.

Watson, Roderick. "Postcolonial Subjects? Language, Narrative Authority and Class in Contemporary Scottish Culture." *Hungarian Journal of English and American Studies* 4, no. 1:21–38 (1998).

Whyte, Christopher. "Masculinities in Contemporary Scottish Fiction." *Forum for Modern Language Studies* 4, no. 3:274–285 (1998).

MASTER INDEX

The following index covers the entire British Writers series through Supplement XI. All references include volume numbers in boldface Roman numerals followed by page numbers within that volume. Subjects of articles are indicated by boldface type.

A. *Couleii Plantarum Libri Duo* (Cowley), **II:** 202
A. D. Hope (Hart), **Supp. XI:** 123
"A. G. A. V." (Blunden), **Supp. XI:** 45
A la recherche du temps perdu (Proust), **Supp. IV:** 126, 136
A Laodicean (Hardy), **Retro. Supp. I:** 112, 114
"A Propos of Lady Chatterley's Lover" (Lawrence), **IV:** 106; **VII:** 91
"Aaron" (Herbert), **Retro. Supp. II:** 179
Aaron's Rod (Lawrence), **VII:** 90, 94, 106–107; **Retro. Supp. II:** 230
Abaft the Funnel (Kipling), **VI:** 204
"Abasement of the Northmores, The" (James), **VI:** 69
"Abbé Delille and Walter Landor, The" (Landor), **IV:** 88*n*, 92–93
Abbess of Crewe, The (Spark), **Supp. I:** 200, 201, 210
"Abbey Mason, The" (Hardy), **Retro. Supp. I:** 119
Abbey Theatre, **VI:** 212, 218, 307, 309, 316; **VII:** 3, 6, 11
Abbey Walk, The (Henryson), **Supp. VII:** 146, 147
Abbot, The (Scott), **IV:** 39
Abbott, C. C., **V:** 379, 381
ABC Murders, The (Christie), **Supp. II:** 128, 130, 135
"ABC of a Naval Trainee" (Fuller), **Supp. VII:** 69
"Abomination, The" (Murray), **Supp. VII:** 273
Abyssophone (Redgrove), **Supp. VI:** 236
Abdelazer; or, The Moor's Revenge (Behn), **Supp. III:** 27, 36
Abercrombie, Lascelles, **II:** 247
"Abernethy" (Dunn), **Supp. X:** 77
"Abiding Vision, The" (West), **Supp. III:** 442
Abinger Harvest (Forster), **VI:** 411, 412; **Supp. II:** 199, 223
"Abject Misery" (Kelman), **Supp. V:** 244
Ableman, Paul, **Supp. IV:** 354
Abolition of Man, The (Lewis), **Supp. III:** 248, 255, 257
Abortive (Churchill), **Supp. IV:** 181
About the House (Auden), **Retro. Supp. I:** 13
"About Two Colmars" (Berger), **Supp. IV:** 85
"Above the Dock" (Hulme), **Supp. VI:** 134, 136
"Abraham Men" (Powys), **VIII:** 250

Abridgement of the History of England, An (Goldsmith), **III:** 191
Abridgement of the Light of Nature Pursued, An (Hazlitt), **IV:** 139
Abroad; British Literary Traveling Between the Wars (Fussell), **Supp. IV:** 22
Absalom and Achitophel (Dryden), **II:** 292, 298–299, 304
"Absalom, My Son" (Warner), **Supp. VII:** 380
"Absence" (Jennings), **Supp. V:** 218
"Absence" (Thompson), **V:** 444
"Absence, The" (Warner), **Supp. VII:** 373
Absence of War, The (Hare), **Supp. IV:** 282, 294, 297–298
"Absences" (Larkin), **Supp. I:** 277
Absent Friends (Ayckbourn), **Supp. V:** 2–3, 10, 13, 14
Absent in the Spring (Christie), **Supp. II:** 133
Absentee, The (Edgeworth), **Supp. III:** 154, **160–161,** 165
"Absent–Minded Beggar, The" (Kipling), **VI:** 203
"Absent–Mindedness in a Parish Choir" (Hardy), **VI:** 22
Abstract of a Book Lately Published, A: A Treatise of Human Nature . . . (Hume), **Supp. III:** 230–231
Absurd Person Singular (Ayckbourn), **Supp. V:** 2, 5–6, 9
"Abt Vogler" (Browning), **IV:** 365, 366, 370
Abuses of Conscience, The (Sterne), **III:** 135
Academy (periodical), **VI:** 249
"Academy, The" (Reid), **Supp. VII:** 331
Academy Notes (Ruskin), **V:** 178
Acceptable Sacrifice, The (Bunyan), **II:** 253
Acceptance World, The (Powell), **VII:** 347, 348, 350
"Access to the Children" (Trevor), **Supp. IV:** 504
Accident (Bennett), **VI:** 250
Accident (Pinter), **Supp. I:** 374, 375; **Retro. Supp. I:** 226
Accidental Man, An (Murdoch), **Supp. I:** 227
"Accompanist, The" (Desai), **Supp. V:** 65
"According to His Lights" (Galsworthy), **VI:** 276–277
"Account, The" (Cowley), **II:** 197

Account of Corsica, An (Boswell), **III:** 236, 239, 243, 247
Account of the European Settlements in America, An (Burke), **III:** 205
Account of the Growth of Popery and Arbitrary Government, An (Marvell), **I:** 207–208, 219; **Retro. Supp. II:** 266–268
Account of the Life of Dr. Samuel Johnson . . . by Himself, An (Johnson), **III:** 122
Account of the Life of Mr. Richard Savage, An (Johnson), **Retro. Supp. I:** 142
Account of the Settlement at Port Jackson, **Supp. IV:** 348
Account Rendered (Brittain), **Supp. X:** 45
Ace of Clubs (Coward), **Supp. II:** 155
Achilles (Gay), **III:** 55, 66, 67
Achilles in Scyros (Bridges), **VI:** 83
"Achronos" (Blunden), **Supp. XI:** 45
Ackroyd, Peter, **Supp. VI:** **1–15**
"Acid" (Kelman), **Supp. V:** 245
Acis and Galatea (Gay), **III:** 55, 67
"Across the Estuary" (Nicholson), **Supp. VI:** 216
Across the Plains (Stevenson), **V:** 389, 396
"Act, The" (Harrison), **Supp. V:** 161–162
Act of Creation, The (Koestler), **Supp. I:** 37, 38
Act of Grace (Keneally), **Supp. IV:** 347
"Act of Reparation, An" (Warner), **Supp. VII:** 380
Act of Terror, An (Brink), **Supp. VI:** **55–56,** 57
Act Without Words I (Beckett), **Supp. I:** 46, 55, 57
Act Without Words II (Beckett), **Supp. I:** 46, 55, 57
Actaeon and Diana (Johnson), **I:** 286
Acte (Durrell), **Supp. I:** 126, 127
Actions and Reactions (Kipling), **VI:** 204
Acton, John, **IV:** 289, 290; **VI:** 385
"Ad Amicam"sonnets (Thompson), **V:** 441
Ad Patrem (Milton), **Retro. Supp. II:** 272
Adam and Eve and Pinch Me (Coppard), **VIII:** 85, 88, 89, 91–93
"Adam and Eve and Pinch Me" (Coppard), **VIII:** 90
Adam and Eve and Pinch Me (Rendell), **Supp. IX:** 189, 195
Adam and the Sacred Nine (Hughes), **Supp. I:** 357, 363

"All blue and bright, in glorious light" (Brontë), **V:** 115

"All Day It Has Rained" (Lewis), **VII:** 445

All Day on the Sands (Bennett), **VIII:** 27

"All Flesh" (Thompson), **V:** 442

All Fools (Chapman), **I:** 235, 238, 244

All for Love (Dryden), **II:** 295–296, 305

All for Love (Southey), **IV:** 71

All Hallow's Eve (Williams, C. W. S.), **Supp. IX:** 281, 282, 284, 285

All My Eyes See: The Visual World of G. M. Hopkins (ed. Thornton), **V:** 377n, 379n, 382

All My Little Ones (Ewart), **Supp. VII:** 36

All Ovid's Elegies (Marlowe), **I:** 280, 291, 293

"All philosophers, who find" (Swift), **IV:** 160

All Quiet on the Western Front (Remarque), **VII:** xvi

All Religions Are One (Blake), **III:** 292, 307; **Retro. Supp. I:** 35

"All Saints: Martyrs" (Rossetti), **V:** 255

"All Souls Night" (Cornford), **VIII:** 112

All That Fall (Beckett), **Supp. I:** 58, 62; **Retro. Supp. I:** 25

All the Conspirators (Isherwood), **VII:** 310

"All the hills and vales along" (Sorley), **VI:** 421–422

All the Usual Hours of Sleeping (Redgrove), **Supp. VI:** 230

All the Year Round (periodical), **V:** 42

"All Things Ill Done" (Cameron), **Supp. IX:** 23–24

All Trivia (Connolly), **Supp. III:** 98

All What Jazz: A Record Diary, 1961–1968 (Larkin), **Supp. I:** 286, 287–288

Allan Quatermain (Haggard), **Supp. III:** 213, 218

"Allegiance, An" (Wallace–Crabbe), **VIII:** 315

Allegory of Love: A Study in Medieval Tradition (Lewis), **Supp. III:** 248, 249–250, 265

Allen, John, **IV:** 341, 349–350, 352

Allen, Walter Ernest, **V:** 219; **VI:** 257; **VII:** xvii, xxxvii, 71, 343

Allestree, Richard, **III:** 82

Allott, Kenneth, **IV:** 236; **VI:** xi, xxvii, 218

Allott, Miriam, **IV:** x, xxiv, 223n, 224, 234, 236; **V:** x, 218

All's Well That Ends Well (Shakespeare), **I:** 313, 318

All You Who Sleep Tonight (Seth), **Supp. X:** 283–284, 288

"Allusion to the Tenth Satire of the Second Book of Horace" (Rochester), **II:** 259

Almayer's Folly (Conrad), **VI:** 135–136, 148; **Retro. Supp. II:** 70–71

Almeria (Edgeworth), **Supp. III:** 158

Almond Tree, The (Stallworthy), **Supp. X:** 293–294

"Almond Tree, The" (Stallworthy), **Supp. X:** 293–294, 302

"Almswoman" (Blunden), **Supp. XI:** 42

"Aloe, The" (Mansfield), **VII:** 173–174

Alone (Douglas), **VI:** 293, 294, 297, 304, 305

Alpers, Antony, **VII:** 176

"Alphabetical Catalogue of Names . . . and Other Material Things Mentioned in These Pastorals, An" (Gay), **III:** 56

Alphabetical Order (Frayn), **Supp. VII:** 60

"Alphabets" (Heaney), **Retro. Supp. I:** 131

Alphonsus, King of Aragon (Greene), **VIII:** 139–140

Alps and Sanctuaries (Butler), **Supp. II:** 114

"Alps in Winter, The" (Stephen), **V:** 282

Alroy (Disraeli), **IV:** 296, 297, 308

"Altar, The" (Herbert), **II:** 128

"Altar of the Dead, The" (James), **VI:** 69

"Altarwise by owl–light" (Thomas), **Supp. I:** 174–176

Alteration, The (Amis), **Supp. II:** 12–13

"Alternative to Despair, An" (Koestler), **Supp. I:** 39

Althusser, Louis, **Supp. IV:** 90

Alton, R. E., **I:** 285

Alton Locke (Kingsley), **V:** vii, xxi, 2, 4; **VI:** 240

"Altruistic Tenderness of LenWing the Poet, The" (Cameron), **Supp. IX:** 19

Altus Prosator (tr. Morgan, E.), **Supp. IX:** 169

Alvarez, A., **II:** 125n

Alvíssmál, **VIII:** 231

Amadeus (Shaffer), **Supp. I:** 326–327

Amadis of Gaul (tr. Southey), **IV:** 71

Amado, Jorge, **Supp. IV:** 440

Amalgamemnon (Brooke–Rose), **Supp. IV:** 99, 110–111, 112

Amateur Emigrant, The (Stevenson), **V:** 389, 396

"Amateur Film–Making" (Fuller), **Supp. VII:** 73

Amazing Marriage, The (Meredith), **V:** 227, 232, 233, 234

Ambarvalia: Poems by T. Burbidge and A. H. Clough, **V:** 159–160, 161, 170

Ambassadors, The (James), **VI:** 55, 57–59; **Supp. IV:** 371

"Amber Bead, The" (Herrick), **II:** 106

Amberley, Lady, **V:** 129

"Ambiguities" (Fuller), **Supp. VII:** 73

Ambition and Other Poems (Davies), **Supp. XI:** 102

Ambler, Eric, **Supp. IV:** 1–24

Amboyna (Dryden), **II:** 305

Amelia (Fielding), **III:** 102–103, 105; **Retro. Supp. I:** 81, 89–90

"Amen" (Rossetti), **V:** 256

Amendments of Mr. Collier's False and Imperfect Citations (Congreve), **II:** 339, 340, 350

America. A Prophecy (Blake), **III:** 300, 302, 307; **Retro. Supp. I:** 39, 40–41

America I Presume (Lewis), **VII:** 77

American, The (James), **VI:** 24, 28–29, 39, 67

American Ghosts and Other World Wonders (Carter), **Supp. III:** 91

American Notes (Dickens), **V:** 42, 54, 55, 71

American Scene, The (James), **VI:** 54, 62–64, 67

American Senator, The (Trollope), **V:** 100, 102

American Visitor, An (Cary), **VII:** 186

"Americans in My Mind, The" (Pritchett), **Supp. III:** 316

"Ametas and Thestylis Making Hay–Ropes" (Marvell), **II:** 211

Aminta (Tasso), **II:** 49

"Amir's Homily, The" (Kipling), **VI:** 201

Amis, Kingsley, **Supp. II:** 1–19; **Supp. IV:** 25, 26, 27, 29, 377; **Supp. V:** 206

Amis, Martin, **Supp. IV:** 25–44, 65, 75, 437, 445

"Among All Lovely Things My Love Had Been" (Wordsworth), **IV:** 21

"Among School Children" (Yeats), **VI:** 211, 217

Among the Believers: An Islamic Journey (Naipaul), **Supp. I:** 399, 400–401, 402

Among the Cities (Morris, J.), **Supp. X:** 183

Amores (tr. Marlowe), **I:** 276, 290

Amoretti and Epithalamion (Spenser), **I:** 124, 128–131

Amorous Cannibal, The (Wallace–Crabbe), **VIII:** 319, 320–321

"Amorous Cannibal, The" (Wallace–Crabbe), **VIII:** 319

Amorous Prince, The; or, The Curious Husband (Behn), **Supp. III:** 26

"Amos Barton" (Eliot), **V:** 190

Amours de Voyage (Clough), **V:** xxii, 155, 156, 158, 159, 161–163, 165, 166–168, 170

Amphytrion; or, The Two Sosias (Dryden), **II:** 296, 305

"Ample Garden, The" (Graves), **VII:** 269

Amrita (Jhabvala), **Supp. V:** 224–226

"Amsterdam" (Murphy), **Supp. V:** 326

Amusements Serious and Comical (Brown), **III:** 41

"Amy Foster" (Conrad), **VI:** 134, 148

An Duanaire: An Irish Anthology, Poems of the Dispossessed, 1600–1900 (Kinsella), **Supp. V:** 266

An Giall (Behan), **Supp. II:** 71–73

Anacreontiques (Johnson), **II:** 198

"Anactoria" (Swinburne), **V:** 319–320, 321

"Anahorish" (Heaney), **Retro. Supp. I:** 125, 128

Anand, Mulk Raj, **Supp. IV:** 440

"Anarchist, An" (Conrad), **VI:** 148

Anathemata, The (Jones), **Supp. VII:** 167, 168, 169, 170, 175–178

Anatomy of Exchange–Alley, The (Defoe), **III:** 13

Anatomy of Frustration, The (Wells), **VI:** 228

Anatomy of Melancholy (Burton), **II:** 88, 106, 108; **IV:** 219

Anatomy of Oxford (eds. Day Lewis and Fenby), **Supp. III:** 118

Anatomy of Restlessness: Selected Writings, 1969–1989 (Chatwin), **Supp. IV:** 157, 160; **Supp. IX:** 52, 53, 61

Beaconsfield, Lord, *see* Disraeli, Benjamin

"Bear in Mind" (Cameron), **Supp. IX:** 29

Beardsley, Aubrey, **V:** 318n, 412, 413

"Beast in the Jungle, The" (James), **VI:** 55, 64, 69

Beastly tales from Here and There (Seth), **Supp. X:** 287–288

Beasts and Super-Beasts (Saki), **Supp. VI:** 245, 251

Beasts' Confession to the Priest, The (Swift), **III:** 36

Beatrice (Haggard), **Supp. III:** 213

Beattie, James, **IV:** 198

Beatty, David, **VI:** 351

Beau Austin (Stevenson), **V:** 396

Beauchamp's Career (Meredith), **V:** xxiv, 225, 228–230, 231, 234

Beaumont, Francis, **II: 42–67,** 79, 82, 87

Beaumont, Joseph, **II:** 180

Beaumont, Sir George, **IV:** 3, 12, 21, 22

Beauties and Furies, The (Stead), **Supp. IV:** 463–464

Beauties of English Poesy, The (ed. Goldsmith), **III:** 191

"Beautiful Lofty Things" (Yeats), **VI:** 216; **Retro. Supp. I:** 337

"Beautiful Sea, The" (Powys), **VIII:** 251

Beautiful Visit, The (Howard), **Supp. XI:** 137–138, 140–141, 148–149

"Beautiful Young Nymph Going to Bed, A" (Swift), **III:** 32, 36; **VI:** 256

"Beauty" (Thomas), **Supp. III:** 401–402

Beauty and the Beast (Hughes), **Supp. I:** 347

Beauty in a Trance, **II:** 100

Beautyful Ones Are Not Yet Born, The (Armah), **Supp. X:** 1–6, 12–13

Beauvoir, Simone de, **Supp. IV:** 232

Beaux' Stratagem, The (Farquhar), **II:** 334, 353, 359–360, 362, 364

"Because of the Dollars" (Conrad), **VI:** 148

"Because the pleasure-bird whistles" (Thomas), **Supp. I:** 176

Becket (Tennyson), **IV:** 328, 338

Beckett, Samuel, **Supp. I: 43–64; Supp. IV:** 99, 106, 116, 180, 281, 284, 412, 429; **Retro. Supp. I: 17–32**

Beckford, William, **III:** 327–329, 345; **IV:** xv, 230

Bed Among the Lentils (Bennett), **VIII:** 27–28

"Bedbug, The" (Harrison), **Supp. V:** 151

Beddoes, Thomas, **V:** 330

Beddoes, Thomas Lovell, **Supp. XI: 17–32**

Bedford-Row Conspiracy, The (Thackeray), **V:** 21, 37

"Bedroom Eyes of Mrs. Vansittart, The" (Trevor), **Supp. IV:** 500

Bedroom Farce (Ayckbourn), **Supp. V:** 3, 12, 13, 14

Beds in the East (Burgess), **Supp. I:** 187

Bedtime Story (O'Casey), **VII:** 12

"Bedtime Story for my Son" (Redgrove), **Supp. VI: 227–228,** 236

Bee (periodical), **III:** 40, 179

Bee Hunter: Adventures of Beowulf (Nye), **Supp. X:** 193, 195

"Bee Orchd at Hodbarrow" (Nicholson), **Supp. VI:** 218

"Beechen Vigil" (Day Lewis), **Supp. III:** 121

Beechen Vigil and Other Poems (Day Lewis), **Supp. III:** 117, 120–121

"Beehive Cell" (Murphy), **Supp. V:** 329

Beekeepers, The (Redgrove), **Supp. VI:** 231

"Beeny Cliff" (Hardy), **Retro. Supp. I:** 118

Beerbohm, Max, **V:** 252, 390; **VI:** 365, 366; **Supp. II: 43–59,** 156

"Before Action" (Hodgson), **VI:** 422

Before Dawn (Rattigan), **Supp. VII:** 315

"Before Her Portrait in Youth" (Thompson), **V:** 442

"Before I knocked" (Thomas), **Supp. I:** 175

Before She Met Me (Barnes), **Supp. IV:** 65, 67–68

"Before Sleep" (Kinsella), **Supp. V:** 263

Before the Knowledge of Evil (Braddon), **VIII:** 36

"Before the Mirror" (Swinburne), **V:** 320

"Before the Party" (Maugham), **VI:** 370

Beggars (Davies), **Supp. XI:** 87, 88

Beggars Banquet (Rankin), **Supp. X:** 245–246, 253, 257

Beggar's Bush (Beaumont, Fletcher, Massinger), **II:** 66

Beggar's Opera, The (Gay), **III:** 54, 55, **61–64,** 65–67; **Supp. III:** 195; **Retro. Supp. I:** 80

"Beggar's Soliloquy, The" (Meredith), **V:** 220

Begin Here: A War-Time Essay (Sayers), **Supp. III:** 336

"Beginning, The" (Brooke), **Supp. III:** 52

Beginning of Spring, The (Fitzgerald), **Supp. V:** 98, 106

Behan, Brendan, **Supp. II: 61–76**

Behind the Green Curtains (O'Casey), **VII:** 11

Behn, Aphra, **Supp. III: 19–33**

"Behold, Love, thy power how she despiseth" (Wyatt), **I:** 109

"Being Boring" (Cope), **VIII:** 80

"Being Stolen From" (Trevor), **Supp. IV:** 504

"Being Treated, to Ellinda" (Lovelace), **II:** 231–232

"Beldonald Holbein, The" (James), **VI:** 69

"Beleaguered City, A" (Oliphant), **Supp. X:** 220

"Belfast vs. Dublin" (Boland), **Supp. V:** 36

Belief and Creativity (Golding), **Supp. I:** 88

Belief in Immortality and Worship of the Dead, The (Frazer), **Supp. III:** 176

Believe As You List (Massinger), **Supp. XI:** 185

Belin, Mrs., **II:** 305

Belinda (Edgeworth), **Supp. III: 157–158,** 162

Belinda, An April Folly (Milne), **Supp. V:** 298–299

Bell, Acton, pseud. of Anne Brontë

Bell, Clive, **V:** 345

Bell, Currer, pseud. of Charlotte Brontë

Bell, Ellis, pseud. of Emily Brontë

Bell, Julian, **Supp. III:** 120

Bell, Quentin, **VII:** 35; **Retro. Supp. I:** 305

Bell, Robert, **I:** 98

Bell, Vanessa, **VI:** 118

Bell, The (Murdoch), **Supp. I:** 222, 223–224, 226, 228–229

"Bell of Aragon, The" (Collins), **III:** 163

"Bell Ringer, The" (Jennings), **Supp. V:** 218

"Belladonna" (Nye), **Supp. X:** 198

Bellamira; or, The Mistress (Sedley), **II:** 263

"Belle Heaulmière" (tr. Swinburne), **V:** 327

"Belle of the Ball-Room" (Praed), **V:** 14

Belloc, Hilaire, **VI:** 246, 320, 335, 337, 340, 447; **VII:** xiii; **Supp. IV:** 201

Belloc, Mrs. Lowndes, **Supp. II:** 135

Bellow, Saul, **Supp. IV:** 26, 27, 42, 234

Bells and Pomegranates (Browning), **IV:** 356, 373–374

Belmonte, Thomas, **Supp. IV:** 15

Belsey, Catherine, **Supp. IV:** 164

Belton Estate, The (Trollope), **V:** 100, 101

"Bench of Desolation, The" (James), **VI:** 69

Bend for Home, The (Healy), **Supp. IX:** 95, 96, 98–100, 101, 103, 106

Bend in the River, A (Naipaul), **Supp. I:** 393, **397–399,** 401

Bender, T. K., **V:** 364–365, 382

Bending of the Bough, The (Moore), **VI:** 87, 95–96, 98

Benedict, Ruth, **Supp. III:** 186

Benjamin, Walter, **Supp. IV:** 82, 87, 88, 91

Benlowes, Edward, **II:** 123

Benn, Gotfried, **Supp. IV:** 411

"Bennelong" (Wallace-Crabbe), **VIII:** 319–320

Bennett, Alan, **VIII: 19–34**

Bennett, Arnold, **VI:** xi, xii, xiii, 226, 233n, **247–268,** 275; **VII:** xiv, xxi; **Supp. III:** 324, 325; **Supp. IV:** 229, 230–231, 233, 239, 241, 249, 252; **Retro. Supp. I:** 318

Bennett, Joan, **II:** 181, 187, 201, 202; **V:** 199, 201

Benson, A. C., **V:** 133, 151; **Supp. II:** 406, 418

Benstock, Bernard, **Supp. IV:** 320

Bentham, Jeremy, **IV:** xii, xv, 50, 130–133, 278, 295; **V:** viii

Bentley, Clerihew, **IV:** 101

Bentley, E. C., **VI:** 335

Bentley, G. E., Jr., **III:** 289n, 307

Bentley, Richard, **III:** 23

Bentley's Miscellany (periodical), **V:** 42

Benveniste, Émile, **Supp. IV:** 115

"Benvolio" (James), **VI:** 69

Beowulf, **I:** 69; **Supp. VI: 29–44; Retro. Supp. II:** 298, 299, 305–306, 307

Beowulf (tr. Morgan), **Supp. IX:** 160–162

Christmas Comes But Once a Year (Chettle, Dekker, Heywood, Webster), **II:** 68, 85

"Christmas Day At Home" (Hollinghurst), **Supp. X:** 121

"Christmas Day in the Workhouse" (Wilson), **Supp. I:** 153, 157

"Christmas Eve" (Nye), **Supp. X:** 202, 205

Christmas Eve and Easter Day (Browning), **Retro. Supp. II:** 25–26

"Christmas Garland Woven by Max Beerbohm, A" (Beerbohm), **Supp. II:** 45

Christmas Garland, A (Beerbohm), **Supp. II:** 45, 49

Christmas His Masque (Jonson), **Retro. Supp. I:** 165

Christmas Holiday (Maugham), **VI:** 377

"Christmas Life, The" (Cope), **VIII:** 80

"Christmas Oratorio, A" (Auden), **Retro. Supp. I:** 10–11

Christmas Pudding (Mitford), **Supp. X:** 154–155

"Christmas Storms and Sunshine" (Gaskell), **V:** 15

Christmas–Eve and Easter–Day (Browning), **IV:** 357, 363, 370, 372, 374

Christopher, John, **Supp. V:** 22

Christopher and His Kind (Isherwood), **VII:** 318

"Christopher At Birth" (Longley), **VIII:** 167

Christopher Columbus (MacNeice), **VII:** 406

"Christopher Columbus and Queen Isabella of Spain Consummate Their Relationship" (Rushdie), **Supp. IV:** 452

Christopher Homm (Sisson), **Supp. XI:** 252–253, 263

"Christopher Marlowe" (Swinburne), **V:** 332

Christopher Marlowe in Relation to Greene, Peele and Lodge (Swinburne), **V:** 333

Christ's Hospital, A Retrospect (Blunden), **IV:** 86

"Christ's Hospital Five–and–Thirty Years Ago"(Lamb), **IV:** 42, 76

"Chronicle, The" (Cowley), **II:** 198

Chronicle Historie of Perkin Warbeck, The (Ford), *see Perkin Warbeck*

chronicle history, **I:** 73

Chronicle of Carlingford series (ed. Fitzgerald), **Supp. V:** 98

Chronicle of Friendships, A, 1873–1900 (Low), **V:** 393, 397

Chronicle of Queen Fredegond, The (Swinburne), **V:** 333

Chronicle of the Cid (tr. Southey), **IV:** 71

"Chronicle of the Drum, The" (Thackeray), **V:** 17, 38

Chronicle of Youth: War Diary, 1913–1917 (Brittain), **Supp. X:** 47

Chronicles (Hall), **II:** 43

Chronicles of Barset (Trollope), **Supp. IV:** 231

Chronicles of Carlingford (Oliphant), **Supp. X:** 214, 219

Chronicles of Clovis, The (Saki), **Supp. VI:** 240–243, 245, 249

Chronicles of Narnia, The (Lewis), **Supp. III:** 247, 248, **259–261**

Chronicles of the Canongate (Scott), **IV:** 39

Chroniques (Froissart), **I:** 21

"Chronopolis" (Ballard), **Supp. V:** 22

"Chrysalides" (Kinsella), **Supp. V:** 262

Chrysaor (Landor), **IV:** 96

Church, Dean R. W., **I:** 186

Church and Queen. Five Speeches, 1860–1864 (Disraeli), **IV:** 308

"Church–floore, The" (Herbert), **Retro. Supp. II:** 178–179

"Church Going" (Larkin), **Supp. I:** 277, 279, 280, 285

"Church Service" (Vaughan), **II:** 187

"Church Windows, The" (Herbert), **II:** 127

"Churche–Floore, The" (Herbert), **II:** 126

Church in Crisis, The (Wilson), **Supp. VI:** 305

"Churches of Northern France, The" (Morris), **V:** 293, 306

"Church's Year Book" (Traherne), **Supp. XI:** 268, 272

Churchill, Caryl, **Supp. IV: 179–200**

Churchill, Lady Randolph, **VI:** 349

Churchill, Winston, **III:** 27; **VI:** xv, 261, 274, **347–362,** 369, 385, 392; **Supp. III:** 58–59; speeches, **VI:** 361

Churchill by His Contemporaries (ed. Eade), **VI:** 351*n*, 361

"Church–monuments" (Herbert), **II:** 127

"Church–warden and the Curate, The" (Tennyson), **IV:** 327

"Churl and the Bird, The" (Lydgate), **I:** 57

Chymist's Key, The (tr. Vaughan), **II:** 185, 201

Cibber, Colley, **I:** 327; **II:** 314, 324–326, 331, 334, 337

Cicadas, The (Huxley), **VII:** 199

"Cicero and His Brother" (Landor), **IV:** 90, 91

Ciceronianus (Harvey), **I:** 122

Ciceronis Amor: Tullies Love (Greene), **VIII:** 135, 143

"Cinders" (Hulme), **Supp. VI:** 133, 135–136, 140, **141,** 146

Cinkante balades (Gower), **I:** 56

Cinque Ports, The (Ford), **VI:** 238, 332

Cinthio, Giraldi, **I:** 316; **II:** 71

Circe (Davenant), **II:** 305

"Circe" (Longley), **VIII:** 167

"Circe Truggin" (Powys), **VIII:** 249

Circle, The (Maugham), **VI:** 369

"Circle of Deception" (Waugh), **Supp. VI:** 275

"Circled by Circe" (Gunesekera), **Supp. X:** 86

Circuit of the World, The, *See Heimskringla*

Circular Billiards for Two Players (Carroll), **V:** 273

"Circulation, The" (Traherne), **Supp. XI:** 271

"Circus Animals' Desertion, The" (Yeats), **V:** 349; **VI:** 215; **Supp. III:** 102; **Retro. Supp. I:** 338

"Circus Wheel" (Redgrove), **Supp. VI:** 236

Citation and Examination of William Shakespeare . . . (Landor), **IV:** 100

Cities (Morris, J.), **Supp. X:** 172

"Cities, The" (Russell), **VIII:** 291

Cities, Plains and People (Durrell), **Supp. I:** 126

"Citizen" (Wallace–Crabbe), **VIII:** 311

Citizen of the World, The; or, Letters from a Chinese Philosopher . . . (Goldsmith), **III:** 177, 179, 185, 188–189, 191

City Madam, The (Massinger), **Supp. XI:** 184, 185, 187, 192, 195

"City of Brass, The" (Kipling), **VI:** 203

"City Sunset, A" (Hulme), **Supp. VI:** 136

"City Ways" (Amis), **Supp. II:** 2

City Witt: or, The Woman Wears the Breeches, The (Brome), **Supp. X:** 62

City Wives' Confederacy, The (Vanbrugh), *see Confederacy, The*

"Civilised, The," (Galsworthy), **VI:** 273, 274, 276

Civilization in the United States (Arnold), **V:** 216

Civilization of the Renaissance in Italy, The (Burckhardt), **V:** 342

Civitatis Amor (Middleton), **II:** 3

Cixous, Hélène, **Supp. IV:** 99, 117, 232, 547, 558

"Clachtoll" (MacCaig), **Supp. VI:** 186

Clancy, Laurie, **Supp. IV:** 348

Clapp, Susannah, **Supp. IV:** 164

Clara Florise (Moore), **VI:** 96

Clare, John, **IV:** 260; **Supp. XI: 49–65**

Clare Drummer (Pritchett), **Supp. III:** 313

Clarel (Melville), **V:** 211

"Clarence Mangan" (Kinsella), **Supp. V:** 260

"Clare's Ghost" (Blunden), **Supp. XI:** 44

"Clarice of the Autumn Concerts" (Bennett), **VI:** 266

Clarissa (Richardson), **III:** 80–81, **85–89,** 91, 92, 95; **VI:** 266; **Supp. III:** 30–31; **Supp. IV:** 150; **Retro. Supp. I:** 81

"Clarissa": Preface, Hints of Prefaces and Postscripts (ed. Brissenden), **III:** 86*n*

"Clarissa Harlowe Poem, The" (Ewart), **Supp. VII:** 41

Clark, Kenneth, **III:** 325, 346

Clark, Sir George, **IV:** 290

Clarke, Charles Cowden, **IV:** 214, 215

Clarke, Herbert E., **V:** 318*n*

Clarke, Samuel, **II:** 251

Clarkson, Catherine, **IV:** 49

Classic Irish Drama (Armstrong), **VII:** 14

Classical Tradition, The: Greek and Roman Influence on Western Literature (Highet), **II:** 199*n*

Classics and Commercials (Wilson), **Supp. II:** 57

Comedians, The (Greene), **Supp. I:** 10, 13, 15–16; **Retro. Supp. II:** 162–164

"Comedy" (Fry), **Supp. III:** 201

Comedy of Dante Alighieri, The (tr. Sayers), **Supp. III:** 333, 336, 350

Comedy of Errors, The (Shakespeare), **I:** 302, 303, 312, 321

"Come–on, The" (Dunn), **Supp. X:** 72

Comfort of Strangers, The (McEwan), **Supp. IV:** 390, 396–398, 400, 402

Comforters, The (Spark), **Supp. I:** 199, 200, 201–202, 213

Comic Annual, The (Hood), **IV:** 251, 252, 253–254, 258, 259, 266

"Comic Cuts" (Kelman), **Supp. V:** 256

Comic Romance of Monsieur Scarron, The (tr. Goldsmith), **III:** 191

Comical Revenge, The (Etherege), **II:** 266, 267–268, 271

Comicall Satyre of Every Man Out of His Humour, The (Jonson), **Retro. Supp. I:** 158, 159–160

"Coming" (Larkin), **Supp. I:** 285

"Coming Down Through Somerset" (Hughes), **Retro. Supp. II:** 211–212

"Coming Home" (Bowen), **Supp. II:** 81, 82

Coming of Gabrielle, The (Moore), **VI:** 96, 99

"Coming of the Anglo–Saxons, The" (Trevelyan), **VI:** 393

Coming of the Kings, The (Hughes), **Supp. I:** 347

"Coming to Visit" (Motion), **Supp. VII:** 256

Coming Up for Air (Orwell), **VII:** 281–282

"Commemoration of King Charles the I, martyr'd on that day (King), **Supp. VI:**162

Commendatory Verses Prefixed to Heywood's Apology for Actors (Webster), **II:** 85

Commendatory Verses Prefixed to . . . Munday's Translation of Palmerin . . . (Webster), **II:** 85

"Comment on Christmas, A" (Arnold), **V:** 216

Commentaries of Caesar, The (Trollope), **V:** 102

Commentarius solutus (Bacon), **I:** 263, 272

"Commentary" (Auden), **Retro. Supp. I:** 9

Commentary on Macaulay's History of England, A (Firth), **IV:** 290, 291

Commentary on the "Memoirs of Mr. Fox" (Landor), **IV:** 100

Commentary on the Collected Plays of W. B. Yeats (Jeffares and Knowland), **VI:** 224; VI: 224

Commentary on the Complete Poems of Gerard Manley Hopkins, A (Mariani), **V:** 373n, 378n 382

Comming of Good Luck, The (Herrick), **II:** 107

Commitments, The (Doyle), **Supp. V:** 77, 80–82, 93

"Committee Man of 'The Terror,' The" (Hardy), **VI:** 22

Common Asphodel, The (Graves), **VII:** 261

"Common Breath, The" (Stallworthy), **Supp. X:** 292

Common Chorus, The (Harrison), **Supp. V:** 164

"Common Entry" (Warner), **Supp. VII:** 371

Common Grace, A (MacCaig), **Supp. VI:** **187,** 194

Common Pursuit (Leavis), **VII:** 234, 246

Common Reader, The (Woolf), **VII:** 22, 28, 32–33

Common Sense of War and Peace, The: World Revolution or War Unending (Wells), **VI:** 245

Commonplace and Other Short Stories (Rossetti), **V:** 260

Commonplace Book of Robert Herrick, **II:** 103

"Commonsense About the War" (Shaw), VI: 119, 129

Commonweal (periodical), **V:** 302

Commonweal, The: A Song for Unionists (Swinburne), **V:** 332

"Commonwealth Literature Does Not Exist" (Rushdie), **Supp. IV:** 454–455

Communication Cord, The (Friel), **Supp. V:** 124–125

Communicating Doors (Ayckbourn), **Supp. V:** 3, 9, 11, 12

Communication to My Friends, A (Moore), **VI:** 89, 99

"Communion" (Coppard), **VIII:** 88, 93

"Communist to Others, A" (Auden), **Retro. Supp. I:** 8

"Communitie" (Donne), **Retro. Supp. II:** 89

Companions of the Day (Harris), **Supp. V:** 136, 138

Company (Beckett), **Supp. I:** 62; **Retro. Supp. I:** 29

"Company of Laughing Faces, A" (Gordimer), **Supp. II:** 232

"Company of Wolves, The" (Carter), **Supp. III:** 88

Compassion: An Ode (Hardy), **VI:** 20

"Compassionate Fool, The" (Cameron), **Supp. IX:** 24–25

Compendium of Authentic and Entertaining Voyages, A (Smollett), **IV:** 158

"Competition, The" (Dunn), **Supp. X:** 71

Complaint of Chaucer to His Purse (Chaucer), **I:** 31

Complaint of the Black Knight, The (Lydgate), **I:** 57, 60, 61, 65

Complaint of Venus, The (Chaucer), **I:** 31

Complaints (Spenser), **I:** 124

Compleat Angler, The (Walton), **II:** 131–136, **137–139,** 141–143

Compleat English Gentleman, The (Defoe), **III:** 5, 14

Compleat Gard'ner, The; or, Directions for . . . Fruit–Gardens and Kitchen–Gardens . . . (tr. Evelyn), **II:** 287

Compleat Tradesman, The (Defoe), **Retro. Supp. I:** 63

Compleat Vindication of the Licensers of the Stage, A (Johnson), **III:** 121; **Retro. Supp. I:** 141–142

"Complement, The" (Carew), **II:** 223–224

Complete Clerihews of Edward Clerihew Bentley (Ewart), **Supp. VII:** 43, 46

Complete Collected Essays (Pritchett), **Supp. III:** 313, 315

Complete Collected Stories (Pritchett), **Supp. III:** 312

Complete Collection of Genteel and Ingenious Conversation, A (Swift), **III:** 29, 36

Complete English Tradesman, The (Defoe), **III:** 5, 14

Complete History of England . . . (Smollett), **III:** 148, 149, 158

Complete Little Ones (Ewart), **Supp. VII:** 45

Complete Plays, The (Behan), **Supp. II:** 67, 68, 69, 70, 73, 74

Complete Plays (Kane), **VIII:** 149

Complete Plays of Frances Burney, The (ed. Sabor), **Supp. III:** 64

Complete Poems (Muir), **Supp. VI:** 204

Complete Poems (Day Lewis), **Supp. III:** 130

Complete Poems and Fragments of Wilfred Owen, The (Stallworthy), **VI:** 458, 459; **Supp. X:** 292

Complete Poems of Emily Brontë, The (ed. Hatfield), **V:** 133, 152

Complete Poems of W. H. Davies, The (Davies), **Supp. XI:**95

"Complete Poetical Works of T.E. Hulme" (Hulme), **Supp. VI:** 136

Complete Saki, The (Saki), **Supp. VI:** 240

Complete Short Stories (Pritchett), **Supp. III:** 313

"Complete Stranger" (Dunn), **Supp. X:** 82

Complete Works of John Webster, The (ed. Lucas), **II:** 70n

"Complicated Nature, A" (Trevor), **Supp. IV:** 500

Complicity (Banks), **Supp. XI:** 3–4, 5, 7, 12

Compton–Burnett, Ivy, **VII:** xvii, **59–70;** **Supp. IV:** 506

Comte, Auguste, **V:** 428–429

Comus (Milton), **II:** 50, 159–160, 166, 175; **Retro. Supp. II:** 273–275

Comyns, Barbara, **VIII:** **53–66**

"Con Men, The" (Reading), **VIII:** 267

"Concealment, The" (Cowley), **II:** 196

"Conceit Begotten by the Eyes" (Ralegh), **I:** 148, 149

Concept of Nature in Nineteenth–Century Poetry, The (Beach), **V:** 221n

"Concentration City, The" (Ballard), **Supp. V:** 21

"Concerned Adolescent, The" (Cope), **VIII:** 77

"Concerning Geffray Teste Noir" (Morris), **V:** 293

Concerning Humour in Comedy (Congreve), **II:** 338, 341, 346, 350

"Concerning the Beautiful" (tr. Taylor), **III:** 291

Concerning the Eccentricities of Cardinal Pirelli (Firbank), **Supp. II:** 202, **220–222**

"Concerning the regal power" (King), **Supp. VI:** 158

Concerning the Relations of Great Britain, Spain, and Portugal . . . (Wordsworth), **IV:** 24

Concerning the Rule of Princes (tr. Trevisa), see *De Regimine Principum*

"Concert Party: Busseboom" (Blunden), **VI:** 428

Conciones ad Populum (Coleridge), **IV:** 56

Concluding (Green), **Supp. II: 260–263**

Concordance to the Poems of Robert Browning, A (Broughton and Stelter), **IV:** 373

Concrete Island (Ballard), **Supp. V:** 27, 28

Condemned Playground, The: Essays 1927–1944 (Connolly), **Supp. III: 107–108**

"Condition of England, The" (Masterman), **VI:** viii, 273

Condition of the Working Class in England in 1844, The (Engels), **IV:** 249

"Condition of Women, The" (Oliphant), **Supp. X:** 222

"Condolence Visit" (Mistry), **Supp. X:** 140

Conduct of the Allies, The (Swift), **III:** 19, 26–27, 35; **Retro. Supp. I:** 274, 275

"Coney, The" (Muldoon), **Supp. IV:** 422

Confederacy, The (Vanbrugh), **II:** 325, 336

Confederates, The (Keneally), **Supp. IV:** 346, 348

Conference of Pleasure, A (Bacon), **I:** 265, 271

Confessio amantis (Gower), **I:** 48, 49, 50–56, 58, 321

Confession of My Faith, A, . . . (Bunyan), **II:** 253

"Confessional Poetry" (Harrison), **Supp. V:** 153

Confessions (St. Augustine), **Supp. III:** 433

Confessions of a Justified Sinner (Tennant), **Supp. IX:** 231–232

"Confessions of a Kept Ape" (McEwan), **Supp. IV:** 394

Confessions of a Young Man (Moore), **VI:** 85–86, 87, 89, 91, 96

Confessions of an English Opium–Eater (De Quincey), **III:** 338; **IV:** xviii, 141, 143, 148–149, 150–153, 154, 155

Confessions of an Inquiring Spirit (Coleridge), **IV:** 53, 56

Confessions of an Irish Rebel (Behan), **Supp. II:** 63, 64–65, 71, 75, 76

Confidence (James), **VI:** 67

Confidence Man, The (Melville), **Supp. IV:** 444

Confidential Agent, The (Greene), **Supp. I:** 3, 4, 7, 10; **Retro. Supp. II:** 155–156

Confidential Chats with Boys (Hollinghurst), **Supp. X:** 119, 121–122

Confidential Clerk, The (Eliot), **VII:** 161–162; **Retro. Supp. II:** 132

"Confined Love" (Donne), **Retro. Supp. II:** 89

Confines of Criticism, The (Housman), **VI:** 164

"Confirmation, The" (Muir), **Supp. VI:** 206

"Confirmation Suit, The" (Behan), **Supp. II:** 66–67

"Conflict, The" (Day Lewis), **Supp. III:** 120, 126

Confusion (Howard), **Supp. XI:** 147, 148, 149, 150

Confusions (Ayckbourn), **Supp. V:** 3, 11

Confutation of Tyndale's Answer (More), **Supp. VII:** 245

Congreve, William, **II:** 269, 289, 302, 304, 325, 336, **338–350**, 352; **III:** 45, 62

Coningsby (Disraeli), **IV:** xii, xx, 294, 300–303, 305, 307, 308; **V:** 4, 22

Conjugal Lewdness; or, Matrimonial Whoredom (Defoe), **III:** 14

"Conjugation" (Crawford), **Supp. XI:** 80–80

"Conjugial Angel, The" (Byatt), **Supp. IV:** 153

Connell, John, **VI:** xv, xxxiii

"Connoisseur" (MacCaig), **Supp. VI:** 192–193

Connolly, Cyril, **VI:** 363, 371; **VII:** xvi, 37, 138, 310; **Supp. II:** 156, 199, 489, 493; **Supp. III: 95–113**

Connolly, T. L., **V:** 442*n*, 445, 447, 450, 451

"Connor Girls, The" (O'Brien), **Supp. V:** 339–340

Conny–Catching (Greene), **VIII:** 144

Conquest, Robert, **Supp. IV:** 256

Conquest of Granada by the Spaniards, The (Dryden), **II:** 294, 305

"Conquest of Syria, The: If Complete" (Lawrence), **Supp. II:** 287

Conrad, Joseph, **VI:** xi, **133–150**, 170, 193, 242, 270, 279–280, 321; **VII:** 122; **Retro. Supp. II: 69–83**; list of short stories, **VI:** 149–150; **Supp. I:** 397–398; **Supp. II:** 290; **Supp. IV:** 5, 163, 233, 250, 251, 302, 403

Conrad in the Nineteenth Century (Watt), **VI:** 149

"Conrad's Darkness" (Naipaul), **Supp. I:** 397, 402, 403

Conrad's Prefaces to His Works (Garnett), **VI:** 149

"Conquistador" (Hope), **Supp. VII:** 158

Conscience of the Rich, The (Snow), **VII:** 324, 326–327

"Conscious" (Owen), **VI:** 451

Conscious and Verbal (Murray), **Supp. VII:** 271, 286–287

"Conscious Mind's Intelligible Structure, The: A Debate" (Hill), **Supp. V:** 183

"Conscript" (Larkin), **Supp. I:** 277

Conscription for Ireland: A Warning to England (Russell), **VIII:** 288

Consequently I Rejoice (Jennings), **Supp. V:** 217

Conservationist, The (Gordimer), **Supp. II:** 230–231, 232, 239

"Consider" (Auden), **Retro. Supp. I:** 5

Consider (Rossetti), **V:** 260

Consider Phlebas (Banks), **Supp. XI:** 1, 10, 11–12

Consider the Lilies (Smith, I. C.), **Supp. IX:** 209–210

Considerations Touching the Likeliest Means to Remove Hirelings out of the Church (Milton), **II:** 176

"Considering the Snail" (Gunn), **Supp. IV:** 262–263

"Consolation" (Stallworthy), **Supp. X:** 292

Consolation of Philosophy (Boethius), **I:** 31; **Retro. Supp. II:** 36, 296–297

Consolations (Fuller), **Supp. VII:** 79, 80, 81

Consolidator, The (Defoe), **III:** 4, 13

Constance (Durrell), **Supp. I:** 119, 120

"Constant" (Cornford), **VIII:** 107

Constant, Benjamin, **Supp. IV:** 125, 126, 136

Constant Couple, The; or, A Trip to the Jubilee (Farquhar), **II:** 352, 356–357, 364

Constant Wife, The (Maugham), **VI:** 369

"Constantine and Silvester" (Gower), **I:** 53–54

Constantine the Great (Lee), **II:** 305

"Constellation" (Kelman), **Supp. V:** 255

"Constellation, The" (Vaughan), **II:** 186, 189

Constitutional (periodical), **V:** 19

Constitutional History of England, The (Hallam), **IV:** 283

Constructing Postmodernism (McHale), **Supp. IV:** 112

"Construction for I. K. Brunel" (Morgan, E.), **Supp. IX:** 158

Constructions (Frayn), **Supp. VII:** 51, 53, 58, 64

"Contemplation" (Thompson), **V:** 442, 443

"Contemporaries" (Cornford), **VIII:** 105

Contemporaries of Shakespeare (Swinburne), **V:** 333

"Contemporary Film of Lancasters in Action, A" (Ewart), **Supp. VII:** 44

"Contemporary Sagas", See *Samtíðarsögur*

Continual Dew (Betjeman), **VII:** 365

Continuation of the Complete History, A (Smollett), **III:** 148, 149, 158

Continuous: 50 Sonnets from "The School of Elegance" (Harrison), **Supp. V:** 150

Contractor, The (Storey), **Supp. I:** 408, 416–417, 418

Contrarini Fleming (Disraeli), **IV:** xix, 292–293, 294, 296–297, 299, 308

Contrary Experience, The (Read), **VI:** 416

"Contrasts" (Smith, I. C.), **Supp. IX:** 216

Contre–Machiavel (Gentillet), **I:** 283

Conundrum (Morris, J.), **Supp. X:** 171–174, 179, 184

"Convenience" (Murphy), **Supp. V:** 328

"Convergence of the Twain, The" (Hardy), **II:** 69; **VI:** 16; **Retro. Supp. I:** 119–120

"Conversation of prayer, The" (Thomas), **Supp. I:** 178

"Crowning of Offa, The" (Hill), **Supp. V:** 195

Crowning Privilege, The (Graves), **VII:** 260, 268

"Crowson" (Nye), **Supp. X:** 201

"Croy. Ee. Gaw. Lonker. Pit." (Crawford), **Supp. XI:** 81

Cruel Sea, The (film, Ambler), **Supp. IV:** 3

"Cruelty and Love" (Lawrence), **VII:** 118

Cruelty of a Stepmother, The, **I:** 218

"Cruiskeen Lawn" (O'Nolan), **Supp. II:** 323, **329–333,** 336

Crusader Castles (Lawrence), **Supp. II:** 283, 284

Crux Ansata: An Indictment of the Roman Catholic Church (Wells), **VI:** 242, 244

"Cry Hope, Cry Fury!" (Ballard), **Supp. V:** 26

"Cry of the Children, The" (Browning), **IV:** xx 313

"Cry of the Human, The" (Browning), **IV:** 313

Cry of the Owl, The (Highsmith), **Supp. V:** 173

Cry, The Beloved Country (Paton), **Supp. II:** 341, 342, 343, 344, **345–350,** 351, 354

Cry, the Peacock (Desai), **Supp. V:** 54, 58–59, 75

"Cryptics, The" (Ewart), **Supp. VII:** 39

Crystal and Fox (Friel), **Supp. V:** 118–119

Crystal World, The (Ballard), **Supp. V:** 24, 25–26, 34

C. S. Lewis (Wilson), **Supp. VI:** 304, **305**

Cuala Press, **VI:** 221

"Cub" (Reading), **VIII:** 268

Cub, at Newmarket, The (Boswell), **III:** 247

Cuckold in Conceit, The (Vanbrugh), **II:** 337

"Cuckoo, The" (Thomas), **Supp. III:** 399–400

Cuckoo in the Nest, The (Oliphant), **Supp. X:** 220

Cuirassiers of the Frontier, The (Graves), **VII:** 267

Culture and Anarchy (Arnold), **III:** 23; **V:** 203, 206, 213, 215, 216

Culture and Society (Williams), **Supp. IV:** 380

Cumberland, George, **IV:** 47

Cumberland, Richard, **II:** 363; **III:** 257

Cumberland and Westmoreland (Nicholson), **Supp. VI:** 223

Cunningham, William, **VI:** 385

"Cup Too Low, A" (Ewart), **Supp. VII:** 39–40

"Cupid and Psyche" (tr. Pater), **V:** 351

"Cupid; or, The Atom" (Bacon), **I:** 267

Cupid's Revenge (Beaumont and Fletcher), **II:** 46, 65

Curate in Charge, The (Oliphant), **Supp. X:** 219–220

"Curate's Friend, The" (Forster), **VI:** 399

"Curate's Walk; The," (Thackeray), **V:** 25

Cure at Troy, The (Heaney), **Retro. Supp. I:** 131

Cure for a Cuckold, A (Rowley and Webster), **II:** 69, 83, 85

Curiosissima Curatoria (Carroll), **V:** 274

Curious Fragments (Lamb), **IV:** 79

"Curious if True" (Gaskell), **V:** 15

Curious Relations (ed. Plomer), **Supp. XI:** 225

"Curiosity" (Reid), **Supp. VII:** 330

Curlew River: A Parable for Church Performance (Plomer), **Supp. XI:** 226

"Curse, The" (Healy), **Supp. IX:** 103–104

Curse of Kehama, The (Southey), **IV:** 65, 66, 71, 217

Curse of Minerva, The (Byron), **IV:** 192

Curtain (Christie), **Supp. II:** 124, 125, 134

Curtis, Anthony, **VI:** xiii, xxxiii, 372

Curtis, L. P., **III:** 124*n*, 127*n*

Curtmantle (Fry), **Supp. III:** 195, **206–207,** 208

Custom of the Country, The (Fletcher [and Massinger]), **II:** 66, 340

"Custom–House, The" (Hawthorne), **Supp. IV:** 116

"Customs" (Crawford), **Supp. XI:** 74

Cut by the County (Braddon), **VIII:** 49

"Cut Grass" (Larkin), **Supp. I:** 285

Cut–Rate Kingdom, The (Keneally), **Supp. IV:** 346

Cyclopean Mistress, The (Redgrove), **Supp. VI:** 231

"Cygnus A." (Thomas), **Supp. IV:** 490, 491

Cymbeline (Shakespeare), **I:** 322

Cymbeline Refinished (Shaw), **VI:** 129

"Cynic at Kilmainham Jail, A" (Boland), **Supp. V:** 36

Cynthia's Revels (Jonson), **I:** 346; **Retro. Supp. I:** 158, 160

"Cypress and Cedar" (Harrison), **Supp. V:** 161

Cyrano de Bergerac, **III:** 24

Cyrano de Bergerac (tr.. Fry), **Supp. III:** 195

Cyril Connolly: Journal and Memoirs (ed. Pryce–Jones), **Supp. III:** 96, 97, 112

"Cyril Tourneur" (Swinburne), **V:** 332

D. *G. Rossetti: A Critical Essay* (Ford), **VI:** 332

"D. G. Rossetti as a Translator" (Doughty), **V:** 246

D. H. Lawrence: A Calendar of His Works (Sugar), **VII:** 104, 115, 123

D. H. Lawrence: Novelist (Leavis), **VII:** 101, 234–235, 252–253

Da Silva da Silva's Cultivated Wilderness (Harris), **Supp. V:** 139, 140

Daborne, Robert, **II:** 37, 45

Dad's Tale (Ayckbourn), **Supp. V:** 2

"Daedalus" (Reid), **Supp. VII:** 331

"Daedalus; or, The Mechanic" (Bacon), **I:** 267

Daemon of the World, The (Shelley), **IV:** 209

Daffodil Murderer, The (Sassoon), **VI:** 429

"Daffodil Time" (Brown), **Supp. VI:** 72

Dahl, Roald, **Supp. IV:** **201–227,** 449

Daiches, David, **V:** ix

Daily Graphic (periodical), **VI:** 350

Daily News (periodical), **VI:** 335

Daily Worker (periodical), **VI:** 242

Daisy Miller (James), **VI:** **31–32,** 69

Dale, Colin (pseud., Lawrence), **Supp. II:** 295

Dali, Salvador, **Supp. IV:** 424

Dalkey Archive, The (O'Nolan), **Supp. II:** 322, **337–338**

Dallas, Eneas Sweetland, **V:** 207

"Dalziel's Ghost" (Hill, R.), **Supp. IX:** 114

Damage (film, Hare), **Supp. IV:** 282, 292

Damage (play, Hare), **Supp. IV:** 282, 292

"Damnation of Byron, The" (Hope), **Supp. VII:** 159

Dampier, William, **III:** 7, 24

"Danac" (Galsworthy), *see Country House, The*

Danae (Rembrandt), **Supp. IV:** 89

Dan Leno and the Limehouse Golem (Ackroyd), **Supp. VI:** 10–13

Danby, J. F., **II:** 46, 53, 64

"Dance, The" (Kinsella), **Supp. V:** 271

Dance of Death, The, **I:** 57

Dance of Death, The (Strindberg), **Supp. I:** 57

"Dance the Putrefact" (Redgrove), **Supp. VI:** 234

Dance to the Music of Time, A (Powell), **VII:** xxi, 343, **347–353; Supp. II: 4**

Dancing Hippo, The (Motion), **Supp. VII:** 257

Dancing Mad (Davies), **Supp. XI:** 94

Dancourt, Carton, **II:** 325, 336

"Dandies and Dandies" (Beerbohm), **Supp. II:** 46

Dangerous Corner (Priestley), **VII:** 223

Dangerous Love (Okri), **Supp. V:** 349, 359, 360

Dangerous Play: Poems 1974–1984 (Motion), **Supp. VII:** 251, 254, 255, 256–257, 264

Daniel, **Retro. Supp. II:** 301

Daniel, Samuel, **I:** 162

Daniel Deronda (Eliot), **V:** xxiv, 190, 197–198, 200; **Retro. Supp. II:** 115–116

Daniel Martin (Fowles), **Supp. I:** 291, 292, 293, **304–308,** 310

D'Annunzio, Gabriele, **V:** 310

"Danny Deever" (Kipling), **VI:** 203

Danny, the Champion of the World (Dahl), **Supp. IV:** 214, 223

"Dans un Omnibus de Londre" (Fuller), **Supp. VII:** 80

Dante Alighieri, **II:** 75, 148; **III:** 306; **IV:** 93, 187; **Supp. IV:** 439, 493; **Retro. Supp. I:** 123–124

Dante and His Circle (Rossetti), **V:** 245

"Dante and the Lobster" (Beckett), **Retro. Supp. I:** 19

"Dante at Verona" (Rossetti), **V:** 239, 240

"Dante … Bruno. Vico … Joyce" (Beckett), **Retro. Supp. I:** 17

"Dream of Eugene Aram, The Murderer, The" (Hood), **IV:** 256, 261–262, 264, 267; **Supp. III:** 378

Dream of Fair to Middling Women, A (Beckett), **Retro. Supp. I:** 17

"Dream of France, A" (Hart), **Supp. XI:** 125

Dream of Gerontius, The (Newman), **Supp. VII:** 293, 300, 301

Dream of John Ball, A (Morris), **V:** 301, 302–303, 305, 306

"Dream of Nourishment" (Smith), **Supp. II:** 466

"Dream of Private Clitus, The" (Jones), **Supp. VII:** 175

Dream of Scipio, The (Cicero), **IV:** 189

Dream of the Rood, The, **I:** 11; **Retro. Supp. II:** 302, 307

"Dream Play" (Mahon), **Supp. VI:** 178

Dream State: The New Scottish Poets (Crawford), **Supp. XI:** 67

"Dream Work" (Hope), **Supp. VII:** 155

Dreamchild (Potter, D.), **Supp. X:** 236

"Dream–Fugue" (De Quincey), **IV:** 153–154

"Dream–Language of Fergus, The" (McGuckian), **Supp. V:** 285–286

"Dream–Pedlary" (Beddoes), **Supp. XI:** 30

Dreaming in Bronze (Thomas), **Supp. IV:** 490

"Dreaming Spires" (Campbell), **VII:** 430

"Dreams" (Spenser), **I:** 123

Dreams of Leaving (Hare), **Supp. IV:** 282, 289

"Dreams Old and Nascent" (Lawrence), **VII:** 118

"Dream–Tryst" (Thompson), **V:** 444

Drebbel, Cornelius, **I:** 268

Dressed as for a Tarot Pack (Redgrove), **Supp. VI:** 236

"Dressing" (Vaughan), **II:** 186

Dressing Up—Transvestism and Drag: The History of an Obsession (Ackroyd), **Supp. VI:** 3–4, 12

Dressmaker, The (Bainbridge), **Supp. VI:** 19–20, 24

"Dressmaker, The" (Hart), **Supp. XI:** 132

Drew, Philip, **IV:** xiii, xxiv, 375

"Drink to Me Only with Thine Eyes" (Jonson), **I:** 346; **VI:** 16

Drinkers of Infinity (Koestler), **Supp. I:** 34, 34n

"Drinking" (Cowley), **II:** 198

Driver's Seat, The (Spark), **Supp. I:** 200, 209–210, 218n

"Driving Through Sawmill Towns" (Murray), **Supp. VII:** 271

Droe wit seisoen, 'n (Brink), **Supp. VI:** 50–51

"Droit de Seigneur: 1820" (Murphy), **Supp. V:** 321

Drought, The (Ballard), **Supp. V:** 24–25, 34

"Drowned Field, The" (Hollinghurst), **Supp. X:** 121

"Drowned Giant, The" (Ballard), **Supp. V:** 23

Drowned World, The (Ballard), **Supp. V:** 22–23, 24, 34

Drumlin (ed. Healy), **Supp. IX:** 95

"Drummer Hodge" (Housman), **VI:** 161; **Retro. Supp. I:** 120

Drummond of Hawthornden, William, **I:** 328, 349

Drums of Father Ned, The (O'Casey), **VII:** 10–11

Drums under the Windows (O'Casey), **VII:** 9, 12

Drunken Sailor, The (Cary), **VII:** 186, 191

"Dry Point" (Larkin), **Supp. I:** 277

Dry Salvages, The (Eliot), **V:** 241; **VII:** 143, 144, 152, 154, 155

Dry, White Season, A (Brink), **Supp. VI:** 50–51

Dryden, John, **I:** 176, 327, 328, 341, 349; **II:** 166–167, 195, 198, 200, **289–306,** 325, 338, 340, 348, 350, 352, 354–355; **III:** 40, 47, 68, 73–74, 118; **IV:** 93, 196, 287; **V:** 376; **Supp. III:** 19, 24, 27, 36, 37, 40; **Supp. V:** 201–202

Dryden, John, The younger, **II:** 305

"Dryden's Prize–Song" (Hill), **Supp. V:** 201–202

Du Bellay, Joachim, **I:** 126; **V:** 345

Du Bois, W. E. B., **Supp. IV:** 86

du Maurier, Daphne, **III:** 343; **Supp. III:** **133–149**

du Maurier, George, **V:** 403; **Supp. III:** 133–137, 141

du Maurier, Guy, **Supp. III:** 147, 148

Du Mauriers, The (du Maurier), **Supp. III:** 135–136, 137, 139

Dual Tradition: An Essay on Poetry and Politics in Ireland (Kinsella), **Supp. V:** 272, 273–274

Dubliners (Joyce), **VII:** xiv, 41, 43–45, 47–52; critical studies, **VII:** 57; **Supp. I:** 45; **Supp. IV:** 395; **Retro. Supp. I:** 171–173

"Dubious" (Seth), **Supp. X:** 279

"Duchess of Hamptonshire, The" (Hardy), **VI:** 22

Duchess of Malfi, The (Webster), **II:** 68, 70–73, **76–78,** 79, 81, 82, 84, 85

Duchess of Padua, The (Wilde), **V:** 419; **Retro. Supp. II:** 362–363

"Duddon Estuary, The" (Nicholson), **Supp. VI:** 214

Due Preparations for the Plague (Defoe), **III:** 13

"Duel, The" (Conrad), **VI:** 148

Duel of Angels (Fry), **Supp. III:** 195

"Duel of the Crabs, The" (Dorset), **II:** 271

Duenna, The (Sheridan), **III:** 253, 257, 259–261, 270

"Duffy's Circus" (Muldoon), **Supp. IV:** 415

Dufy, Raoul, **Supp. IV:** 81

Dugdale, Florence Emily, **VI:** 17n

Dugdale, Sir William, **II:** 274

Dugmore, C. W., **I:** 177n

Dujardin, Edouard, **VI:** 87

Duke of Gandia, The (Swinburne), **V:** 333

Duke of Guise, The (Dryden), **II:** 305

Duke of Millaine, The (Massinger), **Supp. XI:** 185

Duke's Children, The (Trollope), **V:** 96, 99, 101, 102

"Duke's Reappearance, The" (Hardy), **VI:** 22

"Dulce et Decorum Est" (Owen), **VI:** 448, 451

"Dull London" (Lawrence), **VII:** 94, 116, 121

"Dulwich Gallery, The" (Hazlitt), **IV:** 135–136

Dumas père, Alexandre, **III:** 332, 334, 339

Dumb Instrument (Welch), **Supp. IX:** 269–270

Dumb Virgin, The; or, The Force of Imagination (Behn), **Supp. III:** 31

Dumb Waiter, The (Pinter), **Supp. I:** 369, 370–371, 381; **Retro. Supp. I:** 222

"Dumnesse" (Traherne), **II:** 189; **Supp. XI:** 274

Dun Cow, The (Landor), **IV:** 100

Dun Emer Press, **VI:** 221

"Dunbar and the Language of Poetry" (Morgan, E.), **Supp. IX:** 160

Dunbar, William, **I:** 23; **VIII:** **117–130**

"Dunbar at Oxinfurde" (Dunbar), **VIII:** 122–123

Duncan, Robert, **Supp. IV:** 269

Dunciad, The (Pope), **II:** 259, 311; **III:** 73, 77, 95; **IV:** 187; **Supp. III:** 421–422; **Retro. Supp. I:** 76, 231, 235, 238–240

"Dunciad Minimus" (Hope), **Supp. VII:** 161

Dunciad Minor: A Heroick Poem (Hope), **Supp. VII:** 161–163

Dunciad of Today, The; and, The Modern Aesop (Disraeli), **IV:** 308

Dunciad Variorum, The (Pope), **Retro. Supp. I:** 238

Dunn, Douglas **Supp. X:** **65–84**

Dunn, Nell, **VI:** 271

Dunne, John William, **VII:** 209, 210

Duns Scotus, John, **V:** 363, 370, 371; **Retro. Supp. II:** 187–188

"Duns Scotus's Oxford" (Hopkins), **V:** 363, 367, 370

Dunsany, Lord Edward, **III:** 340

Dunton, John, **III:** 41

Dupee, F. W., **V:** 31, 45

"Dura Mater" (Kinsella), **Supp. V:** 272

Dürer, Albrecht, **Supp. IV:** 125

"Duriesdyke" (Swinburne), **V:** 333

"During Wind and Rain" (Cornford), **VIII:** 114

"During Wind and Rain" (Hardy), **VI:** 17

Durrell, Lawrence, **Supp. I:** **93–128**

Dusklands (Coetzee), **Supp. VI:** 78–80, 81

"Dusky Ruth" (Coppard), **VIII:** 88, 90, 93

Dusky Ruth and Other Stories (Coppard), **VIII:** 90

"Dust" (Brooke), **Supp. III:** 52

"Dust, The" (Redgrove), **Supp. VI:** 228

"Dust As We Are" (Hughes), **Retro. Supp. II:** 214

Dutch Courtesan, The (Marston), **II:** 30, 40

"Fall in Ghosts" (Blunden), **Supp. XI:** 45

"Fall of a Sparrow" (Stallworthy), **Supp. X:** 294

Fall of Hyperion, The (Keats), **IV:** xi, 211–213, 220, **227–231,** 234, 235

Fall of Kelvin Walker, The (Gray, A.), **Supp. IX:** 80, 85, 89

Fall of Princes, The (Lydgate), **I:** 57, 58, 59, 64

Fall of Robespierre, The (Coleridge and Southey), **IV:** 55

"Fall of Rome, The" (Auden), **Retro. Supp. I:** 11

"Fall of the House of Usher, The" (Poe), **III:** 339

"Fall of the West, The" (Wallace–Crabbe), **VIII:** 321

Fallen Angels (Coward), **Supp. II:** 141, 145

Fallen Leaves, The (Collins), **Supp. VI:** 93, 102

"Fallen Majesty" (Yeats), **VI:** 216

"Fallen Yew, A" (Thompson), **V:** 442

Falling (Howard), **Supp. XI:** 144–146

Falling into Language (Wallace–Crabbe), **VIII:** 323

Falling Out of Love and Other Poems, A (Sillitoe), **Supp. V:** 424

"Fallow Deer at the Lonely House, The" (Hardy), **Retro. Supp. I:** 119

Fallowell, Duncan, **Supp. IV:** 173

"Falls" (Ewart), **Supp. VII:** 39

Falls, The (Rankin), **Supp. X:** 245

False Alarm, The (Johnson), **III:** 121

False Friend, The (Vanbrugh), **II:** 325, 333, 336

"False Morality of the Lady Novelists, The" (Greg), **V:** 7

False One, The (Fletcher and Massinger), **II:** 43, 66

"False though she be to me and love" (Congreve), **II:** 269

Falstaff (Nye), **Supp. X:** 193, 195

Fame's Memoriall; or, The Earle of Devonshire Deceased (Ford), **II:** 100

Familiar and Courtly Letters Written by Monsieur Voiture (ed. Boyer), **II:** 352, 364

"Familiar Endeavours" (Wallace–Crabbe), **VIII:** 317

Familiar Letters (Richardson), **III:** 81, 83, 92

Familiar Letters (Rochester), **II:** 270

Familiar Studies of Men and Books (Stevenson), **V:** 395; **Retro. Supp. I:** 262–263

Familiar Tree, A (Stallworthy), **Supp. X:** 294, 297–298, 302

Family (Doyle), **Supp. V:** 78, 91

Family Album (Coward), **Supp. II:** 153

Family and a Fortune, A (Compton–Burnett), **VII:** 60, 61, 62, 63, 66

Family and Friends (Brookner), **Supp. IV:** 127–129

Family Instructor, The (Defoe), **III:** 13, 82; **Retro. Supp. I:** 68

Family Madness, A (Keneally), **Supp. IV:** 346

Family Matters (Mistry), **Supp. X:** 144, 147–148

Family Memories (West), **Supp. III:** 431, 432, 433, 434

Family of Love, The (Dekker and Middleton), **II:** 3, 21

Family of Swift, The (Swift), **Retro. Supp. I:** 274

Family Prayers (Butler), **Supp. II:** 103

Family Reunion, The (Eliot), **VII:** 146, 151, 154, 158, 160; **Retro. Supp. II:** 132

Family Romance, A (Brookner), *see Dolly*

"Family Sagas", *See Íslendinga sögur*

"Family Seat" (Murphy), **Supp. V:** 328

Family Sins (Trevor), **Supp. IV:** 505

"Family Supper, A" (Ishiguro), **Supp. IV:** 304

Family Tree, The (Plomer), **Supp. XI:** 220

Family Voices (Pinter), **Supp. I:** 378

Famished Road, The (Okri), **Supp. V:** 347, 348, 349, 350, 351, 352–353, 357–359

Famous for the Creatures (Motion), **Supp. VII:** 252

"Famous Ghost of St. Ives, The" (Redgrove), **Supp. VI:** 235–237

Famous History of Sir Thomas Wyat, The (Webster), **II:** 85

Famous Tragedy of the Queen of Cornwall . . . , The (Hardy), **VI:** 20

Famous Victoria of Henry V, The, **I:** 308–309

Fan, The: A Poem (Gay), **III:** 67

Fanatic Heart, A (O'Brien), **Supp. V:** 339

Fancies, Chaste and Noble, The (Ford), **II:** 89, 91–92, 99, 100

"Fancy" (Keats), **IV:** 221

"Fancy, A" (Greville), **Supp. XI:** 111

Fancy and Imagination (Brett), **IV:** 57

Fanfare for Elizabeth (Sitwell), **VII:** 127

"Fanny and Annie" (Lawrence), **VII:** 90, 114, 115

Fanny Brawne: A Biography (Richardson), **IV:** 236

Fanny's First Play (Shaw), **VI:** 115, 116, 117, 129

Fanon, Frantz, **Supp. IV:** 105

"Fanon the Awakener" (Armah), **Supp. X:** 2

Fanshawe, Sir Richard, **II:** 49, 222, 237

Fanshen (Hare), **Supp. IV:** 282, 284

Fanshen (Hinton), **Supp. IV:** 284

"Fantasia" (Redgrove), **Supp. VI:** 231

Fantasia of the Unconscious (Lawrence), **VII:** 122; **Retro. Supp. II:** 234

"Fantasia on 'Horbury'" (Hill), **Supp. V:** 187

Fantastic Mr. Fox (Dahl), **Supp. IV:** 203, 223

fantasy fiction, **VI:** 228–235, 338, 399

Fantasy and Fugue (Fuller), **Supp. VII:** 71–72

Far Cry (MacCaig), **Supp. VI:** 184–185

"Far—Far—Away" (Tennyson), **IV:** 330

Far from the Madding Crowd (Hardy), **VI:** 1, 5–6; **Retro. Supp. I:** 113–114

Far Journey of Oudin, The (Harris), **Supp. V:** 132, 134, 135

Far Journeys (Chatwin), **Supp. IV:** 157

"Fare Thee Well" (Byron), **IV:** 192

Fares Please! An Omnibus (Coppard), **VIII:** 89

"Farewell, A" (Arnold), **V:** 216

Farewell the Trumpets: An Imperial Retreat (Morris, J.), **Supp. X:** 179, 181

"Farewell to Angria" (Brontë), **V:** 125

"Farewell to Essay–Writing, A" (Hazlitt), **IV:** 135

Farewell to Military Profession (Rich), **I:** 312

Farewell to Poesy (Davies), **Supp. XI:** 98

"Farewell to Tobacco" (Lamb), **IV:** 81

Farfetched Fables (Shaw), **VI:** 125, 126

Farina (Meredith), **V:** 225, 234

Farm, The (Storey), **Supp. I:** 408, 411, 412, 414

Farmer Giles of Ham (Tolkien), **Supp. II:** 521

"Farmer's Ingle, The" (Fergusson), **III:** 318

Farmer's Year, A (Haggard), **Supp. III:** 214

Farnham, William, **I:** 214

Farquhar, George, **II:** 334–335, 351–365

Farrell, Barry, **Supp. IV:** 223

Farther Adventures of Robinson Crusoe, The (Defoe), **III:** 13; **Retro. Supp. I:** 71

Farthing Hall (Walpole and Priestley), **VII:** 211

Fascinating Foundling, The (Shaw), **VI:** 129

"Fashionable Authoress, The" (Thackeray), **V:** 22, 37

Fashionable Lover, The (Cumberland), **III:** 257

"Fasternis Eve in Hell" (Dunbar), **VIII:** 126

Fasti (Ovid), **II:** 110n

"Fat Contributor Papers, The" (Thackeray), **V:** 25, 38

Fat Woman's Joke, The (Weldon), **Supp. IV:** 521, 522–524, 525

"Fatal Boots, The" (Thackeray), **V:** 21, 37

Fatal Dowry, The (Massinger and Field), **Supp. XI:** 183, 185

Fatal Gift, The (Waugh), **Supp. VI:** 276

Fatal Inversion, A (Rendell), **Supp. IX:** 201

Fatal Revenge, The; or, The Family of Montorio (Maturin), **VIII:** 200, 207

"Fatal Sisters, The" (Gray), **III:** 141

Fatality in Fleet Street (Caudwell), **Supp. IX:** 35

Fate of Homo Sapiens, The (Wells), **VI:** 228

Fate of Mary Rose, The (Blackwood), **Supp. IX:** 11–12

"Fate Playing" (Hughes), **Retro. Supp. II:** 217

"Fates, The" (Owen), **VI:** 449

Fates of the Apostles, **Retro. Supp. II:** 301

Father and His Fate, A (Compton–Burnett), **VII:** 61, 63

"Father and Lover" (Rossetti), **V:** 260

Forrest, James F., **II:** 245n

Fors Clavigera (Ruskin), **V:** 174, 181, 184

"Forsaken Garden, A" (Swinburne), **V:** 314, 327

Forster, E. M., **IV:** 302, 306; **V:** xxiv, 208, 229, 230; **VI:** xii, 365, **397–413;** **VII:** xi, xv, 18, 21, 34, 35, 122, 144; **Supp. I:** 260; **Supp. II:** 199, 205, 210, 223, 227, 289, 293; **Supp. III:** 49; **Supp. IV:** 440, 489; **Retro. Supp. II:** 135–150

Forster, John, **IV:** 87, 89, 95, 99, 100, 240; **V:** 47, 72

Forsyte Saga, The (Galsworthy), **VI:** xiii, 269, 272, 274; *see also Man of Property, The;* "Indian Summer of a Forsyte"; *In Chancery; To Let*

Fortescue, Chichester, **V:** 76–83, 85

Fortnightly Review (periodical), **V:** 279, 338

Fortunate Isles, and Their Union, The (Jonson), **Retro. Supp. I:** 165

Fortunate Mistress, The: or, A History of . . . Mademoiselle de Beleau . . . (Defoe), **III:** 13

Fortunes and Misfortunes of the Famous Moll Flanders, The (Defoe), *see Moll Flanders*

Fortunes of Falstaff, The (Wilson), **III:** 116n

Fortunes of Nigel, The (Scott), **IV:** 30, 35, 37, 39

Forty New Poems (Davies), **Supp. XI:** 100

Forty Years On (Bennett), **VIII:** 20–21, 22–23

"Forty–seventh Saturday, The" (Trevor), **Supp. IV:** 501

Forward from Liberalism (Spender), **Supp. II:** 488

Fóstbrœðra saga, **VIII:** 239, 241

Foster, A. D., **III:** 345

Foucault, Michel, **Supp. IV:** 442

Foucault's Pendulum (Eco), **Supp. IV:** 116

"Found" (Rossetti), **V:** 240

Found in the Street (Highsmith), **Supp. V:** 171, 178–179

"Foundation of the Kingdom of Angria" (Brontë), **V:** 110–111

Foundations of Aesthetics, The (Richards and Ogden), **Supp. II:** 408, **409–410**

Foundations of Joy, The (Wallace–Crabbe), **VIII:** 318

"Fountain" (Jennings), **Supp. V:** 210, 212

Fountain of Self–love, The (Jonson), **Retro. Supp. I:** 158, 160

Fountain Overflows, The (West), **Supp. III:** 431–432, 443

Fountains in the Sand (Douglas), **VI:** 294, 297, 299, 300, 305

Four Ages of Poetry, The (Peacock), **IV:** 168–169, 170

Four and a Half Dancing Men (Stevenson), **Supp. VI: 264**

Four Banks of the River of Space, The (Harris), **Supp. V:** 137, 140, 142–144

Four Countries (Plomer), **Supp. XI:** 220, 226

Four Day's Wonder (Milne), **Supp. V:** 310

Four–Dimensional Nightmare, The (Ballard), **Supp. V:** 23

Four Dissertations (Hume), **Supp. III:** 231, 238

4.50 from Paddington (Christie; U.S. title, *What Mrs. McGillicuddy Saw*), **Supp. II:** 132

Four Georges, The (Thackeray), **V:** 20, 34–35, 38

Four Hymns (Spenser), **I:** 124

Four Last Things (More), **Supp. VII:** 234, 246–247

Four Lectures (Trollope), **V:** 102

"Four Letter Word, A" (Sisson), **Supp. XI:** 257

Four Loves, The (Lewis), **Supp. III:** 249, 264–265

"Four Meetings" (James), **VI:** 69

Four Plays (Stevenson and Henley), **V:** 396

Four Plays (White), **Supp. I:** 131

Four Plays for Dancers (Yeats), **VI:** 218

4.48 Psychosis (Kane), **VIII:** 148, 149, 150–151, 155, 159–160

Four Prentices of London with the Conquest of Jerusalem (Heywood), **II:** 48

Four Quartets (Eliot), **VII:** 143, 148, 153–157; **Retro. Supp. II:** 121, 130–131; *see also* "The Dry Salvages," "East Coker," "Little Gidding"

"Four Walks in the Country near Saint Brieuc" (Mahon) **Supp. VI:** 168

Four Zoas, The (Blake), **III:** 300, 302–303, 307; **Retro. Supp. I:** 44

Four–Gated City, The (Lessing), **Supp. I:** 245, 248, 250, 251, 255

Foure–footed Beastes (Topsel), **II:** 137

"14 November 1973" (Betjeman), **VII:** 372

Fourteenth Century Verse and Prose (Sisam), **I:** 20, 21

"Fourth of May, The" (Ewart), **Supp. VII:** 36

Fowler, Alastair, **I:** 237

Fowler, H. W., **VI:** 76

Fowles, John, **Supp. I: 291–311**

Foxe, The (Jonson), **Retro. Supp. I:** 163, 164

Fox and the Wolf, The (Henryson), **Supp. VII:** 136, 138, 140

Fox, Caroline, **IV:** 54

Fox, Chris, **Supp. IV:** 88

Fox, George, **IV:** 45

Fox, Ralph, **Supp. IV:** 464, 466

"Fox, The" (Lawrence), **VII:** 90, 91

Fox, the Wolf, and the Cadger, The (Henryson), **Supp. VII:** 136, 140

Fox, the Wolf, and the Husbandman, The (Henryson), **Supp. VII:** 136, 140

"Fox Trot" (Sitwell), **VII:** 131

Foxe, that begylit the Wolf, in the Schadow of the Mone, The (Henryson), see *Fox, the Wolf, and the Husbandman, The*

"Fra Lippo Lippi" (Browning), **IV:** 357, 361, 369; **Retro. Supp. II:** 27

Fra Rupert: The Last Part of a Trilogy (Landor), **IV:** 100

"Fragment" (Brooke), **VI:** 421

"Fragment of a Greek Tragedy" (Housman), **VI:** 156

Fragmenta Aurea (Suckling), **II:** 238

Fragments (Armah), **Supp. X:** 1–6, 12

"Fragments" (Hulme), **Supp. VI:** 137–138

Fragments of Ancient Poetry (Macpherson), **VIII:** 183–185, 187, 189, 194

"Fragoletta" (Swinburne), **V:** 320

"Frail as thy love, The flowers were dead" (Peacock), **IV:** 157

Framley Parsonage (Trollope), **V:** xxii, 93, 101

"France" (Dunn), **Supp. X:** 76

"France, an Ode" (Coleridge), **IV:** 55

"France, December 1870" (Meredith), **V:** 223

"Frances" (Brontë), **V:** 132

Francophile, The (Friel), **Supp. V:** 115

Francillon, R. E., **V:** 83

Francis, Dick, **Supp. IV:** 285

Francis, G. H., **IV:** 270

Francis, P., **III:** 249

"Francis Beaumont" (Swinburne), **V:** 332

Franck, Richard, **II:** 131–132

"Frank Fane: A Ballad" (Swinburne), **V:** 332

Frankenstein; or, The Modern Prometheus (Shelley), **III: 329–331,** 341, 342, 345; **Supp. III:** 355, **356–363,** 369, 372, 385; **Retro. Supp. I:** 247

Frankenstein Un–bound (Aldiss), **III:** 341, 345

Franklin's Tale, The (Chaucer), **I:** 23

Fraser, Antonia, **Supp. V:** 20

Fraser, G. S., **VI:** xiv, xxxiii; **VII:** xviii, 422, 425, 443

Fraser's (periodical), **IV:** 259; **V:** 19, 22, 111, 142

"Frater Ave atque Vale" (Tennyson), **IV:** 327, 336

Fraternity (Galsworthy), **VI:** 274, 278, 279–280, 285

"Frau Brechenmacher Attends a Wedding" (Mansfield), **VII:** 172

"Frau Fischer" (Mansfield), **VII:** 172

Fraud (Brookner), **Supp. IV:** 134

Fraunce, Abraham, **I:** 122, 164

Frayn, Michael, **Supp. VII: 51–65**

Frazer, Sir James George, **V:** 204; **Supp. III: 169–190;** **Supp. IV:** 11, 19

Fred and Madge (Orton), **Supp. V:** 363, 366–367, 372

Frederick the Great (Mitford), **Supp. X:** 167

Fredy Neptune (Murray), **Supp. VII:** 271, 284–286

"Freddy" (Smith), **Supp. II:** 462

Fredolfo (Maturin), **VIII:** 207, 208, 209

Free and Offenceless Justification of a Lately Published and Most Maliciously Misinterpreted Poem Entitled "Andromeda Liberata, A" (Chapman), **I:** 254

Free Fall (Golding), **Supp. I:** 75–78, 81, 83, 85; **Retro. Supp. I:** 98

"Happy old man, whose worth all mankind knows" (Flatman), **II:** 133

Happy Pair, The (Sedley), **II:** 266, 271

"Happy Prince, The" (Wilde), **V:** 406, 419; **Retro. Supp. II:** 365; **Retro. Supp. II:** 365

Happy Valley (White), **Supp. I:** 130, 132–133, 136

Haq, Zia ul–, **Supp. IV:** 444

Hárbarðsljóð, **VIII:** 230

Hard Life, The (O'Nolan), **Supp. II:** 336–337

Hard Times (Dickens), **IV:** 247; **V:** viii, xxi, 4, 42, 47, 59, 63–64, 68, 70, 71

Hardie and Baird: The Last Days (Kelman), **Supp. V:** 256–257

Hardie and Baird and Other Plays (Kelman), **Supp. V:** 256–257

"Hardness of Light, The" (Davie), **Supp. VI:** 109

Hardy, Barbara, **V:** ix, xxviii, 39, 73, 201

Hardy, G. H., **VII:** 239–240

Hardy, Thomas, **II:** 69; **III:** 278; **V:** xx–xxvi, 144, 279, 429; **VI:** x, **1–22,** 253, 377; **VII:** xvi; list of short stories, **VI:** 22; **Supp. IV:** 94, 116, 146, 471, 493; **Retro. Supp. I:** 109–122

"Hardy and the Hag" (Fowles), **Supp. I:** 302, 305

Hardy of Wessex (Weber), **VI:** 21

Hare, J. C., **IV:** 54

Hare, David, **Supp. IV:** 182, **281–300**

"Harem Trousers" (McGuckian), **Supp. V:** 286

Harington, Sir John, **I:** 131

"Hark, My Soul! It Is the Lord" (Cowper), **III:** 210

"Hark! the Dog's Howl" (Tennyson), **IV:** 332

Harlequinade (Rattigan), **Supp. VII:** 315–316

Harlot's House, The (Wilde), **V:** 410, 418, 419

Harm Done (Rendell), **Supp. IX:** 189, 196, 198, 199, 201

"Harmonies" (Kinsella), **Supp. V:** 271

"Harmony, The" (Redgrove), **Supp. VI:** 236

"Harmony of the Spheres, The" (Rushdie), **Supp. IV:** 445

Harness Room, The (Hartley), **Supp. VII:** 132

Harold (Tennyson), **IV:** 328, 338

Harold Muggins Is a Martyr (Arden and D'Arcy), **Supp. II:** 31

Harold the Dauntless (Scott), **IV:** 39

Harold's Leap (Smith), **Supp. II:** 462

Haroun and the Sea of Stories (Rushdie), **Supp. IV:** 433, 438, 450–451

Harriet Hume: A London Fantasy (West), **Supp. III:** 441–442

Harrington (Edgeworth), **Supp. III:** 161–163

Harriet Said? (Bainbridge), **Supp. VI:** 17, **19**

Harriot, Thomas, **I:** 277, 278

Harris, Frank, **VI:** 102

Harris, Joseph, **II:** 305

Harris, Wilson, **Supp. V:** 131–147

"Harris East End" (MacCaig), **Supp. VI:** 182

Harrison, Frederic, **V:** 428–429

Harrison, Tony, **Supp. V:** **149–165**

Harry Heathcote of Gangoil (Trollope), **V:** 102

"Harry Ploughman" (Hopkins), **V:** 376–377

Harsh Voice, The (West), **Supp. III:** 442

Hart, Kevin, **Supp. XI:** **123–135**

Hartley, David, **IV:** 43, 45, 50, 165

Hartley, L. P., **Supp. VII:** **119–133**

Hartmann, Edward von, **Supp. II:** 108

"Harvest Bow, The" (Heaney), **Supp. II:** 276–277

Harvest Festival, The (O'Casey), **VII:** 12

"Harvesting, The" (Hughes), **Supp. II:** 348

Harvey, Christopher, **II:** 138; **Retro. Supp. II:** 172

Harvey, Gabriel, **I:** 122–123, 125; **II:** 25

Harvey, T. W. J., **V:** 63, 199, 201

Harvey, William, **I:** 264

"Has Your Soul Slipped" (Owen), **VI:** 446

Hashemite Kings, The (Morris, J.), **Supp. X:** 175

"Hassock and the Psalter, The" (Powys), **VIII:** 255

Hastings, Warren, **IV:** xv–xvi, 271, 278

Hatfield, C. W., **V:** 133, 151, 152, 153

Háttatal, **VIII:** 243

Haunch of Venison, The (Goldsmith), **III:** 191

Haunted and the Haunters, The (Bulwer-Lytton), **III:** 340, 345

"Haunted House, The" (Graves), **VII:** 263

"Haunted House, The" (Hood), **IV:** 261, 262

Haunted Man and the Ghost's Bargain, The (Dickens), **V:** 71

"Haunter, The" (Hardy), **VI:** 18; **Retro. Supp. I:** 117

Haunter of the Dark, The . . . (Lovecraft), **III:** 345

Hávamál, **VIII:** 230, 232

Have His Carcase (Sayers), **Supp. III:** 345–346

Having a Wonderful Time (Churchill), **Supp. IV:** 180, 181

Haw Lantern, The (Heaney), **Supp. II:** 268, **279–281;** **Retro. Supp. I:** 131–132

Hawaiian Archipelago, The (Bird), **Supp. X:** 19, 24–26, 28

Hawes, Stephen, **I:** 49, 81

"Hawk, The" (Brown), **Supp. VI:** 71

Hawk in the Rain, The (Hughes), **Supp. I:** 343, 345, 363

"Hawk in the Rain, The" (Hughes), **Supp. I:** 345; **Retro. Supp. II:** 200, 202–204

"Hawk Roosting" (Hughes), **Retro. Supp. II:** 204

Hawkfall (Brown), **Supp. VI:** 69

Hawkins, Lewis Weldon, **VI:** 85

Hawkins, Sir John, **II:** 143

Hawksmoor (Ackroyd), **Supp. VI:** 6–7, 10–11

Hawthorne, Nathaniel, **III:** 339, 345; **VI:** 27, 33–34; **Supp. IV:** 116

Hawthorne (James), **VI:** 33–34, 67

Haxton, Gerald, **VI:** 369

Hay Fever (Coward), **Supp. II:** 139, 141, **143–145,** 148, 156

Haydon, Benjamin, **IV:** 214, 227, 312

Hayes, Albert McHarg, **Retro. Supp. II:** 181

"Haymaking" (Thomas), **Supp. III:** 399, 405

"Haystack in the Floods, The" (Morris), **V:** 293

Hayter, Alethea, **III:** 338, 346; **IV:** xxiv–xxv, 57, 322

Hazard, Paul, **III:** 72

"Hazards of the House" (Dunn), **Supp. X:** 68

Hazlitt, William, **I:** 121, 164; **II:** 153, 332, 333, 337, 343, 346, 349, 354, 361, 363, 364; **III:** 68, 70, 76, 78, 165, 276–277; **IV:** ix, xi, xiv, xvii–xix, 38, 39, 41, 50, **125–140,** 217; **Retro. Supp. I:** 147; **Retro. Supp. II:** 51, 52

"He" (Lessing), **Supp. I:** 244

He Came Down from Heaven (Williams, C. W. S.), **Supp. IX:** 284

He Knew He Was Right (Trollope), **V:** 98, 99, 102

"He Revisits His First School" (Hardy), **VI:** 17

"He saw my heart's woe" (Brontë), **V:** 132

"He Says Goodbye in November" (Cornford), **VIII:** 114

He That Will Not When He May (Oliphant), **Supp. X:** 220

"He Thinks of His Past Greatness . . . When a Part of the Constellations of Heaven" (Yeats), **VI:** 211

"He thought he saw a Banker's Clerk" (Carroll), **V:** 270

"He Wonders Whether to Praise or to Blame Her" (Brooke), **Supp. III:** 55

Head to Toe (Orton), **Supp. V:** 363, 365–366

"Head Spider, The" (Murray), **Supp. VII:** 283, 284

Heading Home (Hare), **Supp. IV:** 288, 290–291

Headlong (Frayn), **Supp. VII:** 64, 65

Headlong Hall (Peacock), **IV:** xvii, **160–163,** 164, 165, 168, 169

Healers, The (Armah), **Supp. X:** 1–3, 6–11, 13

Healing Art, The (Wilson), **Supp. VI:** **299–300,** 301, 303, 308

Health and Holiness (Thompson), **V:** 450, 451

"Healthy Landscape with Dormouse" (Warner), **Supp. VII:** 380

Healy, Dermot, **Supp. IX:** **95–108**

Heaney, Seamus, **Supp. II:** **267–281;** **Supp. IV:** 410, 412, 416, 420–421, 427, 428; **Retro. Supp. I:** 123–135

Hear Us O Lord from Heaven Thy Dwelling Place (Lowry), **Supp. III:** **281–282**

Hearing Secret Harmonies (Powell), **VII:** 352, 353

"Hears not my Phillis, how the Birds" (Sedley), **II:** 264

Heart and Science (Collins), **Supp. VI:** 102–103

"Heart, II, The" (Thompson), **V:** 443

Heart Clock (Hill, R.), **Supp. IX:** 111

"Heart Knoweth Its Own Bitterness, The" (Rossetti), **V:** 253–254

"Heart of a King, The" (Plomer), **Supp. XI:** 226

Heart of Darkness (Conrad), **VI:** 135, **136–139,** 172; **Supp. IV:** 189, 250, 403; **Retro. Supp. II:** 73–75

"Heart of John Middleton, The" (Gaskell), **V:** 15

Heart of Mid–Lothian, The (Scott), **IV:** xvii, 30, 31, 33–34, 35, 36, 39; **V:** 5

Heart of the Country, The (Weldon), **Supp. IV:** 526–528

Heart of the Matter, The (Greene), **Supp. I:** 2, 8, 11–12, 13; **Retro. Supp. II:** 157–159

Heart to Heart (Rattigan), **Supp. VII:** 320

Heartbreak (Maitland), **Supp. XI:** 165

Heartbreak House (Shaw), **V:** 423; **VI:** viii, xv, 118, **120–121,** 127, 129; **Retro. Supp. II:** 322–323

Heartland (Harris), **Supp. V:** 135, 136

Hearts and Lives of Men, The (Weldon), **Supp. IV:** 536

"Heart's Chill Between" (Rossetti), **V:** 249, 252

"Heat" (Hart), **Supp. XI:** 132

Heat and Dust (Jhabvala), **Supp. V:** 224, 230, 231–232, 238

Heat of the Day, The (Bowen), **Supp. II:** 77, 78, 79, 93, 95

"Heather Ale" (Stevenson), **V:** 396

Heather Field, The (Martyn), **IV:** 87, 95

"Heaven" (Brooke), **Supp. III:** 56, 60

Heaven and Earth (Byron), **IV:** 178, 193

Heaven and Its Wonders, and Hell (Swedenborg), **Retro. Supp. I:** 38

Heavenly Foot–man, The (Bunyan), **II:** 246, 253

Heaven's Command: An Imperial Progress (Morris, J.), **Supp. X:** 173, 179–180

Heaven's Edge (Gunesekera), **Supp. X:** 85–86, 96–100

"Heber" (Smith), **Supp. II:** 466

Hebert, Ann Marie, **Supp. IV:** 523

Hebrew Melodies, Ancient and Modern . . . (Byron), **IV:** 192

"Hebrides, The" (Longley), **VIII:** 168–169

Hecatommitthi (Cinthio), **I:** 316

Hedda Gabler (Ibsen), **Supp. IV:** 163, 286

"Hedgehog" (Muldoon), **Supp. IV:** 414

"Hee–Haw" (Warner), **Supp. VII:** 380

Heel of Achilles, The (Koestler), **Supp. I:** 36

"Heepocondry" (Crawford), **Supp. XI:** 76

Hegel, Georg Wilhelm Friedrich, **Supp. II:** 22

Heiðreks saga, **VIII:** 231

"Height–ho on a Winter Afternoon" (Davie), **Supp. VI:** 107–108

"Heil Baldwin" (Caudwell), **Supp. IX:** 38

Heilbrun, Carolyn G., **Supp. IV:** 336

Heimskringla, **VIII:** 235, 242

Heine, Heinrich, **IV:** xviii, 296

Heinemann, William, **VII:** 91

"Heiress, The" (McGuckian), **Supp. V:** 282

Heit, S. Mark, **Supp. IV:** 339

"Hélas" (Wilde), **V:** 401

Helen (Scott), **Supp. III:** 151, **165–166**

Helena (Waugh), **VII:** 292, 293–294, 301

Hélène Fourment in a Fur Coat (Rubens), **Supp. IV:** 89

Hellas (Shelley), **IV:** xviii, 206, 208; **Retro. Supp. I:** 255

Hellenics, The (Landor), **IV:** 96, 100

"Helmet, The" (Longley), **VIII:** 176

Héloise and Abélard (Moore), **VI:** xii, 88, 89, **94–95,** 99

"Helplessly" (Smith, I. C.), **Supp. IX:** 217

Hemans, Felicia, **IV:** 311

Hemingway, Ernest, **Supp. III:** 105; **Supp. IV:** 163, 209, 500

Hemlock and After (Wilson), **Supp. I:** 155–156, 157, 158–159, 160, 161, 164

Hello, America (Ballard), **Supp. V:** 29

"Hen Woman" (Kinsella), **Supp. V:** 266–267

Henceforward (Ayckbourn), **Supp. V:** 3, 10, 11, 13

"Hendecasyllabics" (Swinburne), **V:** 321

"Hendecasyllabics" (Tennyson), **IV:** 327–328

Henderson, Hamish, **VII:** 422, 425–426

Henderson, Hubert, **VII:** 35

Henderson, Philip, **V:** xii, xviii, 335

Henderson, T. F., **IV:** 290n

Hengist, King of Kent; or, The Mayor of Quinborough (Middleton), **II:** 3, 21

Henley, William Ernest, **V:** 386, 389, 391–392; **VI:** 159; **Retro. Supp. I:** 260, 264

Henn, T. R., **VI:** 220

"Henrietta Marr" (Moore), **VI:** 87

Henrietta Temple (Disraeli), **IV:** xix, 293, 298–299, 307, 308

"Henrik Ibsen" (James), **VI:** 49

Henry Esmond (Thackeray), *see History of Henry Esmond, Esq. . . . , The*

Henry for Hugh (Ford), **VI:** 331

"Henry James" (Nye), **Supp. X:** 201

Henry James (ed. Tanner), **VI:** 68

Henry James (West), **Supp. III:** 437

"Henry James: The Religious Aspect" (Greene), **Supp. I:** 8

"Henry Petroski, The Pencil. A History. Faber and Faber, £14.95" (Dunn), **Supp. X:** 79

"Henry Purcell" (Hopkins), **V:** 370–371; **Retro. Supp. II:** 196

Henry Reed: Collected Poems (Stallworthy), **Supp. X:** 292

Henry II (Bancroft), **II:** 305

Henry IV (Shakespeare), **I:** 308–309, 320

Henry V (Shakespeare), **I:** 309; **V:** 383; **Supp. IV:** 258

Henry VI trilogy (Shakespeare), **I:** 286, 299–300, 309

Henry VI's Triumphal Entry into London (Lydgate), **I:** 58

Henry VIII (Shakespeare), **I:** 324; **II:** 43, 66, 87; **V:** 328

"Henry VIII and Ann Boleyn" (Landor), **IV:** 92

Henry Vaughan: Experience and the Tradition (Garner), **II:** 186n

Henry's Past (Churchill), **Supp. IV:** 181

Henryson, Robert, **Supp. VII:** **135–149**

Henslowe, Philip, **I:** 228, 235, 284; **II:** 3, 25, 68

Henty, G. A., **Supp. IV:** 201

"Her Second Husband Hears Her Story" (Hardy), **Retro. Supp. I:** 120

Her Triumph (Johnson), **I:** 347

Her Vertical Smile (Kinsella), **Supp. V:** 270–271

Her Victory (Sillitoe), **Supp. V:** 411, 415, 422, 425

Herakles (Euripides), **IV:** 358

Herbert, Edward, pseud. of John Hamilton Reynolds

Herbert, Edward, *see* Herbert of Cherbury, Lord

Herbert, George, **II:** 113, **117–130,** 133, 134, 137, 138, 140–142, 184, 187, 216, 221; **Retro. Supp. II: 169–184**

Herbert of Cherbury, Lord, **II:** 117–118, 222, 237, 238

Herbert's Remains (Oley), **Retro. Supp. II:** 170–171

Hercule Poirot's Last Case (Christie), **Supp. II:** 125

"Hercules" (Armitage), **VIII:** 12

"Hercules and Antaeus" (Heaney), **Supp. II:** 274–275

Hercules Oetaeus (Seneca), **I:** 248

"Here" (Larkin), **Supp. I:** 279, 285

"Here and There" (Dunn), **Supp. X:** 77–78

"Here Be Dragons" (Dunn), **Supp. X:** 72

Here Comes Everybody: An Introduction to James Joyce for the Ordinary Reader (Burgess), **Supp. I:** 194, 196–197

Here Lies: An Autobiography (Ambler), **Supp. IV:** 1, 2, 3, 4

"Heredity" (Harrison), **Supp. V:** 152

Heretics (Chesterton), **VI:** 204, 336–337

Hering, Carl Ewald, **Supp. II:** 107–108

Heritage and Its History, A (Compton–Burnett), **VII:** 60, 61, 65

Hermaphrodite Album, The (Redgrove), **Supp. VI:** 230

"Hermaphroditus" (Swinburne), **V:** 320

Hermetical Physick . . . Englished (tr. Vaughan), **II:** 185, 201

Hermit of Marlow, The, pseud. of Percy Bysshe Shelley

"Hero" (Rossetti), **V:** 260

"Hero and Leander" (Hood), **IV:** 255–256, 267

Hero and Leander (Marlowe), **I:** 234, 237–240, 276, 278, 280, 288, **290–291,** 292; **Retro. Supp. I:** 211

Hero and Leander, in Burlesque (Wycherley), **II:** 321

"Hero as King, The" (Carlyle), **IV:** 245, 246

Hero Rises Up, The (Arden and D'Arcy), **Supp. II:** 31

"Heroine, The" (Highsmith), **Supp. V:** 180

Herodotus, **Supp. IV:** 110

Heroes and Hero–Worship (Carlyle), **IV:** xx, 240, 244–246, 249, 250, 341

Heroes and Villains (Carter), **Supp. III:** 81, 84

Heroic Idylls, with Additional Poems (Landor), **IV:** 100

"Heroic Stanzas" (Dryden), **II:** 292

Heroine, The; or, The Adventures of Cherubina (Barrett), **III:** 335

"Heron, The" (Nye), **Supp. X:** 205

Heron Caught in Weeds, A (Roberts, K.), **Supp. X:** 273–275

Herrick, Robert, **II: 102–116,** 121

Herself Surprised (Cary), **VII:** 186, 188, 191–192

"Hertha" (Swinburne), **V:** 325

Hervarar saga, See Heiðreks saga

"Hervé Riel" (Browning), **IV:** 367

Herzog, Werner, **IV:** 180

"Hesperia" (Swinburne), **V:** 320, 321

Hesperides, The (Herrick), **II:** 102, 103, 104, 106, 110, 112, 115, 116

Hester (Oliphant), **Supp. X:** 217–218

"Hester Dominy" (Powys), **VIII:** 250

Hexameron; or, Meditations on the Six Days of Creation, and Meditations and Devotions on the Life of Christ (Traherne), **Supp. XI:** 268, 269, 277–278

Heyday of Sir Walter Scott, The (Davie), **Supp. VI:** 114–115

Heylyn, Peter, **I:** 169

Heywood, Jasper, **I:** 215

Heywood, Thomas, **II:** 19, 47, 48, 68, 83

"Hexagon" (Murphy), **Supp. V:** 328

Hibberd, Dominic, **VI:** xvi, xxxiii

Hide, The (Unsworth), **Supp. VII:** 354, 356

"Hide and Seek" (Gunn), **Supp. IV:** 272

Hide and Seek (Collins), **Supp. VI:** 92, 95

Hide and Seek (Rankin), **Supp. X:** 244, 246, 248–250

Hide and Seek (Swinburne), **V:** 334

"Hidden History, A" (Okri), **Supp. V:** 352

Hidden Ireland, The (Corkery), **Supp. V:** 41

"Hidden Law" (MacCaig), **Supp. VI:** 186

Higden, Ranulf, **I:** 22

Higgins, F. R., **Supp. IV:** 411, 413

"Higgler, The" (Coppard), **VIII:** 85, 90, 95

Higgler and Other Tales, The (Coppard), **VIII:** 90

High Island: New and Selected Poems (Murphy), **Supp. V:** 313, 315, 316, 324–325

"High Life in Verdopolis" (Brontë), **V:** 135

"High wavering heather . . . " (Brontë), **V:** 113

High Windows (Larkin), **Supp. I:** 277, 280, **281–284,** 285, 286

Higher Ground (Phillips), **Supp. V:** 380, 386–388

Higher Schools and Universities in Germany (Arnold), **V:** 216

"Higher Standards" (Wilson), **Supp. I:** 155

Highet, Gilbert, **II:** 199

Highland Fling (Mitford), **Supp. X:** 152–154

"Highland Funeral" (MacCaig), **Supp. VI:** 193

Highland Widow, The (Scott), **IV:** 39

Highlander, The (Macpherson), **VIII:** 181–182, 190

Highly Dangerous (Ambler), **Supp. IV:** 3

High–Rise (Ballard), **Supp. V:** 27

High Summer (Rattigan), **Supp. VII:** 315

Highsmith, Patricia, **Supp. IV:** 285; **Supp. V: 167–182**

"Highwayman and the Saint, The" (Friel), **Supp. V:** 118

Hilaire Belloc (Wilson), **Supp. VI:** 301–302

Hilda Lessways (Bennett), **VI:** 258; **Supp. IV:** 238

Hill, G. B., **III:** 233, 234n

Hill, Geoffrey, **Supp. V: 183–203**

"Hill, The" (Brooke), **Supp. III:** 51

Hill of Devi, The (Forster), **VI:** 397, 408, 411

"Hill of Venus, The" (Morris), **V:** 298

Hill, Reginald, **Supp. IX: 109–126**

Hilton, Walter, **Supp. I:** 74

Hind, The, and the Panther (Dryden), **II:** 291, 292, 299–300, 304

Hinge of Faith, The (Churchill), **VI:** 361

Hinman, Charlton, **I:** 326–327

Hinton, William, **Supp. IV:** 284

"Hints" (Reading), **VIII:** 265–266

Hints Towards the Formation of a More Comprehensive Theory of Life (Coleridge), **IV:** 56

Hippolytus (Euripides), **V:** 322, 324

Hips and Haws (Coppard), **VIII:** 89, 98

Hireling, The (Hartley), **Supp. VII:** 129–131

"His Age, Dedicated to his Peculiar Friend, M. John Wickes" (Herrick), **II:** 112

His Arraignment (Jonson), **Retro. Supp. I:** 158

"His Chosen Calling" (Naipaul), **Supp. I:** 385

"His Country" (Hardy), **Retro. Supp. I:** 120–121

His Darling Sin (Braddon), **VIII:** 49

"His Fare–well to Sack" (Herrick), **II:** 111

"His Father's Hands" (Kinsella), **Supp. V:** 268

"His Last Bow" (Doyle), **Supp. II:** 175

"His Letanie, to the Holy Spirit" (Herrick), **II:** 114

His Majesties Declaration Defended (Dryden), **II:** 305

His Majesty Preserved . . . Dictated to Samuel Pepys by the King . . . (ed. Rees–Mogg), **II:** 288

His Noble Numbers (Herrick), **II:** 102, 103, 112, 114, 115, 116

"His Returne to London" (Herrick), **II:** 103

His Second War (Waugh), **Supp. VI:** 274

Historia naturalis et experimentalis (Bacon), **I:** 259, 273

Historia regis Henrici Septimi (André), **I:** 270

Historiae adversum paganos (Orosius), **Retro. Supp. II:** 296

"Historian, The" (Fuller), **Supp. VII:** 74

"Historian of Silence, The" (Hart), **Supp. XI:** 132

Historical Account of the Theatre in Europe, An (Riccoboni), **II:** 348

Historical Register, The (Fielding), **III:** 97, 98, 105; **Retro. Supp. I:** 82

Historical Relation of the Island of Ceylon, An (Knox), **III:** 7

"Historical Sketches of the Reign of George Second" (Oliphant), **Supp. X:** 222

"Historical Society" (Murphy), **Supp. V:** 322

"History" (Macaulay), **IV:** 284

History and Adventures of an Atom, The (Smollett), **III:** 149–150, 158

History and Adventures of Joseph Andrews and of His Friend Mr. Abraham Adams (Fielding), **Retro. Supp. I:** 80, 83–86

History and Management of the East India Company (Macpherson), **VIII:** 193

History and Remarkable Life of . . . Col. Jack (Defoe), *see Colonel Jack*

History Maker, A (Gray, A.), **Supp. IX:** 80, 87–88

History of a Good Warm Watch–Coat, The (Sterne), *see Political Romance, A*

"History of a Piece of Paper" (Sisson), **Supp. XI:** 248

History of a Six Weeks' Tour Through a Part of France . . . (Shelley and Shelley), **IV:** 208; **Supp. III:** 355

"History of Angria" (Brontë), **V:** 110–111, 118

History of Antonio and Mellida, The (Marston), *see Antonio and Mellida*

History of Brazil (Southey), **IV:** 68, 71

History of Britain . . . , The (Milton), **II:** 176

History of British India, The, (Mill), **V:** 288

History of Dorastus and Fawni, The (Greene). *See Pandosto: or, The Triumph of Time*

History of England (Hume), **II:** 148; **IV:** 273; **Supp. III:** 229, 238–239

History of England, An (Goldsmith), **III:** 180, 181, 189, 191

History of England, The (Trevelyan), **VI:** xv, 390–391, 393

History of England from the Accession of James II, The (Macaulay), **II:** 255; **IV:** xx, 272, 273, 280, 282, **283–290,** 291

History of England in the Eighteenth Century (Lecky), **Supp. V:** 41

House of Dolls, The (Comyns), **VIII:** 53, 65

"House of Dreams, The" (Thomas), **Supp. IV:** 493

House of Fame, The (Chaucer), **I:** 23, 30; **Retro. Supp. II:** 38–39

House of Hospitalities, The (Tennant), **Supp. IX:** 239

House of Life, The (Rossetti), **V:** 237, 238, 241, 242, 243, 244, 245

House of Pomegranates, A (Wilde), **V:** 419; **Retro. Supp. II:** 365

House of Seven Gables, The (Hawthorne), **III:** 339, 345

House of Sleep, The (Kavan), **Supp. VII:** 212–213

House of Splendid Isolation (O'Brien), **Supp. V:** 341–344

House on the Beach, The (Meredith), **V:** 230–231, 234

House on the Strand, The (du Maurier), **Supp. III:** 138, 139, 140, 141, 147

House of Titans and Other Poems, The (Russell), **VIII:** 277, 290, 292

"House of Titans, The" (Russell), **VIII:** 290

"House We Lived In, The" (Smith, I. C.), **Supp. IX:** 214

House with the Echo, The (Powys), **VIII:** 248, 249, 254

"Household Spirits" (Kinsella), **Supp. V:** 272

Household Words (periodical), **V:** xxi, 3, 42

Householder, The (Jhabvala), **Supp. V:** 227–228, 237

Housman, A. E., **III:** 68, 70; **V:** xxii, xxvi, 311; **VI:** ix, xv–xvi, **151–164,** 415

Housman, Laurence, **V:** 402, 420

Housman: 1897–1936 (Richards), **VI:** 164

How About Europe? (Douglas), **VI:** 295, 305

"How Are the Children Robin" (Graham), **Supp. VII:** 115

How Brophy Made Good (Hare), **Supp. IV:** 281

How Can We Know? (Wilson), **Supp. VI:** 305

"How Distant" (Larkin), **Supp. I:** 284

"How Do You See"(Smith), **Supp. II:** 467

How Far Can We Go? (Lodge; U.S. title, *Souls and Bodies*), **Supp. IV:** 366, 368, 371, 372, 375–376, 381, 408

How He Lied to Her Husband (Shaw), **VI:** 129

How I Became a Holy Mother and Other Stories (Jhabvala), **Supp. V:** 235

"How I Became a Socialist" (Orwell), **VII:** 276–277

How It Is (Beckett), **Supp. I:** 43, 50, 52, 54–55, 58

"How It Strikes a Contemporary" (Browning), **IV:** 354, 367, 373

How Late It Was, How Late (Kelman), **Supp. V:** 243, 252–254

How Lisa Loved the King (Eliot), **V:** 200

"How Many Bards" (Keats), **IV:** 215

"How Pillingshot Scored" (Wodehouse), **Supp. III:** 449–450

How Right You Are, Jeeves (Wodehouse), **Supp. III:** 460, 461, 462

"How Sleep the Brave" (Collins), **III:** 166

"How soon the servant sun" (Thomas), **Supp. I:** 174

"How Sweet the Name of Jesus Sounds" (Newton), **III:** 210

How the "Mastiffs" Went to Iceland (Trollope), **V:** 102

How the Other Half Lives (Ayckbourn), **Supp. V:** 2, 4, 9, 11, 12

How the Whale Became (Hughes), **Supp. I:** 346

"How They Brought the Good News from Ghent to Aix (16—)" (Browning), **IV:** 356, 361

How this foirsaid Tod maid his Confession to Freir Wolf Waitskaith (Henryson), see *Fox and the Wolf, The*

"How to Accomplish It" (Newman), **Supp. VII:** 293

How to Become an Author (Bennett), **VI:** 264

"How to Kill" (Douglas), **VII: 443**

How to Live on 24 Hours a Day (Bennett), **VI:** 264

How to Read (Pound), **VII:** 235

How to Read a Page (Richards), **Supp. II:** 426

How to Settle the Irish Question (Shaw), **VI:** 119, 129

"How to Teach Reading" (Leavis), **VII:** 235, 248

"How would the ogling sparks despise" (Etherege), **II:** 268

"How You Love Our Lady" (Blackwood), **Supp. IX:** 9

Howard, Elizabeth Jane, **Supp. XI: 136–151**

Howard, Henry, earl of Surrey, *see* Surrey, Henry Howard, earl of

Howard, R., **V:** 418

Howard, Sir Robert, **II:** 100

Howards End (Forster), **VI:** viii, xii, 397, 398, 401, **404–406,** 407; **Supp. I:** 161; **Retro. Supp. II:** 143–145

Howarth, R. G., **II:** 69

Howe, Irving, **VI:** 41

Howells, William Dean, **VI:** 23, 29, 33

Howitt, William, **IV:** 212

Hrafnkels saga, **VIII:** 242

Hubert De Vere (Burney), **Supp. III:** 71

Huchon, René, **III:** 273n

Hudibras (Butler), **II:** 145

Hudson, Derek, **V:** xi, xxviii, 263, 274

Hudson, W. H., **V:** 429

Hudson Letter, The (Mahon), **Supp. VI:** 175–176

Hueffer, Ford Madox, *see* Ford, Ford Madox

"Hug, The" (Gunn), **Supp. IV:** 274–275, 276, 277

Huggan, Graham, **Supp. IV:** 170

Hugh Selwyn Mauberley (Pound), **VI:** 417; **VII:** xvi

Hughes, Arthur, **V:** 294

Hughes, John, **I:** 121, 122; **III:** 40

Hughes, Ted, **Supp. I: 341–366; Supp. IV:** 257; **Supp. V:** xxx; **Retro. Supp. I:** 126; **Retro. Supp. II: 199–219**

Hughes, Thomas, **I:** 218; **V:** xxii, 170; **Supp. IV:** 506

Hughes, Willie, **V:** 405

Hugo, Victor, **III:** 334; **V:** xxii, xxv, 22, 320; **Supp. IV:** 86

Hugo (Bennett), **VI:** 249

Huis clos (Sartre), **Supp. IV:** 39

Hulme, T. E., **VI:** 416; **Supp. VI: 133–147**

Hulse, Michael, **Supp. IV:** 354

"Human Abstract, The" (Blake), **III:** 296

Human Age, The (Lewis), **VII:** 80

Human Face, The (Smith, I. C.), **Supp. IX:** 221–223

Human Factor, The (Greene), **Supp. I:** 2, 11, 16–17; **Retro. Supp. II:** 165–166

"Human Life, on the Denial of Immortality" (Coleridge), **Retro. Supp. II:** 65

Human Machine, The (Bennett), **VI:** 250

Human Odds and Ends (Gissing), **V:** 437

"Human Seasons, The" (Keats), **IV:** 232

Human Shows, Far Phantasies, Songs and Trifles (Hardy), **VI:** 20

Human Voices (Fitzgerald), **Supp. V:** 95, 100, 103

"Humanism and the Religious Attitude" (Hulme), **Supp. VI:** 135, 140

"Humanitad" (Wilde), **V:** 401–402

Humble Administrator's Garden, The (Seth), **Supp. X:** 281

"Humble Petition of Frances Harris" (Swift), **III:** 30–31

Humboldt's Gift (Bellow), **Supp. IV:** 27, 33, 42

Hume, David, **III:** 148; **IV:** xiv, 138, 145, 273, 288; **V:** 288, 343; **Supp. III: 220–245**

Humiliation with Honour (Brittain), **Supp. X:** 45

"Humility" (Brome), **Supp. X:** 55

Humorous Day's Mirth, A (Chapman), **I:** 243, 244

Humorous Lieutenant, The (Fletcher), **II:** 45, 60–61, 65, 359

Humours of the Court (Bridges), **VI:** 83

Humphrey Clinker (Smollett), **III:** 147, 150, **155–157,** 158

"Hunchback in the Park, The" (Thomas), **Supp. I:** 177, 178

"Hundred Years, A" (Motion), **Supp. VII:** 266

Hundredth Story, The (Coppard), **VIII:** 89

Hungarian Lift–Jet, The (Banks), **Supp. XI:** 1

"Hunger" (Lessing), **Supp. I:** 240

Hungry Hill (du Maurier), **Supp. III:** 144

Hunt, John, **IV:** 129, 132

Hunt, Leigh, **II:** 332, 355, 357, 359, 363; **IV:** ix, 80, 104, 129, 132, 163, 172, 198, 202, 205–206, 209, 212–217, 230, 306; **Retro. Supp. I:** 183, 248

Hunt, Violet, **VI:** 324

Hunt, William Holman, **V:** 45, 77–78, 235, 236, 240

Hunt by Night, The (Mahon), **Supp. VI:** 173–174, 177

Jocelyn (Galsworthy), **VI:** 277

"Jochanan Hakkadosh" (Browning), **IV:** 365

Jocoseria (Browning), **IV:** 359, 374

"Joe Soap" (Motion), **Supp. VII:** 260–261, 262

Joe's Ark (Potter, D.), **Supp. X:** 229, 237–240

"Johann Joachim Quantz's Five Lessons" (Graham), **Supp. VII:** 116

"Johannes Agricola in Meditation" (Browning), **IV:** 360

Johannes Secundus, **II:** 108

"John Betjeman's Brighton" (Ewart), **Supp. VII:** 37

John Bull's Other Island (Shaw), **VI:** 112, **113–115; Retro. Supp. II:** 320–321

John Caldigate (Trollope), **V:** 102

"John Clare" (Cope), **VIII:** 82

John Clare: Poems, Chiefly from Manuscript (Clare), **Supp. XI:** 36, 63

John Clare by Himself (Clare), **Supp. XI:** 51

"John Fletcher" (Swinburne), **V:** 332

John Gabriel Borkman (Ibsen), **VI:** 110

"John Galsworthy" (Lawrence), **VI:** 275–276, 290

John Galsworthy (Mottram), **VI:** 271, 275, 290

"John Galsworthy, An Appreciation" (Conrad), **VI:** 290

"John Gilpin" (Cowper), **III:** 212, 220

John Keats: A Reassessment (ed. Muir), **IV:** 219, 227, 236

John Keats: His Like and Writings (Bush), **IV:** 224, 236

John Knox (Muir), **Supp. VI:** 198

"John Knox" (Smith, I. C.), **Supp. IX:** 211–212

"John Logie Baird" (Crawford), **Supp. XI:** 71

John M. Synge (Masefield), **VI:** 317

John Marchmont's Legacy (Braddon), **VIII:** 44, 46

"John Norton" (Moore), **VI:** 98

"John of the Cross" (Jennings), **Supp. V:** 207

"John Ruskin" (Proust), **V:** 183

John Ruskin: The Portrait of a Prophet (Quennell), **V:** 185

John Sherman and Dhoya (Yeats), **VI:** 221

John Thomas and Lady Jane (Lawrence), **VII:** 111–112

John Woodvil (Lamb), **IV:** 78–79, 85

Johnnie Sahib (Scott), **Supp. I:** 259, 261

Johnny I Hardly Knew You (O'Brien), **Supp. V:** 338, 339

Johnny in the Clouds (Rattigan), see Way to the Stars, The

Johnson, Edgar, **IV:** 27, 40; **V:** 60, 72

Johnson, James, **III:** 320, 322

Johnson, Joseph, **Retro. Supp. I:** 37

Johnson, Lionel, **VI:** 3, 210, 211

Johnson, Samuel, **III:** 54, 96, **107–123,** 127, 151, 275; **IV:** xiv, xv, 27, 31, 34, 88n, 101, 138, 268, 299; **V:** 9, 281, 287; **VI:** 363; **Retro. Supp. I: 137–150;** and Boswell, **III:** 234, 235, 238, 239, 243–249; and Collins, **III:** 160, 163, 164, 171, 173; and Crabbe, **III:** 280–282; and Goldsmith, **III:** 177, 180, 181, 189; dictionary, **III:** 113–116; **V:** 281, 434; literary criticism, **I:** 326; **II:** 123, 173, 197, 200, 259, 263, 293, 301, 347; **III:** 11, 88, 94, 139, 257, 275; **V:** 101; on Addison and Steele, **III:** 39, 42, 44, 49, 51; **Supp. IV:** 271

Johnson, W. E., **Supp. II:** 406

Johnson over Jordan (Priestley), **VII:** 226–227

"Joker, The" (Wallace–Crabbe), **VIII:** 315–316

"Joker as Told" (Murray), **Supp. VII:** 279

Joking Apart (Ayckbourn), **Supp. V:** 3, 9, 13, 14

Jolly Beggars, The (Burns), **III:** 319–320

"Jolly Corner, The" (James), **Retro. Supp. I:** 2

Jonah Who Will Be 25 in the Year 2000 (film), **Supp. IV:** 79

Jonathan Swift (Stephen), **V:** 289

Jonathan Wild (Fielding), **III:** 99, 103, 105, 150; **Retro. Supp. I:** 80–81, 90

Jones, David, **VI:** xvi, 436, 437–439, **Supp. VII: 167–182**

Jones, Henry Arthur, **VI:** 367, 376

Jones, Henry Festing, **Supp. II:** 103–104, 112, 114, 117, 118

Jonestown (Harris), **Supp. V:** 144–145

Jonson, Ben, **I:** 228, 234–235, 270, **335–351; II:** 3, 4, 24, 25, 27, 28, 30, 45, 47, 48, 55, 65, 79, 87, 104, 108, 110, 111n, 115, 118, 141, 199, 221–223; **IV:** 35, 327; **V:** 46, 56; **Supp. IV:** 256; **Retro. Supp. I: 151–167**

Jonsonus Virbius (Digby), **Retro. Supp. I:** 166

Jonsonus Virbius (King), **Supp. VI:** 157

Joseph Andrews (Fielding), **III:** 94, 95, 96, 99–100, 101, 105; **Retro. Supp. I:** 80, 83–86

Joseph Conrad (Baines), **VI:** 133–134

Joseph Conrad (Ford), **VI:** 321, 322

Joseph Conrad (Walpole), **VI:** 149

Joseph Conrad: A Personal Reminiscence (Ford), **VI:** 149

Joseph Conrad: The Modern Imagination (Cox), **VI:** 149

Joseph Conrad and Charles Darwin: The Influence of Scientific Thought on Conrad's Fiction (O'Hanlon), **Supp. XI:** 197

"Joseph Grimaldi" (Hood), **IV:** 267

"Joseph Yates' Temptation" (Gissing), **V:** 437

Journal (Mansfield), **VII:** 181, 182

Journal, 1825–32 (Scott), **IV:** 39

Journal and Letters of Fanny Burney, The (eds. Hemlow et al.), **Supp. III:** 63

Journal of Bridget Hitler, The (Bainbridge), **Supp. VI:** 22

Journal of a Dublin Lady, The (Swift), **III:** 35

Journal of a Landscape Painter in Corsica (Lear), **V:** 87

Journal of a Tour in Scotland in 1819 (Southey), **IV:** 71

Journal of a Tour in the Netherlands in the Autumn of 1815 (Southey), **IV:** 71

Journal of a Tour to the Hebrides, The (Boswell), **III:** 117, 234n, 235, 243, 245, 248, 249

Journal of a Voyage to Lisbon, The (Fielding), **III:** 104, 105

Journal of Beatrix Potter from 1881 to 1897, The (ed. Linder), **Supp. III: 292–295**

"Journal of My Jaunt, Harvest 1762" (Boswell), **III:** 241–242

Journal of Researches into the Geology and Natural History of the various countries visited by HMS Beagle (Darwin), **Supp. VII:** 18–19

Journal of the Plague Year, A (Defoe), **III:** 5–6, 8, 13; **Retro. Supp. I:** 63, 73–74

Journal to Eliza, The (Sterne), **III:** 125, 126, 132, 135

Journal to Stella (Swift), **II:** 335; **III:** 32–33, 34; **Retro. Supp. I:** 274

Journalism (Mahon), **Supp. VI:** 166

Journalism for Women: A Practical Guide (Bennett), **VI:** 264, 266

Journals and Papers of Gerard Manley Hopkins, The (ed. House and Storey), **V:** 362, 363, 371, 378–379, 381

Journals 1939–1983 (Spender), **Supp. II:** 481, 487, 490, 493

Journals of a Landscape Painter in Albania etc. (Lear), **V:** 77, 79–80, 87

Journals of a Landscape Painter in Southern Calabria . . . (Lear), **V:** 77, 79, 87

Journals of a Residence in Portugal, 1800–1801, and a Visit to France, 1838 (Southey), **IV:** 71

Journals of Arnold Bennett (Bennett), **VI:** 265, 267

"Journals of Progress" (Durrell), **Supp. I:** 124

"Journey, The" (Boland), **Supp. V:** 41

"Journey Back, The" (Muir), **Supp. VI:** 207

Journey Continued (Paton), **Supp. II:** 356, 359

Journey from Cornhill to Grand Cairo, A (Thackeray), see Notes of a Journey from Cornhill to Grand Cairo

Journey from This World to the Next (Fielding), **Retro. Supp. I:** 80

Journey into Fear (Ambler), **Supp. IV:** 11–12

"Journey of John Gilpin, The" (Cowper), see A John Gilpin"

"Journey of the Magi, The" (Eliot), **VII:** 152

Journey Through France (Piozzi), **III:** 134

Journey to a War (Auden and Isherwood), **VII:** 312; **Retro. Supp. I:** 9

Journey to Armenia (Mandelstam), **Supp. IV:** 163, 170

"Journey to Bruges, The" (Mansfield), **VII:** 172

Journey to Ithaca (Desai), **Supp. V:** 56, 66, 73–74

Meredith et la France (Mackay), **V:** 223, 234

"Meredithian Sonnets" (Fuller), **Supp. VII:** 74

Meres, Francis, **I:** 212, 234, 296, 307

Merie Tales, The, **I:** 83, 93

Meriton, George, **II:** 340

Merkin, Daphne, **Supp. IV:** 145–146

Merleau–Ponty, Maurice, **Supp. IV:** 79, 88

Merlin (Nye), **Supp. X:** 195

"Merlin and the Gleam" (Tennyson), **IV:** 329

Mermaid, Dragon, Fiend (Graves), **VII:** 264

Merope (Arnold), **V:** 209, 216

"Merry Beggars, The" (Brome), **Supp. X:** 55

Merry England (periodical), **V:** 440

Merry Jests of George Peele, The, **I:** 194

Merry Men, and Other Tales and Fables, The (Stevenson), **V:** 395; **Retro. Supp. I:** 267

Merry Wives of Windsor, The (Shakespeare), **I:** 295, 311; **III:** 117

Merry–Go–Round, The (Lawrence), **VII:** 120

Merry–Go–Round, The (Maugham), **VI:** 372

Mescellanies (Fielding), **Retro. Supp. I:** 80

Meschonnic, Henri, **Supp. IV:** 115

Mespoulet, M., **V:** 266

"Message, The" (Donne), **Retro. Supp. II:** 90

"Message, The" (Russell), **VIII:** 280–281

"Message Clear" (Morgan, E.), **Supp. IX:** 165

"Message from Mars, The" (Ballard), **Supp. V:** 33

Messages (Fernandez), **V:** 225–226

"Messdick" (Ross), **VII:** 433

Messenger, The (Kinsella), **Supp. V:** 269–270

"M. E. T." (Thomas), **Supp. III:** 401

Metamorphoses (Ovid), **III:** 54; **V:** 321; **Retro. Supp. II:** 36, 215

Metamorphoses (Sisson), **Supp. XI:** 253

Metamorphosis (Kafka), **III:** 340, 345

Metamorphosis of Pygmalion's Image (Marston), **I:** 238; **II:** 25, 40

"Metaphor Now Standing at Platform 8, The" (Armitage), **VIII:** 5–6

Metaphysical Lyrics and Poems of the Seventeenth Century (Grierson), **Retro. Supp. II:** 173

Metempsycosis: Poêma Satyricon (Donne), **Retro. Supp. II:** 94

"Methinks the poor Town has been troubled too long" (Dorset), **II:** 262

"Method. For Rongald Gaskell" (Davie), **Supp. VI:** 106

Metrical Tales and Other Poems (Southey), **IV:** 71

Metroland (Barnes), **Supp. IV:** 65, 66–67, 71, 76

Mew, Charlotte, **Supp. V:** 97, 98–99

Meynell, Wilfred, **V:** 440, 451

MF (Burgess), **Supp. I:** 197

"Mianserin Sonnets" (Fuller), **Supp. VII:** 79

Micah Clark (Doyle), **Supp. II:** 159, 163

"Michael" (Wordsworth), **IV:** 8, 18–19

Michael and Mary (Milne), **Supp. V:** 299

Michael Robartes and the Dancer (Yeats), **VI:** 217; **Retro. Supp. I:** 331–333

"Michael X and the Black Power Killings in Trinidad" (Naipaul), **Supp. I:** 396

Michaelmas Term (Middleton), **II:** 3, 4, 21

Michelet, Jules, **V:** 346

Microcosmography (Earle), **IV:** 286

Micro–Cynicon, Six Snarling Satires (Middleton), **II:** 2–3

Midas (Lyly), **I:** 198, 202, 203

"Middle Age" (Dunn), **Supp. X:** 80

Middle Age of Mrs Eliot, The (Wilson), **Supp. I:** 160–161

Middle Ground, The (Drabble), **Supp. IV:** 230, 231, 234, 246–247, 248

Middle Mist, The (Renault), see *Friendly Young Ladies, The*

"Middle of a War" (Fuller), **VII:** 429; **Supp. VII:** 69

Middle Passage, The (Naipaul), **Supp. I:** 386, 390–391, 393, 403

"Middle–Sea and Lear–Sea" (Jones), **Supp. I:** 176

Middle Years, The (James), **VI:** 65, 69

"Middle Years, The" (Ewart), **Supp. VII:** 39

"Middle Years, The" (James), **VI:** 69

Middlemarch (Eliot), **III:** 157; **V:** ix–x, xxiv, 196–197, 200; **Supp. IV:** 243; **Retro. Supp. II:** 113–114

Middlemen: A Satire, The (Brooke–Rose)), **Supp. IV:** 99, 103

Middleton, D., **V:** 253

Middleton, Thomas, **II:** 1–23, 30, 33, 68–70, 72, 83, 85, 93, 100; **IV:** 79

Midnight All Day (Kureishi), **Supp. XI:** 160

"Midnight Hour, The" (Powys), **VIII:** 256

Midnight Oil (Pritchett), **Supp. III:** 312, 313

Midnight on the Desert (Priestley), **VII:** 209, 212

"Midnight Skaters, The" (Blunden), **VI:** 429; **Supp. XI:** 45

Midnight's Children (Rushdie), **Supp. IV:** 162, 433, 435, 436, 438, 439–444, 445, 448, 449, 456; **Supp. V:** 67, 68

"Midsummer Cushion, The" (Clare), **Supp. XI:** 60

"Midsummer Holiday, A, and Other Poems" (Swinburne), **V:** 332

"Midsummer Ice" (Murray), **Supp. VII:** 278

Midsummer Night's Dream, A (Shakespeare), **I:** 304–305, 311–312; **II:** 51, 281; **Supp. IV:** 198

"Mid–Term Break" (Heaney), **Retro. Supp. I:** 125

Mid–Victorian Memories (Francillon), **V:** 83

Mightier Than the Sword (Ford), **VI:** 320–321

Mighty and Their Full, The (Compton–Burnett), **VII:** 61, 62

Mighty Magician, The (FitzGerald), **IV:** 353

Miguel Street (Naipaul), **Supp. I:** 383, 385–386

"Mike: A Public School Story" (Wodehouse), **Supp. III:** 449

Mike Fletcher (Moore), **VI:** 87, 91

"Mildred Lawson" (Moore), **VI:** 98

Milesian Chief, The (Maturin), **VIII:** 201, 207

Milestones (Bennett), **VI:** 250, 263, 264

Milford, H., **III:** 208n

"Milford: East Wing" (Murphy), **Supp. V:** 328

Military Memoirs of Capt. George Carleton, The (Defoe), **III:** 14

Military Philosophers, The (Powell), **VII:** 349

"Milk–cart, The" (Morgan, E.), **Supp. IX:** 168

Mill, James, **IV:** 159; **V:** 288

Mill, John Stuart, **IV:** 50, 56, 246, 355; **V:** xxi–xxii, xxiv, 182, 279, 288, 343

Mill on the Floss, The (Eliot), **V:** xxii, 14, 192–194, 200; **Supp. IV:** 240, 471; **Retro. Supp. II:** 106–108

Millais, John Everett, **V:** 235, 236, 379

Miller, Arthur, **VI:** 286

Miller, Henry, **Supp. IV:** 110–111

Miller, J. Hillis, **VI:** 147

Miller, Karl, **Supp. IV:** 169

"Miller's Daughter, The" (Tennyson), **IV:** 326

Miller's Tale, The (Chaucer), **I:** 37

Millet, Jean François, **Supp. IV:** 90

Millett, Kate, **Supp. IV:** 188

Millionairess, The (Shaw), **VI:** 102, 127

"Millom Cricket Field" (Nicholson), **Supp. VI:** 216

"Millom Old Quarry" (Nicholson), **Supp. VI:** 216

Mills, C. M., pseud. of Elizabeth Gaskell

Millstone, The (Drabble), **Supp. IV:** 230, 237–238

Milne, A. A., **Supp. V:** 295–312

"Milnes, Richard Monckton" (Lord Houghton), *see* Monckton Milnes, Richard

Milton (Blake), **III:** 303–304, 307; **V:** xvi 330; **Retro. Supp. I:** 45

Milton (Meredith), **V:** 234

"Milton" (Macaulay), **IV:** 278, 279

Milton, Edith, **Supp. IV:** 305–306

Milton, John, **II:** 50–52, 113, **158–178,** 195, 196, 198, 199, 205, 206, 236, 302; **III:** 43, 118–119, 167n, 211n, 220, 302; **IV:** 9, 11–12, 14, 22, 23, 93, 95, 185, 186, 200, 205, 229, 269, 278, 279, 352; **V:** 365–366; **Supp. III:** 169; **Retro. Supp. II:** 269–289

Milton's God (Empson), **Supp. II:** 180, **195–196**

Milton's Prosody (Bridges), **VI:** 83

Mimic Men, The (Naipaul), **Supp. I:** 383, 386, 390, 392, 393–394, 395, 399

Orwell, George, **III:** 341; **V:** 24, 31; **VI:** 240, 242; **VII:** xii, xx, **273–287;** **Supp. I:** 28*n*; **Supp. III:** 96, 107; **Supp. IV:** 17, 81, 110–111, 440, 445

Osborne, John, **VI:** 101; **Supp. I: 329–340; Supp. II: 4,** 70, 139, 155; **Supp. III:** 191; **Supp. IV:** 180, 281, 283

Osbourne, Lloyd, **V:** 384, 387, 393, 395, 396, 397

Oscar Wilde. Art and Egoism (Shewan), **V:** 409, 421

O'Shaughnessy, Arthur, **VI:** 158

Osiris Rising (Armah), **Supp. X:** 1–2, 11–12, 14

Othello (Shakespeare), **I:** 316; **II:** 71, 79; **III:** 116; **Supp. IV:** 285

"Other, The" (Thomas), **Supp. III:** 403

"Other Boat, The" (Forster), **VI:** 406, 411–412

Other House, The (James), **VI:** 48, 49, 67

Other House, The (Stevenson), **Supp. VI:** 263–265

"Other Kingdom" (Forster), **VI:** 399, 402

Other People: A Mystery Story (Amis), **Supp. IV:** 26, 39–40

Other People's Clerihews (Ewart), **Supp. VII:** 46

"Other People's Houses" (Reid), **Supp. VII:** 336

Other People's Worlds (Trevor), **Supp. IV:** 501, 506, 511–512, 517

Other Places (Pinter), **Supp. I:** 378

"Other Tiger, The" (tr. Reid), **Supp. VII:** 332–333

"Other Times" (Nye), **Supp. X:** 198–199

Other Tongues: Young Scottish Poets in English, Scots, and Gaelic (ed. Crawford), **Supp. XI:** 67

Other Voices (Maitland), **Supp. XI:** 165

"Others, The" (Ewart), **Supp. VII:** 39, 40

Otho the Great (Keats and Brown), **IV:** 231, 235

Otranto (Walpole), *see Castle of Otranto, The*

"Otter, An" (Hughes), **Retro. Supp. II:** 204–205

"Otters" (Longley), **VIII:** 174

Ouch (Ackroyd), **Supp. VI:** 3–4

Ounce, Dice, Trice (Reid), **Supp. VII:** 326

Our Betters (Maugham), **VI:** 368, 369

"Our Bias" (Auden), **VII:** 387

Our Corner (periodical), **VI:** 103

Our Country's Good (Keneally), **Supp. IV:** 346

Our Exagmination Round His Factification for Incamination of Work in Progress (Beckett et al.), **Supp. I:** 43*n*

Our Exploits at West Poley (Hardy), **VI:** 20

"Our Father" (Davie), **Supp. VI:** 113

"Our Father's Works" (Blunden), **Supp. XI:** 42

Our Family (Hood), **IV:** 254, 259

Our First Leader (Morris, J.), **Supp. X:** 186

Our Friend the Charlatan (Gissing), **V:** 437

"Our Hunting Fathers" (Auden), **VII:** 108

Our Man in Havana (Greene), **Supp. I:** 7, 11, 13, 14–15; **Retro. Supp. II:** 161

"Our Mother" (Kinsella), **Supp. V:** 263

Our Mother's House (Gloag), **Supp. IV:** 390

Our Mutual Friend (Dickens), **V:** xxiii, 42, 44, 55, 68–69, 72; **Supp. IV:** 247

Our Old Home (Hawthorne), **VI:** 34

"Our Parish" (Dickens), **V:** 43, 46

Our Republic (Keneally), **Supp. IV:** 347

"Our Parish" (Dickens), **V:** 43, 46

Our Spoons Came From Woolworths (Comyns), **VIII:** 56–58

"Our Thrones Decay" (Russell), **VIII:** 285

"Our Village—by a Villager" (Hood), **IV:** 257

Our Women: Chapters on the Sex–Discord (Bennett), **VI:** 267

Out (Brooke–Rose)), **Supp. IV:** 99, 104, 105–106

"Out and Away" (Kavan), **Supp. VII:** 202

Out of Bounds (Stallworthy), **Supp. X:** 292–293

Out of India (Jhabvala), **Supp. V:** 235–236

Out of India (Kipling), **VI:** 204

Out of Ireland (Kinsella), **Supp. V:** 271

"Out of Ireland" (Kinsella), **Supp. V:** 271

Out of the Picture (MacNeice), **VII:** 405

Out of the Red, into the Blue (Comyns), **VIII:** 63

Out of the Shelter (Lodge), **Supp. IV:** 364, 365, 370–371, 372

"Out of the signs" (Thomas), **Supp. I:** 174

Out of the Silent Planet (Lewis), **Supp. III:** 249, 252–253

Out of the Whirlpool (Sillitoe), **Supp. V:** 411

Out of This World (Swift), **Supp. V:** 437–438

Outback (Keneally), **Supp. IV:** 346

"Outcast, The" (Tennyson), **IV:** 329

Outcast of the Islands, An (Conrad), **VI:** 136, 137, 148; **Retro. Supp. II:** 71

Outcasts, The (Sitwell), **VII:** 138

Outcry, The (Julia), **VI:** 67

"Outdoor Concert, The" (Gunn), **Supp. IV:** 269

Outer Planet, The (Nicholson), **Supp. VI:** 217

Outidana, or Effusions, Amorous, Pathetic and Fantastical (Beddoes), **Supp. XI:** 28–29

Outline of History: Being a Plain History of Life and Mankind, The (Wells), **VI:** 245

Outlines of Romantic Theology (Williams, C. W. S.), **Supp. IX:** 275, 284

"Outlook, Uncertain" (Reid), **Supp. VII:** 330

Outlying Stations, The (Warner), **Supp. XI:** 298

"Outpost of Progress, An" (Conrad), **VI:** 136, 148

Outriders: A Liberal View of Britain, The (Morris, J.), **Supp. X:** 175

"Outside the Whale" (Rushdie), **Supp. IV:** 455

"Outskirts" (Kureishi), **Supp. XI:** 156

"Outstation, The" (Maugham), **VI:** 370, 371, 380

"Outward Bound" (Morgan, E.), **Supp. IX:** 167

"Ovando" (Kincaid), **Supp. VII:** 225

"Over Mother, The" (McGuckian), **Supp. V:** 288

"Over Sir John's Hill" (Thomas), **Supp. I:** 179

Over the Frontier (Smith), **Supp. II:** 462, 474

"Over the Hill" (Warner), **Supp. VII:** 380

"Over the Hills" (Thomas), **Supp. III:** 400

"Over the Rainbow" (Rushdie), **Supp. IV:** 434

Over the River (Galsworthy), **VI:** 272, 275

Over the River (Gregory), **VI:** 318

Over to You: Ten Stories of Flyers and Flying (Dahl), **Supp. IV:** 208–211, 213

Overbury, Sir Thomas, **IV:** 286

"Overcoat, The" (Gogol), **III:** 340, 345

Overcrowded Barracoon, The (Naipaul), **Supp. I: 384**

"Overcrowded Barracoon, The" (Naipaul), **Supp. I:** 402

"Overloaded Man, The" (Ballard), **Supp. V:** 33

Overruled (Shaw), **VI:** 129

"Overture" (Kinsella), **Supp. V:** 270–271

"Overtures to Death" (Day Lewis), **Supp. III:** 122

Overtures to Death (Day Lewis), **Supp. III:** 118, 127–128

Ovid, **II:** 110*n*, 185, 292, 304, 347; **III:** 54; **V:** 319, 321

"Ovid on West 4th" (Mahon), **Supp. VI:** 176

"Ovid in the Third Reich" (Hill), **Supp. V:** 187

Ovid's Art of Love Paraphrased (Fielding), **III:** 105

Ovid's Banquet of Sense (Chapman), **I:** 237–238

Ovid's Epistles, Translated by Several Hands (Dryden), **Supp. III:** 36

Ovid's Fasti (tr. Frazer), **Supp. III:** 176

Owen, Wilfred, **VI:** xvi, 329, 416, 417, 419, 423, **443–460; VII:** xvi, 421; list of poems, **VI:** 458–459; **Supp. IV:** 57, 58

"Owen Wingrave," (James), **VI:** 69

"Owl, The" (Thomas), **VI:** 424; **Supp. III:** 403–404

"Owl and Mouse" (Smith, I. C.), **Supp. IX:** 218

"Owl and the Pussy–cat, The" (Lear), **V:** 83–84, 87

Owls and Artificers (Fuller), **Supp. VII:** 77

Owners (Churchill), **Supp. IV:** 179, 180, 181–182, 198

"Oxen, The" (Hardy), **VI:** 16

Oxford (Morris, J.), **Supp. X:** 176, 178

Oxford Book of English Verse, The (ed. Quiller–Couch), **II:** 102, 121

"Remembering the 90s" (Mahon), **Supp. VI:** 177

"Remembering the Thirties" (Davie), **Supp. VI:** 106

"Remembrances" (Clare), **Supp. XI:** 52

Remembrances of Words and Matter Against Richard Cholmeley, **I:** 277

Reminiscences (Carlyle), **IV:** 70n, 239, 240, 245, 250

"Reminiscences of Charlotte Brontë" (Nussey), **V:** 108, 109, 152

Reminiscences of the Impressionistic Painters (Moore), **VI:** 99

Remorse (Coleridge), **IV:** 56

Remorse: A Study in Saffron (Wilde), **V:** 419

"Removal from Terry Street, A" (Dunn), **Supp. X** 69–70

Renaissance: Studies in Art and Poetry, The (Pater), *see Studies in the History of the Renaissance*

Renan, Joseph Ernest, **II:** 244

Renault, Mary, **Supp. IX: 171–188**

Rendell, Ruth, **Supp. IX: 189–206**

Renegade Poet, And Other Essays, A (Thompson), **V:** 451

Renegado, The (Massinger), **Supp. XI:** 184, 185, 195

"Renounce thy God" (Dunbar), **VIII:** 122

"Repeated Rediscovery of America, The" (Wallace–Crabbe), **VIII:** 319

"Repentance" (Herbert), **II:** 128

Repentance of Robert Greene, The (Greene), **VIII:** 132, 134

"Rephan" (Browning), **IV:** 365

Replication (Skelton), **I:** 93

Reply to the Essay on Population, by the Rev. T. R. Malthus, A (Hazlitt), **IV:** 127, 139

"Report from Below, A" (Hood), **IV:** 258

"Report on a Threatened City" (Lessing), **Supp. I:** 250n

"Report on an Unidentified Space Station" (Ballard), **Supp. V:** 33

"Report on Experience" (Blunden), **VI:** 428;**Supp. XI:** 39

Report on the Salvation Army Colonies (Haggard), **Supp. III:** 214

"Report to the Trustees of the Bellahouston Travelling Scholarship, A" (Gray, A.), **Supp. IX:** 79–80, 82, 90

"Reported Missing" (Scannell), **VII:** 424

Reports on Elementary Schools, 1852–1882 (Arnold), **V:** 216

Reprinted Pieces (Dickens), **V:** 72

Reprisal, The (Smollett), **III:** 149, 158

Reproof: A Satire (Smollett), **III:** 158

"Requiem" (Maitland), **Supp. XI:** 177

"Requiem" (Stevenson), **V:** 383; **Retro. Supp. I:** 268

"Requiem" (tr. Thomas), **Supp. IV:** 494–495

"Requiem for the Croppies" (Heaney), **Retro. Supp. I:** 127–128

"Requiescat" (Arnold), **V:** 211

"Requiescat" (Wilde), **V:** 400

Required Writing (Larkin), **Supp. I:** 286, 288

"Re–Reading Jane" (Stevenson), **Supp. VI:** 262

Rescue, The (Conrad), **VI:** 136, 147

Resentment (Waugh), **Supp. VI:** 270

"Resignation" (Arnold), **V:** 210

"Resolution and Independence" (Wordsworth), **IV:** 19–20, 22; **V:** 352

"Resound my voice, ye woods that hear me plain" (Wyatt), **I:** 110

Responsibilities (Yeats), **VI:** 213; **Retro. Supp. I:** 330

"Responsibility" (MacCaig), **Supp. VI:** 189

Responsio ad Lutherum (More), **Supp. VII:** 242–243

Ressoning betuix Aige and Yowth, The (Henryson), **Supp. VII:** 146, 147

Ressoning betuix Deth and Man, The (Henryson), **Supp. VII:** 146, 147

Restoration (Bond), **Supp. I:** 423, 434, 435

Restoration of Arnold Middleton, The (Storey), **Supp. I:** 408, 411, 412–413, 414, 415, 417

"Resurrection, The" (Cowley), **II:** 200

Resurrection, The (Yeats), **VI:** xiv, 222

"Resurrection and Immortality" (Vaughan), **II:** 185, 186

Resurrection at Sorrow Hill (Harris), **Supp. V:** 144

Resurrection Men (Rankin), **Supp. X:** 245, 256–257

Resurrection of the Dead, The, . . . (Bunyan), **II:** 253

"Retaliation" (Goldsmith), **III:** 181, 185, 191

"Reticence of Lady Anne, The" (Saki), **Supp. VI:** 245

"Retired Cat, The" (Cowper), **III:** 217

"Retirement" (Vaughan), **II:** 187, 188, 189

"Retreat, The" (King), **Supp. VI:** 153

"Retreate, The" (Vaughan), **II:** 186, 188–189

"Retrospect" (Brooke), **Supp. III:** 56

"Retrospect: From a Street in Chelsea" (Day Lewis), **Supp. III:** 121

"Retrospective Review" (Hood), **IV:** 255

"Return, The" (Conrad), **VI:** 148

"Return, The" (Muir), **Supp. VI:** 207

"Return, A" (Russell), **VIII:** 284

"Return, The" (Stallworthy), **Supp. X:** 298

Return from Parnassus, The, part 2, **II:** 27

"Return from the Freudian Islands, The" (Hope), **Supp. VII:** 155–156, 157

"Return from the Islands" (Redgrove), **Supp. VI:** 235

Return of Eva Peron, The (Naipaul), **Supp. I:** 396, 397, 398, 399

Return of the Druses, The (Browning), **IV:** 374

"Return of the Iron Man, The" (Hughes), **Supp. I:** 346

Return of the King, The (Tolkien), **Supp. II:** 519

Return of the Native, The (Hardy), **V:** xxiv, 279; **VI:** 1–2, 5, 6, 7, 8; **Retro. Supp. I:** 114

Return of the Soldier, The (West), **Supp. III:** 440, 441

Return of Ulysses, The (Bridges), **VI:** 83

Return to Abyssinia (White), **Supp. I:** 131

Return to My Native Land (tr. Berger), **Supp. IV:** 77

Return to Night (Renault), **Supp. IX:** 175

Return to Oasis (Durrell), **VII:** 425

"Return to the Council House" (Smith, I. C.), **Supp. IX:** 214

Return to Yesterday (Ford), **VI:** 149

Returning (O'Brien), **Supp. V:** 339

"Returning, We Hear the Larks" (Rosenberg), **VI:** 434–435

Revaluation (Leavis), **III:** 68; **VII:** 234, 236, 244–245

"Reveille" (Hughes), **Supp. I:** 350

Revelations of Divine Love (Juliana of Norwich), **I:** 20–21

Revenge for Love, The (Lewis), **VII:** 72, 74, 81

Revenge Is Sweet: Two Short Stories (Hardy), **VI:** 20

Revenge of Bussy D'Ambois, The (Chapman), **I:** 251–252, 253; **II:** 37

Revenger's Tragedy, The, **II:** 1–2, 21, 29, **33–36,** 37, 39, 40, 41, 70, 97

Revengers' Comedies, The (Ayckbourn), **Supp. V:** 3, 10

Reverberator, The (James), **VI:** 67

"Reverie" (Browning), **IV:** 365

Reveries over Childhood and Youth (Yeats), **VI:** 222

Reversals (Stevenson), **Supp. VI:** 255–256

"Reversals" (Stevenson), **Supp. VI:** 256

Review (periodical), **II:** 325; **III:** 4, 13, 39, 41, 42, 51, 53

"Review, The" (Traherne), **Supp. XI:** 273

Review of some poems by Alexander Smith and Matthew Arnold (Clough), **V:** 158

Review of the Affairs of France, A . . . (Defoe), **III:** 13; **Retro. Supp. I:** 65

Review of the State of the British Nation, A (Defoe), **Retro. Supp. I:** 65

"Reviewer's ABC, A" (Aiken), **VII:** 149

Revised Version of the Bible, **I:** 381–382

Revolt in the Desert (Lawrence), **Supp. II:** 288, 289–290, 293

Revolt of Aphrodite, The (Durrell), *see Tunc; Nunquam*

Revolt of Islam, The (Shelley), **IV:** xvii, 198, 203, 208; **VI:** 455; **Retro. Supp. I:** 249–250

"Revolt of the Tartars" (De Quincey), **IV:** 149

"Revolution" (Housman), **VI:** 160

Revolution in Tanner's Lane, The (Rutherford), **VI:** 240

Revolution Script, The (Moore, B.), **Supp. IX:** 141, 143

Revolutionary Epick, The (Disraeli), **IV:** 306, 308

Revolving Lights (Richardson), **Retro. Supp. I:** 313–314

Revue des Deux Mondes (Montégut), **V:** 102

"Revulsion" (Davie), **Supp. VI:** 110, 112

"Rex Imperator" (Wilson), **Supp. I:** 155, 156

"Two Kitchen Songs" (Sitwell), **VII:** 130–131

"Two Knights, The" (Swinburne), **V:** 315, 333

Two Letters on the Conduct of Our Domestic Parties (Burke), **III:** 205

Two Letters on the French Revolution (Burke), **III:** 205

Two Letters . . . on the Proposals for Peace (Burke), **III:** 205

Two Letters . . . to Gentlemen in the City of Bristol . . . (Burke), **III:** 205

Two Lives (Seth), **Supp. X:** 290

Two Lives (Trevor), **Supp. IV:** 516

Two Magics, The (James), **VI:** 52, 69

Two Mice, The (Henryson), **Supp. VII:** 136, 137, 140

Two Noble Kinsmen, The (Shakespeare), **I:** 324, 325; **II:** 43, 66, 87

Two of Us, The (Frayn), **Supp. VII:** 57

"Two Old Men Outside an Inn" (Cornford), **VIII:** 113

Two on a Tower: A Romance (Hardy), **VI:** 4, 5, 20; **Retro. Supp. I:** 114

Two or Three Graces (Huxley), **VII:** 201

Two Paths, The (Ruskin), **V:** 180, 184

"Two Peacocks of Bedfont, The" (Hood), **IV:** 256, 267

Two People (Milne), **Supp. V:** 310

"Two Races of Men, The" (Lamb), **IV:** 82

"Two Spirits, The" (Shelley), **IV:** 196

Two Stories: "Come and Dine" and "Tadnol" (Powys), **VIII:** 248

"2000: Zero Gravity" (Motion), **Supp. VII:** 266

"2001: The Tennyson/Hardy Poem" (Ewart), **Supp. VII:** 40

Two Thieves, The (Powys), **VIII:** 248, 255

Two Thousand Seasons (Armah), **Supp. X:** 1–3, 6–11, 13

Two Towers, The (Tolkien), **Supp. II:** 519

Two Voices (Thomas), **Supp. IV:** 490

"Two Voices, The" (Tennyson), **IV:** 329

"Two Ways of It" (MacCaig), **Supp. VI:** 187

Two Women of London: The Strange Case of Ms. Jekyll and Mrs. Hyde (Tennant), **Supp. IX:**238–239, 240

Two Worlds and Their Ways (Compton-Burnett), **VII:** 65, 66, 67, 69

"Two Year Old" (MacCaig), **Supp. VI:** 192

"Two Years Old" (Cornford), **VIII:** 113

Two–Part Inventions (Howard), **V:** 418

"Two–Party System in English Political History, The" (Trevelyan), **VI:** 392

"Two–Sided Man, The" (Kipling), **VI:** 201

Twyborn Affair, The (White), **Supp. I:** 132, 148–149

"Tyes, The" (Thomas), **Supp. III:** 401

"Tyger, The" (Blake), **III:** 296; **Retro. Supp. I:** 42–43

Tyler, F. W., **I:** 275n

Tylney Hall (Hood), **IV:** 254, 256, 259, 267

Tynan, Katherine, **V:** 441

Tynan, Kenneth, **Supp. II:** 70, 140, 147, 152, 155; **Supp. IV:** 78

Tyndale, William, **I:** 375–377

"Typhoon" (Conrad), **VI:** 136, 148

Tyrannicida (tr. More), **Supp. VII:** 235–236

Tyrannick Loce; or, The Royal Martyr (Dryden), **II:** 290, 294, 305

"Tyre, The" (Armitage), **VIII:** 11

"Tyronic Dialogues" (Lewis), **VII:** 82

Udolpho (Radcliffe), *see Mysteries of Udolpho, The*

Ugly Anna and Other Tales (Coppard), **VIII:** 89

"Uist" (Crawford), **Supp. XI:** 81

Ukulele Music (Reading), **VIII:** 265, 268–269, 270, 271

"Ula Masondo" (Plomer), **Supp. XI:** 218

Ulick and Soracha (Moore), **VI:** 89, 95, 99

"Ultima" (Thompson), **V:** 441

"Ultima Ratio Regum" (Spender), **Supp. II:** 488

Ultramarine (Lowry), **Supp. III:** 269, 270, **271–272,** 280, 283, 285

Ulysses (Butler), **Supp. II:** 114

Ulysses (Joyce), **V:** 189; **VII:** xv, 42, 46–47, 48–52;**Retro. Supp. I:** 169, 176–179; critical studies, **VII:** 57–58; **Supp. IV:** 87, 370, 390, 426

"Ulysses" (Tennyson), **IV:** xx, 324, 328, 332–334

"Umbrella Man, The" (Dahl), **Supp. IV:** 221

"Un Coeur Simple" (Flaubert), **Supp. IV:** 69

Un Début dans la vie (Balzac), **Supp. IV:** 123

"Unarmed Combat" (Reed), **VII:** 422–423

"Unattained Place, The" (Muir), **Supp. VI:** 206

Unbearable Bassington, The (Saki), **Supp. VI: 245–248**

Unbeaten Tracks in Japan (Bird), **Supp. X:** 19, 29–30

"Unbidden Guest, The" (Powys), **VIII:** 251

"Unbuilders, The" (Crawford), **Supp. XI:** 70

Uncensored (Rattigan), **Supp. VII:** 311

"Unchangeable, The" (Blunden), **Supp. XI:** 43

Unclassed, The (Gissing), **V:** 437

Unclay (Powys), **VIII:** 256

Uncle Bernac (Doyle), **Supp. II:** 159

Uncle Dottery: A Christmas Story (Powys), **VIII:** 248

"Uncle Ernest" (Sillitoe), **Supp. V:** 414

Uncle Fred in the Springtime (Wodehouse), **Supp. III:** 460–461

Uncle Silas (Le Fanu), **III:** 345; **Supp. II:** 78–79, 81

Uncle Vanya (tr. Frayn), **Supp. VII:** 61

Unclouded Summer (Waugh), **Supp. VI:** 274

Uncollected Essays (Pater), **V:** 357

Uncollected Verse (Thompson), **V:** 451

Uncommercial Traveller, The (Dickens), **V:** 72

Unconditional Surrender (Waugh), **VII:** 303, 304; see also Sword of Honour trilogy

Unconscious Memory (Butler), **Supp. II:** 107–108

Unconsoled, The (Ishiguro), **Supp. IV:** 301, 302, 304, 305, 306–307, 314–316

"Uncovenanted Mercies" (Kipling), **VI:** 175

"Under a Lady's Picture" (Waller), **II:** 234–235

"Under Ben Bulben" (Yeats), **VI:** 215, 219–220; **Retro. Supp. I:** 338

"Under Brinkie's Brae" (Brown), **Supp. VI:** 64

"Under Carn Brea" (Thomas), **Supp. IV:** 492

Under Milk Wood (Thomas), **Supp. I:** 183–184

Under Plain Cover (Osborne), **Supp. I:** 335–336

Under the Greenwood Tree: A Rural Painting of the Dutch School (Hardy), **VI:** 1, 2–3, 5, 20; **Retro. Supp. I:** 112–113

Under the Hill (Beardsley), **VII:** 292

Under the Hill (Firbank), **Supp. II:** 202

Under the Microscope (Swinburne), **IV:** 337; **V:** 329, 332, 333

Under the Net (Murdoch), **Supp. I:** 220, 222, 228, 229–230

Under the Sunset (Stoker), **Supp. III:** 381

Under the Volcano (Lowry), **Supp. III:** 269, 270, 273, **274–280,** 283, 285

Under the Reservoir (Redgrove), **Supp. VI:** 236

Under Western Eyes (Conrad), **VI:** 134, 144–145, 148; **Retro. Supp. II:** 81–82

"'Under Which King, Bezonian?'" (Leavis), **VII:** 242

Under World (Hill, R.), **Supp. IX:** 120, 121

Undergraduate Sonnets (Swinburne), **V:** 333

Underhill, Charles, *see* Hill, Reginald

"Understanding the Ur–Bororo" (Self), **Supp. V:** 401–402

Undertones of War (Blunden), **VI:** 428, 429; **Supp. XI:** 33, 36, 38, 39–41, 47

Underwood (Jonson), **Retro. Supp. I:** 166

Underwood, Dale, **II:** 256n

Underwoods (Stevenson), **V:** 390n, 395; **Retro. Supp. I:** 267–268

Undine (Schreiner), **Supp. II: 444–445**

"Undiscovered Planet, The" (Nicholson), **Supp. VI:** 217

"Undressing" (Nye), **Supp. X:** 198, 200

Undying Fire, The (Wells), **VI:** 242

Unequal Marriage; or, Pride and Prejudice Twenty Years Later, An (Tennant), see *Unequal Marriage: Pride and Prejudice Continued, An*

Unequal Marriage: Pride and Prejudice Continued, An (Tennant), **Supp. IX:** 237–238, 239–240

"Unfinished Draft, An" (Beddoes), **Supp. XI:** 30